SOCIAL
PSYCHOLOGY

SOCIAL PSYCHOLOGY

H. Andrew Michener
University of Wisconsin, Madison

John D. DeLamater
University of Wisconsin, Madison

Shalom H. Schwartz
Hebrew University of Jerusalem

Under the general editorship of
Robert K. Merton
Columbia University

HARCOURT BRACE JOVANOVICH, PUBLISHERS

San Diego   New York   Chicago   Atlanta   Washington, D.C.
London   Sydney   Toronto

Preface

This textbook grew out of our experiences in teaching introductory social psychology at the University of Wisconsin, Madison. Each of us, teaching the course independently, found that none of the available textbooks offered what we needed. Although some texts provided competent coverage of empirical research, most of these were written from a psychological perspective and emphasized intrapsychic processes rather than social interaction and group processes. Other available texts, while stressing social and group processes, provided little or no coverage of research findings; they covered theories and concepts rather than empirical research. Missing was a book that had both a sociological emphasis and careful coverage of the empirical results generated by social psychologists. This is our attempt to correct the deficiency.

In writing this book, we have drawn on theories developed by all types of social psychologists—those with sociological, psychological, and even anthropological perspectives. In contrast to other texts, we have stressed the impact of social structure and group membership on the social behavior of individuals. At the same time, we have covered the intrapsychic processes of cognition, perception, and learning that underlie social behavior. Throughout the book we have used the results of empirical research—surveys, experiments, and observational studies—to illuminate these processes.

Because this book relies on a sociological perspective, sociology instructors should find it especially appropriate. At the same time, it should appeal to psychology instructors who are interested in an integration of the various disciplines of social psychology. Coverage in the book is broad, and a diversity of topics is discussed. Social psychology is truly interdisciplinary in many respects, and there is growing interest among all social psychologists in such traditional sociological topics as language, gender roles, impression management, intergroup relations, and the impact of social structure on the individual.

CONTENT AND ORGANIZATION. The book opens with a chapter on theoretical perspectives in social psychology, which provides the groundwork for all that follows. The remainder of the book is divided into four parts. Part one focuses on socialization. It covers such topics as self and identity, learning and socialization during childhood, and the social influences that shape the life of the individual.

Part two is concerned with social interaction, the core of social psychology. Each of these chapters discusses how persons interact with others and how they are affected by this interaction. These chapters cover such topics as communication, attitudes, social influence, social perception, self-presentation, altruism and aggression, and interpersonal attraction.

Part three provides extensive coverage of groups, including group cohesiveness and conformity to norms, status processes in interaction, and leadership and group productivity.

Part four, society and social behavior, considers the relations between individuals and the wider societal context. These chapters treat the emergence and resolution of intergroup conflict, the impact of the social structure on the individual, deviant behavior, collective behavior, and social movements.

EASE OF USE. An introductory course in social psychology could be organized in many different ways. For this reason, we have written each chapter as a self-contained unit. Later chapters do not presume that the student has read earlier ones. This enables instructors to assign chapters in whatever sequence they wish.

To help make the material interesting and accessible to students, the introductory section of each chapter poses four to six thought-provoking questions. These questions provide the agenda of issues discussed in the chapter. The remainder of the chapter consists of four to six major sections, each addressing one of these issues. A summary at the end of each chapter has a similar organization. Thus, each chapter poses several key questions about a topic, and then considers each question in a framework that makes it easy for students to learn the major ideas.

In addition, this text includes other learning aids. Tables are used to clarify the results of important studies. Figures are used to illustrate important social psychological processes. Carefully chosen photographs dramatize essential ideas from the text, and boxes in each chapter highlight interesting or controversial issues and studies and also discuss the applications of social psychological concepts to daily life. Key terms and concepts appear in boldface type and are summarized at the end of each chapter. An appendix of research methods and a glossary of key terms are included at the end of the book.

Although this is a new book, many of its chapters have been classroom-tested. Preliminary versions of chapters were used in teaching introductory social psychology classes, both in sociology and in psychology. Students are perhaps the best source of information as to whether a book is interesting and clear. Their feedback helped greatly to improve the book's presentation, pace, style, and interest.

ACKNOWLEDGMENTS. Many of our colleagues reviewed one or more chapters of the book and provided useful comments and criticisms. We extend thanks to:

Robert F. Bales, Harvard University; Philip W. Blumstein, University of Washington; Marilyn B. Brewer, University of California at Los Angeles; Bella DePaulo, University of Virginia; Glen Elder, Jr., University of North Carolina at Chapel Hill; Viktor Gecas, Washington State University; Allen Grimshaw, Indiana University; Elaine Hatfield, University of Hawaii–Manoa; George Homans, Harvard University; Michael Inbar, Hebrew University of Jerusalem; Edward Jones, Princeton University; Lewis Killian, Univeristy of Massachusetts; Melvin Kohn, Department of Mental Health; Robert Krauss, Columbia University; Marianne LaFrance, Boston College; Patricia MacCorquodale, University of Arizona; Armand Mauss, Washington State University; Douglas Maynard, University of Wisconsin, Madison; John McCarthy, Catholic University of America; Kathleen McKinney, Oklahoma State University; Howard Nixon, II, University of Vermont; Pamela Oliver, University of Wisconsin, Madison; James Orcutt, Florida State University; Daniel Perlman, University of Manitoba; Jane Allyn Piliavin, University of Wisconsin, Madison; Michael Ross, University of Waterloo, Ontario; Melvin Seeman, University of California at Los Angeles; Roberta Simmons, University of Minnesota; Sheldon Stryker, Indiana University; Robert Suchner, Northern Illinois University; James Tedeschi, State University of New York–Albany; Elizabeth Thomson, University of Wisconsin, Madison; Mark P. Zanna, University of Waterloo; Morris Zelditch, Jr., Stanford University; Louis Zurcher, University of Texas.

Responsibility for any mistakes that may remain rests wholly with the authors.

Eight people contributed enormously by translating our illegible scribbles and halting dictation into typed manuscript. We express thanks to Mary Anderson, Hani Davis, Mary Donohue, Gail Glasser, Elizabeth Harries, Mary Herzog, Shiela Jacobson, and Judith Landau.

Numerous professionals at Harcourt Brace Jovanovich contributed to the process of turning the manuscript into a book. In the early stages, persons in HBJ's New York office who contributed to the project included Peter Dougherty, Judith Greissman, and Clare Thompson. More recently, the project has benefited from the work of several people on HBJ's staff in San Diego. Marcus Boggs has been a continuing source of support as our acquisitions editor. Nancy Hornick, through her diligent work as manuscript editor, has improved the book's clarity and conciseness. Don Fujimoto, Avery Hallowell, and Mike Yazzolino developed the design and artwork. Our appreciation to them all.

Last, we express our gratitude to those who are close to us. They endured our absence when we were working on the book, listened to our complaints, provided helpful advice when asked, and shared our joy as we achieved milestones.

H. Andrew Michener
John D. DeLamater
Shalom H. Schwartz

Contents

4 Continuity and Change Through the Life Course

5 Symbolic Communication and Language

11 Interpersonal Attraction 321

12 Group Cohesiveness and Conformity 355

SOCIAL PSYCHOLOGY

Chapter 1
Introduction to Social Psychology

Introduction

—Why are some persons effective leaders and others not?

—What makes people fall in love? What makes them fall out of love?

—Why is it so easy to achieve cooperation between persons in some instances, but so difficult in others?

—What effects do major life events like getting married, having a child, or losing one's job have on physical health, mental health, and self-esteem?

—What causes conflict between groups? Why do some conflicts persist far beyond the point where participants can expect to achieve any real gains?

—Why do some people conform to norms and laws, whereas others violate them?

—Why do people present different images of themselves in various situations? What determines the particular images they present?

—What causes harmful or aggressive behavior? What causes altruism?

—Why are some groups so much better at doing their work than others?

—What causes people to develop unique conceptions of themselves? How do these self-concepts change?

—Why are some persons more persuasive and influential than others? What techniques do they use?

—Why do stereotypes persist even in the face of information that obviously contradicts them?

Questions such as these have probably puzzled you, just as they have perplexed others down through the ages. You might think about these questions merely because you want to understand better the social world around you. Or you might want the answers for more practical reasons, such as increasing your own effectiveness and influence in day-to-day social situations.

Answers to questions such as these come from various sources. Personal experience is one such source. Answers obtained by this means are often insightful, but they are usually limited in scope and generality. Occasionally they are even misleading. Another source is informal knowledge or advice from others. Again, answers obtained by this means are sometimes reliable, sometimes not. A third source is thinkers of various orientations—philosophers, novelists, poets, and men and women of practical affairs—who over the centuries have written about these issues. To a remarkable degree, their answers have filtered down and are available today in the form of sayings or aphorisms that comprise common-sense knowledge. Common sense covers a wide range of topics. We are told, for instance, that punishment is essential to successful childrearing ("Spare the rod and spoil the child") and that joint effort is an effective way to accomplish large jobs ("Many hands make light work"). Principles such as these may reflect certain truths, and they appear to provide guidelines for action.

Although commonsense knowledge has certain merits, it also presents some difficulties, not the least of which is that it often contradicts itself. For example, we are told that persons who are similar will like one another ("Birds of a feather flock together"), but also that persons who are dissimilar will like each other ("Opposites attract"). We learn that groups are wiser and smarter than individuals ("Two heads are better than one"), but also that problem solving by groups entails many compromises and inevitably produces mediocre results ("A camel is a racehorse designed by a committee"). Each of these seemingly contradictory statements may hold true under particular conditions. But without a clear statement of when they apply and when they do not, aphorisms ultimately provide little insight regarding relations among people. They provide even less guidance in situations where we need to make decisions. (For example, when facing a choice that entails risk, what should we believe—"Nothing ventured, nothing gained" or "Better safe than sorry"?)

If sources such as personal experience and commonsense knowledge have limited value, how are we to achieve an understanding of social interaction and relations among persons? Are we forever restricted to intuition and speculation, or is there a better alternative?

One answer to this problem is that offered by **social psychology.** Social psychologists propose that accurate and comprehensive knowledge about social behavior can be obtained by applying the methods of science to these issues. That is, by taking systematic observations of behavior and formulating theories that are subject to test and disconfirmation, we can attain a valid understanding of human social relations.

One objective of this book is to summarize many of the facts discovered through systematic social psychological research. To set the stage for this presentation, this chapter will first describe the core concerns of social psychology and provide a formal definition of the field. This definition will indicate in general terms what social psychology does and does not include. Second, we will summarize some of the broad theories (called theoretical perspectives) within social psychology today. These theories recur throughout this book, and provide useful frameworks for understanding relations among people. Third, we will consider the question, "Is social psychology a science?", and to answer it we will review the properties that characterize any science and then examine social psychology in light of them.

What Is Social Psychology?

Core Concerns of Social Psychology

There are several ways to characterize social psychology. Perhaps the most direct approach is to describe the things social psychologists actually study. Social psychologists investigate human behavior, of course, but their primary concern is human behavior in a social context. There are four *core concerns* or

major themes within social psychology. There are (1) the impact that one individual has on another individual; (2) the impact that a group has on its individual members; (3) the impact that individual members have on the group; and (4) the impact that one group has on another group. The four core concerns are shown schematically in Figure 1.1.

The first concern, the effect of one individual on another, is perhaps the most researched topic within social psychology. When the behavior of one person produces an immediate change in the behavior of a second person, we speak of *social influence*. For example, a bank robber brandishing his pistol is obviously exercising influence over the teller's behavior when he issues the threat, "Put the money in this sack. Don't hit the alarm button. Do as I

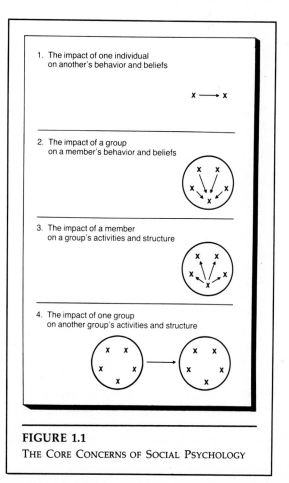

FIGURE 1.1
THE CORE CONCERNS OF SOCIAL PSYCHOLOGY

say and you won't get hurt." In other situations, the effects of one person on another's behavior can be more subtle. Merely staring at a stranger across a room, for example, may make that person uncomfortable enough to change seats or leave the room.

Beyond influencing others' overt behavior, one person may also affect another's psychological state. By this we mean that one person may affect another's beliefs and attitudes about the world. These attitudes, of course, may pertain to objects or people. *Interpersonal attitudes* such as liking, disliking, loving, and hating hold the interest of social psychologists, as do the behaviors they spawn (helping, hurting, and so on). Under certain circumstances, one person may try intentionally to change another's beliefs and attitudes, a process usually referred to as *persuasion.* For example, Carol might try to persuade Debbie that nuclear power plants are dangerous and therefore undesirable. Carol's persuasion attempt, if successful, would likely be reflected in Debbie's future actions (such as picketing nuclear power plants) or in her verbal behavior (advocating non-nuclear power). Social psychologists are interested in the conditions under which such changes in personal beliefs and attitudes occur.

The second concern of social psychology is the impact of a group on the behavior of its individual members. Individuals typically belong to many different groups—families, work groups, seminars, and clubs. Consequently, they spend many hours interacting with others in group contexts. To regulate the behavior of their members, groups usually establish norms or rules. One consequence of social interaction in groups is *conformity,* the process by which a group member adjusts his or her behavior to bring it into line with group norms. Much of our behavior in groups is influenced by norms. For example, college fraternities and sororities have norms—some formal and some informal—that stipulate how members should dress, what meetings they should attend, whom they can date and whom they should avoid, how they should behave at parties, and so on.

Groups also exert substantial, long-term influence on their members through a process called *socialization.* Simply stated, this means that groups regulate what their members learn. They do this so that the members will be adequately trained to enact the roles they play in society. Socialization shapes the knowledge, values, and skills of group members. One product of socialization is language skills. Children in Italian families are taught Italian, not Greek or Japanese, to prepare them for life in Italy. Likewise, students in medical school are taught thousands of technical terms—virtually an entire new language—to prepare them for professional responsibilities. Another product of socialization is a person's religious beliefs and attitudes; these generally reflect the views held by groups to which he or she belongs today or belonged in the past. Socialization not only molds members' values and attitudes on a wide variety of issues, but it also affects their views of themselves. It allows members to regulate their own behavior and to participate effectively in group activities.

The third concern of social psychology is the impact of individual members on the activities and structure of the groups to which they belong. Just as any group will influence the behavior of its members, these persons in turn may influence or redirect the group itself. One way of doing this is by *innovation,* which involves introducing changes in group norms or culture that are accepted by others members. Another way of doing this is by *leadership,* which involves the enactment of several functions (planning, organizing, controlling) necessary for successful group performance. Without effective leadership, coordination among members will be lacking and the group will drift or fail. Leadership, of course, depends primarily on the initiative, insight, and risk-taking propensity of individuals. Through leadership and innovation, individual members can exert a substantial impact on the group.

The fourth concern of social psychology is the impact of one group on the activities and structure of another group. Relations between two groups may be friendly or hostile, cooperative or competitive. This relationship can affect the structure and activities of each. Of special interest is *intergroup conflict*, with its accompanying tension and hostility. Violence may flare up, for instance, between two teenage street gangs disputing territorial rights or between racial groups competing for scarce jobs. Conflicts of this type affect the interpersonal relations between groups as well as within each group. Social psychologists have long been interested in the emergence, persistence, and resolution of intergroup conflict.

A Formal Definition of Social Psychology

As indicated in the above discussion, social psychology is a broad field covering many topics. In essence, *social psychology may be defined as that field which systematically studies the nature and causes of human social behavior.*

Note certain features of this definition. First, it indicates that the main concern of social psychology is human social behavior. This includes many things—the activities of individuals in the context of others, the processes of social interaction between two or more persons, and even the relationships between individuals and the groups of which they are part.

Not only is social psychology concerned with the nature of social behavior, but also with the causes of such behavior. That is, it seeks to discover the conditions that produce any given social behavior. At its simplest, a causal statement takes the form, "Whenever X occurs, then Y occurs." In social psychology, however, few causal statements are this elementary or unconditional. More typical are qualified statements like, "Whenever conditions A, B, C, and D are present and X occurs,

then Y occurs." Such statements obviously are more restricted in generality and explanatory power. Causal statements are the important building blocks of theory, and theory in turn is crucial for the prediction and control of social behavior.

Finally, the definition indicates that social psychologists approach the study of social behavior in a systematic fashion. They rely explicitly on a research methodology when taking observations of social behavior. This methodology, which is scientific in character, includes formal procedures such as experimentation, structured observation, and sample surveys to test theories of social behavior. A more detailed description of this research methodology appears in the Appendix.

Relation to Other Fields

Social psychology bears a close relationship to several other fields, especially sociology and psychology. To understand this relationship, first consider these other fields.

Sociology is the scientific study of human society. It includes topics such as social institutions (family, religion, and politics), stratification within society (class structure, race and ethnicity, sex roles), basic social processes (socialization, interaction, social control), and the structure of social units (groups, networks, formal organizations, and bureaucracies).

In contrast, *psychology* is the scientific study of the individual and individual behavior. This behavior may be social in character, but it need not be. Psychology includes such topics as human learning, perception, memory, intelligence, emotion, motivation, and personality.

Social psychology bridges the gap between sociology and psychology. In fact, it is sometimes viewed as an interdisciplinary field. Both sociologists and psychologists have contributed to social psychological knowledge. Social psychologists working in the sociological tradition rely primarily on sample surveys and other systematic observational techniques to gather data. The subject that interests them most is the relationships between individuals and the groups to which they belong. This leads to an emphasis on such processes as socialization, conformity and deviation, social interaction, leadership, recruitment to membership, cooperation and competition, and the like. Social psychologists working in the psychological tradition rely heavily on laboratory experimental methodology. Their primary concern is how an individual's behavior and internal states are affected by social stimuli (often other persons). This includes such topics as person perception and attribution, attitudes and attitude change, personality differences in social behavior, social learning and modeling, altruism and aggression, and so on.

Thus, sociologically oriented and psychologically oriented social psychologists differ in their outlooks and concerns. As might be expected, this leads them to formulate different theories and to conduct different research programs. Yet in the end these differences are best viewed as complementary rather than as conflicting. Social psychology as a field is richer for them.

Theoretical Perspectives in Social Psychology

Yesterday was a bad day for Roger. First thing in the morning, Roger went to work and told his boss that he would not be able to complete his project on schedule. The boss got furious, screamed at Roger, and told him to complete the work by Monday—or else! Roger was not entirely sure what to make of the older man's behavior, but he decided to take the threat seriously. That evening, talking with his girlfriend Alice, Roger announced that he could not take her out to a party on Friday evening as originally planned because he had to work overtime at the office to complete the project. Alice immediately got mad at Roger and threw a pan at him. By now, Roger was very upset.

Reflecting on these events, Roger noticed that they had some features in common. To explain the behavior of his boss and his girlfriend, he formed a general proposition: "If you fail to deliver on promises and block someone's goals, he or she will get mad at you." He was happy with this theory until he read a curious newspaper story: "MAN IS FIRED FROM JOB, THEN SHOOTS HIS DOG." Roger wondered about this event, and then concluded that his own theory needed revision. The new version included several propositions: "If someone's goals are blocked, he or she will become frustrated. If someone is frustrated, he or she will become aggressive. If someone is aggressive, he or she will attack either the source of the frustration or a convenient surrogate."

On an informal basis, Roger is starting to do the same thing that social psychologists do more systematically. Working from some observed facts regarding social behavior, Roger is attempting to formulate a theory to explain what he has observed.

Defined in general terms, a **theory** is a set of interrelated propositions that organizes and explains a set of observed facts. Theories are not meant to be about particular events but about whole classes of events. Moreover, as the example of Roger indicates, a theory goes beyond mere observable facts because it postulates (causal) relations between concepts. If a theory is valid, it enables its user to explain the phenomena under consideration and to make predictions regarding events not yet observed.

Theory is a crucial element in social psychology. The field includes not one, but a large number of them. It is useful to treat these theories as falling into several categories. Some social psychological theories are scientific or causal in character. Typically, theories of this type are narrow and tightly focused; they seek to explain the conditions that give rise to some specific form of social behavior. For example, one such theory attempts to explain how people will react if they are treated unfairly or inequitably. Another theory specifies the conditions under which contact between members of different racial groups will cause stereotypes to fade or disappear. Theories of this type are presented in various places throughout this book.

In addition, social psychology includes other theories that are much broader in scope. Theories of this type make sweeping assumptions about human nature and offer general explanations of a wide range of diverse social behaviors. Broad theories of this type are termed **theoretical perspectives.**

Theoretical perspectives have a particular value. By adopting specific assumptions regarding human nature, a theoretical perspective provides a lens (or point of view) through which we can examine a wide range of social behaviors. Any lens (such as a microscope or telescope) provides a sharp and penetrating focus on certain features of reality. In the same way, a theoretical perspective—by emphasizing certain notions and downplaying others—enables us to "see" features of social behavior not otherwise apparent. Of course, no two theoretical perspectives emphasize exactly the same concepts and processes; each perspective will highlight different features of a given social situation. The fundamental value of theoretical perspectives lies in their generality; they provide a frame of reference in terms of which we can observe a wide range of social situations and behaviors.

Like many fields of study, social psychology includes several distinct theoretical perspectives. Four of the more important ones are (1) role theory, (2) reinforcement theory, (3) cognitive theory, and (4) symbolic interactionist theory. Each of these perspectives will be discussed.

Role Theory

Several months ago, Barbara was asked to participate in a stage production of Molière's comedy *The Learned Woman*. She was offered the role of Martine, a kitchen servant who is dismissed from her job for using poor grammar. Barbara enthusiastically accepted the offer and learned her part well. The theatre group presented the play six times over a period of three weeks. Barbara played the role of Martine in the first four shows, but then she got sick. Fortunately, another woman (Barbara's understudy) was able to substitute as Martine during the final two shows. Barbara's performance was very good, but so was the understudy's. In fact, one critic wrote that it was difficult to tell them apart.

Barbara's friend, Craig, is more interested in football than in theatre. A member of the college football team, Craig plays the position of fullback. Although very large and strong, he is only a third-stringer. The coach has sent him in to play in several games, but he still makes mistakes. He has the unfortunate habit of fumbling the ball, usually at the worst possible moment. Craig believes, however, that with another year's experience and some improvements in his technique, he will be able to perform better than the other fullbacks and win a place in the team's starting lineup.

Although active in different arenas, Craig and Barbara have something in common: they are both performing roles. When Barbara appears on stage, she performs the role of kitchen servant. When Craig appears on the football field, he performs the role of fullback. In both cases, their behavior is guided by a set of culturally specified plans or blueprints. Barbara's role is very specific; her part calls for her to say certain things and perform certain actions at specified points in the plot. There is little room for her to improvise or deviate from her lines. Craig's role is also quite specific. He has to carry out certain assignments on each of the plays run by his team. Although he still makes mistakes, he tries hard to perform his role.

In everyday life, we all perform roles. Anyone who holds a job can be viewed as performing a role. For example, an advertising executive's job description does not dictate exactly what lines are to be spoken, but it will certainly specify what goals must be accomplished and what performances are required to attain these goals.

Role theory (Biddle and Thomas 1966; Sarbin and Allen 1968; Heiss 1981) is based on a theatrical metaphor. It holds that a substantial proportion of observable, day-to-day social behavior is simply persons carrying out their roles, much as actors carry out their roles on the stage or ballplayers theirs on the field. The following propositions are central to the role theory perspective:

1. People do not usually live in social isolation; instead, they spend much of their lives participating as members of groups and organizations.

2. Within these groups people occupy distinct positions (kitchen servant, fullback, advertising executive, and so on).

3. Each of these positions entails a **role**, which is a set of functions performed by the person on behalf of the group. A person's role is defined by how other group members expect him or her to perform.

4. These expectations are formalized as **norms,** which are rules specifying how a person should and should not behave.

5. In most cases, individuals perform in accordance with prevailing norms. In other words, people are conformists; they try to meet the expectations held by others.

6. Group members evaluate an individual's performance to determine whether it is aligned with the norms and they respond accordingly. If the individual meets the role expectations held by others, then he or she will be rewarded. If, on the other hand, he or she fails to perform as expected, then group members will embarrass, punish, or even expel that person

from the group. The anticipation that sanctions will be applied by others helps to insure that persons perform as expected.

Role theory implies that when we are given information about the role expectations for a specified position, we should be able to predict a significant portion of the behavior of the person occupying that position. Moreover, role theory implies that to change a person's behavior, it is necessary either to modify the expectations that define the person's role or to shift the person into an entirely different role. For example, if the football coach shifted Craig from fullback to tackle, Craig's behavior would quickly change to match the role expectations of his new position.

Role theory maintains that a person's role determines not only behavior, but also beliefs and attitudes. In other words, individuals bring their attitudes into congruence with the expectations that define their roles. A change in role would lead to a change in attitude. One illustration of this appears in a well-known study of factory workers (Lieberman 1965). In the initial stage of this study, researchers measured the attitudes of workers in a midwestern home-appliance factory toward union and management policies. During the following year, a number of these workers changed roles. Some were promoted to the position of foreman, a managerial role. Others were elected to the position of shop steward, a union role.

About a year after the initial measurement, workers' attitudes were reassessed. The attitudes of persons who had become foremen or shop stewards were compared to those of workers who had not changed roles. The recently promoted foremen expressed more positive attitudes than the nonchangers toward the company's management and the company's incentive system (which paid workers in proportion to what they produced). Similarly, recently elected shop stewards expressed more positive attitudes than the nonchangers toward the union and favored an incentive system based on seniority, not pro-

On the assembly line, these men perform tasks and enact roles specified by their work group.

ductivity. In effect, the workers' attitudes shifted to fit their new roles, as predicted by role theory.

Thus, in general, the roles that people occupy not only channel their behavior but also shape their attitudes. Roles can also influence the values that people hold and even affect the direction of their personal growth and development. These topics are discussed in more depth in chapters 4 and 16.

Despite its usefulness, role theory runs into problems with respect to certain kinds of social behavior. Foremost among these is **deviant behavior,** which is any behavior that violates or contravenes the norms defining a given role. Virtually all forms of deviant behavior, whether simply a refusal to perform as expected or something more serious like commission of a crime, are disruptive to ongoing interpersonal relations. The occurrence of deviant behavior poses a challenge to role theory, because it flies in the face of the assumption that people conform to norms. Of course, a certain amount of deviant behavior can be explained by the fact that people are sometimes ignorant of the norms or may face conflicting and incompatible expectations from several other people. In general, however, deviant behavior is an unexplained and problematic exception from the standpoint of role theory. Chapters 12 and 17 discuss the conditions that give rise to deviant behavior, as well as the reactions of others to such behavior.

However, even critics of role theory acknowledge that a substantial portion of all social behavior can be explained in terms of conformity to established role expectations. But role theory does not and cannot explain how role expectations come to be what they are in the first place. Nor does it explain when and how role expectations change. Without accomplishing these tasks, role theory can provide no more than a partial—and ultimately incomplete—explanation of social behavior.

Reinforcement Theory

Reinforcement theory is based on the premise that social behavior is governed by external events, especially rewards and punishments. One illustration of this comes from a study by Verplanck (1955). The point of this study was to show that the course of conversation between persons can be altered by the use of social approval (a reward). Students working with Verplanck sought out situations in which each could be alone with another person and conduct a conversation. During the first 10 minutes, the student engaged the other in polite but neutral chitchat; the student was careful neither to reject nor to support opinions expressed by the other. During this period the student privately noted the number of opinions expressed by the other and recorded this information unobtrusively by doodling on a piece of paper.

After this initial period, the student shifted behavior and indicated approval whenever the other ventured an opinion. The student expressed approval by saying such things as "I agree," "That's so," or "You're right," or by smiling and nodding in agreement. The student continued this for 10 minutes, all the while noting the number of opinions mentioned by the other. The result of this behavior was to substantially increase the rate at which the other expressed opinions.

Next, the student shifted behavior again, and suspended rewards. Any opinions expressed by the other were met with noncommittal remarks or subtle disagreement. As before, the number of opinions was recorded.

The results of the study are clear-cut. All persons increased the rate at which they expressed opinions during the "reward period" as compared with the initial period. Then, during the "extinction period" (when the student suspended approval), about 90 percent reduced the rate at which they expressed opinions. Their behavior was substantially influenced by social approval.

Reinforcement theory has a long tradition, beginning with research by Pavlov (1910) and Thorndike (1913) and evolving through the work of Allport (1924), Hull (1943), and Skinner (1953, 1971). The reinforcement perspective holds that social behavior is determined primarily by external events, not by internal psychological states. Thus the central concepts of reinforcement theory refer to events that are directly observable. Any event that leads to an alteration or change in a behavior is called a **stimulus.** For example, a traffic light that changes to red is a stimulus, as is a wailing tornado siren. The change in behavior induced by a stimulus is called a **response.** Drivers respond to red lights by stopping; families respond to tornado sirens by rushing to their basements for shelter. The concept of **reinforcement** refers to anything that strengthens a response. In Verplanck's study, for example, the students' social approval was a reinforcement that strengthened the response of expressing opinions.

Reinforcement theory has been used to explain many processes of interest in social psychology. Reinforcement theory has made especially important contributions in two areas—social learning and social exchange.

SOCIAL LEARNING THEORY. The basic proposition of social learning theory is that a person learns (that is, acquires new responses) through the application of reinforcement. The name given to this process is **conditioning.** Specifically, if a person performs a particular response, and if this response is then reinforced, the response is strengthened. The person will be more likely to emit the same response again. For example, if a young child, Karl, helps his father rake the leaves, and if his father reinforces this behavior with approval or money, then Karl will be increasingly inclined to help with yard work in the future.

A closely related process, *discrimination learning*, occurs when a person comes to identify the exact conditions under which a response will be reinforced. For example, Karl has learned that if his mother rings the dinner bell (a stimulus), he should respond by coming indoors, washing his hands, and sitting in the appropriate place at the table. His mother will then put food on his plate (a reinforcer). He has also learned, however, that if he performs the response (washing his hands and sitting down) without first hearing the stimulus (dinner bell), his mother will merely tell him that he's too early and cannot have food until later. He has further discovered that a partial response (sitting down at the table without first washing) is met not with food but with reprimands to wash up. Thus, through discrimination learning, Karl understands that reinforcement (food) is obtained only by making the full response in the presence of the bell stimulus.

Although conditioning is the most fundamental mechanism of learning, people frequently acquire new responses through the process of **imitation** (Bandura 1962, 1977). Certainly children learn many things by imitating their parents or older siblings. Adults also learn from one another by this means. Imitation differs from conditioning in that the learner neither performs a response nor receives any reinforcement. Instead the learner watches another person's response and observes whether that person receives any reinforcement.

For example, a young girl might observe that her older sister puts on makeup before going out with friends and that she is rewarded (with social approval) for doing this. Noting the connection between the response

(applying makeup) and the subsequent reinforcement from others, she might infer that if she behaves like her older sister, she will receive reinforcement herself. Thus, she may mimic or copy her sister's behavior and apply cosmetics.

In sum, social learning theory holds that persons acquire new responses both through conditioning and through imitation. In this way, the theory can explain how persons acquire complex responses such as those learned during socialization. Chapters 3 and 4 discuss this in more detail.

SOCIAL EXCHANGE THEORY. Another theory based on the principle of reinforcement is **social exchange theory** (Homans 1961, 1974; Kelley and Thibaut 1978; Emerson 1981). Social exchange theory uses the concept of reinforcement to explain stability and change in interaction between individuals. It assumes that individuals have freedom of choice and often face social situations in which they must choose among alternative actions. Any action provides some rewards and entails some costs. Rewards can assume many forms; they include not only money, goods, and services, but also prestige, status, and approval by others. The theory posits that individuals are hedonistic—they try to maximize rewards and minimize costs. Consequently, they will choose whatever actions produce the best profits (profits = rewards − costs).

Social exchange theory maintains that people will establish stable relationships only if they find it profitable to continue their exchange of goods and/or services. An individual judges the attractiveness of a relationship by comparing the profits it provides against the profits available in other, alternative relationships. The profit available in the best alternative relationship is termed the individual's **comparison level for alternatives.** To illustrate this concept, suppose that an engineer employed by an aircraft manufacturer is offered a highly attractive, profitable

An auctioneer solicits bids at a thoroughbred auction. The horse will be sold to the highest bidder. An exciting form of social exchange, auctions are used to determine prices in circumstances where no one knows beforehand what an item is worth.

job by a competing firm. The new job entails some additional responsibilities, but it also pays a much higher salary and provides more benefits. This job offer has the effect of substantially increasing the engineer's comparison level for alternatives. In this case, exchange theory predicts that the engineer will either leave her job for the new one, or will stay with her current employer and be pro-

moted to a new position with higher rewards (more salary, benefits, and so on).

These ideas apply not only to work relations but also to personal relations. For instance, a recent study of heterosexual couples in long-term dating relationships shows that rewards and costs can explain whether persons stay in or leave such relationships (Rusbult 1980, 1983). Results of this study indicate that persons are more likely to stay when their partner is physically and personally attractive, when the relationship does not entail undue hassle (high monetary costs, broken promises, arguments), and when romantic involvements with attractive outsiders are not readily available. In other words, they are more likely to stay when the rewards are high, the costs are low, and the comparison level for alternatives is low. Findings of this type are predicted by exchange theory.

Exchange theory also predicts the conditions under which persons will try to change or restructure their relationships. Central to this is the concept of **equity** (Homans 1961; Adams 1963). Equity prevails in a relationship when people feel that the rewards each of them receives are proportional to the costs they each bear. For example, a supervisor may earn more money than a line worker and receive better benefits on the job. But the worker may still feel that the relationship is equitable because the supervisor bears more responsibility and has a higher level of education.

When equity is absent—that is, when people feel their relationship is inequitable—the relationship is potentially unstable. Persons find inequity difficult to tolerate—they feel cheated or exploited and become angry. Exchange theory predicts that people will try to modify an inequitable relationship. Most likely, they will attempt reallocation of the costs and rewards so that equity is established.

Despite its usefulness in illuminating why relationships change and how people learn, reinforcement theory has been criticized on various grounds. One criticism is that reinforcement theory portrays persons primarily as reacting to environmental stimuli, rather than as initiating behavior based on imaginative or creative thought. Thus, the theory does not account for creativity, innovation, and invention. A second criticism is that reinforcement theory largely ignores or downplays other motivations. It characterizes social behavior as hedonistic, with persons striving to obtain rewards or maximize profits. Thus, it cannot easily explain selfless behavior such as altruism and martyrdom. Despite its limitations, reinforcement theory has enjoyed substantial success in explaining how persons learn new behaviors and influence the behavior of others. Ideas based on reinforcement and exchange theory are discussed throughout this book, especially in chapters 3, 7, 9, 11, and 13.

Cognitive Theory

The basic premise of **cognitive theory** is that the mental activities of the individual are important determinants of behavior. These mental activities, called **cognitive processes,** include perception, reasoning, memory, problem solving, decision making, and the like. Cognitive theory does not deny the importance of external stimuli, but it maintains that the link between stimulus and response is not automatic or mechanical. Instead, the individual's cognitive processes intervene between external stimuli and behavioral responses. According to cognitive theory, the mind not only interprets the meaning of stimuli but also selects the actions made in response to stimuli.

Cognitive theory stresses that people do more than react to their environment; they actively structure their world. People are highly selective in perceiving the environment. Because they cannot possibly attend to all the stimuli that surround them, they select only those that are important or useful to them. Other stimuli are ignored. Moreover, persons choose the categories or concepts they will use to interpret the stimuli. One implication of this, of course, is that several individuals can form dramatically different impressions of a single complex stimulus.

Consider, for example, what happens when several people view a vacant house displaying a bright "for rent" sign. When a building contractor passes the house, he scrutinizes the construction closely. He sees lumber,

Persons view a diamond in different ways. To a diamond merchant, it is a marketable piece of hard carbon with various attributes—color, clarity, cut, and carat. To this woman, it symbolizes enduring love.

bricks, shingles, glass—and some repairs that should soon be made. Another person, a potential renter, sees the house very differently. He notes that it is located close to his job and wonders whether the neighborhood is safe and whether the house is expensive to heat. The realtor trying to rent the house construes it in still different terms—cash flow, occupancy rate, depreciation, mortgage, and amortization. One of the kids living in the neighborhood has yet another view: noting that no one has lived in the house for several months, he is convinced the house is haunted.

Cognitive theorists (Krech and Crutchfield 1948; Lewin 1951; Neisser 1967; Markus and Zajonc 1985) depict humans as active not only in selecting and interpreting images, but also in such other aspects of information processing as thinking, planning, decision making and problem solving. The emphasis on the processing of information reflects the influence of the early Gestalt movement in psychology (Koffka 1935; Kohler 1947). Central to Gestalt psychology is the principle that people respond to configurations of stimuli rather than to a single, discrete stimulus. In other words, people understand the meaning of a stimulus only by viewing it in the context of an entire system of elements in which it is embedded. To comprehend any part, one must look at the whole. A chess master, for example, would never assess the importance of a chess piece on the board without considering its location and strategic capabilities vis-à-vis all the other pieces on the board; a valid assessment could not be made otherwise.

One concept central to this perspective is **cognitive structure,** which broadly refers to any form of organization among cognitions. Because a person's cognitions (that is, concepts, beliefs, and attitudes) are interrelated, cognitive theory gives special emphasis to exactly how they are structured or organized. One way to study this organization is to investigate the changes that occur in cognitions when approach under attack or strain. The changes that result will reveal something about their underlying structure or organization.

An important principle emerging from this approach is the **principle of consistency** (Heider 1958; Newcomb 1968). This principle maintains that, if a person holds several ideas that are incongruous or inconsistent with each other, discomfort or conflict will be experienced and one or more of the ideas subsequently will be changed to render them consistent. Only by changing ideas and making them consistent will the internal conflict be resolved. As an illustration, suppose you hold the following cognitions about your friend Jeff: (1) Jeff has been a good friend for six years; (2) You dislike hard drugs and the people who use them; and (3) Jeff has recently started using hard drugs. These cognitions are obviously interrelated, and they are also incongruous with one another. The principle of consistency predicts that some change in cognitions will likely occur. That is, you will change either your negative attitude toward drugs or your positive attitude toward Jeff, or possibly you will intervene and try to change Jeff's behavior. Social psychologists have developed several theories based on the general notion of consistency. The *theory of cognitive dissonance* and *balance theory* are two examples. Each is discussed in Chapter 6.

Cognitive theorists maintain that a person's ideas are causal factors in behavior. They criticize reinforcement theorists for overplaying the importance of direct linkages between stimulus and response and for neglecting conscious deliberation and thought. Cognitive theorists argue that cognitive processes intervene between stimulus and response. Thus two people can react to a single stimulus in different ways, depending on the meanings they ascribe to it. A stockholder, for example, noting that the price of his company's stock is falling sharply in reaction to lower earnings, might panic and sell all his holdings; another stockholder, interpreting the company's prospects differently, might react to the decline by buying more at what she considers a bargain price. Different interpretations produce divergent responses.

Cognitive theory has made many important contributions to social psychology. It treats such diverse phenomena as self-concept (Chapter 2), perception of persons and attribution of causes (Chapter 8), attitude change (Chapter 6), helping and aggression (Chapter 10), and intergroup stereotypes (Chapter 15). This perspective has produced many insights and striking predictions regarding individual and social behavior.

One drawback of cognitive theory is that, while dealing with phenomena that are highly complex, it necessarily simplifies—and sometimes oversimplifies—the ways in which people process information. Another drawback is that cognitive phenomena are not directly observable (that is, they are located "in the head" of the individual, and thus must be inferred from behavior); this means that compelling and definitive tests are often difficult to conduct. Overall, however, the cognitive perspective is among the more popular and productive approaches within social psychology.

Symbolic Interactionist Theory

A fourth perspective in social psychology is **symbolic interactionism** (Mead 1934, 1938; Blumer 1969; Shibutani 1961; Kuhn 1964; Stryker 1980). Like the cognitive perspective, symbolic interactionism stresses cognitive processes (thinking, reasoning, planning), but places more emphasis on interaction between persons.

The basic premise of symbolic interactionism is that human nature and social order are products of communication among people. In this perspective, a person's behavior is constructed through give-and-take during interaction with others. Thus, behavior is not merely a response to stimuli; nor is it an expression of inner biological drives, profit-maximization, or conformity to norms. Rather, a person's behavior emerges through communication and interaction with others.

People succeed in communicating with one another only to the extent that they ascribe similar **meanings** to objects. The meaning of an object to a person depends not so much on the properties of the object itself, but on what the person might do with the object. In other words, an object takes on meaning only in relation to a person's plans. A wine merchant, for example, might see a glass bottle as a container for his product; an interior decorator might see it as a vase for some paper flowers; a man in a drunken brawl might see it as a weapon with which to hit his opponent.

Symbolic interactionist theory views humans as goal-seeking and proactive. Persons formulate plans of action to achieve their goals. Many plans, of course, can be brought to realization only through cooperation with other people. To establish cooperation with others, meanings of things must be shared and consensual. If the meaning of something relevant is unclear or involves differences, an agreement must be developed through give-and-take before cooperative action is possible. For example, if a man and woman have just begun to date one another, and he invites her up to his apartment, exactly what meaning does this proposed visit have? One way or another, they will have to achieve some agreement regarding the purpose of the visit before cooperative action is possible. A symbolic interactionist would describe this as developing a consensual **definition of the situation.** The couple might achieve this through explicit negotiation or even through nonverbal communication. But without agreement on the definition of the situation, the woman will have difficulty in deciding whether to accept the invitation, and cooperative action will be impossible.

Symbolic interactionism portrays social interaction as having a tentative, developing quality. To fit their actions together and achieve consensus, persons interacting with one another must continually negotiate new meanings or reaffirm old meanings. Each person plans some actions, tries them out, and then adjusts his or her plans and behaviors in response to the other. Thus, social interaction inherently has some degree of unpredictability and indeterminacy.

Central to social interaction is the process of **role taking,** in which one individual interacting with another imagines how he or she looks from the other person's standpoint. For example, if an employee is seeking a raise in salary, he might first imagine how his boss would react to one type of request or another. To do this, he might draw on knowledge of his past interactions with her, as well as what he has heard from others about her reactions to such requests. By viewing his own action from her standpoint, he may be able to anticipate what type of request is most likely to achieve the desired effect. If he then actually makes a request of the type he expects her to approve, and if she reacts as expected, his role taking has succeeded. Thus, through this role-taking process, cooperative interaction is established.

For interaction to proceed smoothly, a person must achieve consensus with respect to his or her **self** and the identity of others. For each person there must be an answer to the question, "Who am I in this situation, and who are the other people?" Only when this question is answered consensually can persons understand the implications (meanings) that others have for their own plans of action.

Sometimes a person's self is very unusual, with the result that interaction becomes awkward, difficult, or even impossible. One example is Cervantes's tale of a man, temporarily deranged, who thought he was made of glass (Shibutani 1961). His conception of himself created problems both for him and for others. Whenever people came near, he screamed and implored them to keep away for fear they would shatter him. He refused to eat anything hard and insisted upon sleeping in beds of soft straw. Concerned that loose tiles might fall on him from the rooftops, he walked only in the middle of the street. Once, when a wasp stung him in the neck, he did not swat it away because he was afraid of smashing himself. Since glass is transparent while skin is not, he claimed that his body's unusual construction enabled his soul to perceive things more clearly than others, and he offered to assist persons perplexed by difficult problems. Gradually he developed a reputation for astonishing insight, and many persons came to him seeking advice. In the end, a wealthy patron hired a bodyguard to protect him from outlaws

Easy, fluid communication between two persons requires a high degree of consensus regarding personal identities and the meaning of symbols.

and mischievous boys who threw stones at him.

These days, of course, it is unlikely that we would meet such a person. But we might encounter persons who believe they are unusually fragile or remarkably strong or superhumanly intelligent or in contact with the supernatural. Persons with unusual self-concepts can create problems in social interaction because they make it difficult to achieve consensus regarding identities. Cooperative action is virtually impossible without such consensus, for people will simply not know what to expect from individuals who insist they are Napoleon, Goldilocks, or Superman.

The self occupies a central place in symbolic interactionist theory because social order is hypothesized to rest largely upon self-control. Coordination between individuals is possible because each person controls himself from within. The individual strives to maintain self-respect in his own eyes, but because he is continually engaging in role taking, he sees himself from the standpoint of the other persons with whom he interacts. Thus, he can maintain self-respect only by meeting the standards of others.

Of course, the individual cares more about the opinions and standards of some persons than of others. The persons whose opinions he cares most about are termed **significant others.** Typically, these are persons who control important rewards or who occupy central positions in groups to which the individual belongs. Because their standards are valued, significant others will have relatively more influence over the individual's behavior.

In sum, the symbolic interactionist perspective has several strong points. It recognizes the importance of the self in social interaction. It stresses the central role of symbolic communication and language in personality and society. It explicitly treats the processes involved in achieving consensus and cooperation. And it illuminates why people try to maintain face and avoid embarrassment. Many of these topics are discussed in detail in later chapters. The self is discussed in Chapter 2, symbolic communication and language are taken up in Chapter 5, and self-presentation and impression management are treated in Chapter 9.

Critics of symbolic interactionism have pointed out its various shortcomings. One criticism concerns the balance between rationality and emotion. Some critics argue that this perspective overemphasizes rational, self-conscious thought and deemphasizes unconscious or emotional states. A second criticism concerns the implicit model of the individual. In symbolic interactionist theory, the individual appears to be a particular personality type (the "other directed" person) who is concerned primarily with maintaining self-respect by meeting others' standards. A third criticism of symbolic interactionism is that is places too much emphasis on consensus and cooperation, and neglects conflict. The perspective does recognize, however, that interacting persons may fail to reach consensus, despite their best efforts to achieve it. The symbolic interactionist perspective is at its best when analyzing fluid, noncommittal encounters and at its worst when analyzing self-interested behavior or emotionally committed relationships.

A Comparison of Perspectives

The four theoretical perspectives discussed above differ in the issues they address and the issues they choose to ignore. They also differ with respect to the variables they each consider important and those they treat as irrelevant or incidental. In effect, each perspective makes different assumptions about social behavior.

In this section, we will compare the various perspectives in terms of four dimensions: (1) the theory's central concept or focus; (2) the primary social behaviors explained by the theory; (3) the theory's basic assumptions regarding human nature; and (4) the factors that, according to the theory, must change in order to produce a change in a person's behavior. Table 1.1 summarizes this comparison by showing the position of each perspective on each of these dimensions.

CENTRAL CONCEPTS. Each of the four theoretical perspectives places primary emphasis on different concepts. Role theory places emphasis on roles, which are defined by group members' expectations regarding performance. Reinforcement theory explains observable social behavior in terms of the relationship between stimulus and response and the application of reinforcement. Cognitive theory stresses the importance of cognitions and cognitive structure in determining behavior. Symbolic interactionist theory emphasizes the self and role taking as crucial to the processes of social interaction.

BEHAVIORS EXPLAINED. Although overlapping to some degree, the four theoretical perspectives differ with respect to the behaviors or outcomes they attempt to explain. Role theory places greatest emphasis on behavior in role and on the attitude change that results from occupying roles. Reinforcement theory focuses on the acquisition of new response patterns (that is, learning) and on the impact that

TABLE 1.1
Comparison of Theoretical Perspectives in Social Psychology

	Role Theory	Reinforcement Theory	Cognitive Theory	Symbolic Interaction Theory
Central Concepts	Role	Stimulus-Response, Reinforcement	Cognitions, Cognitive Structure	Self, Role taking
Primary Behaviors Explained	Behavior in role	Learning of new responses; exchange processes	Formation and change of beliefs and attitudes	Sequences of acts occurring in interaction
Assumptions about Human Nature	People are conformist and behave in accordance with role expectations	People are hedonistic; their acts are determined by patterns of reinforcement	People are cognitive beings who act on the basis of their cognitions	People are self-monitoring actors who use role taking in interaction
Factors that Produce Change in Behavior	Shift in role expectations	Change in amount, type, or frequency of reinforcement	State of cognitive inconsistency	Shift in others' standards, in terms of which self-respect is established

rewards and punishments have on social interaction. Cognitive theory centers primarily on the mediating effect that cognitions have on a person's overt response to social stimuli, but it also treats changes in beliefs and attitudes. Symbolic interactionism is concerned primarily with sequences of behaviors occurring in interaction among people.

ASSUMPTIONS ABOUT HUMAN NATURE. The four theoretical perspectives differ also with respect to their fundamental assumptions regarding human nature. Role theory, for instance, assumes that people are largely conformist. It views people as characteristically acting in accord with role expectations held by group members. In contrast, reinforcement theory views people's acts—what they learn and how they perform—as determined primarily by patterns of reinforcement. Cognitive theory stresses that people perceive, interpret, and make decisions about the world. They

formulate concepts and develop beliefs, and they act on the basis of these structured cognitions. Symbolic interactionist theory assumes that the person is a conscious, self-monitoring being who uses role taking to achieve goals in interactions with others.

CHANGE IN BEHAVIOR. The four theoretical perspectives differ in their conception of what produces change in behavior. Role theory maintains that, to change someone's behavior, it is necessary to change the role he or she occupies. Different behavior will result when the person shifts roles, because the new role will entail different expectations. Reinforcement theory, in contrast, argues that change in behavior results from changes in the type, amount, and frequency of reinforcement received. Cognitive theory maintains that change in behavior results from changes in beliefs and attitudes; it further postulates that changes in beliefs and attitudes result from efforts to resolve inconsistency or internal conflict among cognitions. Symbolic interactionism holds that people try to maintain self-respect by meeting the standards of others; it also stresses that the issue of which standards are relevant is usually resolved through negotiation. To produce change in behavior, the standards held by others and accepted as relevant must shift first. A person would detect this shift in standards (by role taking) and consequently change behavior.

Is Social Psychology a Science?

Social psychology is that field which systematically studies the nature and causes of human social behavior. The field includes not only theoretical perspectives, but also predictive theories and a large body of accumulated facts obtained through empirical investigation. But one can still ask whether social psychology is truly a science. That is, can we consider social psychology to be a scientific field in the same sense that we might consider physics or biology to be scientific?

Characteristics of Science

Any scientific field rests on three basic assumptions. First, there is a real, external world that exists independent of the way we experience it. This world is subject to investigation by observers. Second, scientists assume that relations in this world are organized in terms of cause and effect. This assumption—which in practice is a working hypothesis—is termed the **principle of determinism.** In its starkest form, this principle holds that there are discoverable causes for all events in a science's domain of interest. Third, scientists assume that knowledge concerning this external world is objective; facts can be discovered by one scientist and then verified by others.

In addition to these assumptions, any field that is a science has certain characteristics or hallmarks. These include the following:

1. Any science is based on *observation of facts.* No field without observation can be a science. This means that "armchair" disciplines lacking practitioners who take observations cannot be scientific fields.

2. Any science uses an explicit, formal *methodology.* This methodology is a set of procedures that must be followed by scientists when establishing facts as known. Because any investigator in the field can use this methodology, one scientist's findings can in principle be verified by others.

3. Any science involves the *cumulation of facts.* That is, once relationships are observed to exist in the world, this knowledge is never lost. Of course, facts sometimes undergo reinterpretation of meaning, but the essential information is still available.

4. Any science includes a body of *theory.* This consists of at least one (but often many) theories that serve to systematize and organize empirical observations. Theory also serves to guide new, empirical investigation.

5. After it attains a reasonable level of development, any science provides at least some degree of *prediction and control* over selected aspects of the environment.

If you hold up a well-developed natural science such as physics or biology against this list, you will see immediately that it has all these hallmarks. These sciences are based on observation of the world, have a formal methodology to guide research, have an accumulation of many facts, possess a body of well-developed theory, and provide at least a moderate degree of prediction and/or control regarding selected aspects of the world.

Social Psychology as a Science

Can social psychology be considered a science? That is, if we hold it up against these criteria, will it measure up?

Social psychology certainly has some of the hallmarks of science. For instance, consider the first hallmark—reliance on empirical observation. Clearly, social psychology is based on empirical observation and classification of facts. The field consists of many thousands of empirical studies. Social psychology also meets the second hallmark, for it relies upon widely shared methodological procedures for conducting empirical investigation. Among the most widely employed methods within social psychology are experimentation and systematic sample surveys. (See the Methods Appendix at the back of this book for more details on methodology in social psychology.)

It is also fair to say that social psychology meets the third hallmark, the cumulation of observed facts. Social psychologists continue to gather facts regarding the conditions under which specific behaviors occur. Of course, more is known about some types of behavior than others, but increasingly sophisticated studies have continued to expand the frontiers of knowledge regarding social behavior.

Social psychology also tests moderately well against the fourth criteria, the reliance on theory. While social psychology has no single, unified theory covering all phenomena in the field, it does include several broad theoretical perspectives (such as those reviewed above). It also has numerous limited or "middle-range" theories that make predictions regarding specific types of social behavior under restricted conditions. We will encounter many of these limited theories in subsequent chapters of this book.

If any problem arises for social psychology as a science, it is primarily with respect to the fifth hallmark. This hallmark holds that, after attaining a reasonable level of development, any science should be able to provide some useful degree of prediction and/or control with respect to the phenomena investigated by the field. There is some question whether social psychology can accomplish this feat.

Although social psychology does fairly well in "explaining" social behavior (that is,

identifying the conditions under which various forms of social behavior occur), it does less well in predicting future events or in providing a basis for control of behavior. Of course, it is possible to point to some successes in prediction and control. For example, political election forecasts based on sample surveys have been fairly accurate in recent years, and programs for modification of interpersonal behavior based on reinforcement principles have proved effective. Nevertheless, social psychology does not excel in prediction and control; certainly it is no match for the mature physical sciences in this respect.

Part of the problem stems from the nature of social psychological theory. Few of the existing theories that make explicit predictions have much generality. They cover only limited ranges of phenomena, or apply only under very restrictive (and sometimes artificial) conditions. Often, the theories fail to predict accurately when attempts are made to apply them to new settings.

If the problem ran no deeper than this, we might be optimistic that social psychology will someday be able to predict behavior successfully. We might conclude that all social psychology needs is better, more refined theories. To some degree this is true, but unfortunately the problem is more complex.

As noted above, any science is based on the principle of determinism; it assumes the world is organized in terms of cause and effect. Science tries to develop laws based on the notion that if X causes Y on one occasion, then X will again cause Y on some similar occasion in the future. Although the assumption of determinism works well for physical phenomena, it may not work as well for human or social behavior. Human beings are conscious and self-aware, and they are capable of exercising some control over their own behavior. Unlike atoms or rocks, they are capable of making decisions and suddenly changing their behavior if they want to. In other words, they have a measure of free will. For this reason some theorists have argued that there will never be anything approaching true "universal laws" describing social behavior. Certainly it is difficult to reconcile the scientific assumption of determinism with the concept of human free will. Of course, this problem is not unique to social psychology. It besets all the social sciences.

As we have shown, social psychology displays many of the characteristics of the more mature physical sciences. It is based on observation of the social world and relies on a formal methodology to guide research. It has accumulated many descriptive facts regarding human social behavior, and it possesses bodies of formal theory. Nevertheless, it has not yet had the same degree of success in prediction and control as the mature physical sciences. Although it does offer compelling explanations for many types of observed social behavior, it has provided only a modest degree of predictability and control of social behavior.

Summary

This chapter considers the fundamental characteristics of social psychology as well as important theoretical perspectives in the field.

WHAT IS SOCIAL PSYCHOLOGY? There are several ways to characterize social psychology. (1) One way is to list the core concerns of social psychology. These concerns are the impact of one individual on another's behavior and beliefs, the impact of a group on a member's behavior and beliefs, the impact of a member on the group's activities and structure, and the impact of one group on another group's activities and structure. (2) By definition, social psychology is that field which systematically studies the nature and causes of human social behavior. (3) Social psychology has a close relationship with other social sciences, especially sociology and psychology. Although they emphasize different issues, both psychologists and sociologists have contributed to social psychology.

THEORETICAL PERSPECTIVES IN SOCIAL PSYCHOLOGY. A theoretical perspective is a broad theory based on particular assumptions about human nature that offers explanations for a wide range of social behaviors. In this chapter four theoretical perspectives were discussed: role theory, reinforcement theory, cognitive theory, and symbolic interactionist theory. (1) Role theory is based on the premise that people conform to norms defined by the expectations of others. It is most useful in explaining the regular and recurring patterns apparent in day-to-day activity. (2) Reinforcement theory assumes that social behavior is governed by external events, especially rewards and punishments. Reinforcement is useful in explaining not only how people learn but also when social relationships will change. (3) Cognitive theory holds that such processes as perception, memory, reasoning, and decision making are significant determinants of social behavior. The theory relies on the principle of consistency to explain attitude change. Differences in cognitions help to illuminate why persons may behave differently in a given situation. (4) Symbolic interactionist theory holds that human nature and social order are products of communication among people. It stresses the importance of the self, of role taking, and of consensus in social interaction. It is most useful in explaining fluid, contingent encounters among people. (5) These four perspectives can be usefully compared and contrasted in terms of their central concepts, the behaviors they explain, their assumptions about human nature, and their treatment of change in behavior.

IS SOCIAL PSYCHOLOGY A SCIENCE? (1) To answer the question whether social psychology is a science, we must first identify the hallmarks that characterize any science. There are five: scientists engage in empirical observation of the world, use a formal research methodology, cumulate knowledge of facts, develop formal theories to explain facts, and employ these theories to provide some degree of prediction and control. (2) Social psychology meets the first four of these hallmarks, but falls somewhat short of meeting the fifth. To date, social psychology has provided only a modest degree of predictability and control over human social behavior.

Key Terms and Concepts

Social Psychology

Theory

Theoretical Perspective

Role Theory

Role

Norm

Deviant Behavior

Reinforcement Theory

Stimulus

Response

Reinforcement

Conditioning

Imitation

Social Exchange Theory

Comparison Level for Alternatives

Equity

Cognitive Theory

Cognitive Processes

Cognitive Structure

Principle of Consistency

Symbolic Interactionism

Meaning

Definition of the Situation

Role Taking

Self

Significant Others

Principle of Determinism

Part 1

Socialization

Chapter 2

Self and Identity

Introduction

"Who am I?" "Is this really me?" "Who do I want to be?" Few human beings in Western societies live out their lives without pondering such questions. The search for self-knowledge and for a meaningful identity is pursued eagerly by some, desperately by others. College students in particular are often preoccupied with discovering who they are.

Each of us has unique answers to these questions, answers which reflect our **self-concepts,** the various thoughts and feelings we have about ourselves. Responses of a nine-year-old boy and a female college sophomore to the question "Who am I?" are presented in Box 2.1. Before reading on, take a few moments to respond to this question yourself in the space provided. Then consider the ways that social psychologists' ideas about self and identity relate to your own self-conception.

Five major questions will be addressed in this chapter:

1. What is the self and how does it arise? Our ability to answer the question "Who am I?" demonstrates that we can distinguish self from others and reflect upon our unique qualities, actions, and feelings. The self arises as we become aware of our uniqueness and learn to plan, observe, guide, and evaluate our own behavior.

2. How do we acquire unique identities? **Identities** are the categories we use to specify who we are, to locate ourselves in the world relative to others. The examples in Box 2.1 (including your own responses) reveal that each person has a unique set of identities. Our identities are self-concepts that specify the ways we relate to people in the social world. Josh identifies himself as Louis's little brother and as a skater. Arlene includes among her identities people-watcher and sister. This chapter examines the ways our specific identities develop and change over time.

3. How do our identities guide our planning and behavior? Identities are the objects we perceive when we reflect on who we are. But they are also sources of motivation. Our specific identities determine our plans, aspirations, and behavior. For example, when choosing college courses or deciding how to spend Saturday night, Arlene is guided by one or more of her identities as creator, people-lover, music enthusiast, and so on. We will examine the ways our identities influence the particular self we enact in different situations.

4. How does self-awareness influence the ways we think and feel? The ways we think about events and remember them depends upon their relevance to the self. When we are self-aware, our identities have a greater impact on our behavior. Self-awareness also influences the sensations we recognize and the emotions we experience.

5. Where do the feelings of evaluation that inevitably accompany thoughts about ourselves come from and how do they affect our behavior? How do we protect our self-esteem against attack?

The Nature and Genesis of Self

The Self as Source and Object of Action

We can behave in a wide variety of ways toward other persons. For example, if Bob is having coffee with Carol, he can perceive her, evaluate her, communicate with her, motivate her to action, control her, and so on. What is interesting to note, however, is that Bob can also act in the same fashion toward himself—that is, he can engage in self-perception, self-evaluation, self-communication, self-motivation, and self-control. Behavior of this type, in which the individual who acts and the individual toward whom the action is directed are one and the same, is termed *reflexive behavior.*

Box 2.1
MEASURING SELF-CONCEPTS

In order to study self-concepts, we need ways to measure them. Many methods have been used. For example, one approach asks people to check those adjectives on a list (intelligent, aggressive, trusting, and so on) that describe them (Sarbin and Rosenberg 1955). In another approach, people rate themselves on pairs of adjectives (strong–weak, good–bad, active–passive): Are they more like one of the adjectives in the pair or more like its opposite (Osgood, Suci, and Tannenbaum 1957)? Another technique developed by Miyamoto and Dorbusch (1956) asks people whether they have more or less of a characteristic (self-confidence, likeableness) than members of a particular group (such as fraternities, sororities, and so on). In yet another technique, people sort cards containing descriptive phrases (interested in sports, concerned with achievement) into piles according to how accurately they think the phrases describe them (Stephenson 1953).

Each of these popular methods provides respondents with a single, standard set of categories to use in describing themselves. Using the same categories for all respondents makes it easy to compare the self-concepts of different people. These methods have a weakness, however. They do not reveal the unique dimensions that individuals use in spontaneously thinking about themselves. For this purpose, techniques that ask people simply to describe themselves in their own words are especially effective (Bugenthal and Zelen 1950; Kuhn and McPartland 1954; McGuire and McGuire 1982).

Below are instructions for the "Who Am I?" technique for measuring self-concepts (Gordon 1968). You can try this test yourself:

In the 15 numbered blanks write 15 different answers to the simple question "Who am I?" Answer as if you were giving the answers to yourself, not to somebody else. Write the answers in the order they occur to you. Don't worry about "logic" or "importance."

I AM

1. _____	6. _____	11. _____
2. _____	7. _____	12. _____
3. _____	8. _____	13. _____
4. _____	9. _____	14. _____
5. _____	10. _____	15. _____

Below are responses obtained from two persons, Josh and Arlene.

Josh: A nine-year-old male	Arlene: A female college sophomore
a boy	a person
do what my mother says, mostly	member of the human race
Louis's little brother	daughter and sister
Josh	a student
have big ears	people-lover
can beat up Andy	people-watcher
play soccer	creator of written, drawn, and spoken (things) creations
sometimes a good sport	music enthusiast
a skater	enjoyer of nature
make a lot of noise	partly the sum of my experiences
like to eat	always changing
talk good	lonely
go to third grade	all the characters in the books I read
bad at drawing	a small part of the universe, but I can change it
	I'm not sure?!

For example, if Bob is a student facing a deadline for an important term paper, he engages in the reflexive process of self-control when he pushes himself ("Complete that history paper now"). He engages in self-motivation when he makes a promise to himself ("You can break for pizza and beer when you finish"). Both of these processes are part of the self. To have a self is to have the capacity to engage in reflexive actions, to plan, observe, guide, and respond to our own behavior (Mead 1934; Bandura 1982).

By definition, the **self** is the individual viewed as both the source and the object of reflexive behavior. Clearly, the self is both active (the source that initiates reflexive behavior) and passive (the object toward which reflexive behavior is directed). William James, the philosopher-psychologist who first emphasized this distinction (1890), labelled the active aspect of the self the "I" and the object of self-action the "Me." Building upon James's ideas, G. H. Mead (1934) described the "I" and the "Me" as alternating phases of every action involving the self.

It is useful to think of the self as a continuing process. Action involving the self begins with the "I"—Bob gets angry, for example ("Outrageous assignment"). In the next moment that action becomes the object of self-reflection, hence part of the "Me"—Bob becomes aware of his own anger ("Wow, you're furious"). Next, Bob responds actively to this self-awareness, again an "I" phase ("I won't write the paper"). This action, in turn, becomes the object to be judged, again a "Me" ("She'll flunk me"). Then an active "I" ("OK, I'll try") is followed by a self-reflective "Me" phase ("Keep going"), as Bob exercises the self-control needed to keep himself writing. The "I" and "Me" phases continue to alternate as every new action (I) becomes in the next moment the object of self-scrutiny (Me). Through these alternating phases of self we initiate, judge, and continuously guide our own behavior.

Mead's description portrays self-action as guided by an internal dialogue. People engage in conversations in their minds as they regulate their behavior. They use words and images to symbolize their ideas about themselves, other persons, their own actions and others' probable responses to them. This description of the internal dialogue suggests that there are three capacities human beings must acquire in order to engage successfully in self-action. They must (1) develop an ability to differentiate themselves from other persons; (2) learn to see themselves and their own actions as if through others' eyes; and (3) learn to use a symbol system or language for inner thought. We will examine, in turn, how children come to differentiate themselves and how they learn to view themselves from others' perspectives. We will also note how language learning is intertwined with acquiring these two capacities.

Self-Differentiation

In order to take the self as the object of our action, we must—at a minimum—be able to recognize ourselves. That is, we must distinguish our own faces and bodies from those of others. This may seem elementary, but infants are not born with this ability. At first they do not even discriminate the boundaries between their own bodies and the environment. With cognitive growth, continuing tactile exploration of their bodies, and social experience with caretakers who treat them as distinct beings, infants gradually discover their physical uniqueness. Studies of when children can recognize themselves in a mirror suggest that most children are able to discriminate their own image from others' by about 18 months (Lewis and Brooks 1975; Bertenthal and Fischer 1978).

Mastery of language is critical in childrens' efforts to differentiate themselves as distinctive social objects (Denzin 1977). Learning one's name is one of the earliest and most important steps in acquiring a self. Children come to identify themselves as unique objects

To take the self as the object of our action, observing and modifying our own behavior, we must be able to recognize ourselves. Although infants are not born with this ability, they acquire it quickly.

toward which action is directed because they are regularly named and thereby singled out from other objects. As Allport put it: "By hearing his name repeatedly the child gradually sees himself as a distinct and recurrent point of reference. The name acquires significance for him in the second year of life. With it comes awareness of independent status in the social group" (1961:115).

A mature sense of self entails recognizing that our thoughts and feelings are our private possessions. Young children often confuse processes that go on in their own minds with external events (Piaget 1954). They locate their own dreams and nightmares, for example, in the world around them. The distinction between self and nonself sharpens as social

experience and cognitive growth bring children to realize that their own private awareness of self is not directly accessible to others. By about age four, children report that their thinking and knowing goes on inside their heads. Asked further, "Can I see you thinking in there?" they generally answer "no," demonstrating their awareness that self-processes are private (Flavell, Shipstead, and Croft 1978).

Changes in the way children talk also reveal their dawning realization that the self has access to private information. During their first years of talking, children's speech patterns are the same whether they are talking aloud to themselves or directing their words to others. Gradually, however, they begin to distinguish speech for self from speech for others (Vygotsky 1963). Speech for self becomes abbreviated until it is virtually incomprehensible to the outside listener, while speech for others becomes more elaborated over time. "Cold" suffices for Amy to tell herself she wants to take off her wet socks. But no one else would understand this without access to her private knowledge. When addressing others, Amy would expand her speech to include whatever private information they need to understand ("Gotta change my wet socks. They're making me cold."). This reflects her growing awareness that each self has its own unique store of knowledge.

Role Taking

Recognizing that one is physically and mentally differentiated from others is only one step in the genesis of self. Once we can differentiate ourselves from others we can also recognize that each person sees the world from a different perspective. The second crucial step in the genesis of self is to adopt these different perspectives in our imaginations, to "take the role of the other."

Here, too, language plays a critical part, for language is a major component of thought. In earliest childhood, thought is probably a jumble of visual images and auditory symbols. Gradually, verbal symbols add flexibility to the inner dialogue of thought. They enrich children's capacities to represent complex ideas in their minds and enable them to converse with themselves in ever more elaborate thought processes (Vygotsky 1963).

Contrast the thoughts of a child of one and a child of nine as they seek their objectives. The one-year-old is incapable of adopting the perspectives of others, whereas the nine-year-old has an expanding capacity for role taking. When one-year-old Lisa sees an ice cream cone, she is likely to tug at her mother's skirt and point. If ignored, she may cry or scream. Years later, at age nine, Lisa might generate a strategy based on the following internal dialogue: "Pointing won't help, she's busy talking. I'll tug her sweater. No, she'll get mad. I'll say I'm hungry. No, she'll say supper's in an hour. I'll suggest buying ice cream for dessert. She'll like that." Lisa's greater effectiveness at nine derives from her ability to adopt her mother's perspective as well as her own.

Role taking is the process of imagining another person's attitudes and thereby anticipating that person's behavior. Through role taking we see the world and ourselves from others' perspectives. By nine, Lisa can imagine her mother's attitudes toward her own actions and anticipate her mother's responses to her. Lisa can therefore select behaviors likely to produce desirable outcomes. Lisa uses her role-taking skill to manipulate her mother's perception of the situation. Of course, role taking is often not perfect. Sometimes we misjudge others' probable responses to us because we are ignorant of or misinformed about their true attitudes.

Role taking is crucial to the genesis of self because through it the child learns to respond reflexively. Imagining others' responses to the self, children acquire the capacity to look at themselves as if from the outside. Recognizing that others see them as objects, children can become objects (Me) to themselves (Mead 1934). They can then act toward themselves to praise ("That's a good girl"), to reprimand ("Stop that!"), and to control their own behavior ("Wait your own turn").

C. H. Cooley (1908) noted a close tie between role taking and language skills long ago. One of the earliest signs of role-taking skills is the correct use of the pronouns *you* and *I*. To master the use of these pronouns requires taking the role of self and of the other simultaneously. Almost all children firmly grasp the use of *I* and *you* by the middle of their third year (Clark 1976). This suggests that children are well on their way to effective role taking at this age. Observations of preschoolers at play reveal complex uses of pronouns and perspectives (Denzin 1977).

TABLE 2.1
SIGNIFICANT OTHERS MENTIONED IN SELF DESCRIPTIONS AS A FUNCTION OF AGE

	Ratio of the Frequency of Mentioning		
Age Group	*1* *Parents* *vs.* *Teachers*	*2* *Brothers and Sisters* *vs.* *Friends and Fellow Students*	*3* *Nonfamily Members* *vs.* *Extended Family*
7 years	1.7 to 1	1.7 to 1	4 to 1
9 years	1 to 1.4	1 to 1.4	8 to 1
13 years	1 to 1	1 to 1	13 to 1
17 years	1 to 2.3	1 to 2.3	49 to 1

Note: 560 boys and girls in this study were asked: "Tell us about yourself." The children's responses suggest that their self-definitions in terms of other people tend to shift away from family members with age—from parents to teachers (Column 1), from brothers and sisters to friends and fellow students (Column 2), from extended family members (cousins, aunts, uncles) to nonfamily members (Column 3). Seven year olds, for example, mentioned parents almost twice as often as teachers, while 17 year olds mentioned teachers more than twice as often as parents (Column 1).

Source: adapted from McGuire and McGuire (1982).

The Social Origins of Self

Our self-concepts are produced in our social relationships. Throughout life, as we meet new people and enter new groups, our self-concepts are modified by the feedback we receive from others. This feedback is not an objective reality that we can grasp directly. Rather, we must interpret others' responses in order to figure out how we appear to them. We then incorporate others' imagined views of us into our self-concepts.

To dramatize the idea that the origins of self are social, Cooley (1902) coined the term "looking-glass self." The most important looking glasses for children are their parents and immediate family, and later their playmates. They are the child's **significant others,** the people whose reflected views have greatest influence on the child's self-concepts. As we grow older, the widening circle of friends and relatives, school teachers, clergy, doctors, and fellow workers provides our significant others. The changing self-concepts we acquire through our lives depend on the social relationships we develop (see Table 2.1).

PLAY AND THE GAME. Mead (1934) identified two sequential stages of social experience leading to the emergence of the self in children. He called these stages *play* and *the game.* Each stage is characterized by its own form of role taking.

In the play stage, young children imitate the activities of people to whom they have been exposed. Through such play, children learn to organize different activities into meaningful roles (nurse, doctor, fire fighter). For example, using their imaginations, children carry sacks of mail, drop letters into mailboxes, greet homeowners, and learn to label these activities as fitting the role "mail carrier." At this stage, children take the roles of the others one at a time. They do not recognize that each role is intertwined with others. Playing mail carrier, for example, the child does not realize that mail carriers also have bosses to whom they must relate. Nor do

By playing complex games, children learn to organize their actions into meaningful roles and to imagine the viewpoints of the different game players at the same time. These experiences teach them how to coordinate effectively with others and to follow social rules.

children in this stage understand that the same person simultaneously holds many roles—that mail carriers are also parents, store customers, and golf partners.

The game stage comes later, when children enter into organized activities such as complex games of house, school, and team sports. These activities demand interpersonal coordination because the various roles are differentiated. Role taking at the game stage requires children to imagine the viewpoints of several others at the same time. For Ellen to play shortstop effectively, for example, she must adopt the perspectives of the infielders and of the base runners as she fields the ball and decides where to throw. In the game,

children also learn that different roles relate to each other in specified ways. Ellen must understand the specialized functions of each position, the ways the players in different positions must coordinate their actions, and the rules that regulate baseball.

THE GENERALIZED OTHER. Repeated involvement in organized activities lets children see that their own actions are part of a pattern of interdependent group activity. This experience teaches children that organized groups of people share common perspectives and attitudes. With this new knowledge, children construct what Mead calls a **generalized other**—a conception of the attitudes held in common by the members of the organized groups with whom they interact. When we imagine what "the group" expects of us, we are taking the role of the generalized other. We are also concerned with the generalized other when we wonder what "people" would say, or what "society's standards" demand. As children grow older they control their own behavior more and more from the perspective of the generalized other. This helps them to resist influence from specific others who just happen to be present in the situation at the moment.

Over time children internalize the attitudes and expectations of the generalized other, incorporating them into their self-concepts. But building up self-concepts involves more than accepting the reflected views of others. It is often fraught with confusion and turmoil. We may misperceive or misinterpret the responses that others direct to us, for example, due to our less than perfect role-taking skills. Others' responses may themselves be contradictory or inconsistent. We may also resist the reflected views we perceive because they conflict with our prior self-concepts or with our direct experience. A boy may reject his peers' view that he is a sissy, for example, because he previously thought of himself as brave and could still visualize his experience of beating up a bully.

SELF-EVALUATION The views of ourselves that we perceive from others usually imply positive or negative evaluations. These evaluations also become part of the self-concepts we construct. Actions that others judge favorably produce self-concepts about which we feel good. In contrast, when others disapprove or punish our actions, the self-concepts we derive are negative. Our self-evaluations are based on our interpretations of the feedback we receive from others.

Identities: The Self We Know

In Box 2.1 Arlene described herself as a person, member of the human race, daughter, and people-lover. This is the self she knows, a self that includes specific identities. When we think of our identities, we are actually thinking of various plans of action that we expect to carry out. When Arlene identifies herself as a student, for example, she has in mind that she plans to attend classes, write papers, take exams, and so on. If Arlene does not follow through on these plans, she will have to relinquish her student identity. Each of us has a self we know, one that includes identities that we and others ascribe to us. These identities indicate our plans and allow us and others to anticipate how we will behave.

In this section we will consider several questions about the self we know: (1) How do our experiences in society influence the identities we include in this self? (2) What aspects of self do people note in their actual self-descriptions? (3) How do the aspects of self that people note vary from one situation to another? (4) What evidence is there that the self we know is based on the reactions we perceive from others?

Role Identities

Each of us occupies numerous positions in society—student, friend, son or daughter, customer. Each of us therefore enacts many different social roles. We construct identities by observing our own behavior and the responses of others to us as we enact these roles. For each role we enact, we develop a somewhat different view of who we are. In this way, we develop multiple identities. Because these identities are concepts of self in specific roles, they are called **role identities.** The role identities we develop depend upon the social positions available to us in society. As a result, the self we know is linked to society fundamentally through the roles we play. It reflects the structure of our society and our place in it (Burke and Tully 1977; Gordon 1976; McCall and Simmons 1978; Stryker 1980; Turner 1978).

Do societal role expectations strictly dictate the contents of our role identities? Apparently not. Consider, for example, the expectations for the instructor role. Some instructors deliver lectures while others lead discussions; some encourage questions while others discourage them; some assign papers and others do not. As this example indicates, role expectations usually leave individuals room to improvise their own role performances. It is probably more accurate to think of people as "making" their roles—that is, shaping them—rather than as conforming rigidly to role expectations (Turner 1978).

Several influences affect the way we make the roles we enact. A general framework is set by the conventional role expectations in society. In the role of student, for example, we must submit assigned papers. Within this general framework, we fashion our actual role performances to reflect our personal characteristics and competencies (selecting topics that interest us and are likely to highlight our strengths and cover our weaknesses). We also mold our role performances to impress our audience (writing in the style the instructor prefers). Finally, we adjust our different performances to maintain some consistency among them (trying for a level of quality consistent with our other course work). Since each person makes roles in a unique, personal fashion, we each derive somewhat different role identities even if we occupy similar social positions. Consequently, our role identities as

TABLE 2.2

WHO AM I? SELF-DESCRIPTIONS OF HIGH-SCHOOL STUDENTS

Type of Response (example)	Percent Who Mentioned
Role Identities	
Age group (teenager, 15-year-old)	82
Student role (freshman, student)	80
Sex (a boy, daughter)	74
Abstract category (a person, human)	41
Participant in activities (hiker, poet)	31
Membership in actual group (on the football team)	17
Kinship role (sister, husband)	17
Name (Claire, Mark)	17
Territoriality, citizenship (a Bostonian)	16
Religion (Catholic, Lutheran)	11
Personal Qualities	
Interpersonal style (introverted, cool, friendly)	59
Emotional, psychological style (moody, optimistic, in love)	52
Body image (good-looking, 112 lbs.)	36
Preferences: judgments, tastes, likes (loves Bach, hates abstract art)	27
Material possessions (owns a Porsche)	5
Self-Evaluations	
Sense of competence (creative, always making mistakes)	36
Sense of self-determination (ambitious, self-starter)	23
Sense of moral worth (trustworthy, evil)	22
Sense of unity (mixed up, a whole person)	5

Note: Responses of 157 high-school students to the "Who Am I?" questionnaire illustrate the types of self-concepts that constitute the self we know.

Source: adapted from Gordon (1968).

student, friend, team player, and so on, differ from the role identities of others who also occupy these same positions.

Actual Self-Descriptions

If the self we know consists of role identities, people's actual self-descriptions should reflect their major social roles. Do they? To answer this question, we examine responses people give to the "Who am I?" questionnaire. These responses reveal three general types of self-description: role identities, personal qualities, and self-evaluations (Gordon 1968).

ROLE IDENTITIES. In describing themselves, most people mention their major social roles (age group, student, or work role). This is demonstrated in the responses of high-school students in Table 2.2, as well as responses from other large samples. Most respondents spontaneously list their role identities as members of occupational, educational, or family groups among their first self-descriptions. They also frequently mention identities as members of various other social categories such as religion, activity, group, race, and so on. There is usually substantial public agreement about the role identities a person claims (Kuhn and McPartland 1954).

The other two types of self-description—personal qualities and self-evaluations—refer to conceptions of self that others may dispute or ignore. Our conceptions of how moody we are, how moral, or how competent are not matters of public consensus. These self-concepts express the personal idiosyncratic variation in our self-descriptions.

PERSONAL QUALITIES. In describing their personal qualities, people mention most frequently the styles of interpersonal behavior (introverted, cool) that distinguish the way they fashion their unique role performances. People also mention the emotional or psychological styles (optimistic, moody) that characterize these performances. Individual preferences point to specific ways people express their role identities. For example, a person who sees herself as a musician expresses this role identity differently depending on whether she prefers Bach or hard rock. Body image, the aspect of self we recognize earliest, remains important throughout life. Beyond this, our self extends to include our material possessions, such as our clothing, house, car, records, and so on (James 1890).

SELF-EVALUATIONS. The third type of self-description refers to the ways we evaluate ourselves. We form these self-evaluations when reflecting upon the adequacy of our role performances, upon the extent to which we live up to the role identities to which we aspire. Our evaluations most commonly focus on our competence, self-determination, moral worth, or unity. Self-evaluations also influence the ways we express our role identities. A musician, for example, will pursue opportunities to perform in public more persistently if she sees herself as competent than if she thinks she is never quite good enough. Self-evaluations are so important that the concluding section of this chapter will be devoted to them.

The Situated Self

If we were to describe ourselves on several different occasions, the identities, personal qualities, and self-evaluations mentioned would not remain the same. This is not due to errors of reporting. Rather, it demonstrates that the aspects of self that enter our awareness and matter to us most depend on the situation. The term **situated self** has been coined to express this idea (Hewitt 1976). The situated self is the subset of self-concepts chosen from our identities, qualities, and self-evaluations that constitutes the self we know in a particular situation.

The self-concepts most likely to enter into the situated self are those distinctive in the setting and relevant to the ongoing activities. Consider a black woman for whom being black and being a woman are both important self-concepts. When she interacts with black men, she is more likely to think of herself as a woman; when she interacts with white women, she is more likely to be aware that she is black. Thus self-concepts that are distinctive or peculiar in the social setting tend to enter into the situated self (McGuire and McGuire 1982). The activities in which we are engaged also determine the self-concepts that constitute the situated self. A job interview, for example, draws attention to our competence; a fraternity party makes our body image more salient. The self we experience in our imaginings and in our interactions is always situated because setting characteristics and activity requirements make particular self-concepts distinctive and relevant.

Tests of the Interactionist Approach to Self-Concept Formation

Thus far, we have shown how we base our self-concepts on the reactions we perceive from others during social interaction. How does this approach stand up against evidence from naturalistic studies? Early tests of this approach (Miyamoto and Dornbusch 1956; Quarantelli and Cooper 1966) compared people's self-ratings on various qualities (intelligence, self-confidence, physical attractiveness) with the views of themselves that they perceived from others. The studies also compared self-ratings with actual views of others.

Results of these studies support the assertion that it is the perceived reactions of others,

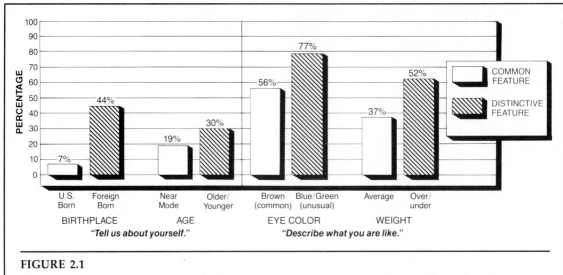

FIGURE 2.1

PERCENTAGE OF STUDENTS WHO MENTION A FEATURE SPONTANEOUSLY AS PART OF THEIR SELF-CONCEPT

A group of 252 sixth-graders from 10 classrooms were asked to describe themselves. Students mentioned a particular feature (for example, birthplace) more often if that feature distinguished them from their classmates. Because these are characteristics on which we stand out from our social groups, attracting more notice and social comment, we are more likely to build them into our self-concepts.

Source: adapted from McGuire and Padawer-Singer (1976).

rather than their actual reactions, that are crucial for self-concept formation (Cooley 1902). Self ratings were considerably more closely related to the perceived ratings of others than to the others' actual ratings. Why is this so? Three reasons are especially important. First, others rarely provide full, honest feedback about their reactions to us. Second, the feedback we do receive is often inconsistent and even contradictory. Third, the feedback is frequently ambiguous and difficult to interpret. It may be in the form of gestures (shrugs), facial expressions (smiles), or remarks that can be understood in many different ways. For these reasons, we may know little about others' actual reactions to us. Instead, we must rely upon our perceptions of others' reactions to construct our self-concepts (Schrauger and Schoeneman 1979).

Evidence that self-concepts are related to the perceived reactions of others does not demonstrate that self-concepts are actually formed in response to these perceived reactions. One study does suggest such an impact of the perceived reactions of others on self-concepts. The study (Mannheim 1966) asked college dormitory residents to describe themselves and also to report how they thought others viewed them. Several months later, self-concepts were measured again. In the interim, students' self-concepts had moved closer to the views they had originally thought that others held. Change toward the perceived reactions of others had indeed occurred.

According to the interactionist approach, those of our features that attract attention during social interaction are the ones that should become self-concepts. Others are most likely to notice and respond to features that distinguish us from our social groups—our weight if we are obese or skinny, our ethnic identity if we are foreign born. These same distinctive features are also the ones we are most likely to note when we compare ourselves to others. We should therefore tend more to mention a feature when describing ourselves if that feature is distinctive.

Studies using the "Who am I?" technique in India and in the United States support this prediction. In both countries, members of minority religious groups (Christians, Muslims, Sikhs in India; Catholics and Jews in the United States) mentioned their religious identity three times as often as members of majority religious groups (Driver 1969; Kuhn and McPartland 1954).

American sixth-graders also tend to pick features that distinguish them when asked to describe themselves (McGuire and Padawer-Singer 1976). Students mention their age, birthplace, sex, hair color, eye color, or weight more frequently when that feature places them in the minority of their class, or when they differ substantially on it from their class average (Fig. 2.1). These findings support the interactionist approach to self-concept formation because they demonstrate that *socially distinctive* features are especially important in self-identification.

Identities: The Self We Enact

How does the self influence the planning and regulation of social behavior? The general answer to this question is that we are motivated to plan and to perform behaviors that will confirm and reinforce the identities we wish to claim for ourselves (Burke and Reitzes 1981; Backman and Secord 1968). In elaborating upon this answer, we will examine three more specific questions: (1) How are behaviors linked to particular identities? (2) Of the different identities available to us, what determines which ones we choose to enact in a situation? (3) How do our identities lend unity and consistency to our behavior?

Identities and Behavior

At first glance, the link between identities and behavior appears straightforward. A person who wants to claim a particular identity

chooses to perform behaviors that express that identity. For example, if Roberta wishes to claim a feminine identity she will perform feminine behaviors and avoid masculine behaviors. When others recognize Roberta's behavior as feminine they will react in ways that confirm and support her feminine identity.

But what if a person does not know which behaviors others consider feminine, or if she disagrees with their notions of feminine behavior? Does being feminine require Roberta to lose a tennis match to her date, or to express sympathy rather than anger when her friend spills coffee on her sweater? That will depend upon the meanings of a feminine identity and the meanings of these different behaviors to Roberta and to her friends.

This example demonstrates that the link between identities and behaviors is through their common meanings (Burke and Reitzes 1981). If members of a group agree on the meanings of particular identities and behaviors, they can regulate their own behavior effectively. They can plan, initiate, and control behavior to generate the meanings that establish the identities they wish to claim. If the meanings of an identity or of particular behaviors are a matter of dispute, however, people have difficulty establishing their preferred identities. If Roberta sees no connection between competitiveness and femininity, for example, she will have trouble establishing a feminine identity in the eyes of friends who think being feminine means being noncompetitive.

When we travel, change schools or jobs, or move into new groups, we come into contact with individuals who do not share all the same meanings with us, because their backgrounds or cultures differ from ours. We may then be unable to predict whether performing a particular behavior will confirm an identity or undermine it. Only by learning the meanings that prevail in our surroundings can we select behaviors that will confirm the identities we wish to claim.

Choosing an Identity to Enact

Each of us has many different identities. Each identity suggests its own lines of action. These lines of action are not all compatible, however, nor can they all be pursued simultaneously in a single situation. If you are at a wedding reception, for example, you might wish to claim an identity as an eligible dating partner, as an aspiring psychotherapist, or as an amateur guitarist. These identities suggest different, even conflicting, ways of relating to the other guests. What influences the decision to enact one rather than another identity? Below are several ways we determine such choices (McCall and Simmons 1978).

NEED FOR IDENTITY SUPPORT. First, we are likely to enact those of our identities that most need support at the moment because they have recently been challenged. Say we have recently had difficulty getting a date. We then choose actions calculated to elicit responses indicating we are an attractive dating partner. We also tend to enact identities likely to bring intrinsic gratifications (such as a sense of accomplishment) and extrinsic rewards (such as praise) that we especially need or miss at the moment. For example, if, after hours of solitary study, we feel a need for relaxed social contact, we might seek gratification by enacting our guitarist identity and singing with the wedding guests.

SITUATIONAL OPPORTUNITIES. Second, our choice of identity depends upon the opportunities we perceive for profitably enacting an identity in a particular situation. Regardless of what we need or desire, situations let us enact only some identities profitably, not others. If no one wants to tell us their troubles, there is no opportunity to enact an aspiring therapist identity.

A study of racial values, attitudes, and behavior among white Canadian college students vividly demonstrates that, given the situational opportunity, we enact the identities that are most in need of support (Dutton and Lake 1973). Researchers selected subjects on the basis of their earlier statements that they valued equality highly and that they viewed themselves as free of racial prejudice. They invited students individually to the research site, and connected them to a rigged lie detector. The lie detector purportedly revealed to the students their true attitudes by measuring psychological changes in response to seeing slides of interracial scenes. For half the students, the lie detector "revealed" strong negative reactions, implying that they were prejudiced against blacks and threatening their identity as egalitarian. The other students were told their responses were typical of unprejudiced individuals.

Upon leaving the research site, each student was approached either by a white panhandler or a black panhandler. The black panhandler received substantially more money from students whose egalitarian identity had been threatened than from those told their responses indicated no prejudice. The white panhandler received the same moderate amount of money from both groups of students. These results, shown in Figure 2.2, suggest that the threatened students went out of their way to prove they were not racially prejudiced when given the chance to help a black. They perceived the situation as an opportunity to reaffirm their recently challenged egalitarian identity.

THE HIERARCHY OF IDENTITIES. The many different role identities we enact do not share equal importance for us. Rather, we organize them into a hierarchy of relative importance. This hierarchy is a third influence on our decision to enact one or another identity (McCall and Simmons 1978; Stryker 1980). First, the more important an identity is to us, the more frequently we choose to perform activities which express that identity (Stryker and Serpe 1981). Second, the more important an identity, the more likely we are to perceive that situations offer opportunities to enact that identity. Only a person for whom the aspiring

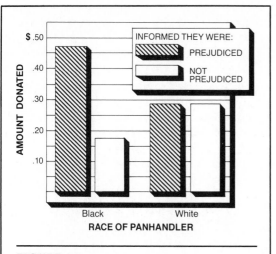

FIGURE 2.2

Acting to Reaffirm Threatened Identities

White students' self-identities as egalitarians were either threatened by false feedback from a lie detector, indicating that they were racially prejudiced, or confirmed by feedback that they were not prejudiced. Following the lie detector test, students were solicited either by a black or a white panhandler. Those who were approached by the black panhandler after their egalitarian identity had been threatened donated the most money. In this way they "proved" they were not racially prejudiced and reaffirmed their recently threatened egalitarian identity. Donations to the white panhandler were unaffected by the feedback about prejudice. These results demonstrate how the desire to affirm threatened identities influences behavior.

Source: adapted from Dutton and Lake (1973).

therapist identity is important, for example, will perceive a wedding reception as a chance to counsel people about their problems. Third, we are more active in seeking out opportunities to behave in terms of important identities (searching for guests willing to discuss their anxieties). Fourth, we conform more with the role expectations attached to the identities that we consider the most important (listening sympathetically and probing gently, as a therapist supposedly should).

Several factors determine the relative importance we attach to each of our role identities: (1) the resources we have invested in constructing the identity (time, effort, and money expended, for example, in learning to be a sculptor); (2) the extrinsic rewards that enacting the identity has brought (purchases by collectors, acclaim by critics); (3) the intrinsic gratifications derived from performing it (the sense of competence and aesthetic pleasure obtained when sculpting a human figure); (4) the amount of self-esteem staked on enacting the identity well (To what extent has a positive self-evaluation become tied to being a good sculptor?). As we engage in interaction and experience greater or lesser success in performing our different identities, their relative importance to us shifts.

Each of us is part of a network of social relationships. These relationships may stand or fall on whether we continue to enact particular role identities. The more numerous and significant the relationships that depend upon enacting an identity, the more committed we become to that identity (Stryker 1980). A famous sculptor, for example, can maintain rewarding relationships with purchasers, critics, art dealers, museum directors, and the general public only if he continues to sculpt. He has a strong commitment to his sculptor identity. A businesswoman who recently began to dabble in sculpting would have little commitment to her sculptor identity. She would lose few, if any, significant relationships by quitting her new hobby.

The more commitment we have to a role identity, the more important that identity will be in our hierarchy. For instance, adults for whom participating in religious activities was crucial for maintaining everyday social relationships ranked their religious identity as relatively important compared with their parent, spouse, and worker identities (Stryker and Serpe 1981). Similarly, the importance rank that undergraduates gave to various identities (student, friend, son/daughter, athlete, religious person, and dating partner) depended

The more important an identity is to us, the more consistently we act to express it, regardless of others' reactions. Are any of your identities so important that you would let yourself express them the way these Hassidic Jews do?

upon the importance to them of the social relationships maintained by enacting each identity (Hoelter 1983).

Identities as Sources of Unity and Consistency

Although the self includes multiple identities, people usually experience themselves as a unified entity. Our most important identities provide consistent styles of behavior and priorities that lend continuity and unity to our behavior. In this way, the importance hierarchy aids us to construct a unified sense of self from our multiple identities.

The importance hierarchy of identities also influences the consistency of our behavior across situations and across time. We behave consistently when we seek to express the same identity in different situations. To be consistent, we must monitor our behavior and regulate it to be sure it confirms the chosen identity. We are especially likely to monitor and regulate behavior intended to express important identities (Santee and Jackson 1979). As a result, people expect to behave more consistently with their important identities, and they generally do so (Bem and Allen 1974; Markus 1977). Imagine that an identity as "expert driver" is important to Steve, for example, but unimportant to Craig. Steve, but not Craig, would insist on driving whatever the occasion.

Behavior is likely to be *in*consistent when it is based upon unimportant identities. We make no persistent efforts to behave consistently with identities low in our hierarchy. When unimportant identities are at stake, we readily switch from one to another to maximize profit in the situation. Craig might volunteer to drive, for example, if driving lets him choose a destination he especially wants. He might read the map for someone else, if he believes a navigator identity will win admiration.

When life changes destabilize the importance hierarchy of our identities, we lose a crucial basis for self-organization and for planning our behavior. This occurs especially during periods in our lifetime such as adolescence and retirement when our social relationships, role opportunities, and abilities change rapidly. We are then liable to feel a weakened sense of unity, confusion about how to behave. This has been called an "identity crisis" (Erikson 1968). In order to overcome such confusion, we must reorganize our identity hierarchy, giving greater importance to identities based on our newly available or remaining social positions. A retiree may successfully reorganize the hierarchy, for example, by upgrading identities based on new hobbies (gardener) and on continuing social ties (witty conversationalist).

The Self in Thought and Feeling

Most of us are preoccupied by our own thoughts, feelings, and information that is especially relevant to us. The "cocktail party phenomenon" demonstrates this self-interest. At a noisy, crowded party you can often barely hear the conversation you are directly involved in. But should someone mention your name, even halfway across the room, you are likely to hear it and immediately to shift your attention in that direction. Experimental research has confirmed this power of self-relevant information to grab our attention (Moray 1959).

In this section we will discuss three ways in which the self affects our thoughts and feelings. These include (1) the impact of information's relevance to the self on memory and judgment; (2) ways that focusing attention on the self influence the relationship between our identities and our behavior; (3) ways the self influences the emotions we experience.

Memory and Judgment

In a recent study, a group of dating couples met for a discussion. Afterward, each member of the group was asked to recall what was said during their meeting. Responses indicated that they remembered their own remarks best, the remarks of their partners (an extension of the self) next best, and the words of strangers least (Brenner 1976). Results of this study demonstrate that our memory for events is better the more they relate to our selves. Relating information to the self has also been shown to enhance learning and memory for factual material. We remember a list of personality traits better, for instance, if we think about how each trait applies to us while trying to memorize the list (Rogers 1977).

Recent psychological theory and research regarding the influence of self on thinking has introduced the concept of **self-schema** (Greenwald and Pratkanis 1984). The self-schema is the active structure of ideas and knowledge we have about ourselves that we use in processing information (Markus 1977). Our important identities are central elements in our self-schema. Consequently, research on the effects of self-schema suggests ways in which important identities influence our judgment and our interpretation of information.

The influences of self-schema on our judgments are due to special features of self-related knowledge (Markus and Sentis 1982). Our knowledge about ourselves is particularly rich and complex, compared with what we know about other objects. This richness and complexity derive from several facts: We think about ourselves on virtually every occasion; self thoughts are especially vivid; and they are often infused with emotion. Repeated thinking about our selves creates detailed and elaborate mental connections among our self-con-

Box 2.2
WHEN DO I FEEL TRUE TO MYSELF?

If, in response to a skiing invitation, you said, "I'd love to, but I want a good grade on the exam I'm preparing for," would that express who you really are? Or would you feel you were sacrificing your real self to external demands? What if you said "I'd love to. Forget the exam. Let's go!" Would that be more truly you? Or would you feel you had surrendered yourself to an uncontrolled, alien impulse? These questions raise the problem of authenticity, the problem of whether we feel true to ourselves when we act.

Our feelings of authenticity do not depend on the actual links between self and behavior. Rather, they depend on our personal beliefs about the nature of the self. Do we believe that our self is anchored more in our internal impulses, or is it more the product of our ties to social institutions like the family, school, or job? According to Turner (1976), individuals locate the self at different points along a continuum from impulse to institution.

Individuals who tend to anchor the self in impulse believe they are being true to themselves only when they act spontaneously to express their own desires, ignoring societal standards and others' demands. These individuals feel most authentic when they abandon inhibitions, follow their impulses, and draw close to others by honestly revealing intimate feelings. For them, the self must be discovered within. If forced to play roles that conflict with their impulses, these individuals feel like hypocrites. They experience the social order as a set of frustrating rules and repressive norms that block the true expression of self.

In contrast, individuals who tend to anchor the self in ties to institutions see the self as something that must be developed and maintained through planful action. They feel they must create a worthy self through disci-plined acts of will, through striving to live up to standards of success and of morality. These individuals feel most authentic when they are in full control of their faculties so that they can behave according to plans, not impulses. They feel like hypocrites when they violate important standards. They experience the social order as the source of important values, such as integrity, courage, or achievement around which they can construct a true, worthy self.

Turner cites a substantial shift in American society from the institutional to the impulsive emphasis in recent decades. For example, an emphasis on impulse guides the flourishing movement devoted to discovering and liberating the socially repressed selves of minorities, youth, and women. Literary themes and child-rearing values increasingly emphasize freedom for impulse. And the growing reliance on psychotherapy to release the self from socially imposed constraints indicates an increasing rejection of the anchoring of self in ties to social institutions. Changes in the responses of students on the "Who Am I?" test also reflect a shift away from institution to impulse. More recently, personal attitudes, feelings, and desires have become increasingly important (Zurcher 1977; Snow and Phillips 1982).

The shift to impulse poses a problem for universities, which encourage students and faculty to strive to create true, worthy selves through standards of academic excellence. Students and faculty who see their true selves in impulse expression experience universities as frustrating and irrelevant to their true concerns. One expression of this dissatisfaction is the demand by students for courses appealing to impulse and self-discovery. Perhaps this tension between impulse and institution exists on your campus or in your personal life.

cepts. It also builds associations in our minds between self-related ideas and the events we encounter in our environment. These associations are readily activated whenever we encounter similar events in the future.

Compare Sara, for whom an athlete identity is important, with Maggie, who does not think about herself as either athletic or nonathletic. Sara will judge more quickly and confidently whether traits like agile, clumsy, muscular, and puny apply to her than will Maggie. She will also reject more strongly information purporting to show that she is either more coordinated than she had previously thought or less. In short, people are quicker and more certain when judging and interpreting information related to their important identities.

These identities also influence the ways people view others. When forming impressions, people seek out information that is particularly relevant to identities they consider important for themselves. For example, Sara might examine others' behavior for signs of their athletic talent and interests. People also discern finer variations in the behavior of other people when that behavior is relevant to their own important identities. Thus Sara will notice especially subtle differences in others' agility and physical coordination. Individuals for whom an athletic identity is unimportant would probably overlook these differences.

In processing information, we use the interrelated mental categories we have created through prior thought and experience. The important identities and other interrelated self-concepts constituting our self-schema provide a finely tuned set of mental categories that we can use to process new information. By employing these self-related categories, we seek out, perceive, judge, and remember information more effectively.

Effects of Self-Awareness

While eating with friends, reading a book, or participating in conversation, your attention is usually directed toward the objects, people, and events that surround you. But what happens if—upon looking up—you discover a photographer, lens focused on you, snapping away? Or what if you suddenly notice your image reflected in a large mirror? In such circumstances most of us become self-conscious. We enter a state of **self-awareness**—that is, we take the self as the object of our attention, and focus on our own appearance, actions, and thoughts. This corresponds to the "Me" phase of action (Mead 1934).

Numerous circumstances cause people to become self-aware: seeing our reflection in a mirror, facing a camera, hearing our voice on tape, encountering unfamiliar tasks and surroundings, or blundering in public. Mirrors, cameras, and recordings of our own voice cause self-awareness because they directly present the self to us as an object. Unfamiliarity and blundering also cause self-awareness because they disrupt the smooth flow of action and interaction. When this happens, we must attend to our own behavior more closely, monitoring its appropriateness and bringing it into line with the demands of the situation. In general, anything that reminds us that we are objects of others' attention will increase our self-awareness.

How does self-awareness influence behavior? When people are highly self-aware, they are more likely to behave honestly, helpfully, and industriously than when they are not self-aware. Self-awareness motivates people to close the gap between behavior and ideals. In general, people who are self-aware act in ways more consistent with personal and social standards (Wicklund and Frey 1980; Wicklund 1982). Their behavior is controlled more by the self. In the absence of self-awareness, behavior is more automatic, habitual, or driven. Society gains control over its members through the self-control individuals exercise when they are self-aware (Shibutani 1961). This is because the standards people conform to are largely learned from significant groups in society. Self-awareness is thus often a civilizing influence.

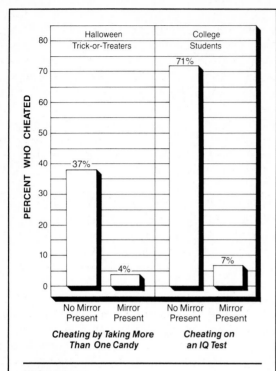

FIGURE 2.3

SELF-AWARENESS:
A CIVILIZING INFLUENCE ON BEHAVIOR

When we are in a state of self-awareness, we are more likely to behave in a manner that corresponds with prevailing social standards, or with the personal standards built into our identities. This is illustrated by the effects of the presence of a mirror—which increases self-awareness—on cheating. Halloween trick-or-treaters over age eight, instructed to take only one candy, cheated much less if exposed to a mirror while reaching into the candy bowl. The presence of a mirror also reduced cheating by college students who were given a chance to cheat by continuing work on an intelligence test beyond the time limit.

Source: adapted from Beaman et al. 1979; Diener and Wallbom 1976.

from a bowl. They were first asked their name and age and told, "You may take one of the candies." This instruction defined taking extra candies as "cheating." Self-awareness was raised for half the children. While reaching for the candy, they saw themselves in a large mirror. The presence of the mirror reduced cheating to one-tenth the level of violations exhibited in the absence of the mirror (Fig. 2.3). Evidence on cheating by college students also suggests that self-awareness increases conformity (Diener and Wallbom 1976). These and other studies show that important aspects of our identities—such as being honest—have more impact on our behavior when we are self-aware.

The most widely endorsed theory to explain these effects of self-awareness assumes that attention to self leads to self-evaluation (Wicklund 1975). We evaluate ourselves by comparing our current or planned behavior to our ideal standards or to the standards salient in the situation. Because our behavior typically falls short of our ideals, this comparison arouses self-dissatisfaction. In order to reduce this dissatisfaction, we first attempt to escape self-awareness (fleeing the scene, covering our face or ears, and so on). If this is impossible, we try to reduce self-dissatisfaction by controlling and modifying our behavior to make it consistent with desirable standards.

When social standards and internalized standards correspond, an increase in self-awareness brings behavior closer to ideals. But what if social standards conflict with internalized standards, as when groups pressure individuals to change their attitudes or to violate their personal standards? When this happens, the impact of increased self-awareness depends upon whether our attention is drawn to the public, social aspects of self or to the private, covert aspects of self (Scheier and Carver 1981).

If we attend to public aspects of self (the way our behavior appears to others, our mannerisms, our public image), we respond more to group influence and adhere less to our

A study of trick-or-treaters illustrates the impact of self-awareness on conformity to standards (Beaman et al. 1979). Children arriving at various homes on Hallowe'en were sent into the living room alone to collect candy personal standards. Attending to private aspects of self (our personal values, attitudes, and internalized standards) has the opposite effect: we guide our behavior more by personal standards and yield less to group influence. In studies demonstrating these opposite effects, cameras were used to induce public self-awareness, and to increase social responsiveness at the expense of self-direction. Mirrors were shown to induce private self-awareness—to increase self-direction at the expense of social conformity (Scheier and Carver 1983).

These findings suggest that groups enhance their social control over individual behavior when they expose individuals to conditions like an attentive audience, unfamiliar circumstances, and socially awkward tasks that increase awareness of the public self. Interestingly, these are precisely the conditions used so effectively by cults. Self-awareness is thus a double-edged sword: If we focus on our internalized standards, it increases independence and self-directed behavior, whereas if we focus on our public image, it increases conformity.

Self Influences on Emotions

At first, knowing how we feel appears to be a straightforward matter. We know whether we are happy or sad because we feel these emotions directly. But the matter is more complex than this. When we feel tightness in the stomach and sweaty palms, how do we know immediately whether we are happy or sad, fearful or in love? Closer examination suggests that the emotions we recognize are often merely plausible explanations we generate for physiological reactions. Whether we interpret our clenched teeth as a sign of fear or of sexual excitement depends on whether we are watching a horror film or an erotic movie.

COGNITIVE LABELLING THEORY. According to the cognitive labelling theory, emotions do not happen to the self. Rather, we ourselves actively construct and label our emotions (Schachter 1964). The theory proposes that we form our emotions in a three-step sequence:

1. An event in the environment produces a physiological reaction.
2. We notice the physiological reaction and search for an appropriate explanation.
3. By examining situational cues (What was happening when I reacted?), we find an emotion label (joy, disgust) for the reaction.

The theory further assumes that arousal is a generalized state, so that different emotions are not physiologically distinguishable. This implies that general arousal can signify virtually any emotion, depending on the situation.

In one study (Schachter and Singer 1962), researchers gave students an injection of epinephrine, a drug that produces heightened physiological arousal, as part of a study of drug effects on vision. They informed one group of students that this injection would probably cause them to experience a pounding heart, flushed face, and trembling (Informed Group). They told a second group nothing about the drug's side effects (Ignorant Group). All students then waited with a confederate who was hired by the researchers. The confederate behaved either euphorically (shooting crumpled paper at a waste basket, flying paper airplanes, playing with a hula hoop), or angrily (reacting with hostility to items on a questionnaire and finally tearing it up).

According to the theory, students in the Informed Group had no need to seek an emotional label because they knew their symptoms were drug induced. Students in the Ignorant Group, however, lacked an adequate explanation for their symptoms. As a result, they would search the environment for cues to help them label their feelings. Results confirmed these predictions. Students in the Ignorant Group adopted the label for their arousal suggested by the environment. That is, those in the Ignorant Group who waited with the euphoric confederate described themselves as happy, while those who waited with the angry confederate described themselves as angry. The self-descriptions of the Informed Group, on the other hand, were largely unaffected by the confederate's behavior.

Numerous later studies have expanded these findings to additional emotions (Kelley and Michela 1980). They show that people who are unaware of the true cause of their physiological arousal can be induced to view themselves as anxious, guilty, amused, or sexually excited by placing them in environments that suggest these emotions (Dienstbier 1978; Dutton and Aron 1974; Zillman 1978). As the theory predicts, environmental conditions influence people to mislabel their physiological arousal only when they are not aware of its true origins.

Later research suggests that the emotional label sometimes precedes the awareness of arousal (Kemper 1978; Leventhal 1980; Pennebaker 1980). We begin with a belief that we are experiencing a particular emotion, and only then search our bodily sensations for signs that will verify our belief. If environmental cues give us reason to believe we are angry, we attend to our flushed face and racing heart and verify our anger. If the cues suggest we are happy, we attend to our feelings of alertness and trembling and confirm our happiness. At any given time, our physiological state may afford evidence to support several emotion labels.

This extension of cognitive labelling theory suggests two ways in which role identities may influence the emotions and sensations we experience. First, particular role identities direct attention selectively to particular sensations. Hypochondriacs verify their identity as sickly by attending to their stuffed noses, raspy throats, and uneven pulse, while people who view themselves as healthy tend to overlook these same physical signs. Second, role identities imply how sensations should be interpreted. The pounding heart that accompanies a drop to earth from an airplane signifies thrill to a veteran skydiver but terror to a novice paratrooper. Each interprets the same physical sign in line with his or her role identity.

SENTIMENTS. Most of the emotions we have discussed (such as fear, joy, anger) are a response to immediate situations and tend to fade quickly when arousal subsides. Complex feelings like grief, love, jealousy, or indignation, however, arise out of our enduring social relationships. These socially significant feelings are called **sentiments** (Cooley 1902; Gordon 1981; Turner 1970). Each is a pattern of sensations, emotions, actions, and cultural beliefs appropriate to a social relationship. Sentiments such as grief, loyalty, envy, and patriotism develop around our attachments to family, friends, fellow workers, and country.

Sentiments reflect the nature of our social relationships and the changes in them. Grief and nostalgia reflect social losses; jealousy and envy reflect problems over control of possessions; indignation and resentment reflect betrayal of commitments. We label our feelings with the culturally appropriate sentiment to make sense of our diverse emotional responses. For example, Mark's joy in Laurie's presence, his sorrow in her absence, his anger when she is criticized, and his fear when threatened with her loss make sense if he labels his feeling "love." Like simpler emotions, sentiments are produced by cognitive labelling. In choosing a sentiment label, however, we take into account all the information we have about our enduring relationship.

As we develop our role identities we also learn which sentiments are appropriate to them (Denzin 1983). By expressing appropriate sentiments, we affirm or modify our identities and the social relationships in which they are embedded. To affirm our identity as a romantic partner, for example, we must express love, jealousy, anxiety, tenderness, and ecstasy, all at the appropriate times and places.

Not everyone can win an Olympic gold medal. But for all of us an inner sense of self-esteem depends on experiencing ourselves as causal agents who make things happen, who overcome obstacles and attain goals.

EMOTION WORK. On occasion, the self takes an especially direct, active role in the control of emotions. At one time or another most of us have psyched ourselves up, forced ourselves to have a good time, tried to feel grateful, and fought back our disappointment. These are all instances of **emotion work,** attempts to change the intensity or quality of our feelings to bring them into line with the requirements of the occasion (Hochschild 1979). Emotion work is needed when we find that we are in violation of **feeling rules**—rules that dictate what people with our identities ought to feel in a given situation. These rules sometimes require feelings we are not experiencing.

There are two basic kinds of emotion work: (1) evocation of feelings that are not present but should be; (2) suppression of feelings that are present but should not be. For example, a flight attendant is expected to feel calm and cheerful as she relates to passengers. But suppose the flight attendant is paralyzed by fear upon learning that her plane has been highjacked. She must then work directly on her own emotions to recapture at least some of the calm demanded by her role. She must evoke feelings of calmness and suppress feelings of fear.

Among the methods used to evoke suitable emotions and suppress unsuitable ones are adopting appropriate postures, shaping our facial expressions, breathing quickly or deeply, and thinking appropriate thoughts. Emotion work modifies our actual feelings. An alternative strategy, employed when we are not personally committed to the identity to which the feeling rules apply, is to control only the outward expression of our feelings (Gordon 1981).

Self-Esteem

Do you have a positive attitude about yourself, or do you feel you do not have much to be proud of? On the whole, how capable, successful, significant, and worthy are you? Answers to these questions reflect our overall self-esteem, our general evaluation of ourselves.

Self-esteem is the evaluative component of the self-concept (Gergen 1971; Gecas 1972).

After examining the components and measurement of self-esteem, this section will address three questions: (1) What are the major sources of self-esteem? (2) How is self-esteem related to behavior? (3) What techniques do we employ to protect and enhance our self-esteem?

What Is Self-Esteem?

COMPONENTS OF SELF-ESTEEM. Our overall self-esteem depends upon how we evaluate our numerous, specific role identities. We evaluate each as relatively positive or negative. You may consider yourself a competent athlete, for example, but an incompetent debater, a worthy friend, but an unworthy son or daughter. According to theory, our overall level of self-esteem is the product of these individual evaluations, with each identity weighted according to its importance (Rosenberg 1965; Sherwood 1965).

Ordinarily, we are unaware of precisely how we combine and weight the evaluations of our specific identities. If we weight our positively evaluated identities as more important, we can maintain a high level of overall self-esteem while still admitting to certain weaknesses. If we weight our negatively evaluated identities heavily, we will have low overall self-esteem even though we have many valuable qualities.

MEASUREMENT OF SELF-ESTEEM. We can further clarify this concept by looking at three methods for measuring self-esteem. One approach, using direct self-evaluations (Rosenberg 1965), asks respondents whether they agree or disagree with statements such as: (1) I certainly feel useless at times. (2) On the whole I am satisfied with myself. (3) I have a number of good qualities. (4) I wish I could have more respect for myself. Each answer reveals direct evaluations of competence, power or control on the one hand, or of moral and social worth or acceptance on the other.

A less direct approach to measuring self-esteem asks people to accept or reject factual rather than explicitly evaluative self-descriptions. Consider the following items from the Coopersmith Self-Esteem Inventory (1967): (1) I'm pretty sure of myself. (2) I have a low opinion of myself. (3) I'm easy to like. (4) I give in easily. On the surface, these descriptions are factual. This approach assumes, however, that all respondents evaluate particular descriptions either positively (items 1, 3) or negatively (items 2, 4). Self-esteem is considered higher the more that people accept positive descriptions and reject negative ones.

A third approach derives from the idea that self-esteem depends on the correspondence between actual self-perceptions and ideals (James 1890; Cohen 1959; Sherwood 1965). In line with this idea, respondents furnish two separate but parallel self-descriptions, one of their actual self and one of the self they aspire to be. A self-esteem score is then derived from the discrepancy between these self-descriptions. Small actual-ideal discrepancies point to high self-esteem, larger discrepancies to lower self-esteem.

These three self-report approaches are the most popular because they measure self-esteem as a reflexive process of self-evaluation. Unfortunately, the scores obtained may be distorted by individuals' desire to present a favorable image of themselves. Nonetheless, these approaches have proven very useful in our understanding of self-esteem (Wells and Marwell 1976).

Sources of Self-Esteem

Why do some of us enjoy high self-esteem while others suffer low self-esteem? To help answer this question, consider three major sources of self-esteem—family experience, performance feedback, and social comparison.

FAMILY EXPERIENCE. As might be expected, parent–child relationships are important for the development of self-esteem. Based on an extensive study of the family experiences of fifth- and sixth-graders, Coopersmith (1967) concluded that four types of parental behavior promote higher self-esteem: (1) showing acceptance, affection, interest, and involvement in children's affairs; (2) firmly and consistently enforcing clear limits on children's behavior; (3) allowing children latitude within these limits and respecting initiative (children setting their own bedtime and participating in making family plans); (4) favoring noncoercive forms of discipline (denying privileges and discussing reasons, rather than punishing physically). Findings from a representative sample of 5,024 New York high-school students corroborate these conclusions (Rosenberg 1965).

Family influences on self-esteem confirm the interactionist idea that the self-concepts we develop mirror the view of ourselves communicated by significant others. Children who see that their parents love, accept, care about, trust, and reason with them come to think of themselves as worthy of affection, care, trust, and respect. But why is discipline related to high self-esteem? Perhaps because parental limits paired with reasoning provide evidence of parental concern and interest. Firm management may also promote self-esteem because it creates a more orderly, predictable environment where children can interact more successfully and feel more capable and in control.

Research also suggests that self-esteem is produced by the reciprocal influence of parents and their children on each other. Children with higher self-esteem exhibit more self-confidence, competence, and self-control. Such children are probably easier to love, accept, reason with, and trust. Consequently, they are likely to elicit responses from their parents that further promote self-esteem.

PERFORMANCE FEEDBACK. Our everyday successes and failures influence self-esteem by providing us with frequent feedback about the quality of our performances. We derive an inner sense of self-esteem from experiencing ourselves as active causal agents who make things happen in the world, who attain goals and overcome obstacles (Cooley 1902; Franks and Marolla 1976). Such self-esteem is based on our sense of efficacy—of competence and power to control events (Bandura 1982). People who hold low power positions (such as clerks, unskilled workers) have fewer opportunities to develop efficacy-based self-esteem because such positions limit their freedom of action. Even so, people seek ways to convert almost any kind of activity into a task against which to test their efficacy and prove their competence (Gecas and Schwalbe 1983). In this way they obtain performance feedback useful for building self-esteem.

SOCIAL COMPARISON. In order to interpret whether performances represent success or failure, we must often compare them with our own goals and self-expectations or with the performances of others. Getting a B on a math exam, for example, would raise your sense of math competence if you had hoped for a C at best, but shake you if you were counting on an A. The impact of the B on your self-esteem would also vary depending on whether most of your friends got A's or C's.

Social comparison is crucial to self-esteem because the feelings of competence or worth we derive from a performance depend in large part on whom we and others compare us with. Even our own personal goals are largely derived from our aspirations to succeed in comparison with people whom we admire. We are most likely to receive evaluative feedback from others in our immediate social context— our family, peers, teachers, and work associates. We are also most likely to compare ourselves with these people and with others who are similar to us (Festinger 1954; Rosenberg and Simmons 1971).

A study of job applicants clearly demonstrates the effect of social comparison on self-esteem (Morse and Gergen 1970). After each applicant had completed a set of forms, including a self-esteem scale, another applicant entered the waiting room. For half the participants, the second applicant wore a dark business suit, carried an attaché case, and commu-

Box 2.3
MINORITY STATUS AND SELF-ESTEEM

Members of racial, religious, and ethnic minorities may have special problems in developing a reasonable level of self-esteem. Because of prejudice, minority group members are likely to see a negative image of themselves reflected in others' appraisals. When they make social comparisons of their own economic, occupational, and educational success with that of the majority, they are bound to compare unfavorably. Therefore, we might assume that members of minority groups will interpret their performances and achievements as evidence of their basic lack of worth and competence.

For example, note the following statement to the United States Supreme Court:

"As minority-group children learn the inferior status to which they are assigned and observe that they are usually segregated and isolated from the more privileged members of their society they react with deep feelings of inferiority and with a sense of personal humiliation" (Clark 1963).

Is this hypothesis true? Hundreds of studies have sought to determine whether minority status undermines self-esteem in America (Wylie 1979). Surprisingly, the vast majority of studies offer little support for the conclusion that minorities (racial, religious, or ethnic) have appreciably lower self-esteem. A number of the best-controlled studies suggest that minorities may even have somewhat higher self-esteem (Bachman 1970; Rosenberg and Simmons 1972; Simmons et al. 1978; Trowbridge 1972).

Close examination of these studies reveals that reflected appraisals from significant others and social comparisons of success do indeed affect minority group members. For example, the self-esteem of black school children is strongly related to their perception of what their parents, teachers, and friends think of them. In everyday life, however, appraisals and social comparisons are usually not negative (Barnes 1972; Rosenberg 1973, 1981; Yancey, Rigsby, and McCarthy 1972). Living in segregated neighborhoods, minority-group children usually see themselves through the unprejudiced eyes of their own group, not the eyes of the dominant majority. In contrast, blacks attending largely white schools and Catholics growing up in non-Catholic neighborhoods—circumstances likely to produce negative reflected appraisals—do tend to have lower self-esteem than majority groups (Rosenberg and Simmons 1972). In effect, segregation insulates minority children from regularly comparing themselves with more successful majorities.

When social comparisons with majorities are made, their impact on self-esteem depends on who is blamed for failures. Minorities can protect their self-esteem by blaming the system of discrimination rather than themselves for their lesser accomplishments. Indeed, minority statuses such as race, religion, and ethnicity show virtually no association with overall self-esteem (Jacques and Chason 1977). Social failure affects self-esteem only when people attribute it to poor individual achievement (Rosenberg and Pearlin 1978).

nicated an aura of competence. The remaining participants each waited with an applicant who wore a smelly sweatshirt and no socks, and appeared dazed. Several minutes later, while still in the presence of the highly impressive or unimpressive competitor, applicants completed additional forms, including a second self-esteem scale. Applicants exposed to the obviously inferior competitor revealed a substantial increase in self-esteem from the

Elated with their school's victory, these fans are proud to be students at the University of Missouri. They boost their own self-esteem by identifying with their school team. But following a defeat, fans are likely to avoid loss of self-esteem by identifying less with their team.

first to the second self-esteem measurement; among those faced with the impressive competitor, self-esteem dropped substantially.

Losing one's job is interpreted as a serious failure in our society. A national survey of American employees reveals that job loss undermined self-esteem, but the size of the drop depended on social comparison. In neighborhoods with little unemployment, persons who lost their jobs suffered a large drop in self-esteem. In neighborhoods where many others were unemployed too, the drop was less. This difference points to the importance of the immediate social context for defining success/failure (Cohn 1978).

Self-Esteem and Behavior

Self-esteem interests social psychologists because people with high self-esteem behave quite differently from those with low self-esteem. Research findings indicate that high self-esteem is generally associated with active and comfortable social involvement, whereas low self-esteem is a depressing and debilitating state (Coopersmith 1967; Rosenberg 1979; Wylie 1979).

Compared with those low in self-esteem, children, teenagers, and adults with higher self-esteem are socially at ease and popular with their peers. They are more confident of their own opinions and judgments, and expect they will be well received and successful. They are more vigorous and assertive in their social relations, more ambitious, and more academically successful. During their school years, those with higher self-esteem participate more in extracurricular activities, are elected more frequently to leadership roles, show greater interest in public affairs, and have higher occupational aspirations. On psychiatric examinations and psychological tests they appear healthier, better adjusted, and relatively free of symptoms.

The picture of people with low self-esteem forms an unhappy contrast. People low in self-esteem tend to be socially anxious and ineffective. They view interpersonal relationships as threatening, feel less positively toward others, and are easily hurt by criticism. Lacking confidence in their own judgments and opinions, they yield more readily in the face of opposition. They expect others to reject them and their ideas, and have little faith in their ability to achieve. In school, they set lower goals for themselves, are less successful academically, less active in the classroom and in extracurricular activities, and less popular. People with lower self-esteem appear more depressed and express more feelings of unhappiness and discouragement. They more frequently manifest symptoms of anxiety, poor adjustment, and psychosomatic illness.

Most of these contrasts are drawn from comparisons between naturally occurring groups of people who report high or low self-esteem. It is therefore difficult to determine whether self-esteem causes these behavior differences or vice versa. For example, high self-esteem may enable people to assert their opinions more forcefully, and thus to convince others. But the experience of influencing others, in turn, may increase self-esteem. Thus, reciprocal influence, rather than causality from self-esteem to behavior, is probably most common.

The relationships of self-esteem to social behavior are not always straightforward. Studies of the relationship between self-esteem and susceptibility to persuasion illustrate this complexity. Several show that people who report high self-esteem are more resistant to persuasion (see Janis 1954). Other studies show that persuasion is more effective with people high in self-esteem (Nisbett and Gordon 1967). To explain these contradictory results, McGuire (1969) suggests that self-esteem affects two different processes involved in persuasion—understanding the message and yielding to others. Low self-esteem tends to interfere with understanding, especially when it is difficult or threatening to understand. Once the message is understood, however, low self-esteem is conducive to yielding. Results of later studies support this explanation (Leventhal 1970; Zellner 1970).

Protecting and Enhancing Self-Esteem

Ordinarily, we seek to maintain a positive evaluation of our own worth and competence. To this end, we strive—while enacting our various role identities—to meet or surpass our own standards for achievement and to elicit supportive responses from others. Inevitably, however, we fail to live up to all our idealized self-expectations and to impress others sufficiently to obtain the full role support we desire. Here, four different techniques used to protect or enhance self-esteem will be examined (see McCall and Simmons 1978; Rosenberg 1979; Secord and Backman 1974).

MANIPULATING APPRAISALS. We choose to associate with people who support our role performances and communicate favorable appraisals, and avoid people who do not see us the way we see ourselves. This enables us to conclude: "Others think highly of me." For example, a study of interaction in a college sorority revealed that women associated most frequently with those who they believed saw them most as they saw themselves (Backman and Secord 1962). Such selective interaction practically ensures that we will receive favorable appraisals.

Another way to enhance our self-esteem is by interpreting others' appraisals as more favorable than they actually are. Such distortion occurs even among people who interact frequently. For instance, soldiers and human relations trainees tend to overestimate their peers' ratings of their qualities (Reeder, Donahue, and Biblarz 1960; Sherwood 1965). Similarly, people often overestimate how highly others regard their own racial, religious, ethnic, and occupational groups. (Rosenberg 1979).

SELECTIVE INFORMATION PROCESSING. Another way we enhance our self-esteem is by attending more to those occurrences that reflect favorably on our merits and virtues. This is known as selective information processing. Psychiatric attendants focus more on their contributions to alleviating patients' suffering, for example, than on the cleanup and housekeeping activities that occupy most of their time (Simpson and Simpson 1959). We also protect our self-esteem by taking credit for successes but denying responsibility for failures and for the ill-effects of our actions (Bradley 1978). We attribute good grades to our ability and effort, for example, and poor grades to bad luck, external pressures, or other extenuating circumstances. Memory also acts to protect self-esteem. We recall our good, responsible, and successful activities more often than our bad, irresponsible, and unsuccessful ones. We also enhance esteem by remembering our own contributions to joint efforts (preparing a project, preserving a relationship) as greater than others' contributions (Ross and Sicoly 1979).

SELECTIVE SOCIAL COMPARISON. When we lack objective standards for evaluating ourselves, we engage in social comparison (Festinger 1954). By carefully selecting others with whom to compare ourselves, we can further protect our self-esteem. We usually compare ourselves with persons who are similar in age, sex, occupation, economic status, abilities, and attitudes

(Suls and Miller 1977; Walsh and Taylor 1982). We tend to avoid comparing ourselves with the class valedictorian, homecoming queen, or star athlete, thereby forestalling a negative self-evaluation.

Once people make a social comparison, they tend to overrate their relative standing (Felson 1981). This is illustrated by self-ratings obtained from a large sample of American adults (Heiss and Owens 1972). Only 2 percent rated themselves "below average" as parents, spouses, sons or daughters, or in the qualities of trustworthiness, intelligence, and willingness to work.

SELECTIVE COMMITMENT TO IDENTITIES. Still another technique involves committing ourselves more to those self-concepts in which we excel and downgrading those in which we fall short. This protects overall self-esteem because self-evaluation is based most heavily on those identities and personal qualities we consider most important. In one study, adults estimated how good they were on 16 qualities and stated how much they cared about each (see Table 2.3). Results show that, in general, people were more likely to consider a quality important if they thought they excelled in it (Rosenberg 1979).

People tend to enhance self-esteem by assigning more importance to those identities (religious, racial, occupational, family) they consider particularly admirable (Hoelter 1983). They also increase or decrease identification with a social group when the group becomes a greater or lesser potential source of esteem (Tesser and Campbell 1983). Students, for example, are more apt to wear clothing that displays university affiliation following a football victory rather than a defeat. They also identify more with their school when describing victories ("We won") than defeats ("They lost"), thereby enhancing or protecting self-esteem (Cialdini et al. 1976).

All four techniques for protecting self-esteem described here portray human beings as active processors of social events. People do

TABLE 2.3
IMPORTANCE TO SELF AND SELF-ESTIMATED GOODNESS OF "WORKING WITH HANDS"

Self-Estimated Goodness	Importance to Self		Number
	Great Deal	*Some or Little*	*Number*
Very Good	68%	32%	533
Fairly Good	27%	73%	392
Poor	6%	94%	224

Note: 1,149 Chicago adults were asked to rate such qualities as honesty, kindness, likeability, and being realistic. The responses for 16 qualities showed a pattern similar to that illustrated here for "working with hands." People rated those qualities they believed they excelled in as more important to self. In this way they protected and enhanced their self-esteem.

Source: adapted from Rosenberg (1979).

not accept social evaluations passively or allow self-esteem to be buffeted by the cruelties and kindnesses of the social environment. Nor do successes and failures directly affect self-esteem. The techniques described here testify to human ingenuity in selecting and modifying the meanings of events in the service of self-esteem.

Summary

The self is the individual viewed both as the source and the object of reflexive behavior.

THE NATURE AND GENESIS OF SELF. (1) We experience the self as source when we plan, observe, and control our own behavior. We experience the self as object when we think about who we are. (2) Newborns lack a sense of self. Later, they come to recognize that they are physically separate from others. As they acquire language they learn that their own thoughts and feelings are also separate. (3) Through role taking, children come to see themselves through others' eyes. They can then observe, judge, and regulate their own behavior. (4) Children construct their identities based on how they imagine they appear to others. They also develop self-evaluations based on the perceived judgments of others.

IDENTITIES: THE SELF WE KNOW. The self we know includes multiple identities. (1) Each identity is linked to one of the social roles we enact. At the same time, we shape it to fit our own unique qualities. (2) Role identities are the self-concepts individuals mention most often when describing themselves. They also mention personal qualities and self-evaluations. (3) The self we know varies with the situation. We attend most to those aspects of our selves that are distinctive and relevant to the ongoing activity. (4) We form self-concepts primarily in response to the perceived reactions of others. Because we notice and react to features that distinguish people from their social groups, such features are especially likely to become important self-concepts.

IDENTITIES: THE SELF WE ENACT. The self we enact expresses our identities. (1) We choose behaviors in order to evoke responses from others that will confirm particular identities. To confirm identities successfully, we must share with others our understanding of what these behaviors and identities mean. (2) We choose which identity to express based on that identity's need for support, situational opportunities for enacting it, and its relative importance to us. The relative importance of an identity depends on the resources invested in constructing that identity, and the benefits tied to enacting it. (3) We gain a sense of personal unity and lend consistency to our behavior over time by striving persistently to enact important identities.

THE SELF IN THOUGHT AND FEELING. The self affects both thought and feeling. (1) We learn and remember information better if it relates to the self. We seek out, perceive, and judge information more effectively if it relates to our important identities. (2) When attention is drawn to the self, we become self-aware and take greater control over our behavior. We then conform more with our own personal standards and with salient social standards. (3) The emotions we experience also depend on the self. Our identities cause us to notice particular sensations and influence the interpretations and emotional labels we apply to them. When our emotions seem socially inappropriate, we try to modify our feelings.

SELF-ESTEEM. Self-esteem, the evaluative component of self, is essential to most people. (1) Overall self-esteem depends on the evaluations of our specific role identities. Self-reports are a general method for measuring self-esteem. (2) Self-esteem derives from three sources: family experiences of acceptance and discipline, direct feedback on the effectiveness of actions, and comparisons of our own successes and failures with those of others. (3) People with higher self-esteem tend to be more popular, assertive, ambitious, academically successful, better adjusted, and happier. (4) We employ numerous techniques to protect and enhance self-esteem. For example, we seek favorable reflected appraisals, process information selectively, overestimate our relative worth compared to similar others, and attribute greater importance to qualities in which we excel.

Key Terms and Concepts

Self-Concept

Identity

Self

Role Taking

Significant Others

Generalized Other

Role Identity

Situated Self

Self-Schema

Self-Awareness

Sentiments

Emotion Work

Feeling Rules

Self-Esteem

Chapter 3
Childhood Socialization

Introduction

Perspectives on Socialization

The Developmental Perspective
The Social Learning Perspective
The Interaction of Development and Learning
The Impact of Social Structure

Agents of Childhood Socialization

Family
Peers
School

Processes of Socialization

Observational Learning
Instrumental Learning
Internalization

Outcomes of Socialization

Gender Roles
Linguistic and Cognitive Competence
Knowledge of Social Rules
Achievement and Work Orientations

Summary

Key Terms and Concepts

Introduction

A change has come over me. I do things differently from the way I used to. The change has been subtle, slow, but other people have noticed it as well. My wife complains, but it's not my fault. I am suffering from creeping Harry Cohenism.

Harry Cohen is my father. For years, this was nothing more than a statement of fact. He is my father and I am his son and other than that, we had very little in common. He could spell and I could not. He could do math in his head and I could not. He could not sleep well or at all past 6 A.M. and I could sleep soundly and forever and he was always, but always, way older than I was.

Now, however, we are both the same age—middle-aged. He is upper middle-aged, and I am younger middle-aged, but we are essentially the same age.

I sleep like him now. I used to sleep like me—deeply and endlessly. When I was a kid, this would drive my father mad. He would look at me sound asleep in my bed at, say, 1 o'clock in the afternoon, and explode with frustration: "Get up, get up!" He could not understand how anyone could sleep so late. I could not understand how anyone could not. Sleeping, in fact, was one of the very few things I did really well. I excelled at sleeping.

But no more. I wake up at 6 in the morning. My eyes open and that is it. I try to go back to sleep, but I cannot. I lie and look at the clock and wait for the sun to come up, but there is no going back to sleep. For a long time, I worried that something was wrong with me. I could not figure out what was happening, and then it occurred to me. I was becoming my father.

I know that by all logic I should be becoming my mother, too. After all, half my genes are hers and, knowing her, they are the dominant ones. But for some reason, I feel that her genes declared themselves early and that from here on out it is my father who is taking over.

After all, it is my father and not my mother who falls asleep in front of the television set. It is my father and not my mother who gets bogged down in detail in the middle of telling a story. And it is my father who will tell you the same story twice—only each time a little bit differently. I am even beginning to like opera.

For a time, I thought that I was my own man, that I could be exactly what I wanted to be. I recognize now that there is such a thing as a genetic manifest destiny—a case of the future really being the past. I don't have any problems with that, though. My father is a grand man—sweet and sensitive and smart. I didn't realize it until recently, but in many ways we're a lot alike—not like my son. Boy, can that kid sleep!

I wonder where he gets it from.

—RICHARD COHEN

Richard Cohen expresses well one of the striking features of social life. There is a great deal of continuity from one generation to the next, continuity in both physical characteristics and in behavior. Genetic inheritance is one source of continuity. But a major contributor to intergenerational similarity is **socialization,** "the ways in which individuals learn skills, knowledge, values, motives, and roles appropriate to their position in a group or society" (Bush and Simmons 1981).

How does an infant become "human"—that is, an effective participant in society? The answer is through socialization. As the infant grows she learns how to interact with others. Like all of us, Richard Cohen learned to speak English, a prerequisite for participation in our society. We learned basic interaction rituals, such as greeting a stranger with a handshake and a loved one with a kiss. We also learned the socially accepted ways to achieve various goals, both material (food, clothing, and shelter) and social (the respect, love, and help of others). It is obvious that socialization makes us like most other members of society in important ways. It is not so obvious that socialization also produces our individuality. The self, and the capacity to engage in self-oriented acts discussed in the preceding chapter, are a result of socialization. Richard Cohen's appreciation for opera, for example, reflects his unique socialization by his father.

This chapter will examine childhood socialization. By "childhood" we mean the period from birth to adolescence. Childhood is a social concept, shaped by historical, cultural, and political influences (Denzin 1977). In contemporary American society, we define children as immature, in need of training at home and of a formal education. Chapter 4 examines the continuing socialization of adolescents and adults.

The discussion here focuses on four questions:

1. What are the basic perspectives in the study of socialization?
2. What are the socializing agents in contemporary American society?
3. What are the processes through which socialization occurs?
4. What are the outcomes of socialization in childhood?

Perspectives on Socialization

At the beginning of this chapter, Richard Cohen attributes the similarity between himself and his father to "genetic manifest destiny." What is the more important influence on behavior—nature or nurture, heredity or environment? This question has been especially important to those who study the child. Although both are influential, one view emphasizes biological development (heredity), whereas another emphasizes social learning (environment).

The Developmental Perspective

The human child obviously undergoes a process of maturation. He or she grows physically, develops motor skills in a sequence that appears to be relatively uniform, and begins to engage in various social behaviors at about the same age as most other children.

Some theorists view socialization as largely dependent upon processes of physical and psychological maturation, which are biologically determined. Gesell and Ilg (1943) have documented the sequence in which motor and social skills develop and the ages at which each new ability appears in the average child. They view the development of many social behaviors as primarily due to physical and neurological maturation; thus, caregivers can facilitate but are not responsible for the occurrence of many behaviors which others might consider outcomes of socialization. For example, toilet training requires voluntary control over sphincter muscles and the ability to recognize cues of pressure on the bladder or lower intestine. According to developmental theory, when children around age 2½ develop these skills, they will learn by themselves without environmental influences.

Table 3.1 indicates sequences of development of various abilities that have been identified by observational research. The ages indicated are approximate; some children will exhibit the behavior at younger ages, while others will do so later.

As an example, consider the development of responsiveness to other persons. At as early as 4 weeks, many infants respond to close physical contact by relaxing. At 16 weeks, babies can discriminate the human face and usually smile in response. They also show signs of recognition of the voice of their usual caregiver. By 28 weeks, the infant clearly differentiates faces and responds to variations in facial expression. At one year, the child shows a variety of emotions in response to behavior by others. He or she will seek out interaction with adults or with siblings by crawling or walking to them and tugging on clothing. Thus recognition of, responsiveness to, and orientation toward adults seem to follow a uniform developmental pattern. From a developmental viewpoint the ability to interact with others depends in part on the development of visual and auditory discrimination.

Developmental explanations can be provided for very complex phenomena. Piaget

TABLE 3.1
THE PROCESS OF DEVELOPMENT

	16 Weeks	28 Weeks	1 Year	2 Years	3 Years
Visual Activity	Follows objects with eyes Eyes adjust to objects at varying distances	Watches activity intently Hand-eye coordination	Enjoys watching moving objects (like TV picture)	Responds to stimuli in periphery of visual field Looks intently for long periods	
Interpersonal	Smiles at human face Responds to caregiver's voice Demands social attention	Responds to variation in tone of voice Differentiates people (fears strangers)	Engages in responsive play Shows emotions, anxiety Shows definite preferences for some persons	Prefers solitary play Rudimentary concept of ownership	Can play cooperatively with older child Strong desire to please Sex differences in choice of toys, materials
Vocal Activity	Vocalizes pleasure (coos, gurgles, laughs) Babbles (strings of syllablelike sounds)	Vocalizes vowels and consonants Tries to imitate sounds	Vocalizes syllables Practices two to eight known words	Vocalizes constantly Names actions Repeats words	Uses three-word sentences Likes novel words
Bodily Movement	Can hold head up Can roll over	Can sit up	Can stand Can climb up and down stairs	Can run Likes large-scale motor activity— push, pull, roll	Motion fluid, smooth Good coordination
Manual Dexterity	Touches objects	Can grasp with one hand Manipulates objects	Manipulates objects serially	Good control of hand and arm	Good fine-motor control —uses fingers, thumb, wrist well

Source: adapted from Arnold Gesell and Frances Ilg, Infant and Child in the Culture of Today *(New York: Harper and Row, 1943) and Frank Caplan, ed.,* The First Twelve Months of Life *(New York: Grosset and Dunlap, 1973).*

(1965) proposed that moral judgment is the result of a process of sequential development in the child's reasoning abilities. His theory is based on conversations with children of various ages. To study moral judgment, a child is given the following pair of stories:

A. A little boy who is called John is in his room. He is called to dinner. He goes into the dining room. But behind the door there was a chair, and on the chair there was a tray with 15 cups on it. John couldn't have known that there was all this behind the door. He goes in; the door knocks against the tray; bang go the 15 cups and they all get broken.

B. Once there was a little boy whose name was Henry. One day when his mother was out he tried to get some jam out of the cupboard. He climbed onto a chair and stretched out his arms. But the jam was too high up, and he couldn't reach it and have any. While he was trying to get it, he knocked over a cup. The cup fell down and broke.

The child is then asked, "Which child is naughtier? Why?"

Based on the children's responses, Piaget identified three stages of moral development. The first stage is called *moral realism*. In this stage acts are judged solely on the basis of the amount of damage done. Children say that John is naughtier than Henry, because John broke 15 cups. At this stage, morality involves obedience to the rules the child has been taught by parents. At about age seven, children gradually move into the second stage, called *moral relativism*. They take into account the intentions of the individual in evaluating the morality of an act. Children at this stage say John was not as naughty as Henry because John broke the cups by accident. At about age eleven, children enter a third stage, *moral independence*. In this stage they recognize and apply abstract moral or ethical principles to particular acts.

Critics of developmental models believe that the maturity of the child is not of basic importance to socialization. They agree that demands made by caregivers must be appropriate to the child's degree of physical and neurological development. Demands made before the child is capable of responding to them will create difficulty. So maturity does set limits on the speed and sequencing of outcomes of the socialization process, but it is not primarily responsible for those outcomes.

The Social Learning Perspective

While the developmental perspective focuses on the unfolding of the child's own abilities, a second perspective emphasizes the child's acquisition of cognitive and behavioral skills from the environment. Successful socialization requires that the child acquire considerable information about the world. First, many physical or natural realities must be learned (Baumrind 1980), such as what animals are dangerous and which things are edible. Children must also learn about the social environment. They must learn the language used by people in their environment in order to communicate their needs to others. They also need to learn the meanings their caregivers associate with various actions. As noted earlier, children need to learn to identify the kinds of persons encountered in the immediate environment. They need to learn what behaviors they can expect of people, as well as the expectations for their own behavior.

Within this perspective, socialization is primarily a process of children learning "the meanings that are shared in the groups in which they are reared" (Shibutani 1961). Such variation in meanings gives groups and subcultures (and societies) their distinctiveness. In our society, many groups sharply differentiate male and female. Males have traditionally been defined as aggressive, independent, and action-oriented, while females have been defined as passive, dependent, and nurturant. Many groups also associate specific meanings with persons from other ethnic or religious groups. For example, many whites perceive blacks as less ambitious, more likely to engage in aggressive or violent behavior, and less intelligent than whites (see Chapter 6). Conversely, whites often view persons of Oriental descent as more intelligent and more family-oriented than whites.

This viewpoint emphasizes the adaptive nature of socialization. The infant learns the verbal and interpersonal skills necessary in order to interact successfully with others. Having acquired these skills, children can perpetuate the meanings that distinguish their social groups, and even add to or modify these meanings by introducing innovations of their own.

Responsiveness to another person develops early in life. By 16 weeks of age, a child smiles in response to a human face. By 28 weeks, a child can distinguish caregivers from strangers.

The Interaction of Development and Learning

Recent research on socialization takes into account both the importance of developmental processes and the influence of social learning. The developmental age of the child obviously determines which acts the child can perform. Infants less than six months old cannot walk. All cultures have adapted to these developmental limitations by coordinating the performance expectations placed on children with maturation of their abilities. At the same time, developmental processes are not necessarily sufficient for the emergence of complex social behavior. In addition to developmental readiness, social interaction—learning—is necessary for the development of language. This is illustrated by the case of Isabelle who lived alone with her deaf-mute mother until the age of six and one-half. When she was discovered, she was unable to make any sound other than a croak. Yet within two years after she entered a systematic educational program, her vocabulary numbered more than 1,500 words and she had the linguistic skills of a six-year-old (Davis 1947).

Developmental processes produce a readiness to perform certain behaviors. The content of these behaviors is determined primarily by social learning, that is, by cultural influences. This malleability allows a society or subculture to create distinctive speech and behavior patterns. Consider, for example, why most Americans are right-handed. For years it was assumed that there was a neurological basis for this distinctive trait. In fact, handedness may be influenced by social pressures and social learning. Furniture (such as desks), machinery (such as automobile and airplane controls), and many other cultural tools and products are made for right-handed persons. As soon as children enter school, teachers may begin to pressure them to use their right hands. It may be that these social influences account in part for our distinctive handedness.

The Impact of Social Structure

Socialization is not a random process. Teaching new members the rules of the game is too important to be left to chance. Socialization is organized according to the sequence of roles that newcomers to the society ordinarily pass through. In American society, these include familial roles, such as son or daughter, and roles in educational institutions, such as preschooler, elementary school student, and high-school student. Distinctive socialization outcomes are sought among those who occupy each of these roles. Thus young children are expected to learn language, and basic norms governing such diverse activities as eating, dress, and bowel and bladder control. Preschool programs will not enroll a child who has not learned the latter.

Furthermore, social structure designates the persons or organizations responsible for producing desired outcomes. In a complex society such as ours, there is a sequence of roles and a corresponding sequence of agents. These are age-linked roles; we expect transitions from one to another to occur at certain ages. Thus a child is an elementary student from ages six to twelve; we expect elementary school teachers to teach the basics to their students. Next the child moves into the role of a junior-high-school student, where a new group of socializing agents is encountered. Next the adolescent becomes a high-school student with yet another group of agents who further develop knowledge and abilities.

This view is sociological; it considers socialization as a product of group life. It calls our attention to the changing content of and responsibility for socialization throughout the individual's life. This viewpoint underlies the discussion both in this chapter and the next.

Agents of Childhood Socialization

Socialization has four components. It always involves:

1. someone who serves as a source of what is being learned;
2. a learning process;
3. a person who is being socialized; and
4. something that is being learned.

We refer to these four components as *agent, process, target,* and *outcome.* This section will consider the three primary agents of childhood socialization—family, peers, and school. Subsequent sections will focus on the processes and outcomes of childhood socialization.

Family

At birth, the human infant is completely dependent on others. The child's survival depends on others fulfilling his physical and emotional needs. This dependency makes the child amenable to socialization.

At birth, infants are primarily aware of their own bodies. Hunger, thirst, or pain create unpleasant and perhaps overwhelming bodily tension. The infant's primary concern is to remove these tensions, and satisfy bodily needs. In order to meet the infant's needs, adult caregivers must learn to read the infant's signals accurately (Ainsworth 1979). At the same time, infants begin to perceive their principal caretakers as the source of satisfaction. As a result, infants develop a very strong emotional attachment to their caregivers.

Face-to-face interaction is important in the development of the caregiver-infant relationship (Ainsworth 1979). Close bodily contact seems to be essential; infants relax in response to being held tightly, and relaxed infants eat better. The feeding process provides a regular basis for physical touching. These early experiences are truly interactive. The caregiver's response to the infant will vary depending upon the character of the child's vocalizations, the time since last feeding, and knowledge of this particular child (Bell 1979). The adult is learning how to care effectively for this infant, and the infant is forming a strong attachment to the caregiver.

IS A MOTHER NECESSARY? Does it matter who responds to and establishes a caring relationship with the infant? Must there be a single principal caretaker in infancy and childhood in order for effective socialization to occur? Because the mother is the usual caregiver in our culture, an important aspect of this question is whether a mother's absence, or day care, is detrimental to socialization.

Psychoanalytic theory (Freud) asserts that an intimate emotional relationship between infant and caregiver (almost always the mother at the time Freud wrote) is essential to healthy personality development. This was one of the first hypotheses to be studied empirically. To examine the effects of the absence of a single, close caregiver on children, researchers have studied infants who are institutionalized. In the earliest reported work, Spitz (1945, 1946) studied an institution in which six nurses cared for 45 infants less than 18 months old. Although the infants' basic biological needs were met, they had little contact with the nurses, and there was little evidence of emotional ties between nurses and infants. Within one year, the infants' scores on developmental tests fell dramatically from an average of 124 to an average of 72. Within two years, one-third had died, 9 had left, and the 21 who remained in the institution were severely retarded. These findings dramatically support the hypothesis that an emotionally responsive caregiver is essential.

Infants raised in institutions show two types of deficits. One deficit is socioemotional: such infants are apathetic, showing little or no emotional response to adults in their environ-

ment (Goldfarb, 1943). The absence of emotional expression by caregivers toward infants probably retards development of the infants' emotional responsiveness. The second deficit is cognitive. There is progressive impairment of intellectual functioning in institutionalized infants (Goldfarb 1943; Spitz 1945); as they grow, they fall progressively farther behind in verbal and other abilities. This appears to reflect the lack of sensory stimulation (color, sound, and movement) in institutional environments.

The findings of research on institutionalized children led to the conclusion that infants need a secure **attachment**—a warm, close relationship with an adult that produces a sense of security and provides stimulation—in order to develop the interpersonal and cognitive skills needed for proper growth (Ainsworth 1979).

Could the argument be taken one step further? Can these studies be interpreted as indicating that infants need "a warm, intimate, and continuous relationship with a *mother*" (Bowlby 1965)? Perhaps only in the mother-infant relationship can the sense of security and emotional warmth and responsiveness necessary to development occur. Other potential caretakers may have less emotional interest in the infant and may not provide adequate substitutes. This position clearly implies that (1) mothers should remain in the home and care for their children instead of working outside the home and (2) day care centers will have detrimental effects on child development.

The assertion that mothers are the crucial caregivers remained unchallenged until the early 1970s. The women's movement has rejected the traditional division of labor between male and female, which gives women the responsibility of child care. In addition, more and more women with children are employed full- or part-time outside the home. According to the Bureau of Labor Statistics, 57 percent of the women in two parent families with preschool children are working. These women, who are vitally concerned with the effects of day or child care on children, have questioned the need for the mother to be continuously present in the young child's environment.

Some continue to believe that the biological mother should be the primary caregiver because she is "primed hormonally as well as psychologically to care for the young she bears" (Baumrind 1980). Others, however, think that other family members—fathers, grandparents, aunts, or uncles—are equally capable of forming the necessary attachment with the child. Most writers agree that such a relationship is especially important during the first three years of life; research indicates that this is the time when language, basic intellectual skills, and emotional development flourish (B. White 1975). Some investigators believe that day care during this period is detrimental. "I firmly believe that most children would get off to a better start in life when they spend the majority of their waking hours being cared for by their parents and by other family members than they would in any form of substitute care" (Miller 1981). There is no empirical evidence that day care programs have negative effects on development (Etaugh 1980). However, the research conducted so far has been limited to studies of high-quality day care programs affiliated with colleges and universities, so we must be cautious in drawing conclusions.

FAMILY COMPOSITION. Does the makeup of the family affect the way in which parents socialize children? Research suggests that the answer is yes.

A recent study compared 52 sets of male twins and 44 "singleton" boys aged two-and-one-half (Lytton, Conway, and Sauvé 1977). Data collection involved interviews with parents and observation of parent-child interaction in the home and in the laboratory. Twins received less verbal interaction (per child) than single children. Parents gave twins fewer directions and stated fewer rules, and were less likely to follow up to see whether the boy(s) had completed the directions. Twins and singletons also differed in their behavior. The quantity and quality of speech of the twins was lower than that of the singletons. Twins also showed stronger needs for contact or affiliation with parents. Parents of twins obviously have less time per child, and the reduced rates of interaction appear to influence both verbal and emotional development.

The size of the family also influences patterns of authority. As more children are born, authority becomes centralized in the parents and the rules applied to children's behavior become more formal (Clausen 1966). A study of high-school students found that those from larger families more often reported that their parents were autocratic and that their parents did not explain the rules to which the children were subjected (Elder and Bowerman 1963). At the same time, children from larger families are more likely to experience independence, as parental attention is spread over more children. Older children are more likely to experience the responsibility and authority that accompanies taking care of younger siblings.

SOCIAL CLASS AND SOCIALIZATION TECHNIQUES. One of the most important influences on socialization is social class. In the United States, the lower and middle classes differ in their discipline techniques. The expectations of parents, and their attitudes about child-rearing, are major influences on the techniques employed (Bronfenbrenner 1958). Educated persons are more likely to rely on the opinion of experts (such as Dr. Spock) in books about child rearing. A survey of recent parents found that virtually all couples read at least one such "primer" on how to parent (Clarke-Stewart 1978). As parental education increased, so did the number of books read.

Since 1945, child-rearing books have advised parents to rely on reasoning rather than physical punishment when children violate norms. If the more educated read more of these books, we would expect them to follow this advice more closely than less educated parents. Several studies support this hypothesis; there is a negative relationship between social class and the use of physical punishment (Gecas 1979). Although middle- and upper-class parents tend to rely on reasoning, they are even more likely to use love-withdrawal, techniques such as shame and guilt. Such a parent responds to a rule violation by saying, "I'm ashamed of you," or "Good children don't do things like that." These techniques are obviously based on the child's emotional attachment to the parent.

Kohn (1969) argues that the goal of discipline varies with social class. Middle-class parents are likely to pay attention to intentions and punish intentional rule violations but not accidental ones. In working-class families, children are more likely to be punished for acts with harmful consequences, regardless of intentions. Research generally supports these hypotheses (Gecas 1979). In a study of parents of third graders (Gecas and Nye 1974), both husbands and wives were asked, "If your child is playing and accidentally breaks something that you value, what would you do?" and "If your child intentionally disobeys after you have told him to do something, what would you do?" The indicator for social class was based on the husband's occupation, which was either white-collar or blue-collar. White-collar parents frequently reported they would respond differently to the two situations, whereas blue-collar parents were more likely to report similar responses.

Thus, socioeconomic status is a major influence on discipline techniques; higher status parents are more likely to use psychological influence, and to base rewards and punishments on the child's intentions.

Peers

As the child grows, peers become increasingly important socializing agents. The peer group differs from the family on several dimensions. These differences influence the type of interaction and thus the kinds of socialization that occur.

The family consists of persons who differ in status or power, while the peer group is composed of status equals. From an early age the child is taught to treat parents with respect and deference. Failure to do so will probably result in discipline, and the adult will use the incident as an opportunity to instruct the child about the importance of deference (Denzin 1977). Interaction with peers is more open and spontaneous; the child does not need to be deferential or tactful. Thus, children at the age of four bluntly refuse to let children they dislike join their games. Flat refusals are unlikely in interaction with adults, because four-year-olds have learned that parents punish such behavior. They may say things that adults consider insulting, such as "You're ugly," to another child.

Membership in a particular family is ascribed, whereas peer interactions occur on a voluntary basis (Gecas 1981). Thus, peer groups offer the first experiences in exercising choice over whom the child relates to. The opportunity to make such choices contributes to the child's sense of social competence, and allows interaction with other children who complement the developing identity.

Unlike the child's family, peer groups in early and especially middle childhood (ages 6 to 10) are usually homogeneous in regard to sex and age. Peer associations make a major contribution to the development of the child's identity. In peer interaction, the role of friend is acquired, contributing to greater differentiation of the self (Denzin 1977). Peer and other relationships found outside the family provide a basis for establishing independence; the child ceases to be exclusively involved in the role of offspring, sibling, grandchild, and cousin. These alternate, nonfamilial identities may provide a basis for actively resisting parental socialization efforts (Stryker and Serpe 1982). For example, a parent's attempt to enforce certain rules may be resisted by the child whose friends make fun of children who behave that way.

School

Unlike the peer group, school is expressly designed to socialize children. In the classroom, there is typically one adult and a group of children of similar age. There is a sharp status distinction between teacher and student. The teacher determines the skills to be acquired, and relies heavily on instrumental learning, using such reinforcers as praise, blame, and privileges to shape student behavior (Gecas 1981). School is the child's first experience with formal and public evaluation of performance. Every child's behavior and work is evaluated in terms of the same standards, and the judgments are made publicly to others in the class, as well as to parents.

Schools are expected to teach reading, writing, and arithmetic. But they do much more than that. Teachers use the rewards at their disposal to reinforce certain personality traits, such as punctuality, perserverence, and tact. Schools teach children which selves are desirable and which are not. Thus children learn a vocabulary they are expected to use in evaluating themselves and others (Denzin 1977). The traits chosen are those thought to facilitate social interaction throughout life in a particular society. In this sense, schools civilize children.

The school facilitates the use of social comparison as an influence on behavior. Because the teacher makes public evaluations of the children's work, each can judge performance relative to others. These comparisons are especially relevant to the child because of the relative homogeneity of the classroom group. Even if the teacher deemphasizes a child's low score on the spelling test, the child interprets the performance as a poor one relative to those of classmates. A consistent performance will affect a child's image of self as a student.

Processes of Socialization

How does socialization occur? Frequently, it involves learning. We will examine three types that are especially relevant: observational learning, shaping, and instrumental learning. Another process, called internalization, is also important.

Observational Learning

Children at age four love to play "dress-up." Boys put on sport coats and drape ties around their necks; girls put on skirts, step into high-heeled shoes, and totter around the room. Through observing adults, children have learned the patterns of appropriate dress in their society. Observational learning can also be involved in acquiring interpersonal skills. Children often learn interactive rituals, such as shaking hands or waving goodbye, by watching others perform the behavior and then doing it on their own.

Observational learning, or modelling, refers to the acquisition of behavior based on observation of another person's behavior and of its consequences for that person (Shaw and Costanzo 1982). Many behaviors and skills are learned this way. The importance of this type of learning is often masked because it is combined with direct instruction. The major advantage of modelling is its greater efficiency compared to trial and error learning. If children learned to write by simply attempting to make letters, much of their time and effort would be wasted, in the sense that many of the characters they made would not be recognizable as letters. By providing written models that they can copy, and with which they can compare their productions, the process is made much more efficient.

Does observational learning lead directly to performance of the learned behavior? No; research has shown that there is a difference between learning a behavior and performing it. People can learn how to perform a behavior by observing, but they may not perform the act

Modelling is an important process through which children learn the behaviors considered appropriate by their social groups.

until the appropriate opportunity arises. A great deal of time may elapse before the observer is in a situation where the eliciting stimulus is present. A parent in the habit of muttering "damn" when he spills something may, much to his chagrin, hear his three-year-old say "damn" the first time she spills milk. Children may learn through observation many associations between situational characteristics and adult behavior, but may not perform these behaviors until they occupy adult roles and find themselves in such situations.

Even if the appropriate stimulus occurs, people may not perform behaviors learned through observation. An important influence is the consequences experienced by the model following the model's performance of the behavior. In one study (Bandura 1965), nursery school children watched a film in which an adult (model) punched, kicked, and threw balls at a large, inflated rubber Bobo doll. Three versions of the film were shown to three groups of children. In the first, the model was rewarded for his acts: a second adult appeared and gave the model soft drinks and candy. In the second version he was punished: the other adult spanked him with a magazine. In the third version, there were no rewards or punishments. Subsequently, each child was left alone with various toys, including a Bobo doll. The child's behavior was observed through a one-way mirror. Children who observed the model who was punished were much less likely to punch and kick the doll than the other children.

Did the children in the other two groups not learn the aggressive behaviors, or did they learn them by observation but not perform them? In order to answer this question, the experimenter returned to the room and offered the child a reward for each act of the model that he or she could reproduce. Following this offer, children in all three groups were equally able to reproduce the acts performed by the model. Thus, a child is less likely to perform an act learned by observation if the model experienced negative consequences.

Whether children learn from observing a model also depends on the characteristics of the model. Children are more likely to imitate high status and nurturant models than models who are low in status and nurturance (Bandura 1969). Preschool children given dolls representing peers, older children, and adults, consistently chose adult dolls as people they would go to for help and older children as people to go to for teaching (Lewis and Brooks-Gunn 1979). Children also are more likely to model themselves after nurturant persons than cold and impersonal others. Thus socialization is much more likely to be effective when the child has a nurturant, loving primary caregiver.

In many situations, children observe the behavior of more than one person. In a complex society, there are often differences in adults' responses to a particular situation. What happens when children see models who respond in different ways? In one study, second- and third-graders observed one model

Box 3.1
CHILD ABUSE

A nine-month-old is brought to an emergency room severely bruised and suffering from a concussion. A two-year-old is found locked in a closet, severely malnourished and covered with what appear to be cigarette burns. A mother is charged with murder; she allegedly smothered her three-year-old son with a pillow. On October 21, 1975, Glenda Abbey appeared on television in Washington, D.C., and tearfully appealed for help in finding her four-year-old son, Sean. The next day she was charged with murder; she allegedly tied a 33-pound concrete block to his body and threw him in the Potomac River (Wilkinson 1980).

A common reaction to incidents such as these is "How could someone do that?" One answer is that child abuse reflects the lack of attachment between the infant and the primary caregiver. Recent work suggests that both the infant and caregiver are genetically programmed to become attached to each other. A major component of this programming is a responsiveness by the mother to infant communication. When the mother is unresponsive or inappropriately responsive, normal maternal behavior does not occur, and abuse may result (Ainsworth 1980).

Research in this area employs observation of mother–infant interaction both in the home and the laboratory. In the laboratory setting a common procedure is to separate the child from the mother, and then observe their behavior when they are reunited. Separation activates the infant's need for attachment, the quality and intensity of which can be assessed by observing the reunion. Using this technique with children in their first year of life, three types of mother–infant bonds have been identified. The first and most common is the secure attachment. These children actively seek proximity and renewed contact with the mother, and express pleasure at the reunion. Home observation indicates that these moth-

ers are sensitive to infant signals, and respond quickly and sympathetically to their distress.

The other two types of bonds are anxious attachment. These children show distress at separation but are not happy when their mothers return. In the home, they display less pleasure in being held, but cry when put down. These children are less responsive to strange adults and to other children. There are two variants to anxious attachment. The ambivalent child mixes approach behavior with resistance to contact. At times they express anger at contact with the mother. The mothers of these infants tend to respond slowly when their children are distressed. The other variant is termed avoidance because these children avoid contact in situations where other infants seek it. Home observations indicate that their mothers consistently reject the child, due to feelings of irritation and resentment. The mothers view the responsibility for child care as interfering with their own interests and activities. These mothers have a strong aversion to close bodily contact and tend to be unexpressive emotionally (Main 1973).

Evidence that attachment deficits are related to abuse comes from research on older children who have been abused. Abused children respond to other children and adults in ways strikingly similar to the avoidant child (George and Main 1979). They approach caregivers less frequently, more frequently avoid other persons, and more often threaten or assault others.

Why are some mothers abusive? Research (DeLozier 1979) reveals that abusing mothers often experienced threats, severe discipline, or actual abandonment as children. At the time of their own child's birth they reported feeling isolated, frightened, and angry. This led to continuing anger and resentment of the child. Mothers who report above average levels of conflict with the spouse, who are full-time housewives with two or more children, and who experience psychological stress are more likely to engage in severe violence toward a child (Gelles 1980).

Child abuse, like other socialization outcomes, is the result of an interactive process. Abusive parents typically abuse only one of their children. Children who are more difficult to cope with are more likely to be abused. Abuse is more frequent for infants born prematurely or with mental or physical handicaps. Especially fussy, irritable infants are also more likely to be abused (Walters and Walters 1980). Thus, infants who are especially diffi-

cult to care for may elicit abusive responses from caregivers who are angry and resentful toward the child.

Most of the research on abuse looks at the mother–infant relationship. This is partly due to the fact that mothers are more likely to be abusive (Gelles 1980). Women are more likely to bear the primary responsibility for child-rearing, so they are likely to experience anger and frustration toward children. Also, because mothers are more likely to be blamed by others if children misbehave, they may react more negatively to misbehavior than fathers.

making two choices or two models each making one choice (Fehrenbach, Miller, and Thelen 1979). The model(s) selected one from a set of 10 colored squares; they either chose the same color every time, or alternated between two colors. The children were then given 20 opportunities to choose one of the colors. The measure of modelling was the number of times children chose the same color as the model (either of the alternatives chosen by models in the inconsistent conditions).

As indicated in Table 3.2, children rarely imitated one or two models who made inconsistent choices. While they were more likely to make the same choice when one model behaved consistently, the largest effect was obtained when two models consistently chose the same alternative. These results suggest that

attempts to teach a specific behavior will be much more effective when parents and other caregivers behave consistently.

Instrumental Learning

When you got dressed this morning, chances are you put on a shirt or blouse with several buttons, and pants, a dress, or a skirt that had hooks and a zipper. Observation of adults during childhood probably helped you to learn how to get dressed. But mastering buttons, hooks, and shoelaces undoubtedly took considerable time, trial and error, and slow progress accompanied by praise from adults. **Instrumental learning** refers to the acquisition of behavior based on the rewards or punishments that the learner experiences following performance of the behavior.

TABLE 3.2

MATCHED RESPONSES BY CHILDREN TO CONSISTENT OR INCONSISTENT MODELS

Condition	Mean Number of Responses (20 Opportunities)
Two models, consistent choices	10.56
Two models, inconsistent choices	2.06
One model, consistent choices	4.63
One model, inconsistent choices	2.56

Source: adapted from Fehrenbach, Miller, and Thelen 1979, Table 1.

The most important process in the acquisition of many skills is a type of instrumental learning called shaping (Skinner 1953, 1957). **Shaping** refers to learning in which an agent initially reinforces any behavior that remotely resembles the desired response and subsequently requires increasing correspondence between the learner's behavior and the desired response before providing reinforcement. Shaping thus involves an agent who wants to teach a specific response, and a learner who is able to produce relevant behaviors.

The degree of similarity between desired and observed responses required by the agent depends in part on the child's past performance. In this sense, shaping is interactive in character. In teaching children to clean their rooms, parents initially reward them for picking up their toys. When children show they can do this consistently, parents may require that the toys be replaced on certain shelves as the condition for a reward. Shaping is more likely to succeed if the level of performance required is consistent with the child's abilities. Young children who are developmentally unable to perform complex activities can be rewarded for performing simple but related behaviors. Thus, a two-year-old may be praised for drawing lines with crayons, whereas a five-year-old is expected to draw recognizable objects or figures. Thus, shaping as a socialization process corresponds with the fact that the child's motor and intellectual abilities develop gradually.

REINFORCEMENT. The first statement of the influence of rewards on behavior is called the "law of effect": "An act followed by satisfaction is more likely to recur than is an act that is followed by discomfort" (Thorndike 1907). Contemporary psychologists refer to such satisfaction as positive reinforcement, and to discomfort as negative reinforcement. There are two broad classes of reinforcement, primary and secondary (Skinner 1953).

One basis for learning is an association between behavior and the satisfaction or dissatisfaction of biological needs—for food, water, and sexual gratification, for example. The reduction or satisfaction of biological needs is termed **primary reinforcement.** Any behavior that results in primary reinforcement will gradually increase in frequency. This is undoubtedly the process by which some learning occurs in infancy. Infants learn that a particular action—a high-pitched cry, for example—will be followed by a caregiver's appearance and the subsequent satisfaction of hunger. The act of crying is thus reinforced, and when the infant subsequently experiences the same inner discomfort (the same stimulus), the act of crying is repeated. Caregivers respond to the vocalization because it signals to them that the infant is hungry. This is the child's earliest experience of social interaction; an act by the child (crying) is followed by an act of the caregiver (feeding) that is a meaningful response to the child's behavior (Fafouti-Milenkovic and Uzgiris 1979).

The constant association of the caregiver's presence with the satisfaction of biological hunger eventually makes the mere presence of the caregiver reinforcing for the child. When we consistently associate reinforcers (behaviors) that satisfy biological needs with other stimuli, these other stimuli may themselves become reinforcing. The use of a stimulus that has become rewarding through association with primary reinforcers is termed **secondary reinforcement.**

Social approval is a generalized secondary reinforcer because children learn that approval of parents and siblings is associated with the satisfaction of biological needs. Over time, approval becomes reinforcing in its own right. Obtaining social approval from one's family and later from friends is a major motivator of human action. As the child moves into peer groups, the school, and other social situations, he or she will engage in a wide variety of behaviors in order to earn the approval of other persons.

Box 3.2
THE HIDDEN COSTS OF REWARD

Do rewards always increase the likelihood that a child will repeat the behavior?

We usually assume that the effects of reinforcement on behavior are positive, that rewarding someone for a behavior will make that person more likely to repeat it. Usually that assumption is correct, but there are exceptions to the rule. Depending upon the nature of the reward and of the behavior, reinforcement can produce a decrease in the likelihood that the behavior will be repeated.

Behavior may result from two kinds of motivation (Deci 1975). **Extrinsically motivated behavior** is engaged in in order to obtain an external reward such as food or money or praise. **Intrinsically motivated behaviors** are those performed in order to achieve an internal state that the individual finds rewarding. Extrinsic behavior is a means to an end; intrinsic behavior is enacted for its own sake. Many people work in order to earn money, whereas painting a picture, completing a crossword puzzle, or solving a riddle may be rewarding in and of themselves.

Research suggests that providing an extrinsic reward for intrinsically motivated behaviors may reduce the frequency or quality of the activity. One study employed three groups of preschool children who had demonstrated high levels of interest in drawing (Lepper, Greene, and Nesbit 1973). The first group was told they would get a certificate (symbolic reward) if they completed the task. The second group was simply given the certificate after they finished. Those in the control group neither expected nor received the reward for drawing. Children who expected the reward spent less time drawing during a subsequent free-play period. In subsequent research using a similar design, investigators offered children either money, a symbolic reward, or verbal praise (Anderson, Manoogian, and Reznick 1976). Whereas both monetary and symbolic reinforcement reduced interest in the task, verbal praise produced an increase in time spent in the task during the free period.

Why do symbolic rewards have a different effect than verbal praise? It has been suggested that extrinsic rewards serve two functions, either a controlling function that maintains or changes behavior, or an information function that indicates how well the person is doing (Deci 1975). Tangible rewards such as money may serve a controlling function, while verbal praise may provide information that motivates further behavior. These hypotheses were tested by rewarding preschool and elementary school children with pretzels or stars, or verbal praise for a maze performance task (Dollinger and Thelen 1978). Consistent with prior research, pretzels and stars earned upon completion of the task reduced intrinsic motivation, while verbal praise during the task which conveyed information about the quality of task performance did not affect interest.

A review of research in this area (Condry 1977) suggests that at age five, children become aware that sometimes they do things because they want to and other times they do them because people promise them rewards. When the child is intrinsically motivated, the self is centrally involved. The focus and pace of activity are determined by the child. The child assesses performance in terms of internal standards. When someone else introduces extrinsic rewards, the child focuses effort in the direction desired by the adult. Such activity involves the self to a much smaller degree, and is evaluated in terms of the standards of the person providing the reward.

Money is an important type of secondary reinforcement in many societies. How does money become a reinforcer? Children learn that the satisfaction of many needs, biological and otherwise, can be obtained through money. Parents who are besieged by requests for the latest toy, doll, or breakfast treat stress the fact that such things cost money. A major focus of many second- and third-grade curricula is the identification of coins of different denominations, and the things that one can acquire if one has enough money. In adolescence, many peer groups introduce young people to the belief that possession of certain clothing, records, and cars, all of which cost money, is socially desirable. Thus the importance of obtaining money and its value for attaining approval and status are explicitly taught to children.

PUNISHMENT. Punishment is one of the major child-rearing practices used by parents. Up to 90 percent of parents questioned in surveys reported that they punished their children occasionally (Sears, Maccoby, and Levin 1957). The punishment is frequently physical; in a survey of 1,146 families, 71 percent of the parents reported slapping or spanking children (Gelles 1980). **Punishment** is an unpleasant event which follows a response and reduces the frequency with which it occurs. But does it work?

Research indicates that punishment is effective in some circumstances but not others. One influence on its effectiveness is timing. In a study of fourth- and fifth-grade boys, each was presented with a pair of toys and told to select one of the pair. The punishment consisted of saying, "No. That's for the older boys." The time between the act and the occurrence of punishment was systematically varied. In one group, the boys were reprimanded just as they touched the toys. In another, the reprimand was given after the boy picked up the toy. In a control group, the boys were warned prior to their choice not to touch one

of the pair. The researchers then measured the boys' behavior when they were subsequently left alone with the two toys. Boys who had been reprimanded just as they picked up the toy were least likely to play with the toy. The results suggest that the longer the delay between act and punishment, the less effective the punishment will be (Aronfreed and Reber 1965).

In addition, the effectiveness of punishment may be limited to the situation in which it is given. Punishment tends to suppress behavior only as long as the conditions under which it was administered remain in force. Since punishment is usually administered by someone, it may be effective only when that person is present. This probably accounts for the fact that when their parents are absent children may engage in activities which their parents had earlier punished (Solomon 1964; Parke 1969, 1970).

A third influence on the effectiveness of punishment is the nature of the relationship between teacher and learner. Punishment delivered by an adult who behaves warmly and supportively toward the child appears to be more effective than that given by a cold and distant person (Aronfreed 1968; Parke 1967).

A fourth factor is whether punishments are accompanied by a reason or explanation (Parke 1969). By providing children with some understanding of why they should not engage in the behavior, explanations help children to exercise greater self-control. Punishment without a reason may only inhibit the particular act. Providing a reason allows the child to generalize the prohibition to a class of acts and situations. Yelling "No!" as a child reaches out to touch the stove may suppress that behavior. Telling the child not to touch it because it is "hot" enables him to learn to avoid hot objects generally.

Finally, consistency between the reprimands given by parents and their own behavior makes punishment more effective than if parents do not "practice what they preach" (Mischel and Liebert 1966).

Shaping is the process through which many complex behaviors are learned. Initially the socializer (teacher or parent) rewards behavior that resembles the desired response. Once the child begins to learn, greater correspondence between the behavior and the desired response is required to earn the reward.

SELF-REINFORCEMENT AND SELF-EFFICACY. Children learn hundreds if not thousands of behaviors via instrumental learning. The performance of some of these behaviors will remain dependent on extrinsic motivation—that is, on whether someone else will reward appropriate behaviors or punish inappropriate ones. The performance of other activities becomes independent of extrinsic rewards and punishments. As children are socialized, they learn not only specific behaviors but also performance standards. Children learn not only to write, but to write neatly. These standards become part of the self; having learned them, the child uses them to judge his own behavior, and thus becomes capable of **self-reinforcement** (Bandura 1978). The child who has drawn a house and comes running up to her father with a big smile saying, "Look what I drew," has already judged the drawing as a good one. If her father agrees, standards and self-evaluation are confirmed.

Moreover, experiences with an activity over time create self-perceptions of efficacy at that activity (Bandura 1982). If the individual executes an activity successfully, that experience contributes to a sense that the person is competent at it. That, in turn, makes the individual more likely to seek out opportunities to engage in that behavior. The greater one's sense of efficacy, the more effort one will expend at a task and the greater one's persistence in the face of difficulty. A young girl who perceives herself as a good basketball player is more likely to try out for a team. Conversely, experiences of failure to perform a task properly, or of the failure of the task to produce the expected results, creates the perception that one is not efficacious. Perceived lack of efficacy is likely to lead to avoidance of the task. A boy who perceives himself as poor at spelling will probably not enter the school spelling bee.

Internalization

Often we feel a sense of moral obligation and feel that we should perform some behavior. At other times we experience a strong internal feeling that a particular behavior is wrong, that we should not engage in it. Usually guilt is experienced if these moral prescriptions or prohibitions are violated.

Internalization is the process by which behavioral standards initially external to the person (for example, held by parents) become internal and subsequently guide the person's behavior. An action is based on internalized standards when the person engages in it without considering possible rewards or punishments. Various explanations have been offered of the process by which internalization occurs, but all of them agree that children are most likely to internalize the standards held by more powerful or nurturant adult caregivers.

Internalization is an important socializing process. It results in the exercise of self-control; people conform to behavioral standards even when there is no surveillance of their behavior by others, and therefore no rewards for that conformity. People who are widely admired for taking political or religious actions that are unpopular, for standing up for their beliefs, often do so because those beliefs are internalized.

Outcomes of Socialization

Socialization efforts are directed toward the acquisition of particular skills, knowledge, or behavior. This section will discuss several outcomes of the process, including gender roles, linguistic and cognitive competence, knowledge of social rules, and orientation toward work and achievement.

Gender Role

"It's a boy!" "Congratulations; you have a girl!" Such a pronouncement by a birth attendant may be the single most important event in a person's life. In large part, the gender assigned to the infant at birth has a major influence on the socialization of that child.

Every society has differential expectations for the characteristics and behavior of males and females. In our society, men have traditionally been expected to be competent—competitive, logical, able to make decisions easily, ambitious; women have been expected to be high in warmth and expressiveness—gentle, sensitive, tactful (Broverman et al. 1972). Parents employ these as guidelines in socializing their children, and differential treatment

begins at the moment of birth. Male infants are handled more vigorously and roughly, whereas females are given more cuddling (Lamb 1979). Boys and girls are dressed differently from infancy, and may be given different kinds of toys to play with.

In addition, mothers and fathers differ in the way they interact with infants. Mothers engage in behavior oriented toward fulfilling the child's physical and emotional needs (Baumrind 1980), whereas fathers engage the child in rough and tumble, physically stimulating activity (Walters and Walters 1980). Thus, almost from birth, infants are exposed to models of masculine and feminine behavior. At about age one, fathers begin to pay special attention to their sons and reduce the interaction with their daughters (Lamb 1979). At the same time the child increasingly prefers the same-sex parent. More frequent interaction with and a preference for the same-sex parent may account for Richard Cohen's observation that he is much more like his father than his mother.

By age two, the child's gender identity—perception of self as male or female—is firmly established (Money and Ehrhardt 1972). Boys and girls show distinct preferences for different types of play materials and toys by this age. Between the ages of two and three, differences in aggressiveness become evident, with boys displaying more physical and verbal aggression, and behaving more aggressively in play (Maccoby and Jacklin 1974). By age three, children more frequently choose same-gender peers as playmates; this increases opportunities to learn gender-appropriate behavior via modelling (Lewis and Brooks-Gunn 1979). By age four, the games typically played by boys and girls differ; groups of girls play house, enacting familial roles, while groups of boys play cowboys.

Parents are an important influence on the learning of **gender role,** the expectations associated with one's gender. Children learn appropriate behaviors by observing their parents' interaction. Children also learn by interacting with parents, who reinforce behavior consistent with parental expectations and punish behavior inconsistent with these standards. The child's earliest experiences in relating to members of the other gender occur in interaction with the opposite-gender parent. A female may be more likely to develop the ability to have warm, psychologically intimate relationships with males if her relationship with her father was of this type (Appleton 1981).

Boys are not all alike in our society; neither are girls. The specific behaviors and characteristics that the child is taught depend partly upon the gender role expectations held by the parents. These in turn depend upon the network of extended family—grandparents, aunts and uncles, and other relatives—and friends of the family. The people in these networks are influenced by the institutions to which they belong. Churches and work organizations influence interactional networks which in turn influence the identities available to us and our expectations about how people should behave (Stryker and Serpe 1982). Persons active in the Catholic church may have different gender-role expectations than persons belonging to the Quaker religion.

Schools also teach gender roles. Reading and telling stories is a common activity in preschool and first-grade classes; many of these stories portray males and females as different. Men are rulers, adventurers, and explorers; women are wives (Weitzman et al. 1972). As children learn to read, the books they are given elaborate the child's notion of gender roles. Stories such as *Snow White* clearly convey the expectation that men work outside the home and women do the housework. Teachers also contribute to socialization by rewarding appropriate gender role behavior; they tend to reinforce aggressive behavior in boys and dependency in girls (Serbin and O'Leary 1975).

Linguistic and Cognitive Competence

Another important outcome of socialization is the ability to interact effectively with others. We shall discuss two specific competencies: language and the ability to cognitively represent the world.

LANGUAGE. Language is the major means by which members of groups or societies communicate. Therefore, learning language is a prerequisite for full and effective participation in social groups (Shibutani 1961). Three main components of language are: the sound system (phonology); the words and their associated meanings (morphology or lexicon); and rules for combining words into meaningful utterances (syntax or grammar). Learning a language involves mastering each of these components (Miller and McNeill 1969).

Chronologically, infants master sounds first. In the first year of life, children babble; they emit a vast range of sounds, many of which are not part of their parent's language. Increasingly, however, their vocalizations are restricted to those which are meaningful. Three of the socialization processes discussed earlier contribute to learning phonology. Observation is important because children imitate the sounds they hear from family members. Instrumental learning is also an important part of the acquisition of language. When children experience discomfort, they make sounds in order to attract a caregiver to remove the discomfort. The removal of discomfort reinforces those vocalizations that precede it. Shaping also occurs; as the child vocalizes, parents respond positively to some sounds, and ignore others. Initially, a mother may respond to "ma"; her response, via a smile, touch, or words is reinforcing; over time, she may progressively limit her response to "ma-ma."

At about one year of age, children begin to master the second component. They verbalize meaningful single words. Such utterances have much broader and diverse meaning for the child than for adults. For example, when a fifteen-month-old says "car," the child may mean "I see the car," "I want to go for a ride in the car," "Here comes a car," or "Give me my toy car." An adult caregiver is faced with the task of determining the child's meaning. The adult often engages in a trial-and-error process, offering several responses in succession until the child seems satisfied. Children's discovery that others do not initially respond "correctly" from their perspective motivates them to improve the precision of their speech, that is, to expand the number of words they employ in communication (Miller and McNeill 1969). Thus, language acquisition proceeds via children's desire to satisfy their needs, and adults' demands for greater articulateness before granting such satisfactions.

Sometime between 18 and 24 months of age, children begin to speak two- or three-word sentences. Examples of such sentences include "See truck, Mommy," and "There go one." Such speech is "telegraphic"—that is, the number of words is greatly reduced relative to adult speech (Brown and Fraser 1963). At the same time, such utterances are clearly more precise than the single-word utterances of the one-year-old child.

Once children begin to utter simple sentences, we can study the acquisition of the third component of language, grammar. How do children acquire the rules for combining words into meaningful sequences? Important data were obtained by studying the speech of a 27-month-old boy named Adam (Brown and Bellugi 1964). Adam used three classes of words: nouns, verbs, and "pivots"—or modifiers such as "a," "my," or "more" (Braine 1963). Theoretically, these three classes of words could be combined into nine types of sentences containing two words (2^3) and 27 types containing three words (3^3). But of these 36 possible types, only four types of two-word sentences and eight types of three-word utterances using Adam's vocabulary were grammatically permissible in the English language. Amazingly, all of Adam's sentences recorded by the researchers were of the permissible types. He did not utter even one combination that is not allowed in English grammar. He was not stringing words together at random;

he was adhering strictly to acceptable patterns.

How can a young child make grammatically correct sentences? Consider two possible explanations. First, sounds, words, and meaning may be acquired by instrumental learning through imitation and shaping by adults (Skinner 1957; Staats 1968). But Adam had only recently begun to use three-word sentences, and *none* of them exhibited the nonconforming or random sequencing one would expect if he had to learn the rules of grammar. In addition, children are often observed producing grammatically correct novel sentences that they have never heard before.

A second explanation assumes that children's grammatical ability is derived at least in part from a biological predisposition to acquire language (Chomsky 1965). Everyone may be born with neural structures that enable the person to recognize certain universal features of speech. Once the children identify those features in the language spoken around them, they are able to produce grammatically meaningful sentences. This neural structure allows the child to order words correctly; the culture, communicated by parents and other socializing agents, provides the particular sounds and words (Miller and McNeill 1969). While the exact role of neural structures in language acquisition is not clear, the rapidity with which children develop linguistic competence suggests that such structures exist. Learning, of course, also plays a major role.

Another process contributing to the development of linguistic competence is expansion. Adults often respond to children's speech by repeating it in expanded form. In response to "Eve lunch," the mother might say "Eve is eating lunch." One study of two mothers showed that they expanded 30 percent of the utterances of their two-year-old children (Brown 1964). Adults probably expand on the child's speech in order to determine the child's specific meaning. The fact that adults do this indicates that they assume children can comprehend more complex utterances than the children spontaneously emit. Research evidence supports this assumption (Fraser, Bellugi, and Brown 1963). Speech expansion contributes to language acquisition by providing children with a model of how to convey more effectively the meanings they intend.

The next stage of language development is highlighted by the occurrence of "private speech," in which children talk loudly to themselves, often for extended periods of time. Private speech begins at about age three, increases in frequency until age five, and disappears by about age seven. Such talk serves two functions. First, it contributes to the child's developing sense of self. Private speech is addressed to the self as object, and often includes the application of meanings to the self such as "I'm a girl." Private speech also plays an important part in the child's developing awareness of the environment. Much of this talk consists of naming aspects of the physical and social environment. The repeated use of these names solidifies the child's understanding of the environment. Children also often engage in appropriate actions as they speak, reflecting their developing awareness of the social meanings of objects and persons. Thus, a child may label a doll a "baby" and dress it and feed it.

Gradually the child begins to engage in dialogues, either with others or with the self. These conversations reflect the ability to adopt a second perspective. This ability partly reflects increasing awareness of others and of the world. Thus, at age six, when one child wants a toy that another child is using, the first child frequently offers to trade. She knows that the second child will be upset if she merely takes the toy. This movement away from a self-centered view may also reflect maturational changes. Additionally, dialogues require meshing the child's own speech and action with that of another; thus, behavior is becoming more genuinely interactive.

By the age of six, most children make statements that reflect an understanding of the reasons for actions and the likely responses of others. ("Daddy will be mad if I don't clean up.") At this age, children are able to see their behavior from the perspective of others, and to use language to regulate their behavior (Luria and Yudovich 1971).

Although most children in the United States learn to speak English, there are large differences in the way they talk. Accents, vocabulary, and grammatical forms vary from person to person. These variations are not random. Each family and neighborhood has particular social class, ethnic, and other characteristics that influence the language taught to children. Imagine a child who is playing noisily near the telephone when it rings. One mother says "Be quiet." Another says "Please be quiet for a minute; I have to answer the phone" (Hess and Shipman 1965). These responses reflect very distinct linguistic styles (Bernstein 1961a, 1961b), to be discussed in Chapter 5. A specific child's speech reflects the language used by parents, peers, and later, the teachers with whom the child comes into contact.

COGNITIVE COMPETENCE. Children must develop the ability to think as well as talk. They need to represent what goes on around them in their own minds so that they can think about it. The ability to represent reality mentally is closely related to the development of language.

The child's basic tasks are (1) to learn the regularities of the physical and social environment, and (2) to store past experience in a form that can be used in current situations. We employ three modes of storing information about the environment (Bruner 1964). The first is *enactive*, the representation of past events in our musculature. Examples include the behaviors necessary to maintain one's balance while riding a bicycle, and the representation of routes that we drive frequently as a series of turns and directions. We perform these automatically; we are often unable to describe verbally exactly what we do. The second mode is *iconic* representation, in which we retain a concrete image of the object or event. Our ability to remember faces is an example of iconic representation. The third is the *symbolic* mode, in which an arbitrary symbol represents the event, object, or person. Language is a particularly useful symbol system because it allows us to represent abstract as well as concrete phenomena, and because we can combine words to represent a wide range of phenomena effectively.

Normally, we use all three modes. Very little is known about the development of enactive and iconic modes of storing information. As the child learns words—category labels—these may facilitate iconic representation. "Dog" may elicit a mental picture of the family's purebred Irish setter. But at what age do children begin to use symbolic representation? An ingenious research design has been used to answer this question (Bruner and Kenney 1966). A set of drinking glasses of different sizes and shapes was presented to the child. The glasses were arranged in three rows with three glasses in each row. Then the glasses were scrambled and the child was asked to reproduce the original order. Children of five, six, and seven years of age were able to do so with few errors. The children were able to reproduce the order correctly because they remembered a visual image of the way the glasses were initially arranged. This is iconic representation. Next, one glass was placed in a different location than it had occupied originally. The children were then asked to order the other eight glasses using that glass as a reference point. Most seven-year-old children could do so, while most five- and six-year-olds could not. The results suggest that seven-year-olds were employing symbolic representations.

In a complex society, there are so many physical objects, animals, and persons that it is not possible to remember each as a distinct entity. Things must be categorized into more general groupings, such as birds, dogs, houses, and girls. We employ a superordinate dimension that ignores differences on more specific dimensions. The ability to utilize general categories can be studied by asking children to sort objects, pictures, or words into groups. Young children (aged six to eight) rely on visual features such as color or word length and sort objects into numerous categories. Older children (aged ten to twelve) increasingly use functional or superordinate categories such as "foods" and sort objects into fewer groups (Olver 1961; Rigney 1962). Clearly, the child becomes increasingly adept at classifying diverse objects and treating them as equivalent.

These skills are very important in social interaction. It is the ability to group objects, persons, and situations that allows one to determine how to behave toward them. Society, via language, provides us with the appropriate categories (Shibutani 1961). In addition, we are taught norms that define appropriate and inappropriate behaviors toward members of each category. Both the categories and the norms must be learned by children in order for them to interact effectively with others.

The learning of categories of persons and their associated meanings is especially important to smooth interaction. Even very young children differentiate persons by age. By about two years of age, children correctly differentiate babies and adults when shown photographs. By about five, children employ four categories: "little children," "big children," "parents" (ages 13 to 40), and "grandparents" (age 40+) (Lewis and Brooks-Gunn 1979). Another commonly used set of categories involves religion. Children's conceptions of members of various denominations have been studied by asking a child "What is a Jew?" or "What is a Catholic?" (Elkind 1961, 1962, 1963). At age six, the typical response is "a person." At eight, children refer to behavior ("A person who goes to temple"). At age ten, children focus on more abstract differences in beliefs ("A person who believes in one God"). The increasing abstractness of these responses with age clearly parallels the increasing use of superordinate principles discussed above.

As children learn to group objects into meaningful categories, they learn not only the categories, but also how others feel about such persons. Children learn not only that Catholics are people who believe in the Trinity of Father, Son, and Holy Ghost, but also that their parents like or dislike Catholics. Thus, children acquire positive and negative attitudes toward the wide range of social objects they come to recognize. The particular categories and evaluations children learn are influenced by the social class, religious, ethnic, and other subcultural groupings to which those who socialize them belong.

CAUSAL ATTRIBUTION. "If you don't eat your dinner, you can't have dessert." Many children experience this cause and effect relationship. But at what age do they really understand that whether they eat dinner determines whether they get ice cream? Can they make accurate judgements of cause and effect? A basic aspect of causal relationships is that they proceed in one direction, the cause preceding its effect(s) in a series of events. Research suggests that preschool age youngsters understand the principal of unidirectionality. Children were shown pictures of three events: (1) "Scott cried"; (2) "Scott pulled the dog's tail"; (3) "The dog bit Scott." They were then asked why the dog bit Scott, and asked to point to either event 1 or event 2. Three-year-olds were able to accurately identify event 2 as the cause (Kun 1978).

We frequently need to know why someone has engaged in a behavior, so that we can respond appropriately. If someone does you a favor, your reaction will vary depending on whether you think the action was voluntary, or performed because a third party promised to reward the actor. Like other cognitive processes, the ability to make attributions about others' intentions or motives develops as the child matures. This is clearly demonstrated in a study of kindergarten, first- and second-grade children, and college students. Each subject listened to two stories that described a boy playing with a toy. In one story, the child had chosen to play with the toy. In the other, the child was portrayed as externally constrained; half of the subjects were told his mother had told him to play with it, and the other half were told she had offered him a reward (some cake) if he would do so. After listening to both stories, each subject was asked which boy "really wanted" to play with the toy. The kindergarten children reported that the child who was constrained was more motivated to play with the toy. They saw the external constraint as adding to the internal motivation of the child, and producing greater desire to play with the toy. First- and second-graders said that the child who had chosen to play with the toy had a greater desire. These older children and especially the college students believed that the command or reward was an alternative to rather than a supplement to the child's intrinsic motivation (Karniol and Ross 1976).

Knowledge of Social Rules

In order to interact effectively with others, people must also learn the social rules that govern interaction, and adhere to them. Beliefs about which behaviors are acceptable and which are unacceptable for specific persons in specific situations are **norms.** Conformity to norms makes society possible. If each of us behaved in whatever ways we wished, social interaction would be unpredictable and chaotic. Coordinated activity would be very difficult, and we would find it hard or impossible to achieve our goals. Therefore, each group, organization, and society develops rules governing behavior.

LEARNING NORMS. How do children acquire the notion of norms, and learn the specific norms that apply to them? Within days of their birth, children discover that certain vocalizations attract the caregiver's attention to their needs. The effectiveness of these vocalizations is due to norms. The social conventions that specify the meanings of vocalizations, their ordering in speech, and the appropriateness of particular words in particular settings all pre-exist the child. An American child learns to say

At school, children get their first exposure to universal norms—behavioral expectations that are the same for everyone. Although parents and friends treat the child as an individual, teachers are less likely to do so.

"please," a French child to say *"s'il vous plaît,"* and a Serbian child to say *"molim te."* In every case, the child is learning the value of conforming to arbitrary norms governing requests. Learning language therefore trains the child to conform and serves as a model for the learning of other norms. Gradually, through instrumental as well as observational learning, the child learns the generality of the relationship between conformity to norms and the ability to interact smoothly with others and achieve one's own goals.

Children learn many basic social norms in the family setting. The norms governing bodily display, dressing, and eating are acquired fairly early and continually reinforced. As early as two years of age, the child begins to engage in various interpersonal activities toward parents and siblings, including assertive and aggressive behaviors like hitting and kicking. The reactions of other family members to these actions are the major vehicle by which children learn norms regarding behavior toward others. If parents and siblings consistently punish physical aggressiveness, children will cease to employ it.

What influences which norms children will learn? The general culture is one influence. All American children learn to cover most parts of the body with clothing. The position of the family within the society is another influence. Parental expectations reflect social class, religion, and ethnicity. Thus, the norms taught vary from one family to another. Interestingly, parents often hold norms that they apply distinctively to their own children. Mothers and fathers expect certain behaviors of their own sons or daughters, but may have different expectations for other people's children (Elkin and Handel 1978). They may expect their children to be more polite than other children in interaction with adults. Also, parental expectations are not constant over time; they change as the child grows older. Parents expect greater politeness from a ten-year-old than from a five-year-old. Finally, parents adjust their expectations to the particular child. They take into account level of ability and past experiences relative to other children. Parents expect better performance in school from a child who has done well in the past compared to one who has had problems in school. In all of these ways, each child is being socialized to a somewhat different set of norms.

When children begin to engage in cooperative play, at about four years of age, they begin to experience normative influence by peers. The expectations of age mates differ in two important ways from those of parents. First, children bring different norms from their separate families and therefore introduce new expectations to the child. Thus, through peers, children first become aware that there are other ways of behaving. In some cases, peers' expectations conflict with those of parents. For example, many parents do not allow their children to play with toy guns, knives, and swords. Through involvement with their peers, children may become aware that other children routinely play with such toys. As a result, the child will experience normative conflict. Thus children discover that they need to develop strategies for resolving such conflicts at an early age.

Another way that peer group norms differ from parental norms is that the former reflect a child's perspective (Elkin and Handel 1978). Many parental expectations are oriented toward socializing the child for adult roles. Children react to each other as children and are not concerned with long-term outcomes. Thus, peers encourage impulsive spontaneous behavior rather than behavior directed toward long-term goals. Peer-group norms emphasize participation in group activities, whereas parental norms may emphasize homework and other educational activities that may contribute to academic achievement.

When children enter school, they are exposed to a third major socializing agent, the teacher. In school, the child is first exposed to "universalistic" rules, norms that apply equally to all the children. The teacher is much less likely than the parents to make allowances for the unique characteristics of the child; children must learn to wait their turn, to control impulsive and spontaneous behavior, and to work without a great deal of supervision and support. In this regard, the school is the first of many settings where the individual is treated as a member of a group rather than as a unique individual.

Teachers use a variety of symbolic rewards (such as stars and smiling faces) and punishments (such as "time outs" or temporary exclusion from group activities) to enhance learning. How do these different types of teacher response affect the child's desire to learn? The earlier discussion of intrinsic and extrinsic motivation suggests that the impact of these responses will depend on whether they are experienced as external constraints controlling behavior, or as signs indicating the child's success or failure. Teachers who use rewards to control children's behavior may also be undermining the child's intrinsic interest in school related activities.

A study of 36 classes of fourth-, fifth-, and sixth-graders (Deci, Nezlek, and Sherman 1981) investigated the possibility that teachers' rewards undermine children's intrinsic interest in school. Questionnaires measuring intrinsic and extrinsic orientation toward schoolwork and self-esteem were completed by 610 children. Children were asked whether they preferred:

1. challenge (intrinsic motivation) or easy work (extrinsic);
2. to work to satisfy their own curiosity or to please the teacher;
3. to work independently or with the teacher's help;
4. to rely on their own versus the teacher's judgment.

Then, teachers' orientations were measured by presenting a series of vignettes; each one described a problem that regularly arises in school. Potential responses included:

1. utilizing rewards or punishments (high control orientation);
2. encouraging the children to take a specific action;
3. encouraging the children to work out a solution (high autonomy).

The teacher rated the acceptability of each response to each of eight situations. As predicted, the students of teachers who were oriented toward controlling the child's behavior had lower intrinsic motivation scores and lower self-esteem. The measures were taken twice, six weeks after school started in the fall, and seven months later. Surprisingly, the correlation was as strong in October as it was in May. The findings suggest that, within just six weeks, teachers' orientations toward control have a pronounced effect on students' intrinsic interest in school, an effect that persists throughout the school year.

Thus, school is the setting in which children are first exposed to more universalistic norms, and the regular use of symbolic rewards. Such settings become increasingly important in adolescence and adulthood, in contrast to the individualized character of familial settings.

MORAL DEVELOPMENT. We not only learn the norms of our social groups, but we also develop the ability to evaluate behavior in specific situations by applying certain standards. The process through which children become capable of making moral judgments is termed **moral development.** It involves two components: 1) the reasons why one adheres to social rules; and 2) the bases used to evaluate actions by self or others as good or bad.

How do children evaluate acts as good or bad? One approach to answering this question is to ask children to evaluate a behavior, and then to ask them why they did so. This approach was used by Jean Piaget (1965), whose theory of the development of moral judgment was described earlier. Essentially Piaget proposes three bases for making moral judgments: amount of harm/benefit, actor's intentions, and the application of agreed upon rules or norms.

Kohlberg (1969) extended Piaget's work by analyzing in greater detail the reasoning by which people reach moral judgments. He presents stories involving conflict between human needs and social norms or laws. For example:

> In Europe, a woman was near death from cancer. One drug might save her, a form of radium that a druggist in the same town had recently discovered. The druggist was charging $2,000, ten times what the drug cost him to make. The sick woman's husband, Heinz, went to everyone he knew to borrow the money, but he could only get together about half of what it cost. He told the druggist that his wife was dying and asked him to sell it cheaper or let him pay later. But the druggist said, "No." The husband got desperate and broke into the man's store to steal the drug for his wife.

Respondents are then asked: Should Heinz have done that? Was Heinz right or wrong? What obligations did Heinz and the druggist have? Should Heinz be punished?

Kohlberg proposes a developmental model with three levels of moral reasoning, each level involving two stages. This model is summarized in Table 3.3.

Kohlberg argues that the progression from Stage 1 to Stage 6 is a standard or universal one, and that all children begin at Stage 1 and progress through the stages in order. Practically no one reasons consistently at Stage 6, and relatively few regularly use Stage 5 considerations. Most people usually reason at Stages 3 or 4. Several studies have shown that such a progression does occur (Kuhn, Langer, Kohlberg and Haan 1977). If the progression is universal, then children from different cultures should pass through the same stages in the same order. Again, data suggest that they do (White, Bushnell and Regnemer 1978). On the basis of such evidence Kohlberg claims that this progression is the natural human pattern of moral development. He also

TABLE 3.3
KOHLBERG'S MODEL OF MORAL DEVELOPMENT

Preconventional Morality:
*Moral judgment based on external,
physical consequences of acts.*

Stage 1.   Obedience and punishment orien-
            tation. Rules are obeyed in order
            to avoid punishment, trouble.
Stage 2:   Hedonistic orientation. Rules are
            obeyed in order to obtain rewards
            for the self.

Conventional Morality:
*Moral judgment based on social
consequences of acts.*

Stage 3:   "Good boy/nice girl" orientation.
            Rules are obeyed to please others,
            avoid disapproval.
Stage 4:   Authority and social-order
            maintaining orientation. Rules are
            obeyed to show respect for
            authorities and maintain
            social order.

Postconventional Morality:
*Moral judgments based on universal
moral and ethical principles.*

Stage 5:   Social-contract orientation. Rules
            are obeyed because they represent
            the will of the majority, to avoid
            violation of rights of others.
Stage 6:   Universal ethical principles. Rules
            are obeyed in order to adhere to
            one's principles.

Source: adapted from Kohlberg (1969) Table 6.2.

believes that attaining higher levels is better or more desirable.

What determines how far people progress in the sequence of moral development? One variable is culture. Adults in societies without written languages tend to respond to the moral dilemmas using Stage 1, 2, or 3 reasoning (C. White 1975). Adults in more technologically developed societies are more likely to use Stage 4, 5, or 6 principles. Kohlberg argues that a written language is essential to the

ability to think abstractly; if people cannot engage in abstract, symbolic thought, they cannot use these principles in reaching moral judgments.

While moral development is an interesting topic of study in its own right, other investigators have explored the relationship between moral judgment and behavior. Two studies of cheating in schoolwork, one involving sixth-graders (Krebs 1967) and one involving college students (Schwartz, Feldman, Brown, and Heingartner 1969), found that those whose moral development had reached higher stages were less likely to cheat. Participants in political activities such as demonstrations and sit-ins often claim their behavior is based on moral principles. But is it? A study by Haan, Smith, and Block (1968) explores the relationship between political activities and moral development in young adults. The results are depicted in Table 3.4 (none of the subjects were classified as being in Stage 1, which is consistent with their age). In general, the highest rates of political activity are found among subjects who used level 3 reasoning. In most instances, there is a consistent increase from those classified in Stage 3 to those classified in Stage 6 in the percentage reporting an activity. At the same time, a high percentage of subjects at Stage 2 reported participation in the various activities.

Many of the subjects reported involvement in a sit-in at the University of California at Berkeley. As Kohlberg might predict, the reasons why people reported participating in it varied by level of moral thought. Preconventional subjects said they did so because the protest was an opportunity to improve their status in their peer groups. Postconventional subjects viewed their participation as growing out of their commitment to individual civil liberties. In general, the conventional subjects avoided the sit-in because it constituted a confrontation with legitimate authorities. These differences in the reasons given by subjects at different levels are consistent with the theory; they also demonstrate that moral judgment is

TABLE 3.4

RELATIONSHIP BETWEEN MORAL DEVELOPMENT AND SOCIOPOLITICAL ACTIVITY

| | | Percent Reporting Activity | | | | | | | | | |
| | | Men | | | | | Women | | | | |
Activity	*Stage*	*2*	*3*	*4*	*5*	*6*	*2*	*3*	*4*	*5*	*6*
Picket		56	12	9	44	75	0	8	13	44	55
Sit-in		25	5	5	27	31	14	7	4	26	27
Petition Work		25	14	18	35	38	0	4	10	35	18
Attend Meetings		62	46	41	60	69	40	33	48	56	63
Distribute Literature		44	11	20	42	50	20	10	21	44	55
Demonstrate		56	14	8	48	75	20	11	10	47	55
Peace March		56	12	5	40	62	0	11	10	44	64

Source: adapted from Haan, Smith, and Block (1968) Table 7.

the outcome of an interaction between the characteristics of a situation and the level of moral thought achieved by those present.

Kohlberg's formulation is an impressive attempt to specify a universal model of moral development. At the same time, there are limitations to it. His model has been criticized as sexist, as not applicable to the processes women use in moral reasoning (Gilligan 1982). Furthermore, like Piaget, there is little interest in the influence of social interaction on moral reasoning. Instead, Kohlberg locates the determinants of moral judgment within the individual. Both models also view moral judgment as a process of applying some broad criterion to a specific situation, whether the criterion is avoidance of punishment or a moral principle.

In response to these limitations, Haan (1978) has proposed a model of interpersonal morality. Many moral decisions and actions result from negotiations among people in which the goal is to achieve a "moral balance." Participants attempt to balance situational characteristics, such as the options open to them, with their individual interests, to arrive at a decision that allows them to preserve their sense of themselves as moral persons. Hearing that a sit-in is planned, for example, the individual makes a tentative decision based not only on his or her commitment to civil liber-

ties or conventional authorities, but also on his or her sense of what a moral person would do. This tentative decision influences subsequent discussions about the sit-in with other persons. The final decision about the action taken is influenced by these interactions.

Haan (1978) studied six adolescent friendship groups as they participated in a series of games that involved making moral decisions. For example, a man who had been declared dead returns home and finds his wife has remarried. Participants varied in their initial reactions, and in their beliefs about what the man should do. The group interactions generally led to an agreement that a particular action would be "moral" in that situation. Such an agreement constitutes a moral balance; it balances the realities of the situation and the group members' preferences for action. An individual's moral principles are only one influence on the outcome.

There probably are situations in which a single individual must reach a moral decision and does so by applying general principles without regard to features of the setting. In such instances, Kohlberg's model may be quite applicable. At other times, we reach moral decisions through a process of interaction with others, or include our expectations of the behavior of others and characteristics of the setting in our own decision making. These decisions are likely to be compromises with principles rather than their mechanical application. In such settings, Haan's concept of moral balance may be more applicable than Kohlberg's model.

Achievement and Work Orientations

One of the persistent questions about human behavior is what guides its direction and explains its intensity. All of us observe that both we and other people choose between alternatives, appear fairly consistent in our behavior across situations, and often persist in attempting to achieve a goal even in the face of adversity. Social psychologists employ the concept of motivation to account for these phenomena. **Motive** refers to a disposition within the person that produces behavior directed toward goals; social motives are those developed in interaction with other persons.

THE ACHIEVEMENT MOTIVE. One of the most widely studied motives is the **achievement motive,** a conscious or unconscious desire to reach high standards of excellence (McClelland 1961). The strength of this motive is positively related to academic performance, even among people who are equal in intellectual ability. It is also positively associated with the tendency to engage in entrepreneurial activity, including taking risks when the outcome is under one's control. People with high levels of this motive are more likely to engage in innovative activity, and to try to anticipate future events.

The achievement motive develops early in the person's socialization. Differences between children in the strength of the motive are evident at five years of age (McClelland 1958). Moreover, achievement scores of six-year-old children are positively related to the scores of the same persons as adults (Moss and Kagan 1961).

Various techniques for measuring achievement motivation have been developed. The most common involves analyzing the stories people write to describe what is happening in pictures of people they are shown. For example, look at the drawing in Figure 3.1. What is happening here? What is the boy thinking? What will happen? Two stories (adapted from McClelland 1961) written by others are (1) "A boy in a classroom is daydreaming. He is recalling an incident which was more fun than being in school. He will probably get called upon to recite and be embarrassed." (2) "The boy is a student taking an exam. The exam is two-thirds over and he is thinking about his answers. He can't remember some of the material. He will miss most of the items he can't remember and be disgusted with himself for not learning them."

The stories written by people are analyzed to determine the extent to which they portray characters as striving to achieve some standard. In Story 1, for example, there is no mention of standards of excellence or achievement. Story 2, by contrast, is rich in achievement imagery. How much concern with achievement and meeting standards of excellence is evident in the story you created? In

FIGURE 3.1
WHAT DO YOU THINK IS HAPPENING IN THIS PICTURE?

research settings, each story is given a score based on the total number of achievement-related ideas contained in it; this measure is termed an *n achievement* score, or *n ach.*

The strength of this motive is a result of two factors. One is the emphasis on excellence and success in childhood socialization (Rosen and D'Andrade 1959). Parents and others who reward children for successfully competing against some standard are contributing to the development of this motive. The second factor is the extent to which parents train their children to be independent (Winterbottom 1958). Children need autonomy in order to display achievement-oriented behavior.

Since the strength of the achievement motive is determined by socialization practices, social groups emphasizing excellence and independence should produce children with high levels of achievement motivation. This hypothesis was tested by studying members of six ethnic groups in the northeastern United States: blacks, French-Canadians, Greeks, Italians, Eastern European Jews, and native-born white Protestants. Interviews were conducted with 427 mother-son pairs and the six groups were compared on both achievement motive and occupational aspirations. Greek, Jewish, and Protestant mothers set high goals for their sons, had high standards for their actual performance, and expected independent behavior. In keeping with these socialization goals, their boys had high levels of the achievement motive. French-Canadian and Italian mothers were lower on all these characteristics. Black mothers had high standards and encouraged independence, and their sons had high achievement scores, but both mothers and sons had low vocational aspirations (Rosen 1959).

It has frequently been noted that children from some ethnic groups do not perform well in school. These results for blacks, however, do not suggest that their relative failure is due to low levels of need achievement, nor to the lack of parental encouragement to achieve.

A study of black and Chicano elementary-school students from a low income neighborhood tried to pinpoint the relationship between achievement motive, aspirations, and school performance. Both parents and children had high educational aspirations. At the same time, parents believed that doing well in school would not lead to better jobs or a higher standard of living for their children. Parents believed that discrimination was pervasive and that it severely limited their own as well as their children's opportunities. They therefore discouraged their children from expecting occupational success. As a result, children did not take schooling seriously and did not try to excel academically even though they had high aspirations. Teachers, observing the poor performance of the children, came to expect them to fail. Finally, local employers discriminated against blacks and Chicanos, and justified this discrimination in part on the basis of the poor educational performance of members of these minorities (Ogbu 1974).

Thus, high levels of the achievement motive and high educational aspirations do not necessarily result in high academic performance. In addition to motivation, one must expect high performance to be rewarded; one must believe that there is an opportunity to realize one's aspirations. Thus performance depends both on motivation and on the perceived "payoff" from that performance (McClelland and Winter 1969).

ORIENTATIONS TOWARD WORK. Work is of central importance in social life. The maintenance of society depends on directing the efforts of its members toward performing necessary tasks. In recognition of the importance of work, occupation is a major influence on the distribution of economic and other resources. In addition, we identify others by their work; its importance is evidenced by the fact that one of the first questions we ask a new acquaintance is, "What do you do?"

Given its importance, most adults are motivated to work at jobs that provide economic and perhaps other rewards. Therefore, it is not surprising that a major part of socialization is the learning of orientations toward work. By the age of two, the child is aware that adults "go work," and asks why. Adults respond with a variety of concrete answers, such as "Mommy goes to work to earn money." The child in turn learns that money is needed to obtain food, clothing, and toys. The child of a physician or nurse might be told that mommy goes to work to help people who are ill. Thus, from an early age the child is being taught the social meaning of work.

The nature of occupations varies tremendously. One dimension on which jobs differ is closeness of supervision; a self-employed auto mechanic has considerable freedom while an assembly-line worker may be closely supervised. The nature of the work varies; mechanics deal with things, salespersons deal with people, attorneys deal with ideas. Finally, occupations such as attorney require self-reliance and independent judgment, whereas an assembly-line job does not. So the meaning of work depends on the type of job the individual has. Adults in different occupations should have different orientations toward work, and these orientations should influence how they socialize their children. Based on this hypothesis, extensive research on social class differences in the values conveyed through socialization has been conducted in two countries (Pearlin and Kohn 1966; Kohn 1969). Fathers are given a list of traits, including good manners, success, self-control, obedience, and responsibility, and asked to indicate how much they value each one for their children. Underlying these specific characteristics a general dimension, "self-direction versus conformity" is usually found. Data from fathers of three- to fifteen-year-old children indicate that the emphasis on self-direction and reliance on internal standards increases as social class increases.

These differences in the evaluations of particular traits reflect differences in the conditions of work. In general, middle-class occupations involve the manipulation of people or symbols, and the work is not closely supervised. Thus, these occupational roles require people who are self-directing, and who can make judgments based on knowledge and internal standards. Working-class occupations are more routinized, and more closely supervised; thus, they require workers with a conformist orientation. Kohn argues that fathers value those traits in their children that the father associates with success in his occupation.

Do differences in the value parents place on self-direction influence the kinds of activities they encourage their children to participate in? A study of 460 adolescents and their mothers (Morgan, Alwin, and Griffin 1978) examined how maternal emphasis on self-direction affects the young person's grades in school, choice of curriculum, and participation in extracurricular activities. The researchers reasoned that parents who value self-direction will encourage their children to take college-preparatory courses, because a college education is a prerequisite to jobs that provide high levels of autonomy. Similarly, they expected mothers who value self-direction to encourage extracurricular activities, because such activities provide opportunities to develop interpersonal skills. The researchers did not expect differences in grades, however. The results confirmed all three predictions. Thus, parents who value particular traits in their children do encourage activities that they believe are likely to produce those traits.

Summary

Socialization is the process through which infants become effective participants in society. It makes us like all other members of society in certain ways (shared language), as well as distinctive in other ways (musical preferences).

PERSPECTIVES ON SOCIALIZATION. (1) One approach to the study of socialization emphasizes biological development; it views the emergence of interpersonal responsiveness, and the development of speech and of moral judgment as influenced by maturation. (2) The other approach emphasizes learning, the acquisition of skills from other persons. Society organizes this process by making certain agents responsible for particular types of socialization of specific persons.

AGENTS OF CHILDHOOD SOCIALIZATION. There are three major socializing agents in childhood. (1) The family provides the infant with a strong attachment to one or more caregivers. This bond seems to be necessary in order for the infant to develop interpersonal and cognitive skills. The absence of attachment may contribute to abuse of the child by adults. Family composition, size, and social class all influence socialization by influencing the amount and kind of interaction between parent and child. (2) Peers provide the child with equal status relationships and are an important influence on the development of self. (3) Schools teach skills—reading, writing, and arithmetic—as well as traits like punctuality and perseverance.

PROCESSES OF SOCIALIZATION. Socialization is based on three different processes of learning. (1) We learn many behaviors and skills by observation. We may not perform these, however, until we are in the appropriate situation. (2) Instrumental learning, the association of rewards and punishments with an act, is a second basis for learning both behaviors and performance standards. Studies of the effectiveness of various child-rearing techniques indicate that rewards do not always make a desirable behavior more likely to occur and punishments do not always eliminate an undesirable act. Through instrumental learning, children develop the ability to judge their own behaviors and to engage in self-reinforcement. (3) Socialization also involves internalization, the acquisition of behavioral standards and making them part of the self. This process enables the child to engage in self-control.

OUTCOMES OF SOCIALIZATION. (1) The child gradually learns a gender role, the expectations associated with being male or female. Whether the child is independent or dependent, aggressive or passive, depends on the expectations communicated by parents, kin, and peers. (2) Language is another outcome; it involves learning both words and the rules for combining them into meaningful sentences. Related to the learning of language is the development of thought, and the ability to group objects and persons into meaningful categories. (3) The learning of social norms involves parents, peers, and teachers as socializing agents. More generally, children learn that conformity to norms facilitates social interaction. Children also develop the ability to make moral judgments. (4) Children acquire motives, dispositions that produce sustained, goal-directed behavior. One such motive is the desire to achieve high standards of excellence, the achievement motive. Orientations toward work are influenced primarily by parents; middle-class families seem to emphasize self-direction while working-class families emphasize conformity.

Key Terms and Concepts

Socialization

Attachment

Observational Learning

Instrumental Learning

Shaping

Primary Reinforcement

Secondary Reinforcement

Extrinsically Motivated Behavior

Intrinsically Motivated Behavior

Punishment

Self-Reinforcement

Internalization

Gender Role

Norm

Moral Development

Motive

Achievement Motive

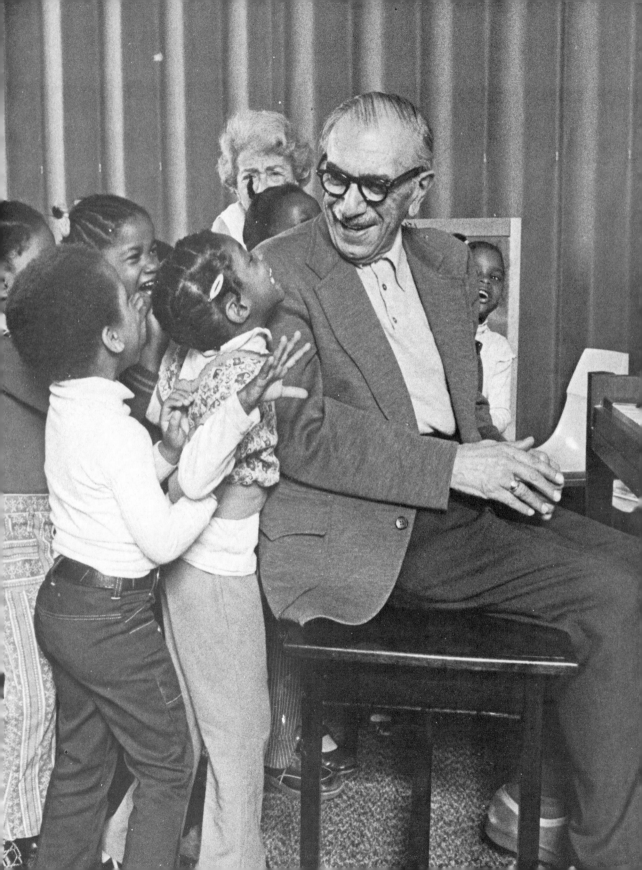

Chapter 4
Continuity and Change Through the Life Course

Introduction

"I still can't get over Liz," said Sally. "I sat next to her in almost every class for three years, and still I hardly recognized her. Put on some weight since high school, of course, and dyed her hair. But mostly it was the defeated look on her face. When she and Hank announced they were getting married they were the happiest couple ever. But that lasted long enough for a baby. Then years of underpaid jobs. She works part-time in sporting goods at Sears now. Had to take that job when her real estate work collapsed in the recession. Pity, just when she was beginning to get on her feet!"

Jim had stopped listening. How could he get excited about Sally's Central High School reunion—people he'd never met? But Sally's mind kept racing. A lot had happened in 20 years:

John — Still bigger than life. Football coach at the old school and assistant principal too. Must be a fantastic model for the tough kids he works with. That scholarship to Indiana was the break he needed.

Frank — Hard to believe he's in a mental hospital! He started okay as an engineer. Severely burned in a helicopter crash and then hooked on pain killers. Just fell apart. And we voted him Most Likely to Succeed.

Andrea — Thinking about a career in politics. She didn't start college until her last kid entered school. Now she's an urban planner in the mayor's office. Couldn't stop saying how she feels like a totally new person.

Tom — Head Nurse at Westside Hospital's emergency ward. Quite a surprise. Last I heard he was a car salesman. Started his nursing career at 28. Got the idea when lying in the hospital for a year after a car accident.

Julie — Right on that one, voting her Most Ambitious. Finished Yale Law, clerked for the New York Supreme Court, and just promoted to senior partner with Wine and Zysblat. Raised two kids at the same time. Having a husband who writes novels at home made life easier. Says she was lucky things were opening up for women just when she came along.

Linda — Too bad she quit journalism school to put her husband through med school. She was a great yearbook editor. Still, says she enjoys writing stories as a stringer for the News. Leaves time for family and travel.

Sally's reminiscences show how different lives can be, and how unpredictable. When we think about people like Liz or Tom or Frank, change seems to be the rule. There is change throughout the life course for all of us. But there is continuity too. Julie's string of accomplishments is based on her continuing ambition, hard work, and competence. John is back at Central High, once a football hero, now the football coach. Though not a journalist as planned, Linda writes occasionally for a paper; and she may yet develop a serious career in journalism over the next 20 years. Even Frank had started on the predicted path to success before his tragic helicopter crash.

As we look into the future, we cannot project with any certainty what will happen to us. But people's lives have patterns that allow us to make sense of them. Each of us will experience a life characterized both by continuity and by change. This chapter will examine the different forms that life courses take, and the important influences that shape them.

Components of the Life Course

Lives are too complex to study in all their aspects. Consequently we start by identifying the three main components of the life course on which we will concentrate: (1) career roles, (2) identity and self-esteem, and (3) stress and satisfaction. Career roles are the sequence of activities people engage in during their lifetimes. Identity and self-esteem refer to the conceptions of self that develop and change as people carry out these activities. Stress and satisfaction point to the emotional responses of people to the varied experiences of their lives. By examining these components, we will trace the continuities and changes that occur in what we do (career), who we are (identity and self-esteem), and how we feel (stress and satisfaction).

CAREERS. A **career** is a sequence of roles, each role with its own set of activities. We can view our lives as a set of intertwining careers in the worlds of work, family life, school, social participation, and so on (Abeles, Steel, and Wise 1980). Our most important careers are in three major social domains: work, family and friends, and education. The idea of careers comes from the work world, where it refers to the sequence of jobs held. Liz's work career, for example, consisted of a sequence of jobs as waitress, checkout clerk, clothing salesperson, real-estate agent, and sporting-goods salesperson.

The careers of one person differ from those of another in several ways—in the roles that make up the careers, in the order in which the roles are performed, and in the timing and duration of role-related activities. For example, one person's family career may consist of roles as infant, child, adolescent, spouse, parent, grandparent, and widow, while another's family career includes roles as divorcee or stepsister but excludes the parent role. The order of roles also may vary. "Parent before spouse" has very different consequences from "spouse before parent." In addition, the timing of career events is important. Having a first child at 36 has different life consequences than having a first child at 18. Finally, the duration of enacting a role may vary. For example, some couples end their marriages before the wedding champagne has gone flat, whereas others go on to celebrate their golden wedding anniversary.

Societies provide structured career paths that determine the options available to individuals and constrain their choices. The cultural norms, social expectations, and laws that organize life in a society make various career options more or less attractive, accessible, and necessary. In the United States, for example, educational careers are socially structured so that virtually everyone attends kindergarten, elementary school, and at least a few years of high school. Thereafter, educational options are more diverse—night schools, technical and vocational schools, apprenticeships, community colleges, universities, and so on. But individual choice among these options is also socially constrained. The norms and expectations of our social groups strongly influence our educational careers.

Market conditions also affect individual career paths. The availability of jobs affects whether individuals choose to enter the labor market, join the army, or continue their education beyond high school—just as the market of available marital partners (during war or peace-time, for example) influences both the timing and the likelihood of marriage.

A person's total life course consists of intertwined careers in the worlds of work, family, and education (Elder 1975; Neugarten and Hagestad 1976). The shape of the life course derives from the contents of these careers, from the way they intermesh with each other, and from their interweaving with those of family members. Sally's classmates, Julie and Andrea, enacted similar career roles: both finished college, held full-time jobs, married, and raised children. Yet the courses of their lives were very different. Julie juggled all these roles simultaneously, helped by a husband who was able to work at home. Andrea waited until her children were at school before continuing her education and then adding an occupational role. In sum, the different content, order, timing, and duration of intertwining careers make each person's life course unique.

IDENTITY AND SELF-ESTEEM. As we engage in career roles, we observe our own performances and other peoples' reactions to us. Using these observations, we construct our **identities**—our sense of who we are, what we can do, and where we stand relative to others. Inevitably, too, we evaluate our performances and thereby gain or lose self-esteem. Identities and self-esteem are crucial guides to behavior, as discussed in Chapter 2. We therefore take identities and self-esteem as the second component of the life course.

STRESS AND SATISFACTION. Feelings of stress and emotional upset or of satisfaction and happiness accompany virtually all career activities. These feelings reflect how we experience the quality of our lives; thus stress and satisfaction are seen as the third component of the life course. These feelings vary in their intensity in response to life course events. Levels of stress, for example, change as career roles become more or less demanding (parenting roles become increasingly demanding as children enter adolescence), as different careers compete with each other (family versus occupational demands), and as unanticipated setbacks occur (one's employer goes bankrupt). Levels of satisfaction vary as career rewards change (salary increases or cuts), and as we cope more or less successfully with career demands (meeting sales quotas, passing exams) or with life events (a heart attack or skiing accident).

The major components of the life course have been identified: career roles, identity and self-esteem, and stress and satisfaction. Our examination of the life course will be organized around four broad questions:

1. What are the major influences leading to progression through the life course? That is, what causes people's careers to follow the paths they do?

2. How do people cope with repeated transitions through the life course? How do they prepare for and adapt to them?

3. What are the typical courses of life for men and women in American society? What happens when people depart from the typical patterns?

4. In what ways do historical events and trends modify the typical life course pattern? How have events such as wars and

trends such as the increasing employment of women influenced the career paths, the identities and self-esteem, and the stress and satisfaction of individuals?

Influences on Life Course Progression

Imagine yourself 60 years from now as you review the course of your life. As you identify the major episodes along your unique path from birth to old age, you are likely to pinpoint specific life events—encounters with people who became important to you, accidents or illnesses, major successes or failures at school or work. **Life events** are episodes that mark transition points in our lives. They provoke coping and readjustment (Danish, Smyer, and Nowak 1980; Hultsch and Plemons 1979). For many young people, for example, the move from home to college is a life event marking a transition from adolescence to young adulthood. This move initiates a period during which students work out new behavior patterns and revise their self-expectations and priorities.

This section will consider the three major influences on the life course: biological aging, social age-grading, and historical trends and events. These influences act upon us through specific life events (Brim and Ryff 1980). Some life events are carefully planned—a trip to Europe, for example. Other events, no less important, occur by chance—like meeting one's future spouse in an Amsterdam hostel (Bandura 1982).

Biological Aging

Throughout the life cycle we undergo biological changes in body size and structure, in the brain and central nervous system, in the endocrine system, in our susceptibility to various diseases, and in the acuity of our sight, hearing, taste, and so on. Changes are rapid and dramatic in childhood. Their pace slows considerably after adolescence, picking up again in old age. Even in the middle years, however, biological changes may have substantial impacts. The shifting hormone levels associated with menstrual periods in women and with aging in men and women, for example, are thought by many to affect mood and behavior (Bardwick 1971; Doering 1980; Hoyenga and Hoyenga 1979).

Biological aging is inevitable and irreversible. But it is only loosely related to chronological age. Biological puberty may come at any time between 8 and 17, for example, and serious decline in the functioning of body organs may begin before age 40 or after age 85 (Heron and Chown 1967). The neurons of the brain die off steadily throughout life and do not regenerate. Yet intellectual functioning, long assumed to be determined early in life and to decline with aging, is now known to increase as well as decrease over the life course (Baltes, Reese, and Lipsitt 1980). Even in old age, mental abilities and performances may improve with opportunities for learning and practice (Baltes and Willis 1982).

Biologically based capacities and characteristics limit what we can do. Their impacts on the life course depend, however, upon the social significance we give them. How does the first appearance of gray hair affect careers, identities, and stress, for instance? For some this biological event is a painful source of stress. It elicits dismay, sets off thoughts about mortality, and instigates desperate attempts to straighten out family relations and to make a mark in the world before it is too late. Others take gray hair as a sign to stop worrying about trying to look young, to start basing their priorities on their own values, and to demand respect for their experience. In a similar manner, the impacts of other biological changes on the life course—such as the growth spurt during adolescence or menopause in middle age—also depend on the social significance given them.

Social Age Grading

Which members of a society are supposed to raise children and which are supposed to be cared for by others? Who should attend school

and who should work full-time? Who should be single and who should marry? Age is the primary criterion that every known society uses to assign people to such activities and roles (Riley, Johnson, and Foner 1972). Throughout life, individuals move through a sequence of age-graded social roles. Each role consists of a set of expected behaviors, opportunities, and constraints. Movement through these roles shapes the course of life.

Each society prescribes a customary sequence of age-graded activities and roles. Table 4.1 presents a sampling of widely held age norms for transitions between roles in the domains of family, education, and work. The findings indicate that there were fairly sharply defined age norms for several role transitions in the early 1960s when these data were gathered. The desirable ages for some transitions have changed in recent years, and the amounts of agreement have undoubtedly changed. Preferred marriage ages may be later, for example. Whatever the specific content of current age norms, however, people continue to be aware that norms exist. As a result, age norms serve as a basis for planning, as prods to action, and as brakes against moving too fast (Neugarten and Datan 1973).

Pressure to make the expected transitions between roles at the appropriate times transforms the life course into a series of normative life stages. A **normative life stage** is a discrete period in the life course during which individuals are expected to perform the set of activities associated with a distinct age-related role. The fact that the order of the stages is prescribed means that people try to shape their own lives to fit socially approved career paths. In addition, people perceive deviations from expected career paths as undesirable. Insofar as individuals follow customary paths, their ages roughly locate them in normative life stages. Transitions from one life stage to another influence the person in three ways: they change the roles available for building identities, modify the allocation of privileges and responsibilities, and alter the socialization experiences to which the person is exposed.

TABLE 4.1

AGE NORMS FOR ROLE TRANSITIONS

Age Norm Question	Age Range	Percent Who Mention an Age in This Range Spontaneously	
		Men (N = 50)	Women (N = 43)
Best age for a man to marry	20–25	80	90
Best age for a woman to marry	19–24	85	90
Best age for most people to finish school and go to work	20–22	86	82
When most men should be settled into a career	24–26	74	64
When most men should hold their top jobs	45–50	71	58
When most people should become grandparents	45–50	84	79
When most people should be ready to retire	60–65	83	86

Note: A representative sample of middle-class American men and women, age 40 to 70, shows considerable agreement. Essentially the same pattern of agreement was also found in other samples, ages 20 to 80.

Source: adapted from Neugarten, Moore, and Lowe (1964).

BUILDING IDENTITIES. Since our identities are built around the roles we enact, role transitions often produce identity change. The period between ages 20 and 24, for example, brings substantial, sometimes wrenching changes in self-conceptions. Those who marry, start their first job, or have their first child are likely to begin to view themselves as spouses and parents responsible for others rather than as students relatively free of responsibility or as dependent children. Much smaller changes in identity are likely for those whose roles change less, who remain single, or who pursue graduate studies.

ALLOCATING PRIVILEGES AND RESPONSIBILI-TIES. The shape of the life course is further affected by normative life stages because societies use age-graded social positions to allocate privileges and responsibilities to individuals (Eisenstadt 1956; Sorokin 1947). For example, our age largely determines whether or not we can be employed for pay or tried in a court. It also determines whether we are too young to

drive a car, or too old. The specific ages granting access to privileges (holding political office) and imposing responsibilities (serving in the military) vary with the community, society, and even through history. This variability makes it apparent that chronological age itself does not determine the allocation of privileges and responsibilities. Rather, allocation depends upon the social definition of age-appropriate roles and activities.

SHAPING SOCIALIZATION EXPERIENCES. Role transitions also bring with them changes in the nature of socialization experiences. As we assume adult roles, socialization agents place less emphasis on teaching ideal standards of morality and performance, and more on teaching ways to find realistic, workable compromises between contradictory demands. The content of socialization tends to shift from regulating biological drives in childhood, to instilling broad values in adolescence, to transmitting specific role-related norms for behavior in adulthood (Brim 1966). The nature of socialization relationships also changes as we grow older. These relationships become less emotionally charged and less central in our lives. The power differences between socializee and socializing agents also diminish as we grow older and move into most higher education and occupational organizations. As a result, adults are more able to resist socialization than children (Mortimer and Simmons 1978).

Historical Trends and Events

Recall that Sally's classmate, Julie, attributed her rapid rise to senior law partner to lucky historical timing. Julie applied to Yale Law School shortly after the barriers to women had been broken, and she sought a job just when affirmative action came into vogue at the major law firms. Sally's friend Liz attributed her setback as a real estate broker to an economic recession coupled with high interest rates that crippled the housing market. As the experiences of Julie and Liz illustrate, historical trends and events are another major influence on the life course. The lives of individuals are shaped by *trends* that extend across historical periods (such as increasing equality of the sexes and improved nutrition) and by *events* that occur at particular points in history (such as recessions, wars, and earthquakes).

Historical trends and events can change the very patterns of biological aging and of age-graded role transitions. Consider, for example, the effects of the historical trend toward improved nutrition and health care. This trend has brought on puberty earlier, lengthened the period of fertility, extended the years of gainful labor, and increased the proportion of elderly in the population. Or consider some effects of an historical event— war. Wars force children to grow up without fathers, women to assume tasks previously managed by men, and men to quit school to become soldiers. Historical trends and events make the individual life course much less predictable than we might expect.

BIRTH COHORTS. To aid in the understanding of how historical events and trends influence the life courses of individuals, social scientists have developed the concept of cohorts (Ryder 1965). A **birth cohort** is a group of people who were born during the same period. The period could be one year or several years, depending on the issue under study. What is most important about a birth cohort is that its members are all approximately the same age when they encounter particular historical events. The birth cohort of 1960, for example, was three years old when President Kennedy was assassinated, eight years old when the Vietnam War protests heated up, fifteen years old during Watergate, and twenty-two years old when unemployment rose in 1982.

A person's membership in a specific birth cohort locates that person historically in two ways. First, it points to the trends and events the person is likely to have encountered. Second, it indicates approximately where an individual is located in the sequence of normative life stages when historical events occur. Life-stage location is crucial because historical events or trends have different impacts on individuals who are in different life stages.

To illustrate, consider the effects of a cutback in funding to support graduate studies in counseling and social work. Such a cutback would have quite different impacts on the cohort of current college seniors as compared with the freshman cohort, or with the cohort of those who completed graduate training five years ago. For some seniors, this historical event might mean switching professional goals, or taking a job and postponing graduate school. The freshman cohort, however, probably would be minimally affected by this historical event. And the cohort that had completed graduate school five years earlier might even benefit because future competition in its profession would be reduced.

Of course, not all members of a cohort experience historical events in the same way. A cutback in funds would strongly affect only those members of the senior cohort who were planning careers in counseling or social work, not those planning to become lawyers or stockbrokers. Thus, differential vulnerability to historical events causes differences within a single cohort, as well as between cohorts.

Placement in a birth cohort also affects access to opportunities. Members of large birth cohorts, for example, are likely to be disadvantaged throughout life. They begin their education in overpopulated classrooms. They then must compete for scarce openings in professional schools and crowded job markets. And, as they age, they face reduced retirement benefits because their numbers overwhelm the Social Security system. Table 4.2 presents various examples of how the same historical

events affect members of cohorts in distinct ways. These historically different experiences mold the unique values, ideologies, personalities, and behavior patterns that characterize each cohort through the life course. Within each cohort there are differences too. For example, war led to a father's absence for some children but not for others.

COHORTS AND SOCIAL CHANGE. Due to differences in their experiences, each birth cohort ages in a unique way. Each cohort has its own set of collective experiences and opportunities. As a result, cohorts differ in their career patterns, attitudes, values, and self-concepts. As cohorts age, they succeed one another in fill-

TABLE 4.2

HISTORY AND LIFE STAGE

Historical Event	Cohort of 1937–38		Cohort of 1957–58	
	Life Stage When Event Occurred	Some Life Course Implications of the Event	Life Stage When Event Occurred	Some Life Course Implications of the Event
World War II (1939–45)	Childhood	For many, father absent in the military. Emerging political views influenced by pride in America's world role.		
Baby Boom (1955–60)	Young adulthood	Early marriage; early childbearing; more children.	Infancy	Member of large cohort. Educated in crowded schools.
Vietnam War (1964–73)	Young adulthood	For draftees, disrupted family and occupational life. For others, increased occupational chances and advancement.	Childhood	For some, father absent in the military. Emerging political views influenced by doubts about America's world role.
Recession (1981–83)	Middle adulthood	Financial pinch in sending children to college. Increased wives' employment to sustain living standards.	Young adulthood	Delayed marriage and childbearing. Competition for few jobs in large cohort. Unemployment, blocked occupational chances.

ing the social positions in the family, political, economic, and cultural institutions. Power is transferred from members of older cohorts with their historically based outlooks to members of younger cohorts with different outlooks. In this way, the succession of cohorts produces social change. It also gives rise to intergenerational conflict around issues on which successive cohorts disagree (Elder 1975; Keniston 1971; Mannheim 1953 [1928]).

In this section, we have provided an overview of changes during the life course. Based on this discussion, it is useful to think of ourselves as living simultaneously in three types of time, each deriving from a different source of change. As we age biologically, we move through "developmental time" in our own biological life cycle. As we pass through the intertwined sequence of roles in our society, we move through "social time." And as we respond to the historical events that impinge upon our lives, we move together with our cohort through "historical time."

Coping with Life Course Transitions

As we progress through the life course, we are confronted with numerous transitions with which we must cope. Transitions are seldom easy. Becoming a parent, starting a job, divorcing one's mate—all such transitions bring people face to face with new challenges and social expectations. They often require substantial changes in our plans, behavior, and sense of who we are.

Many transitions are normative—that is, they are expected at a prescribed time or age. Entering high school and college, marriage, childbirth, promotion into responsible jobs, and retirement are all normative transitions. In contrast, other transitions are non-normative and unexpected. Non-normative transitions may be caused by events in individual lives (being orphaned by a car accident) or by events on the wider historical scene (being

drafted into military service). People can anticipate and plan for normative transitions; but non-normative transitions usually catch them unprepared, making coping especially difficult (Brim and Ryff 1980). This section examines factors that influence our success in coping with transitions: anticipatory socialization, severity of change, social support, and personal resources and competence.

Anticipatory Socialization

One way people prepare for transitions is by **anticipatory socialization**—activities that provide people with knowledge, skills, and values of a role they have not yet assumed. The teenager learning about sexual activity from the boasts of an older friend or from an X-rated movie is engaging in anticipatory socialization. So is the aspiring diplomat or politician who attends closely to the behavior of Henry Kissinger or Ronald Reagan in a television interview. Anticipatory socialization contrasts with explicit training because it is not intentionally designed as role preparation by socialization agents (Clausen 1968; Heiss 1981).

Three factors influence the effectiveness of anticipatory socialization in easing life course transitions (Bush and Simmons 1981; Thornton and Nardi 1975). First is the visibility of the future role. Anticipatory socialization usually prepares children more effectively for the parent than for the spouse role, for example. Children see the parent role directly when interacting with their own parents; but important aspects of interaction among spouses occur when children are away or asleep.

Second is the accuracy with which a future role is presented. The interactions between spouses that children do observe are often laundered to hide negative feelings and conflict, resulting in poor anticipatory socialization.

Third is the certainty or agreement regarding the expectations associated with a future role. Anticipatory socialization for old age is difficult, for example, because we lack clear,

Through anticipatory socialization, individuals acquire skills, knowledge, and values of roles they hope to assume in the future. Highly visible aspects of roles (make-up) are much easier to acquire than hidden aspects (attitudes toward husbands).

agreed norms for how the elderly should behave (Rosow 1974; Matthews 1979). Should they "ease up and accept dependence gracefully," or "stay active and insist on their independence?"

Successful anticipatory socialization entails goal setting, planning, and preparation for future roles. Only by setting at least tentative occupational and family goals during our teenage years, for example, can we effectively plan our educational and social lives. Preparation occurs through part-time jobs, special courses, reading, talking with informed individuals, and so on. People also prepare for transitions by trying out elements of their anticipated roles. This is what couples planning marriage are doing when they take joint vacations, live together for a trial period, and share purchases.

Unanticipated transitions and transitions that turn out unexpectedly require a reassessment of goals. In order to cope effectively, people who, for example, inherit great wealth, flunk out of professional school, or experience a bitter divorce must shift their life course goals.

Severity of Change

The more severe the losses a transition brings, the more difficult it is to cope with that transition. The severity of change experienced, however, depends not so much on the absolute amount of loss. More important is the perceived change in the relationship between one's expectations or aspirations and one's resources (Thomas and Znaniecki 1974). A job layoff may reduce the monetary resources of all employees equally, for example. The severity of the transition to unemployment will be greater, however, for those who aspire to a higher standard of living and for those who build their public identity entirely around their jobs.

Even normative transitions are difficult when there is **role discontinuity**—that is, when the values and identities associated with a new role contradict those of earlier roles (Benedict 1938). Upon entering a discontinuous role, we must revise our former expectations and aspirations. Retirement, for example, often creates role discontinuity. During their working years, adult males are expected to strive for autonomy and productivity, and to build their identities around their work. Retirement introduces contradictory expectations for most men. They must now assume more dependent and less productive roles, and rebuild their identities around these discontinuous roles (Mortimer and Simmons 1978).

When people confront severely problematic transitions, they become more consciously purposeful about their coping behavior. People may develop and execute new plans that they had never thought about before. Faced with hopeless unemployment, for example, families may decide to emigrate, and husbands and wives may agree to split temporarily and find jobs in different cities. Such drastic solutions to severe change illustrate coping by sacrificing short-term satisfactions to pursue long-term goals.

Social Support

Though we move through the life course as individuals, our lives are usually interdependent with others. We can therefore draw upon social support when confronting transitions. Social support, in the form of advice, emotional and material aid, increases our ability to cope successfully with transitions. The negative impact on mental health of such nonnormative events as illnesses, accidents, and job loss is less, for instance, when family and friends provide social support (Eaton 1978; Howe 1981; Pearlin et al. 1981). In order to help their members, families reallocate their resources and reorganize their activities. Parents lend money to young couples to help them manage the economic pressures of the child-rearing years. Wives and children take

jobs and redistribute household responsibilities to maintain the family economy when men are fired, or become disabled (Moen, Kain, and Elder 1982).

Normative transitions of particular social importance are sometimes marked by **rites of passage**—special public ceremonies or rituals in which the individual's new status is affirmed (Glaser and Strauss 1971; Van Gennep 1960). Christenings, bar mitzvahs, graduations, marriage ceremonies, and retirement parties are common rites of passage in American society. They signify both to the individual and to others that the person now has a new identity and that new behaviors, rights, and duties are appropriate. These ceremonies serve as social occasions for giving emotional support, advice, and material aid to those adopting new roles.

Rites of passage are especially valuable when people are reluctant to make a role transition because it requires taking on onerous responsibilities or giving up power, freedom, or pleasures. Graduations, weddings, and retirement parties mark transitions of this type. The public affirmation of the transition propels the person forward despite any reluctance, and inhibits later backsliding.

Personal Resources and Competence

Personal resources such as intellectual ability and emotional and physical health also influence success in coping with transitions. A woman's ability to cope with childbirth, for example, is related to these personal resources. If she is a member of a couple with higher education, occupational standing, and marital quality, she will cope better with the pain of childbearing, and enjoy the rewarding aspects of childbirth more (Entwisle and Doering 1981). In addition, successful coping depends on our sense of competence or efficacy—our confidence that we can control events and determine their outcomes. If we feel *in*competent, we are unlikely to make the effort to utilize our personal resources and skills (Bandura 1977; Elder 1984).

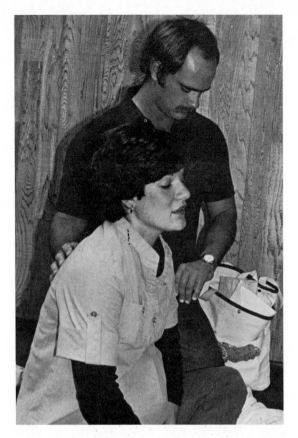

A woman whose husband helps her prepare for childbirth will probably cope better with the stressful transition to motherhood than a woman whose husband provides less social support.

Coping with earlier stressful transitions prepares individuals for subsequent life adaptation. We assess and react to new situations in light of our personal biographies. Earlier experiences of failure reduce an individual's sense of competence or efficacy (Duncan and Morgan 1980). Such experiences may leave people with a sense of helplessness and dread in facing new transitions. Success in earlier coping increases individuals' sense of competence, makes them more optimistic, and strengthens their adaptive skills.

A study of women born at the turn of the century demonstrates the interplay across the life course of personal resources, sense of com-

petence, and coping with transitions (Elder and Liker 1982). The researchers reasoned that middle-class women should cope more successfully with difficult transitions than working-class women because members of the middle class tend to have better personal resources (such as health and intellectual training). They therefore hypothesized that exposure to severe economic deprivation during early adulthood would strengthen the ability of middle-class women to cope with subsequent losses, but weaken the ability of working-class women. This hypothesis was confirmed. Exposure to hardship during the Depression was associated with increased emotional vitality and self-efficacy among middle-class women 40 years later, when they confronted the losses associated with old age. Earlier hardship was associated with subsequent helplessness and diminished self-confidence among working-class women. These findings support the idea that outcomes of earlier transitions shape the personal resources and sense of competence we bring to later transitions.

Stages in the Life Course: Age and Sex Roles

People in every society experience a fairly standard sequence of normative life stages. For most people, movement through developmental time and social time follows one of a few common patterns. We will now examine some typical life-course patterns in American society and some important variations on these patterns, and comment on experiences that distinguish males and females as well as experiences common to both sexes. This comparison is necessary since every known society uses sex as well as age to assign people to roles (Linton 1942; Riley, Johnson, and Foner 1972).

Every society expects certain role behaviors, values, and attributes of males and others of females. Differences in expectations are least pronounced for very young children, increase through adolescence, and become even sharper in young adulthood. Before children are 10, for example, similar amounts of self-reliance, obedience, and leadership are usually expected of both girls and boys. By age 20, however, males and females typically face sex-differentiated expectations for these and other attributes as well as for choices of college major, occupation, and life style (Stoll 1978). Expectations remain strongly differentiated by sex throughout adulthood. With retirement and old age, expectations for males and females become more similar again.

The four postchildhood stages are shown in Table 4.3. Each stage is labelled according to the major social task or challenge that characterizes it. The labels point to the fact that these stages are socially derived rather than the direct products of biological or cognitive development (Havighurst 1948). In discussing each stage, we will focus on each of the major components of the life course we have identified—careers, identity and self-esteem, stress and satisfaction. We will also note the role transitions inherent in moving through these stages and will consider how people cope with the problems posed by these transitions.

Stage I: Achieving Independence

Most college students are currently in the stage of achieving independence. This is a period of transition from lives centered psychologically and economically around parents to lives in which we stand on our own. This stage challenges us to disengage from parents and take responsibility for our own choices and our own futures. For both men and women, achieving independence means taking actions that are competent, persevering, and task-oriented. In addition, women—but not men—tend to view the expression of warmth, kindness, and empathy as signs of independence (Johnson et al. 1975). In contrast, there is evidence that, as college men become more competent and task-oriented, they see themselves as increasingly less warm, open, and

TABLE 4.3
POSTCHILDHOOD LIFE STAGES

Stage	Major Challenge	Conventional Labels	Age Range
I	Achieving independence	Youth, Late adolescence	16–23
II	Establishing work and family commitments	Young adulthood	18–40
III	Performing adult roles	Adulthood, Maturity, Middle age	35–70
IV	Coping with loss	Late maturity, Old age	60–90

Note: The overlap in ages between the stages shows that age is only a rough indicator of life stage.

interested in others (Mortimer, Finch, and Kumka 1982).

Several major social transitions are typically associated with this life stage: leaving one's home, leaving school, entering the work force, getting married, and establishing an independent household. A century ago these transitions were usually spread over many years, occurring one at a time in a fixed order. More recently these transitions have been compressed into the age range from 17 to 25 for most American youth. Individuals are freer now to choose when to make each transition; but they are constrained in these choices by the requirements of getting a formal education and preparing for an occupation. Individuals who make transitions too early or too late pay a price. Being out of step leads to lost income, and lost occupational and marital opportunities (Hogan 1981; Modell, Furstenberg and Hershberg 1976).

CAREERS. During this stage individuals explore the fit between their personal abilities and interests on the one hand, and available work options on the other. Following high school, many youths join the work force in unskilled or semiskilled jobs (as sales and check-out clerks, construction workers, waiters, and so on). Others, especially minority group members in large cities, are frustrated in their search for jobs. They find only sporadic employment during this life stage. Still others enter military service. About half of all youths attend college; but most work at least part-time as well (Sweet, In press). As a result, the vast majority of youths try out a variety of jobs during this life stage, acquiring skills and preferences that eventually lead to more permanent employment.

College students benefit from institutional support in their movement toward independence. College provides a partially protected environment in which one can develop self-reliance with the support of peers. College also instills in many students the motivation to pursue long-range, socially approved goals—such as working eight years to earn an advanced degree—even if this is not personally attractive. Such motivation is very helpful in the struggle for occupational success (Becker 1964). The academic interests of students often reflect the sex typing of subject areas (physics and engineering for males, humanities and social work for females). Sex-differentiated preferences for subjects arise in high school when boys or girls see particular subjects as useful in their future occupational choices (Hilton and Berglund 1974).

The ultimate goal for most men and women is to establish a long-term, intimate relationship with a member of the opposite sex. During this stage, however, close personal relationships are often quite different for men and women (Stockard and Johnson 1980). Male peer groups frequently view women as sex objects to be pursued and conquered. This pursuit initially takes the form of a shared game among peers that builds their ingroup solidarity. Consequently, the first men to become seriously involved emotionally with women feel pressure from their peers not to break this solidarity. The conventions of dating encourage men to take the initiative and women to be more passive and dependent. This pattern fosters a sense of autonomy among men, but it inhibits the achievement of independence among women.

For women, the pursuit of a husband reduces the importance of their closest friendships (Bernard 1981). Women compete with each other in making themselves attractive to men. Producers of hair rinses, skin creams, and other beauty products capitalize on this competition. For a number of women, this behavior is aimed at attracting desirable marital partners who can support them financially (Udry 1974). Although women spend much of their time with individual males, they are not welcomed into the world of male friendships. During this life stage, the prevailing relationship between young women and men has often been of sex object to money machine (Stockard and Johnson 1980). As women become less financially dependent on men, however, this type of relationship is likely to become less prevalent.

IDENTITIES AND SELF-ESTEEM. A central challenge of this life stage is to solidify a personal identity—to develop a firm sense of continuity and direction in one's life (Erikson 1968). Because men and women face different adult role expectations, they tend to build their identities on different bases. National surveys reveal that males tend to construct their identities around their anticipated or actual occupational roles. By anchoring their identities in their own vocational choices, young men can gain a concrete sense of self-direction (Douvan and Adelson 1966; Lowenthal, Thurnher, and Chiriboga 1975).

In contrast, most females in recent decades have tended to construct their identities around their anticipated roles as wives and mothers. Young women's identity commitments may be more tentative and ambiguous than men's because the exact nature of a woman's future roles depends so much upon whom she will marry. It can be adaptive for young women to hold back from firm identity commitments and to maintain flexibility regarding goals. Young women thus avoid prematurely narrowing the range of their potentially compatible marital partners and retain the capacity to adjust to their husband's goals (Angrist and Almquist 1975; Sales 1978). Nonetheless, an increasing number of young women, especially the daughters of happily employed mothers, have recently begun to anchor their identities in their own vocational aspirations (Zuckerman 1981).

Studies of self-evaluation during this life stage show that self-esteem may drop after high school as youths struggle to achieve independence. Illustrating this drop, a sample of male college undergraduates from Michigan rated themselves as less competent, successful, active, and strong in their senior year than they did in their freshman year (Mortimer, Finch, and Kumka 1982). Self-esteem rises later, when people successfully adapt to family and work roles (Haan and Day 1974; Hess and Bradshaw 1970). For the Michigan sample, self-ratings rose over the 10 years following college graduation.

STRESS AND SATISFACTION. Both men and women experience this period of rapid transitions as relatively stressful. Women are considerably more likely than men to feel frightened, to feel that life is hard, and to feel financially insecure (Campbell, Converse, and Rogers 1968). These sentiments may well reflect the fact that young women have less control than men over the important directions their lives are taking. Once they set their life directions by marrying, however, the stress women feel is usually reduced. Women who seriously pursue occupational goals at this time may experience social disapproval.

Socially important role transitions are often marked by rites of passage—public ceremonies that affirm the individual's new status. These ceremonies signify both to the individual and to others that he or she now has a new identity and that new behaviors, rights, and duties are now appropriate.

The lives of successful career women in the 1970s usually included at least one strong nontraditional figure—a working mother, egalitarian father, supportive teacher or relative—who provided encouragement and helped the woman to withstand this added source of stress (Huston-Stein and Higgins-Trenk 1978).

Both overall life satisfaction and satisfaction with specific aspects of life tend to be lower for women and men during this life stage than during most later stages (Campbell et al. 1976; Gould 1978; Lowenthal et al. 1975). Individuals in this stage are unsure of their objectives, of their abilities, and of their futures. Aspirations for occupational and marital success may be high, but individuals worry about translating their dreams into realities. As people make firm career commitments and solidify their identities, moving into the next stage, life satisfaction increases.

Box 4.1
SEX STEREOTYPES AND SEX DIFFERENCES: MYTH OR REALITY?

We are all taught that some behaviors are more appropriate for males, while others are more appropriate for females. Not surprisingly, many people come to believe that males and females have different personality traits. What are the traits believed to be typical of each sex? Do females and males really differ on these traits, or are these sex stereotypes a myth?

The best known series of studies on sex stereotyping of personality characteristics began by asking male and female college students to list all the ways they thought men and women differed psychologically (Broverman et al. 1972). The researchers then listed each trait that the students mentioned at least twice on a scale that looked like this:

Not at all Aggressive						Very Aggressive
1	2	3	4	5	6	7

Various groups of adults, ages 17 to 60, then indicated how much they thought each item characterized adult men and adult women. In numerous studies, people cited consistent differences between males and females for 20 traits (see page 111). To see how aware you are of these stereotypes, indicate with a check whether you think a trait is usually seen as more typical of men or of women. Note also whether you consider each trait a desirable one for an adult to have or an undesirable one.

Broverman and her associates (1972) found that both men and women agree on the stereotypes and on the desirability of each trait. The first five traits listed were seen as more typical of men, the next ten as more typical of women, and the last five as more typical of men. That is, men were seen as more independent, aggressive, and ambitious, women as more passive, emotional, and easily influenced. In general, men were perceived as stronger and more confident than women, and women as weaker and more expressive than men.

The reachers also found that most traits stereotyped as masculine were evaluated as desirable, whereas most traits stereotyped as feminine were evaluated as undesirable. In other words, traits associated with men were usually considered to be better. Did your evaluations of trait desirability favor the male stereotyped traits? If not, you may fit a trend among the educated toward valuing some of the traditionally feminine traits (emotional) more positively and some of the traditionally masculine traits (ambitious) more negatively (Der-Karabetian and Smith 1977; Pleck 1976). This trend means that even if sex stereotypes persist, women may be evaluated less negatively than before.

Do men and women actually differ in the ways suggested by these stereotypes? The picture is still far from clear. There appear to be some real differences between males and females in social behavior. But the stereotypes exaggerate both the number and size of the differences. Here is a summary of some major conclusions reached in critical surveys of the research:

AGGRESSION. Males are indeed more physically aggressive than females. Starting with more hitting and shoving at age two or three, and progressing through more physical fights, violent crime, and spouse-beating, males exhibit more physical aggression through the life course. This difference appears in many different cultures, suggesting that biological factors may be involved. Note, however, that even though males are more likely to initiate physical aggression, females are no less aggressive than males when they are directly provoked and when aggression is socially acceptable (Frieze et al. 1978; Maccoby and Jacklin 1974).

EMOTIONALITY. The stereotype holds that women are more fearful, anxious, and easily upset than men. The majority of more than 30 studies on this topic based on people's descriptions of their own and others' traits supports this stereotype. Women and girls tend to describe themselves as more fearful and anxious, and other raters also tend to describe women as more anxious than

	STEREOTYPICAL BELIEFS ABOUT MEN AND WOMEN									
	Most Typical of		Desirable				Most Typical of		Desirable	
Trait	*Men*	*Women*	*Yes*	*No*	*Trait*		*Men*	*Women*	*Yes*	*No*
Independent	—	—	—	—	Excitable in minor crises		—	—	—	—
Aggressive	—	—	—	—	Aware of others' feelings		—	—	—	—
Ambitious	—	—	—	—	Submissive		—	—	—	—
Strong	—	—	—	—	Strong need for security		—	—	—	—
Blunt	—	—	—	—	Feelings easily hurt		—	—	—	—
Passive	—	—	—	—	Self-confident		—	—	—	—
Emotional	—	—	—	—	Adventurous		—	—	—	—
Easily influenced	—	—	—	—	Acts as a leader		—	—	—	—
Talkative	—	—	—	—	Makes decisions easily		—	—	—	—
Tactful	—	—	—	—	Likes math and science		—	—	—	—

men. However, studies in which researchers observe how people actually behave in fear-arousing situations, and that measure physiological signs of emotionality (pulse, heartbeat, respiration), have revealed no consistent differences between males and females. Taken together, the evidence on emotionality is inconclusive: women may score higher than men on self-reports of emotionality because women are given more freedom and encouragement to express their feelings in our society (Frieze et al. 1978; Tavris and Offir 1984).

DEPENDENCY. Included in the stereotype that women are more dependent is the idea that women rely more on others for protection and help, and are more easily influenced and persuaded. The evidence offers only weak support for this stereotype. Young girls and boys do not differ in clinging to their parents, resisting separation, or wandering about freely. Studies of adult behavior indicate that women are slightly more likely than men to accept suggestions, comply with requests, and be persuaded in face-to-face interaction. These small gender differences are probably largely due to the fact that women more often hold low status positions, and that women are assumed to have lower status if no status indications are available. When face-to-face pressure is absent, and when men and women are equally familiar with the topics at issue, gender differences in persuasibility virtually disappear (Eagly 1978, 1983; Karabenick 1983).

SOCIABILITY. Are women more interested in people, friendlier, and more capable of establishing interpersonal relationships than men? Recent evidence suggests that neither men nor women consistently seek more social contact. The number of friends people have depends mainly on opportunities to meet and spend time with others, not on gender. Thus, college women and men—having equal social opportunities—have about the same number of friends. The same holds for unmarried women and men. Young married women whose social contacts are typically more confined tend to have fewer friends. The studies revealed differences in the quality of male and female friendships, however. Same-sex friendships tend to be more intimate and spontaneous for women than for men. Women are more likely to talk about their feelings and concerns, men to engage in activities such as sports (Caldwell and Peplau 1982; Fischer 1980; Rubin 1983).

Research on other social behaviors and on intellectual abilities have revealed few differences between males and females, except those that emerge after age 10 (such as females' greater verbal ability, males' greater visual-spatial ability). Future research may reveal additional differences, however. The causes of most of the differences we observe in the everyday behavior of men and women are clear; they are the product of socialization, of responses to social expectations, and of the channeling of opportunities in the family, school, and workplace.

Stage II: Establishing Family and Work Commitments

During their twenties and early thirties, most men and women hold worker, spouse, and parent roles. The central challenge of this stage is to establish oneself firmly in these roles—to forgo other options and commit one's energy, time, and self-definition to a particular job and to a particular mate. Priorities must also be set between work and family roles. Women usually give first priority to their roles as wife and mother, men to their work roles.

CAREERS. During the past century the family careers of over 90 percent of Americans have included marriage. Young adults are marrying later now than in recent decades (Table 4.4). In 1980, half of the women had married by age 22.1 and half the men had married by age 24.4. Men and women were marrying at about the same ages in 1980 as they did in the early 1900s. What is not yet clear is whether the proportion who will never marry is increasing.

Obtaining a college education usually delays marriage about two years or more for women and one year for men (Marini 1978). The expanding premarital period of adulthood is being filled increasingly by the less permanent commitment of cohabitation. In recent years, probably one-third of young adults live with a member of the opposite sex for a period of six months or more before marriage (Cherlin 1981). Though the proportion who marry eventually may not be changing, remaining single for an extended period has now become a viable life style (Bernard 1981).

Divorce rates reveal that many young adults have difficulties establishing firm family commitments. If recent trends continue, about half of those who marry this year will eventually divorce, most within the first 10 years of marriage. But people who get divorced typically remarry, and they tend to do so within three years. As a result, most divorces and remarriages occur before people reach age 35 (Cherlin 1981).

The most striking transition of this stage is the transition to parenthood. For more than 20 percent of couples, the first child arrives within seven months of marriage. These couples face the strains of simultaneous transitions to marriage and to parenthood. The couples also suffer ill-effects because they make these transitions in a non-normative sequence (Hogan 1981). Most couples wait two to three years after marrying before having their first child. During this time, couples develop priorities, life styles, and commitments to each other. When the first child arrives, these commitments must be revised to cope with the child's needs. Thus the transition to parenthood causes great role discontinuity. Two to three years later the typical couple has a second and—if current trends continue—last child.

TABLE 4.4

PERCENT OF MEN AND WOMEN MARRIED BY VARIOUS AGES AT THREE DIFFERENT PERIODS

	Women				Men		
Age	1960	1970	1980	Age	1960	1970	1980
18	24	18	12	18	5	5	3
22	75	66	52	22	48	48	31
25	87	86	72	25	72	73	57
29	91	92	85	29	84	86	76

Source: adapted from Cherlin (1981).

The vast majority of men work full-time throughout this life stage, barring problems of unemployment or disability. Employment is less regular for women. Most women work full-time until they have a child, stay home to care for their very young children, and return to work shortly thereafter. Statistics for women's employment in 1980 reflected this pattern. Over 89 percent of childless women aged 25–34 (single or married), but only 41 percent of women with children under age three, were in the labor force. Regular jobs outside the home were held by 51 percent of those with children three to five years old and 62 percent of women with children aged six to seventeen. Many women with young children choose to stay home. But women are also constrained to stay home because their housework load typically doubles with the birth of a child and because child care is both difficult to arrange and expensive. Moreover, despite calls for role sharing, few husbands help significantly with housework and child care (Bernard 1975; Moore and Sawhill 1978).

The occupational experiences of women and men are likely to be very different. More than half of all women employees do clerical (secretarial, typing, bookkeeping, cashier) and service (retail sales, waiting tables, health service assistance) work. Men are much more likely to be craftsmen and foremen, managers and administrators, or to work in wholesale. Although more women than men work in the professions, women are more often in low status professions. Thus, most professional women work in elementary school teaching and nursing, whereas most professional men work in high school and college teaching, medicine, dentistry, law, and science.

The distribution of occupations by gender indicates that men enjoy more prestige and power in their jobs, and earn substantially higher incomes than women. Men are much more likely than women to be in occupations where movement upward through an organizational hierarchy is common. As a result, men are more likely than women to gain occupational status and achieve greater responsibili-

Money, power, excitement—yes! Women? Try to find one. Despite progress toward equality, men continue to occupy better paid and higher powered jobs. Women who build their identities around their work are therefore at a distinct disadvantage.

ty, authority, and sharply higher earnings as they age from their twenties to their forties (Sweet, In press).

The number of women in such previously male-dominated occupations as accounting, law, physical science, and university teaching is increasing rapidly. Nonetheless, the "pay gap" between women and men has actually increased. From the 1950s to the 1980s, the median salary of full-time female workers declined from about 66 percent to less than 60 percent of the median salary for men (Knudsen 1969; *Newsweek* 1983). A substantial part of this gap is due to discrimination (Featherman and Hauser 1976).

IDENTITIES AND SELF-ESTEEM. Men committed to a particular line of work become increasingly caught up in their occupational careers during this stage. Men build their identities around their performance at work and around the future advancement they anticipate. They are likely to think of themselves as "rising junior executives." "budding craftsmen," "maturing scholars," or "salesmen on the move." Success

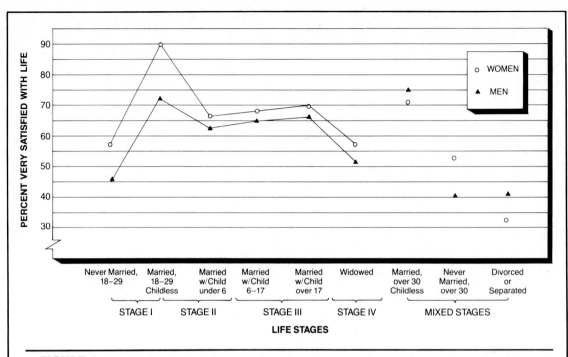

FIGURE 4.1

SATISFACTION OVER THE LIFE COURSE

A national sample of Americans responded to the question: "How satisfied are you with your life as a whole these days?" Responses were scaled from 1 (completely dissatisfied) to 7 (completely satisfied). This chart shows the percentages of men and women who indicated that they were very satisfied (by choosing 6 or 7 on the scale). The sample has been divided into life-cycle categories based on age, marital status, and age of youngest child. The first six categories, arranged in sequence from the left, represent the standard life-course pattern, beginning with young unmarried status, through marriage and parenthood, to widowhood. The curves connecting the responses of these groups show the trends of satisfaction across the life course. The final three categories represent people who diverge from the common pattern. The chart also shows the match between the life-cycle categories and the life stages.

Source: adapted from Campbell et al. 1976:398.

in their occupational careers brings a rise in self-esteem during this stage. In contrast, men who fail to establish themselves in a work career by the end of this stage experience confusion about their identities and have relatively low self-esteem (Riley et al. 1969; Van-Maanen 1976).

Most women become increasingly committed to their families during this stage. Even if they are employed, married women tend to build their identities primarily around their relationships to their husbands and children.

They are likely to think of themselves as wives and mothers, as persons who try to provide a pleasant, supportive home for their children and husbands. Women who enter business and the professions often do construct firm identities around their occupational careers. They are sometimes hindered in this, however, by the treatment they receive as a minority in the upper reaches of large organizations. Women are more often excluded from informal male peer networks and find it harder to be taken seriously than men (Kanter 1976).

It is apparently more difficult to build a sense of self-esteem on work as a homemaker than on work outside the home (Mackie 1983). There are no clear criteria for judging quality homemaking and no raises or promotions to signify a job well done. In contrast, outside jobs usually provide supportive social contacts, and the regular paycheck indicates that other people value one's work. Thus, even the low prestige jobs that many women hold can bolster self-esteem. The effects of outside work on self-esteem show up in a survey of working-class women. Three out of four housewives felt incompetent at running their homes, whereas over half the employed wives said they were "extremely good at their jobs," and not one said she felt incompetent (Ferree 1976). A study of educated middle-class women also showed the effects of work on self-esteem: housewives said they felt "worthless" almost twice as often as employed wives (Shaver and Freedman 1976).

STRESS AND SATISFACTION. Marriage brings a dramatic drop in feelings of stress for most women, but an increase in stress for men. Recently married husbands are more likely than their wives to feel rushed, to feel life is hard, and to worry about paying their bills. The birth of a first child increases stress to the highest level in the life course for both husbands and wives. Strain between spouses increases. Parents of children under age six are the most likely to believe they do not understand each other well and to admit that they disagree (Campbell et al. 1976).

Levels of satisfaction are only partly determined by stress; hence patterns of satisfaction differ somewhat across the life course. Figure 4.1 portrays satisfaction levels for men and women in different life-cycle stages. Young married women report higher levels of satisfaction with their lives than any other group. Men are also unusually happy during the childless married years. The arrival of children reduces satisfaction, especially among women. When young children are present, there is less satisfaction with standards of living, with savings, with housing, and with the marriage relationship. It is the divorced and separated men and women who are the least satisfied, however.

Stage III: Performing Adult Roles

What is the major challenge around which people your parents' age organize their lives? For most adults, the major challenge from their late thirties until into their sixties is to put their lives to a useful purpose—to make a meaningful social contribution (Erikson 1968). Of course, few people talk about making "meaningful social contributions." Instead, people try to be good workers, parents, and spouses; that is, they try to meet high standards for performance in the adult roles to which they are committed.

CAREERS. Most men and childless career women spend the first part of this stage working their way up the occupational ladder. Devoting themselves primarily to their jobs, they seek the increased responsibility, respect, and financial rewards available in their occupations. At some point in their forties or fifties many workers recognize that their occupational life has reached a plateau that may extend to retirement. Taking stock of where they are, these workers often become less concerned with their own achievements and more interested in promoting others (Gould 1978; Lowenthal et al. 1975). Thus lawyers, machinists, managers, or researchers who earlier enjoyed the guidance of mentors, may now take pleasure in guiding younger associates themselves. They may also concern themselves more with the social values of their occupations—with fairness and safety in the work setting, or with the politics and ethics of their professions.

Workers who are inclined toward greater self-determination may respond to the occupational plateau by pursuing new experiences and challenges. Some seek jobs similar to their current ones in firms or institutions where the path to further advancement is still open (such as leaving one automobile company for another, or a local government job for one in Washington). Others return to school or study on their own in order to launch new careers (such as switching from teaching to stock brokerage, or from banking to public law). Starting one's own business, moonlighting at a second job, and turning a hobby into a money-maker are other self-determining responses at this life stage. Career switching in middle adulthood has become easier in the United States, because there is an increasing cultural emphasis on self-realization and a growing tolerance for varied occupational alternatives for both men and women (Sarason 1977).

Most employed mothers devote themselves primarily to their families when their children are young. Even those whose professional careers were built on extended training and personal investment—lawyers, doctors, and professors—tend to compromise their work commitments in favor of family requirements. Studies of married professionals reveal that the wife, not the husband, stays home when a child is sick or when the baby-sitter does not show up. And few professional women bring work home, unlike their husbands (Poloma 1972). Such compromises cause married women to fall behind men in their work careers. As a result, these women may pursue occupational advancement and personal achievement most intensively during their forties and fifties, after their children become teenagers. Paradoxically, this may be just when their husbands are beginning to feel less driven.

Women who had stayed home to raise children usually seek greater involvement in the wider community when their youngest child enters high school. Volunteer work attracts women who have little financial need or women whose husbands object to their holding a job. Women who seek jobs at this stage are often at a disadvantage: they have no established record of reliable employment, nor have they developed marketable skills for over a decade. Consequently, they must often settle for jobs that are below their educational level and less than fulfilling (Sewell, Hauser, and Wolf 1980).

Men change little in their family roles during this lengthy stage. For women, however, the departure of their youngest child from the home may mark a major transition. At this point the "basic tasks of womanhood, as defined in American society, those of bearing and rearing children, are completed" (Lopata 1971:41). Women who have devoted themselves exclusively to child rearing may feel useless when their children no longer need them, and they may become deeply depressed (Bart 1975). But because most women today are involved in nonfamily activities and careers by this transition point, they react to the "empty nest" in a more positive way (Radloff 1980). Though some feel depressed initially, they tend to adjust quickly and to experience a sense of relief at their reduced family responsibilities. Many women feel more free, self-directed, and open to opportunity after their children leave home than ever before (Lowenthal et al. 1975; Neugarten 1968; Rubin 1979).

IDENTITIES AND SELF-ESTEEM. It is widely assumed that men continue to anchor their identities in their occupational roles throughout this midlife stage. In the absence of studies that follow the same individuals over many years, this assumption is based on theory and in-depth interviews. The level of men's self-esteem is thought to depend primarily upon their relative occupational success. People commonly gauge their success by whether they receive promotions and raises early, late, or on time compared to others in similar occupational roles (Levinson 1978; Lowenthal et al. 1975).

Women presumably anchor their identities primarily in their family roles. Loss of the maternal role when children leave home might therefore weaken a woman's sense of

TABLE 4.5
Effects of Marriage and Employment on Identity and Self-Esteem of Educated Middle-Aged Women

	% Housewives (N = 29)	% Married Professionals (N = 25)	% Single Professionals (N = 27)
Identity			
Feelings of uncertainty about who you are and what you want:			
Hardly ever	34	64	58
Fairly often	66	36	42
Feeling lonely:			
Hardly ever	28	72	27
Sometimes to often	72	28	73
Self-Esteem			
Self-evaluated competence in five areas (domestic, social, child care, cultural, intellectual):			
Poor to average	31	4	15
Average to good	55	42	31
Good to very good	14	54	54
Feels "not very" attractive to men:	61	12	58

Note: Housewives who were interviewed had graduated with honors from the University of Michigan 15 to 25 years earlier. The employed single or married professionals held Ph.D.s or M.D.s, and were matched with housewives of similar age.

Source: adapted from Birnbaum (1975).

identity temporarily and undermine her self-esteem. But the ensuing period of freedom is usually accompanied by an expanding sense of competence, maturity, and self-assurance (Kuhlen 1964; Neugarten 1968). Menopause was also once thought to weaken women's self-assurance and esteem. Perhaps this was true when menopause signified the end of childbearing—the loss of what was considered women's most important capacity. But menopause no longer has this social meaning because women end childbearing earlier today and cultivate alternative roles around which to build identities. There is even cross-cultural evidence that following menopause, women become more assertive, dominant, and autonomous; whereas men at this age become more nurturant and affiliative (Freedman 1979; Guttman 1977; Lowenthal et al 1975).

Being employed increases the self-esteem of married women (Kessler and McCrae 1982). In particular, women who complete college and work as professionals have a firmer sense of identity and higher self-esteem. This was illustrated in a study which compared the sense of identity and self-esteem of a group of married female professionals, single female professionals, and housewives (Birnbaum 1975; see Table 4.5). Single professionals resembled married professionals on both dimensions, although the group of singles felt as lonely and unattractive as did housewives. The responses of each group suggest that (1) professional employment contributes to a firmer identity and sense of competence, and (2) the combination of employment and marriage combats feelings of loneliness and being unattractive to men.

STRESS AND SATISFACTION. For both married men and married women Stage III is a period of declining psychological stress. For parents the following types of stress are greatest when children are under six, and decline steadily as children grow older: feeling tied down, feeling life is hard, worrying about having a nervous breakdown, and—especially—worrying about finances (Campbell et al. 1975).

The drop in stress levels at this stage fits with a general theory about "life cycle squeeze" as a determinant of stress and satisfaction (Wilensky 1961). The idea of **life cycle squeeze** refers to the fact that in certain life stages, financial and family burdens are typically great while job status and rewards are low. This produces an unfavorable balance between aspirations and resources. Life cycle squeeze is relatively low among young singles and childless couples. It increases sharply for couples with preschool children, producing the increased stress and dissatisfaction noted above. During Stage III, life cycle squeeze eases: workers' earnings and status rise toward their peak while family and financial burdens lessen. This leads to decreased stress and increased life satisfaction. If people are divorced, separated, widowed, or retired, they commonly experience the imbalance of resources and aspirations that characterizes life cycle squeeze. Surveys reveal that life satisfaction, stress, and happiness generally rise and fall together with the experience of life cycle squeeze (Estes and Wilensky 1978).

Although life cycle squeeze eases as the midlife stage progresses, two other sources of stress gradually increase: physical illness and the death of parents or close friends. People aged 45 to 64 reported three times more anxiety about physical illness than people aged 21 to 34 in one national survey (Gurin, Veroff, and Feld 1960). In a more recent study, women's reports of deteriorating health (eyesight, hearing, teeth, hair, and so on) increased greatly after age 45 (Rossi 1980). The death of a parent or close friend can be stressful because it increases one's own sense of mortality, deprives one of important roles as child or friend, may increase fears about health, and may impose added financial burdens. But the disruption of day-to-day living resulting from parental death is seldom severe. This is because elderly parents rarely play a central role in the lives of their adult children in our society (Kalish 1976).

Stage IV: Coping with Loss

Most of us will enter the final life stage during our sixties. Retirement or the onset of a major physical disability are the key markers of the transition into this stage. The central challenge of this stage for older adults is to cope with a series of practically unavoidable losses: loss of one's occupational role through retirement, of significant relationships through death, and of health, energy, income, and independence. Despite the severity of these losses, most older people say they are quite satisfied with life and that they are coping fairly well (Harris 1982).

Most people who reach age 65 in the United States today spend as many years in this final stage of life as they spent in childhood and adolescence. Men who reach 65 can expect to live another 14 years, women another 18.

Through many of these years, older people can actively enjoy a wide range of activities because most remain reasonably healthy at least until age 75. Yet the aged, as a group, are often mistakenly believed to be narrow-minded, unteachable, not very bright, uninterested in sex, and not good at getting things done (Harris 1975). Thus, in addition to coping with losses, older people must often cope with **ageism**—prejudice and discrimination against the elderly based on negative beliefs about aging.

Box 4.2

THE MIDLIFE CRISIS: HOW NORMAL? HOW NECESSARY?

It is widely believed that some time between age 35 and 44 most of us—especially men—will pass through a period of severe inner turmoil. If we open ourselves to the inevitable questions and repressed self-doubts this period raises, we will emerge with renewed vigor and authenticity to face the second half of our lives. If we fail to confront our inner worries and dissatisfactions and to reassess profoundly our past commitments and behavior, we will lose vitality and remain constricted in our actions during our remaining years. This **midlife crisis** is the critical stage of transition into middle age, when people become aware that time is running short, that unless they make changes in their personal relations, in their work, and in themselves, it will be too late.

The midlife crisis has been discussed in social science research (Gould 1978, Levinson 1978), popularized in the bestseller *Passages* (Sheehy 1976), and discussed on countless talk shows. When a Wisconsin psychiatrist set up a "midlife crisis hotline," his phone rang off the hook. Despite the widespread acceptance of this concept, many remain skeptical (Brim 1976; Bush and Simmons 1981). The existence and nature of the midlife crisis have been established primarily through in-depth interviews and discussions with highly educated men. This research may be biased, however, because the interviews have been carried out and interpreted by researchers who assumed that adulthood consists of a series of discrete stages and transitions.

The major concerns that have been raised regarding the midlife crisis revolve around two questions:

1. Is a midlife crisis a normal, virtually universal part of aging for men?
2. Is it necessary for a vital, healthy later adulthood?

In exploring these questions, researchers began by developing an inventory of the problems that men undergoing a midlife crisis presumably experience according to the literature (Costa and McCrae 1980). They identified types of problems (such as inner turmoil, change in time perspective, increased awareness of the repressed parts of self, marital and job dissatisfaction). Members of a first sample ($N = 233$) reported whether they were experiencing these problems by completing a questionnaire. In order to determine whether the problems presumably typical of the midlife crisis became more frequent or intense between the ages of 35 and 45, the researchers compared various age groups between 33 and 79. To their surprise, there were no age differences at all in the number or intensity of problems reported. Replicating this study with a second sample ($N = 315$), the researchers again found no differences between age groups.

What do these findings mean? Apparently a midlife crisis is not a universal, normal part of aging associated with any one period in adulthood. But is a midlife crisis necessary for later health and vitality? Some additional findings suggest that the answer is "no." Men who reported many of the problems presumably associated with the midlife crisis also scored high on a neuroticism questionnaire. These same men had also scored high on neuroticism 10 years earlier. This strongly suggests that the current crises of these men were "simply one more incident in a life-long history of maladjustment" (Costa and McCrae 1980:84).

Results of these studies suggest that men (and women) do confront problems with their work and family commitments, identities, and self-evaluations through adulthood. But, contrary to popular dramatization, people do not struggle intensely with all of these problems at any single adult stage. In fact, a struggle of crisis proportions is neither common in the general population nor a sign of future vitality.

CAREERS. Most older people maintain strong primary relationships. More than half the elderly live with their spouses and marriage continues to be their most important social tie. But the marital relationship often becomes more egalitarian in this stage. Women typically continue the shift toward greater assertiveness and independence begun in the preceding life stage, and men continue their shift toward greater nurturance and expressiveness (Guttman 1977). Retirement adds to equality by reducing differences between spouses' activities. The happiest marital relationships among the elderly are those characterized by relative equality, mutual emotional support, and flexible sharing of household tasks (Sinnot 1977).

Death of one's spouse is the most severe trauma the elderly confront. Women are typically widowed because they have longer life expectancies than their husbands. Half of married women lose their husbands by age 70. When husbands outlive their wives, they usually become widowers only after age 85. Death of a spouse causes many types of loss. It severs the deepest of emotional bonds, takes away the main companion in day-to-day activities, frustrates the fulfillment of sexual needs, removes the key significant other for affirming one's identity, and—especially for women—produces economic loss.

How well a widow copes with her husbands' death seems to depend on her social class background. The initial loss is more disruptive for middle-class women than for working-class women. This is because middle-class women usually share more aspects of their lives with their husbands (friends, intellectual, cultural, and political interests). In the long term, however, middle-class widows adjust better. They tend to have a more secure income, a larger network of friends, more education, and better job skills. All of these aid middle-class widows in reestablishing satisfactory social relations and an independent sense of self. Lacking these assets, working-class widows are more likely to remain isolated and lonely (Lopata 1979).

Although there are a few tragic exceptions, older Americans—married or not—are rarely abandoned by their families. In fact, more than half see at least one of their adult children almost every day, and the vast majority have contact with a child or sibling every week (Harris 1982; Shanas 1979). The image of the elderly as isolated in institutions such as nursing homes is inaccurate. Only about one in four is likely to spend *any* part of this life stage in an institution (Tobin 1980). Very few older people live *with* their adult children; but this reflects preference for independence on both sides, not the lack of an emotional bond. When the need arises, adult children provide the overwhelming proportion of personal care (Steere 1981).

Occupations, the second main career line, come to an end for most older people with retirement between ages 60 and 65. Ideally, retirement would be a gradual process loosely linked to aging, since occupational abilities and inclinations diminish only gradually. People who have control over giving up their occupational careers (for example, top management and the self-employed) do indeed withdraw more gradually (Hochschild 1975). Retirement brings many losses; income, prestige, one's sense of competence and usefulness, and one's social contacts may all decline. Retired persons may need to fill free time, develop new everyday routines, and—if married—adjust to spending more time with their spouses. Men experience substantial role discontinuity upon retiring. Women tend to experience less discontinuity because they retain at least their homemaking responsibilities.

The main fear of retirees is that they will be cut off from social participation. Does this happen? As a rule, people continue the level of social involvement they developed in their preretirement years. Those who were constantly busy and involved with people find new outlets in voluntary activities, hobbies, and social visits. Individuals who were uninvolved remain so. Few withdraw further (Palmore 1981).

Reduced financial resources do, however, disrupt social participation, especially among the working class (Robson 1982). Retirees who must worry about finances hesitate to spend money traveling to visit friends and entertaining them. Nor can they buy "proper" clothes or tickets for social events. Working-class couples also have more difficulty with the increased presence of retired husbands in the home. Because they are accustomed to exclusive control over the household, working-class wives tend to experience this as an irritating invasion. Middle-class wives are more likely to welcome the added companionship (Kerckhoff 1966).

IDENTITIES AND SELF-ESTEEM. Retirement, widowhood, and declining health deprive people of many of the central roles and relationships around which their identities have been built. Considering these losses, identity change in this stage is less than one might expect (Atchley 1980). The relative stability of identities is due primarily to the fact that older people continue to think of themselves in terms of their former roles. Though retired, individuals still think of themselves as nurses, accountants, or musicians, for example. Though widowed, they remain "John's wife" or "Sarah's husband" in their own eyes. Identities are also preserved because many personal qualities remain stable. Individuals are likely to see themselves as unchanged in their honesty, outspokeness, religiousness, and so on.

Neither widowhood nor retirement alone do serious damage to self-esteem (Atchley 1980). Several aspects of aging are, however, associated with self-esteem loss. Whatever deprives older people of their independence and of control over their own lives—such as ill-health or falling into poverty—weakens self-esteem. Moving into an institution or family residence where one becomes highly dependent also undermines self-esteem if caretakers make all the decisions for an older person. These well-meaning actions commu-

Despite the losses associated with old age, most elderly people say they are quite satisfied with life. As long as they stay healthy and independent, most elderly people maintain their social involvements, activities, and self-esteem.

nicate the assumption that the older person is mentally and physically incompetent.

STRESS AND SATISFACTION. Fear of death is not a major source of stress for older people. Most accept its inevitability. The three main sources of stress are perceived financial difficulties, failing health, and reduced social activity (Atchley 1980; Palmore 1981). Anxiety over financial difficulties is particularly high among widows. Financial anxiety also plagues retired persons whose incomes are fixed in periods of rapid inflation. Stress from failing health rises throughout this life stage, especially after age 75. Older people become anxious and depressed when they experience reduced energy levels, lack of motivation, memory loss, a slowdown in their ability to process information, and chronic or acute diseases. Depression induced by ill-health is often misdiagnosed as mental deterioration and confusion. As a result, depressed older people often fail to receive the psychotherapeutic treatment that could restore them to alertness and satisfactory functioning.

A widely publicized theory of adjustment to aging, **disengagement theory,** holds that withdrawal from social commitments is inevitable with aging, and that withdrawal promotes satisfaction with life because it frees up time and energy for introspection (Cumming and Henry 1961). The evidence, however, contradicts this theory. First, disengagement is not inevitable. Older people whose social and occupational opportunities permit usually remain engaged. Thus, elderly carpenters continue their cabinetmaking and emeritus professors continue their research and writing. Second, life satisfaction is more often associated with engagement than with disengagement. With few exceptions, older people who are more involved in social activities and relationships report higher levels of satisfaction (Maas and Kuypers 1974; Palmore 1981).

Historical Variations

Throughout this chapter, we have based our description of stages in the life course on recent findings and on projected future trends. But historical events—wars, depressions, medical breakthroughs—change life courses. And historical trends—fluctuating birth and divorce rates, rising education, varying patterns of women's work—also influence the life courses of individuals born in particular historical periods.

No one can predict with confidence the future changes that will result from historical trends and events. What can be done is to examine how major events and trends have influenced life courses in the past. Two examples will be treated: the historical trend toward greater involvement of women in the occupational world, and the effects of the Great Depression and subsequent wars on the lives of men. The goals of this section are: (1) to emphasize the fact that historical trends continually influence the typical life course; and

(2) to illustrate how to analyze the links between historical events and the life course.

Women's Work: Sex-Role Attitudes and Behavior

At their graduation exercises in 1955, the women of Smith College were launched into the adult world with the following advice from Adlai Stevenson (Senator, U.N. Ambassador, and Presidential candidate): A women's place in politics is to "influence man and boy" through the "humble role of housewife." Misguided as these remarks may sound today, they probably struck a responsive chord in most of the audience; for during the 1950s, it was widely accepted that "there is some work that is men's and some that is women's, and they shouldn't be doing each other's" (Thornton and Freedman 1979).

SEX-ROLE ATTITUDES. In the past three decades, attitudes toward women's roles in the world outside the family have changed dramatically. The historical trend in attitudes has been away from the traditional division of labor (paid occupations for men and homemaking for women) to a more egalitarian view. But much of this change did not occur until well into the 1960s.

Consider some of the following statements of sex-role attitudes. Do you agree with them?

(a) It is better if the man is the achiever outside the home and the woman takes care of home and family.
(b) Most of the important decisions in life should be made by the man of the house.
(c) If her husband can support the family, a woman should not work for pay.
(d) It is wrong for a woman to be very active in clubs, politics, and other outside activities before her children are grown.
(e) Preschool children are likely to suffer if their mother works.

These are paraphrases of attitude statements included in one or more large-scale

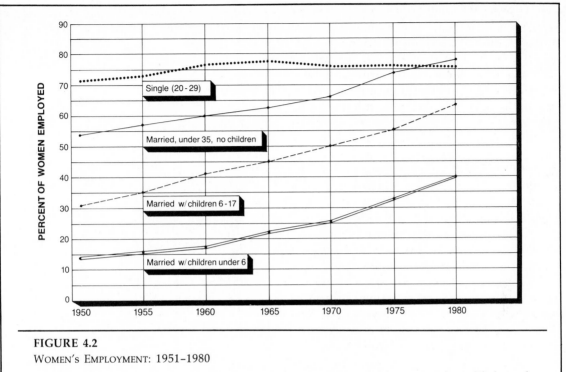

FIGURE 4.2

Women's Employment: 1951–1980

The percentage of married women who are employed has risen steadily since 1950. Young single women have maintained virtually the same high level of employment throughout this period. In each year, women with young children were least likely and childless married women were most likely to be employed.

Source: adapted from Sweet, 1985.

surveys of adult women during the 1960s and 1970s. In the 1960s, about two-thirds or more of women surveyed agreed with these statements. However, by the late 1970s, three of these attitudes had become minority views (b, c, d), and statements (a) and (e) were endorsed only by about half the women. This shift from traditional to egalitarian sex-role attitudes has been quite strong among women (Cherlin 1981; Mason and Bumpass 1975; Spitze and Huber 1980; Thornton and Freedman 1979).

Work Force Participation. This historical trend is not limited to attitudes. Women's actual participation in the work force has been on the increase for almost a century. Figure 4.2 shows the percent of women employed outside the home since 1951. The proportion of married women who are employed has been growing steadily, with a slight acceleration of growth between 1970 and 1980. Among young single women, the employment level, which was already very high in 1951, has remained high. The proportion of women who work during pregnancy and who return to work while their child is still an infant has also grown steadily over this time period (Sweet 1985.)

Why have women joined the work force in ever greater numbers throughout the twentieth century? Has the spread of egalitarian attitudes been an important source of influence? Probably not. The idea that wives and mothers should not work except in cases of extreme need was widely held until the 1940s. Yet women's employment increased steadily between 1900 and 1940. The change in sex-role attitudes occurred largely in the 1970s, yet women's employment rose rapidly during the two decades preceding these attitude changes. It therefore seems likely that sex-role attitude changes have not been a cause of the increased employment of women, but a response to it—an acceptance of what more and more women were in fact doing.

What, then, are the causes? Perhaps most convincing is the argument that the types of industries and occupations that demand female labor are the ones that have expanded most rapidly in this century. Light industries like electronics, pharmaceuticals, and food processing have grown rapidly, for example, and service jobs in education, health services, secretarial and clerical work have multiplied. Many of these occupations were so strongly segregated by sex that men were reluctant to enter them (Oppenheimer 1970). In addition, male labor has been scarce during much of the century due to rapidly expanding industry and commerce. The majority of the slack was taken up by a large pool of unemployed married women. These women could be pulled into the work force at a lower wage because they were often supplementing a family income.

Other factors that may have promoted the increased employment of women include rising divorce rates, falling birth rates, rising education levels, and the invention of labor-saving devices for the home. None of these factors alone can explain the continuing rise in the employment of women over the whole century. However, at one time or another each of these factors probably strengthened the historic trend, along with changes in sex-role attitudes.

The specific changes in women's work behavior demonstrate that the timing of a person's birth in history greatly influences the course of his or her life. Whether you will join the work force depends in part on historical trends during your lifetime. So does the likelihood that you will get a college education, marry, have children, divorce, die young or old, and so on.

Effects of Historical Events: The Great Depression

> The city had been shaken for nearly six years by a catastrophe involving not only people's values, but in the case of many, their very existence. Unlike most socially generated catastrophes, in this case virtually nobody in the community had been cushioned against the blow; the great knife of the depression had cut down impartially through the entire population, cleaving open the lives and hopes of rich as well as poor. The experience had been more nearly universal than any prolonged recent emotional experience in the city's history; it had approached in its elemental shock the primary experiences of birth and death.
>
> —Lynd and Lynd, *Middletown in Transition*

The Great Depression, commencing with the stock market crash of 1929, and stretching through the 1930s, brought heavy economic loss and suffering to many American families. Only about half the population was spared severe misfortune. In a series of studies, a group of researchers analyzed the impact of deprivation during the depression on life courses. They traced the lives of men over a 40-year period, from their birth in the 1920s into adulthood (Elder 1974; 1980; 1981; Elder and Rockwell 1979a; 1979b).

In a study of this kind, researchers might contrast the life courses of deprived and non-deprived individuals who were the same age when deprivation hit. This would be a comparison *within* a birth cohort. But we also want to know if the effects of deprivation were the same whether an individual was two years old or fourteen when the depression began. To discover such age-linked differences in the effects of historical events requires compari-

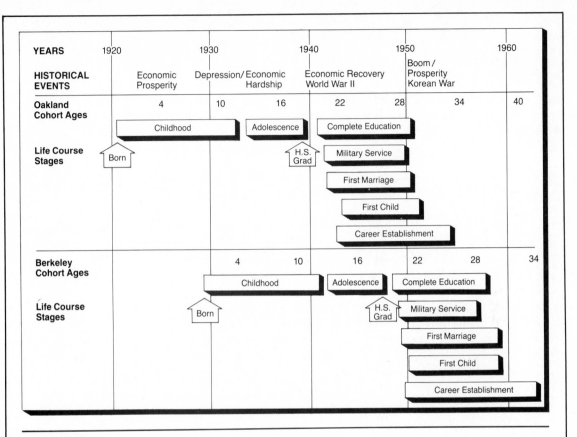

FIGURE 4.3

<small>HISTORICAL TIME, DEVELOPMENTAL TIME, AND SOCIAL TIME IN THE LIVES OF TWO COHORTS</small>

Historical events intersected differently with the lives of two birth cohorts of men from the San Francisco Bay area. The Oakland cohort (born 1920–21) spent their childhood in a period of prosperity and their adolescence in a period of deprivation. Drafted into the military shortly after graduating from high school to serve in World War II, these men returned from the service to expanding educational and career opportunities. The Berkeley cohort (born 1928–29) knew no early prosperity and spent their childhood in a period of deprivation. Too young to serve in World War II, this cohort spent its adolescence in a period of economic recovery fueled by the war. After graduating high school, these men served in the Korean War, returning to a booming economy that offered abundant career opportunities. Of course, not all families were equally deprived in the Great Depression.

Source: adapted from Elder 1974; 1981; Elder and Rockwell 1979a.

sons *between* birth cohorts. With this purpose, Elder and a group of researchers (1980; 1981) compared the impact of the depression on two different birth cohorts with similar backgrounds from the San Francisco Bay area. Boys from Berkeley (born 1928–29) were in their early childhood years during the height of the depression. Boys from Oakland (born 1920–21) were in their early adolescence. Figure 4.3 shows the intersection of economic events and wars with the life stages of these two cohorts. Boys whose families lost at least 34 percent of their income between 1929 and 1933 were defined as "deprived." Others were considered relatively nondeprived because there was an overall 25 percent drop in the cost of living at that time.

How was this major historical event linked to individual biographies? Berkeley children and Oakland adolescents experienced the drastic income loss of their families most immediately through three changes in family life:

1. *Change in the household economy.* Responsibilities for earning income from jobs and budgetary management fell more on mothers and adolescent boys and less on fathers.

2. *Redistribution of power and influence.* Mothers increased their relative decision-making power at the expense of fathers, parental control over children decreased, and fathers became less attractive models for their sons.

3. *Greater social and psychological strain.* Parent–child and husband–wife conflict rose as status differences became ambiguous; family members became more irritable and handled their feelings and relationships less effectively.

We will now examine how the Great Depression, working first through these three family changes, affected the careers, work and family values, self-evaluations and psychological adjustment of men in the Berkeley and Oakland cohorts.

Boys in the Berkeley cohort were young children when their families encountered the depression. Because they were still highly dependent on their parents' care and nurturing, the Berkeley boys were especially vulnerable to the family instability, conflict, and emotional strain caused by economic deprivation. The Oakland boys, in contrast, were past this very vulnerable life stage when their families encountered the depression. These differences suggest that deprivation should have been more harmful to the young Berkeley cohort than to the older Oakland cohort

because they were at a more vulnerable age when their lives were disrupted. Data gathered during the adolescence of each cohort support this hypothesis (Table 4.6).

ADOLESCENCE. Among the vulnerable Berkeley cohort, deprivation resulted in poorer grades, lower self-esteem, assertiveness, ambition, and goal-direction, heightened feelings of victimization by life circumstances, and greater sensitivity to being judged. In contrast, the Oakland adolescents showed no ill-effects of earlier deprivation. In fact, deprived Oakland boys were quicker to form occupational interests and goals, because they had taken on more adult responsibilities during the Depression.

YOUNG ADULTHOOD. All but a handful of the Oakland cohort served in World War II, and most of the Berkeley cohort served in the Korean War. Deprivation influenced the Berkeley boys to enter the armed forces at an earlier age because deprivation reduced their chances of attending college or settling in an occupation, the two major reasons to defer military service. A tuition-free education at a California state college was available to members of both cohorts. Yet, earlier family deprivation reduced the chances of graduating from college—especially for the Berkeley men who had performed poorly in high school and had lower aspirations.

In the Berkeley cohort, men from deprived families married and had their first child substantially later than their nondeprived counterparts. This delay probably reflected a bitter lesson learned from the disrupted childhood life of their own families: that is, it is unwise to undertake the responsibilities of wife and children until one is financially secure. Deprived Oakland men committed themselves to work and established stable careers, while deprived Berkeley men drifted between different jobs unless they attended college. The contrasting effects of deprivation in the two cohorts reflects the occupational goals and interests,

TABLE 4.6

EFFECTS OF DEPRIVATION DURING THE GREAT DEPRESSION ON TWO BIRTH COHORTS OF MALES

Life Course Outcomes	1920-21 Cohort (Oakland)	1928-29 Cohort (Berkeley)
Adolescence		
(1) Social adjustment	No effect	D poorer than ND
(2) Psychological adjustment	No effect	D poorer than ND
(3) Academic achievement	No effect	D poorer than ND
(4) Formation of occupational interests and goals	D earlier than ND	Unavailable
(5) Ambition and aspirations	D higher than ND	D lower than ND
Young Adulthood (age 18–30)		
(1) College completion	D slightly less than ND	D much less than ND
(2) Age at entry into army	No effect — World War II	D younger than ND — Korean War
(3) Age at marriage	No effect	D two years older than ND
(4) Age at birth of first child	No effect	D three years older than ND
(5) Establishing a stable occupational career	D earlier than ND	D greater difficulty than ND (unless D attended college)
Middle Adulthood (age 40)		
(1) Social and psychological adjustment	D better than ND if from middle class. No effect if from working class	*D worse than ND
(2) Occupational status attained	No effect	D lower than ND (unless D attended college)
(3) Work values	*D more concerned with job security than ND	*D more concerned with job security than ND
(4) Family values	*D more concerned with family security than ND	*D more concerned with family security than ND

Key: D—Men from families that were economically *deprived* during the Great Depression.

ND—Men from families that were *not deprived*.

No Effect—Deprived members of the birth cohort did not differ from nondeprived members on this outcome.

*—This effect occurred only for deprived men whose adult work life was unsuccessful.

Note: Economic deprivation during the depression had a more negative impact on the life course outcomes of the 1928–29 birth cohort because they were at a younger, more vulnerable age when their lives were disrupted.

Source: adapted from Elder (1974, 1981); Elder and Rockwell (1979a).

self-confidence, and ambition with which deprived men from the two cohorts began their occupational careers.

MIDDLE ADULTHOOD. By the time these men reached 40, their adult experiences largely determined whether effects from the depression persisted. Deprived Berkeley men continued to show impairments in social and psychological adjustment only if their adult work life had been troubled. These deprived men described themselves as more anxious; they consumed more alcohol, used psychotherapy more often, and were more likely to be divorced. The picture for the Oakland cohort was strikingly different. Men from the deprived middle class were freer of psychological symptoms and more able to cope with challenges than any other group. These surprising gains associated with deprivation suggest that a successful struggle to overcome adversity can actually enhance a person's psychological health and adaptiveness.

The expanding economy enabled most men from deprived families to overcome earlier handicaps to occupational attainment. In the Berkeley cohort, however, deprived men who did not make it to college never fully recovered from the weak start of their occupational careers. In both cohorts, the unsuccessful sons of deprived parents had work values that were distinctive in emphasizing job security, income, pensions, and unwillingness to take risks to get ahead. The family values of these men were also distinctive. They emphasized the comforts of family life and the notion of home as a refuge. The work and family values of the unsuccessful deprived men reflect a combination of what was missing in the families of their childhood and what the men now needed because of their troublesome work life.

From this study, we draw several general conclusions:

1. The greater the exposure of individuals to a historic event, the greater its impact on their lives. For example, the depression

had more influence on individuals whose families suffered deprivation than on individuals whose families were spared deprivation.

2. Historical events influence individuals by changing everyday interactions, socialization experiences, and/or life chances. The depression influenced men from deprived families by increasing family conflict, weakening parental control over children, and reducing chances for obtaining a college education.

3. The life stage of the individual modifies the impact of a historical event. Men exposed to deprivation as young children (Berkeley) were more severely impaired in their life careers than men exposed during early adolescence (Oakland).

4. A person's later life experiences can change or erase the effects of earlier exposure to historical events. Adult occupational success erased the adolescent psychological deficits of deprived Berkeley men.

Summary

The life course consists of a set of intertwining careers—sequences of roles and activities—in the worlds of work, education, and family and friends. Identities, self-esteem, and the stress and satisfaction we experience throughout life depend upon career activities and success.

INFLUENCES ON LIFE COURSE PROGRESSION. There are three major influences on progression through the life course. (1) The biological growth and decline of body and brain set limits on what we can do. The impacts of biological developments on the life course, however, depend on the social meanings we give them. (2) Each society has a customary, normative sequence of age-graded roles and activities. This normative sequence largely determines the bases for building identities, the responsibilities and privileges, and the socialization experiences available to individuals of different ages. (3) Historical trends and events modify an individual's life course. The impact of a historical event depends upon the person's life stage when the event occurs.

COPING WITH LIFE COURSE TRANSITIONS. Transitions between roles confront us with the need to modify our plans, behavior, and identities throughout the life course. Several factors influence success in coping with transitions. (1) Anticipatory socialization—acquiring knowledge, skills, and values of future roles—is especially effective for transitions we expect. (2) The severity of change and its effect on the relationship between one's resources and aspirations make coping more difficult. (3) Social support, in the form of advice, emotional and material aid, increases ability to cope. (4) Personal resources, such as intellectual ability, emotional and physical health, and a sense of competence developed through past coping, enhance adaptability to transitions.

STAGES IN THE LIFE COURSE: AGE AND SEX ROLES. Four broad life stages characterize the life course beyond childhood. (1) Achieving independence (age 16 to 23) entails numerous crucial transitions in education, work, and family life. Stress is high and satisfaction with life relatively low during this stage. Young men tend to emphasize jobs in building their identities; young women emphasize family ties. (2) Establishing firm family and work commitments (age 18 to 40) through marriage and work careers is the norm. The patterns and timing of family and work careers have undergone major changes in recent decades. For most men, identity and self-esteem are tied to occupational success; for most women, family remains central. Satisfaction rises with marriage, but birth of a first child increases stress and reduces satisfaction. (3) Performing adult roles competently (age 35 to 70) leads to an occupational plateau for most men, who then seek other challenges. Most women turn more to occupational advancement or to community involvements as family demands recede. Self-esteem is supported by occupational achievement for both women and men. Stress eases during this stage because resources grow faster than needs. (4) Coping with loss (age 60 to 90) is the key challenge for the elderly. Most cope well with retirement and even with death of a spouse, unless or until they experience financial difficulties, failing health, or reduced social participation. As long as the elderly retain independence, their self-esteem remains stable and their identities change little.

HISTORICAL VARIATIONS. The historical timing of one's birth influences the life course through all stages. (1) Over the past 30 years, women's participation in the work force has increased dramatically and attitudes towards women's employment have become much more favorable. The likelihood that women will experience pressures and opportunities to work outside the home is now greater at every life stage. (2) Economic deprivation during the Great Depression had long-term impacts on the careers, values, and adjustment of men over the next 30 years. These effects depended both on the social life stages and personal resources of the men and their families when first exposed to deprivation and on later life experiences.

Key Terms and Concepts

Career

Identities

Life Event

Normative Life Stage

Birth Cohort

Anticipatory Socialization

Role Discontinuity

Rites of Passage

Midlife Crisis

Life Cycle Squeeze

Ageism

Disengagement Theory

Part 2

Social Interaction

Chapter 5

Symbolic Communication and Language

Introduction

Communication is a basic ingredient of every social situation. Imagine playing a game of basketball or buying a pair of shoes without some form of verbal or nonverbal communication. Without it, interaction breaks down and the goals of any social encounter are foiled. Indeed, it would be impossible to arrange commercial transactions, trials, birthday parties, or any other social occasion without communication. In its absence, people have no sense of what a social situation is all about. What, then, *is* this crucial social behavior?

Communication is the process whereby people transmit information about their ideas and feelings to one another. We communicate through spoken and written words, through voice qualities and physical closeness, through gestures and posture. Often communication is deliberate: we smile, clasp our beloved in our arms and whisper, "I love you." Other behavior communicates unintentionally. If we forget a birthday or become totally absorbed in a book, for example, a sensitive partner may interpret our behavior as communicating lack of affection.

Because people do not share each other's experiences directly, they must convey their ideas and feelings to each other in ways that others will notice and understand. **Symbols** are the forms used to represent our ideas and feelings, thoughts, and intentions. Symbols can represent our experiences in a way that others can perceive with their sensory organs—through sounds, gestures, pictures, even fragrances. But to interpret symbols as they are intended, their meanings must be socially shared. Thus to communicate successfully we must master the ways for expressing ideas and feelings that are accepted in our community.

Symbols are arbitrary stand-ins for what they represent. Green could as reasonably stand for "stop" as for "go," the sound *luv* as reasonably for negative as for positive feelings. The arbitrariness of symbols may become painfully obvious when we travel in foreign countries. We are then likely to discover that the words and even the gestures we take for granted fail to communicate accurately. A North American who makes a circle with thumb and index finger to express satisfaction to a waiter may be in for a rude surprise if he is eating at a restaurant in Ghana, where the waiter may interpret his gesture as a sexual invitation. In Venezuela, it may be interpreted as a sexual insult! The traveler may then have serious difficulties straightening out these misunderstandings because he and the waiter lack a shared language of verbal symbols to discuss them.

Communication is rarely a process of consciously translating ideas and feelings into symbols and then transmitting these symbols in hopes that others will interpret them correctly. Most communication occurs without any self-conscious planning. As we communicate with others, we usually produce our ideas and thoughts as we go along. In fact, we often learn about our own thoughts and feelings only when we express them to others. Sometimes we are surprised to discover what we ourselves think and feel as we communicate.

Language and nonverbal forms of communication are amazingly complicated. They must be understood and used with flexibility and creativity. Most of us fail on occasion to communicate our ideas and feelings with accuracy or to understand others' communications as well as we might wish. Yet, considering the problems a communicator must solve, most people do surprisingly well. This chapter begins with an examination of language, moves on to nonverbal communication, then analyzes the mutual impacts of communication and social relationships on each other. Finally, this chapter considers the delicate coordination involved in our most common social activity—conversation. In doing so it addresses the following questions:

1. What is the nature of language, and how is it used to grasp meanings and intentions?

2. What are the major types of nonverbal communication, and how do they combine with language to convey emotions and ideas?

3. How do social relationships shape communication, and how does it in turn express or modify those relationships?

4. What rules and skills do people employ to maintain a smooth flow of conversation and to avoid disruptive blunders?

Language and Verbal Communication

Although people have created numerous symbol systems (mathematics, music, painting), language is the main vehicle of human communication. All peoples possess a spoken language. There are thousands of different languages in the world. This section addresses several crucial questions regarding the role of language in communication: What is the nature of language as a symbol system? What is meaning in language? How do people attain mutual understanding through language use? How are language and thought related to one another?

Language as a Symbol System

Little is known about the origins of language (Lieberman 1975), but humans have possessed complex spoken languages since earliest times (Kiparsky 1976). **Spoken language** is a socially acquired system of sound patterns with meanings agreed on by the members of a group. We will examine the basic components of spoken language as well as some of the advantages of language use.

BASIC COMPONENTS. Consider the following statement of one roommate to another: "Wherewereyoulastnight?" What the listener hears is a string of sounds much like this, rather than the sentence, "Where were you last night?" Spoken languages include sounds, words, meanings, and grammatical rules. To understand a string of sounds and to produce an appropriate response, people must recognize the following components: (1) the distinct sounds of which the language is composed (the phonetic component); (2) the combination of sounds into words (the morphologic component); (3) the common meanings of the words (the semantic component); and (4) the conventions for putting words together built into the language (the syntactic component, or grammar). We are rarely conscious of manipulating all these components during conversation, though we do so regularly and with impressive speed.

Unspoken languages, such as Morse code, computer languages, and the sign languages of the deaf lack a phonetic component, although they do possess the remaining components of spoken language. People who use sign languages, for example, use upper body movements to signal words (morphology) with shared meanings (semantics), and they combine these words into sentences according to rules of order (syntax). For a communication system to be considered a language, morphology, semantics, and syntax are all essential. Linguists study these components, seeking to uncover the rules that give structure to language. Social psychologists are more interested in how language fits into social interaction and influences it, and in how language expresses and modifies social relationships (Giles, Hewstone, and St. Clair 1981).

ADVANTAGES OF LANGUAGE USE. Words—the symbols around which languages are constructed—provide abundant resources with which to represent ideas and feelings. The average adult native speaker of English knows the meanings of some 35,000 words, and actively uses close to 5,000. Because it is a symbol system, language enhances our capacity for social action in several ways. First, it frees us from the constraints of responding only to the here and now. Using words to symbolize objects, events, or relationships we can think about them in retrospect, and plan future responses to them. We can happily

These apes seem to be carrying on a lively conversation. How similar is their communication to human language? Although researchers hotly debate this question, they do agree that animal communication lacks the flexibility and creativity of human language.

relive or anticipate events such as ski trips, and we can brood on events such as rejection by a friend, reinterpreting their meanings and planning steps to prevent their recurrence.

Second, language allows us to communicate with others about experiences we do not share directly. You cannot know directly the joy and hope your friend feels at bearing a child, nor her grief and despair at her mother's death. Yet she can convey a good sense of her emotions and concerns to you through words, even in writing, because these shared symbols elicit the same meanings for you both. Thus, through language, we convert what would otherwise be unique individual experiences into shared experiences.

Third, language enables us to transmit, preserve, and create culture. Through the spoken and written word, vast quantities of information pass from person to person and from generation to generation. Language is an indispensable tool for transmitting knowledge, beliefs, and practices. Language also enhances our ability to go beyond what is already known and to add to the store of cultural ideas and objects. Working with linguistic symbols, people generate theories, design and build new products, and invent social institutions.

Finally, words used to name an object let us know how to behave toward that object (one might call a person "friend" or "enemy," for example). The behaviors we recognize as appropriate for each object are drastically different depending upon which of these verbal labels is applied. So are the behaviors implied by calling a remark an "insult" or a "joke," or by naming a golden liquid "poison" or "Scotch." The label applied to an object tells us how to relate to it.

Box 5.1
ANIMAL AND HUMAN COMMUNICATION: A COMPARISON

Speech is a uniquely human activity. Still, numerous animals have ways of communicating. Bees communicate about the locations of nectar sources by performing elaborate dances. Ants communicate chemically by laying down trails for other ants to follow.

Against the backdrop of animal communication the qualities of human language stand out more clearly. Unlike language, these varieties of animal communication are not symbolic. Each one is linked genetically to specific, physically present events. These nonsymbolic modes of communication cannot be used either to think about present or future, or to communicate new ideas.

Some animals use sounds as one means of communication. Recordings of the sounds animals make under natural conditions suggest that birds and mammals have vocabularies ranging between five and thirty distinct calls. The small number of natural animal calls contrasts sharply with the thousands of words in human speech. Most scientists believe that animal calls are largely instinctive, automatic responses to pleasant or fearful situations—expressions of pleasure, alarm, warning, and so on (Miller 1981). With rare exceptions, animal calls, unlike human vocabularies, are not learned. Nor can they be applied to novel situations.

The absence of developed speech among animals does not necessarily signify a lack of complex communication. Communicating mainly through sight, smell, and touch, for example, the intelligent apes maintain an elaborate social organization. The possibility that they could be taught to communicate with symbols captured the imagination of scientists and stimulated numerous frustrating attempts to teach the apes language. Eventually, researchers recognized that these attempts were doomed to failure because chimps lack the vocal apparatus necessary to produce human speech.

Noting that chimps in the wild are responsive to gestures, scientists next tried to teach them American Sign Language (ASL), a gestural language of the deaf. These efforts were much more successful. Several chimps have mastered and used hundreds of ASL signs (Gardner and Gardner 1980). More important, chimps have generalized these signs to objects other than the ones used in training and even to absent objects. For example, the chimp Washoe learned the sign for "open" in connection with a particular door, later generalized it to other doors, then to closed containers, and eventually to a water faucet. This certainly looked like symbol use.

The next step was to ask whether chimps could combine signs into meaningful sequences, another crucial feature of human language. Washoe's first combination of signs occurred at the age of 20 months. By the time she was three, the Gardners had recorded well over 300 combinations. This rate of development is much slower than for children. Still, it suggests that chimps may have some ability to produce new meanings by combining signs.

Could chimps master the even more developed language skill of ordering signs according to rules of syntax? This problem was tackled using a different method (Premack and Premack 1984). A chimp named Sarah was taught to form sequences with various plastic tokens she had learned to associate with different objects (foods, colors, actions, relations, and so on). During these experiments, Sarah also followed instructions presented in complex sequences of tokens. For example, in response to "Red on green if-then Sarah take apple; green on red if-then Sarah take banana," Sarah took the apple rather than the banana that was available when a red card was on top of a green card.

What can we conclude from such studies? Enthusiasts conclude that apes are really capable of understanding human language and engaging in symbolic communication. Apes will never speak, but they are capable of manipulating abstract symbols, if only at an elementary level. Human symbolic communication is a great advance, but it separates us from other organisms only in degree (Meddin 1979).

Critics, on the other hand, are not convinced (Sebeok and Umiker-Sebeok 1980; Terrace 1984). They argue that ingenious stimulus-response training and constant signalling by their teachers enables apes to imitate some of the outward forms of language. But, they say, the key features of language are missing. Critics see no evidence that apes use signs as symbols—recognizing their arbitrary relationship to objects. They view the apes'

responses to sequences of signs as based on rote learning not on applying syntactic rules. Finally, critics claim that apes do not combine signs spontaneously to produce new meanings; they only imitate or respond to prompting by their trainers.

Whichever argument is correct, all agree that animal communication lacks the infinite flexibility and creativity of human language. Moreover, field studies indicate that animals make no natural use of symbols to communicate, whereas the use of symbols is central to natural human communication.

Linguistic Meaning

"That's a great deal to make one word mean," Alice said in a thoughtful tone.

"When I make a word do a lot of work like that," said Humpty Dumpty, "I always pay it extra."

"Oh!" said Alice. She was too much puzzled to make any other remark.

—LEWIS CARROLL, *Through the Looking Glass*, 1872

Meaning is one of the most puzzling and controversial terms in the study of language, yet also one of the most central. We talk in order to express the meanings of our thoughts, and we listen in order to discover the meanings of what others say. A commonsense theory is that the meaning of a word is simply what the word refers to. But this theory of meaning is inadequate. First, if meaning equals reference, then all words that refer to the same object should have the same meaning. This is not necessarily so. For example, "the large building," "Merton Hall," and "the library," could all refer to the same place, yet these words obviously have different meanings. Second, a single word may refer to different objects at different times yet retain the same meaning. One such word is "I." "I" refers to Jonathan when he uses it, but to Judy when she uses it. Finally, some words—"the," "although," "ought"—are quite meaningful, yet they do not refer to any object.

Most students of semantics (the study of meanings) agree that the sense of a word is somehow related to the attributes associated with that word. Based on two types of associations, a useful distinction can be made between two types of meanings: denotative and connotative.

DENOTATIVE MEANING. The literal, explicit properties associated with a word as defined in a dictionary are called **denotative meanings.** These are "objective" in the sense that they are shared by many people. The way dictionaries are written provides insight into the nature of denotative meaning. Dictionary writers collect samples of language from literature, the media, and speech, then figure out what meanings are being employed from the context of a given word. In short, they derive the meanings of words from the ways people commonly use them.

We can convey part of the denotative meaning of words that refer to concrete, material objects (elephants, books) by pointing out examples of these objects. But a word means more than any single example can express. "Book," for example, is a symbol that stands for a whole category of related objects that vary in size, shape, color, contents, and so on. Thus, even the words for concrete objects indicate categories that mean much more than one example can convey.

For more abstract words (justice, authority), it is difficult or impossible to find clear examples to which we can point. Such words consist of complex relationships among people, events, activities, and so on. "Authority," for example, means the right and power of one party in a relationship to judge and exact obedience from another party. Some words ("the," "because") arouse no particular thoughts about objects, relationships, or activities in most of us. Their meaning is defined by their function. One function of "the," for example, is to signal that a noun is coming. This is apparent if we contrast the following two sentences: "The dress burns" and "Dress the burns."

CONNOTATIVE MEANING. The **connotative meaning** of a word includes all the personal associations and emotional responses that an individual has to that word. Warm, happy feelings that some people associate with the word "home," for example, are connotative meanings. For other people, "home" may conjure up coldness or suffocation. Connotative meanings are personal; they are not part of the dictionary definitions of words. Words with similar denotative meanings may have very different connotative meanings. "Separate" and "segregate," for example, both denote keeping objects apart. Yet "segregate" has negative connotations associated wtih racism, whereas "separate" is emotionally neutral.

When the connotative meanings people associate with words are at variance, communication problems may result (Kuhlman, Miller, and Gungor 1973). For instance, the different connotative meanings that scientists and theologians associated with the key terms "knowledge" and "authority" produced tension and misunderstanding between these two groups (Back, Bunker, and Dunnagen 1972). Scientists felt they could base firm knowledge on the authority of scientific methods; theologians felt that the only absolute basis for firm knowledge was the authority of God. As a result, scientists and theologians had great difficulty communicating about the nature of scientific, moral, or theological truths.

Consider another example. As World War II continued into 1945, American analysts carefully monitored the Japanese emperor's messages to his people. They understood his words as exhorting his people to fight the invaders to the death. This seemingly defiant message, suggesting the war would drag on and casualties mount, weighed heavily in the American decision to drop the atomic bomb. Only later was it learned that the connotative meaning of the emperor's messages for the Japanese was that surrender, though certain, would be honorable. Had the Americans understood this connotation it is conceivable that the bomb might never have been dropped.

MEANING AND CONTEXT. Words have multiple denotative meanings. The word "pen," for example, is both an instrument for writing with ink and a fenced enclosure for pigs. One of the striking characteristics of language is that the more frequently words are used the more meanings they seem to have. One dictionary, for example, lists 80 meanings for "take," 55 for "light," 39 for "charge," but only three for "rudder," and one for "surrey." Although some meanings of a word may be related, other meanings can be very distinct. The senses of "charge" in "Please charge it!" and in "The charge is $20" are related; but its meanings in "Charge the battery," "Who's in charge?" and "Fire as you charge" are quite different.

Given the large number of meanings packed into a single word, there must be ways to decipher the correct meaning in a particular sentence. The key to selecting the correct meaning of a word is *context*. Three types of context are especially important: the context of other words in the sentence, the context of other sentences in the conversation, and the social context of people, situations, and events in which the word is used.

Suppose you heard the sentence "I can't take the bike." What is the meaning of "take" here? If the sentence context included the words "but I'll get there by car," most of us would infer that "take" meant "to ride on." If, instead, the words that followed were "because it's too heavy," we might infer that "take" meant "lift up and carry." The context of sentences could also clarify the meaning of "take." Consider: "He's pulling away. I can't take the bike. I'm too slow." In this context, "take" seems to mean "catch up with." Finally, the social context may clarify word meaning. If one thief mutters to another, "I can't take the bike," as he vainly struggles to cut the chain lock, "take" would seem to mean "get into one's possession."

It should now be apparent that successful communication is much more then transmitting and receiving words with fixed, shared meanings. Conversationalists must select and discover the meanings of words through their context. In ordinary social interaction, the meanings of whole sentences and conversations may be ambiguous. Speakers and listeners must jointly work out these meanings as they go along. This next section will consider how people manage to attain mutual understanding through the use of language.

Language Use as a Social Accomplishment

Virtually all adults have **linguistic competence** in their native language. They know how sounds and meanings go together, and they know the implicit rules that enable them to generate and to understand grammatically acceptable sentences. But linguistic competence does not guarantee that a person will use language well. In normal speech we hesitate, repeat ourselves, mispronounce words, and make grammatical errors. If you listen carefully to a natural conversation, you will notice many errors of performance. Despite these errors, people usually succeed in understanding each other. It is failure to use language in *socially* appropriate ways that most frequently

disrupts communication during interaction. We will therefore examine several social requirements for effective language use.

SOCIOLINGUISTIC COMPETENCE. To attain mutual understanding, language performance must be appropriate to the social and cultural context. Otherwise, even grammatically acceptable sentences will not make sense. "My mother eats raw termites" is grammatically correct and meaningful; it reflects linguistic competence. But as a serious assertion by a North American, this utterance would probably draw amazed looks. Because it expresses an idea that is totally incongruous with American culture, listeners would have difficulty interpreting it. In a termite-eating culture, however, the same utterance would be quite sensible. This demonstrates that successful communication requires **sociolinguistic competence**—knowledge of the implicit rules for generating socially appropriate sentences. Such sentences make sense to listeners, because they fit with the listeners' cultural and social knowledge (Hymes 1974).

The termite example illustrates how a lack of sociolinguistic competence often violates accepted cultural knowledge. Speech that clashes with what is known about the social relationship to which it refers suggests that a speaker is not socially competent (Grimshaw 1981). Speakers are expected to use language that is appropriate to the status of the individuals they are discussing, and to their relationship of intimacy. For example, socially competent speakers would not state seriously: "The janitor ordered the president to turn off the lights in the Oval Office." They know that low-status persons do not "order" those of much higher status; at most they "hint" or "suggest." Referring to a relationship of true intimacy, socially competent speakers would not say, "The lover bullied his beloved." Rather, they would select such socially appropriate verbs as "coaxed" or "persuaded." In short, socially competent speakers recognize that social and cultural constraints make some statements interpretable in a situation and others contrary to common sense.

SPEECH ACTS. Almost all of our speech is intended to have an impact on a listener. We speak in order to accomplish a purpose. To express the idea that speech is a form of social action, we use the term **speech act,** which refers to the smallest unit of verbal social behavior (Austin 1962; Searle 1979). Speakers intend whatever they say to be interpreted as some type of social act: to warn listeners, inform, question, order, accuse, thank, complain, invite, and so on. We attain mutual understanding only when listeners recognize the purposes of the speaker's speech acts. When a question is used, for example, the speaker wants listeners to recognize that the purpose is to request information.

The purpose of a speech act may not be obvious; taken out of context, most statements are ambiguous. For example, what does a speaker who says "John drinks" intend? Is this statement meant to inform us about John, to issue a warning, to pronounce an evaluative judgment, or to suggest a possible drinking partner? No matter how well listeners grasp the literal meaning of a speaker's words, communication has not succeeded unless they also recognize the speaker's intended purpose.

To make sure purpose is understood, we can explicitly indicate the intended speech act. "I must warn you that John drinks" is quite explicit. It is sometimes difficult to make our intentions clear without pointing to them explicitly. That is why we begin statements with phrases like "I authorize" (appoint, nominate, challenge, bet, and so on) that designate our intention. For the most common speech acts, however, each language has standard short forms that designate the intended act implicitly. These standard forms reduce the time and effort needed for communication. In English, for example, there are short forms for telling ("John is waiting"), asking ("Is John waiting?") and ordering ("Wait, John!"). Introductory phrases that normally indicate the speech act intended ("I tell you," "I ask you," "I order you,") are not used in these standard forms. Instead, standard forms employ syntax (word order and verb forms) and intonation to convey their purpose.

So far we have discussed speech acts in which people indicate their intentions directly, either by stating them explicitly or by using standard forms. Most of the time, however, speech is more subtle. We indicate our intentions only indirectly. Suppose, for example, you want someone to open the door. The standard form that directly signals an order is: "Open the door!" But this same intention is often expressed in various indirect ways, including: "Would you mind opening the door?" "The door should be open." "Haven't you forgotten something?" "I'm more comfortable with the door open." Under certain circumstances, each of these indirect speech acts might accomplish the purpose of getting someone to recognize that you want them to open the door.

The alternatives for expressing the same intention differ from one another in politeness, assertiveness, sophistication, friendliness, and so on. Socially competent speakers take such considerations into account when selecting a way to express their intentions. The rich variety of indirect alternatives that speakers can construct makes speech flexible and creative.

Mutual understanding is further complicated because a single statement can be used to express different intentions. For example, what is expressed by "It's too hot in here"? In different situations this sentence might be used indirectly as a request to open or to close the window, a criticism of whoever switched off the fan, a threat to leave a meeting, a demand to stop kissing. How do listeners decide how to interpret this statement? And how can speakers be confident that listeners will understand it as intended? Clearly, speakers rely on appropriate intonation patterns and on the immediate situation to communicate which interpretation is correct. Listeners use this information with some success, but research has only begun to unravel the intriguing ways all this is done (Goodwin 1979; Labov and Fanshel 1977).

UNDERSTANDING AND COOPERATION. Mutual understanding is a cooperative enterprise. Because language does not convey thoughts and feelings in an unambiguous manner, people must work together to attain a shared understanding of each others' utterances (Goffman 1983). A speaker must cooperate with a listener by formulating the content of speech acts in a manner that reflects the listener's way of thinking about objects, events, and relationships. The speaker must also take into consideration the listener's current knowledge. For example, the indirect request "Could you pick up my laundry?" shouted while racing to class, will be effective only if the listener knows where the laundry was left. Is it at the Laundromat or strewn all over the room?

Listeners must cooperate by actively trying to understand. They must go beyond the literal meanings of what they hear to determine what the speaker is really trying to say. Only by making a creative effort to understand can listeners cope successfully with the fact that we often formulate our speech acts indirectly, leave out words ("Paper come?"), abbreviate familiar terms ("See ya in calc."), and make vague references ("He told him he would come later").

According to a theory proposed by Grice (1975), listeners assume that much talk is based on a **cooperative principle.** That is, conversationalists ordinarily assume that the speaker is behaving cooperatively by trying to be (1) informative (giving as much information as is necessary and no more), (2) truthful, (3) relevant to the aims of the ongoing conversation, and (4) clear (avoiding ambiguity and wordiness).

The principle of cooperation is more than a code of conversational etiquette. Often we can reach a correct understanding of otherwise ambiguous talk only by assuming that speakers are indeed trying to satisfy this principle. Consider, for example, how the relevance assumption (3) enables the conversationalists to understand each other in the following exchange:

TONY: I'm exhausted.
RACHEL: There's a bed in my room.

On the surface, Rachel has merely asserted the presence of a bed in her room. By implication, however, she has invited Tony to rest there. But why does she expect that he will understand this? Because she expects him to assume she is adhering to the relevance maxim of the cooperation principle, so her comment must relate to what he said. If so, it probably means the bed was mentioned as a response to his exhaustion. If Rachel was violating the principle and responding irrelevantly, she would be shocked when she later found Tony sprawled on her bed.

The cooperative principle is also crucial for speech forms like sarcasm or understatement to succeed. In sarcasm or understatement, speakers want listeners to recognize that their words mean something quite different from what they seem to convey. One way we signal to listeners that we intend our words to imply something different is by obviously violating certain maxims of the cooperative principle while holding to the rest. Consider Carrie's sarcastic reply when asked what she thought of the lecturer: "He was so exciting that he came close to keeping most of us awake for the first half hour." By flouting the maxim of clarity (responding in an unclear, wordy way) while still being informative, truthful, and relevant, Carrie implies that the lecturer was in fact a bore. Speakers add force and interest to their conversation by such violations of the cooperative principle. Listeners understand the speakers' indirect meanings because they can recognize intended violations against the backdrop of general adherence to the principle.

Thus the successful use of language during interaction is an impressive social accomplishment. To attain mutual understanding, conversationalists must demonstrate sociolinguistic competence—use language appropriate to the cultural and social setting. They must select speech acts that will best express their intentions under the circumstances, directly or indirectly. And they must cooperate in their roles as speakers and listeners: talking in ways that take account of others' current knowledge and perspectives, and listening creatively in order to figure out what others wish to imply through their frequently ambiguous words.

Language and Thought

Language has developed to serve a purpose: to communicate thoughts and feelings. Because of this purpose, the features of language are molded by its uses. The features of a language must enable adults to speak and understand it easily and efficiently. Children must be able to learn it. It must express the ideas people normally want to convey, and it must effectively communicate ideas that are special to a particular social and cultural system. In short, the features of language are shaped by human capacities to process information and by the ideas that arise through exposure to the physical and social environments. This leads to the first question addressed in this section: What features are shared by all languages and why?

There is another side to the relationship between language and thought. Once people have learned a language it wields a power of its own. It aids people in thinking about some ideas and hinders them in thinking about others. In fact, language may mold many aspects of behavior. This leads to the second question: What impacts do the distinctive features of different languages have on the ways speakers think?

LINGUISTIC UNIVERSALS. If languages are molded in part by the capacities, ideas, and experiences all people share, languages should also have certain features in commmon. **Linguistic universals** are features common to all languages. Every language has nouns and verbs, for example, because people must refer to objects and to actions. Certain sets of concepts are so basic that every language has words to express them. Some universal lexical concepts are shown in Table 5.1. The 100 basic concepts listed are likely to be used in everyday speech. They are learned by children at an early age, and are seldom borrowed by one language from another.

Every language appears to have terms that express height, length, and distance, and directions like up/down, front/back, and left/right. The terms for spatial dimensions are universal probably because all human beings use the same basic perceptual capacities to orient themselves in the physical world (Clark and Clark 1977). The universality of experience with time, number, and negativity produces terms to express these abstract concepts in virtually every language. All have ways of distinguishing between present, past, and future, between single and multiple objects, between ideas and their negation ("go" versus "not go") (Greenberg 1966). The origins of these universals lie in basic human capacities for thought about abstract events and relations.

Of most interest to social psychologists are universals rooted in the social and cultural conditions of life. For example, the universal characteristics of families and of human conversations give rise to two sets of linguistic universals; kin terms and pronouns.

Languages invariably enable speakers to distinguish at least three characteristics of relatives: generation, blood relationship, and sex. But the precision with which a language designates particular relatives may vary. In English, "mother-in-law" indicates all these characteristics, while "nephew" designates generation and sex but not blood relationship. We can specify whether or not a nephew is related by blood if we use more complicated constructions ("my nephew through my wife"). In all

TABLE 5.1
SOME UNIVERSAL LEXICAL CONCEPTS

1. I	21. dog	41. nose	61. die	81. smoke
2. thou	22. house	42. mouth	62. kill	82. fire
3. we	23. tree	43. tooth	63. swim	83. ash
4. this	24. seed	44. tongue	64. fly	84. burn
5. that	25. leaf	45. claw	65. walk	85. path
6. who	26. root	46. foot	66. come	86. mountain
7. what	27. bark	47. knee	67. lie	87. red
8. not	28. skin	48. hand	68. sit	88. green
9. all	29. flesh	49. belly	69. stand	89. yellow
10. many	30. blood	50. neck	70. give	90. white
11. one	31. bone	51. breasts	71. say	91. black
12. two	32. grease	52. heart	72. sun	92. night
13. big	33. egg	53. liver	73. moon	93. hot
14. long	34. horn	54. drink	74. star	94. cold
15. small	35. tail	55. eat	75. water	95. full
16. woman	36. leather	56. bite	76. rain	96. new
17. man	37. hair	57. see	77. stone	97. good
18. person	38. head	58. hear	78. sand	98. round
19. fish	39. ear	59. know	79. earth	99. dry
20. bird	40. eye	60. sleep	80. cloud	100. name

Source: adapted from Swadesh (1971).

languages, precise, simple terms are used for the relatives who spend most time together because of caregiving and biological ties—parents, children, siblings, and spouses. This suggests that languages develop kin terms in response to the universal requirements of family interactions.

Similarly, the demands of conversation give rise to a universal set of pronouns. All languages have pronouns that designate the roles of speaker (I), of those addressed (you), and of other participants (he, she, they). Pronoun systems also invariably distinguish singular from plural (I/we, he/they). These features are critical for efficient conversation. Speakers must constantly refer to themselves and to one or more addressees during conversations. Pronouns eliminate the need to repeat names, roles, or other designations of participants each time they are mentioned. "You," for example, is much more efficient than

"John, Mary, Steve, and Ellen." Thus pronouns, like kin terms, take their universal features from the need for effective social interaction.

Just as the common capacities and shared experiences of humankind give rise to linguistic universals, so the different social and environmental experiences of groups lead to differences between languages. Most obvious are variations in vocabulary. The concepts for which a language provides words depend on what speakers like and need to talk about. There are precise words for frequently needed concepts. The Hanunoo, for whom rice is a staple, for instance, have 92 names for rice (Brown 1965). Each name conveys the shape, color, texture, state, and so on, of a different type of rice. This makes communication accurate and easy. To convey the same information in English would not be impossible, although it would be inefficient. Instead of one basic word, English speakers would have to say something like: "the long-grained, brown-flecked, firm, cooked rice."

All languages multiply terms for concepts that are central to daily activities. This principle also applies to subgroups within larger language groups. Groups like surgeons, farmers, sociologists, and cooks each have special vocabularies that are relatively unknown to others. We sometimes refer to these vocabularies disparagingly as "jargons." But jargons enable speakers to perform their tasks more effectively. If a surgeon had to describe the contours of each instrument to the operating room nurse, the waiting patient might bleed to death. The rapid stream of technical terms is much more efficient.

LINGUISTIC RELATIVITY. So far we have discussed the influence of thought and experience on language. What of the reverse? Does the language we speak influence the way we think about and experience the world? The most famous theory on this question—the Sapir-Whorf **linguistic relativity hypothesis**—holds that language "is not merely a reproducing instrument for voicing ideas, but is itself a shaper of ideas, the program and guide for the individual's mental activity" (Whorf 1956). Both strong and weak forms of this hypothesis have been proposed.

According to the strong form of the linguistic relativity hypothesis, language determines our perceptions of reality, so we cannot perceive or comprehend distinctions that don't exist in our own language. Orwell's description of "Newspeak," the language developed by the totalitarian rulers in his novel *Nineteen Eighty-Four*, gives frightening expression to the impact of language on thought:

> Don't you see that the whole aim of Newspeak is to narrow the range of thought? In the end we shall make thoughtcrime literally impossible because there will be no words in which to express it.... Every year fewer and fewer

> words, and the range of consciousness always a little smaller.... The revolution will be complete when the language is perfect.
> —GEORGE ORWELL, *Nineteen Eighty-Four* (1949:46–47)

Orwell's description suggests that language determines thought through the words it makes available to people. We cannot talk about objects or ideas for which we lack words. The ways we think about the world are determined by the way our language slices up reality.

This strong form of the linguistic relativity hypothesis has not fared well in research. Consider some of the evidence. Some languages have only two basic words (dark and white) to cover the whole spectrum of colors. Yet people from these and all other known language groups can discriminate and communicate about whatever large numbers of colors they are shown (Heider and Olivier 1972). Most likely any concept can be expressed in any language, though not with the same degree of ease and efficiency. Before either the object or the word "television" existed, for example, someone undoubtedly referred to the concept of "a device that can transmit pictures and sounds over a distance." When new concepts are encountered, people invent words (laser) or borrow them from other languages ("sabotage" from French, "goulash" from Hungarian).

Although vocabulary does not appear to determine thought, the grammatical rules built into languages might. Grammatical rules of the Navajo language, for example, force attention to the shapes of objects. When Navajo speakers use verbs of handling, they must indicate whether the object is long, short, flexible, rigid, and so on, by attaching suffixes to the verb. Carroll and Casagrande (1958) reasoned that this grammatical requirement should affect the way Navajo speakers think about objects. They proposed that compared with English-speaking children, Navajos would match objects more often on the basis of

Nonverbal cues suffuse words with life, emphasizing them and clarifying their meaning. Nonverbal cues also carry their own message, as the irritated listener on the right makes clear.

shape. When they asked children to pick which two of three different objects went together best, however, there was no evidence that grammatical requirements determined thought. English-speaking children matched objects on the basis of shape just as often as Navajos.

Thus the hypothesis that language determines thought has found little support. But there is considerable evidence for a weaker form of this hypothesis which says: Each language facilitates particular forms of thinking because it makes some events and objects more easily codable or symbolized. The availability of linguistic symbols for objects or events has been shown to have two clear effects. First, it improves the efficiency of communication

about these objects and events, and second, it enhances success in remembering them.

Regarding communication efficiency, recall that the availability of 92 names for rice enabled the Hanunoo to communicate quickly and precisely about their staple food. Similarly, the efficiency of a surgeon's communication depends on specialized vocabulary. To demonstrate the value of language labels for memory, consider a study that measured the effect of language labels on people's ability to remember nonsense shapes (Santa and Ranken 1972). Subjects were exposed to a large number of nonsense shapes that were either labelled verbally or not. Later, when asked to recognize shapes they had seen, subjects recalled shapes better if they had originally been labelled.

Why? The verbal labels probably helped people to discriminate more completely among the shapes and to store them more distinctively in memory.

Based on the accumulated research we can conclude that language is more a reflection of human capacities and culture than a determinant of thought. But language also influences memory and perhaps the efficiency of thought.

Nonverbal Communication

As you stare out the window, you notice two men on the sidewalk engaged in heated conversation. Occasionally you hear the sounds of their voices, though you are unable to make out the words. One older man, dressed in a dark suit, gazes straight at the other and appears to be speaking rapidly in a shrill voice. He emphasizes his points with sharp thrusts of the hands, and leans forward, features tense, occasionally scowling. The younger man, dressed in coveralls, looks away with eyes downcast, stealing an occasional glance at his watch. He clasps his arms across his chest, hands tightly grasping elbows, and scrapes his shoe in a crack in the pavement. After a few minutes, a young woman appears and exchanges greetings with both men. She then moves close to the man in coveralls who turns toward her. The other man steps back, his arms dropping to his sides. A moment later, all three are smiling and the two men shake hands.

Even without access to the verbal content of the interchange in this sketch, most people could make good guesses about the changing emotions the two men experienced, their feelings toward each other, their relative status and power, and their relationship with the woman. A great deal of information is communicated at the nonverbal level. But some ambiguity remains. This section examines three questions concerning nonverbal communication: (1) What are the major types of nonverbal communication? (2) How is emotion communicated through facial expressions? (3) What is

gained and what problems arise because nonverbal and verbal communication are combined in ordinary interaction?

Types of Nonverbal Communication

By one estimate, the human face can make some 250,000 different expressions (Birdwhistell 1970). Combining these with other nonverbal cues, the number of nonverbal communication possibilities is infinite. Four major types of nonverbal cues are described below and summarized in Table 5.2.

PARALANGUAGE. Speaking involves a great deal more than the production of words. Vocal behavior includes loudness, pitch, speed, emphasis, inflection, breathiness, stretching or clipping of words, pauses, and so on. All the vocal aspects of speech other than words are called **paralanguage.** This includes such highly communicative vocalizations as moaning, sighing, laughing, and even crying. Shrillness of voice and rapid delivery, such as those of the dark-suited man in our sketch, communicate tension and excitement in most situations (Scherer 1979). Combined with other nonverbal communications, paralinguistic cues reinforce the expression of anger and superior status. Various uses and interpretations of paralinguistic and other nonverbal cues will be examined later in this chapter. For now, see how many distinct meanings you can give to the sentence, "George is on the phone again" by varying the paralinguistic cues you use.

BODY LANGUAGE. The silent motion of body parts—scowls, smiles, nods, gazing, gestures, leg movements, postural shifts, caressing, slapping, and so on—all constitute **body language.** Because body language entails movement, it is known as *kinesics* (from the Greek *kinein* meaning "to move"). While paralinguistic cues are auditory, we perceive kinesic cues visually. The contrasting body movements of the three people in our sketch were probably particularly useful to you in interpreting their feelings and intentions.

TABLE 5.2
TYPES OF NONVERBAL COMMUNICATION

Type of Cue	Definition	Examples	Channel
Paralanguage	Vocal (but nonverbal) behavior involved in speaking	Loudness, speed, pauses in speech	Auditory
Body language (kinesics)	Silent motions of the body	Gestures, facial expressions, eye gaze	Visual
Interpersonal spacing (proxemics)	Positioning of body at varying distances and angles from others	Intimate closeness, facing head-on, looking away, turning one's back	Primarily visual, also touch, smell, and auditory
Choice of personal effects	Selecting and displaying objects that others will associate with you	Clothing, makeup, room decorations	Primarily visual, also auditory and smell

INTERPERSONAL SPACING. Positioning ourselves at varying distances and angles from others—standing close or far away, facing head-on or to one side, adopting various postures, and creating barriers with books or other objects—also communicates nonverbally. **Interpersonal spacing** cues probably suggested to you, for example, that only the man in the coveralls was romantically involved with the woman in the sketch. Because proximity is a major means of communication between people, this type of cue is also called *proxemics.* When there is very close positioning, proxemics can convey information through smell and touch as well.

CHOICE OF PERSONAL EFFECTS. Though we usually think of communication as expressed through our bodies, people also communicate nonverbally through the personal effects they select: their choices of cars, home decoration, clothing, contact lenses, and—if one believes the commercials—beer. A uniform, for example, may communicate social status, political opinion, life style, and occupation, revealing a great deal about how its wearer is likely to behave (Joseph and Alex 1972). You may have made assumptions about the status and life style of the men in our sketch based on the fact

that one wore a dark suit and the other coveralls. The deliberate use of personal effects to communicate impressions is discussed in Chapter 9.

For the most part, nonverbal cues—like language—are learned rather than innate. As a result, the meanings of particular nonverbal cues may vary from culture to culture. Other features of nonverbal communication may have universal meanings, however. These universals are based in our biological nature. The nonverbal communication of emotion reveals an interesting combination of learned and innate features.

Facial Communication of Emotion

More than 2,000 years ago, the Roman scholar Pliny The Elder said: "The face of man is the index to joy and mirth, to severity and sadness." When we want to hide our feelings, we look away or cover our face. If we must show our face, we try carefully to compose our expressions (Goffman 1959). Our sense that we must shield our natural facial expressions to conceal our true emotions from others suggests that we share two beliefs: (1) people *express* their emotions in distinctive ways on their faces, and (2) observers can accurately

Box 5.2
MALE DOMINANCE IN COMMUNICATION

Asymmetric patterns of verbal and non-verbal communication often reflect status differences between people. Is it therefore surprising to find that asymmetry pervades communication between males and females? Numerous studies offer subtle but convincing evidence of a widespread tendency for males to dominate females in cross-sex communication (Thorne, Kamerae, and Henley 1983). Do any of the following patterns appear in your own interactions?

Regardless of status, women are more likely than men to be addressed by first name rather than by title and last name. This use of lower status address forms for women has been observed in such work settings as hospitals, universities, and news rooms. Men tend to signal dominance through freer staring, pointing, unreciprocated touch, and walking slightly ahead of the women they are with. Women are more likely to avert or lower their eyes, react passively to touch, and move out of a man's way when passing him on the sidewalk (Henley 1977; LaFrance and Mayo 1978; Leffler, Gillespie, and Conaty 1982).

Joking and laughing also reveal asymmetry. Males tell jokes much more often—a sign of high status; but women laugh harder at the jokes—a sign of submissiveness (Coser 1960). Women also tend to be less assertive than men when introducing new topics into a conversation. Women are much more likely to ask a question ("Did you see the report on. . .?") rather than simply to declare their interest in the topic ("There was a report on. . ."). Women also reveal their lower power by checking more frequently whether their conversational partner is still listening. They do this by adding unnecessary questions onto their assertions ("Isn't it?"), and by inserting "You know" into their remarks (Fishman 1978, 1980).

Paralinguistic behavior also suggests that women have less interpersonal power. Women use less intrusive responses than men to indicate attention or agreement during conversation. Women prefer head nods and "M-hmn," rather than the more assertive "yeah" or "right." In conversations between men and women, men interrupt more, but women do not protest; and women hesitate longer after interruptions before starting to talk again (Argyle, Lalljee, and Cook, 1968; Zimmerman and West 1975). Women are more encouraging and supportive listeners; but, contrary to cultural stereotypes, men are generally more talkative (LaFrance and Mayo 1978).

Why do men use higher status, more dominant styles of communication than women? One explanation is based on the assumption that in Western cultures men are socialized from early childhood to be dominant and women to be submissive. As a result, men and women use speech styles that reflect the personalities and self-images they have acquired through socialization (Lakoff 1979).

A second explanation makes no assumption that men and women differ in their personalities. It proposes that the different communication styles are situational adaptations to the gender-linked distribution of power in society. Because women are granted lower status and power than men in most situations, women lack the power needed to control communication through dominant styles. Instead, women tend to adopt verbal and nonverbal styles that enable low-power individuals to gain some control over communication (Fishman 1980; O'Barr and Atkins 1980).

These findings come during a period of social inequality between men and women. Future research will reveal whether this dominance is present in different cultures and settings, and whether it will persist. Both theoretical explanations suggest that if and when women achieve true equality, signs of male dominance in communication styles will disappear.

recognize the emotions others are experiencing. Are these two beliefs correct? This section will address this question and discuss the interplay of innate and cultural influences on the facial communication of emotion.

EMOTIONS EXPRESSED BY THE FACE. Research indicates that people communicate six different emotions by distinctive facial expressions: happiness, sadness, surprise, fear, anger, and disgust (Ekman and Friesen 1975; Harper, Wiens, and Matarazzo 1978). Certain facial features are crucial for the expression of each emotion. Using only the lower face, for instance, nearly everyone in one study was able to identify happiness but was unsuccessful in identifying fear (Ekman, Friesen, and Tomkins 1971). Both fear and sadness are judged best from the eyes/eyelid area (Boucher and Ekman 1975).

By combining elements of the expressions of the six distinctive emotions, and by varying their intensity, we can produce a virtually unlimited number of subtle emotional blends. But only the six primary emotions are recognized with any reliability.

LEARNED OR INNATE? Social psychologists are especially interested in the communication of emotion because it reflects a meeting between biological, social, and cultural influences. Darwin (1872) was the first to propose that facial expressions of emotion are an innately determined part of our biological heritage. If this is so, all peoples of the world should exhibit very similar expressions when experiencing the same emotion. Individuals should also be able to recognize emotions expressed by members of other cultures.

Consider one study intended to test these expectations (Ekman, Sorenson and Friesen 1969). Stories suggesting specific emotions were read to preliterate natives in isolated sections of New Guinea and Borneo. A story suggesting sadness, for example, told of a man whose child had just died. The natives were then shown photos of faces that American college students had identified as expressing the six primary emotions. The natives were asked to choose which photo fit each story. Because they had little or no exposure to Western culture, the natives could not have *learned* to interpret the pictured emotions the same way Americans do. Nonetheless, their choices agreed closely with the emotions identified in each picture by the Americans. This supports the universality of recognition.

To test the universality of expression, photos of individuals from many different cultural groups were shown to members of other groups (Ekman and Friesen 1975). Members of each group successfully recognized the facial emotions expressed by members of other cultural groups. This suggests that all were responding to a common set of facial expressions that represents the primary emotions across cultures. Observations of children who were born blind provide convincing added support for the universality of emotional expression. These blind children, who cannot learn how to express emotions from seeing others, still smile, laugh, and frown much like sighted children (Eibl-Eibesfeldt 1979).

CULTURAL INFLUENCES. What is universal in facial expressions is the particular combination of facial muscles that move when we experience a given emotion. There are strong cultural influences, however, on the actual expression of emotion in everyday interaction. These influences take two main forms. First, through learning, culture helps determine which stimuli evoke particular emotions. Thus, cultural groups differ in the emotions that various odors, sounds, events, and so on evoke in their members. People learn to respond to the smell of manure with disgust or with pleasure, for example. Cultural learning can also influence whether the event of death will elicit sadness or happiness for the deceased.

Second, culture influences the expression of emotion through display rules. **Display**

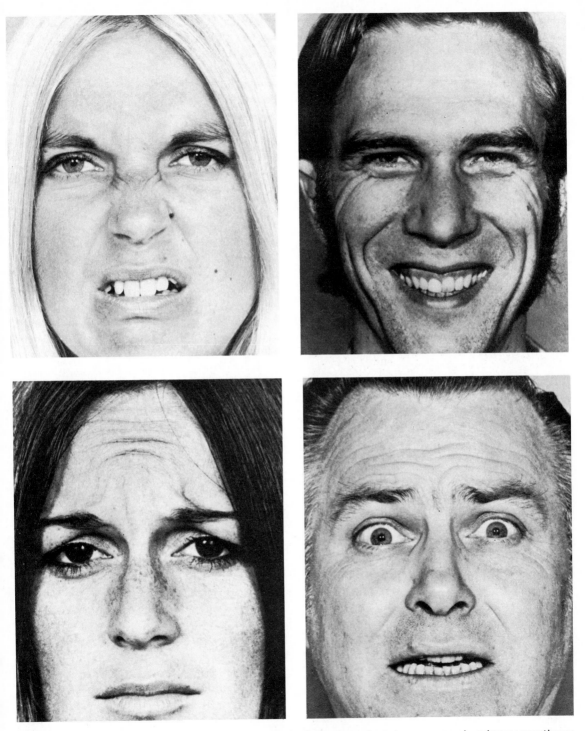

People from many cultures use similar distinctive facial expressions to express six primary emotions: happiness, sadness, surprise, fear, anger, and disgust. Can you identify the emotion expressed in each of the pictures above? Cross-cultural agreement in the expression and recognition of emotions suggests that these basic facial expressions are innate.

rules are culture-specific norms for modifying facial expressions of emotion to make them fit with the social situation (Ekman 1972). Display rules are typically learned in childhood. They become habits that automatically control facial muscles. Display rules may require modifying facial expressions of emotion in one of several ways. They may require (1) greater intensity in the expression of an emotion, (2) less intensity, (3) complete neutralization of the emotional expression, or (4) masking one emotion with a different one. In some Mediterranean cultures, for example, people intensify their display of sadness by exaggerating facial expressions. In contrast, the British are noted for emotional understatement, for deintensifying the display of emotion. Amerian males, until recently at least, have learned to neutralize the expression of sadness and fear in public situations (Ross and Mirowsky 1984). And the Japanese often employ laughing and smiling to cover up anger, sorrow, or disgust (Morsbach 1973).

In response to our earlier question, we can conclude that people do indeed express primary emotions in distinct ways on their faces, and that others can accurately recognize these emotions. These universal features of the facial expression of emotion are innate. In order to communicate emotions effectively in everyday interaction, however, people must learn and employ the display rules of their own culture.

Combining Nonverbal and Verbal Communication

When we speak on the telephone or shout to a friend in another room we are limited to communicating through verbal and paralinguistic channels. When we wave to arriving or departing passengers at the airport we use only the visual channel. Ordinarily, however, communication is multichanneled. Information is conveyed simultaneously through verbal, paralinguistic, kinesic, and proxemic cues. What is gained and what problems are caused by combining different communication channels? If they appear to convey consistent information, they reinforce each other and

communication becomes more accurate. But sometimes the information conveyed through different channels appears inconsistent. This produces confusion and may even arouse suspicion of deception. This section examines some outcomes of apparent consistency and inconsistency among channels.

REINFORCEMENT AND INCREASED ACCURACY. The multiple cues we receive often seem redundant, each carrying the same message. A smile accompanies a compliment delivered in a warm tone of voice; a scowl accompanies a vehemently shouted threat. But multiple cues are seldom entirely redundant. They are better viewed as complementary (Poyatos 1983). The smile and warm tone convey that the compliment is sincere; the scowl and vehement shout imply that the threat will be carried out. Thus multiple cues add information to each other, reduce ambiguity, and increase the accuracy of communication.

Taken alone, each channel lacks the capacity to carry the entire weight of the messages exchanged in the course of a conversation. Paralinguistic and kinesic cues, in particular, suffuse words with life by supporting and emphasizing them. The word "maybe," for example, is a weak way to express doubt unless it is delivered in a slow, deliberate manner and accompanied by raised eyebrows or a shrug. The words "come here" take on meaning either as a coy invitation, frantic demand, or matter-of-fact request depending on the tone of voice and beckoning gesture that accompany them.

By themselves, the verbal aspects of language are insufficient for accurate communication. The importance of paralinguistic cues is illustrated in a study of students from a Nigerian secondary school and teachers college (Grayshon 1980). Although these students took courses in English and knew the verbal language well, they did not know the paralinguistic cues of British native speakers. The students listened to two British recordings with identical verbal content. In one record-

Sign languages enable the deaf to participate fully in communication. Though lacking a system of sounds (phonetics), sign languages possess three of the four basic components of human language—symbols (morphology) with arbitrary meanings (semantics) and rules for combining them (syntax).

ing, paralinguistic cues indicated that the speaker was giving the listener a brush-off. In the other recording, paralinguistic cues indicated that the speaker was apologizing. Of 251 students, 97 percent failed to perceive any difference in the meanings the speaker was conveying. Failure to distinguish a brush-off from an apology could be disastrous in everyday communication. Accurate understanding requires paralinguistic as well as verbal knowledge.

Our accuracy in interpreting events is greatly enhanced if we have multiple communication cues, rather than verbal information alone. The value of a full set of verbal and nonverbal cues in understanding social events was demonstrated in a study of students' interpretations of various scenes (Archer and Akert 1977). Students observed scenes of social interaction that were either displayed in a video broadcast or described verbally in a transcript of the video broadcast. Thus students received either full, multichannel communication or verbal cues alone. Afterward students were

TABLE 5.3

PERCENT OF OBSERVERS ACCURATELY INTERPRETING SOCIAL INTERACTIONS

Interpretation Question (people in scene)	Communication Cues Available		Accuracy for Chance Guesses
	Full AudioVisual (n = 37)	Only Verbal Transcript (n = 76)	
Which man is not married? (three men)	45	18	33
Which woman has no children? (three women)	56	17	33
Friends, acquaintances, or strangers? (one man and one woman)	62	20	33
Who won the poker game? (three men)	63	48	33
Is she speaking to a man or a woman? (one woman on telephone)	87	51	50

Source: adapted from Archer and Akert (1977).

asked to answer questions about what was going on in each scene, questions that required going beyond the obvious facts. Results of the study are shown in Table 5.3. Observers who received the full set of verbal and nonverbal cues were substantially more accurate in interpreting social interactions. Of those provided multichannel cues, 56 percent correctly identified which of three women engaged in a conversation had no children, compared with only 17 percent of those limited to verbal cues. In several cases, judgments based on the single verbal channel were right less often than chance guesses! These findings as well as others convincingly demonstrate the gain in accuracy from multichannel communication.

RESOLVING INCONSISTENCY. At times the messages conveyed by different communication channels may appear inconsistent. This makes interaction problematic. What would you do, for example, if your instructor welcomed you during office hours with warm words, a frowning face, and an annoyed tone of voice? You might well react with uncertainty and caution, puzzled by the apparent inconsistency among the verbal and nonverbal cues you were receiving. You would certainly try to figure out the instructor's "true" feelings and desires, and you might also try to guess why

the instructor was sending such confusing cues.

The strategies people use to resolve apparently inconsistent cues depend upon their inferences about the reasons for the apparent inconsistency (Zuckerman, DePaulo, and Rosenthal 1981). It could be due to the communicator's ambivalent feelings, to poor communication skills, or to an intention to deceive. A large body of research has compared the relative weight we give to messages in different channels when we do not suspect deception.

In one set of studies, people judged the emotions expressed by actors who posed contradictory verbal, paralinguistic, and facial signals (Mehrabian 1972). These studies showed that facial cues were most important in determining which feelings are interpreted as true. Paralinguistic cues were second, and verbal cues were much less important. Later research, exposing receivers to more complete combinations of visual and auditory cues, replicated the finding that people rely more on facial than on paralinguistic cues when the two conflict. This preference for facial cues increases with age from childhood to adulthood, indicating that it is a learned strategy (DePaulo et al. 1978).

People also use social context to help them judge which channel is more credible (Bugenthal 1974). They consider whether the facial expression, tone of voice, or verbal content are appropriate to the particular social situation. If people recognize a situation as highly stressful, for example, they rely more on the cues that seem consistent with a stressful context (a strained tone of voice) and less on cues that seem to contradict it (a happy face or verbal assertions of calmness). In short, people tend to resolve apparent inconsistencies between channels in favor of the channels whose message seems most appropriate to the social context.

If people suspect deception, they do not prefer facial cues in determining someone's "true" feelings. They realize that the face is the most easily "faked" nonverbal channel, and that facial expressions are subject to socially learned display rules. Instead, suspicious observers are influenced more by the less controlled channels such as body movements or tone of voice. Because these channels are normally outside the speaker's awareness, they are less likely to be censored. Even when receivers control both verbal and facial cues, their "true" feelings may leak out nonverbally through body movements and paralinguistic cues (Ekman and Friesen 1969; Zuckerman et al. 1984).

The effects of suspicion on the strategy adopted to resolve apparent inconsistency is nicely demonstrated in the following study (Zuckerman et al. 1982). Observers were told that a speaker never lied, sometimes lied, or very often lied. They were then exposed to apparently inconsistent communications comprised of various combinations of facial, body, and paralinguistic cues. When judging the speaker's feelings, observers who expected no deception were most influenced by facial cues. In contrast, those who were led to suspect deception discounted the messages conveyed by the face and were influenced more by voice and body cues.

Social Structure and Communication

So far this chapter has examined the nature of verbal and nonverbal communication, and some consequences of the fact that everyday communication usually combines the two. But how do social relationships shape communication? And how does communication express, maintain, or modify social relationships? These questions pinpoint social psychology's concern with the reciprocal impacts of social structure and communication on each other. This section examines three aspects of these impacts. First, it discusses the links between styles of speech and position in the stratification system. Second, it examines social norms that regulate interaction distances and some of the outcomes when these norms are violated. Third, it analyzes ways that communication expresses and modifies the two central dimensions of relationships—status and intimacy.

Social Stratification and Speech Style

The way we speak reflects and regulates our social relationships. A major proponent of this view, Basil Bernstein, studied the connections between speech styles and modes of interaction in various social classes, families, and schools in England (1974, 1975). He identified two major speech styles (or "sociolinguistic codes"): a restricted code and an elaborated code. An example of speech in each code will help us to define these two speech styles.

Suppose a child demands to stay up late to watch television. Using the restricted code, a parent might say: "No! *I* say you can't." Using the elaborated code, a parent might reply: "That's probably not a good idea. If you don't sleep now you'll be exhausted tomorrow and you probably won't enjoy the trip we planned."

As these examples demonstrate, the **restricted code** is a concrete and egocentric speech style. It is direct, rooted in the here and now, lacking in qualifications, and emotionally expressive. In contrast, the **elaborated code** is a relatively abstract speech style attuned to the characteristics of the particular listener. It allows for subtle differences in meaning by employing qualifications and extended perspectives on time and events. It encourages listeners to reason for themselves.

Despite the crowded circumstances, the eight people on this bench have maintained some privacy. Strangers feel uncomfortable when they must intrude on each others' personal space. To overcome this discomfort, they studiously ignore each other, avoiding touch, eye contact, and verbal exchanges.

The restricted language code is used in settings that emphasize rigid role definitions and respect for formal social positions. In these settings, people exercise social control through issuing direct commands, demanding obedience, and applying the same rules to everyone. The restricted code does an efficient job of communicating when the aim is to express straightforward expectations authoritatively or with strong feeling. The elaborated code is used in settings that emphasize unique individual characteristics and needs. In these settings, social control is person-oriented. People tailor their demands to one another's capabilities and provide reasons and explanations. Such social relations are found in families or classrooms with flexible or loose role expectations and definitions.

According to this analysis, the mode of social control that prevails in relationships in a cultural group determines the type of language code the group members are likely to acquire. In working-class families, schools, and work settings in Great Britain, for instance, social relationships tend toward rigid, positional control; and the working class socialize toward restricted codes. Middle-class relationships tend toward more flexible, personal control, and socialize toward elaborated codes (Bernstein 1974, 1975). Class differences in speech style have been found in studies of the way mothers talk to their children and answer their children's questions, and in studies of children's speech (Robinson and Rackstraw 1972; Turner 1974).

In interviews about a devastating tornado, American adults also revealed class-connected preferences for restricted versus elaborated codes. Lower-class persons tended to describe the disaster that hit their community entirely through their own eyes. They rarely qualified their statements or provided an abstract overview. Upper middle-class persons tended to describe the disaster from others' viewpoints as well as their own. They set their observations in context for the listener, and explained and qualified their reactions (Schatzman and Strauss 1955).

These ideas and findings have given rise to a sharp, sometimes heated controversy (Edwards 1976). Advocates of so-called **deficit theories** claim that people who use restricted codes are less capable of logical reasoning and abstract thought. They also claim that restricted speech styles are typical of lower-class, black, and other culturally disadvantaged groups in America as well as in Great Britain. Combining these two claims, deficit theorists argue that the children from disadvantaged groups perform poorly in school because their restricted language makes them cognitively inferior. To overcome this deficit, they advocate compensatory education programs to teach disadvantaged children better language use (Bereiter and Engleman 1966).

The strongest criticism of deficit theories has come from Labov (1972b). Based on interviews in natural environments, he demonstrates that "black English," which has been described as restricted and impoverished, is every bit as rich and subtle as standard English. It differs mainly in surface details like pronunciation ("ax" = ask) and grammatical forms ("He be busy" = He's always busy). Nonstandard speech may appear impoverished because nonstandard speakers feel less relaxed in the social contexts where they are typically observed (schools, interviews). Social researchers or other "outsiders" who observe them may also inhibit their language (Grimshaw 1973). When interviewed by a member of their own race, for instance, black job applicants used longer sentences and richer vocabularies, and employed words more creatively (Ledvinka 1971).

Thus speech differences between groups have not been shown to reflect differences in cognitive ability. Nonetheless, members of socially less valued groups do experience more communication problems in social institutions. Recognizing this, they often "correct" their speech to conform with higher prestige usages in appropriate situations (Labov 1972a). The struggle over what language use is "correct" or "preferred" is part of the larger intergroup struggle for power in society. In Quebec, for example, the previously disadvantaged French-speaking community passed laws making French the only official language for use in commerce and education. Through legislating language use they have asserted their power over the formerly dominant English speakers.

Normative Distances for Interaction

American and Northern European tourists in Cairo are often surprised to see men touching and staring intently into each other's eyes as they converse in public. Surprise may turn to discomfort at the closeness of interaction if the tourist must engage the Arab male in conversation. Bathed in the warmth of his breath, the tourist may feel sexually threatened. In our own communities, in contrast, we are rarely made uncomfortable by the overly close approach of another. People apparently know the norms for interaction distances in their own cultures and they conform to them. What are these norms, and what happens when they are violated?

NORMATIVE DISTANCES. Edward Hall (1966) has described four spatial zones that are normatively prescribed for interaction among middle-class Americans. Each zone is considered appropriate for particular types of activities and relationships. *Public distance* (12–25 feet) is prescribed for interaction in formal encounters, lectures, trials, and other public events. At this distance, communication is often one-way, sensory stimulation is very weak, people speak loudly, and they choose language carefully. *Social distance* (4–12 feet) is prescribed for most casual social and business transactions. Here, people speak at normal volume, they do not touch, frequent eye contact is needed to maintain smooth communication, and sensory stimulation is low. *Personal distance* (1½ to 4 feet) is prescribed for interaction among friends and relatives. Here, people speak softly, touch, and receive substantial sensory stimulation by sight, sound, and smell. *Intimate distance* (0 to 18 inches) is prescribed for giving comfort, making love, and aggressing physically. This distance provides intense stimulation from touch, smell, breath, and body heat. It signals unmistakable involvement.

Many studies support the idea that people know and conform to the normatively prescribed distances for particular kinds of encounters (LaFrance and Mayo 1978). When we compare different cultural and social groups, both similarities and differences in distance norms emerge. All cultures prescribe closer distances for friends than for strangers, for example. The specific distances for preferred interactions vary widely, however. Latin Americans, Arabs, Greeks, and French typically use smaller interaction distances than Americans, British, Swiss, and Swedes (Sommer 1969). Females tend to interact with one another at closer distances than males do in various cultures (Sussman and Rosenfeld 1982). Social class may also influence interpersonal spacing. In Canadian school yards, lower-class primary school children were observed to interact at closer distances than middle-class children, regardless of race (Scherer 1974).

Differences in distance norms may cause discomfort in cross-cultural interaction. People from different countries or social classes may have difficulty in interpreting the amount of intimacy implied by each other's interpersonal spacing and in finding mutually comfortable interaction distances. Cross-cultural training in nonverbal communication can reduce such discomfort. For instance, Englishmen were liked more by Arabs with whom they interacted when the Englishmen had been trained to behave nonverbally like Arabs—to stand closer, smile more, look more, and touch more (Collett 1971).

VIOLATIONS OF PERSONAL SPACE. What happens when people violate distance norms by coming too close? In particular, what do we do when strangers intrude upon our personal space?

The earliest systematic examination of this question included two parallel studies (Felipe and Sommer 1966). In one, strangers approached lone male patients in mental hospitals to a point only six inches away. In the other, strangers sat down twelve inches away from lone female students in a university library. The mental patients and the students who were approached left the scene much more quickly than the patients and students who were not approached. After only two minutes, 30 percent of the patients who were intruded on had fled, compared with none of the others. Among the students, 70 percent of those whose space was violated had fled by the end of 30 minutes, compared with only 13 percent of the others. Results of this study are shown in Figure 5.1.

Flight is not the only response to space violation. In addition, people protect their privacy by turning their backs on intruders, leaning away, and placing barriers such as books, purses, or elbows in the intervening space. Only very rarely do people react verbally to space violations (Patterson, Mullens, and Romano 1971).

Violating personal space is uncomfortable for intruders too. Individuals required to pass through the personal space of others who are engaged in conversation feel more awkward and display more unpleasant facial expressions than individuals who merely pass nearby (Efran and Cheyne 1974). Due to their discomfort, people will avoid intruding. They will drink from a water fountain much less frequently, for instance, if someone is standing within a foot of it (Baum, Riess, and O'Hara 1974).

Staring is a powerful way to violate another's privacy without direct physical intrusion. Staring by strangers elicits avoidance responses, indicating that it is experienced as an intense negative stimulus. When stared at by strangers, for instance, pedestrians cross the street faster, and drivers speed away from intersections more quickly (Ellsworth, Carlsmith, and Henson 1972; Greenbaum and Rosenfeld 1978).

Communicating Status and Intimacy

The two central dimensions of social relationships are status and intimacy. Status is concerned with the exercise of power and control. Intimacy is concerned with the expression of affiliation and affection that creates social solidarity (Kemper 1973). Verbal and nonverbal communications express and maintain particular levels of intimacy and relative status in relationships. Moreover, through communication we may challenge existing levels of intimacy and relative status and negotiate new ones (Fishman 1972; Scotton 1983).

Communication can signal our view of a relationship only if people recognize which communication behaviors are appropriate for an expected level of intimacy or status, and which are inappropriate. The following examples suggest that we easily recognize when communication behaviors are inappropriate. What if you: Repeatedly addressed your mother as Mrs. _____? Used vulgar slang during a job interview? Draped your arm around your professor's shoulder as she explained how to improve your test answer? Looked away each time your beloved gazed into your eyes? Each of these communication behaviors would probably make you uncomfortable. They would doubtlessly also cause others to think you inept, disturbed, or hostile. Each behavior expresses levels of intimacy or relative status easily recognized as inappropriate to the relationship. Let us survey systematically how specific communication be-

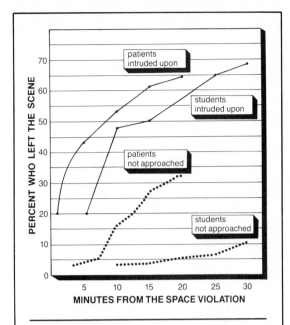

FIGURE 5.1

REACTIONS TO VIOLATIONS OF PERSONAL SPACE

How do people react when strangers violate norms of interpersonal distance and intrude upon their personal space? A common reaction is illustrated here. Strangers sat down twelve inches away from lone female students in a library, or approached lone male patients in a mental hospital to within six inches. Those who were approached left the scene much more quickly than control subjects who were not approached. Violations of personal space often produce flight.

Source: adapted from Felipe and Sommer (1966).

haviors express, maintain, and change status and intimacy in relationships.

STATUS. Forms of address clearly communicate relative status in relationships. Inferiors use formal address (title and last name) for their superiors ("When is the exam, Professor Levine?"), whereas superiors address inferiors with familiar forms (first name or nickname: "On Friday, Daphne"). Status equals use the same form of address with one another. Both use either formal (Ms./Mr.) or familiar forms

(Myra/Ben), depending on the degree of intimacy between them (Brown 1965). When status differences are ambiguous, individuals may even avoid addressing each other directly. They shy away from choosing an address form because it might grant too much or too little status.

A shift in forms of address signals a change in social relationships, or at least an attempted change. In order to promote equality and fraternity, the French Revolutionaries demanded that everyone use only the familiar (*tu*) and not the formal (*vous*) form of the second-person pronoun, regardless of past status differences. Presidential candidates try to reduce their differences with voters by inviting the use of familiar names (Ronnie, Fritz). In cases where there is a clear status difference between people, the right to initiate the use of more familiar or equal forms of address belongs to the superior ("Why don't you drop that 'Dr.' stuff?"). This principle also applies to other communication behaviors. It is the higher status person who usually initiates changes toward more familiar behaviors such as greater eye contact, physical proximity, touch, or self-disclosure.

We each have a repertoire of different pronunciations and dialects, and a varied vocabulary from which to choose when speaking. Our choices of language to use with other people express a view of our relative status and may influence our relationships. People usually make language choices smoothly, easily expressing status differences appropriate to the situation (Gumperz 1976). Teachers in a Norwegian town, for instance, were observed to lecture to their students in the standard language (Blom and Gumperz 1972). When they wished to encourage student discussion, however, they switched to the local dialect, thereby reducing status differences. Note how your teachers also switch to more informal language when trying to promote student participation.

Language choice by bilinguals also expresses status in relationships. Paraguayans speak Spanish with persons of higher status, but switch to the tribal language, Guarani, among equals (Rubin 1962). Bilingual Puerto Ricans in New York use English in the formal, status-differentiated settings of school and work. They typically switch to Spanish with their friends who are status equals (Greenfield 1972).

Paralinguistic cues also communicate and reinforce status in relationships. People of higher status interrupt their partners more during conversations and talk more themselves. Inferiors grant status to others by avoiding interruptions, and by responding with "M-hmn" more frequently at appropriate intervals to indicate they are following the conversation. Among status equals, these paralinguistic behaviors are distributed more equally (LaFrance and Mayo 1978; Leffler, Gillespie, and Conaty 1982).

Body language also serves to express status. When status is unequal, people of higher status tend to adopt relatively relaxed postures with their arms and legs in asymmetrical positions. Those of lower status stand or sit in more tense and symmetrical positions. The amount of time we spend looking at our partner, and the timing, also indicate status. Higher status persons look more when speaking than when listening, whereas lower status persons look more when listening than when speaking. Overall, inferiors look more at their partners, but they are also first to break the gaze between partners. Finally, superiors are much more likely to intrude physically on inferiors by touching or pointing at them (Dovidio and Ellyson 1982; LaFrance and Mayo 1978; Leffler, Gillespie, and Conaty 1982).

Two aspects of interpersonal spacing that clearly influence and reflect status are physical distance and the amount of space each person occupies. Equal status individuals jointly determine comfortable interaction distances and tend to occupy approximately equal amounts of space with their bodies and with the possessions that surround them. When status is unequal, superiors tend to control interaction distances, keeping greater physical distance than equals would choose. Superiors also claim more direct space with their bodies and possessions than inferiors (Hayduk 1978; Gifford 1982; Leffler, Gillespie, and Conaty 1982).

INTIMACY. This second central dimension of relationships is also expressed through communication. One way we signal intimacy or solidarity is by addressing each other with first names. The exchange of title and last names is common for strangers. In other languages, speakers express intimacy by their choice of familiar versus formal second-person pronouns. As noted above, the French can choose between the familiar *tu* or formal *vous*; the Spanish have the familiar *tu* or formal *usted*.

Our choice of language is another way to express intimacy. For example, Paraguayan men usually court women in Spanish; after marriage, they converse with their wives in the tribal language as a sign of increased intimacy (Rubin 1962). Similarly, residents of a Norwegian town were found to use the formal version of their language with strangers and the local dialect with friends. They spoke the formal version when transacting official business in government offices then switched to dialect for a personal chat with the clerk after completing their business (Blom and Gumperz 1972).

The **theory of speech accomodation** (Giles 1980; Beebe and Giles 1984) illustrates an important way that people use verbal and paralinguistic behavior to express intimacy or liking. According to this theory, people express or reject intimacy by adjusting their speech behavior during interaction to converge with or diverge from their partner's. To express liking or evoke approval, they make their own speech behavior more similar to their partner's. To reject intimacy or communicate disapproval, they accentuate the differences between their own speech and their partner's.

Adjustments of paralinguistic behavior demonstrate speech accomodation during conversations (Taylor and Royer 1980; Thakerar, Giles, and Cheshire 1982). Individuals who wish to express liking tend to shift their own pronunciation, speech rate, vocal intensity, pause lengths, and utterance lengths during conversation to match those of their partner. Individuals who wish to communicate disapproval modify these vocal behaviors in ways that make them diverge more from their partner's. Among bilinguals, speech accomodation may also determine the choice of language (Bourhis et al. 1979). To increase intimacy, bilinguals choose the language they believe their partner would prefer to speak. To reject intimacy, they choose their partner's less preferred language.

The use of slang gives strong expression to ingroup intimacy and solidarity. Through slang, group members assert their own shared social identity and express their alienation from and rejection of the outgroup of slang illiterates. At the same time, society tends to adopt slang into the standard language. This blunts its usefulness for affirming ingroup solidarity and makes necessary the constant manufacture of new slang. Middle-class white youths, for example, adopt black slang as a sign of their own rebellion and also out of a desire to identify with the rebellion of alienated blacks. As a result, black slang must continuously undergo renewal to express black solidarity (Drake 1980).

The ways we express intimacy through body language and interpersonal spacing are well recognized. For instance, research supports the folklore that lovers gaze more into each other's eyes (Rubin 1970). In fact, we tend to interpret a high level of eye contact from others as a sign of intimacy. We communicate liking by assuming moderately relaxed postures, moving closer and leaning toward others, orienting ourselves face-to-face, and touching them (Mehrabian 1972). There is an important qualification to these generalizations, however. Mutual gaze, close distance, and touch reflect intimacy and promote it only when the interaction has a positive cast. If the interaction is generally negative—if the setting is competitive, the verbal content unpleasant, or the past relationship antagonistic—these same nonverbal behaviors intensify negative feelings (Schiffenbauer and Schiavo 1976).

Maintaining a Smooth Flow of Conversation

Conversation is a regular daily activity. Yet we all have trouble communicating at times. The list of what can go wrong is long and painful: inability to get started, irritating interruptions, awkward silences, failure to give others a chance to talk, failure to notice that listeners are bored or have lost interest, changing topics inappropriately, assuming incorrectly that others understand, and so on. This section examines the ways people avoid these embarrassing and annoying blunders. To maintain smooth-flowing conversation requires knowledge of certain rules and communication skills that are often taken for granted. We will discuss some of the rules and skills that are crucial for initiating conversations, regulating turn taking, and coordinating conversation through verbal and nonverbal feedback.

Initiating Conversations

Conversations must be initiated with an attention-getting device, a summons to interaction. Greetings, questions, or the ringing of a telephone can serve as the summons. But conversations do not get underway until potential partners signal that they are attending and willing to converse. Eye contact is the crucial nonverbal signal of availability for communication. Goffman (1963) suggests that eye contact places a person under an obligation to interact: when a waitress permits eye contact, she places herself under the power of the eye-catcher.

The most common verbal lead into conversation is a **summons-answer sequence** (Schegloff 1968). Response to a summons ("Joel, you home?" "Yeah.") indicates availability. More importantly, this response initiates the mutual obligation to speak and to listen that produces conversational turn taking. The summoner is expected to provide the first topic—a conversational rule little children exasperatingly overlook. Our reactions when people violate the summons-answer sequence demonstrate its widespread acceptance as an obligatory rule. When people ignore questions, greetings, or other summons, we conclude either that they are intentionally insulting us, socially incompetent, or psychologically absent (sleeping, drunk, crazy).

Examination of how new topics are initiated reveals yet another rule. Strangers are expected to introduce new topics into conversation as questions inviting a response ("You going to the game tonight?"). People who know each other may simply announce a topic ("I'm going to the game tonight!"), claiming the conversational floor and the right of a response (Maynard 1978). Using the socially inappropriate method is likely to fail. A stranger who announces, "I'm going to Chicago for the weekend" is likely to evoke embarrassed silence from others. The same remark by an old friend, in contrast, would produce a flood of suggestions of things to do, places to go, and tales of past visits.

Regulating Turn Taking

A pervasive rule of conversation is to avoid bumping into someone verbally. To regulate turn taking, people use many verbal and nonverbal cues, singly and together, with varying degrees of success (Duncan and Fiske 1977; Kendon, Harris, and Key 1975; Sacks, Schegloff, and Jefferson 1978).

SIGNALING TURNS. Speakers indicate their willingness to yield the floor by looking directly at a listener with a sustained gaze toward the end of an utterance. People also signal readiness to give over the speaking role by pausing, and by stretching the final syllable of their speech in a drawl, terminating hand gestures, dropping voice volume, and tacking relatively meaningless expressions ("you know") on to the end of their utterances. Listeners indicate their desire to talk by inhaling audibly as if preparing to speak. They also tense and move their hands, shift their head away from the speaker, and emit especially loud vocal signs of interest ("Yeah," "M-hmn").

Speakers retain their turn by avoiding eye contact with listeners, tensing their hands and gesticulating, and increasing voice volume to overpower others when simultaneous speech occurs. People who persist in these behaviors are soon viewed by others as egocentric and domineering. They have violated an implicit social rule: "It's all right to hold a conversation, but you should let go of it now and then." (Richard Armour)

Verbal content and grammatical form of speech also provide important cues for turn taking. People usually exchange turns at the end of meaningful speech units after an idea has been completed. First priority for the next turn goes to any person explicitly addressed by the current speaker with a question, complaint, or other invitation to talk. People expect turn changes to occur after almost every question, but not necessarily after other pauses in conversation (Hanni 1980). It is difficult to exchange turns without using questions. When speakers in one study were permitted to use all methods except questions for signaling their desire to gain or relinquish the floor, the length of each speaking turn virtually doubled (Kent, Davis, and Shapiro 1978).

TURN ALLOCATION. Much of our conversation takes place in settings where turn taking is more organized than in spontaneous conversations. In class discussions, meetings, interviews, and therapy sessions, for example, responsibility for allocating turns tends to be controlled by one person, and turns are often allocated in advance. Prior allocation of turns reduces strains that arise from people either competing for speaking time or avoiding their responsibilities to speak. Allocation of turns also increases the efficiency of talk. It can arrange a distribution of turns that best fits the task or situation—a precisely equal distribu-

tion (as for a debate) or just one speaker (as in a football huddle).

Prior allocation of turns influences both how long people talk and the methods they use to extend their turns (Sacks, Schegloff, and Jefferson 1978). With prior allocation, people tend to speak longer during each turn which they lengthen by stringing many sentences together. In spontaneous conversation, turn lengths are ordinarily shorter. When people wish to extend their turns, they increase the complexity of what they say within single sentences. These observations on turn allocating illustrate some of the subtle, taken-for-granted rules that govern everyday conversation.

Feedback and Coordination

We engage in conversation to attain interpersonal goals—to inform, persuade, impress, control, and so on. For this purpose, we shape and reshape our speech in the course of conversation. To do this effectively, we must assess how what we say is affecting our partner's interest and understanding as we go along. Both verbal and nonverbal feedback help conversationalists in making this assessment. Through feedback, conversationalists coordinate what they are saying to each other from moment to moment. Responses called **back channel feedback** are especially important for regulating speech as it is happening. These are the small vocal and visual comments a listener makes while a speaker is talking, without taking over the speaking turn. They include such responses as "Yeah," "M-hmn," short clarifying questions ("What?" "Huh?"), brief repetitions of the speaker's words or completions of his or her utterances, head nods, and brief smiles. When conversations are proceeding smoothly, the fine rhythmic body movements of listeners (swaying, rocking, blinking) are precisely synchronized with the speech sounds of speakers who address them (Condon and Ogston 1967). These automatic listener movements are another source of feedback that indicates to speakers whether they are being properly "tracked" and understood (Kendon 1970).

Both the presence or absence and the timing of back channel feedback influence speakers. In smooth conversation, listeners time their signs of interest, agreement, or understanding to occur at the end of long utterances, or when the speaker turns his head toward them. The absence or mistiming of such listener feedback undermines coordination. It makes speakers uneasy or upset and causes them to hesitate or stop talking (Rosenfeld 1978). Alerted to the possible loss of listener attention and involvement by the absence of feedback, speakers employ attention-getting devices to evoke feedback. One such attention-getting device is the phrase "You know." Speakers frequently insert "You know" into long speaking turns immediately prior to or following pauses if their partner seems to be ignoring their invitation to provide feedback or to accept a speaking turn (Fishman 1980).

When speakers are denied feedback, the quality of their speech deteriorates. They become less coherent and communicate less accurately. Their speech becomes more wordy, less efficient, and more poorly fitted to the specific information needs of their partner (Kraut, Lewis, and Swezey 1982). Lack of feedback causes such deterioration because it prevents speakers from learning several things about their partners. They cannot discern whether their partners (1) have relevant prior knowledge they need not repeat; (2) understand already so they can wrap up the point or abbreviate; (3) have misinformation they should correct; (4) feel confused so they should backtrack and clarify; or, (5) feel bored so they should stop talking or change topics.

The fact that feedback influences the quality of speech has another interesting consequence. Listeners who provide their conversational partners with a lot of feedback also understand their partner's communication more fully and accurately. Through their feedback, active listeners help shape the conversation to fit their own information needs. This

finding reinforces a central theme of this chapter: that communication is a shared social accomplishment.

Summary

Communication is the process whereby people transmit information about their ideas and feelings to one another.

LANGUAGE AND VERBAL COMMUNICATION. Language is the main vehicle of human communication. (1) All spoken languages consist of sounds that are combined into words with arbitrary meanings and put together according to grammatical rules. Language enhances our capacity for social action. It frees us from the here-and-now and allows communication about nonshared experiences. (2) The meanings of words consist of both the properties most people associate with them and the personal responses they evoke in each individual. Most words have multiple meanings. (3) The successful use of language during interaction is a social accomplishment. To attain mutual understanding, conversationalists must use socially appropriate language, express their intentions in ways listeners can recognize, take account of others' current knowledge, and actively work to decipher meanings. (4) All languages share universal features based on human capacities for thought and on common social experience. Each language also has distinctive features that make it easier or more difficult to think about and remember particular ideas.

NONVERBAL COMMUNICATION. A great deal of information is communicated nonverbally during interaction. (1) Four major types of nonverbal communication are paralanguage, body language, interpersonal spacing, and choice of personal effects. (2) People from all cultures express and recognize the same six primary emotions in distinctive facial expressions. During interaction, however, people modify facial expressions of emotion according to cultural display rules. (3) Information is usually conveyed simultaneously through nonverbal and verbal channels. Multiple cues may add information to each other, reduce ambiguity, and increase accuracy. But if cues appear inconsistent, people must determine which cues reveal the speaker's true intentions.

SOCIAL STRUCTURE AND COMMUNICATION. The ways we communicate with others reflect and influence our relationships with them. (1) The more rigid control patterns observed among the lower class foster concrete, direct, egocentric, and emotionally expressive styles of speech. The more personalized control observed among the middle class fosters speech styles that are more abstract, qualified, and attuned to the listeners' unique qualities. (2) The appropriate interaction distances for particular types of activities and relationships are normatively prescribed. Cultural groups differ in their distance norms, making it difficult for individuals of different cultures to find mutually comfortable interaction distances. When strangers violate distance norms, people flee the scene or use other devices to protect their privacy. (3) We express, maintain, or challenge the levels of relative status and intimacy in our relationships through our verbal and nonverbal behavior. Status and intimacy influence and are influenced by forms of address, choice of dialect or language, interruptions, matching of speech styles, gestures, eye contact, posture, and interaction distances.

MAINTAINING A SMOOTH FLOW OF CONVERSATION. Smooth conversation depends on conversational rules and communication skills that are often taken for granted. (1) Conversations are initiated by a summons to interacton. They get underway only if potential partners signal availability, usually through eye contact or verbal response. (2) Conversationalists avoid verbal collisions by taking turns. They signal either a willingness to yield the floor or a desire to talk through verbal and nonverbal cues. In some situations turns are allocated in advance. (3) Effective conversationalists assess their partner's understanding and interest as they go along through vocal and visual feedback. If feedback is absent or poorly timed, the quality of communication deteriorates.

Key Terms and Concepts

Communication
Symbol
Spoken Language
Denotative Meaning
Connotative Meaning
Linguistic Competence
Sociolinguistic Competence
Speech Act
Cooperative Principle
Linguistic Universals
Linguistic Relativity Hypothesis
Paralanguage
Body Language
Interpersonal Spacing
Display Rules
Restricted Code
Elaborated Code
Deficit Theories
Theory of Speech Accomodation
Summons-Answer Sequence
Back Channel Feedback

Chapter 6

Attitudes

Introduction

"Woody Allen movies are great!"

"My Human Sexuality class is really boring."

"I like my job."

"I think government spending causes inflation."

"The law requiring 18 year olds to register is a lousy law."

"Guns don't kill people; people kill people."

What do all of these statements have in common? Each represents an **attitude**, a predisposition to respond to a particular object in a generally favorable or unfavorable way (Ajzen 1982). A person's attitudes influence the way in which he perceives and responds to the world (Allport 1935; Thomas and Znaniecki 1918). Attitudes influence attention: the person who likes Woody Allen movies is more likely to notice news stories about Allen's activities. Attitudes influence behavior: the college student who opposes the draft is more likely to participate in a demonstration against the draft law.

Because attitudes are an important influence on people, they occupy a central place in social psychology. But what exactly is an attitude? What do we mean by a "predisposition to respond"? Further, how do we measure a person's attitudes? We cannot study predispositions directly; instead, we must rely on various measures that reflect a person's attitudes. Moreover, a particular attitude does not exist in isolation. The person who believes that government spending causes inflation has a whole set of beliefs about the role of government in the economy, and this attitude about spending is related to those other beliefs. If attitudes influence behavior, perhaps we can change behavior by changing attitudes. This leads us to ask: How do attitudes change? Politicians, lobbyists, auto manufacturers, and brewers spend billions of dollars every year trying to create favorable attitudes. Even if

they succeed, do these attitudes affect our behavior?

In this chapter we will consider the following questions:

1. What is an attitude? Where do attitudes come from and how are they formed?

2. How do we find out someone's attitudes? How are attitudes measured?

3. How are attitudes organized?

4. Under what conditions do attitudes change?

5. What is the relationship between attitudes and behavior?

The Nature of Attitudes

An attitude exists in a person's mind; it is a mental state. Every attitude is about something, an object. In this section we will consider the components of an attitude, the characteristics of stereotypes, and the sources of attitudes and their functions.

The Components of an Attitude

Consider this statement: "I don't want to go to Human Sexuality class; it's boring." This attitude has three components: (1) beliefs or cognitions; (2) a favorable or unfavorable evaluation; and (3) a behavioral disposition.

COGNITION. Our cognitions, or beliefs, are the ways in which we perceive objects. The person who doesn't like his human sexuality class perceives it as involving certain content, taught by a particular person. We cannot always prove whether particular beliefs are true or false. For example, economists and government officials disagree on whether government spending causes inflation, with both sides equally convinced they are right.

EVALUATION. An attitude also has an affective or evaluative component. "It's boring" indicates that the course arouses a mildly unpleasant emotion in the speaker. Stronger negative emotions include dislike, hatred, or even loathing: "I can't stand punk rock." Of course, the evaluation may be positive: "I like Woody Allen movies," or "This food is terrific." Generally, the evaluative component can be thought of as having both a direction (either positive or negative) and an intensity (ranging from very weak to very strong feelings).

BEHAVIOR. An attitude involves a predisposition to respond or a behavioral tendency toward the object. "I don't want to go" represents a tendency to avoid the class. "I'm going to vote for Steve Smith" indicates an intention to engage in a behavior. Persons having a specific attitude are inclined to behave in some ways toward an object and not in other ways.

RELATIONSHIPS BETWEEN THE COMPONENTS. Cognitive, evaluative, and behavioral components all have the same object, so we would expect them to be organized into a single, relatively consistent whole. At the same time, these three components are distinct; if they were identical we would not need to distinguish among them. This implies that we should be able to measure each component, and that we should find a positive relationship between them.

In order to assess this relationship, researchers took a survey of women's attitudes toward contraceptives (Kothandapani 1971). They classified statements about birth control as representing "feelings," "beliefs and opinions," or "actions." For example, "Birth control causes birth defects" is a belief; "The very thought of birth control disgusts me" is a feeling; and "I would volunteer to speak about the merits of birth control" is an action. Researchers interviewed a group of married black women, none of whom were pregnant at the time. From the women's responses, they constructed measures of each of the components. Results indicated that there was a positive correlation among items that were designed to measure the same component. Measures of the three components were positively associated but the relationships were not as close.

Stereotypes

"Blacks are lazy."
"Jocks are dumb."
"Southerners are bigots."
"Engineering students are bores."
"Sociologists are radicals."

Each of these statements is an example of a particular type of attitude called a stereotype. Originally, the term referred to a rigid and simplistic "picture in the head" (Lippman 1922). In current usage, a **stereotype** is a rigid and simplistic perception of members of one group that is widely shared by others. For example, instead of recognizing variations among blacks in athletic ability, some people believe blacks excel only in athletics. A stereotype is basically cognitive: a belief. When we encounter a member of a particular group, we base our perceptions on our stereotypes. Yet most people are unaware of the impact of stereotypic beliefs on their judgments of others (Hepburn and Locksley 1983).

Most people have stereotypes of members of various racial and ethnic groups. In a 1978 survey, half of the whites said they viewed blacks as less ambitious than whites (lazy), one-third perceived blacks as more violent, and one-quarter saw blacks as less intelligent (*Newsweek*, February 26, 1979). Many people have stereotypes of persons who are Polish or Oriental. Negative stereotypes of Polish people, for example, are reinforced by ethnic jokes that characterize them as stupid or naive. Some stereotypes are positive, however, like the belief that Orientals excel in math. Although many whites have stereotypic views of blacks, the content of those views may vary depending on family background and personal experiences. A white person raised in New York City may view blacks as prone to crime and violence, and as untrustworthy. In the rural South, a white may not associate blacks with crime and violence, but stereotype them as being musically talented.

Stereotypes are often associated with intense emotions. A strong like or a strong dislike for members of a specific group is referred to as **prejudice**. Prejudice and stereotypes go together, with people using their stereotypic beliefs to justify the prejudice toward members of the group. The emotional component of prejudice can lead to intergroup conflict (Chapter 15) or violence directed at members of another group (Chapter 18). Because of its social consequences, researchers have made considerable effort over the past 30 years to find ways to reduce prejudice. Some of that research is reviewed in Chapter 15.

The behavioral component that accompanies negative stereotypes and prejudice toward members of another group is a tendency to **discriminate**, to act in ways that harm such persons or bar them from opportunities. In schools, discrimination can take the form of discouraging members of a group from enrolling in particular classes or programs. In some high schools, women are reportedly discouraged by counselors and teachers from taking algebra and trigonometry courses. In housing, certain persons may be prevented from living in a neighborhood by the unwillingness of owners and real-estate agents to rent or sell to them.

Negative stereotypes, and the prejudices and discrimination associated with them, contribute significantly to social problems. The continuing controversy over busing children to schools, over the availability of abortion for the poor, and over the desirability of welfare and unemployment programs is complicated by attitudes toward the groups affected by such programs. Attitudes toward Communists, Arabs, and Jews influence our foreign policy and public opinion about international issues. Thus there is an attitudinal basis for many of the social issues that we read and hear about in the daily news.

Attitude Formation

"Woody Allen movies are great."
"I like my job."
"Blacks are lazy."
"Southerners are bigots."
"The law requiring 18-year-olds to register is a lousy law."
"Guns don't kill people; people kill people."

Where do attitudes like these come from? How are they formed? The answer lies in the processes of social learning or socialization (discussed in Chapter 3). Attitudes may be formed through reinforcement (instrumental learning), through associations of stimuli and responses (classical conditioning), or by observing others (observational learning).

We acquire an attitude toward Woody Allen's films or our jobs through instrumental learning—that is, based on direct experience with the object. If you experience rewards related to some object, your attitude will be favorable. Thus, if your work provides you with good pay, a sense of accomplishment, and compliments from your co-workers, your attitude toward it will be quite positive. Conversely, if you associate negative emotions or unpleasant outcomes with some object, you will dislike it. For example, repeated exposure to bland, overcooked food leads many students to have a very negative attitude toward dormitory food.

Only a small portion of our attitudes are based on direct contact with some object, however. We have attitudes about many political figures whom we've never met. We have stereotypes of members of certain ethnic or religious groups even though we have never been face to face with a member of those groups. We acquire such attitudes through our interactions with third parties. People learn stereotypes like "blacks are lazy" from their parents, who in turn reward their children for adopting similar attitudes. This is also considered instrumental learning, but in this case, we acquire rewards and punishments through the behavior of a third party.

Friends are another important source of our attitudes. The attitude that the law requiring Selective Service registration is bad, for example, may be learned through interaction with peers. A 1943 study of Bennington College women by Newcomb demonstrates the impact of peers on the political attitudes of college students. Although most of these women were raised in wealthy, politically conservative families, the faculty of Bennington had very liberal political attitudes. The study demonstrated that freshmen who maintained close ties with their families and did not become involved in campus activities remained conservative, whereas women who became active in the college community and who interacted more frequently with other students gradually became more liberal. Presumably, the students at Bennington rewarded the liberal attitudes of their peers.

We acquire prejudices toward a particular group through *classical conditioning,* in which a neutral stimulus gradually acquires the ability to elicit a response through repeated association with other stimuli that elicit that response. Children learn at an early age that "lazy," "dirty," "stupid," and many other characteristics are undesirable. Children themselves are often punished for being "dirty," or hear adults say "don't be stupid!" If they hear their parents (or others) refer to members of a particular group as "lazy," or "stupid," children will increasingly associate the group name with the negative reactions initially elicited by these terms. A number of experiments have shown that classical conditioning produces negative attitudes toward groups (Staats and Staats 1958; Lohr and Staats 1973).

Some attitudes are held primarily or exclusively by members of particular groups or subcultures. Attitudes like "guns don't kill people; people kill people" and "when guns are outlawed, only outlaws will have guns" are widespread among members of the National Rifle Association. Holding such an attitude may be both a prerequisite to acceptance by other group members and a symbol of one's loyalty to the group.

Another source of attitudes is the media,

especially television and films. Here, the mechanism may be observational learning. The attitude that all Southerners are bigots may result primarily from exposure to the media. Because racism and bigotry are unacceptable in our current social and political climate, people who hold such attitudes often attract the attention of the media. Many persons living in the United States have had little contact with Southerners. Consequently, residents of other regions who see or read of incidents in which Southerners express racist or prejudiced attitudes may (erroneously) conclude that all Southerners are bigots.

The Functions of Attitudes

We acquire attitudes through learning. But why do we retain them? One answer is that they serve important functions for us. Each attitude fulfills at least one of four functions or purposes for the individual (Katz 1960).

Some attitudes serve an instrumental function. Obviously, we develop favorable attitudes toward objects that aid or reward us and unfavorable attitudes toward objects that thwart or punish us. People in business generally have favorable attitudes toward Republican candidates because Republican politicians frequently propose legislation that benefits business. Similarly, we like those co-workers and fellow students who help us with our own work, and dislike persons who we perceive as competing with us for scarce resources, whether grades, jobs, or lovers.

Attitudes often serve a knowledge function—that is, they provide us with a meaningful and structured environment. Because the world is too complex for us to understand, we group objects and events into categories and develop simplified (stereotyped) attitudes that allow us to treat individuals as members of the category. Our attitudes about that category (object) provide us with meaning and with a basis for action toward the object. The belief that blacks are untrustworthy leads some whites to be guarded in their interaction with blacks. Reacting to every member of the group

It can be difficult to find out another person's attitudes. But some people help us out by displaying what they believe.

in the same way is more efficient, if less satisfying, than trying to learn about each as an individual.

Some attitudes express the individual's basic values, and reinforce self-image. Many conservatives in our society have negative attitudes toward abortion, racial integration, and equal rights for women. Thus, a person whose self-concept includes conservatism may adopt these attitudes because they express that self-image. The Catholic church positively values having children, and opposes the use of mechanical or chemical means of birth control. A Catholic man may favor large families because that attitude is consistent with these religious values.

Finally, some attitudes protect the person from recognizing certain thoughts or feelings. Some experiences and thoughts threaten our self-image or adjustment. An individual may experience feelings that are unacceptable to him, such as hostility toward his father. If he recognized this hostility, he would feel guilty, because we are taught to love our parents. So instead of acknowledging that he hates his father, he may direct it toward mem-

bers of a minority group, or authority figures such as policemen or teachers. This is one function of prejudice. People who have severe feelings of inferiority may respond by developing attitudes of superiority to others.

In sum, attitudes are psychological entities comprised of cognitive, affective, and behavioral components. These components are interrelated but not identical. Attitudes are learned through direct experience or through interaction with other persons. An individual holds attitudes because they serve one or more functions for him or her.

The Measurement of Attitudes

When you meet someone, you need information about the person in order to interact smoothly. You need to find out her attitudes and how she feels about objects that are relevant to your interaction—the class or workplace where you meet, the persons whom you both know, or the current local or national events. Because attitudes are mental states, they cannot be directly observed. Sometimes we can infer someone's attitudes from some form of display associated with the person. A button that says "No Nukes" indicates that the person wearing it is opposed to nuclear power plants and/or weapons. Slogans printed on T-shirts are another source of information about attitudes. A woman wearing a shirt with the slogan "A woman without a man is like a fish without a bicycle" almost certainly has feminist attitudes about male-female relationships. Bumper stickers are another source of information (Wrightsman 1969). But we cannot rely on these sources because most people we interact with do not put their attitudes on display.

In order to obtain systematic information about the attitude of each person in a group toward some object, we need techniques that will allow us to measure attitudes. Social psychologists have developed a wide variety of methods for measuring attitudes, both direct and indirect.

Direct Methods

The most direct way of finding out someone's attitude is 'to ask a direct question and record the person's answer. This is the way most of us "study" the attitudes of persons with whom we interact. It is also the technique used by newspaper and television reporters. In order to make the process more systematic, social psychologists employ several methods, including the single-item measure, Likert scales, and Semantic Differential techniques (see Box 6.1).

SINGLE ITEMS. The use of just one question to assess attitudes is very common. The item usually consists of a direct positive or negative statement about the object, and the respondent indicates whether she agrees or disagrees, or is unsure. Such a measure is economical; it takes a minimum of time or space to present. It is also easy to score. The major drawback of the

---

Box 6.1
THE MEASUREMENT OF ATTITUDES

Suppose you want to assess attitudes toward premarital sexual behavior. Here are three techniques you could employ.

Single Item

The single item is probably the most common measure of attitudes. An example of this type is:

I think people should wait until they are married to have sex.

___ Yes
___ No
___ Not sure

Likert Scale

The Likert Scale consists of a series of statements about the object of interest. The statements may be positive or negative. The respondent indicates how much he or she agrees with each statement. For example:

1. I think people should wait until they are married to have sex.

___ Strongly agree	$(+2)$
___ Agree	$(+1)$
___ Undecided	(0)
___ Disagree	(-1)
___ Strongly disagree	(-2)

2. I think having sex before marriage strengthens the marriage.

___ Strongly agree	(-2)
___ Agree	(-1)
___ Undecided	(0)
___ Disagree	$(+1)$
___ Strongly disagree	$(+2)$

Semantic Differential Scale

The Semantic Differential Scale consists of a number of dimensions on which the respondent rates the attitude object. For example:

Rate how you feel about premarital sexual intercourse on each of the following dimensions.

good	$(+3)$	$(+2)$	$(+1)$	(0)	(-1)	(-2)	(-3)	bad
weak	(-3)	(-2)	(-1)	(0)	$(+1)$	$(+2)$	$(+3)$	strong
fast	$(+3)$	$(+2)$	$(+1)$	(0)	(-1)	(-2)	(-3)	slow
negative	(-3)	(-2)	(-1)	(0)	$(+1)$	$(+2)$	$(+3)$	positive
light	(-3)	(-2)	(-1)	(0)	$(+1)$	$(+2)$	$(+3)$	heavy
exciting	$(+3)$	$(+2)$	$(+1)$	(0)	(-1)	(-2)	(-3)	boring

single item is that it is not very precise. Of necessity, it must be general, and detects only gross differences in attitude. Using the single-item measure in Box 6.1, we could only separate people into two groups, those who favor premarital abstinence, and everybody else.

LIKERT SCALES. Often we want to know not only how each person feels about an object, but also how each respondent's attitude compares with the attitudes of others. The Likert scale, the technique of summated ratings, provides such information (Likert 1932).

Box 6.1 includes a two-item Likert scale. Each possible response is given a numerical score, indicated in parentheses. We would assess the respondent's attitude by adding his scores for all the items. For example, suppose you strongly agree with item 1 and strongly disagree with item 2; your score would be +4, indicating strong opposition to premarital intercourse. Your roommate might strongly disagree with the statement that people should wait until they are married (−2), and might also not agree that premarital sex strengthens a

marriage (+1); the resulting score of −1 indicates a slightly negative view. Finally, someone who strongly disagrees with item 1 and agrees with item 2 would get a score of −3, and could be differentiated from a person who received a −4.

Typically, a Likert scale includes at least four items. The items should be counterbalanced—that is, some should be written as positive statements and others should be written as negative ones. Our two-item scale in Box 6.1 has this property; one item is positive and the other is negative. The Likert scale allows us to order respondents fairly precisely; items of this type are commonly used in public opinion polls. Such a scale takes more time to administer, however, and involves a scoring stage as well.

SEMANTIC DIFFERENTIAL SCALES. The Semantic Differential scale is quite different in format (Osgood, Suci, and Tannenbaum 1957). Like most attitude scales, the single item and Likert scales measure the *denotative* or dictionary meanings of the object to the respondent.

However, objects also have a *connotative* meaning, a set of psychological meanings that vary from one respondent to another. One person may have had very positive experiences with sexual intercourse, whereas another person's experiences may have been very frustrating. The Semantic Differential scale measures connotative meaning. It presents the respondents with a series of bipolar adjective scales—that is, a scale whose ends are two adjectives having opposite meanings. The person rates the attitude object on each scale. Analyses of such ratings frequently identify three aspects of meaning: evaluation, potency, and activity. Evaluation is measured on scales such as good-bad and positive-negative; potency by weak-strong and light-heavy; and activity by adjective pairs like fast-slow and exciting-boring.

The example in Box 6.1 includes two bipolar scales measuring each of the three dimensions. Scores are assigned to each scale from $+3$ to -3; scores are summed across scales of each type to arrive at evaluation, potency, and activity scores. In the example shown, scores on each dimension could range from -6 (bad, weak, and inactive) to $+6$ (good, strong, and active).

One advantage of this technique is that the researchers can compare an individual's attitudes on three dimensions, allowing more complex differentiation among persons. Another advantage is that it can be used with any object, from a specific person to an entire nation. Its disadvantages include the fact that it often requires more time to administer and to score.

Indirect Methods

All of the methods discussed so far involve asking direct questions. They assume that people will honestly report their attitudes toward the object of interest. But is this assumption valid? Some persons might be uneasy if they were asked questions about their sexual attitudes—or consider the problems of an interviewer asking whites to report their attitudes toward blacks (or vice versa).

Many people with strong prejudices toward other racial or ethnic groups might be unwilling to express those attitudes to a stranger, the interviewer. Furthermore, these methods assume every member of the sample has an attitude; some may not, and yet they may answer direct questions as if they did. If either of these assumptions is false, direct methods will yield erroneous results.

In order to avoid such error, we can measure attitudes indirectly by observing overt behavior. Several researchers have obtained behavioral measures from representative samples.

Suppose your phone rang about 9:00 PM and the caller said: "Hello . . . Ralph's Garage? This is George Williams . . . listen, I'm stuck out here on the parkway . . . and I'm wondering if you'd be able to come out here and take a look at my car?"

You would probably say: "Sorry, this isn't Ralph's Garage."

The caller replies: "This isn't Ralph's Garage! Listen, I'm terribly sorry to have disturbed you, but listen . . . I'm stuck out here on the highway . . . and that was the last change I had. I have bills in my pocket, but no more change to make another phone call . . . Now I'm really stuck out here. What am I going to do now? . . . Listen . . . do you think you could do me the favor of calling the garage and letting them know where I am? I'll give you the number . . . They know me over there."

Would you call? Would it make any difference if the caller sounded white or sounded like a Southern black? Would whether or not you called the garage reflect your attitude toward George Williams?

White persons may be especially reluctant to report prejudice toward blacks if they are asked direct questions. The Wrong Number Technique was developed to provide an indirect method of studying attitudes toward blacks. This particular technique was used to study the attitudes of persons living in Brooklyn (Gaertner and Bickman 1971). Researchers selected subjects from the telephone directory who were living in areas known to be made up almost entirely of black or white residents. They called over 500 whites and 500 blacks and recorded how many of these subjects contacted the garage (actually a confederate of the experimenter, waiting to receive calls). The results showed that whites were more likely to help other whites (65 percent) than blacks (53 percent), whereas blacks were equally likely to help both blacks and whites (63 percent).

Another behavioral indicator is the Lost Letter Technique (Milgram 1972; Schwartz and Ames 1977) in which the experimenter prepares a large number of letters, places them in stamped envelopes, and drops them individually ("lost") in areas of considerable pedestrian traffic. He addresses the letters to organizations with known positions on major issues, such as the National Audubon Society or the National Organization for Women. The experimenter can vary the organization; for example, he can address one-half of the letters to the National Abortion Rights League and the other half to Parents Opposed to Abortion. Or, he can address all letters to the same organization, and vary the neighborhood or city where they are dropped. The behavioral measure is the percentage of letters returned (the letters are addressed to a Post Office Box controlled by the researcher). Mailing a lost letter to an organization presumably indicates a favorable attitude toward that organization. Variation in the return rate is assumed to reflect variation in the attitudes of a particular neighborhood, campus, or other area where the letters were "lost."

A third indirect technique involves littering. As you walk across campus, you are often given a leaflet about a candidate for campus or political office. If it happens to be a candidate you support, you will probably read and perhaps keep the flier. But if you dislike the candidate, you will probably get rid of the flier quickly, perhaps by simply dropping it on the ground. In one study, handbills were placed on windshields of parked cars. As the drivers returned, observers noted whether they kept the flier or dropped it. As each car left the lot, the interviewer measured the driver's attitude by asking direct questions. Results showed there was a strong relationship between dislike of the candidate and littering (Cialdini and Bauman 1981).

Because these indirect methods have not been widely used it is difficult to compare them with direct procedures. There is evidence, however, that indirect procedures are less reliable and less valid than the direct ones (Lemon 1973). In addition, direct techniques are more sensitive to the differences in attitudes between individuals (Petty and Caccioppo 1981). Finally, the available evidence suggests that people do respond honestly to direct questions, even when the questions involve very sensitive topics (DeLamater and McKinney 1982). Unobtrusive methods, such as determining whether "lost" letters are mailed, are a useful approach when it is impossible to ask direct questions, or when there is reason to believe that some persons do not have an attitude.

Attitude Organization and Change

Attitude Structure

Have you ever tried to change another person's attitude toward an object, such as a political candidate, or a racial group, or a behavior such as premarital sex? If you have, you probably discovered that he had a counter argument for every argument you made. He seemed to have quite a few reasons why he felt his attitude was correct. An individual's attitude toward some object usually is not an isolated psychological unit. It is embedded in a cognitive structure, linked with a variety of other attitudes. We can often find out what other cognitive elements are related to a particular attitude by asking the person why he holds that attitude. For example:

Interviewer: "Why do you think premarital sexual intercourse is bad?"

Bill: "Because sex outside of marriage is wrong; it is against the teachings of God, in the Bible."

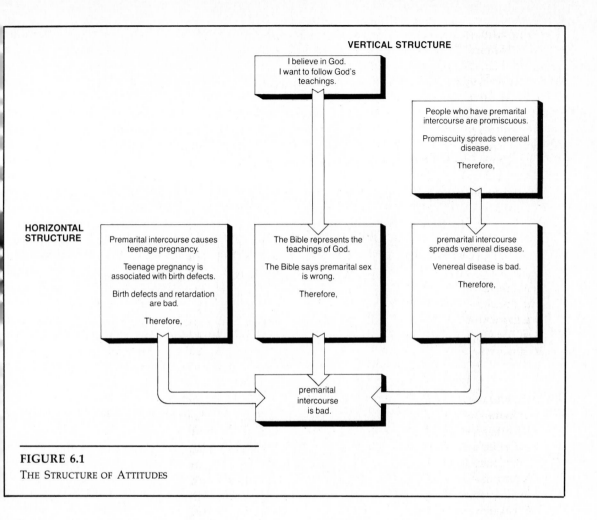

VERTICAL STRUCTURE

I believe in God.
I want to follow God's teachings.

People who have premarital intercourse are promiscuous.

Promiscuity spreads venereal disease.

Therefore,

HORIZONTAL STRUCTURE

Premarital intercourse causes teenage pregnancy.

Teenage pregnancy is associated with birth defects.

Birth defects and retardation are bad.

Therefore,

The Bible represents the teachings of God.

The Bible says premarital sex is wrong.

Therefore,

premarital intercourse spreads venereal disease.

Venereal disease is bad.

Therefore,

premarital intercourse is bad.

FIGURE 6.1
THE STRUCTURE OF ATTITUDES

Interviewer: "Are there any other reasons?"

Bill: "Well, I think people who have sex before marriage are usually promiscuous, and they spread venereal disease."

Interviewer: "Any other reasons?"

Bill: "Um . . . yeah. They may get pregnant, and teen-age pregnancy is really bad."

This exchange illustrates the two basic dimensions of attitude organization, vertical and horizontal structure (Bem 1970).

VERTICAL STRUCTURE. Bill is opposed to premarital sex because it violates his religious beliefs. This suggests that his attitude is embedded in a vertical structure, like that portrayed in the middle of Figure 6.1. His acceptance of what he perceives as the biblical view on premarital intercourse is one source of his attitude. That acceptance, in turn, is based on his belief in God. Thus, Bill's attitude toward premarital sex is not an isolated cognitive element; it is built upon other attitudes. For this reason, it is difficult to change Bill's opposition to premarital sex.

A fundamental or primitive belief, such as a belief in God, is often the basis for a large number of specific attitudes (Bem 1970). For example, Bill probably is opposed to murder, adultery, and other sins mentioned in the

Bible. Changing a fundamental belief may result in widespread changes in the person's attitudes. If Bill comes into contact with members of the Unification Church, they may attempt to persuade him that the Reverend Moon is the only legitimate religious authority. If he is converted, the resulting change in religious beliefs will lead to changed attitudes toward many objects, including family and friends.

HORIZONTAL STRUCTURE. When the interviewer asked Bill why he was opposed to sex before marriage, Bill gave two other reasons. One was his belief that people who engage in premarital sexual intercourse are promiscuous and that promiscuity spreads venereal disease. The other reason was that premarital sex leads to teen-age pregnancy and such undesirable consequences as birth defects. These belief structures are represented in the right-hand and left-hand columns of Figure 6.1. When an attitude is linked to more than one set of underlying beliefs, we describe that attitude as being part of a horizontal structure.

An attitude embedded in a horizontal structure is more difficult to change than one based on a single set of more fundamental attitudes. Even if you show Bill statistical evidence that venereal disease is not associated with premarital intercourse, his religious beliefs and his concern about teen-age pregnancy make it unlikely that this attitude will change.

Thus, attitudes are often embedded within a larger cognitive structure. A particular attitude may rest on one or more vertical structures, and may be linked to several other attitudes to form a horizontal structure. In general, attitudes embedded in such structures will be more resistant to change.

Balance Theory

THE DRIVE TOWARD CONSISTENCY. The elements of cognitive structure are called **cognitions.** A cognition is an individual's perception of his own attitudes, beliefs, and behaviors. Bill perceives himself as someone who believes in

God and follows God's teachings. These two cognitions seem to go together; we are not surprised that Bill perceives both as applying to him. Many of his attitudes are consistent with what he perceives as God's teachings; for example, he has very negative attitudes toward adultery and murder. Given his attitude toward premarital sex, we would expect Bill to abstain from intercourse until he marries, and indeed he has never engaged in that behavior. Thus, Bill's behavior is consistent with his attitudes.

Consistency between a person's cognitions—that is, a person's beliefs, attitudes, and behaviors—seems to be the norm. If you perceive yourself as having liberal political values, you probably favor medical assistance programs for the poor. If you value equal rights for all persons, you probably support school integration, and you may try hard to behave in nonsexist ways when you interact with members of the opposite sex. The observation that most people's cognitions are consistent with one another implies that individuals are motivated to maintain that consistency. Several theories of attitude organization are based on this observation. **Consistency theories** hypothesize that, should inconsistency develop between cognitive elements, people are motivated to restore harmony between elements. One example of this type is balance theory, developed by Heider (1958) and elaborated by Rosenberg and Abelson (1960).

BALANCED COGNITIVE SYSTEMS. Consider the statement "I'm going to vote for Steve Smith; he's in favor of reducing taxes." Balance theory is concerned with cognitive systems like this one. Such systems contain three elements—the speaker, P; another person (Steve Smith), O; and an impersonal object (taxes), X. Two types of relationships may exist between elements. **Sentiment relations** may be either positive (liking, endorsing) or negative (disliking, opposing), symbolized as + or −. **Unit relations** refer to the extent of perceived association between elements. A positive unit relation may result from ownership, a relationship (such as friendship or marriage), or causality. A negative relation indicates dissociation, like that between ex-spouses, or members of groups with opposing interests. A null relation exists when there is no association between elements.

With these terms in mind, we will analyze our example. We can illustrate this system as a triangle, as in Figure 6.2A. Balance theory is concerned with the elements and their interrelations from P's viewpoint. Thus, the speaker favors reduced taxes, perceives Steve Smith as favoring reduced taxes, and intends to vote for Steve. This system is balanced. A **balanced state** is one in which all three relations are positive, or in which one is positive and the

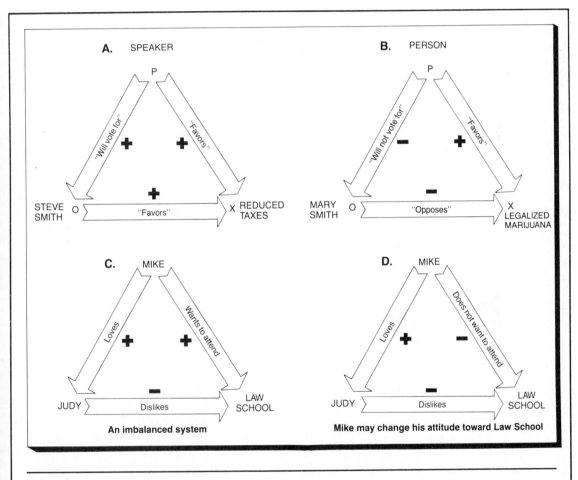

FIGURE 6.2
BALANCED COGNITIVE SYSTEMS AND RESOLUTION OF IMBALANCED SYSTEMS

When the relationships among all three cognitive elements are positive (A), or when one relationship is positive and the other two are negative (B), the cognitive system is balanced. When two relationships are positive and one negative, the cognitive system is imbalanced.

In 6.2C Judy's negative attitude toward law school creates an unpleasant psychological state for Mike. He can resolve the imbalance by deciding he does not want to go to law school (D), by deciding he does not love Judy, or by persuading Judy to like law school.

other two are negative. Consider another example: Suppose you favor legalizing possession of marijuana and candidate Mary Smith wants mandatory prison sentences for its possession. Your cognitions would be balanced if you disliked Mary Smith. This system is shown in Figure 6.2B.

IMBALANCE AND CHANGE. An **imbalanced state** is one in which two of the relationships between elements are positive and one is negative, or in which all three are negative. Consider Judy and Mike, who are seniors in college. They have been going together for three years, and are in love with each other. Mike is thinking about going to law school. Judy doesn't want him to stay in school after he gets his Bachelor's degree. She wants him to get a job so that they can get married. Figure 6.2C illustrates the situation from Mike's viewpoint. It is imbalanced; there are two positive relations and one negative one.

Balance theory assumes that an imbalanced situation like this is unpleasant. When subjects are presented hypothetical triads like those shown in Figure 6.2C and asked to rate each triad, imbalanced triads are rated as less pleasant than balanced ones (Jordan 1953; Price, Harburg, and Newcomb 1966). To restore balance, people will try to eliminate perceived imbalance among cognitions by changing one or another of their attitudes. There are three ways to do this. First, the sign of one of the relations may be reversed (Tyler and Sems 1977). Mike may decide he does not want to attend law school (Figure 6.2D). Alternatively, Mike may decide he does not love Judy, or he may persuade Judy that it is a good idea for him to go to law school. Each of these involves changing one relationship so that there are either zero or two negative relationships.

There are two other ways to restore balance. One is by changing a relation to a null relation (Steiner and Rogers 1963). Mike may decide that Judy doesn't know anything about law school, and that her attitude toward it is

irrelevant. Finally, the person may restore balance by differentiating the attributes of the other person or object (Stroebe et al. 1970). Mike may distinguish between major law schools, which require all the time and energy of their students, and less prestigious ones, which require less work. Although Judy is correct in her belief that they would have to postpone marriage if he goes to Yale Law School, Mike believes that he can go to a local school part-time and also support a wife.

Which technique will be used to remove imbalance? Balance is usually restored the easiest way possible (Rosenberg and Abelson 1960). If one relationship is weaker than the other two, the easiest mode of restoring balance is to change the weaker relationship (Feather 1967). Because Mike and Judy have been seeing each other for three years it would be very difficult for Mike to change his sentiments toward Judy. It would be easier for him to change his attitude toward law school than to get a new fiancée. However, Mike would prefer to maintain their relationship and go to law school. In this case, he may attempt to change Judy's attitude, perhaps by differentiating the object—law schools. If his influence attempt fails, Mike will probably change his own attitude toward law school.

Theory of Cognitive Dissonance

Another major consistency theory is the theory of cognitive dissonance. Whereas balance theory deals with the relationship between three cognitions, dissonance theory deals with consistency between two or more elements. There are three situations in which dissonance commonly occurs: (1) after a decision, (2) when an important belief is disconfirmed, or (3) if one acts in a way that is inconsistent with his beliefs.

POST-DECISIONAL DISSONANCE. Although Susan will begin her junior year in college next week, she will need to work part-time in order to go to school. After two weeks of searching for work, she received two offers. One was a part-time job typing for a faculty member whom she likes that payed $4 per hour with flexible working hours. The other was a job in a restaurant as a cashier that payed $6 per hour and with working hours from 5:00 P.M. to 9:00 P.M. Thursdays, Fridays, and Saturdays. Susan had a hard time choosing. Both jobs are located near campus, and she thinks she would like either one. Whereas the typing job offers flexible hours and easier work, the cashier's job pays more and offers her the opportunity to meet interesting people. Susan chose the cashier's job, and she is experiencing dissonance.

Dissonance theory (Festinger 1957) assumes that there are three possible relationships between any two cognitions. Cognitions are consistent, or *consonant,* if one naturally or logically follows from the other; they are *dissonant* when one implies the opposite of the other. The logic involved is "psycho logic" (Rosenberg and Abelson 1960)—logic as it appears to the individual, not logic in a formal sense. Two cognitive elements may also be irrelevant; one may have nothing to do with the other. In Susan's case the decision to take the cashier's position is consonant with its convenient location, the higher pay, and the opportunities to meet people, but dissonant with the fact that she'll be responsible for hundreds of dollars, and has to work weekend nights (Fig. 6.3).

Having made the choice, Susan is experiencing **cognitive dissonance,** a state of psychological tension induced by dissonant relationships between cognitive elements. The magnitude of dissonance she experiences is based on the proportion of elements that are dissonant with her decision. Because there are three consonant and only two dissonant cognitions, she will experience moderate dissonance. The magnitude is also influenced by the importance of the elements; she will experience less dissonance if it is not important that she has to work every Friday and Saturday, more dissonance if an active social life on weekends is important to her.

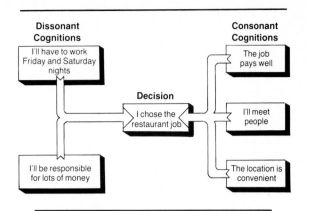

FIGURE 6.3

POST-DECISIONAL DISSONANCE

Whenever we make a decision, there are some cognitions—attitudes, beliefs, knowledge— that are consonant with that decision, and other cognitions that are dissonant with it. Dissonant cognitions create an unpleasant psychological state that we are motivated to reduce or eliminate. In this example, Susan has chosen a job and is experiencing dissonance. Although three cognitions are consistent with her decision, two other dissonant cognitions are creating psychological tension.

Dissonance is an uncomfortable state. To reduce dissonance, the theory predicts that Susan will change her attitudes. She can either change the cognitions themselves, or change the importance associated with the elements involved. It is hard to change the cognitions; she chose the restaurant job, and thereby committed herself to working weekend nights and to being responsible for large sums of money. Alternatively, Susan can change the relative importance of her cognitions. She can emphasize the importance of one (or more) of the consonant cognitions and perceive one (or more) of the dissonant cognitions as less important. Even though she has to work to earn money, she can emphasize the fact that the cashier's job pays well. Although she would prefer to be able to go out on weekends, this is less important because the cashier's job will allow her to meet people.

Box 6.2
WHEN PROPHECY FAILS

PROPHECY FROM PLANET. CLARION CALL TO CITY: FLEE THAT FLOOD. IT'LL SWAMP US ON DEC. 21, OUTER SPACE TELLS SUBURBANITE.

When this headline appeared in the *Lake City Herald* in September of 1955, it caught the attention of several social psychologists. They were interested in how people would respond to the undeniable disconfirmation of an important belief. This headline provided a perfect opportunity to find out (Festinger, Riecken, and Schachter 1956). The newspaper article tells the story of Marian Keech, who had been receiving messages from the planet Clarion predicting that, on 21 December 1955, a great flood would inundate the Western Hemisphere. Marian had attracted a small group of followers. Members of the research team (assuming that the flood would *not* come), joined the group without revealing their professional identities. They tried not to influence the group, but kept careful records of what happened in the three months before and the period after 21 December 1955.

Mrs. Keech continued to receive messages about the flood and about how the faithful could save themselves. The messages promised that a flying saucer would land shortly before the flood to take the faithful to other planets. Eight persons were heavily committed to the belief that the flood would occur. They made public declarations of belief, quit their jobs, and broke up relationships with spouses, friends, or relatives. Seven others were less committed but equally active in the group.

On 14 December, Marian received the first of many specific instructions on how to prepare to leave. Each believer was given a "passport," a piece of blank paper, and a stamped envelope. Subsequent messages told members to remove all metal from the clothing that they would be wearing in the saucers. They were also given passwords to be used in establishing contact with the aliens coming to save them, and instructions to remove all identification from their persons. They were told that an escort would arrive at exactly

---

In a laboratory study of post-decision dissonance, undergraduate women were given a choice between two products: a toaster and a coffee maker, or a stopwatch and a radio. Subjects rated the attractiveness of each item before and after their choice. To reduce dissonance researchers predicted that the women would minimize the importance of cognitions dissonant with the decision—that is, the attractiveness of the chosen object would increase and the attractiveness of the item that was not chosen would decrease. Results verified these hypotheses (Brehm 1956).

DISCONFIRMATION OF A BELIEF. After she accepted the cashier's job, Susan realized she would need some nice clothes to wear at work.

She bought three outfits, which cost her over $200. She told her friends that she would be working on weekend evenings. Three weeks after she started work, the manager called her in and told her that business had fallen off sharply and the restaurant had to cut expenses. Accordingly, he cut back her hours from 12 hours to 6 hours. Susan was very upset. The belief that she would work three nights per week was one basis for her initial decision. That was the reason why she would earn more working in the restaurant. She had also bought three outfits believing she would be working three nights a week.

This illustrates a second situation that may produce dissonance: the disconfirmation of a belief. Four conditions must exist in order for

midnight on 20 December to take them to the flying saucers. Twenty-three persons gathered at Mrs. Keech's home on the evening of 20 December. Midnight came and went. At 12:05 A.M., a message informed the group that there had been a short delay. Irrelevant messages and wandering conversations consumed the next three hours. From 3:00 A.M. to 4:30 A.M. the group tried without success to account for the apparent disconfirmation of their belief. At 4:45 A.M. they received a "Christmas message" informing them that because of their commitment and faithfulness, the earth had been spared.

In the days following the apparent disconfirmation, the behavior of group members changed radically. During the three months prior to 21 December, members had been cold and hostile toward the press, avoiding publicity. Now they called media representatives, made tape recordings for radio broadcast, and wrote press releases. Before the predicted cataclysm, members had sought secrecy and anonymity; now they freely gave information to local citizens about their beliefs and activities. Prior to 21 December, they had not actively recruited new members; now they welcomed visitors, and encouraged them to join. How can we account for this sudden about-face?

The researchers assumed that failure of the rescue and flood to occur produced dissonance. The most committed members had all taken important actions, such as quitting their jobs, based on a belief that had been disconfirmed. The group's members were motivated to reduce this dissonance. Members could not reduce dissonance by denying that they believed the flood would come, nor could they claim the flood occurred. Moreover, they could not deny that they took action such as quitting jobs and ending relationships. They could decide that their belief was mistaken, but that would arouse dissonance with other cognitions such as the belief that they were intelligent people. Alternatively, they could reduce dissonance by persuading themselves that they were right all along, and that their faithfulness had saved the world. Furthermore, if they could convince others to adopt their views, this would affirm their sense that those views were correct. "If more and more people can be persuaded that the system of belief is correct, then clearly it must, after all, be correct" (Festinger et al. 1956). Finally, in order to convince others, they had to seek publicity and make efforts to recruit new members.

disconfirmation to produce dissonance (Petty and Cacioppo 1981). First, the belief must be firmly held. Susan was certain she would be working Thursday, Friday, and Saturday. Second, the person must be committed to the belief; she must have taken action based on it. In this case, Susan chose a job and spent about $200 on clothes. Third, the belief must be specific enough so that events can disconfirm it. Finally, the disconfirmation must occur, and the person must perceive it. The perception that one took action based on the belief is dissonant with the cognition that the belief was disconfirmed.

Three modes of resolving dissonance are common in this situation. First, Susan could quit her job as a cashier. This action would

remove the discrepancy between her acts and her present cognitions that the job involves six hours per week. This mode of resolution is most likely to be employed if the costs of maintaining the original decision are high (Frey 1982). Second, she could change her assessment of how much money she needs to earn; she could decide that working six hours per week will provide her with enough income after all. This changes one of the cognitions that is dissonant with her act. Third, she can become a more committed believer. She may believe that the reduction is temporary, that business will pick up when the weather gets cold, and that the manager will ask her to work Thursday nights as well. This mode is likely only when there is support from others who share this belief (Festinger, Rieck-en, and Schachter 1956). The fact that others made the same choice or share the same belief provides information consonant with one's own choice/belief (Stroebe and Diehl 1981). For example, if Susan spends time with other employees who have been adversely affected by the decline in business, they may support each other in the belief that it is temporary. Her friends and family are more likely to encourage her to use the first or second mode.

COUNTERATTITUDINAL BEHAVIOR. Another way to produce dissonance is to behave in a way that is inconsistent with our attitudes. Such situations may involve forced compliance—pressures on a person to comply with a request to engage in counterattitudinal behavior.

Imagine that you have volunteered to serve in a psychology experiment. You arrive at the lab and are told you are participating in a study of performance. You are given a peg board and told to carefully turn each peg exactly one quarter turn. After you have turned the last peg you are told to start over, to turn each peg another one quarter turn. Later you are told to carefully remove each peg from a peg board, and then to put each peg back. After an hour of such activity, the experimenter indicates that you are finished. The experimenter says, "We are comparing the performance of subjects who are briefed in advance with that of others who are not briefed. You did not receive a briefing. The next subject is supposed to be briefed, but my assistant who usually does this couldn't come to work today." He asks you to help out by telling a waiting subject that the tasks you have just completed were fun and exciting. For your help, he offers you either $1 or $20.

In effect, you are being asked to lie, to say that the boring and monotonous tasks you performed are enjoyable. If you tell the next subject the tasks are fun, your behavior is dissonant with your cognitions that they are boring. In addition, lying to the next subject is dissonant with your belief that you are moral or honest. To reduce dissonance, you can change one of the cognitions. However, you can't change your awareness of what you told the next subject. Therefore, the theory predicts that you will change your attitude toward the task, that you will like it more.

These predictions were tested in a classic experiment by Festinger and Carlsmith (1959). Most of the subjects agreed to brief the next subject. They told him that the tasks were interesting and that they had fun doing them. A secretary then asked each subject to rate the experiment and the task. These ratings provide the measures of the dependent variable. As expected, control subjects who did not brief anyone and were not offered money rated the tasks as very unenjoyable, and did not want to participate in the experiment again.

What about the experimental subjects who lied and had been offered money? For those offered $20, the money provides justification for engaging in counterattitudinal behavior. Therefore, these subjects should also rate the task as unenjoyable and be unwilling to participate again. In the $1 condition, subjects did not have the additional justification provided by being paid $20. Consequently, they should experience dissonance. Because they cannot deny that they lied, they are likely to reduce dissonance by changing their attitude, and increasing their liking for the task and the experiment. Results of the study confirmed these predictions. Subjects in the $20 condition rated the task negatively, whereas those in the $1 condition rated the task and experiment positively.

These results reflect the **dissonance effect:** the greater the reward or incentive for engaging in counterattitudinal behavior, the less the resulting attitude change. The obvious alternative is the **incentive effect:** the greater the incentive for engaging in counterattitudinal behavior, the greater the resulting attitude change.

Under what conditions does each occur? Research suggests that the dissonance effect is more likely when subjects choose (or have the

People use various strategies for handling the dissonance aroused by messages that are inconsistent with their behavior. Faced with these two ads, nonsmokers resolve the inconsistencies by emphasizing the importance of health and denying that smoking leads to fun; smokers resolve the inconsistencies by emphasizing fun and denying their risk of cancer.

illusion of choosing) whether or not to engage in the behavior. In one study (Sherman 1970), subjects were asked to write essays taking a position on current issues that contradicted their own attitudes. They were paid either 50 cents or $2.50 for the essay. In one condition, subjects were allowed to choose whether or not to write the essay; as a result, they experienced the dissonance effect. In the second condition, students were offered no choice. As a result, subjects who received $2.50 wrote longer and more persuasive essays and showed greater attitude change, demonstrating the incentive effect.

Another factor in counterattitudinal behavior is the relative amount of justification for the act (Gerard, Conolley, and Wilhelmy 1974). There are justifications both in favor of and against performing an act. The difference between these is called the *resultant justification*. When the resultant justification is low, a greater attitude change is necessary to reduce dissonance. But as resultant justification increases, attitude change becomes less likely (the dissonance effect). On the other hand, if the resultant justification increases beyond the sufficient amount, attitude change again becomes likely (the incentive effect). These relationships are shown in Figure 6.4. If we apply this to the Festinger and Carlsmith study, we find that subjects who had low justification for lying (those in the $1 condition) had to change their attitude to increase justification, whereas for those in the $20 con-

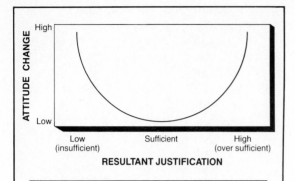

FIGURE 6.4

THE RELATIONSHIP BETWEEN JUSTIFICATION OF COUNTERATTITUDINAL BEHAVIOR AND ATTITUDE CHANGE

When we behave in a way that violates our attitudes, we will have justifications both supporting and opposing our behavior. If we subtract the latter from the former we get the resultant justification. When resultant justification is low, we experience a greater change in attitude in order to reduce the dissonance. At moderate levels of justification, we experience no change in attitude. But as resultant justification increases, attitude change becomes more likely. Thus, the left half of the U-shaped curve represents the dissonance effect; increasing incentive/justification is associated with reduced change. The right half represents the incentive effect; increasing incentive/justification is associated with increasing change.
Source: adapted from Gerard, Conolley, and Wilhelmy (1974).

dition, the money provided adequate justification, making an attitude change unnecessary.

Thus, dissonance does not always occur (Wicklund and Brehm 1976). In order for the individual to experience dissonance, the person must be committed to a belief or course of action (Brehm and Cohen 1962). In addition, the person must believe she chose to act or acted voluntarily, and is thus responsible for the outcome of her decision (Linder, Cooper, and Jones 1967). Consider Susan's position, the student who chose the cashier's job. If the owner of the restaurant were Susan's father and he demanded she work for him, she would

have had little or no post-decision dissonance. Moreover, in instances where an act is dissonant with the individual's cognitions, the person may not experience dissonance (Calder, Ross, and Insko 1973).

Also, dissonance does not always lead to attitude change. Instead it may be reduced by engaging in behavior that ameliorates the psychological tension. In a recent study it was found that consumption of beer and its effects helped to eliminate dissonance (Steele, Southwick, and Critchlow 1981).

Is Consistency Inevitable?

If our beliefs and behavior were always consistent, all of our cognitions would be in harmony. Obviously, that is not the case. Practically every adult in the United States knows that cigarette smoking is related to lung cancer, yet millions continue to smoke. Most of us overindulge in a favorite food (pizza, chocolate) or beverage (Mountain Dew, beer) at least occasionally, even though we know it is not healthy to do so. When we do, our behavior is inconsistent with the belief that overindulgence is unhealthy. How is it that people can hold mutually inconsistent cognitions?

For one thing, many of our cognitions never come into contact with each other; we may never become aware that our contradictory cognitions are in fact related. Thus, many people who have a very positive attitude toward nature flock to Yosemite National Park and are unaware that their behavior is overtaxing the park. One reason that this happens is because much of our behavior is mindless. Because we don't think about our actions, we are unaware that they are inconsistent with our beliefs (Triandis 1980). The cigarette smoker often lights up without consciously thinking about the act. Sometimes he is surprised to find a lit cigarette in the ashtray, reflecting his lack of awareness of the act of smoking. Thus, the relationship between the act and one's knowledge is often not salient to the person.

Another reason why inconsistency occurs is that each belief, attitude, or self-perception is embedded in a larger structure of consistent, related attitudes, beliefs, and self-perceptions. For example, Bill's attitude toward premarital sexual intercourse discussed earlier was embedded in a structure of other attitudes and values. Although two attitudes may be inconsistent, each may be related to several other consonant attitudes. To change one or the other would create new inconsistencies. In effect, people tolerate some inconsistencies in order to avoid others.

An interesting example involves members of a black community in a midwestern city. Many blacks have been active in local politics, consistently supporting equal opportunity legislation, nondiscrimination in employment and housing, and equal treatment of blacks by police and other community agents. These cognitions share a high degree of consistency. Many of these people belong to the same Methodist church. Some of the most prominent are church deacons and consistently support its activities. But this church has a strict theological prohibition against women preachers that denies female members access to the pulpit. So far church deacons have turned down the requests of three women for nondiscriminatory treatment. Although this behavior is dissonant with their commitment to equal opportunity, the deacons tolerate this dissonance, because they are not prepared to revise many religious beliefs and practices in order to remove the inconsistency.

At the other end of the scale are isolated cognitive units called **opinion molecules** (Abelson 1968). Each opinion molecule consists of a fact or an item of information, a feeling or emotion, and a "following"—that is, a sense that other people hold the same opinion. For example, "Premarital sex causes teenage pregnancy. I think young people today are too promiscuous, and so do a lot of my friends." Because opinion molecules are isolated, we are rarely aware that they are inconsistent with other cognitive elements. They are

also usually immune to argument. They provide the individual with something to think and say about the topic, and may be routinely injected into the conversation when the opportunity arises.

In sum, we prefer consistency among our cognitions. Should inconsistencies arise, we are motivated to change our attitudes or behavior in order to restore harmony. Not all of our cognitions are consistent, however. Inconsistency persists for a variety of reasons, either because we may not be aware of imbalance or dissonance, because restoring consistency between some cognitions would create other inconsistencies, or because some cognitive elements are isolated opinion molecules.

The Relationship Between Attitudes and Behavior

Do Attitudes Predict Behavior?

We have just seen how behavior can affect our attitudes, and how people sometimes change their attitudes when their behavior appears to contradict them. However, most people think of attitudes as the source of behavior. For example, we often assume that when we know a person's attitude toward an object (another person, volleyball, or Woody Allen movies), we can predict how that person will behave toward that object. If you know someone enjoys volleyball, you would expect her to accept your invitation to play volleyball with friends. When we are able to predict another person's responses, we can decide how to behave toward that person in order to achieve our own goals. But can we predict someone's behavior if we know their attitudes?

In 1930, the social scientist Richard LaPiere traveled around the United States by car with a Chinese couple. At that time, there was considerable prejudice against the Chinese, particularly in the western part of the country. The three travelers stopped at more than 60 hotels, auto camps, and tourist homes, and more than 180 restaurants. They kept careful notes about how they were treated. In only one place were they denied service. Later, LaPiere sent a questionnaire to each place asking whether they would accept Chinese guests. He received responses from 128 establishments; 92 percent of them indicated that they would *not* serve Chinese guests (LaPiere 1934).

Most studies have found only a modest correlation between attitude and behavior (Wicker 1969). The correlation (*r*) is a measure of the relationship between two variables and may range from −1.00 to +1.00. If the correlation is zero, there is no relationship. If one variable increases as the other gets bigger, the correlation is positive. For example, height and weight are positively correlated. A survey of 33 studies of attitudes and behavior found the average correlation between these two variables to be +.30 or less. This suggests that we need to define and measure attitudes and behavior more carefully, and that our behavior is influenced by variables other than attitudes. Subsequent work suggests that four variables influence the relationship between attitudes and behavior: (1) the correspondence between attitude and behavior; (2) the characteristics of the attitude; (3) the activation of the attitude; and (4) situational constraints on behavior. Each of these variables is considered below.

Correspondence

Attitudes are more likely to predict behavior when the two are at the same level of specificity (Schuman and Johnson 1976). For example, suppose you have invited a casual acquaintance to dinner and you want to plan the menu. You know that she is Italian, so she probably likes Italian food. But can you predict with confidence that she will eat green noodles with red clam sauce? Probably not. A favorable attitude toward a type of cuisine does not necessarily mean that the person will eat every dish of that type. Yet many studies

have attempted to predict from the general attitudes of people toward blacks specific behaviors such as willingness to have one's photograph taken with particular blacks in particular settings (Green 1972). Not surprisingly, the relationship between attitude and behavior was weak.

A general attitude is a summary of many feelings about an object under a variety of conditions, or about a whole class of objects. Logically, it should not necessarily predict behavior in any particular single situation. On the other hand, it might predict a composite measure of a number of relevant behaviors. For example, even though someone might object to being photographed with a black in a way that implies that they were on a date, he might engage in other problack behaviors.

Can we predict whether people will engage in various environmentally oriented behaviors if we know their attitudes toward environmental quality? To answer this question, researchers distributed a questionnaire, including a 16-item Likert scale, to measure attitudes toward conservation and pollution. Between three and eight months later, they contacted subjects three times and asked them to participate in various environmental projects. The projects included signing and circulating copies of three petitions, participating in a litter pick-up program and recruiting a friend to do so, and participating for up to eight weeks in a recycling program. The results are shown in Table 6.1. The first column of numbers displays the relationship between the general attitude measure and individual behaviors. These correlations range from .12 to .57; 7 of the 14 correlations are about .30, the magnitude noted by Wicker (1969). When the researchers combined the 14 individual behavioral measures into 3 categories, the attitude-behavior correlations improved somewhat (middle column). When they created a composite "behavioral index" and correlated this with the general attitude measure, the relationship increased. Thus,

TABLE 6.1

CORRELATION BETWEEN SUBJECTS' ENVIRONMENTAL ATTITUDES AND BEHAVIORAL CRITERIA

Single Behaviors	r	Categories of Behavior	r	Behavioral Index	r
Offshore oil	.41	Petitioning behavior scale (0–4)	.50	Comprehensive behavioral index	.62
Nuclear power	.36				
Auto exhaust	.39				
Circulate petitions	.27				
Individual participation	.34	Litter pick-up scale (0–2)	.36		
Recruit friend	.22				
Week 1	.34	Recycling behavior scale (0–8)	.39		
Week 2	.57				
Week 3	.34				
Week 4	.33				
Week 5	.12				
Week 6	.20				
Week 7	.20				
Week 8	.34				

Note: $N = 44$.

r = correlation.

Source: adapted from Weigel and Newman 1976.

general attitudes can predict a general measure of relevant behaviors (Weigel and Newman 1976).

What about predicting a specific behavior, such as whether your Italian guest will eat green noodles and red clam sauce? Just as general attitudes best predict a composite index of behavior, we need a specific measure of attitude to predict a specific behavior. We can think of each as having four elements: an action (eating), target (green noodles and red clam sauce), context (in your home), and time (tomorrow night). The greater the degree of *correspondence*—that is, the number of elements that are the same in the two measures—the better we can predict behavior from attitudes (Ajzen and Fishbein 1977).

A study of birth control use by 244 women (Davidson and Jaccard 1979) demonstrates that attitudinal measures which exhibit correspondence with the behavioral measure are better predictors of behavior. In this study, the behavior of interest was whether women used birth control pills during a particular two-year period. Attitude was measured in four ways. The measure of the women's general attitude toward birth control had only one element in common with the behavior (target); the correlation between this attitude measure and behavior was a modest .323, as shown in Figure 6.5. When the attitude measure had two elements in common with the behavior (target and action), the correlation rose to .525. Finally, an attitude measure that included three elements (target, action, and time)—"Do you plan to use birth control pills in the next two years?"—was most highly correlated with the behavioral measure.

Earlier in this chapter we mentioned that most establishments in LaPiere's study which served the Chinese couple later said they would not. The lack of a relationship between

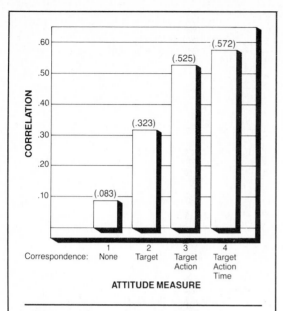

FIGURE 6.5

CORRELATIONS OF ATTITUDE MEASURES THAT
VARY IN CORRESPONDENCE WITH BEHAVIOR

Every behavior involves a target, action, context, and time. In order to predict behavior from attitude, the measures of attitude and behavior should correspond—that is, involve the same elements. The larger the number of elements in common, the greater the correlation between attitude and behavior. Researchers obtained four measures of attitudes toward birth control from 244 women: (1) general attitude toward birth control; (2) attitude toward birth control pills; (3) attitude toward using pills; and (4) attitude toward using pills in the next two years. The behavioral measure was actual use of pills during the two-year period. Note that as correspondence increased from zero to three elements, the correlation between attitude and behavior also increased.

Source: adapted from Davidson and Jaccard (1979).

asked whether Chinese guests would be served. Thus, there was correspondence between the measures on only one element—the action—which may account for the discrepancy LaPiere found between attitude and behavior.

Characteristics of the Attitude

The relationship between attitude and behavior is also affected by the nature of the attitude. Three characteristics of attitudes that may influence the relationship are (1) whether the attitude is grounded in experience, (2) the certainty with which the person holds it, and (3) whether it is stable over time.

DIRECT EXPERIENCE. If you have a positive attitude toward tennis based on having played the game, and your roommate has a positive attitude based on hearing you rave about it, which of you is more likely to accept an invitation to play? One study (Regan and Fazio 1977) provides an answer to this question. The behavior of interest was the proportion of time spent playing with several kinds of puzzles. Subjects in the direct experience condition played with sample puzzles, while those in the indirect experience condition were given only descriptions of the puzzles. Researchers then asked subjects to complete attitude measures, and subsequently gave them an opportunity to play with the puzzles. They discovered that the average correlation between attitude and behavior was much higher for subjects who had direct experience.

There are several reasons why attitudes based on direct experience are more predictive of subsequent behavior (Fazio and Zanna 1981). The best predictor of behavior is past behavior; the more frequently you have played tennis in the past, the more likely you are to play in the future (Fredricks and Dossett 1983). An attitude is a summary of a person's past experience; thus, one grounded in direct experience predicts future behavior more accurately. In addition, direct experience makes more information available about the object itself (Kelman 1974). This makes the

attitude and behavior in LaPiere's study may be due to lack of correspondence. The behavioral measure was whether a particular Oriental couple (target) was served (action) in a particular restaurant or hotel (context) on a particular day (time). However, LaPiere's questionnaire measuring attitude simply

This clinic has been the scene of demonstrations both for and against abortions. Although most Americans have attitudes about abortion, only a minority act on their beliefs. People who are more certain of their attitudes, whether pro or con, are more likely to engage in such behavior.

attitude more accessible and more likely to influence behavior.

CERTAINTY. Suppose you ask two friends which candidate they like in the upcoming presidential election. One replies, "I'm voting for X," and the other says, "Well, maybe I'll vote for Y." Which person's behavior do you think you could predict? In general, the more certain the person is of his attitude the more likely it is to influence behavior. Studies of voting behavior find that many of the errors in predictions occur among those who report indifference to the election—that is, people who have weak or uncertain attitudes (Schuman and Johnson 1976). In one study, researchers measured people's attitudes before an upcoming election. Subjects completed a 15-item Likert scale, and also indicated how certain they were of each response (Sample and Warland 1973). For each subject, two mea-

sures were constructed, one of attitude and one of certainty. The 243 subjects were divided into high and low certainty groups. Researchers noted how subjects voted in the election, 15 days after completing the questionnaire. Among subjects who were more certain of their attitudinal responses, the attitude-behavior correlation was .47, whereas among those who were less certain the correlation was .06. The average for all subjects was the usual .29.

The certainty with which an attitude is held depends partly on whether it is based on direct experience. Attitudes based on direct experience with the object, as opposed to information obtained from others, may be held with greater certainty. The person who has direct experience has more information about the object, and thus a more clearly defined attitude. The attitude may also be more resistant to change (Fazio and Zanna 1981).

TEMPORAL STABILITY. Most studies attempting to predict behavior from attitudes measure people's attitude first and their behavior weeks or months later. A modest or small correlation may mean there is little relationship. Or it could mean that people's attitudes may have changed in the interim period. If the attitude changes after it is measured, the person's behavior may be consistent with his attitude at the time, even though it appears inconsistent with our measure of his attitude. Thus, in order to predict behavior from attitudes, the attitudes must be stable over time.

In general, we would expect that the longer the period between measurement of attitude and of behavior, the more likely the attitude will change, and the smaller the attitude-behavior relationship. In a study designed to test this possibility (Schwartz 1978) an appeal was mailed to almost 300 students to volunteer as tutors for blind children. Earlier, students had filled out a questionnaire measuring general attitudes toward helping as well as questions about tutoring blind children. Some students had filled out the questionnaire six months before, some three months before, and some both three and six months earlier; still others had not seen the questionnaire. The correlation between attitude toward tutoring and actually volunteering was greater over the three-month period than over six months. Thus, to avoid problems of temporal instability, the amount of time between the measurement of attitudes and of behavior should be brief.

In addition, this study found that the correlation between specific attitude and behavior was greater when the general attitude toward altruism was stable over time than if the general attitude was unstable. This suggests that we can predict behavior more accurately in areas where people have well organized and strongly held general attitudes.

Thus, characteristics of attitudes influence the degree to which we can predict behavior. Our ability to predict will be greater if the attitude is based on direct experience with the object, if it is held with certainty, and if it is stable over time.

Activation of the Attitude

Each of us has thousands of attitudes. Most of the time a particular attitude is not within our conscious awareness. In order for an attitude to influence behavior, it must be **activated,** that is, brought from memory into conscious awareness (Zanna and Fazio 1982).

An attitude is usually activated by exposure of the person to the object, particularly if the attitude was originally formed through direct experience with the object (Fazio, Powell, and Herr 1983). Earlier sections of this chapter may have activated your attitudes toward many objects, such as Woody Allen's films, premarital sexual activity, birth control, Italian food, and tennis. If you are reading this book at home and look at the television set, attitudes toward various programs may be activated. Thus, one way to activate attitudes is to arrange situations in which relevant objects are present. Soft lighting, a fire in the fireplace, and glasses of wine are all associated with seduction; we often set up these cues in the hope of eliciting our partner's positive attitudes toward romantic and sexual activity.

Once activated, the person needs to decide what those attitudes imply, and use this to guide his behavior. There appear to be systematic differences in the extent to which people use information about their internal states to guide behavior in *self-monitoring* (Snyder 1979). In any setting, people are motivated to behave appropriately. Some rely on situational cues; they are referred to as being high in self-monitoring. Others rely on information about their inner states, including attitudes; these people are low in self-monitoring. Persons who rely on internal information should exhibit greater attitude-behavior consistency than those who utilize situational cues. Experimental data support this prediction (Snyder and Tanke 1976; Ajzen, Timko, and White 1982).

Another influence on the relationship between attitudes and behavior is the extent to which the individual accepts responsibility for his own behavior. Some people are very concerned about the consequences of their behavior and feel personally responsible for the outcome of their actions. Such persons are low in *responsibility denial*. Others feel that they are not responsible for the consequences of their acts; these individuals are high in responsibility denial. People low in responsibility denial are more likely to attend to their attitudes and use them as guidelines for their behavior. This prediction was tested in the study of 300 undergraduates cited earlier. The questionnaire that the students completed three and six months prior to receiving the request to tutor blind children included a measure of responsibility denial. The students were divided into three groups, those who obtained low, moderate, and high scores on responsibility denial. The correlation between attitude toward volunteering and actually doing so was substantial among those with low scores in responsibility denial, and zero among those high in responsibility denial (Schwartz and Howard 1980).

Thus, whether an attitude influences behavior depends in part on (1) whether the attitude is activated, (2) whether the person uses attitudes as guidelines for behavior, and (3) whether the person accepts responsibility for the consequences of his behavior.

Situational Constraints

If you believe that the Reverend Sun Myung Moon is the "True Father" and are attending a service of the Unification Church, your behavior will reflect your attitude. If you believe that the Unification Church, Scientology, and The Way are all dangerous cults and attend a meeting of the Citizens Freedom Foundation, a national group opposed to such cults, your behavior will be consistent with your attitude. Suppose, however, that you are opposed to cults but find yourself in a conversation with three followers of the Reverend Moon. Would you voice your opposition—that is, behave in a manner consistent with your attitudes—or tactfully end the interaction? It will probably depend partly on the strength and certainty of your attitude. If you are strongly opposed to cults, you may speak your mind. But if situational constraints prevent you from expressing your attitude, you may behave in a way that is inconsistent with your beliefs. In LaPiere's study, hotel and restaurant employees confronted by a white man and a Chinese couple may have felt compelled to serve them rather than run the risk of creating a scene by refusing to do so.

Situational constraints influence behavior based on the likelihood that other persons will learn about our behavior. Situational constraints often determine whether our behavior is consistent with our attitudes. In fact, how we behave is frequently a result of the interaction between our attitudes and constraints present in the situation (Warner and DeFleur 1969). This relationship is summarized in Figure 6.6, using attitudes toward cults as an example. A conversation between someone weakly opposed to cults and followers of the Reverend Moon (weak pressures) would be a situation of conflict for the individual, whereas someone strongly opposed to cults is more likely to voice his opposition.

Sometimes we feel constrained by the possibility of others learning of our behavior. At other times those around us exert direct social influence; they communicate specific expectations about how we should behave. When we are expected to behave in ways that are inconsistent with our attitudes, there is a weaker relationship between attitudes and behavior (Frideres 1971; Frideres, Warner, and Albrecht 1971). Consequently, the less visible our behavior is to others, the more likely it is that our behavior and attitudes will be consistent (Acock and Scott 1980).

But what if those whose opinions we value are not actually present? Several studies have assessed the impact of reference groups on the attitude-behavior relationship. Such research

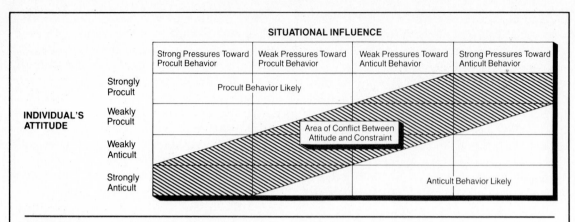

FIGURE 6.6

THE INFLUENCE OF ATTITUDE AND SITUATIONAL CONSTRAINTS ON BEHAVIOR

Our behavior is influenced not only by our attitudes, but also by situational constraints, the behavior of others, or the likelihood that others will find out what we do. When the individual has a strongly held attitude, and situational influences encourage behavior consistent with the attitude, there will be a strong relationship between attitudes and behavior. But when situational influences produce pressure to behave in ways inconsistent with one's attitude, or when the attitude is weak, behavior and attitude are less likely to be consistent.

Source: adapted from Warner and DeFleur (1969, Fig. 3).

involves measuring the subject's attitudes toward some object, and then asking him to indicate the position of various social groups with regard to that object. One study asked students to report their own personal attitudes toward marijuana, as well as the views of their friends and families toward legalization of it. Students were subsequently given an opportunity to vote in a mock election. Results showed that both attitude and the position the person believed his friends had taken were related to how the student voted (Acock and DeFleur 1972). Several other studies report similar findings (Schuman and Johnson 1976).

So far we have suggested that behavior is consistent with attitude unless there are situational constraints on behavior. However, it is possible that social pressures *always* influence how we act and that behavior is always a product of one's attitude and situational pressures (Fishbein and Ajzen 1975, 1981). According to this theory, one's behavioral intention mediates between attitude and behavior. Behavioral intention is determined by one's

attitude (A_B) and subjective norm—one's perception of social constraints (S_N). Attitude refers to positive or negative feelings about engaging in the behavior. *Subjective norm* is the individual's perception of others' beliefs about whether or not certain behavior is appropriate. We can express these relationships mathematically as follows:

Behavior = Behavioral intention
= Attitude + Subjective norm

Suppose Bill has two good friends who are followers of the Reverend Moon. They have been giving him literature and encouraging him to join the Unification Church. In order to predict what Bill will do, we need to know his attitude and his perception of how others will react to his joining this cult. Attitude is the sum of our beliefs (*b*) about the likelihood of various consequences of the act, and our evaluation (*e*), positive or negative, of each consequence:

$$A_B = \Sigma\, b\, e$$

TABLE 6.2

DETERMINING ATTITUDE (A_B) FROM BELIEFS (b) AND EVALUATIONS (e)

Consequences of Joining the Unification Church	Belief (b)	Evaluation (e)	Product ($b \times e$)
(1) Gain a sense of purpose	+3	+3	+9
(2) Have one's physical needs provided for	+3	+1	+3
(3) Loss of relationship with Cindy	+2	−2	−4
(4) Loss of some personal freedom	+1	−3	−3
		Attitude $= \Sigma b \times e = +5$	

For example, Bill has several beliefs about joining the "Moonies." If he joins, he will gain a sense of purpose to his life and his physical needs will be met. At the same time, he would have to end his relationship with Cindy. Also, he had read that ex-cult members claim that they had to relinquish their personal freedom when they joined. These beliefs and their evaluations are shown in Table 6.2. Bill is certain consequences (1) and (2) would occur; hence their value (b) is +3. His evaluation of consequence (1) is very positive (+3), whereas his evaluation of having his physical needs cared for is less positive (+1). He believes it is likely that he will have to give up Cindy (+2), which would be unpleasant (−2). He is skeptical about the claim that he will lose his freedom (+1), although he would be very upset if that occurred (−3). Bill's attitude is +5, the value of $b \times e$.

Subjective norm is the product of normative beliefs (NB)—expectations about how significant others will react—and motivation to comply (MC) with each:

$$S_N = NB \times MC$$

For Bill, the significant others are his parents, his peers, and his girlfriend, Cindy. His parents are strongly opposed to his joining a cult (−3) and he is moderately motivated to comply with their views (+2). He is equally motivated to comply with his friends' views (+2) who strongly favor his joining (+3). And he is highly motivated to comply with Cindy, who opposes his becoming a Moonie. This is summarized in Table 6.3. Thus the value of S_N is

TABLE 6.3

DETERMINING SUBJECTIVE NORM FROM NORMATIVE BELIEFS (NB) AND MOTIVATION TO COMPLY (MC)

Significant Others	NB	MC	NB × MC
Parents	−3	+2	−6
Friends	+3	+2	+6
Cindy	−2	+3	−6
			$S_N = \Sigma(NB)(MC) = -6$

the product of $NB \times MC$, or −6. Behavioral intention is simply attitude multiplied by subjective norm, or $(+5)(-6) = -30$. The model predicts that Bill will not join the Unification Church. Although his attitude toward the behavior is positive, the social pressures are negative.

This model combines several elements discussed earlier in this chapter. It has been used to predict behavior in signing up for a treatment program for alcoholics (McArdle 1972), using birth control pills (Davidson and Jaccard 1979), and smoking (Fishbein 1980). Using quantitative measures of the components of attitudes, it is possible to predict a specific behavior under specific circumstances (Bentler and Speckart 1981). The complexity of the model suggests that any behavior is the result of several influences; attitude is only one.

This model has also been the target of some criticism (Liska 1984), because it assumes that our behavior is largely determined by our intentions. In some situations, our own past behavior may be even more influential than our intentions. For example, whether one has

This Hari Krishna member is passing out literature and seeking new recruits. A person who considers joining the cult will be influenced not only by his or her attitudes, but also by subjective norms—the anticipated reaction of family and friends.

donated blood in the past is a much better predictor of whether one will donate blood in the next four months than his statement about whether he intends to do so (Bagozzi 1981). In effect, much of our behavior is habitual, and may not match our conscious intentions. In spite of our intentions, our behavior may be affected by whether or not we have a vested interest in the outcome of that behavior (Sivacek and Crano 1982). In a study of 79 adult women committed to a six-week weight loss program, the amount of weight actually lost was influenced by the importance each woman placed on physical appearance and on good health (Saltzer 1981).

Summary

THE NATURE OF ATTITUDES.   Attitudes have four characteristics. (1) Every attitude has three components: cognition, an evaluation, and a behavioral predisposition toward some object. (2) A rigid, simplistic attitude toward members of some group that is widely shared by others is called a stereotype. (3) We learn attitudes and stereotypes through reinforcement, through repeated associations of stimuli and responses, and by observing others. (4) Attitudes are useful; they may serve instrumental and knowledge functions, express a person's values, or protect a person's self-image.

THE MEASUREMENT OF ATTITUDES.   There are two types of attitude measures. (1) Direct methods involve asking a direct question and recording the answer. They include the use of single items, Likert scales, and Semantic Differential Techniques. (2) Indirect methods involve observing overt behavior. Such methods are useful when a direct question might elicit a false response. Examples include the "wrong number" and "lost letter" techniques.

ATTITUDE ORGANIZATION AND CHANGE.   An attitude is usually embedded in a larger cognitive structure and is based on one or more fundamental or primitive beliefs. Consistency theories assume that when cognitive elements are inconsistent, individuals will be motivated to change their attitudes or behavior in order to restore harmony. Balance theory assesses the relationship between three cognitive elements and suggests ways to resolve imbalance. Dissonance theory cites three situations in which inconsistency often occurs: after a choice between alternatives, when an important belief is disconfirmed, and when people engage in behavior that is inconsistent with their attitudes. The theory also cites four ways to reduce dissonance: (1) by changing one of the elements, (2) by adding consonant cognitions, (3) by changing the importance of the cognitions involved, or (4) by engaging in behavior that ameliorates psychological tension.

THE RELATIONSHIP BETWEEN ATTITUDES AND BEHAVIOR. The attitude-behavior relationship is influenced by four variables: correspondence, characteristics of the attitude, activation of the attitude, and situational constraints. (1) The relationship is stronger when the measures of attitude and behavior correspond in action, target, context, and time. (2) The relationship is also stronger if the attitude is based on direct experience, is held with certainty, and is stable over time. (3) Several factors determine whether an attitude will influence behavior including whether it is activated, whether the person uses it as a guide for behavior, and whether he accepts responsibility for the consequences of his behavior. (4) Situational constraints may facilitate or prevent the expression of attitudes in behavior. As a result, behavior is frequently the product of one's attitudes and perceptions of social norms. Researchers have identified several exceptions to this rule, however.

Key Terms and Concepts

Attitude
Stereotype
Prejudice
Discrimination
Likert Scale
Semantic Differential Scale
Cognitions
Consistency Theory
Sentiment Relations
Unit Relations
Balanced State
Imbalanced State
Cognitive Dissonance
Dissonance Effect
Incentive Effect
Opinion Molecule
Activation of an Attitude
Situational Constraint

Chapter 7
Social Influence and Persuasion

Introduction

Carol faces a problem. One year ago, shortly after graduating from college, she began work as a technical assistant in a small company. She is reasonably happy with her job—it challenges her abilities and she likes the people— but she is troubled by her low salary. The job did not pay very well at the start, and she still has received no raise. Carol realizes that under company policy she may not get a pay raise for another 12 to 18 months. Carol's boss, Martha, has the authority to grant her a higher salary immediately. Carol broached the issue in a tentative way about a week ago, but Martha did not respond favorably. Carol wonders what to do now.

Thinking the problem over, Carol realizes there are many things she could do. She could go out of her way to be nice to Martha, hoping that Martha might like her better and eventually offer her a raise. She could try to persuade Martha that she is doing more for the company than Martha realized and is therefore underpaid at her present salary. She could threaten to leave the company and find work elsewhere. Or she could ask for additional job responsibilities that would justify a salary increase.

Which of these techniques, if any, should Carol use? She wants a raise, and these influence techniques may help her accomplish that goal. Which will be effective and which will not?

Techniques of Social Influence

To obtain a raise, Carol will have to exert social influence. By definition, **social influence** occurs when one person's behavior causes another person to change an opinion or to perform an action that he or she would not otherwise do. Thus, in social influence, one person (the **source**) intentionally engages in some behavior (persuasion, threats, promises) that causes another person (the **target**) to behave in a manner that is different from what he or she would ordinarily do. In our example,

Carol (the source) is contemplating various techniques she might use to influence Martha (the target) to give her a pay raise. Influence, then, is a causal relationship between the source's behavior and the target's response (Tedeschi, Bonoma, and Schlenker 1972; Gamson 1968).

There are many forms of social influence. Influence attempts may be either open or manipulative (Tedeschi, Schlenker, and Lindskold 1972). Open influence attempts are based on techniques that are apparent to the target— that is, when the target understands that someone is attempting to change his or her attitudes or behavior. Manipulative influence attempts are hidden from the target. Ingratiation and tactical self-presentation are examples of manipulative influence. In this chapter, we will focus on open influence; we will take up manipulative influence in Chapter 9.

There are three basic techniques of open influence—persuasion, threats, and promises. In persuasion, the source uses information and argument to change the target's beliefs and attitudes about a situation. For example, a business executive might try to persuade an oil-drilling contractor by saying, "Why don't you change plans and try to finish drilling the Ewing #3 Well as soon as possible? Otherwise, we will have to wait a long time before getting approval to connect it to a pipeline and we may end up losing money." The executive is trying to change the way the contractor views the situation by presenting special facts.

When using promises and threats, the source does not rely on information and argument. Instead, he manipulates the rewards and punishments available to the target. For example, the business executive might promise the oil-drilling contractor: "If you complete the Ewing #3 Well 30 days ahead of schedule, I'll give you a 5 percent bonus." Alternatively, the executive might threaten: "If you don't complete the well on schedule, I'll deduct 1 percent of your salary for every day that you are late." In making these statements, the source (executive) introduces rewards (5 percent bonus) or punishments (1 percent penalty) into the situation. He does not try to convince the target to view the situation differently. Instead, he changes the situation itself by adding rewards or imposing punishments contingent on the target's performance.

Influence attempts are either successful or unsuccessful. In fact, our everyday attempts at persuasion probably fail more often than they succeed. Even threats and promises do not always achieve their intended effect. Because we all engage in, and are exposed to, influence attempts, we need to understand the conditions under which they prove effective. We will devote the remainder of this chapter to a discussion of open influence and the effectiveness of various influence attempts. Specifically, the following issues are considered:

1. What factors determine whether a persuasive communication will be effective in changing a target's beliefs and attitudes?

2. To what extent are persuasive communications transmitted by the mass media effective in changing the beliefs and attitudes of large numbers of people?

3. Under what conditions do threats and promises prove successful in gaining compliance?

4. What processes are involved in bargaining when two persons have the capacity to reward one another? What tactics can be used in bargaining to secure superior outcomes?

5. What processes are involved in bilateral conflict when two persons have the capacity to punish one another? Under what conditions will the use of threats increase compliance, rather than increase conflict?

Communication and Persuasion

Effectiveness of Persuasion

Day in and day out we are bombarded with persuasive messages. As an example, consider what happens to Steve Maxwell on a typical day. First thing in the morning, Steve's clock radio comes on. Before he can even get out of bed the cheerful voice of the announcer is trying to sell him a new mouthwash. Riding the bus on his way to work, he notices campaign posters on several billboards. A local election is in progress and the candidates are trying to get his vote. At lunch, a friend describes plans to attend a concert the following weekend, and urges him to come along. Later in the day, he listens to an argument from a co-worker who wants to change some of the paperwork procedures in the office. At 5:30 that afternoon, he stops in a store to look for a new pair of shoes. The clerk recommends one type over another, and encourages him to try them on. When he arrives home, Steve opens his mail. One letter is a carefully worded appeal from a charitable organization asking him to volunteer his time. Later that evening, when Steve is watching television, advertisers bombard him with ads for laundry soap, beer, shampoo, and new cars, trying their best to separate him from his money.

All of these communications have something in common. In each and every case, the message seeks to persuade. **Persuasion** may be defined as an effort (by a source) to change the beliefs or attitudes of a target person through the use of information or argument.

Although some attempts at persuasion succeed, many do not. Most persons hearing the morning advertisement on the radio will not purchase the new mouthwash, and probably the majority of those seeing the political billboard will not even vote in the election. In fact, it is remarkable that persuasive communications are effective at all. Instead of changing attitude, the target can respond in a wide variety of ways.

For instance, the target could simply ignore the message. Rather than heed the automobile advertisement or the beer commercial, the television viewer can switch channels. Likewise, in face-to-face interaction, the target can disregard what the source is saying by switching to a different topic of conversation.

Another possible response to a persuasive communication is to suspend judgment. The target might listen to the message but decide to seek additional information before concluding that one viewpoint or another is correct. In this case, the persuasive communication will not lead to immediate attitude change, and may eventually be discarded.

Still another response to a persuasive communication is to derogate the communicator. That is, the target may dismiss the communicator as poorly informed, illogical, or even stupid. ("That politician is still advocating the same ridiculous policy that he supported four years ago. He's no smarter today than he was then.")

The target could also respond by engaging in counter-persuasion. If a TV announcer is trying to sell a case of Miller beer, there is no easy way to argue that Budweiser is better. But in face-to-face interaction the target could certainly attempt to change the source's attitude. ("I don't understand why you think Miller's is good. It tastes awful! Here, try a Bud.")

Thus, there are many ways to respond to a persuasive communication. A change in the target's beliefs and attitudes will occur only occasionally. This leads to a fundamental question: Under what conditions will a persuasive message succeed in changing the target's beliefs or attitudes? For the influencing agent, this is perhaps the most important issue.

Whether a message produces attitude change depends on many factors. These can be organized in terms of the question, "Who says what to whom by what means with what effect?" In other words, the effectiveness of a message depends on who sends it (the communicator or source), what is said (the message content), who receives it (the target audience), and the medium (channel) by which the message is sent. These factors are outlined below:

1. *The communicator*   The expertise, likeableness, and trustworthiness of the person making the influence attempt

2. *The message*   The content and structure of the communication itself

3. *The target audience*   The personality, prior beliefs, and commitments of the persons the persuasive attempt it directed toward

4. *The channel*   The medium used to transmit the message (such as the mass media or face-to-face interaction).

We will now look at how each factor determines efficacy of persuasive communication.

The Communicator

Suppose we ask 25 persons to read a persuasive communication (such as a newspaper editorial) advocating a position on a nutrition-related topic. We tell this group that the message is written by a Nobel Prize-winning biologist. Suppose we ask another 25 persons to read the same message, but we tell them it was written by a cook at a local fast-food establishment. Then we ask both groups to indicate their attitude toward the position advocated in the message. The question is: Which group of persons will be more persuaded by the communication?

Assuming that we assembled the groups at random, the only difference between them is that they ascribe the message to a different source. Thus, any difference in their reaction to the message must be due to the identity of the source. Most likely, the persons who received the message from the prize-winning biologist will be more persuaded than those receiving it from the cook.

Why will this occur? In most cases, the identity of the source provides the target with information above and beyond the content of the message itself. The target uses this information to assess the communicator's credibility. This in turn affects the target's willingness to accept the message. By definition, **communicator credibility** is the extent to which the communicator is perceived by the target audience as a believable source of information. Note that the communicator's credibility is "in the eye of the beholder." A source is credible if the *target* believes that he or she is credible. Thus, a person may be credible for some audiences but not for others.

Many factors influence a communicator's level of credibility, but several seem to be of special importance. These are the communicator's expertise, trustworthiness, and attractiveness.

EXPERTISE. In general, a message from a source having a high level of expertise on the issue at hand will bring about greater attitude change than a similar message from a source having a lower level of expertise (Hovland and Weiss 1951; Maddux and Rogers 1980; Petty, Cacioppo, and Goldman 1981). One reason for this is that recipients may be more accepting of messages from high-credibility sources, whereas they may consider the issue more carefully when receiving a message from a low-credibility source. This is illustrated in one study (Sternthal, Dholakia, and Leavitt 1978) in which subjects were exposed to a message advocating the passage of a Consumer Protection Bill by the U.S. Senate. For some subjects, the message was ascribed to a lawyer educated at Harvard with extensive experience in consumer issues (a high-credibility source). For other subjects, the message was ascribed to a citizen interested in consumer affairs (a low-credibility source). Afterward subjects were asked to express their reaction to the message. In general, subjects who initially opposed the position advocated in the message expressed more unquestioning agreement and less counterargument when the message came from the high-credibility source than when it came from the low-credibility source.

One important factor in communicator expertise pertains to the target's prior involvement with, and knowledge about, the issue at hand. When the target has little involvement or prior knowledge on some issue, messages from highly expert sources produce more attitude change than those from less expert sources. But the more involving the issue, or the more knowledge that the target has about the issue, the less likely that communicator expertise will make any difference in persuasion (Rhine and Severance 1970). This occurs because when involvement and knowledge are high, the content of the message itself

As the automobile owner listens to the message from the garage mechanic, she asseses not only the quality of the argument but also the credibility of the communicator. He may have expertise, but can he be trusted?

becomes the overriding determinant of attitude change (Petty and Cacioppo 1979).

TRUSTWORTHINESS. Although expertise is an important factor in credibility, it is not the only one. Under some conditions, a communicator can be highly expert but still not very credible. As an example, suppose that your car has been running poorly and you take it into a garage for a checkup. A mechanic you have never met inspects your car. He identifies several problems, one of which involves major repair work on the engine. The mechanic offers to complete this work for $380. The mechanic may have a high level of expertise, but can you accept his word that the expensive repair is necessary? How much does he stand to gain if you believe his message?

As this example shows, the target person pays attention not only to a communicator's expertise but also to his or her motives. If the message appears highly self-serving and beneficial to the communicator, the recipient may distrust the communicator and discount the message.

The opposite effect also holds true. Communicators who argue against their own vested interests seem especially trustworthy. For example, if an employee of a local business quietly told you that you should not purchase a product made by her company, but should purchase one made by a Japanese competitor instead, the message would be surprising but also persuasive. Her comment would have more impact than if she had argued for purchasing her own American-made model. A communicator who violates our initial expectations by arguing against her own vested interest will appear particularly trustworthy, and, therefore, is especially persuasive (Walster, Aronson, and Abrahams 1966).

Another factor that affects trustworthiness (and hence credibility) is the social identity of the communicator. A communicator's identity provides many clues regarding his underlying goals and values. A communicator who is perceived as having goals similar to the audience will be more persuasive than a communicator perceived as having dissimilar goals (Berscheid 1966; Cantor, Alfonso, and Zillman 1976). For example, a given policy proposal will probably be received differently by conservative Republicans depending on whether it was made by Ronald Reagan or Jesse Jackson. The political identity of the source reveals much about the source's goals and intentions, and these in turn affect his perceived trustworthiness.

ATTRACTIVENESS. The physical attractiveness of a communicator can affect a message's persuasiveness. Although attractiveness is not as important as expertise or trustworthiness, it nevertheless has some impact on the target. Political parties, for example, have a tendency to select candidates who are physically attractive. Whether or not their abilities and experience suit them for public office, the candidates' good looks may increase their persuasiveness and get them elected. Likewise, television and magazine advertisements for skin cream, panty hose, and so on, employ attractive models as communicators. Advertisers realize that such models are able to hold an audience's attention. This is especially important with messages that are not highly involving and that might otherwise be ignored by the audience.

Physically attractive communicators are influential not only on television, but in face-to-face interactions as well. Attractive communicators are better liked than unattractive ones. Consequently, they will be more effective in changing the target's beliefs and attitudes (Mills and Aronson 1965; Horai, Naccari, and Fatoullah 1974; Chaiken 1979). Attractiveness is especially important when the message is not what the target audience would like to hear. If the message is unpopular, the difference in persuasiveness between an attractive and unattractive communicator will be substantial (Eagly and Chaiken 1975).

The Message

Persuasive communications differ dramatically in their content. Some contain arguments that are highly factual and rational, whereas other communications contain emotional appeals that motivate action by arousing fear or greed. Moreover, messages differ in terms of their detail and complexity (simple versus complex arguments), their strength of presentation (strong versus weak arguments), and their balance of presentation (one-sided versus two-sided arguments). In this section we will discuss the impact of these properties on persuasion, beginning with the question of message discrepancy.

MESSAGE DISCREPANCY. Suppose a woman told you that Elizabeth II, the queen of England, is five feet four inches tall. Would you believe her? What if she said five feet ten inches tall—would you believe that? How about six feet three inches? Or seven feet four inches?

You may not know how tall the queen actually is, but you probably have a rough idea. Although you might believe five feet ten inches, you would probably doubt six feet three inches, and certainly disbelieve seven feet four inches. The message asserting that the queen is seven feet four inches tall is highly discrepant from your beliefs.

By definition, a **discrepant message** is one advocating a position that is different from what the target believes. To bring about a change in beliefs, a message must be at least somewhat discrepant from the target's current position; otherwise it would merely reaffirm what the target already knows. Up to a certain point, greater levels of message discrepancy will lead to greater change in attitudes and beliefs (Jaccard 1981). A message that is moderately discrepant will be more effective in changing a target's beliefs than a message that is only slightly discrepant. Of course, it is possible for a message to be so discrepant that the target will simply dismiss it. To say that the queen of England is seven feet four inches tall is just not believable.

If a message is only slightly discrepant, it may be persuasive whether it comes from a high-credibility source or a low-credibility source. But if the message is highly discrepant, it will be persuasive only when it comes from a high-credibility source. Highly discrepant messages from a low-credibility source are likely to be ineffective because the target will derogate the source. Figure 7.1 summarizes these relationships between message discrepancy, communicator credibility, and attitude change.

Numerous empirical studies report findings consistent with the relationships shown in Figure 7.1 (Aronson, Turner, and Carlsmith 1963; Rhine and Severance 1970). In one experiment, subjects were given a written message on the number of hours of sleep that people need each night to function effectively (Bochner and Insko 1966). In some cases, the message was attributed to a Nobel Prize-winning physiologist (high credibility), and in

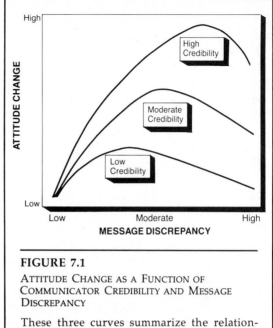

FIGURE 7.1

ATTITUDE CHANGE AS A FUNCTION OF COMMUNICATOR CREDIBILITY AND MESSAGE DISCREPANCY

These three curves summarize the relationship between message discrepancy and attitude change conditional on the credibility of a source. Note that messages from low-credibility communicators produce maximum attitude change at moderate levels of discrepancy, whereas messages from high-credibility communicators produce their maximum attitude change at high levels of discrepancy.

other cases it was attributed to a YMCA director (medium credibility). The arguments contained in the message were identical for all subjects, with one important exception. In some cases the message proposed that people need eight hours of sleep per night, in others the message proposed seven hours, in others six hours, and so on, down to zero hours of sleep per night. Most subjects began the experiment with the idea that approximately eight hours of sleep were needed each night. Therefore, these messages had different levels of discrepancy.

Results of this study show that the more discrepant the position advocated by the highly expert source (Nobel Prize winner), the greater the amount of attitude change. Only when the source argued for the most extreme position (zero hours of sleep) did subjects refuse to believe the message. This same pattern was noted for the medium expert source (YMCA director), except that his effectiveness peaked out at moderate levels of discrepancy (three hours of sleep per night). For very extreme positions (two hours of sleep or less), the medium expert source was less effective. In effect, communicators with high credibility produce maximum attitude change at high levels of discrepancy, while those with medium credibility produce maximum attitude change at moderate levels of discrepancy.

FEAR AROUSAL. Most persuasive communications are based on either rational appeals or emotional appeals. Rational appeals are factual in nature; they present specific, verifiable evidence to support claims. Rational messages are frequently drive-reducing—that is, they address a need already felt by the audience and provide the missing solution (Bauer and Cox 1963). An emotional appeal, however, arouses basic drives and creates a need where none was present.

Perhaps the most common emotional appeals are those involving fear. Fear-arousing messages are especially useful when the source is trying to motivate the target to take some specific action. A political candidate, for example, might warn that if his opponent is elected to office, the nation will find itself embroiled in international conflict. Likewise, an industrial leader may warn that unless steps are taken to impose trade restrictions, American jobs will be lost to foreign compeititon. In each of these cases, the source is using a fear-arousing communication. Messages of this type direct the target's attention to some negative or undesired outcome that is likely to occur unless the target takes certain actions advocated by the source.

In most cases, research shows that communications arousing high levels of fear produce more change in attitude than communications

arousing low levels of fear (Leventhal 1970; Higbee 1969). For example, fear-arousing communications have been effective in persuading people to reduce their cigarette smoking, to drive more safely, to improve their dental hygiene practices, and to change their attitudes toward Communist China (Insko, Arkoff, and Insko 1965; Leventhal and Singer 1966; Berkowitz and Cottingham 1960; Leventhal 1970).

The impact of fear-arousing communications is shown clearly in a study in which college students received messages advocating inoculations against tetanus (Dabbs and Leventhal 1966). These messages described tetanus as being easy to catch and as producing serious (occasionally fatal) consequences. The message also indicated that inoculation against tetanus, which could be obtained easily, provided effective protection against the disease. Depending on experimental treatment, subjects received either high-fear, low-fear, or control communications. In the high-fear condition, the messages described tetanus in extremely vivid terms in order to create a high level of apprehension and fear. In the low-fear condition, the messages carried a less detailed description so that no more than moderate fear would be produced. In the control condition, the message provided little detail about the disease and correspondingly little fear was aroused.

To determine the message's effectiveness, the students were asked how important they thought it was to get a tetanus inoculation and whether they actually intended to get one. Responses showed that students exposed to the high-fear message had stronger intentions to get shots than those exposed to the other messages. Moreover, records kept at the university health service indicated that students receiving the high-fear message were more likely to obtain inoculations during the following month than were students receiving the other messages.

This study demonstrates that fear-arousing messages are effective in changing attitudes.

In general, however, fear-arousing messages are effective only when certain conditions are met. First, the message must assert that if no changes are made in behavior, the target will suffer serious negative consequences. Second, the message must show convincingly that these negative consequences are highly probable. Third, the message must recommend a specific course of action which, if adopted, will enable the target to avoid the negative consequences. Messages that predict negative consequences but fail to assure the target that the consequences can be avoided through action will produce little attitude change or subsequent action. Instead they will leave the target feeling that the negative consequences are inevitable regardless of what he or she may do (Rogers 1975; Maddux and Rogers 1983).

ONE-SIDED VERSUS TWO-SIDED MESSAGES. When a source uses rational rather than emotional appeals, other message characteristics come into play. A common technique in persuasion is the one-sided message. Such a message emphasizes only those points that explicitly support the position advocated by the source. A two-sided message, in contrast, acknowledges that there are opposing viewpoints and then attempts to refute or downplay them. For example, if a man uses a one-sided message to persuade his wife to spend their vacation at the seashore, he would list the reasons for going to the shore and avoid mentioning any reasons for not going. If he used a two-sided message, he would mention both the reasons for going and the reasons for not going, but stress the reasons for going and refute the reasons for not going as invalid or unimportant.

Which is more effective, a one-sided message or a two-sided message? The answer to this question depends heavily on the audience. One-sided messages have the advantage of being uncomplicated and easy to grasp. They are more effective when the audience already agrees with the speaker or is not well-informed about the issue. Two-sided messages have the advantage of making the speaker appear less biased and more trustworthy. They are more effective when the audience is initially opposed to the speaker's viewpoint or is well-informed about alternative positions (Karlins and Abelson 1970; Sawyer 1973).

The Audience

Some persons are easier to persuade than others. That is, a given message from a specific communicator will have more impact on some targets than on others. Although the attributes of the source and the content of the message are important in persuasion, so are the characteristics of the target audience. Two of these characteristics are the level of the target's intelligence and the degree of the target's involvement with the issue.

INTELLIGENCE. Who would be easier to persuade, a genius or an imbecile? Or—to rephrase the question—who would be easier to persuade, someone having high intelligence or someone having low intelligence? The person with low intelligence might yield more readily to an argument, and in this sense, he might be easier to persuade than the target with high intelligence. But what if the low-intelligence person is not able to comprehend the (complex) argument in the first place? Without adequate comprehension, no attitude change can occur. The person with high intelligence may not yield readily to an argument, but at least she will comprehend it.

As this example shows, intelligence and persuasion are related in two distinct ways. Although high intelligence may increase comprehension of an argument and induce higher levels of attitude change, it may also heighten resistance and therefore inhibit or block attitude change (McGuire 1972).

Thus, any consideration of the relation between intelligence and persuasion must take into account message properties. This is illustrated in a study (Eagly and Warren 1976) involving high-school students who took a standard intelligence test (verbal ability). The students were exposed to a persuasive communication. For some this message included several complex (and apparently valid) arguments. For others the message was simple and included no arguments. The results showed that the high-intelligence students displayed greater comprehension for the complex messages and were slightly more persuaded by these arguments than low-intelligence students. At the same time, high-intelligence students were more prone to reject the simple messages than the low-intelligence students.

Thus, a person's intelligence does not of itself determine whether he will be more or less easy to persuade. Much depends on the message itself. Although persons of higher intelligence are better able to resist persuasive communications, they are also better able to understand complex messages, and therefore may be more influenced by such messages than are persons of lower intelligence.

INVOLVEMENT WITH THE ISSUE. Another important aspect of targets of persuasion is the extent of their involvement with a particular issue. Suppose, for example, that someone advocates a fundamental change at your college, such as increasing the number of comprehensive exams required for graduation. The proposed change would take effect in September of next year. Most undergraduates at your college would probably be very involved with this issue, because the change would affect their chances of getting a college degree. Now, suppose the source advocated that the change take place 10 years in the future rather than next September. Students would probably have little interest in this proposal, simply because they would be finishing college long before any changes take effect.

Thus, involvement with the issue affects the way a target person processes a message. When highly involved, a target will be motivated to scrutinize the message closely and to think carefully about its content. Strong arguments will likely produce substantial attitude change, whereas weak arguments will produce little or no attitude change. In contrast, the target who is less involved will be less motivated to scrutinize the message or to think about it carefully. If any change in attitude occurs, it will probably depend more on peripheral factors (such as communicator attractiveness or credibility) rather than on the arguments themselves (Chaiken 1980; Petty, Cacioppo and Heesacker 1981).

In one study, a message similar to that described above was in fact presented to a group of college students (Petty, Cacioppo, and Goldman 1981). The message proposed that college seniors be required to take a comprehensive exam prior to graduation. Three variables were manipulated in this study. The first variable was personal involvement with the issue. Half the subjects were told that the new policy would take effect next year (high involvement); whereas other subjects were told that the policy would take effect 10 years in the future (low involvement). The second variable was the strength of the message's argument. Half the subjects received eight highly persuasive arguments in favor of the proposal; the other subjects received eight specious arguments. The third variable was the expertise of the source. Half of the subjects were told that the source of the message was a professor of education at Princeton University (high-expert source); the other half were told that the source was a student at a local high school (low-expert source).

The results of this study are illustrated in Figure 7.2. In the high-involvement condition, the target's attitude toward comprehensive exams was determined primarily by the strength of the arguments. Strong arguments produced significantly more attitude change than weak ones. The expertise of the communicative source had no significant impact on attitude change. In the low-involvement condition, attitudes were determined primarily by source expertise; the high-expert source produced more attitude change than the low-expert source. The strength of the arguments

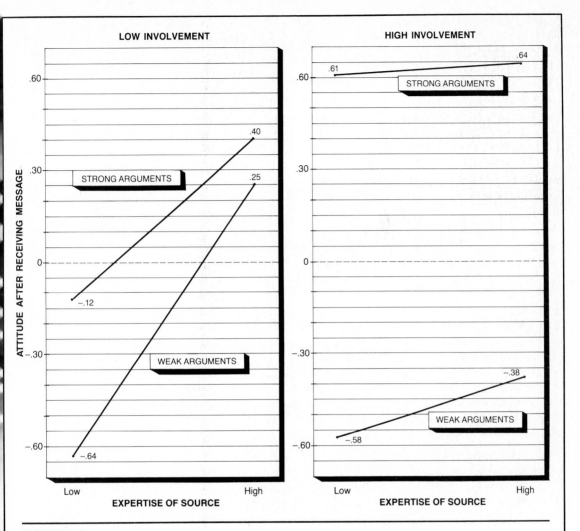

FIGURE 7.2

THE EFFECTS OF PERSONAL INVOLVEMENT ON PERSUASION

In this study, students received a message advocating that college seniors be required to take a comprehensive exam prior to graduation. Half the students were told that the new policy would take effect next year (high involvement), while the others were told the policy would take effect 10 years later (low involvement). Results show that students in the high-involvement condition were af-

fected primarily by the strength of the arguments rather than the expertise of the source, whereas students in the low-involvement condition were more affected by the expertise of the source rather than the strength of the arguments.

Source: adapted from Petty, Cacioppo, and Goldman (1981).

had relatively little effect on this group. Thus, the primary determinant of attitude change depended on the target's involvement with

the issue. For subjects with high involvement, the strength of the argument was more important because subjects cared about the issue. For those with low involvement, peripheral factors (such as communicator expertise) were more important because subjects had little motivation to scrutinize the arguments critically.

Persuasion Via Mass Media

Impact of Media Campaigns

The term *mass media* refers to those channels of communication that enable a source to reach a large audience. Whereas face-to-face communications can reach only a small audience, mass media can influence a large number of people. The most influential mass medium in the United States is television, followed by newspapers, radio, and magazines (Atkin 1981).

A **media campaign** is a systematic attempt by a source to use the mass media to change attitudes and beliefs of a target audience. Media campaigns are common in the industrialized world. They are used by advertisers to sell new products or services, by political parties to sway voters' sentiments, and by public officials to change citizens' behavior ("Help prevent forest fires," "Don't drive if you drink," "Conserve energy," and so on). A huge amount of money is spent on media campaigns. Each year tens of billions of dollars are spent on persuasive communications delivered through the mass media.

Despite the expense, most media campaigns do not produce large amounts of attitude change. In general, persuasive messages sent via mass media have only a small impact on their target audience's attitudes (Klapper 1960; Bauer 1964). Consider, for example, what occurs during presidential campaigns. Soon after the political conventions nominate their candidates in midsummer, most Americans know how they intend to vote in the upcoming November election. Although the parties spend millions of dollars on political advertising during the fall campaign, they will not change many voters' attitudes. In most elections, only about 7 to 10 percent of the voters

change their presidential preferences during a campaign (Berelson, Lazarsfeld, and McPhee 1954; Benham 1965). It is difficult to change political attitudes via the mass media.

Of course, from another perspective, a shift of 7 to 10 percent may be quite significant. Many professional advertisers and politicians are quite satisfied if their media messages can shift public opinion a few percentage points in the intended direction. In a close race, a net gain of 1 or 2 percent might be sufficient to win the election. Thus, even though a media campaign might be considered a failure in terms of producing widespread attitude change, it may also be considered a resounding success from the standpoint of electing a given candidate (Mendelsohn 1973). Even a small amount of attitude change may be sufficient to justify the cost of the media campaign.

Why are media campaigns usually able to produce only small amounts of attitude change? There are several reasons. First, there is the phenomenon of *selective exposure:* many messages do not even reach the audience they are intended to influence. Instead of reaching persons who disagree with the message (and whose opinions might therefore be changeable), many media communications are heard by persons who already agree with the message (and whose opinions will therefore be reinforced, not changed). In most routine media exposure, persons encounter more messages supporting than not supporting their pre-existing attitudes (Sears and Freedman 1967).

Second, even if the intended targets receive messages from the media, they may resist them the same way they reject messages in face-to-face contacts. A target person might disbelieve the media message or derogate the source. Recipients of media communications are not passive. The impact of a message depends heavily on the use that the audience can make of the information (Swanson 1979; Dervin 1981). For example, in selling consumer products persuasion is more effective

Box 7.1
IMMUNIZATION AGAINST PERSUASION

Most people are motivated to defend their attitudes from attack, especially with respect to important issues. If attitudes are based on a high level of information, they may be relatively easy to defend. However, if attitudes are based on little information, they may be vulnerable to attack. Can steps be taken to increase a target person's immunity to persuasion?

One class of beliefs that target persons have difficulty defending is the *cultural truism*. Truisms are beliefs widely accepted by members of a given culture. Examples of American truisms are: "Everyone should brush his teeth after every meal if at all possible"; "The effects of penicillin have been, almost without exception, of great benefit to mankind"; and "Mental illness is not contagious." Because truisms are rarely questioned, people have little practice in defending them against attack.

One theorist (McGuire 1964) proposes that a target person can be "immunized" against persuasion on issues of this type. The immunization treatment consists of giving the target (1) information that is discrepant with the truism, and (2) arguments that refute this discrepant information and support the truism. By exposing a target to weak attacks and allowing the target to refute them, the immunization treatment prepares the target for stronger attacks against the truisms at a later time. This treatment, called a *refutational defense*, is analogous to medical immunization in which a patient is given a small dose of a pathogen so that he can develop antibodies. By exposing the target to small attacks, the immunization builds up the target's resistance to subsequent stronger attacks.

A study by McGuire and Papageorgis (1961) demonstrates the effectiveness of a refutational defense against persuasion. Researchers exposed college students to persuasive messages attacking three different cultural truisms. Two days prior to this attack, the students had received an immunization treatment designed to create resistance to persuasion. For one truism, they received a refutational defense; for the second truism, they received a *supportive defense*—information containing elaborate arguments in favor of the truism; for the third truism, they received *no defense*. Following exposure to the attacks on their attitudes, students rated the extent of their agreement with each of the truisms. They also rated their agreement with a fourth truism, which had not been attacked, and for which no defense had previously been provided. The fourth truism served as a *control*.

Students' final ratings regarding the truisms are indicated in the table below. Results show that the refutational defense provided a high level of resistance to persuasion, whereas the supportive defense provided somewhat less resistance. Students showed least resistance when no defense was provided. In general, these findings demonstrate the effectiveness of the refutational defense in creating resistance against persuasion.

AGREEMENT WITH TRUISMS AFTER ATTACK AS A FUNCTION OF THE TYPE OF DEFENSE PROVIDED BEFORE THE ATTACK*

Type of Defense Provided	Agreement with Truisms
Control (no exposure to attack)	12.62
Refutational defense prior to attack	10.33
Supportive defense prior to attack	7.39
No defense prior to attack	6.64

*Higher scores indicate more agreement with truism after attack.
Source: adapted from McGuire and Papageorgis (1961).

Representatives of an advertising agency meet with clients to review a new media campaign. Even a small amount of attitude change produced by the campaign may be sufficient to justify its cost.

when the target person's involvement with the decision is low and when he perceives relatively small differences among alternative products. In contrast, the impact of the media will be slight when involvement with the decision is high and the differences between products appear clear-cut, (Ray 1973; Chaffee 1981).

Third, even when a target person finds a media message compelling, she may be subject to ·counterpressures that inhibit attitude change (Atkin 1981). Some of these pressures come from social groups (such as families, friends, and co-workers). These groups may exert influence that nullifies the media's impact. In addition, target persons are exposed to conflicting persuasive communications

transmitted over the media. For example, beer advertisements might be very successful if only one manufacturer advertised his product. But because this is not the case, media messages largely offset one another.

Media Effects

It would be inappropriate to conclude that the mass media have no effect whatever on audiences. Although media campaigns are not particularly effective in changing attitudes, they are effective in strengthening pre-existing attitudes. In other words, they reinforce and buttress preferences already held by the target audience. Televised debates between presidential candidates, for example, usually strengthen existing attitudes rather than change them. This was demonstrated in the famous Kennedy-Nixon debates of 1960. Viewers who were pro-Kennedy prior to the first debate concluded that Kennedy had "won" the debate, whereas those who were pro-Nixon concluded that Nixon had "won" (Kraus 1962; Sears and Whitney 1973).

In addition to strengthening pre-existing attitudes, mass media are also successful in creating attitudes toward new objects. Many media campaigns have cultivated new attitudes toward objects that previously were unknown or unimportant to the audience. The "Smokey the Bear" campaign, for example, has been effective in raising peoples' consciousness regarding prevention of forest fires. Businesses also use media campaigns to create positive attitudes toward new products. Commercials promoting the virtues of a sugar-free, caffeine-free cola, for example, are aimed at creating favorable attitudes toward this drink. Obviously the advertisers hope to influence people who drink competing old-line colas.

Media campaigns to create positive attitudes toward new objects are also common in politics. One example is the campaign created for Jimmy Carter shortly before his nomination in 1976 (Patterson 1980). Although Carter had been governor of Georgia, he was not well known outside the South. To win the Democratic nomination for president, Carter needed more name recognition among voters. The solution to this problem was a media campaign based on the theme "Jimmy Who?". By asking this question, the campaign sought first to pique voters' curiosity and later to create a positive view of this unknown candidate.

Threats and Promises

Although persuasion is an important means of influence, it is certainly not the only means. An alternative form of influence involves the use of threats and promises. In using threats and promises, the source is more concerned with changing the target's behavior than with changing the target's beliefs and attitudes. That is, the source's main objective is to achieve compliance from the target.

As an example, consider how Richard Sorenson exercises influence by means of promises. Sorenson, a home owner, lives in a northern state where it snows heavily each winter. One cold January day, a blizzard dumps eight inches of snow on his driveway and sidewalk. Not wanting to shovel snow, he notices that his neighbor's 14-year-old son is outside clearing his own driveway with a snowblower. Sorenson approaches the boy and says, "If you use your snowblower to clear my driveway and sidewalk, I will pay you $5." This is an influence attempt in the form of a promise. Sorenson promises to pay the boy $5 in return for a clear driveway and sidewalk.

Influence based on promises and threats differs from persuasion in a fundamental way. In using persuasion, the source tries to change the way a target person views the situation. Sorenson, for example, might have attempted a persuasive appeal in hopes of modifying the boy's viewpoint ("How about being a good neighbor and plowing out my driveway after finishing yours?"). But in using promises and threats, the source restructures the situation itself. By promising to pay money for a clear driveway, Sorenson has added a new contingency to the situation. He hopes this will affect the boy's behavior.

Effectiveness of Threats and Promises

Before we consider the effectiveness of threats and promises, it may be helpful to define these terms more precisely. A **threat** is a communication from one person (the source) to another (the target) that takes the general form: "If you don't do X (which I want), then I will do Y (which you don't want)" (Boulding 1981; Tedeschi, Schlenker, and Lindskold 1972). The sanction could be almost anything—a physical beating, a monetary fine, the loss of love—provided that the target wishes to avoid it. For example, a boss might say to his employee: "If you don't obtain a new advertising contract from that customer, I'll fire you." If the employee needs his salary to keep food on the table and has no other job prospects, he will certainly take the threat seriously. On the other hand, if the employee hates his boss and has a new job lined up elsewhere, he may not care whether he is fired. In this case, the threat will have little impact because the target has no real need to avoid the sanction.

A **promise** is similar to a threat, except that it involves contingent rewards, not punishments. A person using a promise says: "If you do X (which I want), then I will do Y (which you want)." Notice that a promise involves a reward controlled by the source. Richard Sorenson promises a payment of $5, provided that his 14-year-old neighbor clears the driveway and sidewalk. Promises are frequently used in exchanges, both monetary and nonmonetary.

Threats and promises are often—but not always—effective in gaining compliance from the target. In issuing a promise, the source creates a set of options for the target. Suppose, for example, that the source makes the promise, "If you clear the snow from my driveway with your snowblower, I will pay you $5." In response, the target can (1) comply with the source's request, (2) refuse to comply and let the matter drop, or (3) propose a counteroffer ("How about $7? It's a long driveway and the snow is very deep").

A threat also creates a choice for the target. Once a threat is issued, the target can (1) comply with the threat, (2) refuse to comply, or (3) issue a counterthreat (Boulding 1981).

The range of possible responses to threats and promises raises a fundamental question: Under what conditions will threats and promises be successful in gaining compliance, and under what conditions will they fail? Certain characteristics of threats and promises, such as their magnitude and credibility, affect the probability that the target will comply.

MAGNITUDE OF THREATS AND PROMISES. Late at night, on an isolated street corner, a bandit brandishes a pistol and issues the threat: "Hand over your money or I'll blow you away!" The victim is forced to choose between two undesirable alternatives—losing his money or losing his life. Facing a negative outcome of enormous magnitude, the victim will almost certainly hand over his wallet. However, if the threat were of smaller magnitude, his reaction might be different. A bandit would not get the victim's wallet if, instead of using a gun, he said, "Hand over your money or I'll zap you with this rubber band!" Obviously, the effectiveness of a threat varies directly with the magnitude of the punishment involved.

A similar principle holds true for promises. The greater the magnitude of the reward promised, the greater the probability of compliance (Cozby 1972; Lindskold and Tedeschi 1971). A factory supervisor, for example, might obtain compliance from a worker by saying, "If you are willing to work the late shift next month, I'll approve your request for four extra days of vacation in September." The worker's reaction might be less accommodating, however, if his supervisor said, "If you work the late shift next month, I'll let you take your coffee break five minutes earlier today." The greater the magnitude of the reward promised, the higher the probability that the worker will comply with the supervisor's request.

CREDIBILITY OF THREATS AND PROMISES. Suppose someone says: "If you don't do X (which I want), then I will do Y (which you don't want)." How can you tell whether this threat is credible? Does the person making the threat really mean it, or is he merely bluffing? As the target, you need to know whether to believe the threat. You might comply if the threat is credible, but you certainly do not want to comply if the threat is merely a bluff. Unfortunately, the only way to find out whether a threat is credible is to refuse to comply, which can be risky. If the threat is merely a bluff, it will quickly become evident. But if the threat is real, you will have to suffer the consequences.

Credibility is also a problem for the threatener. Even if he is really bluffing, he wants you to believe that his threat is credible. After all, a successful threat is one that achieves compliance without actually having to be carried out. If you refuse to comply, the threatener must either admit that he is bluffing or incur some costs in carrying out the threat.

The effectiveness of a threat depends both on its credibility and on the magnitude of the expected punishment. According to one theory (Tedeschi, Bonoma, and Schlenker 1972), we can determine the effectiveness of a threat by multiplying the credibility of a threat by its magnitude. The product of these two variables is called the **subjective expected value** (SEV) of the threat:

$$SEV = \text{Credibility of threat} \times \text{Magnitude of punishment threatened}$$

Note that when both credibility and magnitude are high, SEV is also high, exerting a lot of pressure on the target. However, when either the credibility or the magnitude is low, the SEV is low, exerting much less pressure on the target. In deciding whether or not to comply with the threat, a target will unconsciously calculate the SEV. In general, the higher the SEV, the greater the probability of compliance with the threat.

Various empirical studies support the SEV model of threat effectiveness (Bonoma et al. 1970; Faley and Tedeschi 1971). For example, in one laboratory study (Horai and Tedeschi 1969), several pairs of persons were asked to play a game over and over. In each case, one member of the pair was a subject, whereas the other was actually a confederate following a programmed strategy. During each trial, both the subject and the confederate were required to make certain choices. The object of the game was to gain points. Threats could be issued by the confederate, but not by the subject. To gain extra points, the confederate occasionally delivered threats to influence the subject's choice. ("If you do not pick Choice 1 on the next trial, I will take *n* points away from your counter.") The magnitude of the punishment threatened was either high (20 points),

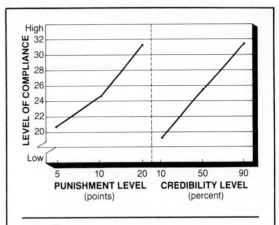

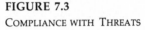

FIGURE 7.3

COMPLIANCE WITH THREATS

Compliance is a function of both the magnitude of the punishment threatened and the credibility of the threat. The greater the punishment threatened, the greater the compliance with the threat. Likewise, the greater the credibility of the threat, the greater the compliance.

Source: adapted from Horai and Tedeschi (1969).

medium (10 points), or low (5 points), depending on experimental treatment. The credibility of the confederate was manipulated by varying the frequency with which he carried out his threats if the subject did not comply. In the high-credibility condition, the confederate carried out his threats 90 percent of the time; in the medium-credibility condition, he carried them out 50 percent of the time; in the low-credibility condition, 10 percent of the time.

The results of this study are shown in Figure 7.3. They indicate that both the magnitude of punishment threatened and the credibility of the source affect the subject's level of compliance. Compliance increased as a direct function of both variables. The greatest amount of compliance occurred under the highest magnitude of punishment and the highest level of credibility. Results of this study support the SEV model.

The demand "Your money or your life" is effective because of the magnitude of the threat and its consequences.

Although the SEV model pertains to threats, it may also be applied to promises. Of course, the relevant variable with respect to promises is the magnitude of reward promised, not the magnitude of punishment threatened. Both reward magnitude and promise credibility affect compliance to promises. Results of one study showed that target persons were more influenced when the reward promised was large rather than small and when the source had some credibility in following through on his promises (Lindskold et al. 1970). Consistent with the SEV view, these conclusions hold true only when the reward promised is greater than the rewards that might be gained from failing to comply.

Problems in Using Threats and Promises

Threats and promises pose certain problems for the user. First, the person using them must achieve credibility in the eyes of the target person. A threat or promise having low credibility will have a low SEV, and therefore a low level of effectiveness. Thus, the source must try to bolster credibility.

To some degree, the credibility of a threat depends on the identity of the source. A threat involving physical violence, for example, will be more credible if it comes from a karate expert wearing a black belt than if it comes from the proverbial 97-pound weakling. In some cases, the source may attempt to manipulate how he is perceived by the target. Thus, bank robbers try to increase compliance with their threats by adopting a sinister appearance, with trench coats and masks. They do not dress like Bozo the Clown.

A second problem for the user of threats and promises is maintaining surveillance over the target's behavior. That is, the source must watch closely to make sure compliance has in fact occurred. The need to maintain surveillance is more troublesome in the case of threats than promises. Not only may the targets of threats fail to comply—they may also attempt to conceal their noncompliance in order to avoid punishment (Ring and Kelley 1963).

The cost of surveillance is one reason why the source might prefer to use persuasion rather than threats or promises. If successful, persuasion requires no surveillance. For example, if an employer uses persuasion and succeeds in changing an employee's mind, she can expect that the employee will carry out the task on his own, without surveillance. This is certainly more convenient and less costly for the employer.

A third problem is that threats may arouse resentment or hostility toward the influencer (Zipf 1960). Promises do not entail this difficulty, because they involve rewards and not punishments. In general, a target will have more positive feelings toward someone who uses promises than someone who uses threats (Rubin and Lewecki 1973). In situations where the source has an ongoing relationship with the target and where maintaining a good relationship might be important, the source may prefer to use promises, not threats.

Box 7.2
"YOUR MONEY OR YOUR LIFE!"

Perhaps the greatest threat that can be made is one against your life. Threats of this type frequently occur during robbery or hold-up attempts involving a lethal weapon, such as a firearm. How do robbery victims react to threats made against their lives?

To answer this question, Luckenbill (1982) studied 201 cases of robbery and attempted robbery that occurred in a Texas city between February 1976 and March 1977. Police records indicated that victims take several factors into account before deciding whether to comply with a threat. First, they consider the source's capacity to inflict serious injury or death. For example, compliance was high (75 percent) when the source had a lethal weapon (a knife or a gun) and was in a position to use it. As two victims noted:

> "I wasn't going to try anything because he had a piece (firearm). When he's got a piece, you give him the money. That's all there is to it. If you try anything, he might shoot you."
>
> "I would've killed him if I could've gotten to my pistol. But . . . I couldn't do a thing, you know. He was standing right there watching me. And his pistol was loaded. I could see the steel bullets in the cylinder. And he was shaking so bad he might've shot me if I tried anything. If I had a clear chance,

you know, I would've nailed him. But hell, I'm not going to risk my life for a few measley bucks."
>
> —Luckenbill 1982, p. 814

When the source had no lethal weapon, compliance was low (5 percent). According to police records, the target opposed the demand for money in almost all cases in which the robber did not have a weapon.

A second factor considered by victims was the source's intent regarding the use of force—that is, whether the source's threat was contingent or noncontingent. If the threat was contingent ("If you don't give me your money, I'll shoot you."), victims assumed that they would not be hurt if they complied. However, if the threat was noncontingent ("I'm going to shoot you and take the money."), most victims concluded that the robber intended to punish indiscriminately. Luckenbill's data show that in cases where the robber issued a noncontingent threat, victims actively opposed the robber, primarily because they feared imminent death.

In general, these findings support the view that compliance to a threat is likely when the subjective expected value (SEV) of the threat is large, provided that compliance with the threat provides an assured means of avoiding punishment.

Bargaining and Negotiation

Up to this point we have considered various techniques of influence—namely, persuasion, threats, and promises. Throughout our discussion we have assumed that one person (the source) attempts to influence another person (the target) in order to change the behavior of that person. In many situations, however, it happens that not one but *both* persons can exercise influence. Whereas person A (the source) may attempt to influence person B (the target), person B (now the source) may also

attempt to counterinfluence person A (now the target). For example, if Hugo threatens Norman, Norman might issue a counterthreat. (Hugo: "Get out of my way or I'll knock you down." Norman: "If you touch me, I'll smash in your face.")

Situations in which both persons exercise influence are often complex. When each person controls rewards valued by the other, the potential for bargaining exists. When each person controls punishments feared by the other, the potential for two-sided threat and the escalation of conflict exists. In this section we will discuss both of these processes beginning with bargaining.

Bargaining in Exchange Relations

An **exchange** is an interaction in which person A gives person B something that B values in return for B giving A something that A values (Emerson 1981; Kelley and Thibaut 1978). The items exchanged can be virtually anything—goods, services, money, or whatever. We see exchanges occurring every day. If you make a purchase in a grocery store, you exchange money for food. Politicians sometimes exchange votes on one issue for those on another issue. In holding a conversation, two persons exchange one type of information for another.

A key issue in exchange is price. Anyone involved in an exchange naturally wants to get the right item without paying too high a price. Some exchanges involve fixed or pre-established prices. For example, the price of food in grocery stores is not usually subject to discussion or haggling. In other situations, however, prices are negotiable. When you go to a used car lot to purchase an auto, the price is certainly open to discussion. Likewise, when you are offered a new job, the price of your services (that is, your salary) may be subject to some bargaining. In cases like this, what really matters is whether the buyer and seller can agree on price.

THE STRUCTURE OF BARGAINING SITUATIONS. The term **bargaining** refers to a process of interaction in which two (or more) persons with different preferences make a sequence of concessions in an attempt to reach an agreement that is mutually acceptable. This agreement specifies how each person will behave in the future—that is, what each person will give and take (Rubin and Brown 1975; Druckman 1977; Morley and Stephenson 1977).

Notice the essential features of a bargaining situation. First, there must be at least two persons, and these persons must have initially different preferences regarding some issue. A car dealer and a customer, for example, may disagree over the price of a car, with the dealer asking $2,995 and the customer offering $2,300. Second, both persons must believe some form of agreement is possible, one that would leave each person better off than if no agreement were achieved. For example, if the dealer and the customer feel that nothing can be gained from bargaining, or if one or both persons believe that an agreement is completely out of reach, then bargaining will not occur. Third, a number of different possible agreements must be attainable through bargaining. In other words, the bargainers must believe that the price or the terms of exchange are genuinely open to discussion. Because the bargainers have opposing preferences many outcomes are possible (Deutsch and Krauss 1960).

People can bargain over anything, but the most common issue in bargaining is price. What price will be paid for a used car? What rent will be paid for an apartment? What salary will be paid for a new job? In some instances, however, the terms of an agreement are more important than the price itself. A labor union, for example, in bargaining against management, may be more concerned with work rules or job security than with wage increases. Similarly, a newly married couple may bargain over role definitions—who will do what around the house.

Bargaining usually consists of tactics whereby each party tries to obtain concessions from the other. A bargainer who obtains concessions while making few concessions himself will consider the outcome favorable. Thus, the bargaining process usually involves a series of concessions leading to a final resolution that both parties find acceptable. Because the resolution is a compromise, neither of the bargainers is likely to be completely satisfied. But to be a true resolution, the agreement must be one that both parties can honor in the future.

THE BARGAINING RANGE. The most fundamental question in bargaining is: What actions will lead to a good outcome? In other words, what moves should a person make in bargaining to obtain a favorable agreement? Although there is no simple formula that will always produce a good outcome, a bargainer's actions can certainly influence the result. Suppose, for example, that you have recently taken a job and you find that you need a car to commute to work. Late one afternoon you go down to Friendly Al's Used Car Lot and take a look around. You observe that Al has many cars on his lot, and you make a mental note that his business must be a little slow this month. Looking over the cars, you spot one you like. The only stumbling block is Al's asking price, painted on the windshield in large white numbers: $2,995.

After checking out the car mechanically, you decide that you want to buy it—but not at Al's price. In order to determine what is possible, you need to know how much flexibility Al has. Suppose that Al paid $1,500 for the car when it originally came onto his lot. He also paid for some minor repairs on the car, and he wants to cover his overhead and to obtain a small profit. This means that he will not accept less than $1,800 for the car; this figure is referred to as Al's **limit.** Because Al would like to sell the car for more than his limit, he has posted an asking price of $2,995 on the windshield. This higher figure is referred to as his **level of aspiration**—the highest price that he thinks he might realistically get for the auto. Al realizes that the actual sale price of the car may fall somewhere between his $1,800 limit and his $2,995 level of aspiration.

As a potential buyer, you also have a limit and a level of aspiration. After checking your finances closely, you figure that the most you could pay for a car at this time is $2,300. This is your limit. You have checked the local newspapers to see what prices other dealers are asking for similar automobiles and noticed that other cars sell for as little as $1,500, although these are a year or two older and possibly in poorer condition. You hope that you can bargain Al down to $1,500. This is your level of aspiration.

Thus, the seller (Al) has a limit of $1,800 and an aspiration level of $2,995. The buyer (you) has a limit of $2,300 and an aspiration level of $1,500. Of course, at the start you do not know Al's limit and he does not know yours. But, obviously, the price of the car has to fall somewhere between $1,800 and $2,300. This is the distance between the two limits, referred to as the **bargaining range.** Al will not accept less than $1,800; you will not pay more than $2,300. In realistic terms, your $1,500 level of aspiration is out of reach. So is Al's asking price. There is no guarantee that an agreement will be reached, although room for negotiation certainly exists.

INITIAL OFFER. When opening serious discussions with Al, what initial offer should you make? You could either make an extremely low offer ($1,500) or you could make your highest possible offer ($2,300). Which offer will lead to the most favorable outcome for you?

If you make a high initial offer ($2,300), it will make an agreement easier to reach. You will probably get the car but the price will be steep. If you make a low initial offer, it is likely to provoke further bargaining and might lead to concessions on Al's part. The problem with a low offer, however, is that Al may become discouraged and break off negotiations. Experimental evidence suggests that an extremely low initial offer is more likely to lead to favorable outcomes for you (the buyer) than a more moderate offer, provided that bargaining is not broken off (Bartos 1974; Benton, Kelley, and Liebling 1972; Harnett and Vincelette 1978).

Why is a low initial offer more likely to produce a favorable outcome? In most cases, it reduces the aspiration level of the other party (Yukl 1974a, 1974b; Liebert et al. 1965). After receiving an extremely low initial offer, the

In negotiating the purchase of a used car, the customer must estimate not only the salesman's level of aspiration but also his limit. Only then does the customer have any real chance of getting a "miracle deal."

other bargainer may conclude that his original aspiration was simply out of reach. He may respond by lowering his demand or making larger concessions than he would otherwise. If this happens, the person making the low initial offer will obtain a favorable outcome.

CONCESSIONS. If you make an initial offer of $1,500 for the automobile, with Al asking $2,995, someone will obviously have to make concessions before an agreement is reached. Bargaining typically involves a sequence of concessions, in which each party reduces its demands and moves in the direction of compromise.

If a bargainer is going to make some concessions, does he gain by making them frequently or infrequently? The answer to this

question, of course, depends on the reaction of the other bargainer. On one hand, the other bargainer might decide to *match* the concession—that is, make a concession in return. For instance, if you raise your offer to Al (say, from $1,500 to $1,700), he might respond by lowering his demand somewhat (from $2,995 to $2,800). Another possible response to concession is *mismatching*, in which the opponent refuses to make a concession in response. For example, if you offered a concession, Al might assume that you are getting weaker and therefore remain firm with his asking price. Both matching and mismatching can occur in negotiations (Pruitt 1981).

Evidence suggests that many bargainers will make concessions in direct response to a concession made by their opponents. Moreover, when one bargainer initiates frequent concessions during negotiations the other bargainer is likely to match with frequent concessions (Chertkoff and Conley 1967; Yukl 1974b). Bargainers are especially likely to make a concession immediately after one has been offered. (Bartos 1974; Hopmann and Smith 1977).

The term **concession magnitude** denotes the average size of a bargainer's concession. For example, if you offered Al a concession by raising your bid from $1,500 to $1,700, and subsequently offered a second concession by raising $1,700 to $2,000, your concession magnitude would be $250. Concession magnitude is an important concept because although bargainers may match in the *number* of concessions made, they frequently mismatch in terms of *magnitude*. Suppose, for example, that you offered your first concession, raising $1,500 to $1,700, and Al responded by lowering his asking price from $2,995 to $2,850. Then you offered a second concession, raising $1,700 to $2,000, and Al responded by lowering $2,850 to $2,700. It is apparent that, although Friendly Al is matching the frequency of your concessions, he is gaining an advantage by failing to match their magnitude. Thus, from your viewpoint, mismatching is undesirable because you will end up paying more for the car.

Evidence indicates that bargainers will attempt to match the concession magnitude of their opponent only under certain circumstances. Concession magnitude is more likely to be matched when a bargainer perceives that the other party is engaging in cooperative behavior because he chooses to, rather than because he has to. In other words, if one party is operating from a position of strength or in terms of some principle, he will be perceived as impervious to pressure or competitive tactics. Any concessions from him will be construed as a conciliatory gesture, and are likely to produce concessions of similar magnitude (Michener et al. 1975; Wall 1977).

Another condition that may lead bargainers to match concession magnitude is the existence of a *prominent solution* (Schelling 1960). This is a bargaining solution that is readily apparent and that logically stands out from other possible solutions. For example, in a territorial dispute, a river running through the property may stand out as a natural boundary and therefore constitute a logical basis for dividing the property. If one bargainer offers concessions that move in the direction of a prominent solution, then the other bargainer may be disposed to match the concession magnitude.

BARGAINING AS PROBLEM SOLVING. Because bargaining involves conflict, many people view it as a battle to be won rather than as a problem to be solved. Yet it is often more effective to adopt a problem-solving orientation when bargaining, because this increases the chances that *all* participants will come out ahead. In adopting this viewpont, the basic objective is to invent **integrative proposals**—alternatives that reconcile bargainers' divergent interests by providing high benefits to both of them (Pruitt 1981).

Consider a husband and wife who are trying to resolve the issue of where to spend their summer vacation (Pruitt 1981). Initially, the husband wants to go to the mountains and the wife wants to go to the seashore, although they both prefer some kind of vacation to none

at all. Rather than digging in their heels, the husband and wife explore the factors that underlie their different preferences. It turns out that the husband prefers the mountains because he likes fishing, hiking, and the attractive mountaintop views. Of these, fishing and hiking have the highest value for him. The wife prefers the seashore because she likes swimming, sunning on the beach, seafood dinners, and the salt air, in that order.

Initially, the husband and wife consider three options—the mountains, the seashore, and no vacation at all. They also begin to consider a fourth option—spend one week in the mountains and one week at the seashore. This fourth option is a compromise, because it lies halfway between the husband's and wife's initial preferences. Although attractive in some respects, it is still not entirely satisfactory. Rather than stop here, the couple continues to work on the problem. By treating their conflict in terms of underlying factors, they try to create new integrative proposals that are superior to the halfway compromise. Suddenly, the wife suggests that they spend their vacation at an inland lake. This would give the husband the chance to fish and hike, and the wife an opportunity to swim, sun, and eat fresh fish. With this integrative proposal, the couple resolves the conflict. Figure 7.4 depicts the five alternatives in terms of their values to husband and wife.

By striving to develop integrative proposals, bargainers may be able to transform a situation from open conflict to problem solving. A constructive resolution is most likely to emerge when bargainers take the following steps: (1) Separate the people from the problem. To avoid the entanglement of egos, the bargainers should ideally see themselves as working side by side, attacking the problem, not one another. (2) Focus on interests, not positions. By exchanging information on underlying values and interests, bargainers will see what conditions must be met by an integrative proposal. (3) Invent new options for mutual gain. Integrative proposals tailored to the underlying values and interests of the

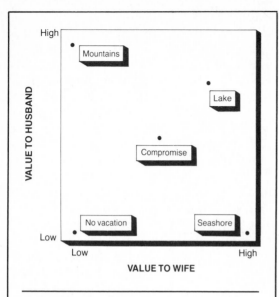

FIGURE 7.4

VACATION ALTERNATIVES

This figure depicts vacation alternatives available to a married couple. The alternatives are displayed in terms of their value to the wife and to the husband. They include a trip to the mountains, seashore, a compromise between the mountains and the seashore, and no vacation. Also shown is a trip to an inland lake, which is an integrative proposal. Because both husband and wife find the lake preferable to the halfway compromise, they agree on this alternative.

Source: adapted from Pruitt (1981).

bargainers are frequently superior to superficial compromises between initial positions. This is shown clearly in the preceding example, where the husband and wife preferred the new option (inland lake) to the halfway compromise between initial positions (one week in the mountains and one week at the seashore). (4) In those extreme cases where interests are directly opposed and integrative proposals cannot be developed, bargainers should insist on objective criteria as a basis for concession. Rather than rewarding intransigent and stubborn behavior with concessions, bargainers should insist that certain criteria (for example,

market value, expert opinion, custom, or law) be met as a condition for concessions. By placing emphasis on objective criteria, rather than on what the bargainers are willing or unwilling to do, neither party need give in to the other. Both can defer to an objectively determined resolution (Fisher and Ury 1981; Pruitt and Lewis 1977; Pruitt and Carnevale 1980).

Bilateral Threat and Escalation

Thus far, we have characterized bargaining as a process of reciprocal influence between two persons. This process may involve a sequence of rigid demands and counterdemands between individuals, or it may involve joint attempts at integrative problem solving. Either way, the influence techniques used are persuasion and promises.

Beyond this, however, the process of bargaining may also involve threats. In some situations, only one bargainer has the capacity to issue threats. This may give him extra leverage in the negotiations. But when *both* persons can issue threats and inflict punishments the situation is considered one of **bilateral threat**. Bargaining of this kind is precarious and may degenerate into open hostility and conflict.

For example, suppose that two persons, Alex and Paul, have reached a deadlock in their negotiations. To coerce a favorable settlement, Alex threatens to inflict punishment if Paul does not make some further concessions. How will Paul respond to this threat? He might decide to comply and offer the settlement. On the other hand, Paul might decide to issue a counterthreat. Paul's counterthreat will probably be larger in magnitude than Alex's because he wishes to deter Alex from carrying out the original threat. The result will be an escalation of the conflict. At this point Alex might back down. But if Alex feels committed to his position, he will have no alternative but to respond with yet another threat. These actions constitute a threat-counterthreat spiral in which bargainers stand firm in their positions and threaten to inflict more and more damage on one another.

A classic laboratory study by Deutsch and Krauss (1960, 1962) demonstrates what can happen when both bargainers have threat capability. This study involves a two-person bargaining simulation in which participants enact the roles of the chief officers of two trucking companies, called Acme and Bolt. Acme's objective is to move its cargo to its destination in one direction over a road displayed on a board in front of the subjects. Bolt's objective is the same, except that it moves its cargo in the opposite direction (Fig. 7.5). Each participant's profits depend on the speed with which he or she moves the truck from start to destination. The experiment involves 20 trips. For each trip, a player earns 60 cents minus 1 cent for each second the cargo is in transit between points.

As Figure 7.5 indicates, Acme and Bolt each have two routes, a long one and a short one. The short route permits the faster trip. The need for bargaining arises because the short route is only one lane wide and will accommodate no more than one truck at a time. If both participants select the one-lane road as their route, they will not be able to move past one another and will waste valuable time. The logical solution to this problem is for participants to take turns using the one-lane road, thereby alternating the loss involved in traveling the longer route.

Participants in this experiment have different threat capabilities. In one experimental condition (bilateral threat), Acme and Bolt control gates that, when lowered, block the other's movement along the one-lane road. In another condition (unilateral threat), only one participant (Acme) controls a gate that could be used to prevent Bolt from taking the short route. In a third condition (no threat), neither Acme nor Bolt controls a gate.

In the original version of this study (Deutsch and Krauss 1960), no verbal communication was permitted among participants. Results showed that bargaining effectiveness decreased when participants had threat capability. In the no-threat condition, the average

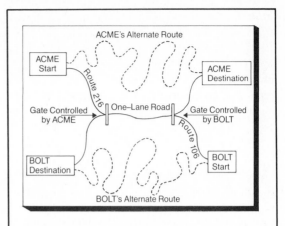

FIGURE 7.5
ROAD MAP OF THE TRUCKING GAME

In this game, the objective of each player (Acme and Bolt) is to move a truck from start to destination as quickly as possible. The one-lane road (center) provides the fastest route, although both players cannot use it simultaneously. When both players control gates, each player can threaten to block the other's access to the one-lane road. Under these conditions (bilateral threat), conflict between players may escalate.
Source: adapted from Deutsch and Krauss (1960).

joint payoff (that is, the payoff to Acme plus the payoff to Bolt) was $2.03, whereas in the unilateral threat condition (one gate) the average joint payoff was −$4.06. In the bilateral threat condition (two gates), the average joint payoff was −$8.75. Thus, the presence of bilateral threat capability in the situation made coordination difficult to establish. When both participants could issue threats, a threat-counterthreat spiral frequently occurred creating a deadlock that wasted valuable time. This resulted in a large negative joint payoff to participants.

Subsequent trucking game experiments investigated threat under conditions where the subjects were able to communicate with each another (Deutsch and Krauss 1962). Subjects were either required to talk to one another on every play (compulsory communication), or they were given the option to talk if they wished to do so (permissive communication). The findings of these experiments showed similar results. Once again, even with communication, the bilateral threat condition provoked worse outcomes than the unilateral or no-threat conditions.

Other studies have investigated the effects of power differences on threats and escalation in a bilateral situation. The major question posed in these studies is: What is the outcome of a bilateral situation in which both persons have some threat capability but one person has greater destructive power?

In general, bargainers with more power than their opponents tend to behave exploitatively, whereas those with less power tend to behave submissively (Rubin and Brown 1975). For one thing, persons who have more power are reluctant to make concessions. Not only may they refuse to initiate concessions, but they may even refuse to match concessions from the low-power bargainer (Smith and Leginski 1970; Michener et al. 1975). In addition, bargainers in a position of high power tend to have high aspirations and to make few concessions, whereas bargainers with low power tend to match any concessions made by the other.

The power of the strong bargainer also has a deterrent effect on his weaker opponent. Because he fears retaliation, the weaker bargainer hesitates to use threats or behave aggressively. The deterrence effect is unmistakable—the aggressive behavior of the low-power person decreases as the punishment magnitude of the high-power person increases (Michener and Cohen 1973).

In general, situations in which both bargainers have threat capability are potentially explosive. Even a single threat or punitive act may set off a threat-counterthreat spiral. One threat provokes another, making any resolution difficult to achieve (Hornstein 1965; Smith and Anderson 1975).

Summary

Social influence occurs when action by one person (the source) causes another person (the target) to change an opinion or to comply with a directive.

COMMUNICATION AND PERSUASION. A common form of social influence is persuasion. Several factors affect the extent to which a persuasion attempt will succeed in changing beliefs and attitudes. (1) Characteristics of the source determine a message's effectiveness. Communicators who are credible (that is, highly expert, trustworthy, and/or attractive) will generally be more persuasive than communicators who are not. (2) Message characteristics also determine a message's effectiveness. Highly discrepant messages are more persuasive when they come from a source having high credibility. Fear-arousing communications (warnings) are most effective when they specify a course of action that can avert impending negative consequences. One-sided messages have more impact than two-sided messages when the audience already agrees with the speaker's viewpoints or is not well-informed about other viewpoints; two-sided messages are superior when the audience is sophisticated and well-informed. (3) Characteristics of the target also determine a message's effectiveness. More intelligent targets are better able to comprehend complex messages than are less intelligent targets, but more intelligent targets may be less willing to yield to a persuasive argument; intelligent targets are most responsive to complex messages containing strong arguments. Involvement with the issue also affects the way a target will process information in a message. Targets who are highly involved with an issue scrutinize messages closely, and are more influenced by the strength of the arguments than by peripheral factors such as communicator attractiveness or credibility.

PERSUASION VIA MASS MEDIA. Numerous persuasive attempts are made every day via the mass media (television, newspapers, radio, and magazines). (1) In general, media campaigns produce only modest amounts of attitude change. This occurs because exposure to media messages is selective, audiences are resistant to influence, and counterpersuasion from competing sources is widespread. (2) Mass media are especially effective in buttressing attitudes that already exist and in creating positive attitudes toward new objects (such as new products or political candidates).

THREATS AND PROMISES. Threats and promises are influence techniques used primarily to achieve compliance from the target person. In using threats and promises, the source alters the environment of the target by directly manipulating reward contingencies. (1) The effectiveness of a threat depends on both the magnitude of the punishment and the probability that it will be carried out. Greater compliance results from high magnitude and high probability. Similar effects hold true for promises, although these involve rewards rather than punishments. (2) Threats and promises pose several problems for the source. For example, the source must maintain surveillance over the target. In addition, threats may arouse resentment or hostility in the target.

BARGAINING AND NEGOTIATION. In many situations, influence is bilateral rather than unilateral. (1) When two persons are able to reward one another, bargaining and negotiation frequently result. Certain tactics may lead to favorable outcomes in bargaining. Among these are the use of a low initial offer and the use of mismatching responses to concessions by the opponent. These tactics are risky, however, and may lead to a stalemate or failure to reach agreement. A superior approach to bargaining, where possible, is to develop integrative proposals that benefit both parties. (2) When each party controls punishments, bargaining may escalate into bilateral threat and conflict. If the two persons have very unequal power, the weaker person will probably hesitate to issue threats and will accommodate the demands of the stronger person instead. But when both parties have equal (or nearly equal) power, the use of threats by one may provoke threats by the other, resulting in an escalation of conflict.

Key Terms and Concepts

Social Influence

Source

Target

Persuasion

Communicator Credibility

Discrepant Message

Media Campaign

Threat

Promise

Subjective Expected Value (SEV)

Exchange

Bargaining

Limit

Level of Aspiration

Bargaining Range

Concession Magnitude

Integrative Proposal

Bilateral Threat

Chapter 8
Social Perception and Attribution

Introduction

It's 10 P.M., and the mental hospital admitting physician is interviewing a respectable-looking man asking for treatment. "You see," the patient says, "I keep on hearing voices." After taking a full history, the physician diagnoses the man as a schizophrenic, and assigns him to the psychiatric award.

In one unusual study (Rosenhan 1973), eight pseudopatients who were actually research investigators gained entry into mental hospitals by claiming to hear voices. During the intake interviews, the pseudopatients gave true accounts of their backgrounds, life experiences, and present (quite ordinary) psychological condition. They falsified only their names and their complaint of hearing voices. Once in the psychiatric ward, the pseudopatients ceased simulating *any* symptoms of abnormality. They reported that the voices had stopped, talked normally with other patients, and made observations in their notebooks. Although some of the other patients suspected that the investigators were not really ill, the staff did not. In fact, one staff report ominously described an investigator's note taking as "patient engages in writing behavior." Even upon discharge, the pseudopatients were still diagnosed as schizophrenic, though now it was "schizophrenia in remission."

A person who presents himself to a mental hospital for admission may pose a difficult problem for the hospital staff. Is he really "mentally ill" and in need of hospitalization, or is he basically "healthy"? Is he no longer able to function in the outside world, or is he merely seeking a break from his work or his family? Or might he be faking?

The staff doctor must determine what kind of person the potential patient really is by gathering information, classifying it as indicating illness or health, combining this information into a general impression, and picking a diagnostic label (schizophrenic, paranoid, mildly depressed) that suggests what form of treatment should be administered. While performing these actions, the staff doctor is engaging in social perception. Broadly defined, **social perception** refers to constructing an understanding of the social world out of the data we obtain through our senses. More narrowly defined, social perception refers to the processes through which we use available information to form impressions of other people, to assess what they are like.

In making the diagnosis, the doctor also engages in attribution. That is, the physician judges the causes of the observed behavior, and infers from this behavior the personal characteristics (attributes) of the actor. **Attribution** is the process through which we link behavior to its causes—to the intentions, dispositions, and events that explain *why* people act as they do.

Social perception and attribution involve more than passively registering the stimuli that impinge upon our senses. Our current expectations and our prior experiences influence what we perceive and how we interpret it. The intake physician, for example, expects to meet people who are mentally ill, not research investigators, and so gathers information and interprets it in ways likely to confirm that expectation.

Our example demonstrates that social perception and attribution can be unreliable. Under some conditions, even a skilled observer can misperceive, misjudge, and reach the wrong conclusions. Once we form a wrong impression—like the staff member who saw "writing behavior" as a symptom of illness—we are liable to persist in our misperceptions and misjudgments. Yet our everyday social perceptions and attributions seem to work fairly well. The impressions we form of others and the judgments we make about the causes of behavior are usually accurate enough to permit smooth interaction.

In this chapter we will take a close look at the processes of social perception and attribution. We will address the following questions:

1. How do we use concepts to make sense of the flood of information that surrounds us? Why do we choose to use particular concepts in a situation, and why do we use stereotypes?

2. How do we form impressions of others? That is, how do we combine the diverse information we receive about someone into a coherent, overall impression?

3. How do we judge the causes of behavior and interpret the meaning of actions we observe? More specifically, when we judge someone's behavior, how do we decide what this behavior reflects about that person or about the situation?

4. What sorts of errors do we make in judging the behavior of others, and why do we make such errors?

Ordering the World

Concepts: What They Are

During most of our waking moments we are bombarded with sounds, colors, patterns of light, smells, pressures against our skin, and numerous other stimuli. Yet this bombardment is seldom the buzzing confusion it might be, because we impose some order on our environment. We perceive sounds as words or music, smells and colors as flowers or food, pressures as handshakes or kisses. The most fundamental point about perception for social psychology is that perceiving an object or an event in the environment involves categorizing (Bruner 1958). In other words, we employ concepts to organize the complex flow of incoming information into useful categories.

A **concept** is an idea that specifies how various objects or events are related or similar to each other. We have concepts of objects that are natural (butterflies) and manufactured (skyscrapers), physically real (hammers) and imaginary (elves). Concepts may refer to actions (flirting) or to feelings (compassion), to categories of people (hairdressers) or to specific individuals (Charlie Chaplin). They may

be as clearly defined as a "cheeseburger" or as loosely defined as "justice."

Functions of Concepts

What are the functions of concepts? First, concepts simplify our task in perceiving the world by grouping together similar experiences. Concepts direct our attention to particular aspects of stimuli and allow us to ignore others. If we perceive a neighborhood as "friendly," for example, we can walk down the street without attending carefully to every look from a passerby.

Concepts also enable us to go beyond the information immediately available in a situation. When we apply a concept to an object or event, we readily infer additional facts about it. When we recognize a discussion as a "bargaining session," we infer that the participants represent groups with conflicting interests. We may also infer that the opening statements are merely initial bargaining positions, that the bargainers are constrained by their group's wishes, and that vicious verbal attacks do not necessarily signify personal animosity.

The fact that concepts allow us to go beyond the information available also helps us know how to relate to objects. In "friendly" neighborhoods, we can smile at strangers, and we need not keep a hand on our wallet or clutch our handbag tightly. We know that it is safe to tell secrets to people who are "trustworthy," and that we had best remain tight-lipped in the presence of "gossips."

Finally, concepts allow us to predict the behavior of particular individuals using our general knowledge about the categories to which they belong. A person who is a "friend" will help change a flat tire; one who is a "vegetarian" will turn down a steak dinner. Without concepts to help us make predictions, we would be overwhelmed by uncertainty.

Choosing Which Concepts to Use

Through social learning we acquire a vast number of concepts for thinking about people.

Because we have thousands of concepts, we can classify people in any number of ways. For example, we might think of the same individual as a male, a midwesterner, a tennis player, or an introvert. What determines which concepts we are most likely to use in a given setting? This question is important, because the choice of concepts influences how we perceive others and how we relate to them. There are four factors that influence our choice of concepts: the purposes of the perceiver, the social context, the salience of the stimuli, and the accessibility of the concepts in memory.

PURPOSES OF THE PERCEIVER. The purposes or goals of the perceiver are one determinant of concept choice (Bruner 1957). We use concepts to determine how people are likely to affect the pursuit of our goals. The airport security guard must decide if rushing travellers are dangerous or safe, require a close search, or merely a cursory check. For this purpose he classifies passersby as tourists or smugglers, terrorists or vacationers. He scrutinizes their behavior for signs of evasiveness, nervousness, or bravado, traits that fit his concept of potentially dangerous persons. In contrast, travellers are more likely to perceive each other using concepts that reveal the potential for rewarding interaction—such as age, sex, physical attractiveness, smoking habits, and so on. These concepts suit a traveller's purposes.

SOCIAL CONTEXT. The social context of a behavior refers to the activities that are appropriate in a given setting, to the roles ordinarily enacted there, and to the people who are present. The social context strongly influences the concepts we use to label people and their behavior. For example, crowded record stores and sunny beaches are very different social contexts. Imagine someone stripping down to a swimsuit, spreading a towel, and stretching out on it. If he is alone on the beach, we might label his behavior "relaxation," and enviously think of him as a vacationer. If he is in the crowded record store, we are likely to label his

behavior "exhibitionism," and wonder whether he is crazy. Thus, we use different concepts to perceive the same behavior, depending on the social context.

SALIENCE OF STIMULI IN THE ENVIRONMENT. Our attention is drawn to things in our environment that stand out as vivid, distinctive, or unexpected. Such stimuli are salient. When perceiving behavior and situations, we tend to use the concepts that are evoked by these stimuli. Consider the use of concepts like "hair color" and "regional origin." In a group consisting entirely of blondes, hair color plays little role in peoples' perception. If a brunette appears, however, hair color becomes a salient concept for classifying people, as all notice her distinctiveness. We rarely use regional origin as a concept to discriminate among people. A man's ten-gallon hat and cowboy boots may capture our attention, however, and evoke regional origin. This may lead us to think about the regional origins of others around us as well.

ACCESSIBILITY IN MEMORY. Finally, our choice among concepts is influenced by the ease with which we can summon each concept from our memories. The more frequently we use particular concepts, and the more recently we have used them, the more accessible these concepts will be (Higgins and King 1981; Tversky and Kahneman 1974; Wyer and Srull 1981). Consider a student who learns that her roommate has broken both legs while mountain climbing. If the student has just spent a weekend discussing with her parents how careless, rash, and foolhardy college students can be, she is more likely to perceive her roommate as "reckless" than as "adventurous." Because concepts related to recklessness were used in the discussion with her parents, "reckless" is more accessible than "adventurous," although it is not necessarily more appropriate.

The effect of accessibility on concept use is especially interesting because it implies that chance events influence which concepts we employ. When we see a hitchhiker, for example, do we think about picking him up in terms of helpfulness and fun or rashness and danger? If we happen to have just visited the "reckless" mountain climber in the hospital, we are more likely to perceive the act of stopping for a hitchhiker as rash or potentially dangerous. Once a concept becomes accessible through its use for one purpose (perceiving a mountain climber), it is more likely to be used even for totally unrelated purposes (responding to a hitchhiker). Anything that heightens a concept's accessibility will increase its use.

Stereotypes of Groups

One way to simplify the complex world of people is to organize them into groups. We talk about Mexicans, blacks, and Catholics; about lawyers, used car salesmen, and college students. For each group, we have a **stereotype,** a fixed set of characteristics we tend to attribute to all group members (Ehrlich 1973; Lippman 1922). Stereotypes enable us to make quick judgments about people when we have only minimal information. They allow us to form impressions of people and to predict their behavior merely by knowing the groups to which they belong. Unfortunately, stereotypes are often negative, leading us to disparage the group stereotyped. And, of course, stereotypes are likely to be inaccurate. We often ignore this possibility, however, especially when making snap judgments.

ETHNIC AND GENDER STEREOTYPES. Some ethnic stereotypes held by Americans might include, for example, the view that Germans are industrious and scientifically minded, Irish quick-tempered, Italians passionate, and Americans materialistic (Karlins, Coffman, and Walters 1969). Racial and ethnic stereotypes have been studied intensively for many years, and the research shows clearly that these stereotypes have undergone change. Few of us now believe, as many once did, that the typical

We can hardly avoid jumping to conclusions about the personalities of these individuals, but are we right? Stereotypes enable us to make quick judgments about people merely by knowing the group they belong to.

American Indian is a drunk, or that the typical Chinese American is conservative. What is less clear, however, is whether these changes mean that stereotypes have actually faded.

Gender stereotypes are mong the most well-known commonly used stereotypes. In most cases, our first observation upon meeting or even just seeing people at a distance is to classify them as male or female. In spite of the women's movement this classification is likely to elicit a rich—though questionable—stereotype. Many men and women consider males more independent, dominant, aggressive, scientific, and stable in handling crises. They see females as more emotional, sensitive, gentle, helpful, and patient (Harrison 1978; Minnigerode and Lee 1978).

How do people view women who struggle against gender stereotypes? Is there a stereotype of feminists? In a study of this question,

Box 8.1
ARE ETHNIC STEREOTYPES CHANGING?

Contact between ethnic groups has greatly increased over the past 50 years. Has this increased contact been accompanied by a reduction in stereotypes? Studies of stereotypes among white Princeton undergraduates over four decades shed some light on this question. In 1932 (Katz and Braly 1933) students were asked to check off the traits on a list that they thought were typical of various groups. This same checklist was presented to Princeton students in 1950 (Gilbert 1951) and in 1967 (Karlins, Coffman, and Walters 1969). The last survey also asked students to rate each trait in terms of its favorableness. The

students' responses for four different groups—Americans, Italians, Negroes, and Jews—are shown below.

At first glance, it may seem that stereotypes have faded over the last 35 years. Compared with 1932 undergraduates, few 1967 undergraduates characterized Americans as industrious or intelligent, Italians as artistic or impulsive, Negroes as superstitious or lazy, and Jews as shrewd or mercenary. Overall, the percentage of undergraduates who agreed with any of the most common stereotypes in 1932 declined substantially.

A closer look at the data, however,

STEREOTYPES OF FOUR ETHNIC GROUPS

		Percent Calling the Trait "Typical"		
		1932	1950	1967
Americans	Industrious	48	30	23
	Intelligent	47	32	20
	Materialistic	33	37	67
	Ambitious	33	21	42
	Progressive	27	5	17
	Pleasure-loving	26	27	28
Italians	Artistic	53	28	30
	Impulsive	44	19	28
	Passionate	37	25	44
	Quick-tempered	35	15	28
	Musical	32	22	9
	Imaginative	30	20	7
Negroes	Superstitious	84	41	13
	Lazy	75	31	26
	Happy-go-lucky	38	17	27
	Ignorant	38	24	11
	Musical	26	33	47
	Ostentatious	26	11	25
Jews	Shrewd	79	47	30
	Mercenary	49	28	15
	Industrious	48	29	33
	Grasping	34	17	17
	Intelligent	29	37	37
	Ambitious	21	28	48

Source: adapted from Karlins, Coffman, and Walters (1969).

reveals that the percentages for some of the traits viewed as "typical" of a group actually increased during this period. For instance, more undergraduates in 1967 said Americans are materialistic and ambitious than did undergraduates in 1932. Likewise, Italians were more frequently viewed as passionate in 1967 than in 1932, Negroes as more musical, and Jews as more intelligent and ambitious. If we pay attention to the type of traits assigned to the various groups, an interesting trend appears. Students have become more positive in their stereotypes of Negroes and Jews, but they have become more negative in their self-stereotypes as Americans.

The trend toward expressing less negative stereotypes of minority groups suggests a possible problem with the checklist method for measuring stereotypes. There has been a growing sensitivity in America to prejudiced statements about minorities. The idea that negative stereotyping of minority groups is bigoted and socially undesirable has become especially strong on college campuses. Perhaps, then, negative stereotypes have not faded; they have merely gone underground.

To address this issue, researchers developed an ingenious method for measuring stereotypes (Sigall and Page 1971). Half their respondents evaluated how characteristic various traits were of white Americans and of blacks using a standard questionnaire procedure. The remaining respondents were wired to a sophisticated-looking machine through bogus electrodes on their forearms. They were persuaded that this "EMG" machine could measure their true, undistorted feelings. Their task, when evaluating the traits typical of groups, was to see how accurately they could sense their own feelings by predicting the EMG readings. Students wired to the EMG were under pressure to respond honestly, because they believed any lying would be detected. Students using the standard questionnaire, however, had no reason to fear detection if they responded in a socially desirable manner.

The results of this study indicate that responses to standard questionnaires or interviews may be biased due to attempts to hide bigotry. In the EMG condition blacks were characterized as having positive traits (honest, sensitive, intelligent) less often than whites, and as having negative traits (lazy, unreliable, stupid, physically dirty) more often than whites. In the standard rating (checklist) condition, blacks were characterized as more honest and sensitive than whites and whites as more lazy, unreliable, and stupid than blacks. Thus, a negative stereotype of blacks emerged only in the honesty-eliciting EMG condition. The stereotype was even partly reversed in the standard rating condition, as if students were bending over backward to present themselves as unprejudiced.

The picture is not entirely discouraging, however. The black stereotype revealed in the EMG condition was still less negative than the Negro stereotype expressed by students in 1932. The researchers conclude that the apparent changes in stereotypes of blacks (Negroes) over four decades probably reflect a "little fading and a little faking." What are the current stereotypes on your campus today? How sure can you be?

researchers gave photographs of 30 women to male and female college students and asked them simply to identify 15 of these women as supporters of the women's liberation movement (Goldberg, Gottesdiener, and Abramson 1975). The women identified as feminists were the least attractive women in the group. To determine whether the implied stereotype that "feminists are unattractive" might have some basis in reality, the researchers asked the 30 women whose photos had been used for their attitudes toward women's liberation. In addition, a group of judges rated the physical attractiveness of each woman's photo. Results showed that the attractiveness ratings of the actual feminists were no different from the ratings of the nonfeminists.

ORIGINS OF STEREOTYPES. In addition to the stereotypes we have described, people regularly attribute characteristics to members of groups defined by occupation, age, hobbies, school attended, and so on. How do various stereotypes originate? One possibility is that stereotypes arise out of direct experience with a member of the stereotyped group (Campbell 1967). We may once have known Italians who were passionate, blacks who were musical, or Japanese who were polite. We then build a stereotype by overgeneralizing: we infer that *all* members of a group share the attribute that we know to be characteristic of particular members. Thus stereotypes may be based on a "kernel of truth."

Another basis of stereotypes may be the need to boost our own self-esteem (Allport 1954). This would explain why most stereotypes are negative. By comparing ourselves with groups of others whom we stereotype as inferior, we can assert our own superiority (Katz 1960). People are also motivated to increase the solidarity of their own group by developing negative stereotypes of groups with whom they compete, whether on the battlefield or in the economic arena.

Recent research suggests, however, that stereotypes arise even in the absence of a kernel of truth or of self-interested motivation. Stereotyping appears to be a natural outcome of social perception. When people have to process and remember a great deal of information about others, they tend to store this information in terms of group categories rather than in terms of individuals (Taylor et al. 1978). In trying to remember what went on in a classroom discussion, you may recall that several women spoke and that a black expressed a strong opinion, even though you cannot remember which women spoke or who the black was. Because people remember behavior by group rather than by individual,

they are likely to form stereotypes of these groups (Rothbart et al. 1978). Remembering that *women* spoke and that a *black* expressed a strong opinion, you might infer that women are talkative in general, and that blacks are opinionated. You would not form these stereotypes if you remembered these characteristics as belonging to unique individuals.

ERRORS CAUSED BY STEREOTYPES. Although some stereotypes may contain a kernel of truth, stereotypes are always overgeneralizations. They therefore inevitably lead to various errors in social perception and judgment. First, stereotypes lead us to assume that all members of a group possess certain traits. Yet—obviously—individual members of a group may vary greatly on any trait. One football player may shoulder you into the stairwell on a crowded bus; another may offer you his seat. Second, stereotypes lead us to assume that all the members of one group differ greatly from all the members of other groups. Football players and ballet dancers, for instance, may be thought to have nothing in common. In fact, among football players as well as among ballet dancers there are individuals who are patient, neurotic, hardworking, intelligent, and so on.

Stereotypes also promote inaccurate perceptions because people mistakenly assume that the salient features they use to distinguish between groups are also the *causes* of all differences between the groups. For example, skin color is a salient feature that leads people to distinguish racial groups. Once people distinguish groups by skin color, they also tend to assume that all other differences between these groups are due to race. Thus, people attribute the fact that whites obtain higher average scores than blacks on standard intelligence tests to race. By focusing on this one salient feature, they ignore other more likely causes such as socioeconomic opportunities, education, and cultural bias in tests.

RESISTANCE TO CHANGE. Stereotypes are resistant to change even in the face of evidence that contradicts them. This is because people tend to welcome evidence that confirms their stereotypes and to ignore or explain away disconfirming evidence (Lord, Lepper, and Mackie 1984; Weber and Crocker 1983). Suppose that Stan stereotypes homosexual males as effeminate, nonathletic, and artistic. If he stumbles upon a homosexual bar, he is especially likely to notice those males who fit this description, thereby confirming his stereotype. What does he make of the masculine-looking, athletic males who are there? There are several ways he can prevent their presence from threatening his stereotype. He might scrutinize them closely for hidden signs of effeminacy; underestimate their number and say they are atypical; comment that they are the exceptions that prove the rule; or even assume that they, like he, are outsiders. Through responses like these, people explain away contradictory information and preserve their stereotypes. Can you think of instances in which you have used such methods to defend stereotypes you hold?

CONCLUSION. We have noted that stereotypes distort our perceptions of others and are sometimes harmful. Yet stereotypes also serve a valuable purpose. As perceivers, we constantly strive to go beyond the information available to us at the moment, and stereotypes help us to do this. They enable us to infer all sorts of facts about a person as soon as we identify the groups of which the person is a member. Without stereotypes, we would be limited to the small amount we know about someone based on our experiences with him or her. Stereotypes enable us to generalize beyond the concrete behaviors and physical characteristics of an individual, and to predict what that individual is likely to do in many other settings. But the information we gain through stereotypes may be invalid. That stereotypes help us to generalize is their blessing; that they also lead us to overgeneralize is their curse.

Forming Impressions

Imagine that one day a faculty member appears in your social psychology class to announce that your regular instructor is away, and, because the department is interested in how students react to different teachers, a guest instructor will teach your class today. To give students some idea of what the guest instructor is like, the faculty member first passes out a short biographical sketch. After the guest instructor leads a 20-minute discussion, you are asked to complete a questionnaire reporting your impressions of him.

This procedure was used as part of an actual study (Kelley 1950). In this field experiment, Kelley distributed two different personality sketches; he gave one sketch to half the class and the other sketch to the other half. Both sketches included identical information. They described the guest instructor as industrious, critical, practical, and determined. The two sketches differed in only one detail—whether they described the instructor as *warm* or *cold*. This one detail profoundly influenced the impressions students formed following the discussion. Those who had read that the guest instructor was *cold* rated him as less considerate, sociable, popular, good-natured, humorous, and humane than those who had read he was *warm*. Because the students all simultaneously observed the same guest instructor engaging in the same classroom behavior, their different impressions could only have been based on the warm/cold trait in the profile they had read earlier.

How could a single variation embedded in otherwise identical profiles have such an impact on impressions of someone's actual behavior? One explanation is that the students had a theory about which traits go with being warm and which go with being cold. The students may have believed, for example, that people who are cold are also inconsiderate and antisocial, whereas people who are warm are also popular and good-natured. The impressions of the students would then have reflected their assumptions about which personality traits typically go together rather than their actual observations of the instructor's behavior.

Implicit Personality Theories

People do make assumptions about how personality traits are related—which ones go together and which do not. These assumptions are called **implicit personality theories** (Bruner and Tagiuri 1954; Schneider 1973). People do not subject their theories about personality to explicit, systematic examination, nor are people typically aware of the contents of these theories—hence the label "implicit." Implicit personality theories can be viewed as a special form of stereotype (Schneider, Hastorf, and Ellsworth 1979). They are stereotypes regarding the set of traits that we assume to be characteristic of all people who have a given trait. Just as we assume that Mexicans have particular attributes, we also assume that "warm" people or "cold" people have particular attributes.

Because we are not conscious of our implicit personality theories, we can draw upon them without realizing it to flesh out our impressions of a person based on just a few bits of information. Instead of withholding judgment until we know more about their relevant traits, we jump to conclusions about others' personalities using our implicit personality theories. Upon learning that a person is pessimistic, for example, we tend to assume that he is also humorless, irritable, and unpopular, even when we lack evidence that he in fact possesses these traits.

MENTAL MAPS. An implicit personality theory is best pictured as a "mental map" of the way we believe traits are related to one another. Traits we believe to be similar to each other are located close together in our mental map, meaning that people who possess one probably possess the other. Traits we believe to be dissimilar, are located far apart, meaning that they rarely occur together in one person. The mental map in Figure 8.1 shows relationships among various traits, or attributes, based on judgments made by college students (Rosenberg, Nelson, and Vivekananthan 1968).

If your own mental map is similar to the one portrayed in Figure 8.1, you are likely to think that people who are wasteful are also unintelligent and irresponsible (see lower left part of map), and that people who are persistent are likely to be determined and skillful (upper right). When you observe that a person has a particular trait, you infer that the person possesses those traits which are close to it on your mental map.

Figure 8.1 neatly clarifies the "warm-cold" findings in Kelley's study. Note the locations of "warm" and "cold" on the map. Now note the other attributes close by. The "warm" instructor was judged as more sociable, popular, good-natured, and humorous than the "cold" instructor because these traits are all located close to "warm" and far from "cold" on many poeple's mental maps.

Attempts to map people's implicit personality theories consistently reveal that traits are organized along two distinct positive-negative dimensions—a social good-bad dimension and an intellectual good-bad dimension. These dimensions are represented by the lines shown in Figure 8.1. "Warm" and "cold" differ mainly on the social dimension, for example, whereas "lazy" and "industrious" differ on the intellectual dimension (Rosenberg and Sedlak 1972). Some traits (such as "important") are good on both the social and the intellectual dimensions, while other traits (such as "unreliable") are bad on both. In fact, there is a general tendency for traits to be either good or bad on both dimensions.

The fact that traits are arranged along good-bad dimensions in implicit personality theories explains a common bias in impression formation. We tend to judge persons who have one good trait as generally good, and those who have one bad trait as generally bad. Once we believe a person has a specific trait we assume the other traits nearby in our mental

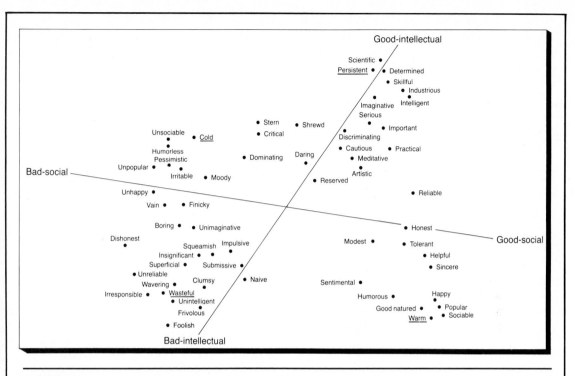

FIGURE 8.1

RELATIONSHIPS AMONG ATTRIBUTES: A MENTAL MAP

Each of us has an implicit theory of personality—a theory about which personality attributes tend to go together and which do not. We can represent our theories of personality in the form of a mental map. The closer attributes are located to each other on our mental map, the more we assume that these attributes will appear in the same person. The mental map shown above is based on the mental maps of many American college students.

Source: adapted from Rosenberg, Nelson, and Vivekananthan (1968).

map also apply to that person. This tendency to perceive personalities as clusters of either good or bad traits is called the **halo effect** (Thorndike 1920).

ORIGINS OF IMPLICIT PERSONALITY THEORIES. Where do our implicit personality theories come from? First, they come from the distilled wisdom of our socializers, who use expressions like, "power corrupts," "ignorance is bliss," and "tall, dark, and (*fill in the blank*)." These expressions tell us which traits go together. Second, and probably more important, the very meanings of words in our language suggest certain relationships. The word "generous" implies both "helpful" and "sympathetic"; "fickle" implies "unreliable" and "unpredictable." As a result, when one word applies to a person, we assume that other words which share similar meanings also apply (Shweder 1977). Third, people we know actually do possess sets of personality characteristics that occur together, further contributing to implicit personality theories (Lay and Jackson 1969; Stricker, Jacobs, and Kogan 1974). For example, skillful people we meet often exhibit determination and intelligence.

INDIVIDUAL DIFFERENCES. Within any single culture and language group, individuals share many socialization experiences and word meanings. Their implicit personality theories therefore share a common core. Yet each of us also has unique experiences that contribute a unique component to our implicit personality theories (Kelley 1955; Rosenberg 1977).

Our unique experiences direct our attention to particular trait categories when we form impressions. For example, when meeting someone, some of us may pay particular attention to physical attractiveness, others to intelligence, others to friendliness, and so on. Suppose that two people meet the same intelligent, friendly individual. If one attends more to intelligence, she is likely to form an impression that the individual is industrious, imaginative, and skillful—all traits associated with intelligence in most people's mental maps. If the other attends more to friendliness, he is likely to form an impression that the individual is popular, good-natured, and warm—traits associated with friendly. Both impressions may be valid, and they are not necessarily contradictory; but they are very different. Thus, people's impressions reflect as much about their own modes of perception as they do about the characteristics of the person being perceived (Higgins, King, and Mavin 1982).

This point was illustrated in a study of summer camp children who were asked to describe their impressions of each other after spending a few weeks together at camp (Dornbusch et al. 1965). When asked to describe their tentmates, each child tended to use his own set of trait categories to describe them all. For example, if Don described Jeffrey using the categories aggressive, excitable, and generous, then Don also tended to use these same traits when describing Larry. Whereas Bob described both Jeffrey and Larry in terms of aggressiveness, humor, and cooperativeness, Jim described them both in terms of humor, confidence, and daring. As this example shows, there is likely to be only limited overlap in the trait categories that different perceivers use to describe the people they meet. As a result, our individual preferences for using particular trait categories substantially influence the impressions we form of others.

Processing Information into Impressions

In everyday life, we often receive a lot of information at once. New experiences with others typically add information to impressions we already hold. Our task as perceivers is to process all this information, to put it together into an overall impression. If your uncle, whom you view as loving and tolerant, criticizes your cousin for his sloppy clothes and stringy hair, how do you make sense of this new information? You might conclude that your uncle's personality is not well-integrated. More likely, however, you would try to understand how this contradictory information fits with your earlier impression of your uncle. In general, people try to integrate the many attributes they perceive in others—to create a unified impression in which seemingly contradictory traits cohere (Asch 1946; Asch and Zukier 1984). For example, you might conclude that your uncle's apparent intolerance was motivated by his love for your cousin and desire to protect him from others' criticism.

Most studies of how we combine information make one assumption: that the overall positive-negative evaluation we make of a person is the most important aspect of our impressions. Although this assumption is limiting, it seems justified by two facts. First, studies of implicit personality theories show that *evaluation* is the most important dimension on our mental maps of personality traits. Second, this evaluative dimension is crucial when we make practical judgments: we reject a job because overall we think it is poor; we invite a new acquaintance to a party because we like her.

Assume that we wish to predict the overall evaluation people would make of someone who is "sincere, friendly, cautious, and dis-

TABLE 8.1

A COMPARISON OF ADDITIVE AND AVERAGING MODELS FOR FORMING IMPRESSIONS

Model	Trait Combinations							
	I		II		III		IV	
Additive	sincere	+3	sincere	+3	serious	+1	serious	+1
	friendly	+2	friendly	+2	irresponsible	−3	irresponsible	−3
	tolerant	+1	tolerant	+1	dishonest	−3	dishonest	−3
			cautious	+1			unimaginative	−1
Overall impression:		+6		+7		−5		−6
Averaging	sincere	+3	sincere	+3	serious	+1	serious	+1
	friendly	+2	friendly	+2	irresponsible	−3	irresponsible	−3
	tolerant	+1	tolerant	+1	dishonest	−3	dishonest	−3
			cautious	+1			unimaginative	−1
Overall impression:		+2.00		+1.75		−1.67		−1.50

honest." First, we can determine how positively or negatively people evaluate each one of these traits. Most college students assign highly positive values to such traits as *sincere* (say +3), less positive values to *friendly* (+2) and *cautious* (+1), and negative values to *dishonest* (−3) (Anderson 1968). Next, we need to find the best way to combine the trait values in order to predict accurately the overall impression people will form.

MODELS OF IMPRESSION FORMATION. Several different models have been proposed to predict the overall favorableness of impressions. According to the **additive model,** we predict best by summing the values of all the single traits. An example of the additive model is shown in the top panel of Table 8.1 with four different combinations of traits. A key feature of the additive model is that when we add traits with a positive value, we increase the favorableness of our overall impression (Column I vs. Column II), whereas when we add traits with a negative value, we decrease favorableness (Column III vs. Column IV).

Another method we could use involves combining all the information we have about a person and *averaging* the values for all the single traits we associate with that person (see

bottom panel of Table 8.1.) In this **averaging model,** the effect of adding new information depends on whether it is more or less favorable than the overall impression we already have. Thus, adding a mildly positive trait to a strongly positive impression makes it less positive (Column I versus Column II), whereas adding a mildly negative trait to a strongly negative impression makes it less negative (Column III versus Column IV).

The bulk of evidence from studies of impression formation supports a refined version of the averaging model called the **weighted averaging model** (Anderson 1981). According to this model, people give more weight to certain types of information and less to others. Several factors influence the weights people assign to information. First, we give greater weight to information obtained from credible sources than to information from less reliable sources. Second, we tend to weight negative attributes more heavily than positive attributes, perhaps because negative information is more striking in a world where people present favorable fronts. Third, we attend more to attributes that are particularly relevant to the judgment at hand—a lawyer's brain rather than her brawn. Fourth, we discount information that is very inconsistent with our previous impressions and stereotypes, or

This man makes a first impression as strong, stern, self-controlled, and daring. First impressions are hard to change because people pay less attention to later information and also tend to interpret it as consistent with their first impression. Told the man is fearful, for example, observers are likely to ignore this information or to interpret it as meaning he shows healthy fear in extremely dangerous situations.

information that is totally redundant with what we already know. Finally, we weight early impressions more heavily than subsequent impressions. We consider the importance of first impressions in more detail below.

FIRST IMPRESSIONS. You have surely noticed the special effort that individuals make to create a good impression when starting a new job, entering a new group, or meeting an attractive potential date. This effort reflects the widely held belief that first impressions are especially important. In fact, this is one case where folk wisdom is supported by a large body of research. Information that is presented early in a sequence is weighted more heavily in impression formation than information presented later. This phenomenon is called the **primacy effect** (Luchins 1957).

What accounts for the power of first impressions? One explanation is that after forming an initial impression of a person, we interpret later information in a way that makes it consistent with our initial impression. Having concluded that your new roommate is neat and considerate, you interpret the dirty socks on the floor the next day as a sign of temporary forgetfulness rather than of sloppiness and lack of concern. This explanation asserts that the existing picture into which new information is placed influences the interpretation of that new information (Asch 1946; Zanna and Hamilton 1977).

A second explanation for the primacy effect is that we attend most carefully to the first bits of information we obtain about a person, but that our attention wanes once we feel we have enough information to make a judgment. It is not that we interpret later information differently; we simply use it less. This explanation assumes that whatever information we attend to most will have the greatest effect on our impressions (Anderson and Hubert 1963; Dreben, Fiske, and Hastie 1979). At this point, there is evidence that both reinterpretation of later information and waning of attention contribute to the power of first impressions.

Under certain conditions, the latest information we acquire exerts the strongest influence on our impressions. This is known as a **recency effect** (Luchins 1957; Jones and Goethals 1971), which occurs when we attend more to later information than to earlier information. We may become suddenly attentive, for example, when a friend reports: "You'll never guess where I saw your roommate last night. . . ." A recency effect is also likely to occur when so much time has passed that we have largely forgotten our first impression, or when we are judging characteristics that we expect to change over time, like moods or certain attitudes. In most everyday interaction, however, the primacy effect prevails.

The primacy effect is a potential cause of social injustice. In a study demonstrating this potential (Jones et al. 1968), subjects observed the performance of a college student on an SAT-type aptitude test. In one condition, the student started off successfully on the first few items, after which his performance deteriorated steadily. In a second condition, the student started poorly then gradually improved. In both conditions, the students answered 15 out of 30 test items correctly. After observing one or the other performance, subjects were asked to rate the student's intelligence and to predict how well he would do on the next 30 items. Remember that overall performance was the same in both conditions. Nonetheless, subjects rated the student who started well and then tailed off as more intelligent than the student who started poorly and improved. They also predicted that the former would do better on the next series. Apparently, subjects gave more weight to the students' performance on the first few items—a clear primacy effect.

Consider the consequences such a primacy effect might have in school. Students who start the semester poorly but then improve will probably be judged more negatively than they deserve to be by teachers and peers. Students with relatively weak backgrounds who are bound to perform poorly at first compared with their better prepared classmates are especially disadvantaged by the primacy effect. And what if a teacher forms an impression about a student before he enters the classroom because he is a member of a stereotyped minority group? The primacy effect will make it extremely difficult for that student to shake the negative first impression others hold.

Impressions as Self-Fulfilling Prophecies

Whether correct or not, the impressions we form of people influence our behavior toward them. Recall, for instance, the students who read that their guest instructor was "warm" or "cold" before meeting him (Kelley 1950). Not only did they form different impressions of the instructor, they also

behaved differently toward him. Those who believed the instructor was "warm" participated more in the class discussion than those who believed he was "cold." In fact the students' participation in class may have influenced the way the guest instructor behaved toward them. He may have acted more warmly toward those who believed he was warm because they participated more in the discussion.

When our behavior toward people reflects our impressions of them, we may cause them to react in ways that confirm our original impressions. If we ignore someone because we think he is dull, for example, he will probably withdraw and add nothing interesting to the conversation. Because our own actions evoke appropriate reactions from others, our initial impressions (correct or incorrect) are often confirmed by the reactions of others. Thus, our impressions may become self-fulfilling prophecies (Merton 1948; Darley and Fazio 1980).

A study of "getting acquainted" conversations between male and female college students demonstrates how impressions may become self-fulfilling (Snyder, Tanke, and Berscheid 1977). The study provided males with a snapshot of either an attractive coed or of an unattractive coed, and asked them to rate her personality. Consistent with a physical-attractiveness stereotype, the snapshot of the attractive woman generated more favorable personality impressions. Each man then engaged in a "get acquainted" phone conversation presumably with the woman in his picture. Men who believed their partner was attractive, spoke with more animation, sociability, and warmth than those who thought their partner was unattractive—evidence that their impressions influenced their own behavior. Although the women knew nothing about their partners' impressions, they responded in a more poised, confident, animated, sociable, sexually warm, and outgoing manner when they were speaking with men who thought they were attractive rather than unattractive. The responses of the women demonstrate the

TABLE 8.2

IMPRESSIONS AS SELF-FULFILLING PROPHECIES IN SCHOOLS AND THE MILITARY

	Sequence of Steps		
	Initial Impression ⟶	*Action* ⟶	*Target's Confirming Reaction*
School	Teachers believe particular students have unusually high potential for intellectual growth, even though these students do not differ from others.	Teachers show greater warmth to students and allow them more time to think when they are unsure of answers.	These particular students raise their scores on intelligence tests over time.
U.S. Army	Company leaders believe groups of enlisted men—especially blacks—are lawless, although they have no objective evidence of lawbreaking.	Company leaders deal harshly with the enlisted men and punish them.	The enlisted men react to punishment with a sense of injustice that spurs them to defiant lawbreaking.

self-fulfilling impact of the men's impressions on their behavior. They also demonstrate the continuous, reciprocal impact that people have on each others' behavior.

Table 8.2 shows the sequence of steps in self-fulfilling prophecies in two important settings—schools and the military. In many studies, students whose teachers believed that they had high potential responded by growing intellectually (Rosenthal 1973; Rosenthal and Rubin 1978). Teachers expressed their positive impressions of students by showing more warmth, closer attentiveness, more frequent contact, and greater persistence in seeking responses to questions (Brophy and Good 1974; Snodgrass and Rosenthal 1982). Another study involving thousands of American soldiers shows that impressions which become self-fulfilling prophecies can also do harm (Hart 1978). In this case, groups of enlisted men, especially blacks, behaved according to the "lawless" steroetype, which their company leaders conveyed to them through imposing unjustified punishments. Thus punishment led to crime.

Attribution: Explaining and Interpreting Behavior

When we interact with other people for the first time, they seldom announce their traits, or provide us with a list of qualities to integrate into our impressions. Rather, we observe words and actions that require interpretation. When a woman performs a favor, does it mean she is generous or manipulative? When she teases a man, does it mean she likes him or that she thinks he's ridiculous? In order to build impressions, we must first figure out *why* people act as they do. Once we have done this, we may be able to predict their future behavior and choose how to act effectively toward them ourselves.

As defined earlier, *attribution* refers to the process through which we link behavior to its causes—to the intentions, abilities, traits, motives, and situational events that explain why people act as they do. Attribution theories focus on the methods we use to interpret other people's behavior and its meaning. They describe how the average person comes to attribute behavior to one or more of its possible causes (Ross and Fletcher 1985).

Most people use commonsense reasoning to understand the causes of behavior. Whether or not their beliefs about behavior are scientifically valid, people act on the basis of these beliefs. Fritz Heider (1944, 1958), whose work stimulated the study of attribution, argued that we must take people's ordinary, commonsense explanations and understandings into consideration if we are to explain human behavior.

Dispositional Versus Situational Attributions

Central to Heider's theoretical analysis of commonsense reasoning is that people, in their efforts to understand the causes of a behavior, subject the events they observe to a kind of psychological analysis. The most crucial decision that observers make is whether to attribute the behavior to the person who performed it (a *dispositional attribution*) or to the surrounding situation (a *situational attribution*).

Consider the attributions you might make upon observing that your neighbor is unemployed. You might judge that he is out of work because he is lazy, irresponsible, or lacking in ability. These are dispositional attributions, because they attribute the causes of someone's behavior to the internal qualities of the person. Alternatively, you might attribute his unemployment to racial discrimination, to the evils of capitalism, or to the poor state of the economy. These are situational attributions, because they attribute the person's behavior to external causes.

DETERMINANTS. What determines whether people attribute an act to a person's dispositions or to the situation? Heider suggests that people consider two factors in making this decision—situational pressures and the actor's intentions. Consider two sets of circumstances in which a man and a woman have sexual intercourse. If the woman succumbed to the act at knifepoint, observers would call this rape, attributing her behavior to overwhelming situational pressures. But suppose there is no knife and the couple are on a date when the alleged rape occurs. What attribution will observers make?

Even when situational pressures are weak (as in the absence of a weapon), an attribution to personal dispositions is uncertain unless observers believe the act is intentional. How do ordinary observers decide whether or not a behavior is intentional? They examine the situation for evidence regarding three questions: (1) How voluntary was the act? (Did the woman or the man initiate physical interaction?) (2) Did the actor engage in other behaviors clearly aimed at the same end? (Did the woman encourage the man's sexual overtures or did she merely agree to a date?) (3) How much effort did the actor exert to perform the act or to avoid the act? (Did the woman go to great pains to be alone with the man or work hard to avoid being alone with him?)

In short, ordinary observers infer intention based on whether an act is voluntary, whether it is goal-directed, and whether a great deal of effort is exerted to perform the act. When observers conclude that an act is intentional, they usually attribute it to the actor's personal dispositions.

SOCIAL CONSEQUENCES. Under certain conditions, the choice between dispositional and situational attribution may have important social consequences. Dispositional attributions define suffering as due to personal problems (Mills 1959) and prescribe solutions through treating individuals (therapy, counseling, handouts). Situational attributions, however, define suffering as a social problem, and prescribe solutions via changes in the social structure (revolutions, job retraining programs, subsidized employment). Consider the fact that most women in Western societies have lower status and lower-paying jobs than most men. If we attribute this fact to women's personal dispositions (fear of success, lack of assertiveness, poorer skills), we would be implying that women should go into psychotherapy, receive assertiveness training, or work harder to improve their skills. If we attribute this fact to sexual prejudice and discrimination in society, we would be implying that societal structures and attitudes are at fault and that reducing discrimination against women in the work-place, providing adequate day-care facilities, changing societal definitions of sex-appropriate roles, and so on, are the appropriate solutions.

A second social consequence of dispositional versus situational attribution concerns the upholding of moral and legal standards of society. If we hold individuals responsible for their own acts, it follows that we should reward them for conformity to social standards and punish them for deviance. Such dispositional attributions support societal standards. If, on the other hand, we attribute acts of crime and violence to the situation—to alienating conditions in inner cities, for example—it is less reasonable to blame the perpetrators and to punish them. Thus, situational attributions may undermine social conformity and morality.

From Acts to Intentions to Specific Dispositions

We have already shown how Heider (1944, 1958) identified the conditions under which we tend to make dispositional attributions. What his theoretical analysis does not explain, however, is which specific dispositions we will choose. Suppose a student protests publicly to a professor that the exam grades in a course are unfairly low. What specific disposition will we attribute to this student? Is the student "courageous," "competitive," "foolish," or what? How do we choose among possible dispositions?

When we try to infer a person's specific dispositions, our perspective is much like that of a detective. According to one theory (Jones and Davis 1965), there are two major steps in the process of inferring personal dispositions.

First, we try to deduce a person's specific intentions from his actions. In other words, we try to figure out what the person originally intended to achieve by performing the act.

From these intentions we then try to infer what personal disposition would cause a person to have such intentions. If we conclude that an act was intended to help, for example, we infer the disposition "helpful." In other words, we attribute a disposition that corresponds with the presumed intention.

In order to figure out a person's intentions, we consider the effects that the person was likely to have anticipated from his action. The student who protested about exam grades, for example, may have anticipated that the professor would respond by raising her grade, raising everyone's grade, reducing the weight of this exam in the course grade, ignoring her protest, criticizing her personally, and so on. We do not consider effects of the action that the actor could neither anticipate nor control. We could infer nothing about the student's intentions or dispositions, for example, if the professor challenged her to a duel, because the student doubtless neither anticipated nor controlled this effect.

The process of inferring dispositions from acts is summarized in Figure 8.2. Panel A traces the general process from the perception of the effects of an action to the inference that a particular effect was intended, to the disposition attributed to the person. Panel B illustrates the process using a concrete example. It lists three effects of the student's public protest. If we infer that the student's intention was to improve everyone's grade, we might conclude that the disposition "concerned for others" corresponds to this intention.

What of the other effects in our example? The effect "professor suffers heart attack" was unanticipated and would therefore probably not influence attribution. But the effect "classmates impressed" presents a problem. What if we inferred that this was what the student really intended to achieve? This would imply

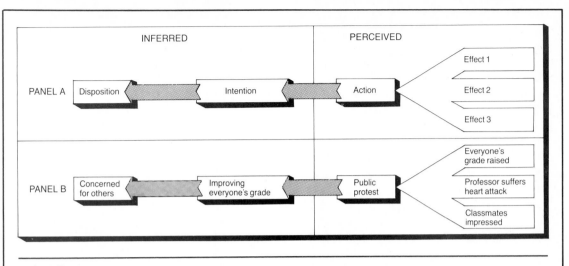

FIGURE 8.2

<small>Attributing Specific Dispositions</small>

The process of attributing a particular disposition to a person entails a sequence of steps. The observer perceives an action together with its effects. From these effects, the observer infers the person's intention—what that person wanted to achieve. From this intention, the observer infers the person's dispositions—the kind of a person that he or she is. For example, persons who observe a student protesting grades in a course might note the three effects of this action listed in Panel B. If they conclude that the student's intention was to improve everyone's grade, they might attribute the disposition "concerned for others" to her.

Source: adapted from Jones and Davis (1965).

the very different disposition of "show-off." The problem is that most acts have multiple effects. A different disposition may correspond to each intended effect. In order to make confident attributions, perceivers must decide which effect(s) the person is really pursuing and which effects are merely incidental. Two main factors influence these decisions. These are the commonality and normativeness of effects (Jones and Davis 1965).

COMMONALITY. Any act that a person chooses to carry out has its own set of effects. The circles shown in Figure 8.3 illustrate a set of effects associated with each of three alternatives. Note that some of these effects are common to more than one alternative. For example, (a) "improving everyone's grade" is common to protesting publicly and circulating a petition. Other common effects are (c) and (f). The remaining effects (b,d,e,g,h) are unique to a particular alternative. These are *noncommon* effects. For example, (d) "impressing classmates with courage" is unique to protesting publicly.

Jones and Davis theorize that observers who are interested in attributing specific dispositions to an actor will try to identify effects that are unique to the action chosen. Only the unique (noncommon) effects may explain why an actor chooses one particular action over the alternatives. For example, noncommon effects of the student's protest are (d) "impressing classmates with courage" and (h) "risks personal criticism by professor." Observers of the student are therefore likely to concentrate on

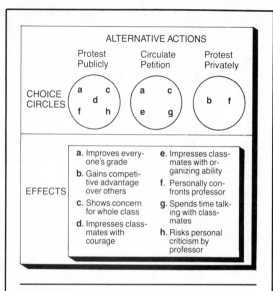

FIGURE 8.3

ATTRIBUTING DISPOSITIONS FROM THE NONCOMMON EFFECTS OF THE ALTERNATIVE CHOSEN

A student who wishes to protest the low grades a professor gives on an exam might protest publicly in class, circulate a petition, or protest privately during the professor's office hours. Each of these alternative actions has a set of effects, represented in the choice circles. Some effects are common to more than one alternative (common effects a,c,f), others are unique to a particular alternative (noncommon effects b,d,e,g,h). Observers are most likely to attribute dispositions to an actor based on the noncommon effects of the alternative chosen.

effects (d) and (h) and to attribute to her dispositions like "courageous" (corresponding to d) or "fearless but foolish" (corresponding to h).

The fewer noncommon effects associated with the chosen alternative, the more confident observers can be about their attributions (Ajzen and Holmes 1976). According to our example, there are two noncommon effects of public protest. Consequently, observers may not be sure whether the student was "courageous" or "fearless but foolish." Had the student chosen to protest privately, however, there would have been only one noncommon effect, (b) "gains competitive advantage." This would have permitted a confident attribution of the disposition "competitive."

NORMATIVENESS. When inferring dispositions, observers also consider the normativeness of behavior. *Normativeness* is the extent to which we expect the average person to perform a behavior in a particular setting. People pursue normative behaviors because their effects are socially desirable. A person who seeks an effect that is socially desirable tells us only that he is "normal." It reveals nothing about his distinctive attributes. The less desirable the effect, however, the more confidently we can base attributions on it. Virtually no student would want a professor to criticize her personally. Hence we are quite confident that a student who knowingly provoked personal criticism is "fearless but foolish." Because impressing one's classmates is a more socially desirable effect, we would be less confident about the "courage" attribution.

Jones and McGillis (1976) have refined the normativeness concept to emphasize the role of expectations. They suggest that the more an action departs from what we would expect, the more confidence we will have in attributing a disposition from that action. Behavior that departs from what we would expect provides information. Socially undesirable effects yield firmer attributions because we do not expect people to pursue such effects. According to this view, unexpected actions that are socially *desirable*—such as extraordinary achievements—will also yield firm dispositional attributions.

This view is particularly useful for understanding how role expectations affect attributions. Actions that conform to role expectations are uninformative about personality dispositions. Actions that violate role expectations, on the other hand, are especially informative. Imagine a business executive preaching capitalism at a stockholders meeting. We cannot be entirely confident whether this view represents his true personal disposition or a role-required performance. We would be more confident in our attribution regarding his attitudes if he preached the opposite view ("share the wealth"). Numerous studies show that nonnormative, unexpected behavior, and especially behavior that violates role expectations, produces more confident inferences about the actor's dispositions (Jones 1979; Jones, Davis, and Gergen 1961; Miller 1976).

Attributing Cause from Different Types of Information

Up to this point we have examined how people make attributions based on single instances of behavior. Often, however, we obtain information about the way a person behaves in a variety of settings. In many cases, we can compare this person's behavior with the behavior of others. These different types of information make many different attributions possible. How do people verify whether they are correctly linking the cause and effect of a behavior? In an extension of Heider's (1958) ideas, Kelley (1967, 1973) addresses this question.

Suppose you hear a presidential candidate deliver a rousing speech favoring a nuclear freeze. To what would you attribute his behavior? Kelley (1967) identifies three potential causes: (1) the *actor*, (2) the *object* of the behavior, and (3) the *context* or setting in which the behavior occurs. For example, you might attribute the speech to the candidate's powerful personality (a characteristic of the *actor*), to the intrinsic value of a nuclear freeze (a characteristic of the *object*), or to the audience's known support for a nuclear freeze (a characteristic of the *context*).

THE PRINCIPLE OF COVARIATION. Kelley argues that when we make causal attributions we analyze information essentially the same way that a scientist would. In other words, we assess whether the behavior occurs in the presence or absence of various potential causes (actors, objects, contexts). In doing so, we use

Is this man really as tough as he looks? Or is he striking a pose to fit his position as a guard? Actions that conform to role expectations reveal little about personality dispositions.

the **principle of covariation:** we attribute the behavior to the potential cause that is present when the behavior occurs and absent when the behavior fails to occur—the cause that "covaries" with the behavior. For example, if you know that the candidate's position shifts from pro- to anti-nuclear freeze depending on the views of his audience, you are likely to attribute his behavior to the audience context.

TYPES OF INFORMATION. To determine whether a behavior is caused by the actor, object, or context we use three types of information: consensus, consistency, and distinctiveness information.

Consensus refers to whether all or only a few people perform the same behavior. For example, do all the other candidates speak in favor of a nuclear freeze (high consensus), or is this the only candidate who does so (low consensus)?

TABLE 8.3

ATTRIBUTING CAUSALITY FROM COMBINATIONS OF INFORMATION

Why does a candidate deliver a rousing speech in favor of a nuclear freeze?

Combination	Type of Information			Attribution
	Consensus	*Distinctiveness*	*Consistency*	
(1) LLH	*Low:* Only this candidate speaks in favor of a nuclear freeze.	*Low:* This candidate speaks in favor of many different objectives.	*High:* Whenever this candidate appears, he speaks in favor of a nuclear freeze.	Actor (candidate's beliefs)
(2) HHH	*High:* All the candidates speak in favor of a nuclear freeze.	*High:* This candidate speaks out only for a nuclear freeze but not for other objectives.	*High:* Whenever this candidate appears, he speaks in favor of a nuclear freeze.	Object (virtues of a nuclear freeze)
(3) LHL	*Low:* Only this candidate speaks in favor of a nuclear freeze.	*High:* This candidate speaks out only for a nuclear freeze but not for other objectives.	*Low:* This candidate speaks in favor of a nuclear freeze before this audience but not before other audiences.	Context (audience's view)

Consistency refers to whether the actor behaves the same way at different times and in different settings. If the candidate speaks in favor of a nuclear freeze throughout the campaign before many different audiences, his behavior is highly consistent, whereas if the candidate supports a freeze in some appearances and opposes it in others, his behavior is low in consistency.

Distinctiveness refers to whether the actor behaves differently toward a particular object than toward other objects. If the candidate rarely takes a strong public stand on controversial issues, his outspoken support for a nuclear freeze is a behavior high in distinctiveness. If he speaks out in the same way on many topics his behavior is low in distinctiveness.

Kelley (1967) notes that people sometimes examine these three types of information deliberately and consciously, but often they do

not even realize they are doing so. The particular combinations of consensus, consistency, and distinctiveness information that people associate with a behavior determine their attributions. Table 8.3 illustrates three combinations of information that are particularly important because they produce clear attributions to (1) the actor, (2) the object, and (3) the context.

People usually attribute a behavior to the actor (the candidate) when the behavior is low in consensus (only this candidate speaks in favor of a nuclear freeze), low in distinctiveness (the candidate also speaks in favor of many other issues), and high in consistency (the candidate gives speeches favoring a nuclear freeze whenever and wherever he appears). The candidate apparently believes in a nuclear freeze, which is why he gave such a rousing speech. In short, the combination of low consensus, low distinctiveness, and high consistency is understood to imply that something about the actor (his beliefs) caused the behavior.

We usually attribute a behavior to the object when the behavior is high in consensus, high in distinctiveness, and high in consistency. The nuclear freeze issue is apparently popular; that is why various candidates all give speeches favoring it. Thus, the high-high-high combination is understood to imply that something about the object (the virtues of a nuclear freeze) rather than something about the actor caused the behavior.

Finally, we tend to attribute a behavior to context when there is a combination of low consensus, high distinctiveness, and low consistency. Perhaps this particular audience or the latest turn in the campaign make a favorable speech desirable. Thus, a low-high-low combination implies that something about the context (the situational demands or opportunities) rather than something about the actor or object caused the behavior.

Numerous studies confirm that people use consensus, consistency, and distinctiveness information much the way Kelley theorized (McArthur 1972, 1976; Pruitt and Insko 1980; Zuckerman 1978). Of course, the combinations of information available sometimes differ from those shown in Table 8.3. In these cases, attributions tend to be more complicated, more ambiguous, and less confident.

CAUSAL SCHEMATA. People often lack the time, motivation, or opportunity to obtain full consensus, distinctiveness, and consistency information. Even when they are limited to partial information, however, people still make attributions. In the absence of full information, people draw on their own implicit theories or preconceptions of what causes what in order to make attributions. Kelley (1972, 1973) called these preconceptions **causal schemata.** The three combinations of information shown in Table 8.3 were identified by Kelley as common causal schemata. Based on their past experi-

ence, people assume the combination LLH implies that characteristics of the actor caused a behavior, whereas the combination HHH implies the object, and LHL implies the context.

Perceivers who have only partial information compare it with their causal schemata and then fill in the missing information. For example, imagine that when you go to buy a jacket the salesperson raves about all the different jackets you try on (low distinctiveness). Because only the LLH schema incorporates low distinctiveness, you assume that this whole schema fits. This schema implies the actor as cause. Consequently, you may attribute the behavior to the salesperson (the desire to make a sale) rather than to your appearance in the jacket.

Alternatively, imagine that several different salespersons rave about one jacket (high consensus). Because high consensus appears only in the HHH schema, you are likely to assume that this whole schema fits. This implies the object as cause, so you may attribute the raves to your appearance in the jacket itself (its stylishness and fit). Research on the use of these and other causal schemata generally supports Kelley's ideas about attribution with partial information (Cunningham and Kelley 1975; Orvis, Cunningham, and Kelley 1975).

Attributions for Success and Failure

For students, football coaches, elected officials, and anyone else whose fate is determined by evaluations of their achievements, attributions for success and failure are vital. Heider's (1958) theoretical distinction between internal and external causes of behavior is the starting point for understanding achievement attributions.

POTENTIAL CAUSES. Observers first decide whether success or failure is due to factors within the person (internal) or the environment (external). Heider suggests two major personal factors—ability and effort, and two major environmental factors—task difficulty and luck. Thus, a tennis player may win a game because she has superior coordination (ability/internal), or because her opponent twists her ankle and must forfeit (luck/external). She may lose because she dosen't chase the hard shots (effort/internal), or because her opponent's game is too strong (task difficulty/external).

In their spontaneous attributions for success and failure, people also mention fatigue, illness, personality, and interest (Elig and Frieze 1979). These are all related to the basic internal causes, ability and effort (Darley and Goethals 1980). Fatigue and illness are seen as undermining ability. Thus, a tennis player may lose because her ability is temporarily undercut by exhaustion from the tough match she played earlier. Personality and interest are seen as enhancing or undermining effort. One tennis player may show persistently low levels of effort because she is lazy, whereas another may chase every shot because she has an intense desire to win.

In addition, we can view each potential cause as either stable or unstable (Weiner 1974; Darley and Goethals 1980). Ability is generally viewed as stable, although it may become unstable due to illness or fatigue. Effort is usually viewed as unstable, although it may also appear stable over time due to personality and persistent interest. Task difficulty often appears stable, but it may become unstable due to the illnesses, fatigue, and changing motivations of other people. Finally, luck, though typically considered unstable, is sometimes viewed as stable ("She has all the luck!") Table 8.4 summarizes the internal/external and stable/unstable distinctions among potential causes of success and failure.

ATTRIBUTION PATTERNS   Attributions to stable causes are more likely to satisfy observers because they make the world appear more predictable and controllable (Heider 1958). Therefore, we are most likely to attribute performance to stable abilities, stable levels of effort or motivation, and, on occasion, to task difficulty (Darley and Goethals 1980). If our tennis player wins consistently, we are most likely to attribute her success to her talent, next to her high level of drive, and less to the low level of her opponents or to her persistent luck.

TABLE 8.4
POTENTIAL CAUSES OF SUCCESS AND FAILURE OF A TENNIS PLAYER

		Stable	Unstable
Internal	Ability	Player is consistently strong and talented or weak and uncoordinated.	Player is "off" due to fatigue or illness that undermines her ability.
	Effort	Player consistently strives to excel or is consistently lazy.	Player makes an unusual effort or fails to concentrate adequately.
External	Task Difficulty	The player's opponents are consistently strong and talented.	Opponent is "off" due to fatigue, illness, or lack of motivation.
	Luck	Lucky breaks always go to this player (or her opponents).	Opponent twists her ankle, ball takes a crazy bounce.

Failing is never pleasant, but its impact may vary. If we attribute our poor performance to lack of effort, we are likely to feel guilt or shame and to renew our efforts. If we attribute it to lack of ability, we may despair and quit trying.

When performances are very inconsistent, attribution to stable causes is more difficult. In these cases, we rely more on unstable causes. For example, we usually attribute fluctuations in effort or motivation and short-term variations in ability to fatigue or illness. What if our tennis player is unbeatable one day and a pushover the next? Following her performance we might comment, "She couldn't get herself up for the game" (effort), or "Her elbow was tender" (ability undermined).

Whether we attribute a performance to internal or external causes depends on how the actor's performance compares with those of others. Extreme or unusual performances produce internal attributions; for example, we would judge a player who wins a tournament as "extraordinarily able," and one who loses to an unseeded player 6–0, 6–0 in the first round as "weak." Average or common performances produce attributions to external causes. If defeat comes halfway through the tournament, we are more likely to attribute it to tough competition or bad luck.

CONSEQUENCES. One reason attributions for performance are important is because they influence our emotional reactions to success and failure as well as our future expectations and strivings. Research is only now clarifying these influences, although certain trends are clear. If we attribute a poor exam performance to lack of ability, we are likely to despair of future success and give up studying. However, if we attribute a poor performance to lack of effort, we may feel shame or guilt, but we are likely to study harder and expect improvement. In contrast, an attribution to bad luck elicits feelings of surprise and promotes little change in study patterns; we may nevertheless expect improved grades. Finally, if we attribute our performance entirely to the fact that the test was too difficult, we tend to become angry, but we do not strive for improvement (McFarland and Ross 1982; Valle and Frieze 1976; Weiner, Russell, and Lerman 1978).

Box 8.2
ATTRIBUTION IN SOCIAL CONTEXTS

Most attribution takes place in social contexts where people must reach *shared* understandings of behavior and events in order to interact effectively. As a result, individuals make different attributions during interaction than they would in isolation. (Crittenden 1983; Ross and Fletcher 1985; Stryker and Gottlieb 1981).

The elaborate, rational analysis of information described by attribution theories is most likely to occur when our primary goal is to understand the *causes* of behavior. But during interaction, people are often concerned with other goals, such as (1) shaping the course of interaction; (2) assessing whether others are likely to help or hinder us in the pursuit of our objectives; and (3) evaluating whether the behavior of others is appropriate to some social standard or norm (Jones and Thibaut 1958; Kruglanski 1980).

When our goal is to shape the course of interaction, we use attributions to influence others' interpretations of reality (Kidd and Amabile 1981). For example, a husband may tell his wife he is tired because of overwork, hoping she will accept this attribution and offer tender loving care. She may reject his attribution and propose another—that he was up too late watching television, for example. To reach shared understandings, interaction partners often negotiate the attributions they will accept and reject (Prus 1975). The attributions individuals communicate may not be the same as the attributions they would have made in isolation. Attributions are sometimes knowingly modified to enhance their acceptability. Anticipating that his wife will reject "overwork," the husband may attribute his tiredness to a virus. But the husband may also believe his modified attribution is "true," because self-interest can directly influence our subjective attributions.

When our goal is to assess whether others will promote our objectives, we tend to make dispositional rather than situational attributions. In particular, we focus on attributes related to our objectives. For example, when negotiating a deal with a used car salesman, we are especially likely to make attributions about his honesty and bargaining ability. We tend to overlook the possible influences of role requirements on his behavior and of constraints imposed by his employer.

When our goal is to evaluate others (What grade does a student deserve on a paper? Does an officeholder deserve our vote?), the person's actual performance is more important to us than the causes of behavior. An outstanding officeholder deserves our vote regardless of whether her success is attributable to ability, motivation, or persistent good luck. The evaluation depends primarily on how the actual performance measures up to relevant standards. Hence, we may invest little effort in causal attribution under these circumstances.

On most days we interact with many of the same people in the same settings—working, studying, eating, relaxing, and so on. During these activities, we may feel we are processing a great deal of information in order to make attributions that guide our behavior. In fact, however, the elaborate information processing described in attribution theories is often unnecessary during routine social behavior. Instead, when we recognize familiar situational cues, we tend to short-circuit elaborate reasoning and follow well-learned scripts. **Scripts** are standard sequences of behavior people have learned to perform virtually automatically with only minimal information processing (Abelson 1976; Langer 1978). Most people have scripts for discussing the weather, for example, and for responding to "What time is it?"

In a demonstration of this process (Langer 1978), a researcher approached individuals about to use a library copying machine with the following request: "Excuse me, I have 5(20) pages. May I use the Xerox machine....?" For one-third of the people this was the whole request (no reason). A second group heard the totally redundant continuation "because I have to make copies" (reason form only), while a third group heard "because I am in a rush" (real reason). The percentage of people agreeing to the request in each condition is shown here.

Note that people agreed more when the request entailed a small cost (5 copies) and when it included a real reason rather than no reason. The interesting people are those who heard words with the form of a reason ("because I have to make copies") that provided no real content. (Why else would one ask to use a Xerox machine?) When the request was large (20 pages), they apparently processed the information sufficiently to notice that no real reason had been given. Hence, they agreed only as frequently as people who were given no reason at all. In contrast, when the request was small, they agreed as often as the people given a real reason. They apparently failed to notice that the form lacked any real content: they performed only the minimal information processing necessary to recognize the familiar form. They followed a script that went something like "request + any reason → agree."

This study and others suggest that people engage in elaborate information processing and attribution when situations are novel, or when enacting a script becomes effortful or is disrupted. Otherwise, people may only do the minimal information processing necessary to settle on an appropriate script.

PERCENTAGE OF PEOPLE AGREEING TO LET ANOTHER USE A XEROX MACHINE			
	Reason Given in Request		
Cost of Request	*No Reason*	*Reason Form Only*	*Real Reason*
Small (5 pages)	60	93	94
Large (20 pages)	24	24	42

Source: adapted from E. J. Langer (1978).

Bias and Distortion in Attribution

According to the picture we have drawn so far, people appear to gather information, form impressions, and interpret behavior in highly rational, if sometimes unconscious, ways. In fact, people often deviate from the logical methods described in attribution theories. They fall prey to biases that distort their judgment. Biases may lead people to misinterpret events, and hence to behave in ways that are personally damaging and socially harmful. In this next section we will consider several major types of bias and distortion in attribution.

The Fundamental Attribution Error

Suppose that someone asks you to read an essay that supports Fidel Castro—or one that opposes him. The person explains that the essay was written by a student who was assigned to take either a pro- or anti-Castro stand, as determined by the instructor. Your task is to infer the writer's true underlying attitude. If you are like most people given this task, you will attribute a strong pro-Castro attitude to the writer of the supporting essay, and a strong anti-Castro attitude to the writer of the opposing essay. But that attribution is biased rather than rational. It ignores the fact that the essay writer had no choice: he was

TABLE 8.5

THE FUNDAMENTAL ATTRIBUTION ERROR: GENERAL KNOWLEDGE RATINGS FOR PARTICIPANTS IN A QUIZ

| | General Knowledge Rating | | Questioner-Contestant Difference |
	Questioners	Contestants	
Observers	82.1	48.9	33.2
Contestants	66.8	41.3	25.5
Questioners	53.5	50.6	2.9

Note: Ratings are based on a 100-point scale of general knowledge.

Source: adapted from Ross, Amabile, and Steinmetz (1977).

assigned the position he took in the essay (Jones and Harris 1967).

The tendency to underestimate the importance of situational influences and to overestimate personal, dispositional factors as causes of behavior is so common that it has been called the **fundamental attribution error** (Ross 1977) The tendency was first identified by Heider (1958), who observed that most people ignore the impact of role pressures and other situational constraints on others and see behavior as caused by people's intentions, motives, or attitudes. This bias is especially dangerous when it causes us to overlook the advantages or disadvantages of power built into social roles. We may incorrectly attribute the failures of persons without power to their personal weaknesses, and the successes of the powerful to their superior capabilities.

This bias was clearly demonstrated in a study (Ross et al. 1977) in which university students were randomly assigned to participate in a quiz in the role of either questioner or contestant. Questioners were instructed to make up 10 challenging questions. They were encouraged to show off their knowledge by composing difficult questions from their own areas of expertise. Following the quiz, participants as well as observers were asked to rate the general knowledge of the questioners and the contestants. Their responses are shown in Table 8.5.

The different performances of contestants and questioners were obviously due to the differences in power built into the roles to which they were randomly assigned. Whereas questioners controlled the outcome, contestants were virtually doomed to fail by the powerlessness of their roles. Still, contestants and observers rated questioners as much more knowledgeable than contestants. They made the fundamental attribution of error of overlooking the impact of situational influences (roles) and attributing the performance to the actor's characteristics (knowledgeability). Only questioners understood their advantage in choosing the questions and were aware of their own ignorance on other topics.

The Focus of Attention Bias

Another common tendency, or bias, is to overestimate the causal impact of whomever or whatever our attention is focused on. One study reports a simple but striking demonstration of this bias (Taylor and Fiske 1978). The study involved six subjects who observed a conversation between two persons. Although all six heard the same dialogue, they differed in the focus of their visual attention. Two observers sat behind speaker A, facing speaker B; two sat behind speaker B, facing speaker A; and two sat on the sides, equally focused on both speakers (see Fig. 8.4). Measures taken after completion of the dialogue showed that observers thought the speaker whom they faced had more influence on the tone and content of the conversation, as well as a greater causal impact on the other speaker's behavior.

Observers who sat on the sides and were able to focus equally on both speakers attributed equal influence to them.

We perceive the stimuli that are most salient in the environment—those that attract our attention—as most causally influential. Thus, we tend to attribute most causal influence to people who are noisy, colorful, vivid, or in motion. We tend to credit the person who talks loudest with leadership abilities, the same way we tend to blame the person who runs past us when we hear a rock shatter a car window. Although salient stimuli may be causally important in some cases, we tend to overestimate this importance (McArthur and Post 1977).

The focus of attention bias suggests one theoretical explanation for the fundamental attribution error. The person who behaves is the active element in the environment, therefore, that person is likely to capture our attention. Because our attention is directed more at people who act than at the surrounding situation, we tend to attribute more causal importance to people than to situations.

The Actor-Observer Difference

Actors and observers make somewhat different attributions for behavior. Observers tend to attribute actors' behavior to internal personal characteristics, whereas actors tend to see their own behavior as due to characteristics of the external situation (Jones and Nisbett 1972). Thus, while other customers in a market may attribute the selection of items in your grocery cart to your personal characteristics (vegetarian, alcoholic, chocolate freak), you will probably attribute the selection to the requirements of your situation (preparing for a party) or to qualities of the items (price or nutritional value).

In one demonstration of the actor–observer difference (Nisbett et al. 1973), male students wrote descriptions explaining why they liked their girlfriends and why they chose their majors. Then, as observers, they explained why their best friend liked his girlfriend and chose his major. When explaining

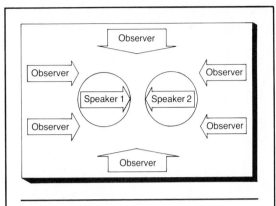

FIGURE 8.4

THE FOCUS OF ATTENTION BIAS

This diagram depicts the seating arrangement for speakers and observers in a study investigating the effect of the focus of visual attention on observers' attributions. Arrows indicate visual focus of attention. Following a conversation between both speakers, observers attributed more influence to the speaker whom they faced than to the other speaker. Observers on the side, however, attributed equal influence to both speakers. This illustrates our tendency to attribute more causal impact to the object of our attention.
Source: adapted from Taylor and Fiske (1978).

their own actions, students emphasized external characteristics, like the attractive qualities of their girlfriends and the interesting aspects of their majors. When explaining the behavior they observed in their friends, they emphasized external characteristics less, but mentioned internal dispositions, like their friends' own preferences and personalities, more.

Two explanations for the actor–observer difference in attribution are that actors and observers have (1) different visual perspectives and (2) different information.

VISUAL PERSPECTIVES. The actor's natural visual perspective is to look at the situation, whereas the observer's natural perspective is to look at the actor. Thus, the actor–observer difference reflects a difference in the focus of attention. Both the actor and observer attribute more causal influence to the source they focus on. If

What are these men looking at? Has someone fallen, jumped, been pushed? Is someone there fighting, playing tennis, making love? The world around us does not make sense automatically. We must construct an understanding of social events and figure out the causes of behavior.

this is true, the actor–observer difference should reverse if the actor sees behavior from the observer's viewpoint and the observer sees the same behavior from the actor's viewpoint. To reverse perspectives, Storms (1973) videotaped a conversation between two people using two separate cameras. One camera recorded the interactions from the visual perspective of the actor, the other from the perspective of an observer. Storms then showed actors the videotape made from an observer's perspective, and he showed observers the videotape made from an actor's perspective. As predicted, reversing visual perspectives reversed the actor-observer difference in attribution.

INFORMATION. A second explanation for the actor–observer difference is that actors have information about their own past behavior

that observers lack. Consequently, observers may make dispositional attributions for actions they mistakenly assume to be typical of the actor's behavior. For example, customers who see a clerk return an overpayment to a customer may assume that the clerk always behaves this way. They may then use this behavior as the basis for a dispositional attribution of honesty. However, if the clerk knows he has often cheated customers in the past, he would probably not interpret his current behavior as evidence of his honest nature.

Even when observers have some information about an actor's past behavior they often do not know how changes in context influence the actor's behavior. This is because observers are usually exposed to an actor in limited contexts. Students may observe a professor deliver witty, entertaining lectures in class week after week, for example. Yet the professor may know that in most other social situations he is shy and withdrawn. As a result, observers (students) may infer dispositions from apparently consistent behavior that actors (the professor) know to be inconsistent across a wider range of contexts.

Motivational Biases

Up to this point, we have considered attribution biases that are based on cognitive factors. That is, we have traced biases to the types of information that perceivers have available, acquire, and process. Motivations—one's needs, interests, and goals—are a second source of bias in attributions. When events affect one's self-interests, biased attribution is likely. Specific motives that influence attribution include the desire to (1) maintain and defend deep-seated beliefs, (2) protect and enhance one's self-esteem, (3) enhance one's sense of control over the environment, and (4) enhance the favorable impression of oneself that others have.

The defense of stereotypes illustrates how people maintain cherished beliefs through biased attribution. People tend to perceive actions that correspond with their stereotypes as caused by the actor's personal dispositions. They may attribute a woman executive's outburst of tears in a crisis to her emotional instability, for example, because that corresponds to the female stereotype. At the same time, people tend to attribute actions that contradict their stereotypes to situational causes. If the woman executive manages the crisis smoothly, people may credit the calming influence of her male assistants. When we attribute behaviors that contradict stereotypes to situational influences, these behaviors reveal nothing new about the persons who perform them. As a result, stereotypes persist even in the face of contradictory evidence (Hamilton 1979).

Attributions for success and failure are also influenced by motivational biases. People tend to take personal credit for acts that yield positive outcomes, and to deflect blame for bad outcomes, attributing them to external causes (Bradley 1978; Zuckerman 1979). Consider a study in which college students were asked to explain the grades they received on three examinations (Bernstein, Stephan, and Davis 1979). Students who received A's and B's attributed their grades much more to their own effort and ability than to good luck or easy tests. However, students who received C's, D's and F's attributed their grades largely to bad luck and the difficulty of the tests. In a similar subtle way, athletes show motivational bias in reporting the outcomes of competitions (Ross and Lumsden 1982). Whereas members of winning teams take credit for winning ("We won"), members of losing teams are more likely to attribute the outcome to an external cause—their opponent ("*They* won," not "We lost").

Various motives may contribute to this bias in attributions of performance. For example, attributing success to personal qualities and failure to external factors enables people to enhance or protect their self-esteem. Regardless of the outcome, they can continue to see themselves as competent and worthy. By avoiding the attribution of failure to personal qualities we also maximize our sense of control. This in turn supports the belief that we can master challenges successfully if we choose to apply ourselves, because we possess the necessary ability. Finally, biased attributions enable people to present a favorable public image and to make a good impression on others. According to Heider (1958), people find an attribution acceptable only when it validates both their wishes and their modes of reasoning. Thus, both motivational and cognitive biases influence attributions.

Summary

Social perception is the process of using information we acquire to construct understandings of the social world and form impressions of people.

ORDERING THE WORLD. (1) We employ concepts to organize the complex flow of incoming information into meaningful categories. (2) Concepts serve several functions. They reduce the effort required for perception, enable us to go beyond the information given, help us to know how to relate to objects, and allow us to predict behavior. (3) Our choice of concepts depends on our purposes as perceivers, the social context, the salience of stimuli in the environment,and the accessibility of concepts in memory. (4) Stereotypes permit us to make quick judgments of people. They arise out of direct experience, the need to boost self-esteem, or the tendency to remember information in terms of group categories. Stereotypes cause errors in perception because they are overgeneralizations. They are often negative and resistant to change.

FORMING IMPRESSIONS. (1) People use implicit personality theories to flesh out impressions of others based on limited information. Most people organize traits along two distinct positive-negative dimensions, both social and intellectual. Impressions may reflect as much about the perceiver's preferences for trait categories as about the person perceived. (2) People try to integrate the bits of information they perceive into a unified impression of others. They apparently average these bits of information together after weighting certain types of information more heavily than other types. Information received early on usually has a more significant impact on impressions than information received later. (3) Impressions become self-fulfilling prophecies when we behave toward others according to our impressions and evoke appropriate reactions from them.

ATTRIBUTION: EXPLAINING AND INTERPRETING BEHAVIOR. Through attribution, people link behavior to its causes. (1) Observers tend to attribute intentional behavior to actors' dispositions rather than to the situation. They infer intentionality if a behavior appears to be voluntary, goal-directed, and effortful. (2) To attribute specific dispositions, observers infer the actor's intention and then attribute the disposition that corresponds best with that intention. Dispositions are inferred from those effects the actor knowingly pursues. (3) Observers who have information about many of an actor's behaviors make attributions to the actor, object of action, or context, depending on which of these causes covaries with the behavior in question. They assess covariation by considering consensus, consistency, and distinctiveness information. (4) Observers attribute success or failure to four basic causes—ability, effort, task difficulty, and luck. Consistent performances are attributed to stable rather than unstable causes, average performances to external rather than internal causes. Attributions for performance influence both emotional reactions to success and failure as well as future expectations and strivings.

BIAS AND DISTORTION IN ATTRIBUTION. (1) A fundamental attribution error is to overestimate the importance of dispositional causes of behavior and underestimate the impact of situational pressures. (2) People also tend to overestimate the causal impact of whatever their attention is focused on. (3) Actors and observers have different attribution tendencies. Actors attribute their own behavior more to characteristics of the external situation, whereas observers attribute the same behavior more to the actor's personal characteristics. (4) Motivations—needs, interests, and goals—lead people to make self-serving, biased attributions. People defend deep-seated beliefs by attributing behavior that contradicts their beliefs to situational influences. People defend and enhance their self-esteem, sense of control, and public image by attributing their failures to external causes and taking personal credit for their successes.

Key Terms and Concepts

Social Perception

Attribution

Concept

Stereotype

Implicit Personality Theories

Halo Effect

Additive Model

Averaging Model

Weighted Averaging Model

Primacy Effect

Recency Effect

Principle of Covariation

Consensus

Consistency

Distinctiveness

Causal Schemata

Scripts

Fundamental Attribution Error

Focus of Attention Bias

Actor-Observer Difference

Chapter 9
Self-Presentation and Impression Management

Introduction

Remember the shabbily dressed street violinist you saw downtown? Your friend remarked on his artistic demeanor and sensitive eyes, and you agreed it was a shame a guy with such talent couldn't afford to study at Juilliard. When people dropped coins into his battered violin case you both felt pleased.

If you lived in New York City, you may have seen 29-year-old Richard Wexler (*Newsweek*, 1978). By day, Richard lives the good life in his classy Manhattan apartment. But come nightfall, the fashionable Wexler kicks off his Italian-made loafers, slips into torn sneakers, tattered jeans, and a frayed shirt, and is transformed into Richie, the ragged street artist. Accompanied by his pedigreed Finnish Spitz dog, Richie hails a cab for Broadway, where he sets up a sign on the sidewalk ("Violinist Needs Money to Further Studies") and serenades theater-goers with sentimental show tunes. On a typical night Richie pulls in more than $300 for an hour's fiddling, enough to buy himself $400 watches and Bermuda vacations.

Richie is a true artist—an artist at managing impressions. He masterfully creates the perception of himself he desires. Richie capitalizes on an important principle in social psychology: the way we perceive people's behavior and the impressions we form based on their behavior largely determine how we act toward them (Asch 1952; Blumer 1962). Because we respond to each other on the basis of our social identities, it is to our advantage to control the self-image we present (Schlenker 1980). Thus, by presenting himself as a "struggling violinist," Richie influences the behavior of passersby and achieves his goal of making lots of money easily.

Although few of us make our living by actively creating a false impression, we all engage in presenting particular images of who we are, whether intentional or not. When we shout or whisper, dress up or dress down, smile or frown, we actively influence how others perceive us and the impressions they form. In fact, presenting some image of ourselves to others is an inescapable aspect of all social interaction. **Self-presentation** refers to all our attempts, both conscious and unconscious, to control the images we project in social interaction. Self-presentation is intertwined with behavior whenever we care about the impressions others have of us (Jones and Pittman 1982). Self-presentation may involve carefully calculated tactics that are designed to make a particular impression. Such intentional use of tactics to manipulate the impressions others form of us is called **impression management.**

This chapter considers the ways in which people actively determine how others perceive them. It examines the following questions:

1. What is the content of self-presentation, what are its goals, and what are the obstacles to successfully achieving these goals?

2. What special impression-management tactics can we use when we want to claim a particular identity such as "overworked employee," "attractive date," "competent student"? Under what conditions do we choose one impression-management tactic over another?

3. How do people unmask the deceptive impression manager?

4. What are the consequences when people fail to project the social identities they desire?

Self-Presentation as an Everyday Necessity

The main goal of self-presentation is to project a particular social identity in a given situation. Thus Richie was concerned with convincing passersby of his identity as a struggling violinist who deserved contributions. But social identities cannot be isolated from the social context. Richie would have failed, for example, had passersby interpreted his performance as part of an advertising campaign for a newly opened Broadway play. In order to communicate social identities successfully, people must have shared understandings about the situation in which the identities are projected. For this reason, successful self-presentation requires efforts to control the definition of the wider situation.

The Definition of the Situation

In order for social interaction to proceed smoothly, people must share a common perception of what is happening between them. In other words, people who are interacting must achieve a shared **definition of the situation**—an agreement about who they are, what their behaviors mean, and what actions are appropriate to their situation. This view—that interaction depends on the shared understandings of social reality—is central to the theory known as *symbolic interactionism* (Mead 1938; Blumer 1962).

Symbolic interactionism assumes that people do not arrive at shared understandings simply by perceiving reality the same way. Rather, people produce shared definitions during interaction by negotiating the meaning of events (McCall and Simmons 1978; Stryker and Gottlieb 1981). In these negotiations people must answer three questions: (1) What type of social occasion is at hand? (2) What identities will be granted? and (3) How much leeway will be given to enact roles in unique individual ways?

FRAMES. The first objective in defining the situation is for people to agree on the type of social occasion at hand. Is it a wedding? Fishing trip? Family reunion? Job interview? The type of social occasion people recognize that they are in is called the **frame** of interaction (Goffman 1974). Each frame, or type of social occasion, is governed by a set of stable, widely known rules or conventions that dictate what kinds of behavior are expected and legitimate, who is likely to be present, and what roles are appropriate. When people recognize a social occasion as a wedding, for example, they immediately know that they are expected to

appear happy, that it is legitimate to kiss the bride, and that the guests are probably relatives and friends of the couple.

The frame of interaction is usually known in advance or else it is quickly discovered. Sometimes, however, the frame of interaction must be negotiated. When a family sends their worrisome teen-ager to a physician for a talk, for example, the discussion may begin with subtle negotiations about whether this is a "psychiatric interview" or merely a "friendly chat." Once negotiated, the frame limits the potential meanings that any particular behavior can have (Gonos 1977). Once the situation is defined as a "psychiatric interview," for example, the jokes the teen-ager tells may now be interpreted as symptoms of illness, not as friendly gestures.

IDENTITIES. The second objective in defining a situation is for people to agree on the identities they will grant each other (McHugh 1968; Perinbanayagan 1974). That is, people must agree on the type of person they will treat each other as being. To a large extent, each person's identity is determined by the frame. For example, a teen-ager in a psychiatric interview can no longer claim an identity as a "well-adjusted, normal kid."

Each person participating in an interaction has a **situated social identity**—a sense of who he or she is in relation to the other people involved in the situation. Identities are "situated" in the sense that they are specific to a particular situation. The identity projected while discussing a film (insightful critic) differs from the identity projected when asking for a loan (reliable friend). These identities are "social" in the sense that they are agreed on for purposes of smooth social interaction, although they are not necessarily accepted privately. In order to avoid unpleasant arguments, for example, you and your friends might relate to one another as if you were more insightful or more reliable than either of you truly believed yourselves to be.

Even if the identity we wish to claim is "true," it may be necessary to dramatize it with

Even if they have done nothing wrong, these teen-agers had best dramatize their innocence by presenting themselves to this policeman with polite deference. True identities may not be self-evident because perceivers are biased by the stereotypes and expectations they bring to a situation.

self-presentation (Goffman 1959). For instance, if adolescents display their usual nonchalant, defiant image when stopped by police they might be arrested, even if they are innocent. They are much more likely to avoid arrest if they dramatize their innocence by presenting a polite, regretful demeanor (Piliavin and Briar 1964). Thus the "true" identity of innocent adolescent must be presented appropriately.

Many of our "true" identities are not self-evident to others. This is because perceptions are based on the stereotypes, implicit personality theories, expectancies, and motivations brought to any situation. People's biases influence the identities they perceive and grant to others. Thus self-presentation may be necessary to overcome biases even when we are establishing our "true" identities.

ENACTED ROLES. The frames and identities people agree on in defining the situation gov-

ern the likely and appropriate roles they may enact. Still, there is room to negotiate the idiosyncratic ways people will actually enact these roles (Turner 1962; Cicourel 1972). People are inclined to enact roles in ways that express their unique personalities.

Consider how different people enact the role of student in a classroom setting. One may participate actively in the discussion, another may listen attentively, a third may take notes, a fourth may read a newspaper, and a fifth may fall asleep. These different role enactments reflect the individual's interests, styles of learning, and reasons for attending the class. Whereas some of these idiosyncratic role enactments are accepted, others may be contested. For example, some instructors may prohibit the reading of newspapers or sleeping in their classes. If the class is to proceed smoothly, the participants must reach an agreement about the range of acceptable role behaviors.

Goals of Self-Presentation

In developing a definition of the situation, we try to manage others' impressions by engaging in tactical self-presentation. The primary goal of self-presentation is to generate impressions that will enable us to obtain favorable outcomes (Jones and Pittman 1982). For example, during a job interview the goal is to win the job and gain the rewards that go with it. A secondary goal of self-presentation—the goal we are most often aware of—is the quest for social approval. Social approval appears to be a major goal because it is so frequently associated with obtaining favorable outcomes. But on the rare occasion when the link of approval to favorable outcomes is reversed, we find that people seek disapproval. For example, when a group of job applicants was told that a personnel manager hired employees he personally *disliked* because they worked out better on a particular job, job applicants presented themselves as holding attitudes opposed to those of the manager, and even criticized his behavior (Jellison and Gentry 1978).

Because rewards usually come with approval, self-presentation typically aims at creating the most highly approved situated identity possible. Selecting the appropriate behaviors to create a favorable identity may require careful planning. First, people must discover those qualities that participants in the interaction are most likely to approve of. Party-goers, for example, must recognize that friendliness is crucial to their situated identity, whereas people engaged in a sales transaction must recognize the importance of honesty. Second, people must anticipate which of various behaviors will be seen as indicating that they possess the qualities approved in that situation. For example, party-goers must anticipate whether or not telling an off-color joke or complimenting the hostess will make them appear friendly. Only after correctly assessing these two aspects of the situation can people confidently choose a behavior appropriate to gain a favorable situated identity.

Often there are norms that dictate how we should present ourselves in order to gain approval. When such norms are obvious, there will be widespread agreement about which behaviors will lead to positive or negative evaluations. Under these circumstances, people find it easy to decide how to behave and to predict others' reactions. When the norms are unclear, however, people do not know how to present themselves, and their behavior is therefore unpredictable (Alexander and Lauderdale 1977).

Social norms, of course, vary from group to group. What happens when one group condones a behavior and another condemns it? Under these circumstances, people tend to enact the behavior they believe will gain the best situated identity in the eyes of the group with whom they are currently interacting. In one study, for instance, University of Virginia undergraduates presented themselves as holding more "hawkish" views when speaking before a pro-Vietnam War audience and more "dovish" views when addressing a pacifist audience (Newtson and Czerlinski 1974). Such evidence suggests that people are capable of being quite fickle even on important issues due to their quest for social approval.

Obstacles to Successful Self-Presentation

People do not always succeed in establishing the situated social identity that they desire. Successful self-presentation has occurred when participants in the interaction respond in a way that fits with the actions used to claim a particular identity—for example, when offers of help are accepted ("altruist"), when romantic embraces are reciprocated ("lover"), and when leadership directives are followed ("leader"). Thus, one's success or failure in establishing a situated social identity depend on the complementary responses of others. This was demonstrated in a study in which students read a paragraph describing a conversation among three persons (Turner and Shosid 1976). One person in the conversation was giving directions to two others about planning a party. When the others accepted these directions—providing a complementary response to his attempted leadership—almost all of the students characterized the person who gave the directions as a "leader or organizer." When identical statements by the would-be leader were not met with a complementary response, almost half the subjects failed to recognize this same person as a leader. Results of this study are shown in Table 9.1.

Why do people sometimes reject the identity claims of others? Three possible reasons are: (1) the identity claims may conflict with the interests of interaction partners; (2) the claims may be inappropriate to the frame of interaction; (3) the claims may arouse suspicion.

CONFLICT OF INTEREST. One obstacle to successful self-presentation is conflict between the goals of the participants in the interaction. In a court of law, for example, a witness for the defense may have difficulty maintaining a social identity as a trustworthy person when faced with the hostile cross-examination of a prosecuting attorney. Less extreme but still troublesome conflicts may occur in many everyday interactions. Consider the student

TABLE 9.1

PERCENT OF OBSERVERS WHO GRANTED DIFFERENT IDENTITIES TO A PERSON WHO DIRECTED OTHERS

	Identity Granted to Person Who Gave Directions		
Responses of Others	"Leader" or "Organizer"	No Clear identity	Negative identity (troublemaker)
Complementary (accept direction)	92%	6%	2%
Not Complementary (reject direction)	56%	36%	8%

Source: adapted from Turner and Shosid (1976).

who discusses his poor examination results with his instructor. By questioning the fairness of the exam or the quality of the grading, the student can present himself as knowledgeable and hard-working, despite his grades. But this self-presentation may conflict with the instructor's identity as a competent preparer of exams and an impartial, careful grader. Hence the student and the instructor may challenge each other's self-presentations.

INAPPROPRIATE CLAIMS. A second obstacle to successful self-presentation arises when an individual claims identities that conflict with the frame of interaction. Flirting with a member of the opposite sex during a funeral, for example, is more likely to create a situated social identity of "uncultured boor" than of "attractive potential date." Claims inappropriate to the interaction frame usually occur when (1) people are ignorant of the rules for behavior on such occasions (never having attended a funeral), or when (2) the need to reaffirm a recently challenged social identity blinds people to the rules (the recently jilted suitor).

SUSPICION. The knowledge that people sometimes intentionally control their appearance raises a third obstacle to successful self-presentation—suspicion. At times people may suspect that the way a person appears—a broad smile, modest remark, desk piled high with books—is contrived to create an impression, rather than being a true expression of that person's character. If contrived, it requires closer scrutiny to determine what it implies about the person's identity. If it is not contrived, it is strong evidence for the person's rightful identity claims. Uncertainty regarding the meaning of appearances arouses suspicion. As a result, even honest identity claims may be rejected because they are perceived as deceptive.

Impression Management as a Tactical Process

Social interaction may be viewed as a kind of drama in which each person performs a "line"—a set of carefully chosen verbal and nonverbal acts (Goffman 1959, 1963, 1967). These acts are selected to communicate the person's definition of the situation and to establish the desired social identity. In order to manipulate impressions, people attempt to control the information others obtain about them. This section examines in detail a variety of impression-management tactics.

Managing Appearances

Consider the planning and control of appearances. Appearances refer to everything about a person that others may observe—clothes, grooming, habits such as smoking or chewing gum, choice and arrangement of personal possessions, and verbal and nonverbal communications. Through the appearances we present, we indicate to others the line of action we intend to pursue and the kind of persons we are (Stone 1962).

We consciously plan appearances to achieve some effect, as when we prepare for a dance or date. We keep these appearances under control, if possible, with quick glances in a mirror or trips to the restroom. The subtle managing of appearances also stands out in preparations for a job interview, as illustrated in a study of female job applicants (von Baeyer, Sherk, and Zanna 1981). In this study, some applicants were led to believe that their male interviewer felt the ideal female employee should conform closely to the traditional female stereotype (passive, gentle, and so on). Other applicants were led to believe that he felt the ideal female employee should be non-traditional (independent, assertive, and so on). Results indicated that applicants managed their appearances to match their interviewer's stereotyped expectations. Those expecting to meet the traditionalist wore more makeup and used a greater number of accessories such as earrings than those planning to meet the non-traditional interviewer.

In everyday interactions we are less aware of planning, but our appearances are hardly left to chance. Managing appearances to present a desired identity influences daily choice of which clothes to wear, whether to clean our room, shave, use perfume, play a rock-and-roll record for a visitor, and so on. We are able to plan appearances successfully because we can take the role of others and anticipate the kinds of responses different appearances will elicit from them.

REGIONS. Goffman (1959) draws a parallel with the notion of front and back stage in theater to illuminate other ways we manage appearances. *Front regions* are settings in which people carry out interaction performances and exert efforts to maintain appropriate appear-

Undertakers employ a wide range of impression-management techniques to create an atmosphere of quiet comfort. Opulent front regions are carefully separated from back regions where teams of workers prepare the deceased for burial in quilted caskets.

ances. In a restaurant dining room, for example, waiters smile and courteously offer to help customers. *Back regions* are settings in which people routinely and knowingly violate the lines they present in front regions. Behind the kitchen doors, those same waiters shout, shove plates, and even mimic their customers.

Back regions are often used to prepare, rehearse, and rehash performances. For example, anticipating dinner with the boss, a couple will take advantage of the privacy of their home to rehearse the topics to discuss. Then—at home after their dinner performance—they will let down their hair in a raucous postmortem. Front and back regions are separated by barriers to perception, like the restaurant's kitchen door and the walls of a home. When performers cross these barriers, their behavior changes—smiles sprout or fade and postures straighten or relax.

The barriers between front and back regions are crucial to successful impression management because they block access to the inevitable violations of impressions that occur during preparation and relaxation. The breakdown of such barriers, for instance, has undermined the ability of national figures to project a leaderlike image in recent years (Meyrowitz 1985). Because the media now expose almost every detail of a president's life, for example, presidents and other officials are often caught off guard. They are seen expressing views and performing actions they would prefer to keep hidden from the public. The slips and inconsistencies that are inevitably revealed undercut the leaders' stature. American presidents may find it difficult to project a heroic identity when the media show one bumping his head on a door (Ford), another nearly collapsing while jogging (Carter), and a third nodding off during an audience with the pope (Reagan). It was much easier to be a hero in the days of Jefferson or Lincoln. Then, reporters were barred from the White House, and the electronic media had yet to penetrate the barriers to the president.

TEAMS. Managing appearances often requires the help of a team, a group of people who cooperate in preparing and maintaining desired impressions. Some teams help to prepare appearances (tailors, barbers, diction teachers, and plastic surgeons), whereas others help to maintain ongoing impression management (hospital and hotel staffs, families). People engaged in teamwork give mutual support to each other's lines of action. This helps them to carry off otherwise difficult encounters successfully.

The operation of an illegal abortion clinic (Ball 1967) illustrates the complex, deceptive use of teamwork and regions to manage appearances. In the 1960s, when abortion was illegal in the United States, abortion clinics had an image of shabby back-alley outfits employing medically unsafe procedures. To overcome this image, the team running a clinic on the Mexican border set up a pleasant waiting room, spic-and-span facilities, and modern-looking equipment. They dressed in laundered, pressed uniforms, and behaved with great respect toward their clients and each other. These appearances created an overwhelming impression of trustworthiness, luxury, and good medical practice—even though the quality of medical care remained inadequate. Had clients been able to penetrate the clinic's back regions, the impression would have faded immediately.

Ingratiation

On most occasions people want to be liked. Not only is it inherently pleasant, but liking may gain us a promotion, a better grade, or a date, and it may save us from being fired, failed, or ignored. How do we persuade others to like us? Often we are sincere in our relations with others; at other times we engage in the impression-management technique called ingratiation (Jones 1964). **Ingratiation** refers to the deliberate use of deception to increase a target person's liking for us in hopes of gaining tangible benefits the target controls. Techniques such as flattery or exaggerating one's admirable qualities are often used to ingratiate oneself.

Ingratiation is based on the idea that targets are more likely to grant benefits to someone they like. People ingratiate themselves with a target only when they think the target has the power to decide whom to benefit. That is, people tend to ingratiate themselves with targets who are not constrained by preestablished regulations but who set their own standards for allocating benefits (Jones et al. 1965). For example, students are less likely to try to ingratiate themselves with instructors who base their grades on objective, multiple choice exams than with instructors who assign papers, and whose grading may be influenced by their liking for a student.

There are three major ingratiation tactics, each of which involves the use of deception. They include opinion conformity (pretending to share the target person's views on important issues), other enhancement (outright flattery or complimenting the target person), and selective self-presentation (exaggerating one's own admirable qualities).

OPINION CONFORMITY. Faced with a target person who has discretionary power, people may ingratiate themselves by expressing agreement on important issues. People tend to like others more if they hold opinions similar to their own (Byrne 1971). But obvious opinion conformity is likely to arouse suspicion. In order to increase their credibility and minimize detection, ingratiators may attempt to mix their opinion conformity on important issues with disagreement on unimportant issues.

Opinion conformity sometimes requires us to tailor the content of the opinions we express to match a target person's general values rather than any specific opinions he or she may hold. Such clever modification of expressed opinions was demonstrated by students who were failing at an experimental task of judging advertising slogans (Jones et al. 1965). Some of the students were led to believe that their supervisor valued friendliness and social compatibility whereas others heard that the supervisor valued efficiency and independence. The students were told that a positive evaluation from their supervisor would help them earn $10. As a result, students shifted their publicly expressed opinions to conform with their supervisor's values. By agreeing with the supervisor, students in the first group implied that they too valued friendliness and compatibility. In contrast, students in the second group expressed less agreement with the supervisor, in order to show their independence and to increase their instructor's liking for them.

OTHER ENHANCEMENT. Flattery is a very common form of other enhancement. But effective flattery cannot be indiscriminate. More than two centuries ago, Lord Chesterfield (1774) asserted that people are best flattered in those

areas in which they wish to excel. This assertion was tested in a study similar to that cited earlier in which students were told that their supervisor valued either efficiency or sociability (Michener, Plazewski, and Vaske 1979). The supervisor was an appropriate target for ingratiation, because the students' possible earnings depended on the evaluations they would receive from her. Before these evaluations were made, the students had a chance to flatter their supervisor. The experimenter asked them to rate her efficiency and sociability on scales that their supervisor would be shown. The results showed that the supervisor's values channeled the form of flattery the students used. Students who believed the supervisor valued efficiency rated her higher on efficiency than on sociability, whereas students who believed she valued sociability rated her higher on sociability than on efficiency. Thus, the students were discriminating in their use of praise. In addition, they avoided extreme ratings that might suggest insincerity.

SELECTIVE SELF-PRESENTATION. A third major form of ingratiation—selectively publicizing one's admirable qualities—is a quick and easy way to generate a desirable public identity. People may mention their honesty, wisdom, friendliness directly—or they may imply their admirable qualities indirectly, by publicly attributing their behavior to appropriate motives (Tetlock 1981). Suppose a student refuses an offer of help on an exam. By publicly attributing this behavior to her sense of fair competition, she can generate an identity as fair and honest. Attributing her refusal to fear of being caught would not have the same identity-enhancing effect.

Selective self-presentation is risky if the target knows enough about us to suspect we are boasting. There is also the danger that future events may prove our claims invalid. People therefore prefer to present self-enhancing descriptions when these risks are minimal— when the target person does not know them

Box 9.1
PLAYING DUMB

Playing dumb is one widely employed ingratiation tactic. By playing dumb people give the target person a sense of superiority by presenting themselves as inferior. Thus, playing dumb is a form of other enhancement. Although popular belief and early research suggest that women are more prone to play dumb (Komarovsky 1946; Wallin 1950), a national survey of American adults indicates otherwise (Gove, Hughes, and Geerkin 1980). Significantly more males than females agreed that they had pretended, at least once, to be less intelligent or knowledgeable than they really were. As shown in the table below, men play dumb more often than women in most situations.

What leads people to "play dumb"? The data indicate that people who use this method are often young, highly educated, of high occupational status, and male. These are certainly not the characteristics usually associated with people who are really inferior. But such people are the ones who are most likely to find themselves in settings where playing dumb may be necessary or appropriate (Gove et al. 1980). Many of these people are located near the bottom of an occupational ladder they aspire to climb, in a setting where intelligence and knowledge are prized. Under these circumstances, a person's relatively low status may require deferring to one's superiors, despite one's own abilities.

In contemporary American society, young, well-educated males are more likely to be channeled into lower status positions in competitive occupations where knowledge is valued and where they are expected to defer to their elders. This is often the fate of junior executives, law clerks, and graduate students, for example. In these situations, people of lower status stand to gain by hiding any intellectual superiority they feel—that is, by playing dumb.

The survey also shows that women play dumb significantly more often than men in relating to their spouses. Perhaps this reflects the continuing cultural expectation that women should refrain from displaying superior knowledge that might challenge their husbands' assumed superiority. Our reasoning about the causes of playing dumb suggests that college educated women probably play dumb more often than women with less education. This is because highly educated women are especially likely to find themselves in school and career settings where knowledge is valued, but deference to superiors is expected.

PERCENT OF PEOPLE WHO REPORTED "PLAYING DUMB"							
			Target Person				
	Overall	*Date*	*Spouse*	*Boss*	*Co-workers*	*Friends*	*Strangers*
Males (1,065)	31.1	8.2	6.0	13.1	14.6	12.6	15.8
Females (1,182)	22.9	9.0	10.0	5.2	6.3	8.7	7.7

Source: adapted from Gove et al. (1980).

and has no way to check their future performances (Schlenker 1975; Frey 1978). For example, people are more likely to boast about themselves to strangers who have no way of checking their stories than to close acquaintances who may learn the truth. People who believe their performances will support boastful claims tend to risk selective self-presentations even when others can check up on their future performances. Bowlers who believe they have a good chance of excelling in a tournament, for example, will often talk about their prowess during prematch discussions. Caution prevails, however, when people believe they will not perform successfully in the future, and when they know others already have negative information about them (Schlenker 1975; Ungar 1980).

Often the target of our selective self-presentation has only partial knowledge about us. For example, the person might think we are sensitive and mature, but know nothing about our creativity and intellectual depth. How do we use selective self-presentation to generate the best possible social identity when a target has partial knowledge?

To answer this question, researchers in one study (Baumeister and Jones 1978) constructed personality profiles consisting of paragraphs portraying students either as sensitive and emotionally mature (good), or as lacking social sensitivity and immature (bad). Researchers told students that the personality profile they received was based on a questionnaire they had completed earlier. Students were also told that their profile had been shown to a partner with whom they would be working later. They were then asked to complete a self-description questionnaire that would also be shown to the partner. This was their opportunity to engage in selective self-presentation. The self-description questionnaire included traits related to maturity and sensitivity as well as traits unrelated to these dimensions. Students who thought their partner had already been shown a "bad" profile described themselves in terms consistent with the partner's knowledge that they were insensitive and immature. However, they compensated for this unfavorable image by presenting themselves in a self-enhancing manner on other, unrelated traits (intelligence, creativity, and reliability). Thus when others had authentic unfavorable information, students did not dispute this information directly. Instead, they

compensated by selective self-enhancement on unrelated dimensions. The self-presentation of students who knew their partner had seen the "good" profile reflected a different tendency. They presented themselves modestly both on the traits related to sensitivity and maturity and on the unrelated traits. This tendency toward modest self-presentations has been observed in several other studies (Jones et al. 1965; Michener et al. 1979).

INGRATIATION AND POWERLESSNESS. Ingratiation is one of the few ways that weak persons can influence powerful targets on whom they depend. The other important modes of influence are usually unavailable to the powerless, who lack material goods to exchange for benefits they desire, superior expertise needed to persuade others, and power to back up threats and make them credible.

Yet the very powerlessness of would-be ingratiators poses a dilemma: the weaker they are, the more they stand to gain by making themselves attractive to their targets, but the more suspicious of deception their targets are apt to become. In other words, the greater the need for ingratiation, the less likely it is to

TABLE 9.2

FAVORABILITY OF SELF-DESCRIPTIONS: MODESTY AND SELF-ENHANCEMENT IN SELECTIVE SELF-PRESENTATION

Target Person's Knowledge of Student	Self-Presentation by Student on:	
	Related Traits (maturity, sensitivity)	Unrelated Traits (intelligence, creativity)
GOOD (sensitive, mature)	Modest −.202	Modest −.104
BAD (insensitive, immature)	Consistent −.265	Self-Enhancing +.571

Note: More positive scores mean more favorable ratings. Scores adjusted to center on zero.
Source: adapted from Baumeister and Jones (1978).

succeed. For this reason, ingratiation tactics must be subtle to conceal ulterior motives and to avoid detection.

Tactical Self-Disclosure

People sometimes engage in **self-disclosure**—the act of revealing personal aspects of one's feelings and behavior to others—in order to establish genuine intimate relations with others (Jourard 1971; Derlega and Chaiken 1975). Yet self-disclosure can also be used as a tactic to control the definition of the situation and to manage impressions. The tactical use of self-disclosure is based on the widely accepted social norm that one person's disclosures should ordinarily be met with disclosures at a similar level of intimacy by another (Ehrlich and Graven 1971). Because people are responsive to this norm, self-disclosure usually triggers reciprocation.

Tactical self-disclosure may be used to achieve any of several goals. First, it can be used to induce others to reveal information one wants for one's own purposes by revealing information about oneself. A stock trader, for example, may reveal her own knowledge or concerns about an investment in order to elicit tips from others regarding that same investment. The information revealed in tactical self-disclosure may be true or false, but in all events it is meant as bait to extract information from others.

A second possible goal of tactical self-disclosure is to develop desired interpersonal relationships. Such relationships may be sought for their own sake, or they may be pursued to take advantage of another's trust. Trust built through self-disclosure can be exploited to obtain a loan, for example, or to set up a victim for a "sting" operation.

Self-disclosure may also be used to obtain social approval. People who reveal private information about themselves often increase their partner's liking for them, especially if the content of the self-disclosure complements what their partner has revealed (Daher and Banikiotes 1976; Davis and Perkowitz 1979). Self-disclosure may also inspire dislike, how-

ever, if it is too intimate for the depth of the relationship (a new acquaintance discussing her deepest anxieties), or if it uncovers dissimilarities with the partner (revealing profound religious yearnings to a nonbeliever) (Cozby 1972; Derlega and Grzelak 1979).

Finally, people may engage in reciprocal self-disclosure in order to create a level of interpersonal openness that permits them to exchange personal information that it is ordinarily inappropriate to publicize. Once people establish their trustworthiness through a sequence of reciprocal self-disclosures, they are free to present self-enhancing information they want others to know ("I was president of my graduating class") without appearing immodest (Jones and Gorden 1972). Likewise, when openness is sufficient, people may reveal potentially damaging information about themselves in order to attain outcomes they long for, such as a homosexual relationship or psychological help.

Aligning Actions

In the course of interaction occasional failures of impression management are inevitable. In pursuit of our goals we may sometimes be caught performing actions that violate group norms (missing an appointment) or contravene laws (running a red light). Such actions potentially undermine the social identities we have been claiming, challenge the definition of the situation we have negotiated, and disrupt smooth interaction. When this occurs, people engage in a variety of **aligning actions**—attempts to define their apparently questionable conduct as actually in line with cultural norms. Aligning actions are tactics intended to repair cherished social identities, restore meaning to the situation, and reestablish smooth interaction (Hewitt and Stokes 1975). Three major types of aligning actions are considered below.

MOTIVE TALK. Our initial reaction to failures of impression management is to request an explanation for someone's unsuitable behavior.

These chess players seem to be building up trust and liking through reciprocal self-disclosure. But self-disclosure can also be used as an impression-management tactic to obtain information and to create a relationship that will later be exploited for personal advantage.

"Why are you late handing in this paper?" an instructor may ask. Explanations of the motives that supposedly underlie behavior are termed **motive talk** (Mills 1940). "I was taking care of my parents who are recovering from a car crash," the student may reply. The explanation of our motives is intended to deny that the behavior has negative implications for the identity in question. Not every motive is equally acceptable. Rather, we must learn **vocabularies of motive**—the sets of explanations regarded as appropriate by particular groups in specific situations (Mills 1940). For example, "God's will" is a good explanation for a priest's celibacy, but it would raise eyebrows if it were used by a labor leader to explain his compromises on a union contract.

DISCLAIMERS. When people anticipate that the actions they will take may be disruptive, they often employ **disclaimers,** verbal assertions intended to ward off any negative implications of these actions in advance (Hewitt and Stokes 1975). Different social conditions require different types of disclaimers.

When individuals are certain that an intended act is discrediting, they use disclaimers to acknowledge that, although the act ordinarily implies a negative identity, theirs is an extraordinary case. For example, before making a bigoted remark, a person may point to his extraordinary credentials: "My best friend is Hispanic, but ... " Similar disclaimers are used prior to acts that would normally undermine one's identity as moral ("I know I'm breaking the rules, but ... ") or as mentally competent ("This may seem crazy to you, but ... "). These disclaimers emphasize that the person is aware that the act could threaten his identity, but that he is appealing to a higher morality or to a superior competence. Still other disclaimers plead for a suspension of judgment until the whole event is clear: "Please hear me out before you jump to conclusions."

When individuals are not certain how others will react, and care little about the potentially threatened identity, they are more likely to preface their actions with hedging remarks: "I'm no expert, but . . . " or "I could be wrong . . . " Such remarks proclaim in advance that possible mistakes or failures should not reflect on one's crucial identities.

ACCOUNTS. When disclaimers are not given or are rejected, accounts are necessary to repair the damage. **Accounts** are the explanations people offer after they have performed acts that threaten their social identities (Scott and Lyman 1968; Schlenker 1980; Tedeschi and Reiss 1980). There are two types of accounts—those that excuse the unsuitable behavior and those that justify it. Excuses minimize one's responsibility by citing uncontrollable events ("My car broke down"), coercive external pressures ("She made me do it"), or compelling internal pressures ("I suddenly felt dizzy"). Presenting an excuse reduces the observer's tendency to hold the actor responsible or to make negative inferences about his character (Riordan, Marlin and Kellogg 1983). Justifications admit responsibility, but, at the same time, they define the behavior as appropriate under the circumstances ("Sure I hit him, but he hit me first") or as prompted by praiseworthy motives ("It was for his own good"). Justifications reduce the perceived wrongness of the behavior.

Accounts are more likely to be accepted when their content appears truthful and conforms with the explanations commonly used for such behavior (Riordan et al. 1983). Even so, accounts are sometimes rejected. Accounts are honored more readily when the person who gives them is trustworthy, penitent, and of superior status, and when the identity violation is not serious (Blumstein, 1974). Thus, we are more likely to accept a psychiatrist's quiet explanation that he struck an elderly mental patient because she kept shouting and would not talk with him than a delinquent's defiant use of the same excuse to explain why he struck an elderly woman.

Altercasting

The tactics discussed so far demonstrate the ways people claim identities and the techniques used to protect them from being discredited. But the actions of one person in an encounter also place limits on who the others can claim to be. Therefore it makes sense to try to impose identities on others that complement those we claim, and to pressure others to enact roles that mesh with the roles we wish to construct for ourselves. **Altercasting** is the use of tactics that impose roles and identities on others. Through altercasting, we cast others into situated roles and identities that are to our advantage (Weinstein and Deutschberger 1963).

In general, altercasting involves treating others as if they already have the roles and identities we wish to impose on them. "After all I've done for you . . . " is a typical altercasting remark. It treats the other as indebted, and thereby sets up the obligation to reciprocate a favor. Teachers engage in altercasting when they tell students, "I know you can do better than that." This remark pressures the student to live up to an imposed identity of competence. Altercasting can also entail carefully planned duplicity. An employer may invite subordinates to dinner, for example, casting them as personal friends in hopes of eliciting employee secrets.

Putting others on the defensive is an especially common form of altercasting: "Explain to the public why you can't control inflation," says the challenger, altercasting the incumbent official as incompetent in running the economy. Should the incumbent rise to his own defense, he admits that the charge merits discussion and that the negative identity may be correct. Should he remain silent, he implies acceptance of the altercast identity because he may be unable to refute it. Putting others on the defensive is a powerful technique used against rivals, because the negative identity it imposes is so difficult to escape.

In order to interact smoothly with each other people must reach a working consensus regarding their situated identities (Goffman 1959). The bargaining of identities is therefore an essential feature of social interaction. In the bargaining process, we concede to others the identities they desire in return for their acceptance of our own identity claims. We also try to deny the identity claims of others that would prevent us from achieving or maintaining our own prized social identities.

The use of altercasting in the give-and-take of identity bargaining is nicely demonstrated in a study of interaction among dates (Blumstein 1975). Women were instructed to claim an identity of "healthily assertive" by altercasting their dates into a more submissive identity. The women did this by making remarks to their dates such as "Must you insist on making all the decisions?" Some of the men conceded the assertive identity claimed by their dates by presenting a self consistent with the altercast ("Sorry I've been so pushy. Whatever you say goes"). Other men rejected their date's assertive identity by altercasting the woman in return, pressuring her to return to a submissive identity ("You always liked me to make the decisions before. What's up?").

This research reveals one of the influences that determine whether people resist altercasting or whether they give in to it. Men who had indicated earlier that dominance was an important part of their self-concept tended to resist their date's altercasting, whereas men who had rated dominance as unimportant tended to accept the submissive identity imposed by the women. In general, we tend to concede identities that are unimportant to our overall self-concept while we reject altercasting aimed at our more central identities.

Unmasking the Impression Manager

Most of us go through life trying to create an impression of ourselves as basically honest, sincere, and truthful. Yet impression management is inherently deceitful. Sometimes the people being deceived have little to gain by questioning the sincerity of others. For instance, morticians may convey an air of sympathy and concern even when they are bored by their client's grief. But mourning relatives would only be more upset by discovering the mortician's true feelings. In other cases, however, unmasking the impression manager is vital for protecting our own interests. In attempting to win a contract, for example, builders may claim to be reliable businessmen and skilled artisans even when they are total frauds. It may be worth thousands of dollars to determine whether the builder's hearty handshake belongs to a fly-by-night operator before making a down payment.

How do people go about trying to unmask the impression manager? In general, they attend to two major types of information—the apparent motives the other person has for an action, and the nonverbal cues that accompany the action.

Assessing Ulterior Motives

When a used car salesman tells us that a battered vehicle with sagging springs was driven only on Sundays by his retired aunt, we are likely to suspect deceit. His ulterior motive is transparent. Ulterior motives that are apparent to the target undermine the success of ingratiation tactics—to say the least. In an early study (Dickoff 1961), for instance, an experimenter praised the performances of her subjects under two different conditions. In one condition, where the experimenter had no apparent ulterior motive, this flattery worked. Subjects liked her better the more she praised them. In the second condition, however, when the experimenter had an obvious ulterior motive (she asked them to volunteer for another experiment), flattery failed to increase their liking for her.

When ulterior motives are apparent, opinion conformity also fails as an ingratiation technique (Jones, Gergen, and Jones 1963; Kraut 1978). Target persons apparently have some understanding of the conditions in which opinion conformity is likely to be used as a technique of impression management. Voters, for example, realize that politicians may falsely state their views in order to create the impression that their opinions are similar to those of the voters. In such conditions, ingratiators are cautious about using opinion conformity because they risk detection (Kauffman and Steiner 1968).

We are especially likely to arouse suspicion when we selectively publicize our admirable qualities. As a result, modest self-presentation may be a safer ingratiation technique than self-enhancement. But does modesty increase others' liking for us? Consider the options available to a person who has succeeded or failed at a task. One who succeeds has the choice between claiming full credit for the success (a self-enhancing response) or disclaiming credit (a modest response). One who fails may deny blame for the failure (self-enhancing) or accept responsibility for it (modesty). Which strategy is more effective?

In a study addressing this question, subjects read about a teacher who had succeeded or failed in teaching his pupil and who gave either a self-enhancing or a modest explanation for the outcome (Tetlock 1980). Subjects liked the teachers more when teachers responded to their success or failure with modest claims. They viewed these teachers as more concerned for others than teachers whose responses were self-enhancing. This finding implies that modesty is a successful ingratiating technique.

In another relevant study, members of a group were asked to evaluate other members following the group's success or failure at a task (Forsyth, Berger, and Mitchell 1981).

Group members reported greater liking for those who took blame for the group's failure or credited others for the group's success (modesty) than for those who blamed others for failure and claimed credit themselves for the group's success (self-enhancement). Taken together, these studies suggest that when observers have objective evidence about someone's performance—whether favorable or unfavorable—modesty is the more effective ingratiation tactic. Self-enhancement tends to reduce others' liking because it is perceived as deceitful impression management (Carlston and Shovar 1983).

Interpreting Nonverbal Cues

It is commonly believed that nonverbal cues—such as the look in people's eyes—are telltale signs of deception. Trial lawyer Louis Nizer (1973), for example, asserts that there are identifiable cues that reveal when witnesses are attempting to deceive jurors. Sigmund Freud (1905) asserted years ago that "He who has eyes to see and ears to hear may convince himself that no mortal can keep a secret. If his lips are silent, he chatters with his fingertips; betrayal oozes out of him at every pore" (*Collected Papers*, Vol. 3, p. 78). Recent research suggests the contrary, however. Results of most experiments reveal that people are not especially adept at using the full range of nonverbal cues to unmask the impression manager.

Perhaps people are more successful at detecting deceit the more nonverbal cues they have available to them. According to this hypothesis, people should detect impression management more readily in face-to-face interaction, when all types of cues are available, than in interaction limited only to auditory cues such as conversing by telephone. This was tested in a study in which undergraduates were instructed to try to give an interviewer the impression that they had either dominant or submissive personalities (Geller 1977). For some of the students the impression they tried to present was deceptive. For others

Box 9.2
BEHAVIOR THAT REVEALS DECEPTION

There are no telltale signs of deception that apply to *all* situations. Nonetheless, people tend to believe that certain behaviors are reliable indicators of deception. For example, we tend to suspect someone who fails to gaze into our eyes, responds particularly slowly to our comments, speaks especially rapidly, fails to smile, or shifts posture frequently. Research, however, disputes these common beliefs about deception (Zuckerman, DePaulo, and Rosenthal 1981).

Although people are often misled, paralinguistic cues such as hesitations and tone of voice are the cues most frequently interpreted correctly as revealing deception (DePaulo, Lanier, and Davis 1983; Zuckerman and Driver 1984). Even these nonverbal behaviors must be interpreted within their social context, however (Krauss 1981). The following study of speech hesitation (Kraut 1978) illustrates how interpretations of deception cues vary according to context.

Half of the subjects in this study heard an applicant for the position of dorm counselor admit to an interviewer that she used marijuana regularly, whereas the other half heard the applicant deny that she ever used marijuana. Before making this statement, the applicant either hesitated, or did not. Subjects judged the applicant as more truthful when she hesitated before admitting use than when she did not hesitate. In contrast, hesitation before denial of marijuana use led listeners to

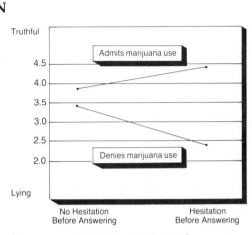

EFFECTS OF SPEECH HESITATION ON JUDGMENTS OF APPLICANTS' TRUTHFULNESS

judge her as more dishonest. Thus, hesitations increased or decreased the perception of deception, depending on the context.

In general, people are better able to interpret various nonverbal cues (pitch, speed of talking, smiling, and so on) when they attend to context. High vocal pitch, for example, often indicates deception, but it may also reflect nervousness if the person is honestly discussing a taboo topic or a self-incriminating event. Thus, like hesitation, high vocal pitch is an unreliable sign of deception. Research has only now begun to identify the contexts in which different behavioral cues signify deception or honest self-presentation.

it expressed their "true" personalities as measured by a self-report questionnaire they had completed earlier. Half of the interviews were conducted face-to-face. For the other half, the interviewer sat in a separate room and communicated by audio hookup. Following the interview, interviewers rated the dominance and submissiveness of the students they had interviewed.

Surprisingly, results showed that interviewers who conversed with subjects over the audio system detected deception better than interviewers who engaged in full face-to-face interaction. In addition, interviewers' ratings of the students' dominance/submissiveness were positively correlated with the students' personality scale scores only when they had been limited to auditory contact and not when they had interacted face-to-face. This finding suggests that interviewers were able to detect the "true" dominance/submissiveness of the impression manager only when limited to auditory cues. When exposed to the full range of nonverbal cues, interviewers were unable to see past the personality presented to them. Similar results were obtained in a study in which observers attempted to detect when people were lying about their opinions and when they were responding honestly in an interview (Krauss, Geller, and Olson 1976).

How can we explain the poorer performance of the interviewers in face-to-face interaction? There are three plausible explanations (Krauss 1981). First, face-to-face interaction may produce information overload. That is, the detector may be flooded with an overabundance of cues—visual, content, and auditory. In dealing with them all simultaneously, the detector may be unable to process any of them efficiently.

Second, in face-to-face interaction behaviors that are visible, such as face and hand movements, tend to attract more attention than auditory cues such as pitch and speed of talking. But visual cues are more readily controlled by communicators than are auditory (Zuckerman et al. 1982). Hence, observers may be deceived more easily because they pay too much attention precisely to those cues that impression managers are most likely to manipulate purposefully (visual cues), and too little attention to the cues under less intentional control (auditory). In one study, when observers in face-to-face interaction were instructed to pay particular attention to auditory cues, they were more successful in discriminating truth from deception (DePaulo, Lassiter, and Stone 1982).

Third, we note that interaction is a two-way street: impression managers also observe the reactions of their audiences. The feedback impression managers receive from their audiences in face-to-face situations is richer than in more limited interaction situations. Using this richer feedback to estimate how well they are succeeding, impression man-agers are more able to fine tune their deceptive communications to be more convincing in face-to-face situations.

Ineffective Self-Presentation and Spoiled Identities

Social interaction is a perilous undertaking—one that is liable to be disrupted at any moment by challenges to one's identity. Some of us manage to recover from ineffective self-presentation, others are permanently saddled with spoiled identities. This section will discuss what happens when impression management fails. First, it considers embarrassment, a spontaneous reaction to sudden or transitory challenges to our identities. Second, it analyzes two deliberate actions aimed at destroying or debasing the identities of persons who fail repeatedly—cooling out and identity degradation. Finally, this section examines the fate of those afflicted with stigma—physical, moral, or social handicaps that may spoil their identities permanently.

Embarrassment and Saving Face

Embarrassment is the feeling we experience when the identity we claim in an encounter is discredited. We feel embarrassed not only when our own identity is sabotaged, but also when the identities of people with whom we are interacting are discredited. Our embarrassment at others' spoiled identities arises from the knowledge that we have been duped about the identities on which we built our interaction (Goffman 1967). For example, someone who claims to be an outstanding ballplayer will feel embarrassed when he drops the first three grounders drilled at him. But the team members who accepted his claims and let him play shortstop in a crucial game will also be embarrassed, because they were foolish enough to believe him.

SOURCES OF EMBARRASSMENT. A study of several hundred cases of embarrassment revealed three conditions that produce this feeling (Gross and Stone 1964). First, people feel embarrassed when they fail to maintain an appropriate identity. This is the plight of the math professor when he discovers that he cannot solve the demonstration problem he has written on the chalkboard. His carefully nurtured identities as a competent mathematician and a well-prepared teacher collapse into embarrassed confusion—and the students who admired his competence share in his discomfort.

Second, embarrassment ensues when people display a lack of poise. They may stumble, spill coffee, barge unawares into places they don't belong, lose control of their equipment (a dentist dropping her drill), of their clothing (a speaker splitting his pants), or even of their own bodies (trembling, burping, and worse). Poise is lost whenever we lose control over those aspects of our self-presentation that we ordinarily manage routinely.

Third, people become embarrassed when their interaction partner deliberately redefines the situation, destroying the identities they have carefully built together. Imagine, for example, a couple involved in a mutual seduction, each partner responding to the other's identity as a romantic lover. Suddenly, one partner launches into a description of her job hunting plans after graduation. In switching identities abruptly, she redefines the situation as a career planning session. This deliberate contradiction of carefully built assumptions embarrasses her partner and destroys his confidence in the predictability of their future interactions.

These three sources of embarrassment are all occasions in which "a *central* assumption in a transaction (is) *unexpectedly* and unqualifiedly discredited for at least one participant" (Gross and Stone 1970:1). Thus, embarrassment arises during social interaction, challenges the identities of participants and the definition of the situation, and makes continued interaction difficult.

RESPONSES TO EMBARRASSMENT. A continuous state of embarrassment is uncomfortable for everyone involved. For this reason, it is usually in everyone's interest to cooperate in

We can read the embarrassment on the face of Police Chief D.R. Sinclair as he announces that one of his own trusted officers has been arrested on a drug charge. People experience embarrassment when an important social identity they claim for themselves or accept in others is discredited.

eliminating embarrassment quickly. Unless their goal is to harm each other, interaction partners typically try to help the embarrassed person restore face. When a party guest trips and falls while demonstrating his dancing prowess, for instance, we might help him save face by remarking that the floor tiles seem to have worked their way loose. Mutual commitment to supporting each other's social identities is a fundamental rule of social interaction (Goffman 1967). That is, we are committed to protecting and restoring the identites of others in the face of threat, just as we are committed to protecting our own identities.

The major responsibility for restoring order lies with the person whose actions produced the embarrassment. As noted earlier, the first line of defense is to provide accounts that realign one's actions with the normative order. People offer excuses that minimize their responsibility or justifications that define their behavior as acceptable under the circumstances. If the audience accepts these accounts, an appropriate identity is restored, and interaction can proceed smoothly. In the interests of eliminating embarrassment, interaction partners may accept accounts that would appear lame to an uninvolved observer. A mother, stung by her college son's failure to come home for the birthday dinner she prepared, may accept his justification—"I was overwhelmed with course work"—even when she suspects he is lying.

When accounts are unavailable or insufficient, people often apologize for their discrediting behavior. By apologizing, people admit that they view their own behavior as wrong. In this way they reaffirm threatened norms and reassure others that they will not violate the norms again. Most important, sincere apologies imply that the discrediting behavior does not fairly represent what the actor is really like as a person (Schlenker 1980). When an apology is accepted, both actor and audience dismiss the discrediting behavior as irrelevant to the actor's "true" social identity. Embarrassment then recedes and the actor's identity is reestablished.

When our behavior discredits a particular, narrow identity, we can save face through an exaggerated reassertion of that identity. A man whose masculine identity is threatened by behavior suggesting he is infantile, for example, might make substantial efforts to reassert his courage and strength. In a test of this hypothesis (Holmes 1971), male subjects were asked to suck on a rubber nipple, a pacifier, and a breast shield (embarrassing experiences). Others were asked to touch surfaces such as sandpaper and cloth. The men were next asked how intense an electric shock they would be willing to endure later in the experiment. Men who anticipated the embarrassing experiences indicated willingness to endure more intense shocks than men who anticipated no threat to their masculinity. By taking the intense shocks, the embarrassed men could

present themselves as tough and courageous, thereby reasserting their threatened masculinity.

Sometimes people embarrass others intentionally and make no effort to help them to save face. In such circumstances, embarrassed persons are likely to respond aggressively. They may vigorously attack the judgment of those who embarrassed them. Alternatively, they may assert that the task on which they failed is worthless or absurd (Modigliani 1971). Retaliation against those who embarrass us is frequently a component of efforts to recover a positive identity (Brown 1968). Retaliation asserts an image of strength and dignity. It also gains revenge, and may forestall future embarrassment by demonstrating the resolve to punish those who would discredit us.

Cooling-Out and Identity Degradation

When people repeatedly or glaringly fail to present appropriate identities or to meet performance standards, others cease to help them save face. Instead, they may act deliberately to modify the offenders' identities or to remove them from their positions in interaction. Failing students are dropped from school, tiresome suitors are rebuffed, schizophrenics are institutionalized. Attempts to modify an offender's identity assume the form either of cooling-out (Goffman 1952) or of degradation (Garfinkel 1956) depending on the social conditions surrounding the failure.

Cooling-out refers to gently persuading the offender to accept a less desirable, though still reasonable, alternative identity. A counselor at a community college may cool-out a weak student by advising her to switch from premed to an easier major, for example, or by recommending that she seek employment after completing community college rather than transfer to the university (Clark 1956). Persons engaged in cooling-out seek to persuade offenders, not to force them. Cooling-out actions usually protect the privacy of offenders, console them, and try to minimize their distress. Thus, the counselor meets privately with the student, emphasizes the attractiveness of the alternative, listens sympathetically to the student's concerns, and leaves the final choice up to her.

Identity degradation involves destroying the offender's current identity and transforming him or her into a "lower" social type. Degradation establishes the offender as a nonperson, an individual who cannot be trusted to perform as a normal member of the social group because of reprehensible motives. This is the fate of the political dissident who is fired from his job, declared a threat to society, and relegated to isolation in a prison or work camp.

Because the offender's loss is severe, it is usually imposed forcibly. Identity degradation often involves a dramatic ceremony—such as a criminal trial or sanity hearing—in which a denouncer acts in the name of the larger society or the law (Scheff 1966). In such ceremonies, persons who had previously been treated as free, competent citizens are brought before a group or individual legally empowered to determine their "true" identity. They are then denounced for serious offenses against the moral order. If the degradation succeeds, the offenders are forced to give up their former identities and to take on new ones as "criminal" or "insane."

Two social conditions strongly influence the choice between cooling-out and degradation: the offender's prior relationships with others and the availability of alternative identities (Ball 1976). Cooling-out is preferred when the offender has had prior relations of empathy and solidarity with others and when alternative identity options are available. Lovers, for example, who have been close in the past can cool their partners out gently by offering to remain friends. Prior relationships entailing little intimacy and the absence of respectable identity alternatives foster degradation. Thus, strangers found guilty of molesting children are transformed into immoral, subhuman creatures.

Professional football and baseball present an interesting contrast in their treatment of players who fail (Ball 1976). Professional football players who do not perform well are usually cooled-out. When cut by their team, they often have acceptable alternatives available to them. They can join another major team or parlay their college education into a reasonable nonfootball job. Degradation is more common for baseball players because they lack respectable alternatives. A drop into the minor leagues produces a sharp loss of status, and baseball players rarely have sufficient education to find a prestigious job outside sports. Cut by their team, baseball players experience social isolation and loss of identity, sometimes referring to themselves as "dead men."

Relationships among peers, families, and within bureaucratic organizations are usually more conducive to cooling-out than to identity degradation. Feelings of solidarity tend to prevail in everyday contacts, and alternative identities are usually available for those who no longer enact their cherished identities successfully. In large organizations, the cooling-out of unsuccessful employees is crucial for smooth functioning. As a result, most of the leading corporations in the United States hire professional consulting firms that specialize in cooling-out employees whom the company wishes to fire. Using "directional counseling," consultants help unsuccessful executives explore appropriate careers and find new jobs.

Stigma: Managing Spoiled Identities

A **stigma** is a characteristic widely viewed as an insurmountable handicap that prevents competent or morally trustworthy behavior. There are three types of stigma (Goffman 1963). First, there are physical handicaps—missing or paralyzed limbs, ugly scars, blindness. Second, there are character defects such as dishonesty, unnatural passions, psychological derangements, or treacherous beliefs. These may be inferred from a known record of imprisonment, sexual abuse of children, mental illness, or radical political activity, for example. Third, there are characteristics such as race, sex, religion, and nationality that are believed to contaminate all members of a group in particular societies.

Once recognized during interaction, all types of stigma spoil the identities of the persons tainted by them. No matter what their other attributes, stigmatized individuals are likely to find that others will not view them as fully competent or moral. As a result, social interaction between "normal" and stigmatized persons is shaky, and frequently experienced as uncomfortable.

SOURCES OF DISCOMFORT. Discomfort arises during interaction between "normals" and stigmatized individuals because both are uncertain what behavior is appropriate. "Normals" may fear, for example, that if they show direct sympathy or interest in the stigmatized person's condition, they will be intrusive ("Is it difficult to write with that artificial hand?"); yet if they ignore the defect, they may make impossible demands ("Would you help me move the refrigerator?"). To avoid being hurt, stigmatized individuals may vacillate between shamefaced withdrawal (avoiding social contact) and aggressive bravado ("I can do anything anyone else can!"). Another source of discomfort for "normals" is fear that being seen with the stigmatized person may discredit them ("If I befriend a convicted criminal, people may wonder about my trustworthiness"). Coming face-to-face with a stigmatized individual may also arouse fear because it may cause "normals" to realize that they themselves are vulnerable ("I too may lose my sanity one day").

EFFECTS ON BEHAVIOR AND PERCEPTIONS. When relating to stigmatized individuals, "normals" tend to alter their usual behavior. They gesture less than usual, exhibit less variability in their behavior, express opinions that reflect their actual beliefs less accurately, and conclude their encounters sooner when interacting with stigmatized others (Kleck 1968). There is also evidence that "normals" tend to speak faster in such interactions, to ask fewer questions, agree less, make more directive remarks, and allow the stigmatized fewer opportunities to speak (Bord 1976). Each of these behaviors diminishes discomfort by limiting the responses of the stigmatized and reducing uncertainty. At the same time, these behaviors have a negative impact on stigmatized persons, by restricting the opportunities of the stigmatized to claim more positive identities.

The mere belief that others think we have a stigma—even when they are mistaken—leads us to perceive them as relating to us in a negative manner. In a dramatic demonstration of this principle (Kleck and Strenta 1980) some female students were led to believe that a woman with whom they would interact had learned that they had a mild allergy (a nonstigmatizing attribute). Other students believed that the woman would view them as disfigured by an authentic-looking scar that had been applied to their faces with stage makeup (a stigmatizing attribute). In fact, the interaction partner had no knowledge of either attribute: In the allergy condition, she had in fact received no medical information. In the scar condition, there was actually no scar to be seen, though the subject did not realize this. The experimenter had removed the scar surreptitiously just prior to the discussion, while presumably applying a moisturizer to it.

Following a six minute discussion, the students described their interaction partners' behavior and attitudes. Those who believed that they had a facial scar remarked more frequently that their partners had stared at them. They also perceived their partners as more tense, more patronizing, and less attracted to them than the nonstigmatized students did. Judges who viewed videotapes of the interactions perceived none of these differences. This is not surprising, since the partner knew nothing about either disability. However, these results indicate that people

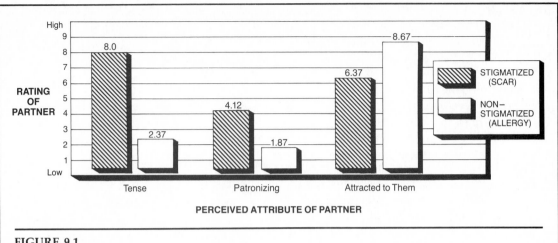

FIGURE 9.1

<small>PERCEPTIONS OF INTERACTION PARTNERS BY STIGMATIZED AND NONSTIGMATIZED INDIVIDUALS</small>

In this study, some female students were led to believe that a large facial scar stigmatized them in the eyes of their female interaction partner. Others were led to believe their partner knew they had a mild allergy—a nonstigmatized characteristic. In fact, interaction partners were unaware of either of these characteristics. Nonetheless, students who believed they were stigmatized perceived their partners as substantially more tense and patronizing and as less attracted to them. This suggests that the mere belief that we are stigmatized leads us to perceive others as behaving negatively toward us.
Source: adapted from Kleck and Strenta (1980).

who believe they are stigmatized tend to perceive others as relating negatively toward them. The findings are illustrated in Figure 9.1.

When people believe they are stigmatized, they tend to *behave* differently too. In one study, for example, one group of mental patients believed the person they were interacting with knew their psychiatric history, whereas another group thought their stigma was safely hidden (Farina et al. 1971). Patients in the first group performed more poorly on a cooperative test and found the task more difficult. Moreover, objective observers of the interaction perceived these patients to be more anxious, more tense, and less well adjusted.

COPING STRATEGIES. Stigmatized persons adopt various strategies to avoid awkwardness in their interactions with "normals" and to establish the most favorable social identities possible. Persons who are handicapped often must

choose between engaging in interaction or concealing their stigma. A stutterer, for instance, may refrain from introducing himself to strangers in order to conceal his stigma. Alternatively, the stutterer may struggle to introduce himself at the risk of drawing attention to his stigma by stumbling over his own name (Petrunik and Shearing 1983). People whose speech reveals their stigmatized foreign origin or lack of education face a similar dilemma when meeting strangers.

Stigmatized persons usually try to induce "normals" to behave tactfully toward them and to build relationships around the untainted aspects of their selves. Their strategies depend on whether their stigma can be defined as temporary—a broken leg or passing bout of depression—or whether it must be accepted as permanent—blindness or stigmatized racial identity (Levitin 1975).

Persons who are temporarily stigmatized focus attention on their handicap, recounting how it befell them, detailing their favorable prognosis, and encouraging others to talk about their own past injuries. In dealings with doctors, nurses, or wardens, they demand treatment as if they were already cured, rejecting their stigmatized roles. They expect to share experiences and intimacies with others as if they were peers. To this end, they employ tactical self-disclosure to elicit reciprocation and they altercast others as equals by asking personal questions.

In contrast, people who are permanently stigmatized try to focus attention on attributes unrelated to their stigma. They often use props to highlight aspects of the self that are unblemished—proclaiming their intellectual interests (carrying a heavy book), political involvements (campaign buttons), or hobbies (a knitting bag) (Davis 1961). The permanently stigmatized try to strike a deal with "normals": They will behave in a nondemanding and nondisruptive manner in exchange for being treated as worthy human beings despite their handicaps. Interaction is most comfortable when they acknowledge their stigma as a minor attribute with which they are coping successfully and about which they are not overly sensitive (Hastorf, Wildfogel, and Cassman 1979).

Studies of interaction between "normal" and stigmatized individuals yield a consistent picture. "Normals" tend to pressure the stigmatized—whether intentionally or unintentionally—to accept and conform to their inferior identities. For example, sighted persons tend to discourage the blind from undertaking such pursuits as sports, politics, and entertaining. Stigmatized individuals are expected to cultivate a cheerful manner, whatever their limitations, avoiding bitterness and self-pity. Many blind persons conform to these expectations, refraining from overt complaint.

Everyone gains some benefit from coping with stigma in these way. Stigmatized persons avoid the constant embarrassment of indelicate questions, inconsiderateness, and awkward offers of help. They gain substantial acceptance and manage to enjoy relatively satisfying interaction in most encounters. "Normals" gain because they can feel superior and be spared facing the true pain and unfairness the stigmatized suffer. In addition, they need not admit to themselves how limited their own tactfulness and tolerance really are. Thus, even identities spoiled by physical, moral, and social handicaps are managed in a way that preserves the social order.

Summary

Self-presentation refers to our attempts, both conscious and unconscious, to control the images we project of ourselves in social interaction.

SELF-PRESENTATION AS AN EVERYDAY NECESSITY. Successful self-presentation requires efforts to control how others define the interaction situation. (1) In defining the situation, people negotiate the type of social occasion they will agree is at hand, the identities they will grant each other, and the amount of leeway they will allow for enacting roles in unique, individual ways. (2) The primary goal of self-presentation is to project an impression of self that will secure or increase one's power to obtain favorable outcomes. Self-presentation typically aims at creating a highly approved social identity because favorable outcomes are usually associated with social approval. (3) Success in self-presentation depends on inducing others to behave in ways that complement our chosen identity. Obstacles to success include conflicts of interest over interaction goals, claiming an identity inappropriate to the setting, and suspicion that the identity one presents is deceptive.

IMPRESSION MANAGEMENT AS A TACTICAL PROCESS. People employ various tactics to manipulate the impressions others form of them. (1) They manage appearances (clothes, habits, possessions, and so on) in order to indicate the kind of person they claim to be. (2) They ingratiate themselves with others through opinion conformity, other enhancement, and selective presentation of their admirable qualities. (3) They engage in self-disclosure, revealing personal information in order to elicit reciprocal disclosure from others or to build interpersonal trust, approval, or closeness which they can later exploit for other purposes. (4) When caught performing socially unacceptable actions, people try to repair their identities through talk that aligns their questionable conduct with cultural norms. They explain their motives, disclaim the implications of their conduct, or offer accounts that excuse or justify their actions. (5) They altercast others, imposing roles and identities that mesh with the identities they claim for themselves.

UNMASKING THE IMPRESSION MANAGER. People attend to two major types of information in detecting deceitful impression management. (1) They assess others' possible ulterior motives. If a person's ulterior motives are apparent, a modest self-presentation is more effective than ingratiation. (2) They scrutinize others' nonverbal behavior. Detection of deceit is better when people concentrate on auditory cues such as tone of voice than when they attend to the full cues of face-to-face interaction.

INEFFECTIVE SELF-PRESENTATION AND SPOILED IDENTITIES. Ineffective self-presentation has several consequences. (1) People experience embarrassment when their identity is discredited. Interaction partners usually help the embarrassed person to restore an acceptable identity. Otherwise, embarrassed persons tend to reassert their identity in an exaggerated manner or to attack those who discredited them. (2) Repeated or glaring failures lead

others to modify the offender's identity through deliberate actions. Others may attempt to cool-out offenders by persuading them to accept less desirable alternative identities, or to degrade offenders' current identities and transform them into "lower" social types. (3) Numerous physical, moral, and social handicaps stigmatize individuals and permanently spoil their identities. Interaction between stigmatized and "normal" persons is frequently awkward and uncomfortable. In general, "normals" pressure stigmatized individuals to accept inferior identities. At the same time, stigmatized individuals seek to build relationships around the untainted aspects of their selves.

Key Terms and Concepts

Self-Presentation

Impression Management

Definition of the Situation

Situated Social Identity

Frame

Front and Back Regions

Ingratiation

Self-Disclosure

Aligning Actions

Motive Talk

Vocabularies of Motive

Disclaimers

Accounts

Altercasting

Embarrassment

Cooling-Out

Identity Degradation

Stigma

Introduction

Item: "A hundred points earns you full membership in the Studded Stompers," explained three male youths arrested for viciously kicking an elderly man into unconsciousness. "Each unprovoked attack on a stranger is worth 10 points." Contrast these aggressive youths with another group of urban teenagers who organize voluntary senior citizen escort programs; they take the elderly shopping, sit in the park or visit museums or theaters with them. "Until these youngsters came along, I almost never left my apartment," one smiling lady reported. "I didn't dare take the subway alone."

Item: On Wednesday, 20 July 1984, James Huberty burst into a McDonald's restaurant carrying a semiautomatic rifle, a shotgun, and a handgun. For the next 90 minutes he fired at people inside and outside of the restaurant, killing 21 people and seriously wounding 20 others. The death toll would have been higher had several people not risked their lives to aid the wounded.

Item: PHYSICIANS EMPLOYED TO MAKE TORTURE MORE EFFECTIVE. Every year headlines like these bring new reports of doctors who dispense drugs that allow torturers to administer more intense shock treatment to their victims. By preventing heart attacks, these doctors block death as an escape. But other physicians leave personal comfort and lucrative practices behind in efforts to relieve human suffering in underdeveloped nations. These doctors subject themselves to primitive living conditions in deserts, jungles, and rain forests in order to treat people afflicted with leprosy, malnutrition, parasitic diseases, and the depredations of war.

The above examples of helping and hurting, altruism and aggression, illustrate an important fact of life: Human beings are capable of vastly different, even opposing, social behaviors. In any situation, some people may help whereas others may cause pain or show indifference. And the same people who behave aggressively in one situation may show compassion in another. The same Nazi doctors who performed cruel experiments on concentration camp inmates labored selflessly to save hospitalized victims of bombings.

The challenge for social psychologists is to explain this variation in human social behavior. When will people help and when will they do harm, and why? Drawing on research and theory, this chapter addresses the following questions:

1. What motivates people to help others?
2. How do characteristics of the situation influence helping?
3. How do emotions affect helping?
4. What motivates people to aggress against others?
5. How do characteristics of the situation influence aggression?
6. How do emotions affect aggression?

In order to address these questions, we need clear definitions of helping and aggression. At first glance two simple definitions seem to fit the behavior in the examples opening this chapter: helping is any behavior that benefits another (Staub 1978), and aggression is any behavior that hurts another (Buss 1961). But these definitions acknowledge only the observable consequences of behavior, ignoring the actor's intentions. Consequently, they often lead to absurd conclusions. For example, according to these definitions, a surgeon might be considered an aggressor if a heart transplant patient died on the operating table, despite heroic efforts to preserve the patient's life; at the same time, a would-be assassin might be considered a helper if the bullet he intended for the president killed the president's chief political rival instead.

Clearly, intentions are important in defining an act as helping or aggression. Intentions are particularly important for social psychologists who are interested in how personal and situational factors together influence decisions to behave. Given this viewpoint, we will use the following definitions of helping and aggression:

Helping is any behavior intended to benefit another. According to this definition, attempts to benefit others that fail (the unsuccessful surgeon, for example) are help; unintended benefits (the would-be assassin) are not. Helping is also sometimes labelled *prosocial behavior*, because helping has positive social consequences and it is approved and encouraged by prevailing social standards. Of course, behavior intended to benefit others is often guided by additional motives. The surgeon, for example, is also motivated to earn a living, to demonstrate competence, and perhaps to achieve social recognition.

Does helping ever occur in the absence of these additional motives? This question is controversial. Some argue that human nature is basically selfish (Phelps 1975); others argue that helping does occur in the absence of external rewards. This type of helping—voluntary, self-sacrificing behavior intended to benefit another with no expectation of external reward—is called **altruism** (Macaulay and Berkowitz 1970).

Aggression is any behavior intended to harm another person, behavior that the target would want to avoid. According to this definition, a bungled assassination is aggression—an act of intended harm that the target wishes to avoid. Heart surgery—approved by the patient and intended as help—is clearly not aggression, even if the patient dies. Note that helping and aggression, as defined here, share four features: (1) Both refer to actual behavior, not to good or evil wishes or hopes. (2) Both may

entail verbal as well as physical benefits or harm. (3) The benefits or harm may affect the target directly, or indirectly by enhancing or damaging the target's possessions or dear ones. (4) Most important, both helping and aggression are intentional—the goal of one to benefit, of the other to harm.

Altruism and the Motivation to Help

There are three main types of motivation for helping. First, our norms define helping as the right thing to do. Second, people help in response to their own feelings of compassion or discomfort, feelings aroused by seeing others in distress. Third, people help because they can obtain rewards and avoid costs. These three types of motivation may operate singly or in combination. Each type motivates some people to help more than others, and each is more important in some situations than in others.

Normative Motivation

People expect each other to help in a wide variety of situations. Thus helping is normative in the sense that it is an approved behavior, supported by social sanctions. From early childhood we are urged repeatedly to act in ways that benefit others. Our helping is praised, our selfishness condemned. Prevailing social norms enable us to anticipate how others will respond to our behavior, and to calculate in advance what the likely social costs and rewards for helping might be. We may also internalize social norms, adopting them as standards for our own conduct. We then feel good or bad about ourselves depending on whether we live up to our internalized standards. People often mention their sense of what they "ought to do"—their norms—when asked why they offer help (Berkowitz 1972).

SOCIAL RESPONSIBILITY. A widely accepted, very general norm that motivates helping is the **social responsibility norm.** It states that individuals should help people who are dependent on them. Several studies show that simply informing individuals that another person—even a stranger—is dependent on them is enough to elicit helping. For example, students worked harder for a supervisor when told that the chances of his winning a prize depended on how hard they worked for him (Berkowitz, Klanderman, and Harris 1964). Researchers eliminated all other sources of motivation for hard work by students. They were offered no material rewards for their work. They also were offered no social rewards, because no one would learn whether they had helped for many weeks. Their supervisor also showed no distress that might arouse the students' feelings of compassion or discomfort. Thus the internalized social responsibility norm was the only apparent motivation for students to help.

Although mere awareness of a stranger's dependency sometimes elicits help, it often fails to do so. Speeding passersby disregard stranded motorists they notice; bystanders watch fascinated but immobile during rapes and other assaults; and thousands of people reject charity appeals every day. Thus, people regularly ignore the social responsibility norm.

Perhaps this norm effectively motivates helping only when people are reminded of it. In a test of this hypothesis (Darley and Batson 1973), theological students were asked to prepare a talk on the parable of the altruistic good Samaritan. On the way to record their talk, the students passed a man slumped in a doorway. Although these students were presumably thinking about the virtues of altruism, they helped the stranger only slightly more than a similar group of students who had prepared a talk on an unrelated topic (careers). A second variable—being in a hurry—had a much stronger impact on the amount of help offered. The findings shown in Figure 10.1 suggest that the social responsibility norm is a weak source of motivation to help, one easily negated by costs of helping.

RECIPROCITY. The **reciprocity norm** states that people should (a) help those who help them and (b) not hurt those who help them (Gouldner 1960). This norm applies to a person who has already received some benefit from another. Small kindnesses that create the conditions for reciprocity are a common feature of family, friendship, and work relationships. People typically report that the reciprocity norm influences their behavior (Muir and Weinstein 1962). But does it really?

Many studies involving both children and adults demonstrate that people are inclined to help those who helped them earlier, in accord with the reciprocity norm (Bar-Tal 1976). Moreover, people try to match the amount of help they give to the quantity they received earlier (Wilke and Lanzetta 1970). By matching benefits, people maintain balance in their relationships and avoid becoming overly indebted to others.

People do not reciprocate every benefit they receive, however. Whether we feel obligated to reciprocate depends on the intentions we attribute to the person who helped us. We feel more obligated to reciprocate if we perceive that the original help was given voluntarily rather than coerced, and that it was chosen consciously rather than accidentally (Goranson and Berkowitz 1966; Greenberg and Frisch 1972). Help that is voluntary increases reciprocity because it implies good intentions.

Reciprocity is also more likely when the original benefit appears to have been tailored specifically to the recipient's preferences. We are more inclined to reciprocate if a friend specially prepared a meal of our favorite dishes, for example, than if he invited us to take potluck. Help that is general, inappropriate, or merely what is required by the helper's role gives no evidence of strong positive intentions. Recipients also consider how much of a sacrifice the helper is making on their

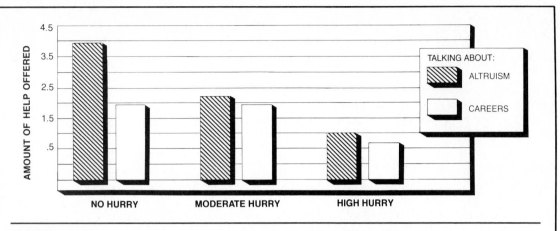

FIGURE 10.1

EFFECTS OF THINKING ABOUT ALTRUISM AND HURRYING ON HELPING

Theological students were asked to prepare a talk either on a topic related to altruism (the parable of the Good Samaritan) or a tropic unrelated to altruism (careers). They were each sent across campus to record the talk, and told either that they were late and should hurry (high hurry), that they should go right over because the assistant was ready (moderate hurry), or that they might as well go now even though the assistant wasn't ready (no hurry). As the students passed through an alley, they encountered a man slumped in a doorway coughing. The victim rated how much help each student offered him on a 5-point scale. Results show that being in a hurry greatly reduced helping. Thinking about altruism had a significant effect only when time pressure was low.

Source: adapted from Darley and Batson (1973).

behalf. They consider not only the size of the benefit but, even more important, the portion of the donor's own resources devoted to the gift. In an experimental demonstration of this idea, students received a gift of 80 cents from their partner in the first round of a game. When they were given the opportunity to reciprocate, students offered much more when they believed their partner had only $1 before making the donation than when they believed their partner had $4 before the donation (Pruitt 1968).

If recipients infer that their benefactors' motives are selfish, they are unlikely to reciprocate. We are especially suspicious of people who are overly generous or who extend help beyond our ability to reciprocate. Exaggerated generosity obligates us to submit to our benefactors' wishes (Greenberg 1980). Gifts we cannot reciprocate threaten our freedom of action.

They arouse an unpleasant emotional state called **psychological reactance** which motivates people to restore their freedom and regain control (Brehm 1972). Not surprisingly, people dislike benefactors they cannot repay. They attribute their benefactors' generosity to selfish, manipulative motives and thereby avoid indebtedness and regain a sense of freedom. This may explain why people in nations that receive large amounts of American foreign aid are hostile to the United States; they may be reacting against constraints of indebtedness (Gergen et al. 1975).

CRITIQUE. Several critics contend that broad social norms like social responsibility and reciprocity are inadequate to explain helping (Latané and Darley 1970; Schwartz 1973). Given the variety of situations people encounter, they claim that such norms are too general to

Despite massive U.S. aid to their country, these people are mocking Uncle Sam. Why? Because people dislike benefactors they cannot repay. They attribute selfish and manipulative motives to rich benefactors in order to avoid uncomfortable feelings of indebtedness and to regain a sense of freedom.

dictate our behavior. Second, if such norms are accepted by almost everyone in society, why do individuals differ in the extent to which they help? Third, the social norms that apply to a particular situation often conflict. Social responsibility may obligate us to help an abused wife, for example, but the widely accepted norm against meddling tells us not to intervene. Finally, while it is always possible to think of some norm that endorses a helping act, how do we know if that norm actually motivated the helper?

PERSONAL NORMS. In response to these criticisms, a different normative theory has been developed (Schwartz 1977; Schwartz and Howard 1981). This theory explains not only the conditions under which norms are likely to motivate helping, but also individual differences in helping in particular situations. Instead of dealing with broad social norms, this theory focuses on **personal norms**—feelings of moral obligation to perform specific actions that individuals generate from their internalized systems of values.

In determining whether feelings of moral obligation motivate helping, researchers measure personal norms as part of a wider survey questionnaire. For example, a survey on medical transplants might ask: "If a stranger needed a bone-marrow transplant and you were a suitable donor, would you feel a moral obligation to donate bone marrow?" This is usually followed up with an apparently unrelated encounter with a representative of an organization who asks these individuals for help. In various studies, individuals' personal norms have predicted differences in their willingness to donate bone marrow, to tutor blind children, to take class notes for students called up for army reserve duty, to work for increased welfare payments for the elderly, and to donate blood.

According to personal norms theory, three phases of decision making precede overt helping: *Awareness*—We notice another's need, think of relevant helping acts, and recognize our own ability to perform some of these acts. *Motivation*—We arrive at a sense of how much we want to perform relevant acts by weighing how well the acts express our internalized moral values and the social and material costs and benefits of these acts. *Defense*—If our motivations for and against helping are nearly equal, we try to reduce our conflict and avoid helping by neutralizing our personal norms. We do this by denying the reality or seriousness of the other's need, denying the feasibility of helping, or denying our own personal responsibility.

Helping is most likely to occur when conditions favor the activation of personal norms and oppose defenses that might neutralize

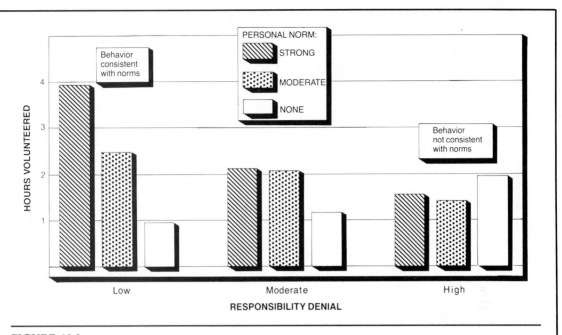

FIGURE 10.2

VOLUNTEERING AS A FUNCTION OF PERSONAL NORMS AND RESPONSIBILITY DENIAL

In a survey on social issues, university students indicated how much of a moral obligation they would feel (personal norm) to read texts to blind children. Three months later, the Director of the Institute for the Blind wrote to the students requesting that they volunteer time for just this purpose. Students who rarely denied responsibility for the consequences of their acts (low responsibility denial) behaved consistently with their personal norms: the stronger their moral obligation, the more they volunteered. Students moderate in responsibility denial showed weak consistency between personal norms and behavior. Students high in responsibility denial showed no consistency between personal norms and behavior. These findings indicate that the impact of our personal norms on helping behavior depends on whether we accept or deny our own responsibility.

Source: adapted from Schwartz and Howard (1980).

personal norms. For example, personal norms predicted quite accurately how often college students would volunteer to tutor blind children for students who tended to accept responsibility for their actions. Among students who tend to deny such responsibility, however, there was no relationship between personal norms and behavior (Schwartz and Howard 1980). Results of this study are illustrated in Figure 10.2. Several other studies reveal that the relationship between personal norms and helping depends on conditions that support norm activation (for example, the tendency to notice others' suffering) and oppose defensive denial of norms (the focus of responsibility on the potential helper) (Schwartz and Howard 1981, 1984).

NORMS AND ALTRUISM. Is normatively motivated helping atruism? Normative explanations of helping point to people's feelings of what they ought to do. These feelings may derive from broad social norms or from a person's own internalized values. Helping that is motivated by the desire to gain the benefits or avoid the costs tied to social norms is not altruism. Helping that is motivated by a person's internalized norms, however, may be altruism, depending on the values that underlie these norms (Schwartz and Howard 1984). If these are values that entail concern for the welfare of others—values like justice and compassion—then the help may be considered altruistic.

Empathy

People often respond to the distress of others on an emotional level. We experience **empathy** when we respond emotionally as if we ourselves were in the same situation as someone else—when another person's pleasure gives us pleasure or another person's pain causes us pain. When we perceive that other people need help, the empathic response is to feel distress ourselves. This can motivate us to relieve others' suffering as well as our own.

The television camera captures Lennie Skutnik rescuing Priscilla Tirado from the icy waters of the Potomac following the crash of an Air Florida jetliner on January 15, 1982. Why did Skutnik dive into the river to save a total stranger? Some call this altruism, behavior motivated by internalized values and empathy. Others question the existence of altruism and look for hidden rewards even in such actions.

The tendency to respond empathically to the perceived emotional states of others is probably biologically based (Hoffman 1977). People of all ages, including one-year-old infants, respond empathically when viewing others in distress. Their empathy is revealed in facial expressions, self-reports of emotion, and measures of physiological arousal. Empathic responses occur very rapidly, and they are largely automatic. Although empathy does not necessarily lead to helping, it does provide a biological basis for helping. Numerous studies have demonstrated that empathic arousal often increases helping (Piliavin et al. 1981)

CONDITIONS THAT PROMOTE EMPATHY. Believing that a victim is similar to oneself—whether in race, sex, personality, or attitudes—promotes empathy. For example, students in one study who observed another student receiving painful shocks when he lost at roulette became more physically aroused if they had been given information that the victim had a personality similar to their own than if they thought the victim was different. Those who were more aroused also donated more of their own money to help the victim (Krebs 1975). When observers take the role of another, imagining how that person feels, rather than simply observing how that person reacts, both empathy and helping behavior increase (Stotland 1969; Harvey et al. 1980, Toi and Batson 1982).

EMPATHY AND ALTRUISM. When empathy motivates us to help, is our real goal selfish—to relieve our own pain aroused through witnessing another's suffering? Or is our helping altruistic, directed toward benefiting another person? Among young children, emphatically motivated helping is probably aimed at benefiting the self. As people grow older, however, feelings of true concern for victims may also emerge, making altruism possible (Hoffman 1981a,b). Adults report two distinct states of emotional arousal while witnessing another's suffering: personal distress–consisting of emotions such as shock, alarm, worry, and upset;

and empathic concern—consisting of emotions such as compassion, concern, warmth, and tenderness (Batson and Coke 1981). Helping in response to emotional arousal is considered altruistic if motivated by empathic concern but not by personal distress.

Is helping in response to empathy ever truly altruistic? One way to answer this question is to examine situations where potential helpers can easily escape personal distress by leaving the situation and where there are no external sanctions for helping. Under these circumstances, feelings of personal distress would motivate escape rather than helping, and there would be no social rewards for helping. Thus helping in response to empathic arousal would be altruistic.

Several experimental and natural field studies have investigated helping in circumstances like these. They have examined contributing to the muscular dystrophy telethon, aiding a master's candidate with her thesis, taking electric shocks in place of a fearful experimental subject, and helping a fellow student catch up on course work (Batson and Coke 1981; Batson et al. 1983; Davis 1983; Toi and Batson 1982). In each of these studies, people who experienced high levels of empathic concern—feelings of compassion, concern, warmth, and tenderness—were the ones most likely to help. These results support the view that empathic concern motivates altruism.

Cost-Reward Motivation

One reason why helping fascinates those who study human motivation is that it seems to defy a widely held assumption about human nature: people are motivated to act in ways that maximize their rewards and minimize their costs. Altruistic helping does defy this assumption. But most helping is not purely altruistic. And some theorists argue that individuals help only when they perceive that the rewards to them for helping outweigh the costs (Lynch and Cohen 1978; Morgan and Leik 1979; Piliavin et al. 1981). The problem lies in revealing the rewards and costs that a potential helper takes into account. In general, the potential helper considers three types: rewards for helping the victim, costs for helping, and costs for not helping.

REWARDS FOR HELPING. The rewards that motivate potential helpers are many and varied. They include admiration and approval from others, thanks from the victim, financial awards and prizes, and feelings of excitement or competence. The rewards people seek through helping reflect their own needs. This is illustrated by a study in which undergraduates were invited to volunteer their assistance in projects such as studying unusual states of consciousness (ESP and hypnosis, for example) or counseling troubled high-school students (Gergen, Gergen, and Meter 1972). Most participants chose to help through activities that satisfied their personal preferences and needs. Those who enjoyed novelty volunteered more frequently to help with the project on unusual states of consciousness. Those who liked close social relationships volunteered more frequently to help troubled high-school students. Thus, the rewards people seek through helping match their own personality needs.

COSTS FOR HELPING. Every helping act imposes costs. These may include the threat of danger, embarrassment, financial costs, time loss, effort expended, exposure to repulsive people and objects, and feelings of inadequacy if help proves ineffective. A study in the New York City subway (Allen 1972) demonstrates the inhibiting impact of such costs on potential helpers. A confederate asked the subject (a passenger) whether the train was going uptown or downtown. The man in the neighboring seat (also a confederate) responded quickly, but gave an obviously wrong answer. The subject could help by correcting this misinformation only at the risk of challenging the misinformer. Whether or not the subjects helped depended on how threatening the

Costs and rewards can strongly influence help-ing. Many people satisfy their own needs through helping—needs for approval, excite-ment, and even financial rewards. Most firefight-ers, for example, report that they enjoy battling fires.

misinformer appeared to be. When the misin-former had loudly threatened physical harm to a person who had just stumbled over his out-stretched feet, only 16 percent helped. When the misinformer insulted and embarrassed the stumbler, 28 percent helped. When there was no reaction to the stumbler, 52 percent helped. Thus, the greater the anticipated cost of antag-onizing the misinformer, the less likely people were to help.

COSTS FOR NOT HELPING. Failure to help also imposes certain costs on potential helpers. Among these are self-blame, public disapprov-al, or condemnation by the victim. Bystanders who fail to help victims may even face crimi-nal prosecution in many European countries. Much helping is simply compliance with social norms to avoid socially imposed costs. Students may donate blood, for example, to avoid condemnation for failing to help their fraternity meet its quota. Employees may authorize payroll deductions for the United Fund to avoid censure by their employers.

Failure to dispel the personal distress from empathic arousal is yet another cost of not helping.

Situational Impacts on Helping

"What time is it?" someone asks; and practi-cally anyone whose watch is working answers helpfully. A child darts from your side into the path of an oncoming car, and you—as virtually anyone would—reach out to grab her. But would you give a dollar to a drunken stranger for a beer? Few people would. And very few of us would intervene in a heated argument between a man and woman we think are married. These examples demonstrate that aspects of the situation have a strong impact on helping. Situations influence our reactions by activating norms, arousing empathy, and pointing to costs and rewards. This next sec-tion considers two aspects of situations that influence helping: characteristics of the needy person, and interactions among bystanders.

Characteristics of the Needy

DO WE KNOW THEM? Some people have a much better chance of receiving help than others. We are especially inclined to help people to whom we feel close. Studies of reactions following natural disasters, for example, indicate that people tend first to aid needy family members, then friends and neighbors, and lastly strangers in the stricken area (Form and Nosow 1958). Relatedness increases helping because ongoing relation-ships create stronger normative obligations, more intense empathy, and entail greater costs when we fail to help. Even the briefest prior encounter with a stranger—merely glimpsing the other—has been found to increase help-ing. This is probably because the earlier encounter generates a visual image of the victim who is suffering, thereby increasing our empathy (Liebhart 1972).

ARE THEY SIMILAR? Because we tend to feel closer to people who are similar to us, we are more likely to help those who resemble us in race, nationality, attitudes, political opinions, ideologies, and even in mode of dress. In one study, for example, a confederate dressed either in jeans and work shirt or in conventional sports clothes and asked college students for a dime to make a phone call. Students complied with the requests more often if the confederate's mode of dress was similar to their own (Emswiller, Deaux, and Willis 1971).

A series of field studies demonstrate that similarity of opinions and political ideologies increases helping (Hornstein 1978). In these studies, New York pedestrians came across "lost" wallets or "lost" letters planted by confederates in conspicuous places. They contained information indicating the original owner's views on the Arab-Israeli conflict, on worthy or unpopular organizations, or on trivial opinion items. The owner's views on these topics either resembled or differed from the views known to characterize the neighborhoods selected. Pedestrians took steps to return the lost objects much more frequently when the owner's views were similar to their own.

ARE THEY DESERVING? Suppose you received a call asking you to help elderly people who had just suffered a reduction in their income after losing their jobs. Would it matter whether they lost their jobs because they were caught stealing and lying or because their work program was being phased out? A study of Wisconsin homemakers who received such a call showed that respondents were more likely to help if the elderly people had become dependent because their program was cut (Schwartz and Fleishman 1978). Potential helpers respond more when the needy persons' dependency is caused by circumstances beyond their control. Such people are true "innocent victims" who deserve help.

Need caused by a person's own misdeeds or failings elicits little help. Contributors to *The New York Times' 100 Neediest Cases* are much less generous, for example, when need can be blamed on the individual's own failures—moral transgressions and psychological

illness—than in cases of need that is clearly considered legitimate—abused children and physical illness (Bryan and Davenport 1968). Need viewed as illegitimate undermines helping in several ways. It inhibits empathic concern, blocks our sense of normative obligation, and increases the possibility of condemnation rather than social approval for helping.

Even in emergencies, potential helpers are influenced by whether they consider a victim deserving. Consider responses to an emergency staged by experimenters in the New York subway (Piliavin, Rodin, and Piliavin 1969). Shortly after the subway train left a station, a young man (confederate) collapsed to the floor of the car and lay staring at the ceiling during the 7½-minute trip to the next station. In one experimental condition, the man carried a cane and appeared crippled. In another condition, he carried a liquor bottle and smelled of whiskey. Bystanders helped the seemingly crippled victim quickly, usually leaping to his aid within seconds, but often left the apparent drunk lying on the floor for several minutes. Much of this difference probably reflects the fact that many people—rightly or wrongly—blame drunks for their own plight.

Interactions among Bystanders

Prior to engaging in a helping act, bystanders go through a sequence of decisions. According to the decision-making theory proposed by Latané and Darley (1970), there are five steps in this sequence. A potential helper must (1) notice that something is happening; (2) decide what's going on (Is someone in trouble? Is it an emergency?); (3) decide whether he or she has the responsibility to act; (4) decide what it is appropriate to do; and (5) decide to implement the chosen behavior. At each step in this decision process, shown in Figure 10.3, potential helpers are influenced by their relations with other bystanders whom they believe to be present.

Consider the tragic murder of Kitty Genovese, an event that inspired the early research on bystander intervention. Shortly

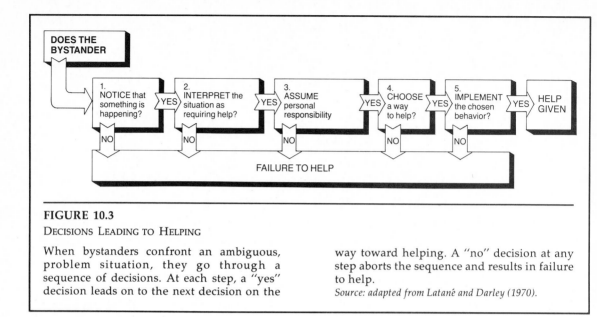

DOES THE BYSTANDER

1. NOTICE that something is happening? — YES — 2. INTERPRET the situation as requiring help? — YES — 3. ASSUME personal responsibility — YES — 4. CHOOSE a way to help? — YES — 5. IMPLEMENT the chosen behavior? — YES — HELP GIVEN

NO / NO / NO / NO / NO

FAILURE TO HELP

FIGURE 10.3

DECISIONS LEADING TO HELPING

When bystanders confront an ambiguous, problem situation, they go through a sequence of decisions. At each step, a "yes" decision leads on to the next decision on the way toward helping. A "no" decision at any step aborts the sequence and results in failure to help.

Source: adapted from Latané and Darley (1970).

before 3:20 A.M. on the 13th of March 1964, Kitty Genovese parked her red Fiat in the lot of the Long Island Railroad station. Although she lived in Kew Gardens, a quiet middle-class residential area, Kitty must have sensed something wrong. Instead of taking the short route home, she started running along well-lighted Lefferts Boulevard. She didn't get far.

Milton Hatch awoke at the first scream. Staring from his window, he saw a woman kneeling on the sidewalk directly across the street, a small man standing over her. "Help me! Help me! Oh God, he's stabbed me," she cried. Leaning out his window, Hatch shouted, "Let that girl alone!" As other windows opened and lights went on, the assailant fled in his car. No one called the police.

With many eyes now following her, Kitty dragged herself along the street, but not fast enough. More than 10 minutes passed before the neighbors saw her assailant reappear, hunting for her. When he stabbed her a second time, she screamed, "I'm dying! I'm dying!" Still no one called the police. Emil Power would have, had his wife not insisted someone else must have already done so.

The third, fatal attack occurred in the vestibule of a building a few doors from Kitty's own entrance. Onlookers saw the assailant push open the building door, though few could hear the weak cry that greeted him. Finally at 3:55, 35 minutes after Kitty's first scream, Harold Klein, who lived at the top of the stairs where Kitty was murdered, called the police. The first patrol car arrived within two minutes, but it was too late (Seedman and Hellman 1975).

Why did no one react sooner? Newspaper editors and psychiatrists called it "bystander apathy" and wrote about urban alienation. Social psychologists, however, theorized that bystanders' failure to intervene in tragic emergencies may be due more to the social influence that bystanders have on each other than to individual callousness (Latané and Darley 1970). To test this idea and to discover the nature of possible bystander influences, researchers conducted a series of laboratory experiments on intervention in emergencies.

In one experiment, the room in which subjects were completing questionnaires gradually filled with smoke (Latané and Darley

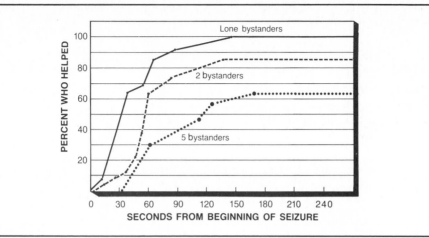

FIGURE 10.4

The Bystander Effect

Students who were engaged in a discussion via intercom of their adjustment to college life heard one participant begin to choke, then gasp and call for help, as if he were undergoing a serious nervous seizure. Students tended to intervene to help the victim most quickly and most often when they believed they were the lone bystander to witness the emergency. More than 90 percent of lone bystanders helped within the first 90 seconds after the seizure. Among those who believed other bystanders were present, however, fewer than 90 percent had helped even after four minutes. The bystander effect refers to the fact that the greater the number of bystanders in an emergency, the less likely it is any one bystander will help.

Source: adapted from Darley and Latané (1968).

1968). In a second experiment, subjects heard a loud crash from the room next door, followed by a woman's screaming, "Oh my God, my foot I . . . I . . . can't move it. Oh my ankle. I . . . can't get this . . . thing off me" (Latané and Rodin 1969). In a third experiment, subjects participating in a discussion over an intercom suddenly heard someone in their group begin to choke, gasp, and call for help, as if gripped by an epileptic seizure (Darley and Latané 1968).

In each experiment, the number of people present when the emergency occurred was varied. Subjects believed either that they were alone with the victim or that one or more others were present. Time and again the same finding emerged: as the number of bystanders increased, the likelihood that any one of them would help decreased. That is, bystanders helped most often and most quickly when they were alone. This finding, called the

bystander effect, is illustrated in Figure 10.4, using data from the nervous seizure experiment.

Three major theoretical processes contribute to the bystander effect: social influence on the interpretation of the situation, evaluation apprehension, and diffusion of responsibility. Each of these processes affects specific steps in the decision-making sequence (see Fig. 10.3).

INTERPRETING THE SITUATION. Emergencies and other situations requiring help are often ambiguous, at least initially. What does smoke pouring through a vent in a room mean? Is a choking, gasping student in real trouble? When faced with ambiguity, people look to the reactions of others for cues about what is going on. Others' reactions influence three steps in the sequence leading to helping. If others appear calm, the bystander may decide that nothing special is happening (Step 1), or that whatever is happening requires no help (Step 2). The failure of others to act also influences the bystander to decide that there is no appropriate way to help (Step 4).

Bystanders often try to appear calm, avoiding overt signs of worry until they see whether others are alarmed. Through such cautiousness they encourage each other to define the situation as nonproblematic. In that way they inhibit each other's helping. The larger the number of apparently unruffled bystanders, the stronger their inhibiting influence on each other. In keeping with this social influence explanation, increasing the number of bystanders does not inhibit individual helping in two conditions: (1) when observation reveals that others are indeed alarmed (Darley, Teger, and Lewis 1973); and (2) when the need for help is so unambiguous that others' reactions are unnecessary to define the situation (Clark and Word 1974).

EVALUATION APPREHENSION. Bystanders are not only interested in others' reactions. They also realize that other bystanders are an audience for their own reactions. As a result, bystanders may feel **evaluation apprehension**—concern about what others expect of them and about how others will evaluate their behavior. Evaluation apprehension *inhibits* helping when bystanders fear that others will view their intervention as foolish or wrong. When they see that other witnesses to an emergency are not reacting (as in the Genovese case), they tend to infer that the others oppose intervention. Evaluation apprehension has its main impact on Step 4, choosing a way to react and Step 5, whether to implement the chosen behavior.

On the other hand, evaluation apprehension *promotes* helping if there are no cues to suggest that other witnesses oppose intervention. Bystanders then tend to assume that others approve intervention. In three laboratory studies demonstrating this effect, bystanders witnessed a convulsive nervous seizure or a violent assault (Schwartz and Gottlieb 1976,

1980). Knowledge that an audience of other bystanders was present led to increased helping when the audio-visual system prevented each bystander from learning how others were reacting.

DIFFUSION OF RESPONSIBILITY. The presence of multiple witnesses also affects the bystander's decision whether to assume personal responsibility for helping (Step 3). Responsibility to intervene is focused 100 percent on a lone bystander, whereas multiple bystanders share the responsibility as well as the blame if the victim is not helped. Hence they are less likely to intervene. ("Why should I help? Let someone else do it.") This process of accepting less personal responsibility because responsibility is shared is called **diffusion of responsibility.** Bystanders sometimes diffuse their own responsibility by wishfully assuming that others have already taken action. Of the 38 witnesses to Kitty Genovese's murder, many claimed that they thought someone else must surely have called the police.

Diffusion of responsibility occurs only when a bystander believes that the other witnesses are capable of helping. We do not diffuse responsibility to witnesses who are too far away to take effective action or too young to cope with the emergency (Bickman 1971; Ross 1971). The tendency to diffuse responsibility is particularly strong if a bystander feels less competent than others who are present. Bystanders helped less, for example, when one of the other witnesses to a seizure was a pre-medical student with experience working in an emergency ward (Schwartz and Clausen 1970).

Emotional States of the Helper

Good Mood

Imagine a day like this: You do better than expected on your last exam; your summer job comes through, paying enough to cover the vacation trip you were planning; the friend

TABLE 10.1

THE EFFECTS OF GOOD MOOD ON HELPING

	Percent Who Helped		
	Picking up papers that had been dropped	*Mailing a "lost" unstamped letter*	*Making a phone call for a stranger*
Ordinary mood	4%	10%	12%
Good mood	88%	88%	83%

Source: adapted from Isen and Levin (1972); Levin and Isen (1975); Isen, Clark, and Schwartz (1976).

you've been trying to persuade to travel with you says "yes"; and the sun is shining. You feel great. According to many studies, you are more likely to help a needy person on this day than when your mood is just fair (Rosenhan et al. 1981). Good moods promote both spontaneous helping and compliance to requests. But moods can pass quickly; and as a person's good mood fades, helping also drops quickly back to normal (Isen, Clark, and Schwartz 1976).

Almost every experience that puts us in a good mood increases the chance that we will help others. Consider a few examples. Suburban school teachers who learned they scored well on a battery of tests donated more to a school library fund than teachers who received no feedback on their performance (Isen 1970). Pay phone users who found a dime in the coin-return slots mailed lost letters they found more frequently than phone users who found no dime (Levin and Isen 1975). People were more likely to help a stranded caller who had dialed the wrong number from a pay phone if they had just received a small gift than if they had received no gift (Isen and Levin 1972). Other mood-enhancing experiences that were shown to increase helping included: recalling happy experiences, reading statements describing pleasant feelings, hearing good news on the radio, listening to soothing music, and enjoying good weather. Some powerful effects of good mood are shown in Table 10.1.

HOW GOOD MOODS PROMOTE HELPING. There are several theoretical explanations for the good mood effect:

1. People in a good mood are less preoccupied with themselves and less concerned with their own problems. This allows people to feel empathy for the needs and problems of others.

2. People in a good mood feel relatively fortunate compared with persons who are deprived. Their good fortune is out of balance with others' need. They restore a just balance by using their resources to help (Rosenhan, Salovey, and Hargis 1981).

3. People in a good mood tend to see the world in a positive light, and try to maintain a warm glow of happiness. If they can relieve others' suffering by helping, they can protect and even increase their positive feelings. At the same time, people avoid helping that is unpleasant or embarrassing because it might ruin their good mood (Cunningham, Steinberg, and Grev 1980; Isen and Simmonds 1978).

Bad Mood

Now imagine a very different day: Your exam grade is lower than expected; your summer job falls through, forcing you to cancel your planned vacation; your friend reacts in anger when you call; and a cold rain soaks you to the bone while you wait for a bus. You feel rotten. In this bad mood, are you more or less likely to help a needy other than when your mood is neutral? Results of many studies reveal that bad mood promotes helping under some conditions but inhibits it under others (Rosenhan et al. 1981).

Three theoretical explanations for the effects of bad mood parallel those for good mood. The first two explanations specify tendencies that inhibit helping, the third shows how bad moods may enhance helping.

1. People in a bad mood become especially concerned about their own worries and problems. Focusing attention on their own needs, they are less likely to notice the needs of others and so less likely to offer help (Thompson, Cowan, and Rosenhan 1981).

2. People in a bad mood see themselves as less fortunate than others. Feeling relatively impoverished, they resist using their own seemingly depleted resources to help another, lest they become even more disadvantaged (Rosenhan et al. 1981).

3. People are motivated to act in ways that make themselves feel better in order to escape bad moods. Because helping is highly valued, people gain praise and boost their low morale by performing helping acts. Thus helping relieves their negative mood (Cialdini, Darby, and Vincent 1973).

What conditions determine whether bad mood inhibits or promotes helping? Research on this question has identified three important conditions. Each condition relates to one of the tendencies outlined above. *Salience of need:* Inhibition of helping due to self-preoccupation and inattention to others' needs is likely when the others' needs do not stand out in a situation (Rogers et al. 1982). *Costs of helping:* The feelings of relative impoverishment associated with bad mood inhibit helping when

the costs for helping are great (Weyant 1978) *Benefits of helping:* Bad mood tends to promote helping acts that promise big boosts to morale through increased self- or public esteem (Weyant 1978).

Guilt

One negative emotional state that consistently increases helping is guilt. Guilt is aroused when we transgress, when we do something we consider wrong. People induced to feel guilty in experiments helped more to make telephone calls for an ecology group, pick up scattered papers, volunteer to participate in experiments, and donate blood, than others not induced to feel guilty (Rosenhan et al. 1981). Guilt-producing transgressions—such as killing a laboratory animal, giving painful electric shocks, lying, damaging expensive machinery—have all led to increased helping. The transgressions have been both intentional and unintentional, public and private, in the laboratory and in the field. They have enhanced spontaneous help and requested help, as well as help that benefits the victim or a third party.

To explain these findings, we might assume that helping allows transgressors to relieve their feelings of guilt in some way. As a socially approved behavior, helping can make up for their bad behavior and boost the transgressors' damaged self-esteem. If this explanation is correct, we would expect that transgressors who find an alternative way to relieve their guilt would help less. Confessing is presumably such an alternative. A study of churchgoers' contributions to charity revealed precisely this effect: the study found that persons who had just gone to confession contributed less to charity than those who had not yet confessed (Harris, Benson and Hall 1975).

The effects of transgression, guilt, and confession on helping have also been studied experimentally. In one laboratory example (Carlsmith, Ellsworth, and Whiteside 1968), subjects were made to feel guilty for ruining an experiment. When these subjects had no opportunity to confess, they helped more on a later task than control subjects who had not transgressed. When the guilty subjects were given an opportunity to confess, however, the increase in helping was eliminated. These and other studies (Cunningham et al. 1980; Regan 1971) support the view that transgression leads to guilt which is then relieved through helping.

Aggression and the Motivation to Harm

Capable as we are of helping, human beings also show a remarkable capacity to harm others. The remainder of this chapter examines aggression. By definition, *aggression* is any behavior intended to harm another, behavior that the target would want to avoid. Our first question concerns the motivation for human aggression: Why do human beings turn against others? Consider three possible answers to this question:

1. People are instinctively aggressive.
2. People become aggressive in response to events that are painful or provoking.
3. People learn to use aggression as an effective means of obtaining what they want.

Aggression as an Instinct

The best known proponent of an instinct theory of aggression was Sigmund Freud (1930, 1950). In Freud's view, we carry within us from the moment of conception both an urge to create and an urge to destroy. The innate urge to destroy, or **death instinct,** is as natural as our need to breathe. This instinct constantly generates hostile impulses that demand release. We release these hostile impulses either by aggressing against others, by turning violently against ourselves (suicide), or by suffering internal distress (physical or mental illness). Because social constraints prevent our releasing hostility in frequent, minor destructive acts, violent aggressive outbursts are virtually inevitable.

Many animal behavior studies conclude that aggression is rooted in instinct. According to Lorenz (1966, 1974), the aggressive instinct has developed in the course of evolution because it contributes to an animal's survival: animals motivated to fight succeed better in protecting their territory, obtaining desirable mates, and defending their young. Through evolution, animals have also developed an instinct to inhibit their aggression once their opponents signal submission, while humans have not. For this reason, humans are more dangerous and destructive than animals.

Because the urge to harm others is genetically determined, instinct theories are pessimistic about the possibility of controlling human aggression. At best, aggression can be partly channeled into approved competitive activities such as athletics, academics, or business. Social rules that govern the expression of aggression are designed to prevent competition from degenerating into destructiveness. Quite often, however, socially approved competition stimulates aggression: soccer fans riot violently, medical students ruin others' laboratory experiments, and business people destroy competitors through ruthless practices. If aggression is instinctive, we should not be surprised that it is always with us.

Despite the popularity of instinct theories of aggression, most social psychologists find them neither persuasive nor useful. Applying observations of animal behavior to humans is hazardous. Moreover, cross-cultural studies suggest that human aggression lacks two characteristics typical of instinctive behavior— universality and periodicity. The needs to eat and breathe, for example, are universal. They are also periodic—rising after deprivation and falling when satisfied. Aggression, in contrast, pervades some individuals and societies but is virtually absent in others. In addition, the occurrence of aggression seems largely governed by specific social circumstances. It shows no periodic rise when people have not aggressed for a long time, or drop after they have recently aggressed. Thus our biological

Box 10.1
HELP: A MIXED BLESSING

How does it feel to receive help? Help demonstrates to the recipient that someone cares, and it relieves need. We might therefore assume that recipients will feel gratitude and joy. But help often brings resentment, hostility, and anxiety. Recipients of aid—both individuals and nations—may come to despise benefactors unless they can eliminate their debt by reciprocating. Why does help have such negative consequences? Because it undermines recipients' self-esteem or national pride, increases their dependency, weakens their future self-reliance, and makes them vulnerable to manipulation by the donor. Thus help is a mixed blessing.

Ideally, help will bolster recipients' own abilities, increase their self-help, and lead to independence. The avowed purpose of foreign aid, for example, is to enable nations to overcome crises and to develop their own resources to cope with future problems independently. The avowed purpose of welfare is to aid impoverished individuals and to help families escape hunger and suffering while they establish themselves as self-supporting. Yet nations and individuals are often reluc-

tant to seek or accept aid because it is given in ways that do not promote these ideals. Instead, help often communicates the message that the recipient is inferior in status and competence (DePaulo and Fisher 1980; Rosen 1984). Accepting help acknowledges failure to display the virtues of self-reliance and achievement admired in Western societies (Weber 1958). The problem is to identify the conditions under which help will have desirable or undesirable impacts on recipients. Several conditions are considered below.

CENTRALITY. Help that implies inferiority in intelligence, competence, morality, or other qualities central to the recipient's self-conception is considered threatening. Help is not threatening when it does not imply any important personal or national inadequacy (Nadler and Fisher 1984a; Tessler and Schwartz 1972). For example, help can be supportive and nonthreatening if need is attributed to uncontrollable or chance factors like a drought, epidemic, or unprovoked attack, or if the aid is defined as enabling one

makeup provides only the capacity for aggression. We must look elsewhere to explain why particular people harm others in particular circumstances.

Aggression as an Elicited Drive

In an early experiment (Barker, Dembo and Lewin 1941), researchers showed children a room full of attractive toys. They allowed some of the children to play with the toys immediately. Others were kept waiting about 20 minutes, looking at the toys, before they were allowed into the room. The children who were made to wait behaved much more destructively when given a chance to play, smashing the toys on the floor and against the walls. This study illustrates aggression as a

direct response to **frustration,** that is, to the blocking of goal-directed activity. By blocking the children's access to the tempting toys, the researchers frustrated them. This frustration elicited an aggressive drive which the children expressed by destroying the researcher's toys.

The most famous theory of aggression as an elicited drive is the *frustration-aggression hypothesis* (Dollard et al. 1939). This hypothesis makes two bold assertions: every frustration leads to some form of aggression, and every aggressive act is due to some prior frustration. In contrast to instinct theories, this hypothesis states that aggression is instigated by environmental events, events external to the person. Several decades of research have led to a modification of the original hypothesis (Berkowitz to overcome a trivial inadequacy in experience or effort.

SIMILARITY. Help that implies an important inadequacy is more threatening when received from those who are similar to us rather than dissimilar in attitudes, knowledge, or background (Nadler and Fisher 1984a). Similarity aggravates recipients' negative self-evaluations because similar helpers are relevant targets for self-comparison. ("If we are both alike, why do I need help while you can give it?") People who receive aid from similar as compared with dissimilar helpers report lower self-esteem, less self-confidence, less intelligence, and more personal threat (De-Paulo, Nadler, and Fisher 1983).

SELF-ESTEEM. People whose self-esteem is high are more threatened by help than those with low self-esteem (Nadler and Mayseless 1983). The inferiority implied by accepting help contradicts the positive self-conceptions of people with high self-esteem. ("How can a capable person like me need help?") Inferiority is consistent with the unfavorable self-conceptions of people with low self-esteem.

THREAT AS A MOTIVATOR. Is the fact that aid threatens a recipient's pride and self-esteem undesirable? Not if we consider the long-term consequences (Nadler and Fisher 1984b). If recipients experience aid as nonthreatening, they feel favorable towards themselves and the helper. But they have little motivation to change. Consequently, they invest little in developing self-reliance and continue to seek help in the future. Nations become dependent satellites and individuals become helpless parasites. In contrast, aid that threatens self generates negative feelings toward the helper as well as the self; but it motivates the recipient to change. This motivation can promote self-help and self-reliance. Both nations and individuals are more likely to invest in developing their own resources and regaining their independence if they feel threatened.

PERCEIVED CONTROL. Threat motivates positive change only when recipients perceive themselves as having some control over their environment. In an uncontrollable environment, threat produces long-term helplessness (Abramson, Seligman, and Teasdale, 1978). In short, recipients shake off their demeaning dependence on charity or foreign aid only when they believe they have a chance to succeed on their own.

1978). First, frustration does not always produce aggressive responses. Frustration sometimes leads to despair, depression, or withdrawal. Second, aggression often occurs without prior frustration. An insulting remark, for example, may elicit an aggressive response even though it blocks no goal-directed activity.

Research on the frustration-aggression hypothesis has generated a broader view of aggression as an elicited drive. Frustration is now viewed as only one of a variety of aversive events that can elicit an aggressive drive. Pain, insults, and physical attacks are other aversive events that may elicit aggression. Current analyses also hold that aversive events do not lead to aggression *directly*. Rather, they create a readiness for aggression by arousing anger. Whether this readiness translates into destructive behavior depends on the situation. Aggressive behavior is more likely, for example, when it is culturally approved, when an appropriate target is available, and when retaliation is unlikely. Some of these situational impacts on aggression are discussed in the section that follows. First, we consider a third source of motivation—rewards.

Aggression as a Rewarding Behavior

Often people behave aggressively because they anticipate that the aggressive act will be rewarding. Gang members mug an elderly woman, stealing her purse to obtain money. A child knocks down another to obtain the toy he desires. Professional killers work for substantial fees. Students destroy library materials to improve their own chances on exams. These and other aggressive acts provide rewards to their perpetrators. According to social learning theory, the expectation of reward is the most important—perhaps the only—motivation for aggression (Bandura 1973). The social learning view holds that aggressive responses are acquired and maintained like any other social behavior through experiences of reward.

If aggression is motivated by the expectation of reward, which aggressive responses, if any, will people perform in a particular situation? This depends on two factors: the range of aggressive responses the person has acquired, and the cost/reward consequences the person anticipates for performing these responses. Unlike animals, humans acquire a wide range of aggressive responses. A person may be skilled, for example, in using a switchblade knife, a Molotov Cocktail, biting sarcasm, or subtle gossip to harm others. People also consider the likely consequences of enacting particular aggressive responses in the current situation. "Will this response gain me the rewards I seek? At what costs?" Answers to these questions largely determine which aggressive act, if any, people perform.

If aggressive acts are acquired and performed because they are rewarding, there is hope that aggression in society can be controlled. Because aggression is learned, for example, child-rearing and socialization techniques that withhold rewards for aggressive acts should reduce aggression. Because the performance of aggression depends on available rewards, social groups can structure situations to make nonaggressive responses more rewarding.

Situational Impacts on Aggression

So far our analysis indicates that situational conditions largely determine whether the motivation to harm will arise and find expression in aggressive acts. This next section will examine four aspects of situations that influence aggression: the reinforcements available, the occurrence of attacks, modelling of aggression by others, and conditions that cause deindividuation.

Reinforcements

Rewards and punishments are two very different types of reinforcement. Whereas rewards intended to encourage aggression are usually successful, punishments intended to inhibit aggression often fail.

REWARDS. Three rewards that promote aggression are direct material benefits, social approval, and attention. The material benefits that large-scale criminals, and even younger bullies, obtain through using violence support their aggression. If benefits are reduced through massive law enforcement or through training the bullied children in karate, this aggressive violence will drop.

Despite the general condemnation of aggression, social approval is a second common reward for specific aggressive acts. Virtually every society has norms approving aggression against particular targets in particular circumstances. Soldiers are honored for shooting the enemy in war, children are praised for defending their siblings in a fight, and almost all of us urge friends to respond aggressively to insults or exploitation on occasion. Attention is a third source of positive reinforcement for aggressive acts. The teenager who aggressively breaks school rules basks in the spotlight of attention even as he is reproached. If we ignored aggressive behavior and rewarded cooperation with attention and praise, would this reduce aggressive acts? This is in fact what researchers found in a study of aggression among 27 male nursery-school children (Brown and Elliott 1965). In this study, teachers selectively ignored aggressive acts and rewarded cooperation with attention and praise. After two weeks, the frequency of verbal and physical aggression declined substantially. Three weeks after these reinforcement tactics were discontinued, however, physical aggression rebounded, while verbal aggression continued to decline. The researchers then asked the teachers again to ignore aggression and reward cooperation. After this second treatment, acts of both physical and verbal aggression declined dramatically. (Even two of the most violent boys in the class became friendly and cooperative.) These findings demonstrate that the careful use of rewarding attention and approval can have powerful effects on aggession. Results of this study are shown in Table 10.2.

PUNISHMENT. Given the widespread use of punishment as a means of controlling aggression, we might assume that punishment or the threat of punishment are effective deterrents. In fact, threats are effective in eliminating aggression only under certain narrowly defined conditions (Baron 1977). For threats to inhibit aggression, the anticipated punishment must be great and the probability that it will be delivered very high. Even so, threatened punishment is largely ineffective when potential aggressors are extremely angry, when they perceive the threatener as angry, and when they have relatively much to gain by being aggressive.

For actual punishment (in contrast to mere threats) to control aggression, certain other conditions must be met (Baron 1977): (1) the punishment must follow the aggressive act promptly; (2) it must be seen as the logical outcome of that act; and (3) it must not violate legitimate social norms. Unless these conditions are met, people perceive punishment as unjustified, and they respond with anger.

The criminal justice system often fails to meet many of these conditions. In most cases, the probability that any single criminal act will be punished is low simply because most criminals are not caught, and punishment rarely follows the crime promptly. Moreover, few criminals see the punishment as a logical or legitimate outcome of their act, and they often have much to gain through their aggression. As a result, the justice system is relatively ineffective in deterring criminal aggression.

TABLE 10.2

REDUCING AGGRESSION IN CHILDREN THROUGH SELECTIVE REINFORCEMENT

Timing of Observations of Children's Behavior	Average Number of Aggressive Acts Observed	
	Verbal	Physical
Before selective reinforcement treatment	22.8	41.2
After first 2-week treatment	17.4	26.0
After 3 weeks of no treatment	13.8	37.8
After second 2-week treatment	4.6	21.0

Source: adapted from Brown and Elliott (1965).

Attacks

Direct verbal or physical attacks provoke aggressive behavior in a variety of situations. Individuals often react sharply to insulting remarks or to the impatient beeping of another driver's horn. Verbal and physical attacks arouse us physiologically. Because we know that our arousal was caused by an attack, we have no difficulty recognizing and labelling it as anger. The typical sequence is: provoking attack → anger → aggressive response. Two factors that modify this sequence are attributions the victim makes for the attack and the victim's belief in reciprocating harm, which are considered next.

ATTRIBUTION FOR THE ATTACK. Although attacks typically produce aggression, we tend to withhold retaliation when we perceive that an attack was not intended to harm us. We are unlikely to respond aggressively, for example, if we see that a man is trying to save a child falling from his grocery cart when he smashes the cart into us. Aggression following an attack is both stronger and more likely when we attribute such actions to the actor's intentions rather than to accidental or legitimate external pressures (Dyck and Rule 1978).

As Little Caesar knew so well, crime does pay. Threats and punishments deter aggression when punishment is prompt and certain and when the rewards of aggression are small. These conditions are rarely met in modern societies, however, where crime thrives.

Attributing an attack to mitigating circumstances could reduce aggressive reactions in one of two ways. It might forestall anger so that the victim does not become motivated to aggress. Alternatively, it might block aggression because the angry victim realizes that social norms condemn retaliating under such circumstances.

In a comparison of these two possibilities, an experimenter provoked subjects by humiliating and insulting them while they performed various tasks (Zillman and Cantor 1976). A second experimenter attributed this attack to external pressures, mentioning that the first experimenter was "really uptight about a midterm he has tomorrow." This external justification was given either prior to the provocation, after provocation, or not at all.

Subjects informed of the mitigating circumstances prior to provocation were much less angry and retaliated less than other subjects. These findings suggest that attribution to mitigating circumstances reduces retaliation by forestalling the arousal of anger. Victims who know that a provocation is due to external pressures are less likely to become angry in the first place. External justifications brought to the victims' attention only after provocation have little power to prevent retaliation once a victim has resolved to strike back (Kremer and Stephens 1983).

NEGATIVE RECIPROCITY AND ESCALATION. Corresponding to the positive norm of reciprocity which supports helping is a negative norm of reciprocity which encourages us to return harm for harm. This norm—"an eye for an eye, a tooth for a tooth"—justifies retaliation for attacks. In a national survey, more than 60 percent of American males considered it proper to respond to an attack on one's family, property, or self by killing the attacker (Blumenthal et al. 1972). Milder attacks called for milder retaliation.

The negative reciprocity norm requires that the retaliation be proportionate to the provocation. Numerous experiments indicate that people tend to match the level of their retaliation to the level of attack (Taylor 1967). In the heat of anger, however, we are likely to overestimate the strength of another's provocation and to underestimate the intensity of our own response. When angry, we are also more likely to misinterpret responses that have no aggressive intent as intentional provocation. Thus even when people strive to match retaliation to provocation, aggression may escalate.

A study of 444 assaults against policemen revealed that escalation of retaliation due to mutual misunderstanding was the most common factor leading to violence (Toch 1969). Typically the police officer began with a routine request for information. The person confronted interpreted the officer's request as threatening, arbitrary, and unfair, and refused to comply. The officer interpreted this noncompliance as an attack on his own authority, and reacted by arresting the suspect. Angered further by the officer's seemingly illegitimate assertion of power, the suspect retaliated with verbal insults and obscenities. From there on the incident escalated quickly. The officer angrily grabbed the suspect, who retaliated by attacking physically. This sequence illustrates how a confrontation can spiral into violent aggression even when the angry participants feel they are merely matching their opponents' level of attack.

Modelling

A third situational factor that promotes aggression is the presence of behavior models.

For example, parents who punish their children physically serve as models of aggressive behavior. Children may not imitate this aggression at home for fear of retaliation. When this fear is removed, however, the child is likely to aggress. Children punished severely for aggression at home are indeed more aggressive outside the home than children punished less severely (Sears et al. 1953).

The following sequence of events at the Woods End protest demonstration illustrates the ways an aggressive model can influence observers:

> Many prominent officials have come to dedicate the Woods End nuclear plant. As the motorcade approaches, hundreds of respectable citizens—business people, professionals, students—surround the cars in protest. At a prearranged signal, the demonstrators abruptly sit down, forcing the motorcade to halt. Tension mounts as demonstrators and police await each others' responses. Suddenly a demonstrator wearing a dark suit leaps to his feet and begins to pound the hood of the first car. A rumor sweeps the crowd: "It's the priest." The police hold back, shouting over their bullhorns for the demonstrators to disperse. Within seconds, hundreds more fists smash against cars.

Aggressive models like the one described here provide three types of information that influence observers. First, through their actions, models demonstrate specific aggressive acts that are possible in the situation. The idea of pounding on the cars, for example, never crossed the minds of most demonstrators until they saw the model do it. The model's acts identified available opportunities for aggressive action.

Second, models provide information about the appropriateness of aggression, about whether it is normatively acceptable in the setting. Models who have high social status or who represent society's moral order are especially likely to be imitated. Their aggression gives legitimacy to the aggression of their imitators. The fact that many demonstrators thought that the model for aggression in our example was a priest encouraged them to imitate him.

Third, models provide information about the consequences of acting aggressively. Observers see whether the model succeeds in attaining goals, whether the behavior is punished or rewarded. Observers are more likely to imitate aggressive behaviors that yield reward and avoid punishment. Hesitation by the police in our example gave demonstrators the impression that smashing cars might go unpunished. Had the police immediately surrounded the aggressive model, observers would probably not have joined in, although they might have erupted in another way.

An aggressive model conveys the message that aggression is acceptable in a particular situation. This message matters little when observers are not motivated to do harm. But people who feel provoked and are inhibiting their desire to aggress, like the initially peaceful demonstrators in our example, tend to lose their inhibitions after observing an aggressive model. They are the most likely to imitate aggression.

Just as aggressive models may increase aggression, nonaggressive models may reduce it. The pacifist tactics of Mahatma Gandhi, who freed India of British colonialism, have been imitated by protestors around the world. Laboratory research has also demonstrated the restraining influence of nonaggressive models. In one study (Baron and Kepner 1970), participants observed an aggressive model deliver many more shocks to a confederate than required by the task. Other participants observed a nonaggressive model who gave the minimum number of shocks required. A control group observed no model. Results showed that subjects who observed the nonaggressive model displayed less aggression than control subjects in a subsequent phase of the experiment, whereas subjects who observed the aggressive model displayed more aggression than the control group. Other research shows that nonaggressive models not only reduce

aggression; they can also offset the influence of aggressive models who are present (Baron 1971).

Deindividuating Conditions

Did the respectable citizens who attended the Woods End demonstration anticipate that they would end up smashing cars, shouting obscene phrases, or defying the police? Surely few expected to behave in such a wild, uninhibited manner. There are times, however, when surrounding conditions reduce a person's self-awareness and lead to impulsive counternormative behavior. People may then behave in a violently aggressive manner they would never have imagined and, when conditions return to normal, they may feel shocked or embarrassed by what they have done.

The temporary loss of self-awareness brought on by situational conditions is called **deindividuation**—the loss of one's sense of individual identity. Several conditions produce deindividuation. Among the most important are anonymity, an undifferentiated crowd, darkness, and consciousness-altering drugs. When no one knows who we are, when we are swallowed up in a faceless crowd, when we cannot see or be seen by others, and when our critical faculties are numbed, our sense of uniqueness and individuality is weakened. In this state we are relatively unconcerned with how we are evaluated by ourselves and others. We are therefore less prone to feel the guilt, shame, or fear that ordinarily regulate our own behavior and make it conform with social and personal standards. Our reduced capacity for self-regulation, in turn, makes us more likely to perform behaviors we would ordinarily inhibit (Diener 1980; Zimbardo 1970).

There is substantial evidence that deindividuating conditions promote aggression (Dipboye 1977; Prentice-Dunn and Rogers 1980). In an early laboratory study, for example, students who were anonymous expressed much more hostility toward their parents than students whose personal identity was stressed (Festinger, Pepitone, and Newcomb 1952).

Swept away by the excitement of a crowd, these men are experiencing a reduced sense of self-awareness that enables them to express aggressive violence they would ordinarily inhibit. When we experience deindividuation, we are capable of uncontrolled behaviors we would never have thought possible.

Among cultures that disguise their warriors before battle (painting face and body, wearing masks or elaborate battle clothes), the warriors are much more likely to kill, torture, or mutilate their enemies in war (Watson 1973). Warriors whose identities are disguised are more deindividuated, hence less inhibited in the expression of violent aggression.

Emotional States of the Aggressor

The previous section demonstrates that situational conditions have a strong impact on aggression. But so far, little attention has been given to the emotional states aroused by these conditions. Aggression can be cold and calculating, but very often it is accompanied by emotional arousal. The next section will consider three aspects of the role of emotion in aggression, including (1) the factors that channel anger into aggressive acts and intensify aggression, (2) how general arousal amplifies aggressive responses, and (3) the release of aggressive emotions through displacement and catharsis.

Angry Arousal

Attack and frustration arouse anger. This angry emotional state in turn prepares the person to behave aggressively. Three factors in a given situation that intensify angry arousal are the strength of frustration, the arbitrariness of frustration, and the aggressive cues available. Each of these factors, discussed below, also increases aggressiveness.

STRENGTH OF FRUSTRATION. The more we desire a goal and the closer we are to achieving it, the more frustrated and aroused we become when we are blocked. If someone cuts ahead of us just as we reach the front of a long waiting line, for example, frustration is strong, and we are likely to become especially angry. According to theory, this intense anger should lead to aggressiveness.

A field experiment based on this idea demonstrates that stronger frustration elicits more aggression (Harris 1974). Researchers recorded the reactions of people when a confederate cut ahead of them in waiting lines to theaters,

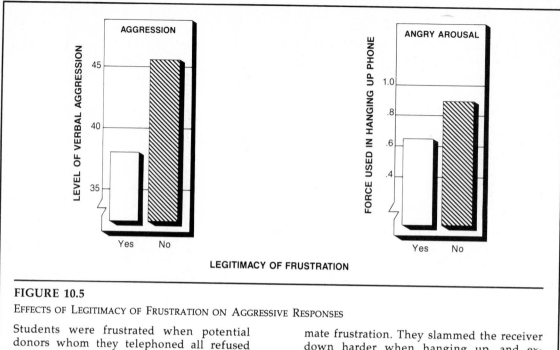

FIGURE 10.5

EFFECTS OF LEGITIMACY OF FRUSTRATION ON AGGRESSIVE RESPONSES

Students were frustrated when potential donors whom they telephoned all refused their appeal for a charity. Half the students heard legitimate reasons for refusal whereas the others heard illegitimate and arbitrary reasons. Those exposed to illegitimate frustration showed a higher level of angry arousal and aggression than those exposed to legiti- mate frustration. They slammed the receiver down harder when hanging up, and ex- pressed more verbal aggression toward poten- tial donors during their conversations. These findings demonstrate that the perceived rea- sons for frustration influence angry arousal and aggression.

Source: adapted from Kulick and Brown (1979).

restaurants, and grocery check-out counters. The confederate cut in front of either the second or the twelfth person in line. As pre- dicted, people at the front of the line responded far more aggressively. They made more than twice as many abusive remarks to the intruder than people at the back of the line.

ARBITRARINESS OF FRUSTRATION. People's per- ceptions of the reasons for frustration mark- edly influence the degree of hostility they feel. People are apt to feel much more hostile when they believe the frustration is arbitrary, unpro- voked, or illegitimate than when they attri- bute it to a reasonable, accidental, or legitimate cause. As a result, arbitrary, illegitimate frus- tration elicits more aggression.

In a study demonstrating this principle, students were asked to make appeals for a charity over the telephone (Kulik and Brown 1979). They were frustrated by refusals from all potential donors (in reality, confederates). In the legitimate frustration condition, poten- tial donors offered good reasons for refusing (such as "I just lost my job"). In the illegitimate frustration condition, they offered weak, arbi- trary reasons (such as "charities are a rip-off"). As shown in Figure 10.5, individuals exposed to illegitimate frustration were more aroused than those exposed to legitimate frustration. They also directed more verbal aggression against the potential donors.

AGGRESSIVE CUES. Whether angry arousal actu- ally leads to aggressive acts depends on the presence of suitable aggressive cues in the environment (Berkowitz 1978). These cues may be necessary to bring the idea of aggression to mind. In their absence, for example, a frustrated, angry homemaker may simply despair and become resigned. Situational cues (sounds from the neighboring apartment of dishes being smashed) may suggest the idea of aggression as well as specific acts that serve as an appropriate means for expressing it (smashing one's spouse's pile of dirty dishes).

Aggressive cues have a second function. They intensify the arousal that an angry person experiences. Seeing a gun or viewing a violent film, for example, may further arouse a frustrated person and make him more aggressive. Substantial cross-cultural evidence shows that people who have been frustrated respond more aggressively when in the presence of a gun than in the presence of neutral objects (Berkowitz and LePage 1967; Frodi 1975). This so-called "weapons effect" occurs when people are already aroused. The sight of weapons intensifies their arousal. The presence of handguns in many homes creates the conditions for a weapons effect, if family members become angry.

General Arousal

It is no surprise that arousal due to provocation leads to aggression. But what of general physiological arousal that has no apparent connection with anger—arousal caused by an ear-splitting rock band, for example, or by strenuous physical exercise? We might not expect such arousal to increase aggression, but numerous studies reveal that virtually any strong sources of physiological arousal can intensify harmdoing responses (Rule, Ferguson, and Nesdale 1980). This includes vigorous exercise, loud noise, competition, stimulating drugs, hard-core pornography, and stimulating music. Because these sources of arousal are so common, their intensifying effect on aggression is important.

AGGRESSION IS THE DOMINANT TENDENCY. General arousal does not cause aggression by itself;

rather, it amplifies aggression when aggression is already the dominant tendency in the situation—that is, when aggression is the natural response because the person has been provoked. If there is no strong tendency to aggression in a situation, general arousal does not promote harmdoing. For example, college students who are provoked by local townspeople respond more aggressively than usual if they are aroused by the noise and excitement of a football game. However, in the absence of provocation, arousal from the game makes them no more aggressive than usual.

In one study illustrating the amplifying effect of general arousal (Zillman, Katcher, and Milavsky 1972), aggression was established as the dominant tendency for half the participants by having a confederate insult them. The others were treated politely. Participants engaged either in an arousing activity (vigorous bicycle pedalling) or in a quiet activity (stringing discs on a wire), and were then given a chance to administer shocks to the confederate. Those who had been provoked earlier retaliated with more intense shocks if they had been exercising. Exercising had no effect on the responses of participants who had not been provoked. In short, arousal amplified harmdoing when aggression was the dominant response.

AROUSAL IS ATTRIBUTED TO PROVOCATION. A second condition necessary for general arousal to amplify harmdoing is that people erroneously interpret arousal as part of their angry feelings—that is, they must misattribute the arousal caused by exercise, noise, and so on, to provocation or frustration (Zillman 1979). When people correctly attribute their exercise-induced arousal to riding a bicycle, for instance, the arousal does not intensify aggression in response to an insult. If enough time has passed so that bicycle riders no longer connect any remaining arousal with exercise, however, this arousal may amplify their feelings of anger and strengthen their aggressive responses. In short, general arousal that is erroneously attributed to provocation intensifies feelings of anger and amplifies aggression.

Emotional Release: Displacement and Catharsis

Infuriated by a day of catering to her boss, Ruth turned on her teen-age son as he drove her home. "Why must you drive like a maniac?" she snapped. Ralph was stunned. He was driving 25 miles per hour and had done nothing to provoke his mother's aggression. Why was he attacked?

DISPLACEMENT. According to instinct and drive theories of aggression, the everyday irritations and provocations we encounter cause a buildup of anger that demands release. We prefer to release this pent-up anger by directly attacking whoever caused it. If we are unable to do this, however, we seek another outlet for our aggressive energy. **Displacement** is the release of pent-up anger in the form of aggression against a target other than the original cause of the anger. Displacement occurs when we cannot identify a tormentor, or when the tormentor is unavailable or is so powerful that fear of retaliation inhibits us (Dollard et al. 1939; Fitz 1976). Ruth's boss was unavailable, and she would not have attacked him anyway for fear of losing her job.

What determines the target of displaced aggression? First, we tend to displace aggression on persons who resemble the source of our anger. Similarity to the original tormentor in appearance, sex, religion, age, and various other characteristics all increase the chances of someone's becoming the target of displaced aggression. Second, we displace aggression more onto potential targets whom we perceive as weak and unable to retaliate. Target weakness and similarity influenced Ruth's displacement of aggression onto Ralph. She chose a target who was weaker than herself and similar in sex to her tormentor. Third, we displace aggression more onto socially sanctioned targets—people who are negatively stereotyped

so that aggression against them is viewed as "justified." Because minority groups are often both negatively stereotyped and weak, they are tempting targets. People who are frustrated by economic or social stress may therefore displace their aggressive energy by inflicting violence on blacks, Hispanics, Jews, and other minorities (Harding et al. 1969).

CATHARSIS. Did Ruth feel better after releasing her anger? She probably did. It is generally thought that letting off steam is better than bottling up hostility. A very old psychological concept, catharsis, captures this idea (Aristotle, *Poetics*, Book 6). **Catharsis** is the reduction of aggressive arousal brought about by performing aggressive acts. The catharsis hypothesis states that we can purge ourselves of hostile emotions by intensely experiencing these emotions while performing aggression. A broader view of catharsis suggests that by observing aggression as an involved spectator to drama, television, or sports we also release aggressive emotions.

Numerous studies support the basic catharsis hypothesis: aggressive acts directed against the source of anger appear to reduce physiological arousal fairly consistently (Geen and Quanty 1977). We usually feel relieved after letting off steam against a tormentor. However, if the person who provoked our anger is relatively powerful, aggression may not bring catharsis because the fear of retaliation keeps us aroused. Aggression against a tormentor is also unlikely to reduce arousal under two other conditions: if we feel our aggression is inappropriate to the situation and will make us look foolish, or if our internalized values oppose the aggression and make us feel guilty about our aggression.

A second hypothesis that extends the original catharsis idea asserts that catharsis reduces subsequent aggression (Dollard et al. 1939; Freud 1950). That is, once people act aggressively and release their angry arousal, they are less inclined to future aggression. This hypothesis underlies advice such as "Put on

Box 10.2
MEDIA VIOLENCE AND AGGRESSION IN SOCIETY

While carrying a 2-gallon can of gasoline back to her stalled car, Evelyn Wagler was cornered by six young men who forced her to douse herself with the fuel. Then one of the men tossed a lighted match. She burned to death. Two nights earlier, a similar murder had been depicted on national television. Four days after the television screening of *Born Innocent*, a 9-year old girl was raped by four teen-agers who reenacted, in detail, a scene from the movie. Violence pervades television: stabbings, shootings, poisonings, and beatings—even cartoon characters torment each other in astonishingly creative ways. In an average week, a viewer can watch 50 to 100 violent deaths during prime time.

Do these presentations of violence encourage viewers to behave aggressively? Is our society more violent because of media violence? These are vexing questions, especially when the average American child spends more time watching television than at any other waking activity (Huston and Wright 1982). By age 16, American children are likely to have seen about 20,000 homicides on television—and aggression on television is modelled by heroes as well as villains. The two incidents cited above suggest that in some cases media violence induces aggression. Yet establishing a causal link between watching television and subsequent aggression has been difficult and highly controversial (Milavsky et al. 1983).

There are four theoretical processes that would explain why exposure to media violence might increase aggressive behavior: (1) *Imitation.* Viewers learn specific techniques of aggression from media models. Social learning through imitation apparently played a part in both violent attacks cited above. (2) *Legitimation.* Exposure to violence that successfully attains goals and has positive outcomes (as in police stories) legitimizes aggression and makes it more acceptable. (3) *Desensitization.* After observing violence repeatedly, viewers become less sensitive to aggression.

This makes them less reluctant to hurt others and less inclined to ease other's suffering. (4) *Arousal.* Viewing violence produces excitement and physiological arousal which may amplify aggressive responses in situations that would otherwise elicit milder anger. Research has shown that all four of these processes operate in linking media violence to aggression (Murray and Kippax 1979).

In hundreds of laboratory and field experiments, children, adolescents, and adults have been exposed to scenarios of aggression, both live and on film. Some of these scenarios have been specially prepared whereas others have been taken from popular television shows. With rare exceptions, these experiments consistently show that observing violence increases subsequent aggression by viewers (Geen 1978; Hearold 1979; Comstock 1984). Experimental studies are crucial in establishing the possibility of a cause-effect link. Still, most experiments expose participants to violence in a concentrated form and measure the effects shortly thereafter. Such studies cannot accurately assess the impact of years of media exposure in everyday life.

Three field experiments conducted in the United States and Belgium (Parke et al. 1977) illustrate the strengths and weaknesses of good experimental research. In each experiment, adolescent male delinquents who lived together in small groups were exposed for a one-week period either to several violent films (such as *Bonnie and Clyde* and *Ride Beyond Vengeance*) or to several nonaggressive films (such as *Ride the Wild Surf* and *The Absent-Minded Professor*). Observers rated the amount of aggression exhibited by each adolescent during the film-viewing week and at least one week before and after this period. They recorded physical threats and attacks, verbal taunts and cursing, as well as attacks against property. The pattern of results from all three experiments shows that adolescent boys who viewed the violent films became more aggressive, especially during the film-viewing week. Physical attacks resembling those seen in the films were the type of aggression that increased most sharply but also faded most quickly. There were indications that the boys who were initially highly aggressive were most vulnerable to the impacts of viewing violence.

These experiments convincingly demonstrate a causal link between viewing violence and aggression. Our ability to generalize from the results of these experiments about the effects of media violence on society, however, is severely limited. Few members of society are exposed to a concentrated, week-long diet of exclusively violent films—and few of us are delinquent adolescents, predisposed to violence. Note also that the observed effects tended to fade away within a week or two. For these reasons, researchers have turned to *correlational studies* that complement the experimental approach in order to assess the impacts of media violence in society.

In one correlational study (Singer and Singer 1981), researchers recorded the television viewing experiences and spontaneous aggression of preschoolers several times over a period of one year. Consistently, aggressive behavior during this period was linked to heavy viewing of aggressive action-adventure programs or cartoons. The level of aggressiveness these children exhibited four to five years later also correlated positively with the amount of violent television they had viewed as preschoolers. A second study (Milavsky et al. 1983) of elementary-school children and teen-agers covered a three-year period. This study revealed a weak positive correlation between watching television violence and subsequent aggression. A third study (Eron 1980, 1982; Eron et al. 1985) examined children's preferences for violent television and their levels of aggression in third grade and again 10 and 21 years later. This study revealed that viewing violent television in third grade correlated positively with later aggression.

The correlations in these studies may reflect a causal impact of viewing violence on subsequent aggression, but correlations do not prove causality. The correlations might also suggest that aggressive children prefer violent programs. The growing body of evidence suggests that the relationship between aggression and television viewing is circular. Because aggressive children are relatively unpopular with their peers, they spend more time watching television. This exposes them to more violence, reassures them that their behavior is appropriate, and teaches them new aggressive techniques. When they then try to use these techniques in interaction with others, they become even more unpopular and are driven back to television—and the vicious cycle continues (Eron 1982; Huesmann 1982; Singer and Singer 1983).

After 20 years of research, most observers agree that viewing media violence does cause later aggression. Although no single study proves this connection beyond a doubt, the combined evidence from hundreds of studies is overwhelming (Comstock 1984; Hearold 1979; Rubinstein 1983). The inevitable question is: Should media violence be censored? Some argue that censorship of the media is a dangerous, antidemocratic step. Others say it depends on how strong the effects of media violence really are. For the general population, the increase in aggression due to media violence is apparently quite small. For those already inclined to violence, it may be greater. But note that even a very small increase spread across millions of viewers would add substantially to violence in society. What, then, should be done about media violence?

the gloves and get the fight over with once and for all." Yet, with few exceptions, performing aggressive acts has been shown to increase future aggression. This is true whether the initial aggression is a verbal attack, a physical attack, or even aggressive play. One particularly telling study, illustrated in Figure 10.6, shows a clear catharsis effect after retaliating against a tormentor followed by increased aggression against that same tormentor (Geen, Stonner, and Shope 1975).

Initial aggression promotes further ag-

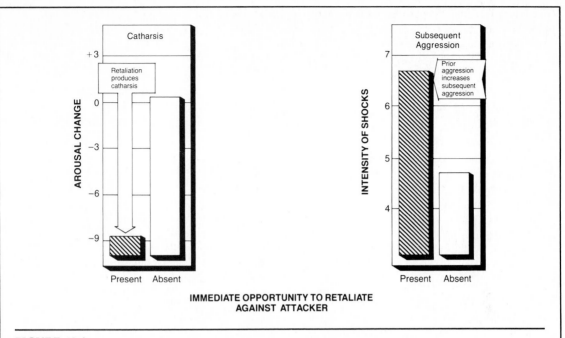

FIGURE 10.6

AGGRESSION, CATHARSIS, AND SUBSEQUENT AGGRESSION

Participants in a learning experiment who were antagonized by a confederate became physically aroused. Some participants had an opportunity to retaliate immediately, whereas others did not. Those who retaliated experienced catharsis—a sharp drop in arousal indicated by a drop in blood pressure. Those who did not retaliate remained aroused (left). Later, both groups of participants had a chance to attack the confederate (right). Those who had retaliated earlier delivered more intense shocks to the confederate than those who had not retaliated earlier. Thus the group that experienced catharsis earlier subsequently behaved more aggressively. These findings contradict the idea that releasing pent-up anger through retaliation reduces future aggression against a target. Instead, catharsis increased subsequent aggression.

Source: adapted from Geen, Stonner, and Shope (1975).

gression in several ways. First, initial aggressive acts produce **disinhibition,** the loosing of ordinary, tight internal controls against socially disapproved behavior. Disinhibition is reflected in the reports of murderers as well as soldiers who comment that killing was difficult the first time, but became easier thereafter. Second, initial aggressive acts serve to arouse our anger even further. Third, they give us experience in harming others. Finally, the catharsis that follows aggression and the plea-sure of thwarting our tormentor reward aggression; and rewarded behaviors are repeated more frequently.

Summary

Helping is behavior intended to benefit others whereas aggression is behavior intended to harm others.

ALTRUISM AND THE MOTIVATION TO HELP. There are three main types of motivation for helping.

(1) Norms define helping as the correct thing to do. The social responsibility norm motivates us to help whoever is dependent on us. The reciprocity norm motivates us to reciprocate intentional benefits. Personal norms, based on internalized values, motivate help when we notice need and feel responsible to relieve it. (2) Empathic arousal in response to others' distress provides a biological basis for helping. Similarity to victims increases empathy. Empathic concern motivates altruism—helping with no expectation of reward. (3) Several cost/reward concerns motivate helping. For example, people seek rewards from helping such as social approval, material gain, and satisfaction of personal needs, whereas they avoid costs such as danger and effort. They also avoid costs imposed for *not* helping such as social and self-condemnation.

SITUATIONAL IMPACTS ON HELPING. The characteristics of the needy and interactions among bystanders are two situational influences on helping. (1) Needy individuals have a better chance of receiving help if they are similar to potential helpers, liked by them, and seen as deserving. (2) Bystanders influence each others' behavior in three ways. First, the reactions of other bystanders affect whether they interpret the situation as requiring help or not. Second, the expectations of other bystanders create evaluation apprehension that may inhibit or enhance helping. Third, the presence of other bystanders fosters diffusion of responsibility which reduces helping.

EMOTIONAL STATES OF THE HELPER. (1) Good moods promote helping because they reduce self-preoccupation, increase feelings of relative good fortune, and are maintained through helping. (2) Bad moods inhibit helping because they increase self-preoccupation and reduce feelings of relative fortune. However, a bad mood enhances helping when need is salient and costs for helping are low. Under these conditions, people will attempt to relieve their bad feelings through helping. (3)

Guilt promotes helping because helping boosts transgressors' esteem.

AGGRESSION AND THE MOTIVATION TO HARM. There are three main theories regarding motivation for aggression. (1) Aggression is based on a biological instinct that generates hostile impulses demanding release. Most social psychologists reject this theory. (2) Aggression is a drive elicited by frustration and other provocations that arouse anger. (3) Aggression is a learned behavior motivated by rewards.

SITUATIONAL IMPACTS ON AGGRESSION. Situational conditions largely determine whether motivation for aggression arises and finds expression. (1) Rewards that encourage aggression include material benefits, social approval, and attention. Punishment and threat effectively inhibit aggression only under narrowly defined conditions. (2) Verbal and physical attacks provoke aggression if they are perceived as intentional. (3) Aggressive models provide information about the available options, normative appropriateness, and consequences of aggressive acts. (4) Deindividuating conditions reduce self-awareness and self-regulation, thereby releasing aggression people ordinarily inhibit.

EMOTIONAL STATES OF THE AGGRESSOR. (1) Factors that intensify angry arousal and increase aggression include the strength and arbitrariness of frustration, and the presence of aggressive cues in a situation. (2) General physiological arousal amplifies aggression when two conditions are met: when aggression is the dominant response in the situation, and when people erroneously attribute their arousal to provocation. (3) People who cannot release anger against the source of provocation displace it as aggression against targets who are similar to the source but weaker, or against socially sanctioned targets, such as minorities. Retaliation usually provides catharsis—relief of angry arousal—but it also promotes subsequent aggression against that same target.

Key Terms and Concepts

Helping

Altruism

Aggression

Social Responsibility Norm

Reciprocity Norm

Psychological Reactance

Personal Norm

Empathy

Bystander Effect

Evaluation Apprehension

Diffusion of Responsibility

Death Instinct

Frustration

Deindividuation

Displacement

Catharsis

Disinhibition

Chapter 11
Interpersonal Attraction

Introduction

Dan was looking forward to the new semester. Now that he was a junior, he would be taking more interesting classes. He walked into the lecture hall, and took a seat halfway down the aisle. As he looked toward the front, he noticed a very pretty young woman taking off

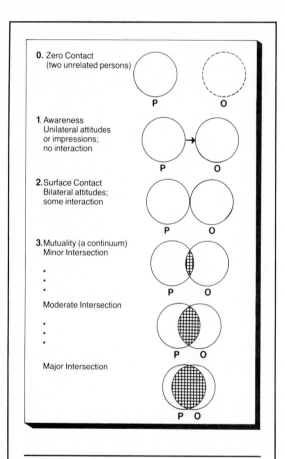

FIGURE 11.1

LEVELS OF PAIR RELATEDNESS

A relationship between two persons develops through a series of stages, or levels. Before it begins, the two are unrelated. The next level occurs when one person becomes aware of the other. The third level involves interaction. Relationships that develop beyond the surface contact stage involve progressively greater mutuality—disclosure of personal information, trust, and interdependence.
Source: adapted from G. Levinger and J.D. Snook (1978).

her coat; as he watched, she sat down in the front row.

Dan noticed her at every class; she always sat in the same seat. One morning he passed up his usual spot and sat down next to her. He asked her how she liked the class. She replied that it was a lot of work. As they talked, they discovered they were from the same city and both were economics majors. When the professor announced the first exam, Dan asked Sally if she would like to study for it with him. They worked together for several hours the night before the exam along with Sally's roommate; Dan and Sally did very well on the test.

The next week he took her to a film on campus. The week after she asked him to a party at her dormitory. That night, as they were walking back to her room, Sally told Dan that her roommate's parents had just separated, and that her roommate was severely depressed. Dan replied that he knew how she felt, because his older brother had just left his wife. Because it was late, they agreed to meet the next morning for breakfast. They spent all day Sunday talking, about love, marriage, parents, and their hopes for the future. By the end of the semester, Sally and Dan were seeing each other almost every day.

The growth of Dan's and Sally's relationship is an example of **interpersonal attraction,** the development of a relationship based on liking, loving, and mutual respect (Backman 1981). Attraction involves increasing intimacy, or pair relatedness, over time as shown in Figure 11.1.

The development and outcome of these relationships involves several stages. This chapter will discuss each of these stages and specifically consider the following questions:

1. Who is available? What determines whom we come into contact with?

2. Who is eligible? Of those available, what determines whom we attempt to establish relationships with?

3. What are the determinants of attraction or liking?

4. How do friendship and love develop between two people?

5. What is love?

6. What determines whether love thrives or dies?

Who's Available?

There may be dozens or thousands of persons who go to school or live or work where you do. Most of them remain strangers, persons with whom you have no contact. Those persons with whom we come into contact, no matter how fleeting, constitute the field of **availables,** the pool of potential friends and lovers (Kerckhoff 1974). What determines who is available? Is it mere chance that George rather than Bill is your roommate, or that Dan met Sally rather than Heather? The answer, of course, is no.

Two basic influences determine who is available. First, institutional structures influence our personal encounters. The admissions office of your school, faculty committees that decide on degree requirements, and the scheduling office, all influence whether Dan and Sally are enrolled in the same classes. Second, individuals' personal characteristics influence their choice of activities. Dan chose to take the economics class where he met Sally because of an interest in that field and the desire to go to graduate school in business. Thus, institutional and personal characteristics together determine who is available.

Given a set of persons who are available, how do we make contact with one or two of these persons? Three influences progressively narrow our choices: routine activities, proximity, and familiarity.

Routine Activities

Much of our life consists of a routine of activities that we repeat daily or weekly. We attend the same classes and sit in the same seats, eat in the same places at the same tables, shop in the same stores, ride the same bus, and work with the same people. These activities provide opportunities to interact with some availables, but not with others. More impor-

tantly, the activity provides a focus for our initial interactions. We rarely establish a relationship by saying, "Let's be friends" at our first meeting. To do so is risky, because the other may decide to exploit us. Or that person may reject such an opening, which may damage our self-esteem. Instead, we begin by talking about something shared—a class, a religion, an ethnic background, or simply the school or the weather.

Most relationships are initiated in the context of routine activities. This was shown clearly in a study of a random sample of college sophomores who described their most recently established heterosexual relationship. Some of the relationships were brand new; others had existed for many months. Thirty-six percent of these relationships began in classes, dorms, clubs, or at work. Thirty-eight percent began with an introduction by a third person. Eighteen percent of the couples met at parties. Only 14 percent met at bars or cocktail lounges. Thus, routine activities, introductions, and socially sanctioned meeting places such as parties are legitimate places for people to initiate contact with each other (Marwell, et al. 1982). Similar studies of the friendship patterns of city dwellers have found that friends are selected from relatives, co-workers, and neighbors (Fischer 1976). Thus, routine activities set limits on the pool of availables.

Proximity

Although routines bring us into the same classroom, dining hall, or work place, we are not equally likely to meet every person who is present. Rather, we are more likely to develop a relationship with someone who is in close physical proximity to us.

In the classroom, seating patterns are an important influence on the development of friendships. One study (Byrne 1961a) varied the seating arrangements for three classes of about 25 students each. At the beginning of the semester, students were assigned seats alphabetically. In one class, they remained in the same seats for the entire semester (14 weeks). In the second class, they were assigned

When we think about where people meet dating partners, we often picture the singles bar. But one study of heterosexual relationships found that relatively few people met their partners in a bar. Much more common were meetings in classes, in dorms, or at work.

new seats halfway through the semester. In the third class, they were reassigned new seats every 3½ weeks. The relationships between students were assessed at the beginning and end of the semester. Few relationships developed among students in the class where seats were changed every 3½ weeks. In the other two classes, students in neighboring seats became acquainted in greater numbers than students in non-neighboring seats. Moreover, by the end of the semester, the relationships between students were closer in the class where seat assignments were not changed.

Similar positive associations between physical proximity and friendship have been found in a variety of natural settings, including dormitories (Priest and Sawyer 1967), married student housing projects (Festinger, Schachter, and Back 1950), and business offices (Schutte and Light 1978).

We are more likely to develop friendships with persons in close proximity because such relationships provide interpersonal rewards at the least cost. First, interaction is easier with those who are close by. It is less costly in terms of time and energy to interact with the person sitting next to you than with someone on the other side of the room. It is obviously less costly to interact with someone who lives on the same floor in your dormitory than a person who lives three floors above you. A second factor is the influence of social norms. In situations where people are physically close or interact frequently—such as in dormitories, classes, and offices—we are expected to behave in a polite, friendly way. Polite, friendly behavior provides increased rewards in these interactions. Failure to adhere to these norms might result in disapproval from others, which increases costs.

Familiarity

As time passes, people who take the same classes, live in the same apartment building, or do their laundry in the same place become familiar with each other. Having seen a person several times, sooner or later we will smile or nod. Repeated exposure to the same stimulus is sufficient to produce a positive attitude toward it; this is called the **mere exposure effect** (Zajonc 1968). In other words, familiarity breeds liking, not contempt. This effect has been demonstrated using a wide variety of stimuli—such as music, visual art, and comic strips—under many different conditions (Harrison 1977).

Does mere exposure influence attraction? The answer appears to be yes. In one experiment, female undergraduates were asked to participate in an experiment on their sense of taste. They entered a series of booths in pairs and rated the taste of various liquids. The schedule was set up so that two subjects shared the same booth either once, twice, five, ten times, or not at all. At the end of the experiment, each woman rated how much she liked each of the other subjects. As predicted, the more frequently a woman had been in the same booth with another subject, the higher the rating (Saegert, Swap, and Zajonc 1973).

Who's Eligible?

We come into contact with many potential partners. Whether a relationship of some type actually develops between two persons depends on whether each is eligible. A person is **eligible** when he or she is both appropriate and desirable for that kind of relationship.

Who's Appropriate?

Appropriateness is defined by social norms. For each type of relationship between persons, norms specify what kinds of persons are allowed to have such a relationship. These norms usually define which persons are appropriate as friends, lovers, and mentors. In American society there is a **norm of homogamy,** a norm requiring that friends, lovers, and spouses be characterized by similarity in age, race, religion, and socioeconomic status (Kerckhoff 1974). Research shows that homogamy is characteristic of adolescent friendship pairs (Kandel 1978) and married couples (Murstein 1980). Differences on one or more of these dimensions make a person less appropriate as a friend, and more appropriate for some other kind of relationship. Thus, a person who is substantially older, but the same in social class and ethnicity, may be appropriate as a mentor, someone who can provide advice about how to manage your career. Potential dates are single persons of the opposite sex who are of similar age, class, ethnicity, and religion.

Norms that define appropriateness influence the development of relationships in several ways. First, each of us uses norms to monitor our own behavior. We hesitate to establish a relationship with someone who is normatively defined as an inappropriate partner. Thus, a low-status person is unlikely to approach a high-status one as a potential friend; the law clerk who just joined a firm will not discuss her hobbies with the senior partner (unless the senior partner asks). Second, if one person attempts to initiate a relationship, the other person will probably refuse to reciprocate. If the clerk did launch into an extended description of the joys of restoring antique model trains, the senior partner would probably politely end the interaction. Third, even if the other person is willing to interact, third parties often enforce the norms that prohibit the relationship (Kerckhoff 1974). Another member of the firm might later chide the clerk for presuming that the senior partner cares about her personal interests.

Who's Desirable?

In addition to social norms that define who is appropriate, individuals also have personal preferences regarding desirability. Someone may be normatively appropriate, but still not appeal to you. Four influences on desirability are physical attractiveness, competence, personality, and similarity. The first three are considered in this section.

PHYSICAL ATTRACTIVENESS. A great deal of evidence suggests that, given more than one potential partner, individuals will prefer the one who is more physically attractive. A study of 752 college freshmen, for example, demonstrates that most individuals prefer more attractive persons as dates (Walster [Hatfield] et al. 1966). As part of the study, freshmen were invited to attend a dance. Prior to the dance, each student had to purchase a ticket; as students waited in line, four ticket sellers secretly rated the person's physical attractiveness as low, average, or high. Before the dance, each student filled out several questionnaires, and was told that dance partners would be selected by the computer. In fact, males and females were paired randomly. The couples arrived at the dance at about 8:00 P.M. and danced until intermission at 10:30 P.M. During the intermission students filled out a questionnaire in which they gave their impressions of their date.

This study tested the **matching hypothesis,** the idea that each of us looks for someone who is of approximately the same level of desirability. The hypothesis predicts that those students whose dates matched their own attractiveness would like their date most. Those whose dates were very different in attractiveness were expected to rate their date as less desirable and less considerate. Surprisingly, the research showed that students preferred a more attractive date, regardless of their own attractiveness. The more physically attractive their partners, the more the students were eager to continue their relationship.

The importance of physical attractiveness in the computer dance study could not have been predicted from reports of men and women about what they look for in a potential date. When asked directly, young people consistently rank character, emotional stability, and various other traits as more important than attractiveness (Berscheid and Walster [Hatfield] 1974b). How then can we explain the importance of attractiveness?

One factor is simply aesthetic; generally we prefer what is beautiful. Although beauty is to some extent "in the eye of the beholder," cultural standards influence our aesthetic judgments. For example, in contemporary American society, a smooth complexion is considered beautiful, whereas in other societies, an elaborate pattern of tattoos on a woman's face might be considered desirable. A second factor is that we anticipate more rewards when we associate with attractive others. A man with an extremely attractive woman attracts more attention and prestige than if he is seen with an unattractive female, and vice versa (Sigall and Landy 1973).

A third reason why we prefer a more attractive person over a less attractive one is the **attractiveness stereotype,** the belief that "what is beautiful is good" (Dion, Berscheid, and Walster [Hatfield] 1972). We assume that an attractive person possesses other desirable qualities. This was demonstrated in one study in which male and female college students were shown three photographs and asked to rate the personality of the person photographed on various dimensions. The people in the photos varied in physical attractiveness; half of the male and female subjects were shown pictures of men whereas the other half were shown pictures of women. Male and female subjects gave similar ratings to both men and women. Physically attractive people were thought to be more sensitive, kind, interesting, strong, modest, and sexually responsive than less attractive persons (Sigall and Landy 1973). They were also considered to be more talented than unattractive people (Landy and Sigall, 1974).

Recall from our earlier story that Dan noticed Sally because she was attractive. Her facial features and coloring fit his standards of beauty. He believes that attractive women are more interesting and sociable, and more rewarding to interact with, demonstrating the attractiveness stereotype. This stereotype influences many of our judgments and behaviors toward others. For example, highly attractive persons are more likely to be recommended for a job (Dipboye, Fromkin, and Wiback 1975), less likely to be considered maladjusted (Cash et al. 1977), and less likely to be considered guilty of a crime (Sigall and Ostrove 1975). When we believe another person possesses certain qualities, those beliefs influence our behavior toward that person so that he behaves in ways that are consistent with our beliefs. In one experiment, males were shown photographs, randomly chosen, of either an attractive woman or an unattractive woman. They were then asked to interact with the woman in the photograph via intercom for 10 minutes. (The woman over the intercom was actually one of several student volunteers.) Each conversation was tape recorded and rated by judges. Women who were perceived as attractive by the men were rated as behaving in a more friendly, likeable, and sociable way, compared to women who were perceived as unattractive. Thus, the men gave the target person opportunities to act in ways that would

Box 11.1
LET'S MAKE A DEAL

Reasonably good-looking professional man, 34, wishes to meet attractive, professional, sensitive woman, 24 to 30, to share interest in music, hockey, people, and conversation. Call _____ or reply to Box 3010.

Attractive Gemini, 36, blond, blue eyes, 5' 7", 125 lbs., tanned, loves sports, playing piano, guitar. Interested in meeting man 26–46, physically fit, financially secure, witty. Reply to Box 2407.

Ads like these can be found in most daily newspapers in the United States. Other papers carry dozens or even hundreds of these ads in each issue. If we look at these ads in terms of what they offer and what they seek we can see that people are seeking a complementary exchange.

One study analyzed 800 such ads in an attempt to identify patterns in the "revelations" and "stipulations" contained in them (Harrison and Saeed 1977). The ads were taken from a national weekly over a six month period. An ad was excluded if the person was under 20 or over 60, or if age was not given. Results of the study showed that most women offered physical attractiveness, and indicated that they were seeking financial security, and an older companion. Conversely, most men offered financial security, and were seeking an attractive, younger woman. Thus each group offered complementary resources.

Results also indicated that people seek partners whose level of social desirability is approximately equal to their own. This supports the *matching hypothesis* (Berscheid et al. 1971). The researchers calculated an "overall desirability score" for both the offerer and the person being sought. Attractiveness, financial security, and sincerity were each worth 1 point on the offerer's index, whereas seeking each of these was worth 1 point on the other index. Points were added to obtain desirability scores, which ranged from 0 to 3. There was a significant correlation between level of desirability offered and level of desirability sought. In addition, most persons who stated they were physically attractive were seeking good-looking partners—evidence of the importance of physical attractiveness.

What kinds of people advertise for partners? You might suspect that these are people who are unable to find partners appropriate to their needs or characteristics in their routine activities. Often they are people who have, or are seeking persons with, atypical characteristics, and are thus less likely to meet eligibles in their immediate environment. Advertisers are often older (40+), members of racial or ethnic minorities (such as Asian-American), religiously devout or Pentecostal, vegetarian, divorced with young children, or physically handicapped. They are seeking persons with specific characteristics—that is, "old-fashioned," nondrinkers, or born-again Christians. By placing ads, people hope to transcend the limits imposed on who's available by proximity and routine activities.

---

confirm their expectations based on the attractiveness stereotype (Snyder, Tanke, and Berscheid 1977).

Each of us knows that physically attractive people may receive preferential treatment. As a result, we spend tremendous amounts of time and money in an effort to increase our attractiveness to others. Men and women purchase clothing, perfumes, colognes, and hair dyes in an effort to enhance their physical attractiveness. Our choice of products reflects current standards of what looks good. Increasingly, people are using cosmetic surgery to enhance their appearance. Plastic surgeons can "lift your face, bob your nose, unbag your eyes, strengthen your chin, pin your ears, tuck your tummy, enlarge your breasts, shape your fanny and smooth your thighs" ("Plastic Surgery Now Commonplace," 1979). In 1984, at least 1.5 million such operations were performed in the United States, costing an estimated 4 billion dollars (Ubell 1985).

Not everyone is favorably predisposed toward attractive persons. Many of us were taught and some of us believe that "Beauty is only skin deep" and "You can't judge a book by its cover." What kinds of people are influenced by another's attractiveness, and what kinds of people "read the book" before making a judgment?

People who hold traditional attitudes toward men and women are those whose judgments are much more likely to be influenced by beauty. In one study (Touhey 1979), students were given the Macho scale, a series of questions used to assess to what degree a person endorses sexist/traditional attitudes. Men and women who obtained high and low scores (a high score reflecting more traditional attitudes) were given photographs and biographical descriptions of several members of the opposite sex. Each subject indicated probable liking for and willingness to date the person in the photograph, and rated the person on various aspects of their characters. Overall, men and women with high Macho scores liked attractive persons more than unattractive ones, whereas low scorers liked attractive and unattractive persons equally well. High scorers rated the attractive person as more dutiful and respecting of authority, a better dancer, and a better potential parent than the unattractive person. The low scorers' overall ratings for attractive versus unattractive persons were not significantly different. After they performed unrelated tasks for 12 minutes, subjects were given another test that measured their ability to recall 20 items of information about the person. Results of this test showed that low scorers recalled more biographical information about the persons than high scorers.

ATTRACTIVENESS ISN'T EVERYTHING. Physical attractiveness may have a major influence on our judgments of others because it is readily observable. If other relevant information is available, it may reduce or eliminate the impact of attractiveness on our judgments. For example, in a classroom or work setting, we often prefer to establish contact with someone who is competent and can give us help. In such cases, information about competence should influence our liking for another person. To determine the influence of such information, researchers asked men and women to rate a stimulus person (female) whose physical attractiveness and competence varied (Solomon and Saxe 1977). Subjects were shown a videotape of an unattractive or an attractive woman, and were either told the woman was very intelligent (grade point average of 3.75, high test scores) or not very intelligent (grade point average 2.25, low test scores). Afterward, subjects were asked to rate the personality of the woman shown on the tape. Subjects gave a more positive rating to women who were described as more intelligent as well as more attractive. In fact, intelligence had greater influence on the personality ratings than did beauty. Moreover, when people are given information about a person's ability before they receive information about physical attractiveness, attractiveness does not influence their judgments of that person's performance (Benassi 1982).

Another influence on liking is information we have about another person's personality. Normally we find out what a person is like slowly, over time. This suggests that although physical attractiveness may be important initially, it becomes less important as we learn more about the other's personal qualities. For instance, if anxiety is an undesirable trait, individuals should report increased liking over time for nonanxious partners. Although individuals may initially like physically attractive, anxious partners, this may change as they learn more about the other person. One study tested this hypothesis by pairing off persons who were high or low in attractiveness and high or low in anxiety levels (Mathes 1975). Each couple had at least five encounters, lasting 40 minutes, and occurring at least one week after the previous encounter. Results of this study showed that over a period of about 4 weeks, both physical attractiveness and anxiety continued to influence liking—that is, more attractive and less anxious partners were liked better over the five encounters. So, although information about personality is important, it does not eliminate the impact of physical attractiveness over time.

Thus physical attractiveness greatly influences our initial impressions of other persons. If it is the only information we have about someone, the attractiveness stereotype leads us to assume that person possesses other desirable traits. But if we also have information about competence or personality, this reduces and may even eliminate the impact of physical attractiveness.

Getting Started

How do we move from the stage of awareness of another person to the stage of contact? Recall that in our introduction Dan noticed Sally at every lecture. Because she was young and not wearing a wedding ring Dan hoped that she was available. She was certainly desirable—she was very pretty, and seemed like a friendly person. How did Dan decide to initiate contact? An important factor in this decision is the availability and desirability of alternative relationships (Backman 1981). Thus, before Dan chose to initiate contact with Sally, he probably considered whether there was anyone else who might be a better choice.

CHOOSING YOUR FRIENDS. We can view each actual or potential relationship—whether involving a friend, co-worker, roommate, or date—as promising rewards but entailing costs. Rewards are the pleasures or gratifications we derive from a relationship. These might include a gain in knowledge, enhanced self-esteem, satisfaction of emotional needs, or sexual gratification. Costs are the negative aspects of a relationship, such as physical or mental effort, embarrassment, and anxiety.

Exchange theory proposes that this is in fact the way people view their interactions (Homans 1961; Blau 1964). People evaluate interactions and relationships in terms of the rewards and costs that each is likely to entail. They calculate likely **outcomes** by subtracting the anticipated costs from the anticipated rewards. If the expected outcome is positive, people are inclined to initiate or maintain the relationship. If the expected outcome is negative, they are unlikely to initiate a new relationship or to stay in a relationship that is ongoing. Dan anticipated that dating Sally would be rewarding; she would be fun to do things with, and others would be impressed that he was dating such an attractive woman. At the same time, he anticipated that Sally would expect him to be committed to her, and that he would have to spend money to take her to movies, plays, and restaurants.

It is not easy to evaluate the outcomes of a relationship. What standards can we use to make such an evaluation? Two standards have been proposed (Thibaut and Kelley, 1959). One is the **comparison level** (CL), which is based on the average of a person's experience in past relevant relationships. Based on this experience, the person expects a certain minimum level of outcomes. Each relationship is evaluated in terms of whether it is above or below that person's CL—that is, better or worse than the average of past relevant relationships. Relationships that fall above a person's CL are satisfying, whereas those that fall below it are unsatisfying.

If this were the only standard, we would always initiate relationships that appear to promise outcomes better than those we already experience, and avoid relationships that appear to promise poorer outcomes. Sometimes, however, we may be inclined to turn down interaction opportunities that appear promising. Or we may remain in a relationship even though we feel that the other person is getting all the benefits. Whether or not this occurs depends on the alternatives available. For this reason, there is a second standard, called the **comparison level for alternatives** (CL$_{alt}$), which is the lowest level of outcomes a person will accept in light of available alternatives. The CL$_{alt}$ varies depending on the outcomes a person believes can be obtained from the best of the available alternative relationships.

Whether or not a person initiates a new relationship will depend on both the CL and CL$_{alt}$. An individual usually avoids relationships whose anticipated outcomes fall below the comparison level. If a potential relationship appears likely to yield outcomes above a person's CL, then initiation will depend on whether the outcomes are expected to exceed the CL$_{alt}$. Dan believed that a relationship with Sally would be very satisfying. He was casually dating two other women, and neither relationship was especially gratifying. Thus the potential relationship with Sally was above both CL and CL$_{alt}$, leading Dan to initiate contact.

Whereas CL is an absolute, relatively unchanging standard, several factors influence a person's CL$_{alt}$, including the extent to which one's routine activities provide opportunities to meet people, the size of the pool of eligibles, and one's skills in initiating relationships. Situational factors are another influence. At a dance, party, or bar, where people hope to initiate relationships, an important situational factor is time. When the party or dance ends or the bar closes, it will no longer be possible to establish contact. This suggests that one's CL$_{alt}$ declines as the evening passes. As the alternatives become fewer, originally less attractive potential partners become more attractive (Pennebaker et al. 1979).

MAKING CONTACT. Once we decide to initiate interaction, the next step is to make contact, which requires getting physically close to the person. At parties and bars, people often circulate, which brings them into physical proximity with many of the other guests.

Once in proximity, strangers frequently use a direct gaze as a signal that they are interested in conversation. In one study, pairs of undergraduates were brought together in a waiting room, and videotaped for five minutes. In the room two chairs were placed side by side with a magazine table in between. Almost every subject gave an initial look at the other subject. If the gaze was mutual, continuous conversation during the five-minute period was very likely; when the gaze was not mutual, conversation was unlikely (Carey 1978). This pattern is probably repeated many times every day in airplanes, on trains and buses, and in classes and waiting rooms.

In most cases, initiation requires an opening line. Usually it is about some feature of the situation. At the beginning of this chapter Dan initiated conversation by asking Sally how she liked the class. Two people participating in a psychology experiment may begin talking by speculating over the real purpose of the experiment. The weather is a widely used topic for openings. The opening line often includes an **identification display,** a signal that we believe the other person is a potential partner in a specific kind of relationship (Schiffrin 1977). Approaching someone in a department store and asking for help clearly communicates your belief that he is an employee. When Dan asked Sally how she liked the class, it conveyed an interest in friendship; a different message would have been sent if he had asked whether she knew the woman sitting next to her. The other person, in turn, decides whether she is interested in that type of relationship; if she is, she engages in an **access display,** a signal that further interaction is permissible. Thus Sally responded warmly to Dan's opening line, encouraging continued conversation.

The Determinants of Liking

Once two people make contact and begin to interact, several factors will determine the extent to which each person will like the other. Four of these are considered in this section, including similarity, complementarity, shared activities, and reciprocity of liking.

Similarity

How important is similarity? Do "birds of a feather flock together"? Or is it more the case that "opposites attract"? These two aphorisms about the determinants of liking are inconsistent. A good deal of research has been devoted to finding out which one is more accurate. On the whole, evidence indicates that birds of a feather *do* flock together; we are attracted to people who are like ourselves. Probably the most important kind of similarity is **attitudinal similarity,** the sharing of beliefs, opinions, likes, and dislikes.

ATTITUDINAL SIMILARITY. A widely employed technique for studying attitudinal similarity is the attraction-to-a-stranger paradigm, initially developed by Byrne (1961b). Potential subjects fill out an attitude questionnaire which measures their beliefs about various topics, such as life on a college campus. Later, subjects receive information about a stranger as part of a seemingly unrelated study. The information they receive describes the stranger's personality or social background and may include a photograph. They also are given a copy of the questionnaire that the subject completed earlier, ostensibly filled out by the stranger. In fact, the stranger's questionnaire is completed by the experimenter who systematically varies the degree to which the stranger's supposed responses match the subject's responses. Subjects are asked how much they like or dislike the stranger, and how much they would enjoy working with him or her.

In most cases, the subject's attraction to the stranger is positively associated with the percentage of attitude statements by the stranger that agree with the person's own attitudes (Byrne and Nelson 1965; Gonzales et al. 1983). We rarely agree with our friends about everything; what matters is that we agree on a high proportion of issues. This relationship between similarity of attitudes and liking is very general; it has been replicated in studies using both men and women as subjects and strangers under a variety of conditions (Berscheid and Walster [Hatfield] 1978).

In the attraction-to-a-stranger paradigm the subject forms an impression of a stranger without any interaction. This allows researchers to determine the precise relationship between similarity and liking. But what would the relationship be if two people were allowed to interact? Would similarity have as strong an effect?

A study attempting to answer this question arranged dates for 44 couples (Byrne, Ervin, and Lamberth 1970). Researchers distributed a 50-item questionnaire measuring attitudes and personality to a large sample of undergraduates. From these questionnaires they selected 24 male-female couples whose answers were most similar (66 to 74 percent identical), and 20 couples whose answers were least similar (24 to 40 percent identical). Each couple was introduced, told they had been matched by computer, and asked to spend the next 30 minutes together at the student union—they were even offered free Cokes. The experimenter rated each subject's attractiveness before they left on their date. When the couple returned, they rated each other's sexual attractiveness, desirability as a date and marriage partner, and indicated how much they liked each other. The experimenter also recorded the physical distance between the two as they stood in front of his desk.

Results of this experiment show that both attitudinal similarity and physical attractiveness influence liking. Partners who were attractive and more similar were rated as more likable. In addition, similar partners were rated as more intelligent and more desirable as a date and marriage partner (see Table 11.1). The couples high in similarity stood closer together after their date than couples low in similarity, another indication that similarity creates liking.

At the end of the semester, 74 of the 88 subjects were contacted and asked whether they (1) could remember their date's name; (2) had talked to their date; (3) had dated him/her; or (4) wanted to date their partner. Researchers compared reports of subjects in the high attractiveness/high similarity condition with those

TABLE 11.1

THE INFLUENCE OF SIMILARITY AND PHYSICAL ATTRACTIVENESS ON LIKING

	Liking/ Desirability Rating	
Physical Attractiveness of Date	*Proportion of Similar Responses*	
	Low	*High*
Male Subjects		
Attractive date	10.55	12.00
Unattractive date	9.89	10.43
Female Subjects		
Attractive date	11.25	12.71
Unattractive date	9.50	11.00

A computer paired 24 couples with a high proportion (66 to 74 percent) of identical answers to a 50-item questionnaire, and 20 couples with a low proportion (24 to 40 percent) of identical responses. Following a 30-minute date, each person rated the likableness and desirability of their date on a scale from 1 to 7. The average of these two ratings is shown by gender and condition. Both men and women liked attractive dates more than unattractive ones, and both liked dates who were more similar.

Source: adapted from Byrne, Ervin, and Lamberth (1970, Table 4).

in the low attractiveness/low similarity condition. Those in the former condition were more likely to remember their date's name, to report having talked to him or her, and to report wanting to date the other person.

The story of Dan and Sally at the beginning of this chapter illustrates the importance of similarity in the early stages of a relationship. After their initial meeting, they discovered they had a number of things in common. They were from the same city. They had chosen the same major and held similar beliefs about their field and about how useful a bachelor's degree would be in that field. Each also found the other attractive; like the subjects in the high attraction/high similarity condition,

Dan and Sally continued to talk after their first meeting.

WHY IS SIMILARITY IMPORTANT? Why does attitudinal similarity produce liking? One reason is cognitive consistency—the desire for consistency between our attitudes and perceptions. The other reason focuses on our preference for rewarding experiences.

Most people desire *cognitive consistency,* consistency between attitudes and perceptions of whom and what we like and dislike. If you have positive attitudes toward certain objects, and discover that another person has favorable attitudes toward those same objects, your cognitions will be consistent if you like that person (Newcomb 1971). When Dan discovered that Sally had a positive attitude toward his major, his desire for consistency produced a positive attitude toward Sally. Our desire for consistency attracts us to persons who hold the same attitudes toward important objects.

This was demonstrated in a study of the friendships that developed among 17 college men who shared a rooming house for a semester (Newcomb 1961). Each man filled out several questionnaires prior to moving into the house. Roommates were assigned by the research staff. During the semester, the men expressed their liking for each other several times. The liking ratings stabilized by the middle of the semester, and they were best predicted by the degree of similarity in attitudes and values. Another study reports similar findings among women (Hill and Stull 1981).

Another reason why we like persons with attitudes similar to our own is because interaction with them provides three kinds of reinforcement. First, interacting with persons who share similar attitudes usually leads to positive outcomes (Lott and Lott 1974). At the beginning of this chapter, Dan anticipated that he and Sally would get along well because they shared similar likes and dislikes. Second, similarity validates our own view of the world. We

According to the matching hypothesis, people seek partners whose level of social desirability is about equal to their own. We frequently encounter couples who are matched—that is, who are similar in age, race, ethnicity, social class, and physical attractiveness.

all want to evaluate and verify our attitudes and beliefs against some standard. Sometimes physical reality provides objective criteria for our beliefs. But often there is no physical standard and so we must compare our attitudes with those of others (Festinger 1954). Persons who hold similar attitudes provide us with support for our own opinions, which allows us to deal with the world more confidently (Byrne 1971). Third, we are attracted to others who share similar attitudes because we expect that they will approve of us. In one experiment, college students were recruited to join groups of strangers. Before the first meeting students were privately informed that based on personality tests, certain other members would probably like them. At the end of the meeting, each person indicated whom he preferred to work with subsequently. Most students chose the person who they had been told would like them (Backman and Secord 1959). In the absence of specific information about

others' feelings, we prefer to develop friendships with those we think will evaluate us favorably (Santee and Jackson 1978).

Complementarity

We have seen that similarity produces liking. Does that mean that *dis*similarity promotes disliking? What about the aphorism "Opposites attract"? This commonsense adage is based on the idea that people are attracted to those whose needs complement their own. Thus, a person with strong needs to dominate, to be in control, should be attracted to a submissive person who will take orders without complaint. A person needing to nurture others by providing love and support should be attracted to one with a strong need to be nurtured.

This theory of complementary needs has been applied to mate selection (Winch 1958), leading to the hypothesis that most people will chose as a mate someone whose needs complement their own. In several studies, results of personality tests given to a small sample of married couples support this hypothesis, although most of the research on mate selection does not (Berscheid and Walster [Hatfield] 1978; Backman 1981).

More recently, it has been suggested that it is not *complementarity* of personal needs that is important, but *role compatibility* (Murstein 1976). As a couple develops their relationship, they must adopt roles that complement each other and fulfill each other's expectations. Thus, a couple with traditional values, in which the man is expected to support the family and take care of the house and the car and the woman is expected to do the housework and raise the children, will find it relatively easy to develop complementary roles. A woman who is committed to a career and hates housework will have a difficult time developing a role to fit her mate's traditional expectations.

Shared Activities

As people interact, they share activities. Recall that after Sally and Dan met, they began to sit together in class and to discuss course work. When the first exam was announced, Dan invited Sally to study for it with him. Sally's roommate was also in the class; the three of them reviewed the material together the night before the exam. Sally and Dan both got A's on the exam, and each felt that studying together helped. The next week they went to a movie together, and several days after that Sally invited Dan to a party.

Shared activities provide opportunities for each person to experience reinforcement—that is, to have positive experiences with the other individual. Some of these reinforcements come from the other person; Sally finds Dan's interest in her very reinforcing. Often the other person is associated with a positive experience, which leads us to like the person (Byrne and Clore 1970). Getting an A on the examination was a very positive experience for Dan and for Sally; the association of the other

person with that experience led to increased liking for the other.

Thus as a relationship develops, the sharing of activities contributes to increased liking. This was shown in a study in which pairs of friends of the same sex both filled out attitude questionnaires and listed their preferences for various activities (Werner and Parmalee 1979). The duration of the friendships varied from three months to twenty years, with an average of five years. Both 13 male and 11 female pairs were included in the study. Results of the study showed much greater similarity between friends in activity preferences than in attitudes. In addition, people were able to predict their friend's activity preferences much more accurately than their friend's attitudes. This suggests that participation in mutually satisfying activities may be a stronger influence on the development and maintenance of friendship than similar attitudes. As Dan and Sally got to know each other, their shared experiences—studying, seeing movies, going to parties—became the basis for their relationship, supplementing the effect of similar attitudes.

Some people are inclined to select friends who share their activity preferences (Snyder, Gangestad, and Simpson 1983). In one study, college students were given a test that measured their tendency toward *self-monitoring*. People who are high in self-monitoring look for cues in the situation to tell them how to behave, whereas those who are low in self-monitoring use their own values and motives to guide their behavior. Each subject was also asked to list the names of seven friends; the researchers combined each of these names with one of eight recreational activities, creating a matrix of seven friends by eight activities. Each student was then asked to indicate the likelihood of engaging in each activity with each friend. Two distinct patterns emerged. People who are low in self-monitoring—that is, whose behavior is primarily influenced by their own values and motives—reported that they were likely to engage in each activity with each friend. Thus their choice of friends seemed to be influenced by *overall* similarity in activity preferences. Students high in self-monitoring—those influenced by situational cues—segregate their friends by activities. They reported that they were likely to engage in an activity with only one or two of their friends. Thus persons high in self-monitoring tend to choose friends who share a high degree of interest in a specific activity but who may be dissimilar on other dimensions.

Reciprocal Liking

One of the most consistent research findings is the strong positive relationship between our liking someone and the perception that the other person will like us in return (Backman 1981). In most relationships, we expect reciprocity of attraction; the greater the liking of one person for the other, the greater the other person's liking in return. But will the degree of reciprocity increase over time, as partners have greater opportunities to interact? To answer this question, one study obtained liking ratings from 48 persons (32 males and 16 females), who had been acquainted for 1, 2, 4, 6, or 8 weeks (Kenny and La Voie 1982). Results showed a positive correlation between liking ratings and reciprocity of attraction increased somewhat from week 1 to week 8. However, because some of the subjects in this study were roommates rather than friends they would be expected to like each other due to the proximity effect. Thus, when roommate pairs were eliminated from the results, the correlation between liking rating increased substantially as expected.

The Growth of Relationships

We have traced the development of relationships from the stage of zero contact (who's available), through awareness (who's eligible) and surface contact (getting started), to mutuality (liking). At the beginning of this chapter we watched Dan and Sally meet, discover that they have similar attitudes and interests, and share pleasant experiences—

such as doing well on an examination, going to a movie, and, later, to a party.

Many of our relationships remain at the "minor" level of mutuality (see Fig. 11.1)—that is, we have numerous acquaintances, neighbors, and co-workers whom we like and interact with regularly, but to whom we do not feel especially close. A few of our relationships grow closer; they proceed through moderate to "major" mutuality. Three aspects of the growth of relationships are examined in this section: self-disclosure, trust, and interdependence. As the degree of mutuality increases between friends, roommates, and co-workers, self-disclosure, trust, and interdependence will also increase.

Self-Disclosure

Recall that when Dan and Sally returned from the party, Sally told Dan that her roommate's parents had just separated, and that her roommate was very depressed. Sally said that she didn't know how to help her roommate, that she felt unable to deal with the situation. At this point, Sally was engaging in **self-disclosure,** the act of revealing personal information about oneself to another person. Self-disclosure usually increases along with mutuality in a relationship. Initially, people reveal things about themselves that are not especially intimate and that they believe the other will readily accept. Over time, they disclose increasingly intimate details about their beliefs or behavior, as well as information that they are less certain the other will accept (Backman 1981).

Self-disclosure increases as a relationship grows. In one study, same-sex pairs of college students were brought into a laboratory setting and asked to get acquainted (Davis 1976). They were given a list of 72 topics, which had been rated earlier by other students on a scale of intimacy from 1 to 11. Subjects were asked to select topics from this list and to take turns talking about each topic for at least one minute's duration while their partner remained silent. The interaction continued until each partner had spoken on 12 of the 72 topics. Results showed that the intimacy of the topic selected increased steadily from the first to the twelfth topic chosen. The average intimacy of topics discussed by each couple increased from 3.9 to 5.4 over the 12 disclosures.

Self-disclosure has to do with content—what a person says. However, each of us has at some time met someone whom we tried to talk to and who simply did not respond, which quickly dampened the desire to get to know that person. This suggests that the mere act of responding to what someone says—whether or not the response is related in terms of content—contributes to the development of a relationship. Both of these variables—whether one person responds and whether the person offers similar information in response to a disclosure—were varied in one study (Davis and Perkowitz 1979). The subjects (96 men and 80 women) were brought into the laboratory individually to interact with a person of the same sex, who was actually a confederate employed by researchers. When the subject spoke, the confederate responded either one-third or two-thirds of the time. These responses were either similar in content to the subject's remarks or different. Later each subject was asked to evaluate the other person (confederate). Subjects who experienced a high rate of response (two-thirds of the time) and high similarity in content (80 percent similar) gave higher ratings to the confederate in terms of attractiveness and perception of others liking him or her, and in terms of feeling that they had become acquainted.

When Sally told Dan about the situation with her roommate, Dan replied that he knew how she felt, because his older brother had just separated from his wife. This exchange reflects reciprocity in self-disclosure; as one person reveals an intimate detail, the other person usually discloses information at about the same level of intimacy (Altman and Taylor 1973). In the Davis study discussed above (1976), each subject selected a topic at the same level of intimacy as the preceding one, or at

the next level of intimacy. However, reciprocity decreases as a relationship develops. Among married couples, a topic introduced by one spouse is quite often of a very different intimacy level than the preceding topic (Morton 1978).

Dan and Sally had known each other several weeks before they told each other about the separations involving someone close to them. What would have happened if one of them had divulged this information the day they met? The fact that disclosures become more intimate over time suggests that an intimate disclosure very early in a relationship may be inappropriate and reduce the discloser's attractiveness. In a laboratory experiment (Wortman et al. 1976), a confederate revealed to some male subjects just two minutes after they had met that his girlfriend was pregnant. Most subjects rated the confederate as immature and phony. When the same disclosure was made after eight minutes of interaction, the confederate was rated as more attractive. Thus, the timing of disclosure may affect the other person's liking for an individual.

Not all people divulge increasingly personal information as you get to know them. You have probably known people who were very open—who readily disclosed information about themselves—and others who said little about themselves. What kinds of people are more likely to engage in self-disclosure? We often think of men as less likely to discuss their feelings than women. Is gender related to degree of self-disclosure? It depends: in casual heterosexual relationships, men are less likely to disclose personal information than women, whereas in intimate heterosexual relationships, men and women do not differ in the degree of self-disclosure (Hatfield 1982). Among dating couples, the amount of disclosure is related more to sex-role orientation rather than gender. Men and women with traditional orientations tend to disclose less to their partners than those with equalitarian orientations (Rubin et al. 1980). Traditional sex roles are more segregated, with each person

Box 11.2
PHYSICAL ATTRACTIVENESS AND SOCIAL INTERACTION

Physical attractiveness is important early in relationships. We prefer attractive people, and we assume that they possess other desirable characteristics. We expect attractive persons to be more sensitive, kind, and interesting (Dion, Berscheid, and Walster [Hatfield] 1972). If we interact with an attractive person in a controlled laboratory setting, we usually give them opportunities to behave in ways that match our expectations—to be open, friendly, and likable (Snyder, Tanke, and Berscheid 1977). But do the attractiveness stereotype and the self-fulfilling prophecy carry over into the ever-changing interactions in our daily lives? Do attractive people have more positive—that is, more frequent, longer, and more intimate—interactions?

To answer this question, a team of six social psychologists studied the interactions of 43 men and 53 women (Reis et al. 1982). All the subjects were seniors in college and lived on campus. Subjects were asked to record a variety of information about every interaction they had lasting 10 minutes or more—who initiated it, its length and intimacy, the degree of disclosure by themselves and others, and its overall quality and satisfaction. They kept records for seven to eighteen days. Immediately following the record-keeping period, the subject was photographed; the photograph showed the subject from head to midthigh region. The photos were rated by students at another university for attractiveness.

Results of this study show that attractiveness was related to quantity of interaction for men but not for women. Attractive men interacted with a larger number of women, and spent more time interacting with women and less time interacting with men than less attractive men. For both men and women, however, attractiveness was related to quality of interaction. More attractive persons reported that their interactions were more intimate and involved more disclosure than less attractive persons.

Other findings suggest that attractive men generally have higher self-confidence and social competence. The authors suggest that this is due to positive feedback—a past history of others liking them and giving them opportunities to display desirable qualities. As a result, attractive men initiate more interactions, are lower in fear of rejection and engage in self-disclosure. Attractive women also have a history of positive feedback. But because they found that men were willing to approach them, they initiated fewer interactions than their less attractive counterparts. In fact, attractive women were lower in self-confidence and social confidence, and lower in trusting men than less attractive women.

In effect, physical attractiveness appears to have beneficial effects on the personal and social abilities of men, but more mixed effects on the social abilities of women.

responsible for certain tasks, whereas equalitarian orientations emphasize sharing. An emphasis on joint activity leads to greater self-disclosure.

The degree of self-disclosure also depends on the personal characteristics of the people involved. Some people are "openers," individuals who elicit intimate disclosures from others. In one study, women were given a questionnaire measuring the degree to which they were "openers." After completing the questionnaire, each woman was asked to interact with a female stranger. Women who were characterized as "openers" were more likely to elicit personal information from the stranger. The same study found differences in the degree to which women disclose personal information (Miller, Berg, and Archer 1983).

Thus, as we get to know someone, we are likely to reveal information about ourselves that increases in intimacy over time. Initially there is reciprocity of self-disclosure, as the other person responds to our disclosures with revelations about himself; but this declines over time. The amount of information revealed depends on the type of relationship and on our beliefs about the appropriateness of disclosure in such relationships.

Trust

Why did Dan confide in Sally that his brother had just left his wife? Perhaps he was offering reciprocity in self-disclosure. Because Sally had confided in Dan, she expected him to reciprocate. But he might not have had he thought that she was engaging in tactical self-disclosure (discussed in Chapter 9). Had he

been suspicious of Sally's motives Dan might not have disclosed information about himself. This suggests the importance of trust in the development of a relationship.

When we **trust** someone, we believe that person is both honest and benevolent (Larzelere and Huston 1980). We believe that the person tells us the truth—or at least does not lie to us—and that his intentions toward us are positive. One measure of interpersonal trust is the Interpersonal Trust Scale reproduced in Table 11.2. The questions focus on whether the other person is selfish, honest, sincere, fair, or considerate. It has been suggested that we are more likely to disclose personal information to someone we trust. The questions in Table 11.2 comprise one measure of interpersonal trust. How much do you trust *your* partner? Answer

---

TABLE 11.2
INTERPERSONAL TRUST SCALE

	Strongly Agree	Agree	Slightly Agree	?	Slightly Disagree	Disagree	Strongly Disagree
1. My partner is primarily interested in his/her own welfare.	_____	_____	_____	_	_____	_____	_____
2. There are times when my partner cannot be trusted.	_____	_____	_____	_	_____	_____	_____
3. My partner is perfectly honest and trustful with me.	_____	_____	_____	_	_____	_____	_____
4. I feel I can trust my partner completely.	_____	_____	_____	_	_____	_____	_____
5. My partner is truly sincere in his/her promises.	_____	_____	_____	_	_____	_____	_____
6. I feel my partner does not show me enough consideration.	_____	_____	_____	_	_____	_____	_____
7. My partner treats me fairly and justly.	_____	_____	_____	_	_____	_____	_____
8. I feel my partner can be counted on to help me.	_____	_____	_____	_	_____	_____	_____

Note: For items 1, 2, and 6, Strongly Agree = 1, Agree = 2, Slightly Agree = 3, and so on. For items 3, 4, 5, 7, and 8 the scale is reversed.

Source: adapted from Larzelere and Huston (1980).

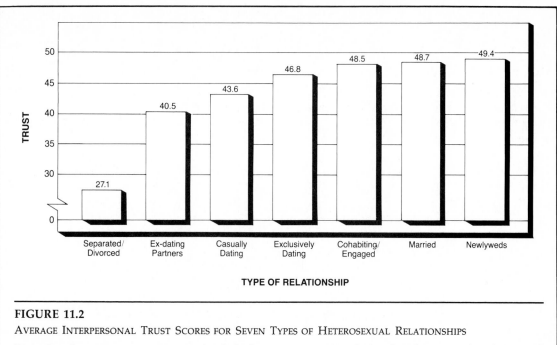

FIGURE 11.2

AVERAGE INTERPERSONAL TRUST SCORES FOR SEVEN TYPES OF HETEROSEXUAL RELATIONSHIPS

Trust involves two components: the belief that a person is honest, and that his or her intentions are benevolent. More than 300 persons completed the Trust Scale (see Table 11.2) for their current or most recent heterosexual partner. Results show that there is a strong relationship between the degree of intimacy in a relationship and the degree of trust.

Source: adapted from Larzelere and Huston (1980, Table 3).

the questions on this scale and determine your score. Higher scores indicate greater trust.

To study the relationship between trust and self-disclosure, researchers recruited men and women from university classes, from a list of people who had recently obtained marriage licenses, and by calling persons randomly selected from the telephone directory.

Each person was asked to complete a questionnaire concerning his or her spouse or current or most recent date. The survey included the Trust Scale reproduced in Table 11.2. Researchers averaged the trust scores for seven types of relationships as shown in Figure 11.2. Note that as the relationship becomes more exclusive, trust scores increase significantly. Is there a relationship between trust and self-disclosure? Each person was also asked how much he or she had disclosed to the partner in each of six areas—religion, family, emotions, relationships with others, school or work, and marriage. Trust scores were positively correlated with disclosure—that is, the more the person trusted the partner, the greater the degree of disclosure.

Interdependence

Earlier in this chapter we noted that people evaluate potential and actual relationships in terms of the outcomes (rewards minus costs) they expect to receive. Dan initiated contact with Sally because he anticipated that he would experience positive outcomes. Sally encouraged the development of a relationship because she, also, expected rewards to exceed costs. As their relationship developed, each discovered that the relationship was reward-ing. Consequently they increased the time and energy devoted to their relationship and decreased their involvement in alternative ones. As their relationship became increas-ingly mutual, Sally and Dan became increas-ingly dependent on each other for various rewards (Backman 1981). The result is strong, frequent, and diverse interdependence (Kelley et al. 1983).

Increasing reliance on one person for gratifications and decreasing reliance on oth-ers is called **dyadic withdrawal** (Slater 1963). One study of 750 men and women illustrates the extent to which such withdrawal occurs. Students identified the intensity of their cur-rent heterosexual relationships, then listed the names of persons whose opinions they consid-ered to be important. They also indicated how important each person's opinions were and how much they had disclosed to that person (Johnson and Leslie 1982). As predicted, the more intimate their current heterosexual rela-tionship, the smaller the number of friends listed by the subjects; there was no change in the number of relatives listed. In addition, as the degree of involvement increased, the pro-portion of mutual friends of the couple also increased (Milardo 1982). Other studies have found that as heterosexual relationships become more intimate, each partner spends less time interacting with friends and relatives (Milardo, Johnson, and Huston 1983).

Interdependence evolves out of the pro-cess of negotiation (Backman 1981). Each per-son offers various potential rewards to the partner; the partner accepts some and rejects others. As the relationship develops, the exchanges stabilize. If a couple shares tradi-tional sex-role orientations, the male will probably pay for their joint activities and drive the car when they are together; a couple that shares equalitarian orientations may contrib-ute equally to the cost of joint activities and alternate driving (Rubin et al. 1980).

A potential reward in many relationships is sexual gratification. As relationships de-

velop and become more mutual, physical inti-macy increases as well. The couple negotiates the extent of sexual intimacy, with the woman's preferences having a greater effect on the outcome (Peplau, Rubin, and Hill 1977). How important is sexual gratification in dat-ing relationships? A study of 149 couples assessed the importance of various rewards in relationships of increasing intimacy (preferred date, going steady, engaged, living together, and married). Among intimate couples, sexual gratification was much more likely to be cited as a major basis for the relationship (Centers 1975). Other surveys indicate that the longer couples have been dating, the more likely they are to engage in sexual intimacy (DeLamater and MacCorquodale 1979).

What Is This Thing Called Love?

It is fair to say that what we feel for our friends, roommates, co-workers, and some of the people we date is attraction. But is that all we feel? Occasionally, at least, we experience something more intense than a positive atti-tude towards others. Sometimes we feel and even say "I love you."

How does loving differ from liking? Much of the research in social psychology on attrac-tion or liking is summarized earlier in this chapter. By contrast, there has been very little research on love. Philosophers and psycholo-gists have proposed various classifications of love over the years (Berscheid and Walster [Hatfield] 1978). Three views of love are con-sidered in this section: the distinction between liking and loving, passionate love, and roman-tic love.

Liking Versus Loving

One of the first empirical studies of love attempts to distinguish between liking and loving (Rubin 1970). Love is something more than liking: it is attachment to and caring about another person (Rubin 1974). Attach-ment involves a powerful desire to be with and be cared about by another person. Caring involves making the satisfaction of another person's needs as significant as the satisfaction of your own.

Based on this distinction, Rubin developed scales to measure both liking and love, which are reproduced in Box 11.3. The Liking Scale (Scale A) evaluates one's dating partner, lover, or spouse on various dimensions—such as adjustment, maturity, responsibility, and likableness. The Love Scale (Scale B) deals with attachment (Items 3, 4, and 9), caring (Items 2, 5, and 7), and intimacy, discussed earlier as self-disclosure (Items 1 and 8). These scales were completed by each member of 182 dating couples, both for their partner and their best friend of the same sex (Rubin 1970). Results showed a high degree of internal consistency within each scale, and a low correlation between scales. Thus the two scales measure different things.

If the distinction between liking and loving is valid, we should find high scores on both liking and love for one's dating partner(s), and a high liking score and lower love score for a (platonic) friend. The average scores of the 182 couples confirmed these predictions. Both men and women reported high and almost equal degrees of liking and loving for partners. Although reported liking for friends was as high as liking for partners, love scores for friends were significantly lower. Subjects indicated whether they were "in love" with their partner, and estimated the probability that they would marry that person. There was a stronger relationship between answers to these questions and love scores than liking scores.

The distinction between liking and loving is important because social norms allow many behaviors between lovers that are not allowed between mere friends. One study (Mack, cited in Levinger 1974) presented 84 college students with a list of activities, and asked how likely a couple was to engage in each one. Four types of relationships were specified: casual acquaintances, good friends, romantically attracted, and in love. The results are shown in Table 11.3. The students felt that most of these activities became more appropriate as the emo-

tional involvement of the couple increased. Thus, as the couple became more emotionally intimate, physical intimacy—holding hands, back rubs, and sexual intercourse—became more appropriate. These differences in norms undoubtedly produce differences in behavior.

Passionate Love

Love certainly involves attachment and caring. But is that all? What about the agony of jealousy and the ecstasy of being loved by another person? A second view of love emphasizes emotions such as these. It focuses on **passionate love,** a state of intense absorption and of intense physiological arousal (Hatfield and Walster 1983).

The concept of passionate love is based on the two-factor theory of emotion (Schachter 1964). According to this theory, the experience of emotion depends on: (1) perceptible physiological arousal, and (2) environmental cues, which we use to determine what emotion is being experienced. Arousal itself may be caused by a variety of factors, including fear, social rejection, frustration, excitement, or sexual feelings. Because arousal is generalized, and its causes complex or ambiguous, an individual must rely on situational cues to determine what emotion is being felt. Thus we experience passionate love when two conditions occur simultaneously: when we experience a state of intense physiological arousal, and when situational cues indicate that love is the appropriate label for that arousal (Berscheid and Walster [Hatfield] 1974a).

There has been no direct empirical test of the two-factor theory of passionate love. However, several studies provide supportive evidence by investigating behavior or feelings related to liking or sexual attraction (Murstein 1980). Arousal in subjects is elicited through fear, frustration, or excitement. At the same time, various situational cues are presented. When the situational cue suggests that passionate love might be the source of their arousal, subjects' feelings and behavior often reflect romantic or sexual attraction.

Box 11.3
LIKING AND LOVING IN PERSONAL RELATIONSHIPS

Liking and loving are different emotions. Think about your closest friend of the same sex (SSF) and your closest dating partner, or lover, or spouse (OSF). Then use this scale to answer each of the statements below.

1	2	3	4	5	6	7	8	9

Not at all true (Disagree completely)	Moderately true (Agree to some extent)	Definitely true (Agree completely)

In the column headed SSF, enter the number that best reflects your answer for your closest friend of the same sex. Then, in the column headed OSF, enter the appropriate number for your closest friend of the opposite sex.

Scale A

	SSF	OSF
1. I think that _____ is usually well-adjusted.	____	____
2. I would highly recommend _____ for a responsible job.	____	____
3. In my opinion _____ is an exceptionally mature person.	____	____
4. I have great confidence in _____'s good judgement.	____	____
5. Most people would react favorably to _____ after a brief acquaintance.	____	____
6. I think _____ is one of those people who quickly win respect.	____	____
7. _____ is one of the most likable people I know.	____	____
8. _____ is the sort of person who I myself would like to be.	____	____
9. It seems to me that it is very easy for _____ to gain admiration.	____	____
TOTAL	____	____

Scale B

	SSF	OSF
1. I feel that I can confide in _____ about virtually everything.	____	____
2. I would do almost anything for _____.	____	____
3. If I could never be with _____, I would feel miserable.	____	____
4. If I were lonely, my first thought would be to seek _____ out.	____	____
5. One of my primary concerns is _____'s welfare.	____	____
6. I would forgive _____ for practically anything.	____	____
7. I feel responsible for _____'s well-being.	____	____
8. I would greatly enjoy being confided in by _____.	____	____
9. It would be hard for me to get along without _____.	____	____
TOTAL	____	____

Now add up the numbers on each scale.

Scale A is a measure of liking. Notice that it asks the extent to which you respect, admire, and have confidence in another person. Often people have about the same (high) degree of liking for their best friends and lovers. Your totals for Scale A may be very similar. Scale B is a measure of love, and inquires about your dependence on, trust in, and feelings of responsibility for another. Usually people report greater love for their opposite-sex friends than for their same-sex friends.

Source: adapted from Zick A. Rubin (1970).

TABLE 11.3

THE RELATIONSHIP BETWEEN ROMANTIC INVOLVEMENT AND BEHAVIOR

	Type of Couple			
Activity	*Casually Acquainted*	*Good Friends, Not in Love*	*Romantically Attracted*	*Much in Love, Fully Committed*
Communication				
smile at each other	89*	98	95	98
stay up late and talk	52	78	79	79
confide in each other	26	69	76	94
Physical Contact				
stand close to one another	51	79	90	93
hold hands	18	44	82	93
give "back rubs"	12	36	76	86
Joint Actions				
study together	55	65	74	82
watch TV together	57	82	79	89
go to parties together	29	61	84	93
prepare meals together	21	47	70	85
go camping together	13	43	54	74
live together	10	33	61	88
have sexual intercourse	3	28	61	79
Shared Ownership				
collect items together	36	51	61	75
exchange clothing	20	43	53	75
Exclusive Commitment				
try to be alone with other	13	25	76	85
refuse to date other persons	3	7	29	90

*Mean percentage of couples at each degree of involvement estimated "to engage in each of the listed behaviors." The raters were 84 college students.

Source: adapted from Levinger (1974).

Imagine that you are hiking in a state park on a warm, sunny day. You come out of a wooded area, and in front of you is a bridge. It is about 450 feet long, and it crosses a canyon more than 200 feet deep. The bridge doesn't look very stable; it is 5 feet wide, and is constructed of boards attached to cables with low wire handrails. As you cross it, the bridge tends to wobble and sway. Chances are that by the time you reach solid ground on the other side you would be experiencing perceptible arousal—at least, that is what two social psychologists hoped when they picked such a site as the location for their experiment (Dutton and Aron 1974).

The control site was another bridge in the same park made of solid wood. It was 10 feet wide with only a 10-foot drop below. The subjects were men between ages 18 and 35 who had just crossed either bridge and were not accompanied by a woman. Researchers varied the gender of the person approaching the subject to manipulate the environmental cue available to the subject. Thus, there were aroused (high bridge) and unaroused (low bridge) men approached by an attractive female or a male. Following this encounter, each subject completed a short questionnaire, which included writing a story about a drawing of a woman; these stories were scored for

America is one of a small number of societies in which love is widely accepted as a basis for getting married. In many other societies, marriages reflect political and economic influences, not romance.

sexual imagery. In addition, the experimenter gave each subject his or her phone number, and noted the percentage of subjects who later phoned the experimenter.

As predicted, subjects who crossed the high bridge (presumed to be aroused) and were approached by the female wrote stories with sexual content and later phoned the experimenter more often than subjects in the other conditions. Subjects who crossed the high bridge and were approached by the male wrote stories with little sexual imagery. In contrast, the stories of men who crossed the low bridge were much less affected by the sex of the experimenter, suggesting that arousal and the cue of an attractive female were both necessary to produce sexual attraction.

The Romantic Love Ideal

The studies and theories of love discussed so far assume that love consists of a particular set of feelings and behaviors. Furthermore, most of us assume that we will experience this emotion toward a member of the opposite sex

at least once in our lives. But these are very culture-bound assumptions. There are societies in which the state or experience we call love is unheard of. In fact, American society is almost unique in accepting love as a major basis for marriage.

In American society we are socialized to accept a set of beliefs about love, beliefs that guide much of our behavior. These five beliefs are known collectively as the **romantic love ideal** (Lantz, Keyes, and Schultz 1975):

1. True love can strike without prior interaction ("love at first sight").

2. For each of us, there is only one other person who will inspire true love.

3. True love can overcome any obstacle ("love conquers all").

4. Our beloved is (nearly) perfect.

5. We should follow our feelings—that is, we should base our choice of partners on love rather than on other (more rational) considerations.

Box 11.4
PLAYING HARD-TO-GET

Have you ever been attracted to someone who seemed uninterested, was usually busy when you called, rarely agreed to go out with you, and was civil but did not encourage you? Sometimes we become obsessed with such persons when realistically we should forget them. Such a person is playing hard-to-get.

Many authorities on how to find a mate claim that playing hard-to-get will inspire more passion in a potential partner than making yourself readily available. According to the two-factor theory, acting aloof and uninterested will frustrate a suitor and increase arousal. Making yourself potentially available, instead of telling the person to get lost, suggests to the suitor that the arousal is due to love for you, not to frustration.

What is the effect of playing hard-to-get on attraction? In one set of studies (Walster [Hatfield] et al. 1973) men were recruited for a computer dating service, and filled out a lengthy questionnaire. Two weeks later they reported to an office, were given the name and phone number of their computer-selected date, and asked to phone her from the office. In reality, each man was given the same number, and his call was answered by a female confederate. In the easy-to-get condition the confederate acted delighted that he had called and readily accepted his request for a date. In the hard-to-get condition, she acted as if she had many dates, and seemed unsure of whether she wanted to go out with him. After the conversation, the men recorded their impressions of the woman they had called. The results showed that the men were highly attracted to the woman regardless of whether she indicated interest in them.

Clearly, the hard-to-get woman was not inspiring passion. At this point, the researchers reconsidered their original hypothesis.

They interviewed men, asking them about the advantages and disadvantages of dating these two kinds of women. The men agreed that a hard-to-get woman was a challenge, was likely to be physically attractive, and that going out with such a woman would boost their egos. But they also thought she was likely to be cold, not very friendly, and that she might humiliate her date. Dating an easy-to-get woman would be more relaxing and friendly, but she might demand too much attention. So what would the perfect date be? The answer: an attractive woman who is easy for the subject to get, but hard for anyone else to get.

This revised hypothesis was tested in the same computer-date setting. The men were each given five folders which included detailed biographies of five different women. The folders also included a copy of each woman's assessment of five men (including the subject) as potential dates. The assessments were systematically varied. One woman was presented as generally easy-to-get—she indicated that she was eager to date all five of the men the computer had paired her with. A second woman was generally hard-to-get, not eager to date any of the five. A third woman was selectively hard-to-get, eager to date the subject but not eager to date any of the other four men. The last two women were controls; no information about their preferences was given. The subject read each of the folders, completed a short questionnaire about his impressions of each, and then picked the one woman he most wanted to date. The data provided strong support for the revised hypothesis. Of the 71 subjects, 42 most wanted to date the selectively hard-to-get woman. The men also expected they would get along with this woman better.

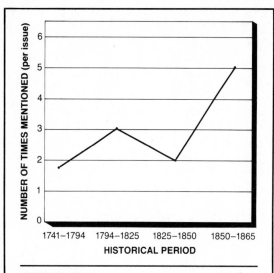

FIGURE 11.3

OCCURRENCE OF THE ROMANTIC LOVE IDEAL IN MAJOR AMERICAN MAGAZINES FROM 1741 TO 1865

One way to measure the influence of the romantic love ideal on American society is to determine the frequency with which it is mentioned in popular magazines. A team of researchers selected a sample of the best-selling magazines from four different historical periods, and counted the number of times each of the five romantic ideals was mentioned—including (1) idealization of the beloved, (2) love at first sight, (3) love conquers all, (4) there is one and only one for each of us, and (5) we should follow our hearts. They discovered that the number of times the ideals were mentioned increased more than 300 percent from 1741–94 to 1850–65.

Source: adapted from Lantz, Keyes, and Schultz (1975); Lantz, Schultz, and O'Hara (1977).

Not everyone fully accepts this romantic love ideal, of course. But it is often expressed in films and novels. Many people admire King Edward VIII of England, who in 1936 gave up the throne, the royal life style, and many of his lifelong friends to marry the American divorcée he loved. Like many others, his mate-seeking behavior was influenced by the romantic love ideal.

This ideal has not always been popular in the United States. A group of researchers conducted an analysis of best-selling magazines published during four historical periods (Lantz, Keyes, and Schultz 1975; Lantz, Schultz, and O'Hara 1977). They counted the number of times that the magazines mentioned one or more of the five beliefs that make up the romantic ideal. The number of times the ideal was discussed increased steadily over time as shown in Figure 11.3. Their findings suggest that American acceptance of the romantic ideal has been gradual over the past 200 years.

Breaking Up

Few things last forever. Roommates who once did everything together lose touch after they finish school. Two women who were best friends gradually stop talking. Couples fall out of love, break up, and divorce. What causes the dissolution of relationships? Research suggests two answers: unequal outcomes, and unequal involvement.

Unequal Outcomes and Instability

Earlier this chapter discussed the importance of outcomes in the establishing and maintaining of relationships. Our decision to initiate a relationship is based on what we expect to get out of it. In ongoing relationships, we can assess our actual outcomes; we can evaluate the rewards we are obtaining relative to the costs of maintaining the relationship.

The comparison level for alternatives (CL_{alt}) is one important standard used in evaluating outcomes. Are the outcomes from this relationship better than those obtainable from the best available alternative? One dimension on which people may evaluate relationships is physical appearance. A relationship with a physically attractive person may be rewarding. Two people who are equally attractive physically will experience similar outcomes on this dimension. What about two people who differ in attractiveness? The less attractive person will benefit from associating with the more attractive one, whereas the more attractive person will experience less positive outcomes. Because attractiveness is a valued asset, the more physically attractive person is likely to find alternative relationships available, and to expect some of them to yield more positive outcomes.

This reasoning was tested in a study of 123 dating couples. Photographs of each person in the study were rated by five men and five women for physical attractiveness, and a relative attractiveness score was calculated for each member of each couple. Both men and women who were more attractive than their partners reported having more friends of the opposite sex (that is, alternatives) than men and women who were not more attractive than their partners. Follow-up data collected nine months later indicated that dating couples who were rated as similar in attractiveness were more likely to be still dating each other (White 1980). These results are consistent with the hypothesis that persons experiencing outcomes below CL_{alt} are more likely to terminate the relationship.

But not everyone compares their current outcomes with those available in alternative relationships. Individuals in the study who were committed—that is, cohabiting, engaged, or married—did not vary in the number of alternatives they reported, and their relative attractiveness was not related to whether they were still in the relationship nine months later. Persons who are committed to each other may be more concerned with equity than alternatives.

Equity theory (Walster [Hatfield], Berscheid, and Walster 1973) postulates that each of us compares the rewards we receive from a relationship to our costs or contributions. In general, we expect to get more out of the relationship if we put more into it. Thus we compare our outcomes (rewards minus costs) to the outcomes our partner is receiving. The theory predicts that **equitable relationships**—those where the outcomes are equivalent—will be stable, whereas inequitable ones will be unstable.

This prediction was tested in a study involving 511 college students who were dating someone at the time (Walster [Hatfield], Walster, and Berscheid 1977). Each student received a list of things that someone might contribute to a relationship, including good looks, intelligence, being loving, being understanding, and helping the other make decisions. Each student then rated the degree to which they and their partners actually contributed each of these things in their relationship. Each student also received a list of potential benefits from relationships and indicated the degree to which they and their partner received each benefit. Researchers calculated each person's benefits and contributions and obtained a measure of outcomes by dividing the benefit score by the contribution score. They divided the total benefits a person perceived the partner was receiving by the total contributions a person perceived the partner was making in order to obtain a perceived outcome-of-partner measure. By comparing person's outcomes with perceived partner's outcomes, the researchers determined whether the relationship was equitable.

Three and one-half months later, students were interviewed in order to assess the stability of their relationships. Stability was determined by whether or not they were still dating their partner, how long they had been going together (or how long they had gone together), and how certain they were that they would be going together the following year. The results clearly demonstrated that inequitable relationships are unstable. The less equitable the relationship was at the start, the less likely the couple was to be still dating 14 weeks later. Furthermore, students who perceived that their outcomes did not equal their partner's outcomes reported that their relationships were of shorter duration, and were much less certain that their relationship would last another year.

Thus, the outcomes experienced in a relationship are one important influence on its stability. If these outcomes are better than a person anticipates getting from alternative relations, and if they are believed equitable relative to those the partner is obtaining, then the person is more likely to remain in the relationship.

Differential Involvement and Dissolution

Are outcomes—that is, rewards minus costs—the only thing we consider when deciding whether or not to continue a relationship? What about emotional attachment or involvement? We often continue a relationship because we love someone, because through interaction over a long period we have developed an emotional commitment to the person, and feel a sense of responsibility for that person's welfare. When the other person is equally committed, the relationship may be quite stable. But if one person is less involved, the relationship may break up.

The importance of equal degrees of involvement is illustrated in another study in which couples were recruited from four col-

leges and universities in the Boston area (Hill, Rubin, and Peplau 1976). Each member of 231 couples filled out an initial questionnaire and completed three follow-up questionnaires, six months, one year, and two years later. At the time the initial data were collected (1972), couples had been dating an average of eight months; most were dating exclusively and 10 percent were engaged. Two years later, researchers were able to determine the status of 221 of the couples. Some were still together, whereas others had broken up.

What distinguished couples who were together two years later from those who had broken up? Some of the major differences are summarized in Table 11.4. Couples who were more involved initially—those who were dating exclusively, who rated themselves as very close, who said they were "in love," and who estimated a high probability that they would get married—were more likely to be together two years later. Of those couples who reported equal involvement in 1972, only 23 percent

TABLE 11.4
DIFFERENTIAL INVOLVEMENT AND DISSOLUTION OF A RELATIONSHIP

Characteristics of Relationships in 1972	Status Two Years Later			
	Women's Reports		Men's Reports	
	Together	Breakup	Together	Breakup
Mean Ratings				
Self-report of closeness (9-pt. scale)	7.9	7.3**	8.0	7.2**
Estimate of marriage probability (as percentage)	65.4	46.4**	63.1	42.7**
Love scale (max. = 100)	81.2	70.2**	77.8	71.5**
Liking scale (max. = 100)	78.5	74.0*	73.2	69.6
Number of months dated	13.1	9.9*	12.7	9.9*
Percentages				
Couple is "in love"	80.0	55.3**	81.2	58.0**
Dating exclusively	92.3	68.0**	92.2	77.5**
Seeing partner daily	67.5	52.0	60.7	53.4
Had sexual intercourse	79.6	78.6	80.6	78.6
Living together	24.8	20.4	23.1	20.4

Note: N = 117 together, 103 breakup for both men and women. Significance by *t* tests or chi-square for together-breakup differences. *p* = probablility of obtaining such a result by chance.
*p < .05.
**p < .01.
Source: adapted from Hill, Rubin, and Peplau (1976).

broke up in the following two years. Of the couples who reported unequal involvement in 1972, 54 percent were no longer seeing each other two years later.

Earlier in this chapter we discussed the importance of similarity in establishing relationships. How important is similarity in determining whether a relationship persists over time? Among the 221 dating couples, stability was associated with similarity in age, educational plans, ability as measured by the Scholastic Aptitude Test, physical attractiveness, and religion. However, both couples who stayed together and those who broke up were initially similar in their sex-role attitudes, approval of premarital sexuality, importance of religion, and in the number of children they wanted. Thus, although attitudinal similarity seems to determine the formation of relationships, it does not distinguish couples whose relationships persist from those whose relationships dissolve.

Not surprisingly, the breakup of a couple was usually initiated by the person who was less involved. Eighty-five percent of those whose relationships ended reported that one person wanted to break up more than did the other. There was also a distinct pattern in the timing of breakups; they were much more likely to occur in May–June, September, and December–January. This suggests that factors outside the relationship such as graduation, moving, and arriving at school lead one person to initiate the breakup.

The dissolution of a relationship is often painful. But breaking up is not necessarily undesirable. It can be thought of as a part of a filter process through which people who are not suited to each other terminate their relationships.

Barriers to Breaking Up

Not all relationships that involve inequity or differential involvement break up. An individual in an unsatisfactory relationship often assesses three aspects of the situation before deciding whether or not to terminate a relationship: the anticipated costs of breaking up, the availability of alternative relationships, and the level of rewards obtained from the relationship in the past.

To assess the costs of breaking up, the individual weighs the costs of an unsatisfactory relationship against the costs of ending that relationship. There are three types of barriers or costs to leaving a relationship: material, symbolic, and affectual (Levinger 1976). Material costs are especially significant for persons who have pooled their financial resources. Breaking up will require agreeing on who gets what, and it may produce a lower standard of living for each person. Symbolic costs include the reactions of others. Will close friends and family members support or criticize the termination of the relationship? These costs probably increase as time and investment in the relationship increase (Backman 1981). Affectual costs involve changes in one's relationships with others. Breaking up may cause the loss of friends, and reduce or eliminate contact with relatives. One may conclude that the costs of breaking up are too great, and stay in the relationship.

A second factor in this assessment is the availability of alternatives. The absence of an attractive alternative may lead the individual to maintain an unrewarding relationship, whereas the appearance of an attractive alternative may trigger the dissatisfied person to dissolve the relationship. A third factor is the level of rewards experienced before the relationship became dissatisfying. If the relationship was particularly rewarding in the past, the individual is less likely to decide to terminate it.

How important are each of these three factors—that is, which factors are most important in determining whether or not a relationship will be terminated? There are four things you can do if you are in an unsatisfying relationship: you can discuss it with your partner, wait for things to improve, neglect your partner, or terminate the relationship. In one study, subjects were given short stories describing relationships in which these three factors varied. They were asked what they would do in each situation (Rusbult, Zembrodt, and Gunn 1982). The lower the prior satisfaction—that is, the less satisfied and less positive their feelings toward and caring for partner—the more likely they were to neglect or terminate the relationship. The less the investment—that is, degree of disclosure and how much a person stands to lose—the more likely subjects were to engage in neglect or termination. Finally, the presence of attractive alternatives increased the probability of terminating the relationship. A subsequent study of ongoing relationships yielded the same results (Rusbult 1983).

A relationship that has been very satisfying in the past, or one in which a person has invested a great deal, will be costly to leave; therefore one is less likely to do so. Moreover, one may remain in a very unsatisfying relationship if there are no attractive alternatives.

Summary

Interpersonal attraction involves the development, maintenance, and dissolution of relationships based on liking and love.

WHO'S AVAILABLE? Institutional structures and personal characteristics influence who is available to us as potential friends, roommates, co-workers, and lovers. Three factors influence whom we select from this pool. (1) Our daily routines make some persons more accessible. (2) Proximity makes it more rewarding and less costly to interact with some people rather than others. (3) Familiarity produces a positive attitude toward those with whom we repeatedly come in contact.

WHO'S ELIGIBLE? Among the availables, we choose those who are appropriate—whose characteristics are consistent with social norms—and desirable. Desirability is influenced by three factors. (1) We prefer a more physically attractive person, both for aesthetic reasons and because we expect to obtain rewards from associating with that person. (2) Information about an individual's competence

influences our judgments in school and work settings. (3) The possession of certain personality traits may make someone especially desirable or undesirable. We choose among those who are eligible based on our expectations about the rewards and costs of potential relationships. We will choose to develop those relationships whose outcomes we expect will exceed both comparison level (CL) and comparison level for alternatives (CL$_{alt}$). We implement our choices by making contact, using an opening line which often indicates the kind of relationship in which we are interested.

THE DETERMINANTS OF LIKING. Many relationships, between friends, roommates, co-workers, or lovers, involve liking. The extent to which we like someone is determined by four factors. (1) The major influence is the degree to which two people have similar attitudes. The greater the proportion of similar attitudes, the more they like each other. Similarity produces liking because we prefer cognitive consistency and because we expect interaction with similar others to be reinforcing. (2) Complementarity, the possession of personal or social characteristics that complement our own, may influence liking in some instances. (3) Shared activities become an important influence on our liking for another person as we spend time with them. (4) We like those who like us; as we experience positive feedback from another, it increases our liking for them.

THE GROWTH OF RELATIONSHIPS. As relationships grow, they change on three dimensions. (1) There may be a gradual increase in the disclosure of intimate information about the self. Self-disclosure is usually reciprocal, with each person revealing something about themselves in response to revelations by the other. (2) Trust in the other person—a belief in his or her honesty and benevolence—also increases as relationships develop. (3) Interdependence for various gratifications also increases, often leading to a decline in reliance on and number of relationships with others.

WHAT IS THIS THING CALLED LOVE? Liking refers to a positive attitude toward an object; love involves attachment to and caring for another person. Love may also involve passionate feelings, a state of intense absorption in the other and of intense physiological arousal. According to the two-factor theory of emotion, the experience of passionate love depends on (1) perceptible physiological arousal, and (2) environmental cues which indicate that the arousal is due to love. The concept of love does not exist in all societies; the romantic love ideal emerged gradually in the United States between 1740 and 1865.

BREAKING UP. There are three influences on whether a relationship dissolves. (1) Breaking up may result if one person feels that outcomes (rewards minus costs) are inadequate. She may evaluate present outcomes against what she thinks could be obtained from an alternative relationship. Alternatively, the person may look at the outcomes her partner is experiencing and assess whether the relationship is equitable. (2) Degree of involvement in a relationship is an important influence on whether it continues. Someone who feels a low level of emotional attachment to, and concern for, the partner is more likely to break up with that person. (3) Barriers to the dissolution of a relationship include the likelihood that eco-nomic and emotional costs will be high, the lack of attractive alternatives, and a high level of prior satisfaction in the relationship.

Key Terms and Concepts

Interpersonal Attraction

Availables

Mere Exposure Effect

Eligibles

Norm of Homogamy

Matching Hypothesis

Attractiveness Stereotype

Outcomes

Comparison Level

Comparison Level for Alternatives

Identification Display

Access Display

Attitudinal Similarity

Self-Disclosure

Trust

Dyadic Withdrawal

Passionate Love

Romantic Love Ideal

Equitable Relationship

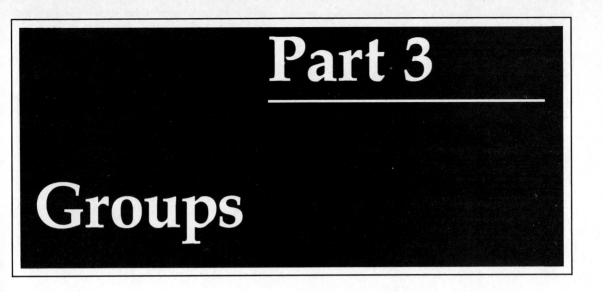

Part 3

Groups

Chapter 12

Group Cohesiveness and Conformity

Introduction

Groups are everywhere. They are one of the most common facts of social life. We all participate in them, and many of us spend a large part of each day engaging in group activities. Families, work groups, sports teams, street gangs, classes and seminars, therapy and rehabilitation groups, classical quartets and rock groups, small military units, neighborhood social clubs, church groups—these are only some of the endless types of groups we encounter.

Groups are important to our life. They provide social support, a cultural framework, and rewards of all kinds. Without them a person would be isolated, unloved, less productive, out of touch with the world, and possibly prone to suicide.

What is a Group?

A **group** is a set of persons who are related to one another as parts of a system. Groups are not merely aggregations of individuals, each pursuing his or her own goals. Rather, groups are organized systems in which relations among persons are structured and patterned.

Although groups can differ with respect to their organization, they all share certain properties or characteristics. These include:

1. *Shared goals* Group members share specific goals, and rely on one another's performances for collective success. Frequently, the goals are ones that the individual cannot attain alone.
2. *Communication* Communication among members may be either unlimited or restricted. But the capacity to communicate—either face-to-face or by other means—must be present for a set of persons to comprise a group.
3. *A structure of expectations or rules* Members uphold certain expectations or rules, called norms, that regulate interaction within the group. Norms coordinate behavior and allocate tasks to individuals within the group.
4. *A conscious identification of members with the group* Individuals who belong to a group develop a concept of themselves as group members. Sometimes these concepts become central to their personal identities.

Given this definition, it is clear that groups are not mere collections of individuals. Not all behaviors in the presence of other people are group interactions; many times individuals interact without common goals or without a set of specific norms to regulate their behavior. A conversation between yourself and an insurance agent who is trying to sell you a policy you don't want would not qualify as a group interaction. There is no shared goal or conscious group identification. Likewise, a theatre crowd escaping in panic from a fire is not a functioning group. The individuals in the crowd have no conscious identification with the mob and, while all doubtlessly wish to escape the fire, they do not share any collective goals.

Persons who interact in a group context will relate to one another as group members, not merely as individuals. Group interaction is based on shared goals, occurs via symbolic communication, is governed by norms, and involves a conscious identification with the group.

Small Groups

The term **small group** refers to a group of persons who are able to interact face-to-face. A group is not considered small if its size precludes interaction among all its members. The term small group is usually reserved for groups ranging from 2 to 20 members (Crosbie 1975). However, a class or discussion group with 30 or even 40 members would qualify as a small group if members could interact directly with each other. For now, when we use the word "group" we will be referring to small groups.

Groups affect our lives in numerous ways. We spend many hours each day interacting with other persons in groups. Most of us belong to family and work groups (or, if in school, to educational groups such as classes and seminars). Groups of this type provide the contacts with friends, relatives, and co-workers that are crucial to our personal welfare.

Groups also influence and channel our behavior. Pressures to conform to group norms lead us to engage in some activities and to shun others. Groups can even affect how we perceive the world, as when we adopt concepts and assumptions that are part of their culture. Members of political or religious groups, for example, may accept the beliefs and stereotypes of these groups as an objective view of reality.

Finally, groups serve as mediators that link individuals to the larger organizations and bureaucracies making up society. People usually relate to bureaucracies as members of groups rather than as individuals. A worker, for example, may be employed by a certain division of General Motors, but she probably spends most of her time working in a small group within the larger organization. Although she will probably have contact with persons elsewhere within GM, it is the co-workers in her own group that provide both support and direction for her activities. Without the benefits of small groups, individuals would have difficulty relating to the larger society.

Issues in the Study of Groups

This chapter will examine the forces that give unity to a group. It addresses the following questions:

1. What factors hold a group together and what factors split it apart? That is, what produces cohesiveness—or the lack of it—in groups?

2. What are group goals? How are they established and maintained? How does the pursuit of group goals contribute to group cohesiveness? What happens to group cohesiveness and integration when a group attains—or fails to attain—its goals?

3. A group cannot function without some minimum level of conformity by its members. How do groups obtain conformity? What factors cause group members to conform in greater or lesser degree?

4. Deviant behavior can threaten group cohesiveness and goal attainment. How do group members react when one of their number deviates from established norms? When does deviant behavior lead to change in group norms?

Group Cohesiveness

The Jaguars are an amateur baseball club with a long record of league championships. The team members are proud of their performance and very committed to continue their winning ways. On the rare occasion when they have a losing streak, the whole team becomes concerned and upset; players voluntarily hold extra practice sessions to sharpen their skills and teamwork. At practice and in games they are a model of coordination—a "finely tuned machine" according to one sportswriter. Though they do not always agree on strategy, the Jaguars seem to resolve their differences constructively. They like each other, and they enjoy traveling to games together and celebrating their victories. They even seem to hold similar attitudes on many things besides baseball. Several of the players consider their teammates best friends, and they spend much of their time off the field together. The Jaguars rarely lose any of their players—even their second-stringers—and everyone turns out for practices and other meetings quite reliably.

Another team in the league is called the Birds. The Birds are a different story. The members are always busy with other activities and hate to spend much time practicing. Something less than a model of competence, the team has occupied last place in the league standings for several seasons. Occasionally the team forfeits a game because it can't even field nine players. When the team does agree to hold a practice, many members forget or don't bother to show up; perhaps this is because they seldom run into one another outside of team activities. Last spring, their planning session dissolved into chaos when the Birds could not agree on how to pay for some new equipment. Ever since then, there has been friction among certain players. The team hasn't even decided whether to participate in the league next year. The members simply have more important things to do with their time.

Perhaps you've experienced groups like these two teams. Being a member of the Jaguars is more demanding, but also much more rewarding. What is the basic difference between the teams? In a word, the Jaguars have a higher level of cohesiveness than the Birds.

Sources of Group Cohesiveness

By definition, **group cohesiveness** refers to the effect of "all forces acting on members to remain in a group" (Festinger 1950, p. 274). In other words, group cohesiveness is the extent to which members are attracted to a group. Our desire to belong to a specific group depends, among other things, on the alternatives available to us. A group will be cohesive only if we find it relatively more attractive than other groups. Although the reasons for this attraction may vary, a highly cohesive group will maintain a firm hold over its members' time and energy.

What gives a group the capacity to attract and hold its members? According to Golembiewski (1962), cohesiveness is based on the following: (1) a member's liking for other group members; (2) a member's commitment to the group's goals and tasks, including sharing in the rewards for success; and (3) the prestige a member gains by virtue of belonging to the group. Each of these factors contributes to a group's cohesiveness.

Attraction and liking among members lead to a high level of group cohesiveness (Back 1951; Lott and Lott 1965). In fact, liking is sometimes regarded as the primary source of

cohesiveness. Another source is the incentive properties of a group—the extent to which it provides various rewards and benefits to members. Thus, a group will be more cohesive to the extent that it provides not only the opportunity to make new friends and participate in social life (Hagstrom and Selvin 1965) but also to pursue personal goals and objectives (Landers and Crum 1971; Anderson 1975).

Consequences of Group Cohesiveness

Does it make a difference whether a group is highly cohesive or not? What are the consequences of group cohesiveness?

A cohesive group is one that members find attractive and wish to belong to. For this reason, we would expect a highly cohesive group to exert more influence over its members than a less cohesive group. Members of a highly cohesive group should be more willing to do whatever is necessary to remain in the group to secure the benefits of membership.

Indeed, research findings indicate that members of highly cohesive groups try to influence other members more and are themselves more influenced (Lott and Lott 1965). Members of highly cohesive groups are also more conforming to collective norms and expectations than are members of less cohesive groups (Wyer 1966; Sakurai 1975).

The patterns of interaction among group members demonstrate the impact of cohesiveness. Given the opportunity, members of highly cohesive groups communicate more than members of less cohesive groups. This has been observed in a wide variety of groups, ranging from student organizations (Lott and Lott 1961) to industrial training groups (Moran 1966). Some of this communication reflects the greater frequency of influence attempts occurring in highly cohesive groups. Moreover, cohesiveness affects not only the amount of interaction, but also its form. Interaction in highly cohesive groups is friendlier, more cooperative, and shows more attempts to reach agreements and to strengthen coordination among members (Shaw and Shaw 1962).

Box 12.1
PRIMARY GROUPS

A **primary group** is a small group that exists long enough to permit the development of strong emotional ties among members. Primary groups are frequently structured so that members perform different tasks. They may also have a distinctive subculture with informal rules that control the actions of members (Dunphy 1972).

Primary groups exist in a variety of forms. The most common in our society are: (1) nuclear families; (2) peer groups (such as children's play groups, teen delinquent gangs, and Wednesday night poker clubs); (3) informal work groups existing in organizational settings (such as factory work groups, classroom groups, and small military units); and (4) groups whose goal is to resocialize their members (such as rehabilitation groups, therapy groups, and self-analytic groups).

Members of a primary group usually possess similar values and attitudes. They care about their mutual friendship. Interaction in primary groups is spontaneous, informal, and personal. This is not to say that it always runs a smooth course. The members of a family can certainly have a heated argument, and children often fight with others in their peer group.

Still, the crucial characteristic of primary groups is that members care about one another as individuals.

Primary groups are often distinguished from *secondary groups*, whose members have few emotional ties with one another and relate in terms of limited roles. Interaction in secondary groups is formal, impersonal, and nonspontaneous. One example would be a formally structured work group in a bureaucratic setting with limited opportunities for personal contact.

Primary groups serve an important function in our urban, bureaucratic society. They provide an arena for friendship and deep personal commitments. They also serve to integrate the individual with larger organizations in society.

This interaction among happy sorority sisters on pledge day reflects a high level of group cohesiveness. Many groups safeguard cohesiveness by selecting new members carefully.

The relationship between group cohesiveness and group productivity may be less obvious. On one hand, there is some evidence that highly cohesive groups work harder and are more productive than less cohesive groups. This has been substantiated by research in military, classroom, and industrial settings. (Goodacre 1951; Shaw and Shaw 1962; Van Zelst 1952a, 1952b). Other studies, however, show that highly cohesive groups are *less* productive (Seashore 1954; Cartwright and Robertson 1961; Warwick 1964). Although these findings appear contradictory, the explanation is logical. Highly cohesive groups obtain more conformity from their members, including conformity to standards of production. However, such groups do not always establish high production standards. If "productivity" is not a goal, members of a highly cohesive group will spend all their time socializing with one another rather than producing.

Group Goals

The Selection of Group Goals

GROUP GOALS AND PERSONAL GOALS. The term **group goal** refers to a desirable outcome that group members strive collectively to bring about. Most groups have at least one major goal, although some pursue several simultaneously. Group goals are a basis for guiding and coordinating the activity of members. They provide a framework for the development of norms and standards within the group.

As an example, consider the goal of a group of skilled workers producing arc welding equipment. Arc welders are devices that fuse together pieces of steel by means of a 6,000-degree electric current; they are used to construct ships, skyscrapers, and oil-drilling rigs. This particular group works for a company whose enlightened owner believes it is good business for workers to share company profits. The owner has designated 50 percent of the profits as a bonus for the workers (on top of base pay). All the workers within the group receive the same bonus, because no individual has all the skills needed to build a welder by himself. The size of the bonus, however, depends on the number of arc welders produced by the group.

When the owner first proposed the bonus, the workers were very enthusiastic. They had some difficulties, however, in agreeing on an appropriate production goal for the group. While one worker proposed 25 units per week, others felt that such a goal was unrealistic. Another worker (who was widely regarded as lazy) proposed 10 units per week. After much discussion and some experimentation, the group settled on 18 arc welders per week as its goal. This goal was attainable and provided an attractive bonus.

It is important to distinguish group goals from personal goals, although the two concepts are related (Mills 1967; Cartwright and Zander 1968). *Personal goals* are outcomes desired by individuals. For example, one individual may want to earn a lot of money; a second may want an opportunity to acquire work experience and additional skills. Very often, individuals belong to a group precisely because it helps them achieve their personal goals. Nevertheless, personal goals and group goals are different. A group goal is not the simple sum of personal goals, nor can it be directly inferred from them. It is a desirable outcome for the group as a whole, not merely for the individual.

If a group is to pursue its goals successfully, there must be goal consensus among its members. **Goal consensus** exists when a substantial proportion of members agree on the group's goal and accept the desirability of trying to achieve it. To develop goal consensus often requires some time. Goal consensus for the arc welders emerged only after members debated among themselves and considered various alternatives. Still, a goal on which there is little agreement has scant chance of being attained.

THEORY OF GOAL SELECTION. Groups differ markedly in the goals they establish. Some groups aspire to high levels of accomplishment, whereas others pursue lesser goals. In other words, groups differ in their levels of aspiration. A group's **level of aspiration** is the difficulty of the goals that members agree to pursue. A group with a high level of aspiration is pursuing a goal that is hard to achieve.

Choosing a group goal is often complex. Members must decide what level of aspiration is suitable based on their needs and capabilities. A team of mountain climbers, for example, might consider climbing several peaks in a mountain range. Group members will doubtlessly consider some peaks more important and worthwhile than others. But the most important goals are often the most difficult. Suppose that the climbers are considering either of two mountains, A or B, as a possible goal. Although Mountain A is very high and snow-capped, it is also dangerous due to ice falls. Several members of an earlier expedition died in an avalanche while attempting to climb to the summit. Mountain B is less imposing, and certainly less dangerous, but still considered worth climbing by the members. None of the mountaineers have ever climbed Mountain A or B, but they firmly believe that Mountain B offers them a higher probability of reaching the top and returning safely than does Mountain A.

Zander (1971, 1977) proposed a theory describing how groups evaluate alternatives when establishing a group goal. According to Zander, we can express the expected value of an alternative as follows:

Expected value of an alternative =
$$\left(\begin{array}{c} \text{perceived probability} \\ \text{of success} \end{array} \times \begin{array}{c} \text{incentive value} \\ \text{of success} \end{array} \right)$$

$$- \left(\begin{array}{c} \text{perceived probability} \\ \text{of failure} \end{array} \times \begin{array}{c} \text{loss incurred} \\ \text{from failure} \end{array} \right)$$

If the climbers used this approach to assess Mountain A, they would find that this alternative has a low expected value. Although the mountaineers agree that climbing A is valuable (that is, has high "incentive value"), they also recognize that the probability of success-fully doing so is low. Moreover, because some climbers might get hurt, the loss incurred from failure would be severe. In contrast, Mountain B has a higher expected value. Although climbing B has slightly lower incentive value than climbing A, there is a much higher probability of reaching the top of B. Any loss incurred from failure would be slight; although the group would waste its time, no members would be hurt.

The theory holds that group members will, in effect, calculate the expected values of both A and B, and then choose the alternative having the highest expected value. Thus, the group will choose Mountain B as the appropriate goal for its expedition.

The Pursuit of Group Goals

GOAL STRIVING. Once a group establishes an appropriate level of aspiration, it can achieve this goal only if its members exercise continued effort and striving. This raises an important question: What factors cause a group to persist toward attaining of its goals?

One factor is the value and importance ascribed to the goal itself. Most groups will work harder to attain goals that are highly valued by their members. Another factor that affects group motivation is the clarity of the path towards the goal. Although group members may know what they want, they may not know the best way of obtaining it. Group motivation is impaired when the path to the goal is unclear. Facing this uncertainty, group members become less enthusiastic, less attracted to their task, and less efficient in their performance (Cohen 1959; Raven and Rietsema 1957).

Another factor that affects group goal striving is feedback. **Feedback** is information received by a group that indicates whether it is progressing satisfactorily toward its goal. If feedback is negative, the group may be headed for failure and group members are likely to change their behavior. Either they will try harder to achieve their goal or they will abandon it for a lesser one. The "try harder" reac-

This team of mountaineers has climbed halfway toward its goal. Careful, realistic choices regarding level of aspiration are crucial in groups such as this one.

tion is most probable when the feedback indicates slight or moderate failure rather than extreme failure (Streufert, Streufert, and Castore 1969). If the feedback indicates that the group is failing completely, the members may simply give up.

The effect of moderately negative feedback is illustrated in a study of an American expedition climbing Mount Everest (Emerson 1966). The expedition took 92 days to climb Everest, which, at 29,028 feet above sea level, is the world's tallest peak. At this altitude, the air is very thin and even the simplest actions require enormous effort and will. A climber can honestly believe he wants to climb Everest very much—but still fail to get out of his sleeping bag soon enough to get important work underway.

As a member of this expedition, the researcher was able to directly observe the group's efforts to reach its goal. His findings suggest that feedback from group leaders to other members was crucial in sustaining the group's motivation. Leaders were selective (sometimes even misleading) in passing along information. They gave negative feedback on the group's progress to dampen overoptimism. This kept the team members challenged so that they exerted their best efforts under the harsh and uncertain conditions. Negative feedback—especially at moderate levels—intensifies group goal striving.

REACTIONS TO GROUP FAILURE. A group that fails repeatedly to achieve its goals has several alternatives available. First, the group might try to retain the original goals while initiating a new and more effective strategy. Alternatively, the group might lower its level of aspiration and pursue more attainable objectives. Or, it may reject its old leaders and find new leadership.

If these changes do not produce satisfactory results, group cohesiveness will deteriorate. Progress in achieving group goals is essential in maintaining positive relations among members (Frye 1966; Streufert and Streufert 1969). Recurring failure will increase frustration and cause members to criticize one another. Members will lower their evaluation of the group, and this in turn may cause them to pursue personal goals that do not contribute to the group's performance or to withdraw from the group entirely. One way or another, failure to meet important group objectives has a corrosive effect on group cohesiveness.

In some cases a group will react to recurring failure not by lowering its level of aspiration or changing its leadership, but by behaving defensively. Members may attempt to avoid embarrassment and to protect themselves by blaming someone else (Deschamps 1972; Zander 1971). This method of deflecting responsibility for failure is known as **scapegoating.** It preserves good relations within the group at the expense of someone else.

The ideal scapegoat is someone who is powerless, different, and easily distinguishable. For this reason, outsiders in weak positions are often chosen as scapegoats. Alternatively, the blame may turn inward, and the group may hold certain highly visible members responsible for the failure of the entire group. Every autumn, for example, about a month before the end of the baseball season, the owner of some losing ball club holds a press conference and announces that he is firing the manager. The reason the team is 37 games out of first place, reporters are given to understand, is that the manager is incompetent. The fans, of course, are delighted to see him go. And, because everyone believes that a new manager cannot possibly lose any more games than his predecessor, tension abates within the group: "Just wait 'til next year."

Conformity in Groups

In order to achieve group goals, members must carry out the appropriate actions. Because a group is a set of persons who relate to one another as parts of a system, the activities of members must be highly coordinated. But coordination does not happen automatically. It can occur only when members conform to group norms and standards. This raises a basic question: What forms of influence within a group produce conformity to group norms?

Informational Influence

Influence within a group may take either of two forms: informational influence or normative influence. By definition, **informational influence** occurs when a person relies on other group members to provide information about reality. This information may serve as a basis for formulating an opinion or for making a decision. Informational influence is common in situations where there are no external or "objective" standards of reference. Under these conditions, individuals will rely on other group members to gain a sense of what is valid or appropriate. Informational influence, then, occurs when a group member faced with uncertainty revises his or her beliefs based on information from other members.

A well-known study by Sherif (1936) demonstrates this process. The study is based on a physical phenomenon termed the **autokinetic effect** (meaning "moves by itself"). The autokinetic effect occurs when a person stares at a stationary pinpoint of light located at a distance in a completely dark room. For most people, the light will appear to move in an erratic fashion. Sherif used the autokinetic effect as a basis for studying informational influence. First, he asked subjects individually to estimate how far the light moved. In making these judgments, subjects were quite literally in the dark—they had no external frame of reference. From their estimates the researcher was able to determine a stable range for each subject. (Remember, however, that the pinpoint of light was not actually moving.) Next, Sherif put two or three of these persons in the autokinetic situation at the same time. Although the estimates they had made earlier when alone were discrepant, the estimates they made in groups converged on a common judgment. Thus, lacking an external frame of reference and being uncertain about their own judgment, group members began to use one another's estimates as a basis for defining reality. Each group established its own (faulty) concept of reality that members used as a frame of reference. Subsequent research (Hood and Sherif 1962) shows that subjects involved in an autokinetic experiment are quite unaware that their judgments are being influenced by other members. Informational influence is often indirect and subtle, but it can be an important source of uniformity in groups.

Normative Influence

Another type of influence that occurs within groups is normative influence. By definition, **normative influence** occurs when someone conforms to group norms in order to receive the rewards and/or avoid the punishments that are contingent on adherence to these expectations. Normative influence is the most fundamental source of uniformity within groups. To understand it more fully, we must look closely at group norms themselves.

NORMS. A **norm** is "an idea in the minds of members in a group, an idea that can be put in the form of a statement specifying what the members or other [individuals] should do, ought to do, are expected to do, under given circumstances" (Homans 1950, p. 123). In general, norms are anchored in a group's values and goals. Norms prescribe behaviors that will lead to attainment of these goals and proscribe behaviors that will hinder their attainment.

Norms apply to almost any behavior imaginable. A work group, for example, may have norms specifying what time workers are expected to show up and how much they are expected to produce. A family may have norms regulating who washes the dishes, as well as who can have sexual relations with whom (incest taboo). A study of several gangs of adolescent boys in the Southwest found that they had norms governing what kinds of information members could reveal to parents and police, how to behave during street fights with rival gangs, and when a member was permitted to steal someone else's girl friend (Sherif and Sherif 1964).

THE RETURN POTENTIAL MODEL. We can think of group norms as having structure and shape. One theoretical approach to the structure of norms is the Return Potential Model (Jackson 1965). This model treats norms as having two dimensions—the *behavior dimension* and the *evaluation dimension*. Both dimensions are shown in Figure 12.1. The behavior dimension specifies the frequency or amount of behavior regulated by the group norm, whereas the evaluation dimension refers to the response to that behavior by other group members. The evaluation of behavior can be positive (approval), indifferent, or negative (disapproval). The curves in Figure 12.1 represent different norms. They show that evaluation is a function of behavior.

Note that the three norms depicted in Figure 12.1 have very different shapes. Let's suppose that Norm A pertains to productive activity in a group of editors working on a magazine. Norm A reflects a situation in which group members encourage and reward higher levels of a given behavior, such as editing more and more pages of manuscript per day. Under this norm, the more pages a member edits, the more she is rewarded. Any member who produces at a very low level on this behavior dimension will receive negative evaluation from other group members. She may be criticized or castigated or perhaps face a monetary punishment. Only by producing at a higher level does she receive a positive evaluation.

Norm B is different, although we can contrast it with the pattern of expectations shown in Norm A. Whereas Norm A basically said "the more the better," Norm B says that there is such a thing as producing *too* much. Under Norm B, a member will be rewarded for producing in the middle range on the behavior dimension. Productivity at very low levels or at very high levels will be negatively evaluated and discouraged. Although one might expect work groups to have norms that look like A, rather than B, this is not necessarily the case. When group members notice that one among them is working much harder than the others, they may disapprove of this "overproduction."

This was illustrated in an early study (Roethlisberger and Dickson 1939) of 14 men, known as the Bank Wiring Group, who assembled banks of telephone switching equipment for the Western Electric Company. The management of the company had recently instituted a wage incentive plan rewarding higher levels of productivity by individual workers. Managers believed that this plan would be effective in increasing the productivity of the Bank Wiring Group. They soon observed, however, that the workers continued to produce at about the same rate as before, despite the opportunity to increase their earnings.

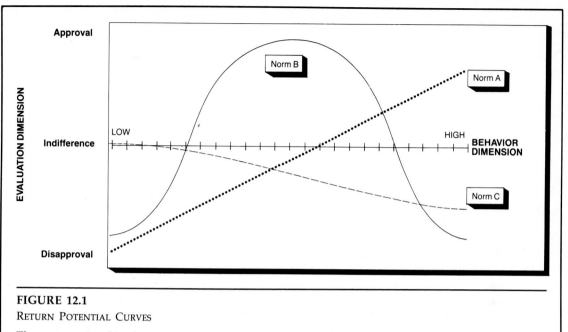

FIGURE 12.1

RETURN POTENTIAL CURVES

The curves in this figure represent three group norms. In each case, varying amounts of behavior are met with some specified amount of approval or disapproval from group members. Under Norm A, for example, low amounts of behavior are disapproved, whereas high amounts are approved. Under Norm B, intermediate amounts of behavior are approved, whereas very low and very high amounts are disapproved. Under Norm C, high amounts of behavior are disapproved, whereas low amounts are neither approved nor disapproved.

Source: adapted from Jackson (1965).

This resulted because the group had a firmly established norm (like Norm B in Figure 12.1) concerning what was "a fair day's work." Group members feared that if they began to produce at higher levels, the company might switch production standards and require higher levels of productivity for lower pay. Therefore, the group enforced its own production norm on individual members. If a man produced too much, he was ridiculed by other members as a "rate buster." If he produced too little, he was disparaged as a "chiseler." If an offender did not respond to these verbal reprimands, he was soon subjected to another form of sanction termed "binging," whereby other members would hit him in the arm. Although this behavior might sound unusual, groups often develop their own special sanctions. What matters to the group is its effectiveness in regulating the behavior of its members.

The norms we have discussed up until this point—Norms A and B—involve both positive and negative evaluation. Other norms, however, pertain to behaviors that group members consider wholly undesirable, represented by Norm C in Figure 12.1. Although group members may tolerate low levels of the undesirable behavior, their reaction quickly becomes more negative as the behavior becomes more frequent or intense. Although a norm like C is unlikely to pertain to productive activities, it might well apply to such behaviors as talking a

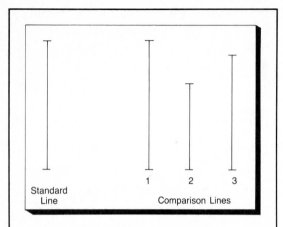

FIGURE 12.2

JUDGMENTAL TASK EMPLOYED IN ASCH CONFORMITY STUDIES

In the Asch paradigm, naive subjects are shown one standard line and three comparison lines. The task is to judge which of the three comparison lines is closest in length to the standard line. By itself, this task appears easy. However, subjects are surrounded by other persons (supposedly also naive subjects, but actually experimental confederates) who publicly announce erroneous judgments regarding the match between lines. Such a situation imposes pressure on the subject to conform to their erroneous judgments.

Source: adapted from Asch (1952).

lot, importuning others, make a nuisance of oneself, and so on. Much of our everyday activity is regulated by norms like this one.

Every norm may be said to specify a **range of tolerable behavior**—that portion of the behavior dimension which members of a group approve and evaluate positively (Sherif and Sherif 1956). For example, in Figure 12.1, Norm A delimits a range of tolerable behavior at the higher end of the behavioral dimension, whereas Norm B delineates a range of tolerable behavior in the middle of the behavioral dimension. Behaviors outside this range are not approved or tolerated. The range of tolerable behavior offers a convenient way to define

the concept of **conformity.** A group member is conforming to a given norm when his or her behavior falls within the range of tolerable behavior.

Another characteristic of a norm is its intensity. The *intensity of a norm* is indicated by the height of the Return Potential Curve from its highest to its lowest point, both above and below the point of indifference. The intensity of a norm reflects the strength of group feelings (whether approval or disapproval) regarding that behavior. In Figure 12.1, group members feel more strongly about the behavior regulated by Norm B than about that regulated by Norm C. Most norms that regulate behaviors crucial to group survival or goal attainment have high intensity, whereas norms about personal discretion or taste (such as style of dress or manner of speaking) have moderate or low intensity.

The Asch Conformity Paradigm

In a series of classic experiments, Asch (1951, 1955, 1956, 1957) investigated conformity within groups. Specifically, he studied the process by which a majority of members pressure an individual to adopt its position. In a laboratory setting, Asch created a situation in which an individual was confronted by a majority who unanimously agreed on a factual matter but were themselves in error. Asch wanted to ascertain whether group pressure could induce an individual to shift his own judgment and conform with the group's erroneous position. The results of his studies show that, within limits, groups can influence members to agree with erroneous judgments.

In a typical Asch experiment, a group of eight persons participates in an investigation of "visual discrimination." In fact, all but one of these persons are confederates working for the experimenter. The remaining individual is a naive subject. In front of the experimental room, large cards display a standard line and three comparison lines, as shown in Figure 12.2. The objective is to decide which of the comparison lines (1, 2, or 3) is the same length as the standard line.

As you can see, the task is very simple and straightforward. One of the comparison lines is the same length as the standard, while the other two are very different. The group repeats this task 18 times using a different set of lines each time. In every case, the standard line matches one of the three comparison lines. Although this task appears easy, it turns out to be quite difficult for the naive subject. During each trial of the experiment, the confederates announce their judgments publicly, one after another. The subject also announces his opinion. In 12 of the 18 trials, confederates give an incorrect response. In the remaining 6 trials, which are neutral, the confederates all respond truthfully.

The purpose of the Asch experiment is to observe how the naive subject behaves during the 12 critical trials. The group is seated so that all of the confederates are asked to respond prior to the real subject. This puts the subject in a difficult position. On the one hand, he knows (or thinks that he knows) the correct response. On the other hand, he hears all the other subjects (whom he believes to be sincere) announcing a different and unanimous judgment.

Results of these experiments indicate that the incorrect opinion expressed by the majority strongly influences the judgments of naive subjects. In the 12 critical trials, nearly one third of the subjects' responses were incorrect (Asch 1957). This compares with an error rate of less than 1 percent in a control condition in which no confederates were present and subjects recorded their judgments privately on paper. Many of the subjects were self-conscious about the discrepancy between the group's judgments and their own. They felt puzzled or under pressure, and tried to figure out what might be happening. Some wondered whether they had misunderstood the experimental instructions; others began to question their eyesight. Even those subjects who did not conform felt some apprehension, but they eventually decided that the problem rested more with the group than with themselves.

In a situation like this, most people find it difficult to remain completely independent of group pressure. Only about 25 percent of Asch's subjects never yielded on any of the critical trials. The rest did conform, either a little or a great deal. From interviews conducted after the experiment, it became clear that this conformity was of a particular type. For the most part, it involved public compliance without private acceptance: although many subjects conformed publicly, they did not believe or accept this judgment privately. Instead, they viewed public compliance as the best choice in a difficult situation.

Factors Affecting Conformity

We have seen that group pressures exert substantial influence on behavior. But an individual's tendency to conform will be greater under some conditions than under others. Below are some of the variables that affect the *amount* of conformity in groups.

UNANIMITY OF THE MAJORITY. Consider the Asch experiment described earlier, in which a single nonconforming member is confronted by a majority. Assume that the majority is unanimous—that is, all the members of the group are united in a position different from the nonconformer's position. In this case, the size of the majority will have an impact on the behavior of the nonconforming member. The pressure for conformity by this member increases with the size of the majority (Asch 1955; Rosenberg 1961). For example, a subject confronted by one other person in an Asch-type situation will continue to answer independently and correctly on nearly all trials. When confronted by two persons, the subject will experience more pressure and will agree with the majority's erroneous answer more of the time. Confronted by three persons, the subject will conform at a still higher rate. In his

Box 12.2
BARRIERS TO INDEPENDENT BEHAVIOR

Conformity to norms is essential to group functioning. Without it, there will be a serious lack of coordination and failure to achieve group goals. Of course, there are many situations in which an individual might desire to act independently rather than to conform to group norms. He or she might disagree with the majority's position and prefer an innovative departure. Nevertheless, groups discourage independent behavior by a variety of means. One review (Hollander 1975) suggests that there are six barriers to independent behavior:

1. *Risk of disapproval from other group members* Most groups establish norms governing central activities. These norms specify a range of tolerable behavior. To the extent that a member's independent behavior falls outside that range, the member risks disapproval from others in the group. By deviating too far, he or she may face outright rejection.

2. *Lack of perceived alternatives* Individuals frequently are unaware of alternatives other than what is specified by group norms. Unless someone else speaks out and proposes alternatives, a member may not realize that he or she has any choice other than conformity.

3. *Fear of disrupting the group's operations* Because group norms usually reflect underlying group goals, individuals know that departing from established norms may rock the boat. Thus, they avoid acting independently out of fear that it may hamper the attainment of group goals.

4. *Absence of communication among group members* Even though a number of members may privately dissent from group standards, they may hesitate to express their reservations publicly. Without communication, they frequently do not know what the other members are thinking. Lacking information that others might join in the nonconforming action, they avoid going out on a limb alone.

5. *No feeling of responsibility for group outcomes* Members who conform may inadvertently cause a group to fail in its objectives. Although they may realize that conformist behavior is producing poor outcomes, they may hesitate to take the initiative to turn the situation around. This is especially common when individuals feel that they are not personally responsible for the group's success or failure.

6. *A sense of powerlessness* If a person feels that he cannot change a situation, he is unlikely to try anything new. The apathy becomes self-fulfilling. No one tries anything different, and, consequently, nothing improves.

These six barriers to independent behavior are powerful contributors to conformity. If several are operating simultaneously, the probability of conformity is further increased.

early studies, Asch (1951) found that conformity to unanimous false judgments increased with majority size up to three members and was essentially constant beyond that point. More recent research (Gerard, Wilhelmy, and Conolley 1968) has questioned the exact point at which the effect of majority size begins to level off. Beyond three of four persons, however, increases in the size of the majority have little added impact.

What happens when the group's majority is not unanimous? Basically, lack of unanimity has a liberating effect on behavior. A subject will be less likely to conform if another member breaks away from the majority (Gorfein 1964; Morris and Miller 1975). One explanation for this is that the member who abandons the majority provides validation and social support for the subject. In an Asch experiment, for example, if one or several members abandon the majority and announce correct judgments, their behavior will reaffirm the subject's own perception of reality.

It appears, however, that *any* breach in the majority—whether it provides social support or not—will reduce conformity pressure (Allen and Levine 1968, 1969, 1971). In one study, subjects participated in groups of five persons, four of whom were confederates. The subjects made judgments on several items. These included visual evaluations similar to those used by Asch, informational items (for example, "In thousands of miles, how far is it from San Francisco to New York?"), and opinion items for which there were no correct answers (Agree or disagree: "Most young people get too much education."). Depending on experimental treatment, subjects were confronted with either a unanimous majority of four persons (the control condition), a majority of three persons and a fourth person who broke from the majority and gave the correct answer (social support condition), or a majority of three persons and a fourth person who broke from the majority but gave an answer that was even more erroneous than that of the majority (extreme erroneous dissent).

The results of this study are shown in Figure 12.3. Note that the control condition, which involved a unanimous majority, produced a very high level of conformity. The social support condition, in which the dissenter joined the subject, significantly reduced conformity. Even in the erroneous dissent condition, when the dissenter gave an answer that was more extreme and incorrect than the majority's, conformity of the subjects declined. Thus, any breach in the majority appears to

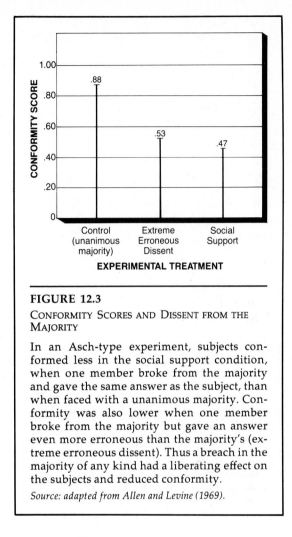

FIGURE 12.3

CONFORMITY SCORES AND DISSENT FROM THE MAJORITY

In an Asch-type experiment, subjects conformed less in the social support condition, when one member broke from the majority and gave the same answer as the subject, than when faced with a unanimous majority. Conformity was also lower when one member broke from the majority but gave an answer even more erroneous than the majority's (extreme erroneous dissent). Thus a breach in the majority of any kind had a liberating effect on the subjects and reduced conformity.

Source: adapted from Allen and Levine (1969).

reduce conformity. However, subjects in the social support and extreme erroneous dissent conditions had very different impressions of dissenters. Under social support, subjects held a positive impression of that person, whereas under extreme erroneous dissent, subjects thought the dissenter was basically a jackass—unlikable, stupid, insincere, and badly adjusted. Either way, the breach in the majority had the same effect: it called into question the correctness of the majority's position and reduced the subject's tendency to conform.

Groups norms can extend to any aspect of behavior, including dress. The Savage Skulls have a different dress code from these corporate executives, but conformity is high within each group.

ATTRACTION TO A GROUP. Members who are highly attracted to a group will conform more to group norms than members who are less attracted to it (Jackson and Saltzstein 1958; Kiesler and Kiesler 1969; Mehrabian and Ksionzky 1970). One explanation for this is that when individuals are attracted to a group, they also wish to be accepted personally by its members. Because acceptance and friendship are strengthened when members hold similar attitudes and standards, individuals highly attracted to a group conform more to the views held by the others (McLeod, Price, and Harburg 1966; Feather and Armstrong 1967). However, attraction to a group will increase conformity only if that conformity is rewarded by group acceptance (Walker and Heyns 1962).

COMMITMENT TO FUTURE INTERACTION. An individual is more likely to conform to group norms when he anticipates that his relationship with the group will be relatively permanent, as opposed to short-term. This was dem-

onstrated in a study that involved groups of five persons who were asked to discuss such problems as urban affairs, international relations, pollution, and population (Lewis, Langan, and Hollander 1972). Some of the participants were led to believe that they would review these problems with group members again in the future, whereas others were not given this expectation. Those who anticipated future interaction conformed more to the majority's opinion than those who did not anticipate future interaction.

Commitment to future interaction affects conformity whether members are attracted to the group or not. For instance, one investigation showed that even if a member does not like the others in the group, he will conform at a high level provided he is already committed to continuing in the group and cannot readily leave or opt out. Such a person is likely to experience distress or dissonance at having to interact with persons he does not like, and he may resolve this by bringing his own attitudes and beliefs into line with group standards

(Kiesler and Corbin 1965; Kiesler, Zanna, and deSalvo 1966).

COMPETENCE. Conformity to group norms is also affected by an individual member's level of expertise relative to that of other members. If a member skilled at the task at hand differs from the majority's view, he will resist pressure to the degree that he believes himself to be more competent than the other group members (Mausner 1954; Ettinger et al. 1971). Interestingly, the extent to which a person *believes* that he is competent may in fact be more important than his actual level of competence (Stang 1972). Persons who in fact are not competent will still resist conformity pressure if they believe they are more skilled than other members. This is because group members who believe themselves to be competent rely less on the judgments of others. When confronted by a majority, they will usually try to persuade other members to change their positions.

GENDER. The gender composition of a group also affects the amount of conformity of its members. The weight of available evidence indicates that, within same-sex groups, females yield more to conformity pressures than males. Although controversial, this finding is based on many different studies conducted during the 1950s, 1960s, and 1970s (see Tuddenham 1958; Endler 1966; Carrigan and Julian 1966). Some studies have shown no difference between the sexes in conformity, but the majority indicate that females conform slightly more than males (Cooper 1979; Eagly and Carli 1981).

Some of this difference may be based on sex-role expectations and gender identity. The traditional female role in the United States rewards submissiveness, nurturance, passivity, and person-orientation—all qualities related to conformity. The traditional male role rewards aggressiveness, assertiveness, dominance, and task-orientation (Wiley 1973). Consequently, standard sex-role expectations may lead to greater conformity among females than males.

Another part of this difference in conformity may be due to the nature of the tasks employed in conformity experiments themselves. Many of the earlier studies employed tasks and opinion items involving male-related activities. Thus, what appears to be sex differences in conformity may actually have resulted from differences in familiarity or competence with the tasks used in some of the experiments.

In a test of this idea (Sistrunk and McDavid 1971), it was reasoned that if women are more conformist on activities regarded as traditionally male, then men might be more conformist on activities regarded as traditionally female. For example, whereas women may be more conformist about such things as cars and politics, men might be more conformist about child care and clothing fashions. Researchers compiled a list of statements, some of which were opinions and others of which were everyday matters of fact. Some of these test items had previously been judged to be of greater interest and familiarity to females, while other items had been judged to be of greater interest and familiarity to males. They presented these items (along with some neutral filler items) to several groups of males and females. Adjacent to each item there appeared some data indicating how the majority of the subjects' peers had responded to each item. This number was manipulated by researchers. The results of this study are shown in Figure 12.4.

On an overall basis, there was no significant difference between males and females in the amount of conformity. However, when we look at the type of item involved, we see that males conformed more than females on the feminine items, whereas females conformed more than males on the masculine items. Both sexes conformed about the same amount on the neutral items. These findings suggest that conformity depends on the nature of the task as well as the gender of the subject. Both

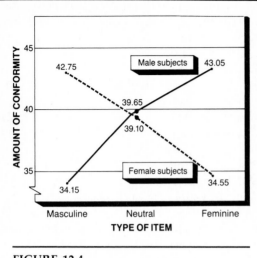

FIGURE 12.4

AMOUNT OF CONFORMITY BY MALES AND
FEMALES AS A FUNCTION OF THE TYPE OF ITEM

Conformity depends not only on gender, but
on the type of item—that is, masculine items
versus feminine items. Females presumably
less familiar or comfortable with masculine
items were shown to conform more on these
items than males. Likewise, males were
shown to conform more on feminine items
than females. These findings suggest that
conformity depends on the nature of the task
as well as the gender of the subject.

Source: adapted from Sistrunk and McDavid (1971).

females and males yield to pressure more
when the task is one with which they are
unfamiliar.

Subsequent research has replicated the
findings of Sistrunk and McDavid, and has
shown that sex-role orientation affects conformity (Goldberg 1974, 1975). In these studies,
women who accepted traditional sex roles conformed more than women who rejected traditional roles or who actively supported the
women's movement. This pattern was particularly marked when the test items were traditionally masculine rather than traditionally
feminine in nature.

Thus, the overall conclusion regarding
gender and conformity is that both task competence and sex-role orientation are mediating

factors in conformist behavior. Early studies
show that women conform more than men,
but this apparently holds true only when the
women accept traditional sex roles or when
they lack competence and familiarity with the
task at hand.

Reactions to Deviance Within Groups

Up to this point we have been looking at
factors that affect the amount of conformity
within groups. We have seen that various
factors affect conformity, such as the size of
the majority and attraction to the group. We
will now consider the opposite of conformity,
known as *deviance*.

Consider the following scene. It is five
o'clock in the morning—still dark outside—
and seven college students are holding a meeting. Everyone is drinking coffee by the gallon
and trying to stay awake. The students have
organized the group as part of one of their
courses: it is responsible for completing a large
project. The school term is nearly over and the
project is due within a week. Unfortunately,
the group is far behind schedule and a major
effort will be needed to meet the project deadline. No one wanted a meeting at this misera-
ble hour of the morning, but there was no
other time when everyone could fit it into
their busy schedules.

The meeting is not progressing well. Two
group members have offered a proposal
regarding the project. Some other members
like the idea, and a consensus is starting to
develop. Their proposal is better than anything else the group has considered. Everybody except a single member, Ben, thinks it
has merit. Although Ben's own suggestions
have not been especially useful, he has nothing but criticism for the idea. Support for the
proposal is strong, but Ben's objections grow
more vigorous. Other members begin to argue
with him because a unanimous vote is necessary before a decision can be reached. The
group is running out of time. The discussion
goes on and on, but Ben won't give an inch.

Soon the sun starts to rise. The majority of the group supports the proposal, but Ben still deviates. Something has to give.

Deviant behavior constitutes a serious problem for the majority. It disrupts normal operations and challenges the group's conception of reality. If allowed to continue unchecked, deviation may eventually cause a group to perform poorly or even to collapse and disband. How will the group's majority cope with deviant behavior such as Ben's? Fundamentally, there are three options available: (1) The majority can try to influence the deviant (using persuasion, threats, and so on) and bring him back within the range of tolerable behavior. (2) The majority can reject the deviant, either by means of outright expulsion from the group or by means of psychological exclusion. (3) The majority can respond to the deviant by changing its own position and moving into line with the deviant's.

Although these responses are diverse, they all constitute attempts by the majority to protect the group's integrity and effectiveness (Festinger 1950; Levine 1980). If the majority of members are committed to the group, they will want the group to continue to exist, to maintain its definition of social reality, and to succeed at its goals. Whatever the form of their reaction to the deviant, members will try to offset the imbalance created by his behavior and to establish a new equilibrium within the group. This section will consider each of the possible responses of the majority.

Pressure to Restore Conformity

When a group first recognizes deviance in a member, it will attempt to increase communication with that person, in hopes of persuading him to conform. Members of the majority will speak to him, remind him of the group's expectations, explain and justify these expectations, and urge him to comply. If he responds by conforming, the problem will be solved and equilibrium will be restored.

If, on the other hand, he refuses to conform and persists in his deviance, the majority will likely apply more pressure. This may involve threats of direct punishment. Whether a deviant will be sanctioned by the majority, and how severely, depends on a number of factors. Most important is the extent to which the deviant's behavior interferes with attainment of important group goals. The majority will be very reluctant to let a deviant member disrupt the group's progress. Behavior that unequivocally prevents the group from attaining its goals—such as violating a central norm—will incite punishment that is both swift and severe (Michener and Burt 1975).

This generalization must be qualified, however, by taking into account the status of the deviant. The term **status** refers to a member's relative standing within the group. It is usually based on the extent to which a member has contributed to attainment of important group goals. Within task-oriented groups, status may affect not only the frequency of participation in discussions, but also the amount of influence over the opinions of others. High-status persons typically participate a great deal and exercise a lot of influence. In some cases, high-status members are given a distinctive title. A foreman in a factory work group, an instructor in a college seminar, a captain in an infantry unit, a prima donna in an opera company are all high-status members of their respective groups.

Thus, the status of the deviant within the group affects the severity of the majority's reaction. Some research indicates that high-status deviant members are punished more severely than low-status members for deviant acts (Wahrman 1970; Hollander and Willis 1967; Sherif and Sherif 1964). Other studies show the opposite effect—that high-status members are punished less severely than low-status members for deviant acts (Blau 1960; Sabath 1964; Gerson 1967). Clearly the relationship between status and sanctioning is complex.

To explain this relationship, one theory (proposed by Sherif and Sherif 1967) holds that both the status of the deviant and the degree of goal interference must be taken into account. According to this theory, high-status

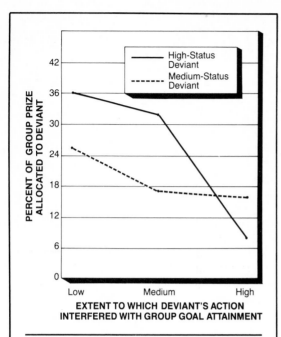

FIGURE 12.5

REACTION TO A DEVIANT AS A FUNCTION OF THE
DEVIANT'S STATUS AND THE INTERFERENCE
INTENSITY OF THE ACT

A deviant group member is punished more
severely—that is, given a smaller share of the
group's prize—when his or her deviant act
interferes substantially with attainment of the
group's goal than when it interferes only
slightly. The status of the deviant within the
group is also taken into account by members
in determining punishment. Compared to the
medium-status deviant, a high-status deviant
is punished less severely for acts of low or
medium interference, but more severely for
acts that greatly interfere with the attainment
of group goals.

Source: adapted from Wiggins, Dill, and Schwartz (1965).

This phenomenon was demonstrated in a
laboratory experiment involving 30 groups of
four persons (Wiggins, Dill, and Schwartz
1965). Each group attempted to solve a series of
intellectual problems and competed against
the other groups in the study for a $50 prize.
One member within each group was made to
appear to have violated work rules, which cost
the group a penalty in points. Depending on
experimental treatment, the point penalty was
either high, medium, or low in magnitude.
When the penalty was high, the violation
virtually wiped out the group's chance of
winning the $50 prize. When the penalty was
medium or low, the violation lessened the
group's chance of winning but did not put
success entirely out of reach. The study also
varied the status of the supposed deviant.
Depending on treatment, the deviant was
either high-status or medium-status. The high-
status member was a person whose performance earlier in the session had been highly
competent and who therefore had contributed
substantially toward attainment of the group's
goal. The medium-status member was one
whose earlier performance had been of average competency.

After completing all the problems, group
members were asked to indicate how they
would distribute the $50 among themselves if
they won the prize. Because each group in this
study included four members, the average
member might expect to win 25 percent of the
prize. However, the actual distribution, which
is shown in Figure 12.5, indicates that group
members sanctioned the deviant by distribut-
ing rewards unequally. The severity of the
sanction depended both on the deviant's status
and the extent to which the deviant act interfered with the group goal. When the deviant
act did not completely block the group's
chance of winning, the high-status deviant
was rewarded more (sanctioned less) than the
medium-status deviant. However, when the
violation seriously interfered with attainment
of the group's goal, the high-status deviant
was rewarded less (sanctioned more) than the
medium-status deviant.

persons are relatively free to violate minor
norms provided they do not interfere with the
attainment of the group's goals. They are not
punished as severely as low-status members
for minor violations. At the same time, high-
status persons are punished more severely
than low-status members if they breach important norms and thereby impede progress
toward the group's goals.

These results indicate that group members are generally reluctant to label a high-status member as deviant. When the consequences of the deviation are minor, they prefer to overlook the matter. However, if the deviant act blocks attainment of the group's goal, the members have little choice; they must label the high-status member a deviant and apply severe sanctions. This phenomenon is called *status liability* to indicate that high-status members are more liable than low-status members for major offenses. Similar findings have been observed in another study (Alvarez 1968).

Rejection of the Deviant

If majority members in a group lack the capability or the inclination to apply pressure to a deviant, they have another option available: they can reject the deviant. Rejection can assume various forms. One of these is expulsion from membership. For example, the majority may pick up the deviant and throw him out the door. Or, in more polite settings, the group may simply not invite the deviant back to their next meeting.

Another form of rejection is psychological isolation. In this case, the majority will ignore the deviant and refuse to interact with him even though he is physically present. Communication with the deviant gradually declines as one member after another comes to view him as a lost cause (Schachter 1951; Sampson and Brandon 1964). Although the amount of interaction is reduced, the level of covert hostility toward the deviant will be high (Orcutt 1973).

Rejection of the deviant is triggered by many of the same factors that produce sanctioning. In fact, rejection and sanctioning often occur at the same time. In the study of status liability discussed above, the majority not only punished the deviate monetarily but also did not want him to participate in their future meetings. Rejection was greatest when the deviant was a high-status member who severely blocked the group's progress. Other studies have shown that rejection, like sanctioning, increases as a deviant takes a more

extreme position from the majority's (Hensley and Duval 1976; Levine, Saxe, and Harris 1976).

Rejection of the deviate is a means of reestablishing equilibrium within the group because it "purifies" the membership. After a deviant is ostracized, only the conforming members remain within the system. This enables the group to retain its integrity as a social unit.

Social Change

Because deviant behavior departs from shared expectations, it challenges the existing social order within a group. Behavior that goes beyond the boundaries of group norms is a potential threat to the group's effectiveness. In some cases, however, an individual will engage in independent behavior not because he wishes to disrupt the group or pursue selfish objectives, but because he wants to change the rules or the procedures used by the group in pursuing its goals. Although well-intentioned, behavior of this type may be viewed as deviant by the majority. What one person (or subgroup) intends as a constructive change or innovation, another may view as a threat to the established order. Any change involves some risks, and the majority's members may prefer to leave well enough alone. In such cases, the majority will attempt to suppress the proposed changes.

Nevertheless, changes in group structure *do* occur, and many times they originate inside the group. This raises a basic question: When is independent, counternormative behavior likely to produce changes rather than meet with suppression by the majority? To answer, we must distinguish between group norms and the goals that underlie those norms. If a member's behavior departs from established norms, but points to new ways to more fully realize the group's goals, the changes may be accepted by group members. On the other hand, if a member attempts to force a change in the group's goals themselves, he or she will likely meet with resistance. Only if a group is drifting aimlessly or has failed repeatedly to achieve its goals will an effort to change goals be favorably received.

Innovative suggestions are more likely to be adopted by the group's majority if they are proposed by a well-established or high-status member. One study indicates that leaders are more able to introduce changes and variations in the group's procedures after they have first demonstrated commitment to the group's norms and values (Merei 1949). High-status members receive less opposition and disapproval than lower-status members for suggesting changes in group plans and discussing group concerns with outsiders (Hollander 1961). This is because high-status members are usually considered more skillful and are more committed to group goals than other members.

Deliberate efforts to bring about social change are made not only by individuals, but also by small subgroups called active minorities. An **active minority** is a subgroup of individuals who adopt a distinct viewpoint on some important issues and who try to persuade the majority to change its own position. While agitating for change within the group, active minorities resist pressure to conform to the majority's position. Very often this creates a high level of conflict between the majority and the active minority.

Because social change can be difficult to achieve, active minorities are not always successful in their efforts to modify group policies or goals. The style of behavior adopted by an active minority is important in determining its success (Moscovici and Faucheux 1972). Several studies have shown that an active minority is more likely to change the opinion of group members if its position is distinctive and consistent over time (Moscovici, Lage, and Naffrechoux 1969; Moscovici and Lage 1976). If the minority is consistent in its position, the majority is less likely to dismiss it as stupid or wayward. Whereas majorities can often gain compliance regardless of members' underlying attitudes, active minorities must truly persuade group members. A consistent position is

persuasive because it implies that the minority is clearheaded, confident, purposive. This is why consistent minorities are more effective than inconsistent ones in changing group norms.

Summary

A group is a set of persons who are related to one another as parts of a system. Groups have certain hallmarks, including goals shared by group members, communication among members, norms that guide members' behavior, and identification of members with the group.

GROUP COHESIVENESS. A highly cohesive group is one that is able to attract and hold its members. (1) Several factors affect a group's cohesiveness. A group will be more cohesive if its members like one another, have a high commitment to the group's goals, and gain prestige by belonging to the group. (2) The level of a group's cohesiveness affects the interaction among members. Members in highly cohesive groups communicate more than those in less cohesive groups; they also exert more influence over one another, and their interaction is friendlier and more cooperative. Highly cohesive groups can be more productive than less cohesive groups, but only if they establish norms requiring a high level of productivity from members.

GROUP GOALS. A group goal is a desirable outcome that members strive collectively to bring about. (1) Groups differ with respect to the difficulty of the goals they choose. The level of aspiration chosen by a group is based on several considerations, including the value of the goal (if attained), the probability of actually reaching the goal, and the loss incurred if the goal is pursued but not achieved. (2) Several factors determine the extent to which a group will persist in pursuit of its goals. Goal striving will be greater if the members see a direct path toward their goal rather than an ambiguous one. Moderate negative feedback strengthens goal striving provided that members still believe their goal is attainable. Extreme negative feedback usually causes members to change or abandon their goal. Recurring failure to achieve goals produces frustration, and may cause members to oust the group's leadership or scapegoat an innocent target.

CONFORMITY IN GROUPS. Group members exert pressures on one another to conform, that is, to behave in accordance with expectations and norms. (1) Informational influence is one type of pressure producing conformity. When no external or objective frame of reference is available, members influence each other by providing information about, and a specific interpretation of, reality. (2) Normative influence is another type of pressure. It entails rewards and/or punishments contingent upon adherence to group norms. The Return Potential Model shows the relationship between behavior and subsequent reward or punishment. (3) The Asch conformity studies use a simple visual discrimination paradigm to investigate conditions that produce conformity in groups. (4) Many factors affect the amount of conformity in groups. First, more conformity occurs when the majority is unanimous than when it is not. Conformity is also greater when members are highly attracted to a group, and especially when conformity leads to liking and acceptance by other members. Another factor affecting conformity is commitment to future interaction; conformity is greater when members believe that their relationship with the group will be relatively permanent. Conformity is also affected by the level of a member's competence or skill; members who oppose the majority's view will resist conformity pressures to the extent that they believe themselves to be more competent than other members. Finally, there is some evidence that gender affects conformity. Females conform more than males, although the magnitude of this difference is small. Recent studies suggest that these differences may be based

not merely on gender but on a person's sex-role orientation and familiarity with the task at hand.

REACTIONS TO DEVIANCE IN GROUPS. Deviant behavior violates group norms, and usually provokes a reaction from the group's majority. (1) The majority may apply pressure on the deviant to conform. This usually involves persuasion or sanctions. The amount of pressure applied will depend on several factors, including the status of the deviant and the severity of the violation. (2) The majority may also reject the deviant through psychological isolation or even expulsion from membership. (3) Finally, the majority may construe the deviant's behavior as a valuable innovation. This reaction is infrequent. However, when it does occur, the majority will change the norms to incorporate (and render acceptable) the deviant's behavior.

Key Terms and Concepts

Group

Small Group

Group Cohesiveness

Primary Group

Group Goal

Goal Consensus

Level of Aspiration

Feedback

Scapegoating

Informational Influence

Autokinetic Effect

Normative Influence

Norm

Range of Tolerable Behavior

Conformity

Status

Active Minority

Introduction

Consider a group of salespersons working for a small California corporation that manufactures laboratory equipment. This group of eleven consists of one vice-president, two managers, and eight salespersons. Their basic goal is to market equipment to industrial laboratories in the northern and southern regions of the state.

The members of this group have different backgrounds and personalities. Even more important, they contribute in different ways to the group's functioning. The vice-president is the dominant member. He has a lot of experience in the industry, having established an outstanding record as a salesman. He is responsible for maintaining the group's sales performance at a high level. In addition, he informs executives in other divisions of the company about ideas regarding new products that might be developed by the company in the future. All important decisions made within the sales group must be approved by the vice-president.

Next in importance are the two managers. Both are experienced and have excellent skills in sales. One manager is responsible for the group's sales performance in the northern region of the state, the other for the southern region. The managers are well-paid, although they receive lower salaries than the vice-president.

The least important members of the group are the eight salespersons. They are responsible for making direct contact with customers in their area and for providing products that meet their customers' needs. Salespersons are younger and less experienced than the managers and vice-president. They are paid partly on salary and partly on commission, but they still earn less than the managers.

Status in Groups

As the above description makes clear, the positions occupied by members of the work group differ substantially from one another. Each position carries a distinct set of role expectations. Moreover, each position can be evaluated by members in terms of its prestige, importance, or value to the group. This evaluation is referred to as the **social status** (or simply *status*) of the position. Within the sales group, the vice-president occupies the position of highest status, because his job is most important. The two managers occupy positions of intermediate status, and the eight salespersons occupy positions of low status. The status structure of the sales group is hierarchical—that is, there are fewer members occupying positions of high status than members occupying positions of low status. The structure of this group is depicted in Figure 13.1.

Note that the concept of status is multidimensional (Kimberly 1970). In other words, positions within a group can be ranked in terms of many different criteria. In this chapter, we shall give special attention to three criteria: (1) the contribution that a member occupying a given position makes toward the group's overall performance; (2) the level of rewards received by that member; and (3) the level of control exercised by that member over group decisions and activities. Although there are exceptions, standing on one of these dimensions usually correlates with standing on the others. That is, a member who enjoys high status on one of these dimensions will probably have high status on the others. The vice-president, for example, contributes the most important skills to the group, receives the greatest rewards, and exercises the highest level of control over important group decisions.

This chapter examines the causes and consequences of status differences among group members. The questions to be addressed include:

1. How do differences in status arise among members in a newly forming group? That is, what processes are involved in status emergence?

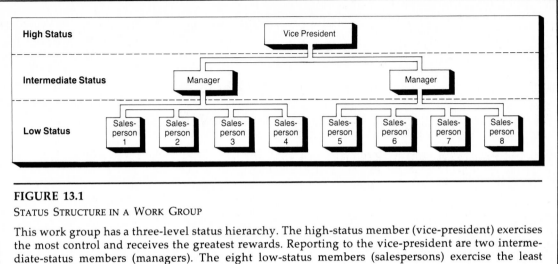

FIGURE 13.1

Status Structure in a Work Group

This work group has a three-level status hierarchy. The high-status member (vice-president) exercises the most control and receives the greatest rewards. Reporting to the vice-president are two intermediate-status members (managers). The eight low-status members (salespersons) exercise the least control and receive the least rewards.

2. In what ways do personal characteristics (such as sex, occupation, education, and race) affect a member's status?

3. In what ways do differences among members in skill and performance affect the rewards received by members? What happens if low contributors receive high rewards, and vice versa? That is, how do members react if reward allocation is inequitable?

4. To what degree are members responsive to legitimate power exercised by group leaders? Under what conditions will members obey legitimate authority, and under what conditions will they refuse to obey?

5. What factors affect the willingness of group members to support the group's leader or cause them to oppose their leader? What circumstances lead to the formation of coalitions that seek to overturn leadership?

Status Emergence in Task Groups

Communication in Task Groups

Consider a group of five undergraduates meeting for the first time. They are members of a task force discussing the case of Johnny Rocco, a delinquent juvenile who has committed a serious crime, but who also comes from an underprivileged background. The group members have been instructed to read a short summary of Johnny Rocco's history, discuss it, and reach a group decision regarding the handling of his case. At one extreme, they might decide that he should be treated leniently, while at the other extreme, they might opt to sanction him severely. The case is complex and ambiguous, and it has no obviously right answer.

This group has been carefully selected to consist of members who are all "equal"—that is, of similar background, social characteristics, and age. All members are of the same sex, and the group has been assigned no formal leader.

When these persons begin their discussion, something interesting happens. The initial equality disappears and distinctions quickly arise among the members. Some participate more than others and exercise more influence regarding the group's decision. Members develop different expectations regarding one another's role in the group, and one or more persons start to provide the group with leadership.

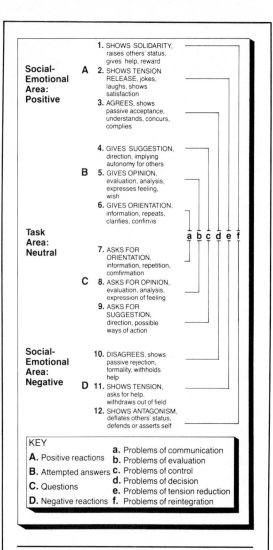

FIGURE 13.2

CODING CATEGORIES IN INTERACTION PROCESS
ANALYSIS

Interaction Process Analysis is a method of
analyzing patterns of communication among
group members. Researchers observe a group
in action and code members' acts into 12
distinct categories. Because these categories
are highly general, they apply regardless of
the specific topic or issue under discussion by
members. Half of the categories pertain to
task or instrumental acts, whereas the other
half pertain to social-emotional or affective
acts.

Source: adapted from Bales (1950).

Suppose we wanted to investigate the process through which these differences emerge
among group members. There are many ways
to do this. One good method is to monitor the
flow of communication among group members. By analyzing the patterns that occur (rate,
direction, and types of messages) we could
obtain a picture of the group's structure. One
problem with this approach is that groups
have different concerns. A group of civil engineers, for example, might want to discuss the
best way to repair an abandoned bridge; a
group of high-school teachers might be concerned with techniques for teaching algebra to
students; a group of basketball players might
ponder a way to increase rebounds and reduce
turnovers. The content of communication will
differ from group to group depending on the
problems or topics of concern. What we need,
then, is a coding system that is general enough
to apply to all groups but specific enough to
break down the flow of communication into
discrete and interpretable acts.

One approach to this is the coding system
called **interaction process analysis** (IPA),
developed by Bales (1950, 1970). The IPA system uses a limited number of categories that
apply to all problem-solving groups. Although
the content may differ from group to group,
any communicative act can be classified into
one of the IPA categories.

The IPA system consists of 12 categories
shown in Figure 13.2. The 12 IPA categories
may be grouped into clusters. The broadest
and most important distinction is that between
social-emotional acts and task acts. **Social-
emotional acts** (categories 1–3 and 10–12) are
emotional reactions, both positive and negative, directed toward other members in the
group. **Task acts** (categories 4–9) are instrumental behaviors that push the group toward
realization of its goals. Another breakdown of
IPA categories is designated by the letters a
through f. These letters represent problems
that confront any newly forming group.
Within the area of task acts are problems of
communication, evaluation, and control. Problems of communication involve analyzing the

situation; problems of evaluation refer to determining members' attitudes toward the situation; and problems of control refer to suggestions for action within a situation. Within the area of social-emotional acts are problems of decision, tension-reduction, and reintegration. Problems of decision refer to acceptance or rejection of proposed courses of action, whereas problems of tension-reduction and reintegration refer to the establishment and maintenance of emotional relations within the group.

In practice, the IPA system might be used as follows: Assume that a task group of seven persons is meeting in a room to discuss a given problem. Members are seated around the table with a number in front of each person. The room itself has one unusual feature—it is equipped with a one-way mirror along one wall so that observers seated behind the wall can monitor the group's interaction. Typically, the observers record the interaction in terms of (1) who speaks to whom and (2) what types of acts are communicated. For example, if Member 2 turned to Member 5 and asked 5's opinion on an issue, the observers would score this by writing "2-5" in IPA category 8. By following this procedure through an entire group session (which might run an hour or two), the observers will obtain a complete record of interaction within the group according to the IPA system.

WHO TALKS IN GROUPS? The IPA system provides a means of observing who talks in groups and what kinds of things they say. Investigators have used it to study a wide variety of problem-solving and discussion groups (Bales and Hare 1965). These studies involve groups of college students, enlisted men, patients undergoing psychotherapy, inmates in a state prison, jurors in mock trials, third-grade boys, and so on. Certain general findings emerge from all these studies. One of the most general is that group members do not participate equally in discussion. Some members talk more than others. Although it can vary, the most talkative person in the group

TABLE 13.1

PERCENTAGE OF TOTAL ACTS INITIATED BY EACH GROUP MEMBER AS A FUNCTION OF GROUP SIZE

Member Number	Group Size					
	3	4	5	6	7	8
1	44	32	47	43	43	40
2	33	29	22	19	15	17
3	23	23	15	14	12	13
4		16	10	11	10	10
5			6	8	9	9
6				5	6	6
7					5	4
8						3

Note: Data are based on a total of 134,421 acts observed via the IPA system in 167 groups consisting of 3 to 8 members.

Source: adapted from Bales (1970, pp. 467–70).

will typically initiate 40–45 percent of all communicative acts. The second most active person will do approximately 20–30 percent of the talking. This pattern is seen clearly in Table 13.1, which summarizes initiated acts for groups ranging from three to eight members. As the size of the group increases, the most talkative person initiates a consistently large percentage of communicative acts, while less talkative persons are crowded out almost completely. This relationship between group size and inequality of participation has been observed in many situations (Stephan and Mishler 1952; Bales and Slater 1955; Bales 1970).

A second basic finding based on IPA is that persons who initiate a great amount of communication also receive a lot in return from other group members. That is, the member who initiates the most communication also receives the most, the member who initiates the second most communication receives second most, and so on (Bales 1953).

A third finding from IPA studies concerns stability of participation: The group member who initiates the most communication during

TABLE 13.2

INTERACTION PROFILE: MEAN PERCENTAGE OF
IPA CATEGORY ACTS

Type of Act (IPA)	Mean Percentage
1. Shows solidarity	2.97
2. Shows tension release	8.17
3. Agrees	10.70
4. Gives suggestion	6.56
5. Gives opinion	22.24
6. Gives orientation	28.72
7. Asks for orientation	5.89
8. Asks for opinion	3.27
9. Asks for suggestion	0.60
10. Disagrees	4.73
11. Shows tension	3.43
12. Shows antagonism	2.41

Source: adapted from Bales and Hare (1965).

the first few minutes of interaction is very likely to continue doing so throughout the life of the group. If a problem-solving group meets for several sessions on successive days, for example, the member who ranked highest in the first session is very likely to rank highest in subsequent sessions. In general, the ranking of members in order of participation is constant over time (Fisek and Ofshe 1970; Fisek 1974).

WHAT TYPES OF ACTS OCCUR IN GROUPS? Up to this point we have considered findings that show differences among group members in the *number* of acts initiated. However, to understand interaction in task-oriented groups, we need to consider not only the quantity of acts, but also the *types* of acts that occur. IPA provides a convenient means of doing this.

As we have noted, the IPA system consists of 12 categories. Six of these pertain to task-oriented acts (categories 4-9), whereas the other six pertain to social-emotional acts (cate-

gories 1-3 and 10-12). Table 13.2 summarizes the typical pattern of acts for many problem-solving groups based on these 12 categories. As this table indicates, about two-thirds of the acts in a group session are task-oriented and about one-third are social-emotional (Bales and Hare 1965). Within the task-oriented categories, the majority of acts fall into categories 4-6 (gives suggestion, gives opinion, gives orientation), while fewer acts fall into categories 7-9 (asks for orientation, asks for opinions, asks for suggestions). Within the social-emotional categories, the majority of acts fall into the positive categories 1-3 (shows solidarity, shows tension release, agrees), and a smaller proportion fall into the negative categories 10-12 (disagrees, shows tension, shows antagonism). Intuitively, this pattern makes sense. The efforts of a problem-solving group would surely be self-defeating if there were more questions than problem-solving attempts and more negative emotional reactions than positive ones.

Of course, we might expect groups to differ in their interaction profiles. Whereas Table 13.2 shows the average or typical interaction profile of a group, consider what happened in an IPA study of Finnish government employees who volunteered to interact in groups of four to six members while drinking brandy and beer (Takala, Pihkanen, and Markkanen 1957). The groups met in a room suitably prepared with tables and tablecloths. Results showed that, compared with normal interaction for these groups measured earlier, the intoxicated groups had low levels of task activity (IPA categories 4-9), and high levels of negative social-emotional activity (especially disagreement and antagonism). These governmental groups had a low level of solidarity even when not intoxicated, so the alcohol may have provided an occasion for voicing latent disagreements. The point to note is that the profile shown in Table 13.2 reflects the *average* problem-solving group, not all groups under all conditions.

Box 13.1
SOCIOMETRY

Interaction Process Analysis (IPA) can be used to measure not only status differences between members but also the flow of conversation in a group. These measurements reveal the naturally occurring communication channels in the group, and therefore provide some insight into group structure.

Communication is only one aspect of group structure, however. Other aspects include patterns of influence (who gives orders to whom) and patterns of attraction (who likes whom). Consider, for instance, the measurement of attraction in groups. One of the first empirical approaches designed to measure patterns of attraction was *sociometry* (Moreno 1934). This technique—which can be used in various groups such as classes, committees, and residential units—is fairly straightforward. Each person in the group is asked to name others in the group whom he or she likes according to some criterion. For example, students in a classroom may be asked whom they want to sit next to, work with, or play with during recess. In residential settings, persons may be asked whom they want to eat with or have as a roommate. Sometimes they are also asked the opposite question: Whom do you dislike, whom do you not want as a roommate? The resulting choices can then be diagrammed in a distinctive figure called a *sociogram*.

Conventionally, each person in a sociogram is represented by a circle. Choices made by persons are represented by arrows; solid arrows indicate a positive choice or liking, whereas broken arrows indicate disliking.

A typical sociogram is displayed below.

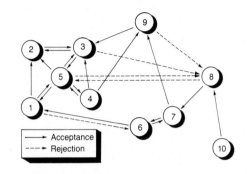

Source: adapted from Jahoda, Deutsch, and Cook (1951).

The distance between circles represents the closeness of a relationship. Two persons who choose one another are positioned close together (see persons 1 and 5 in the sociogram above), whereas two persons who reject one another are far apart (see persons 5 and 8).

Various aspects of group structure can be seen in a sociogram. For instance, person 5, who is liked by many other members, is considered a "star." Person 10, who was chosen by no one, is considered an "isolate." Persons 1, 2, 3, 4, and 5—who chose each other and thus form a tight subgroup—constitute a "clique." Patterns such as these affect the emotional climate in a group. In general, groups characterized by many reciprocal positive choices will have a happy, positive climate. In contrast, groups with several isolates or several distinct cliques usually have a very chilly climate.

Task Leaders and
Social-Emotional Leaders

The IPA system has proved valuable in documenting the emergence of role differentiation and leadership within groups. One study (Bales 1953) investigated a number of five-man groups that met to discuss a problem in a laboratory setting. Group interaction was scored by observers using the IPA system. At the end of the discussion period, members filled out questionnaires in which they were asked to rate each other. Items included such

Members of this airline crew are ranked based on their status. The pilot has greater responsibility and control and receives greater rewards than the co-pilot or navigator. Located elsewhere in the aircraft are the flight attendants, the lowest ranking members of the crew.

questions as: "Who had the best ideas in the group?", "Who did the most to guide the group discussion?", and "Which group member was the most likable?" Typically, there was high agreement among group members in their answers regarding ideas and guidance, although less agreement in their answers regarding liking.

In addition, this study showed a high correlation between participation rank as measured by the IPA system and members' perceptions of one another as measured by questionnaire. The person who initiated the most acts was perceived by others as providing the most guidance and offering the best ideas. In short, the person initiating the most acts was perceived as the group's leader.

But this is not the entire picture. The person initiating the most acts was usually *not* the best-liked member, and indeed was sometimes the most disliked member. The best-liked person was typically the second-highest initiator. Why does this occur?

In general, the highest initiator is someone who drives the group toward attainment of its goals. A high proportion of acts initiated by this person are task oriented (IPA categories 4, 5, 6). For this reason, the high initiator is referred to as the **task leader.** This person contributes many ideas and suggestions, and pushes the group toward achievement of its objectives. However, in the effort to get things done, the task specialist tends to be pushy and openly antagonistic in some instances. He or she makes the most influence attempts and has the most impact on the group's opinion, but this aggressive behavior frequently creates tension. Thus it remains for some other member, called the **social-emotional leader,** to ease the tension and soothe hurt feelings. The acts initiated by this person are likely to be acts showing tension, tension release, and solidarity (IPA categories 11, 2 and 1). The social-emotional leader is the one who exercises tact or tells a joke at just the right moment. This person helps to release tensions and maintain good spirits within the group. Not surprisingly, the social-emotional leader is often the best-liked member of the group.

Thus, in small task-oriented groups, there are two basic leadership functions—getting things done, and keeping relationships pleasant. These will typically be performed by different members. Very frequently these persons work closely together and complement one another. For example, the task and social-emotional leaders tend to interact more with one another and to agree more with each other than with other members of the group (Burke 1968, 1972).

The emergence of distinct task leaders and social-emotional leaders is a common occurrence, although it does not happen invariably. In some groups, both the task and the social-emotional functions are performed by a single member, called a "great man" or "great person." Available data suggest that a single member successfully performs both of these functions in about 15 percent of the cases (Slater 1955). This happens when the high initiator (the task leader) recognizes the importance of attending to the emotional needs of group members. In such cases, there is no need for a separate social-emotional leader (Lewis 1972).

Status Characteristics and Social Interaction

So far we have considered problem-solving groups consisting of members who are initially equal in status. The IPA technique shows that, despite members' initial equality, differences in status quickly emerge within the group setting. Members differ in their rate of participation, influence over group decisions, and the types of acts they contribute.

But what about interaction in a newly formed group whose members are *not* equal? In particular, what about groups that include members of different sexes, races, ages, and occupations? We encounter such groups every day—PTA's, student committees, neighborhood associations, juries, church groups, and

so on. In fact, groups of this type are probably more common than groups consisting of equal-status members.

Individual properties such as race or occupation are referred to as status characteristics. A **status characteristic** is any property of a person around which evaluations and beliefs about that person come to be organized. In addition to race and occupation, properties such as age, sex, ethnicity, education, and physical attractiveness are status characteristics (Berger, Cohen, and Zelditch 1972). Status characteristics involve evaluation that is based to a large degree on cultural stereotypes. In the United States, for example, it is preferable to be male rather than female, an adult rather than a child, white rather than black, and white-collar rather than blue-collar. Although we may not think of ourselves as influenced by someone's age, sex, or race, we are in fact very sensitive to these properties. In group settings, we develop different evaluations of members having different status characteristics (Berger, Rosenholtz, and Zelditch 1980).

Status Generalization

Status characteristics can significantly affect interaction in newly forming groups. Persons with high standing on various status characteristics tend to be accorded high status within such groups. They receive more respect and esteem than other members, and they are chosen more frequently as leaders. Their contributions to group problem solving are evaluated more highly, they are given more chance to participate in discussions, and they exert more influence over group decisions. The process through which differences in members' status characteristics affect group interactions is called **status generalization.** A large number of studies have documented status generalization in group settings (Hurwitz, Zander, and Hymovitch 1960; Berger, Cohen, and Zelditch, 1972; Freese and Cohen 1973).

As an illustration, consider how status generalization can occur in a jury. The members of a jury—who usually differ among

TABLE 13.3

RATES OF PARTICIPATION DURING DELIBERATION BY OCCUPATION AND SEX OF JUROR

Sex	Occupation				
	Proprietor	*Clerical*	*Skilled*	*Laborer*	*Combined Average*
Male	12.9	10.8	7.9	7.5	9.6
Female	9.1	7.8	4.8	4.6	6.6
Combined Average	11.8	9.2	7.1	6.4	8.5

Note: Entries in this table are percentage rates of participation. Since there were 12 persons on a jury, the "average" juror would theoretically have a rate of participation of 8.3 percent. This can be used as a frame of reference against which to compare tabled values. (The "combined-combined" value in the table is 8.5, rather than 8.3, because 26 of 588 jurors in the study were not satisfactorily classified by occupation and are omitted.)

Source: adapted from Strodtbeck, Simon, and Hawkins (1965).

themselves in status characteristics—must discuss a complex problem and come to a group decision. A classic study by Strodtbeck, Simon, and Hawkins (1965) demonstrated that certain status characteristics, such as occupation and sex, can have an impact on jury deliberations. Because the law does not permit the observation of actual jury deliberations, researchers studied mock juries designed to be as authentic as possible. Like real juries, members were selected from the voter registration list in an urban area. The juries consisted of men and women of varying occupational status, including proprietors, clerical workers, and skilled and unskilled laborers. They listened to a tape recording of a trial, after which they were instructed to do everything a real jury does: select a foreman, deliberate on the case, and reach a verdict. Researchers recorded the jurors' deliberations. At the end of the session, jurors completed a questionnaire to indicate their impressions of each other.

From the recording, it was possible to determine which members talked the most. Table 13.3 shows the rates of participation by jury members as a function of their occupation and sex. The results show clearly that men initiated more interaction than women in the mock juries. The data also show the impact of occupational status: The higher the occupational status, the greater the rate of participation. This holds for both males and females.

The questionnaire completed by jurors at the end of the session provided information on their perceptions of one another. Table 13.4 shows the number of votes received by the jury members for being "most helpful in reaching the verdict." This measure reflects the amount of influence each member had over the group decision, as perceived by other members. The findings are very similar to those on the rates of participation. Male jurors were more often perceived as helpful than female jurors, and jurors of high occupational status were more often perceived as helpful than those of lower occupational status. These findings illustrate the status generalization effect.

Another finding concerns the selection of a jury foreman. Jury members chose the foreman before deliberating. Because the foreman's role is task-related, they probably made their choice on the basis of perceived ability. Persons with a high-status occupation (proprietors) were chosen as jury foreman about twice as often as would be expected on the basis of their representation in the sample, whereas persons with low occupational status (unskilled laborers) were chosen only half as often as their representation in the sample would suggest. The impact of occupational status on leadership in groups is substantial.

Overall, this jury study reveals the impact of status generalization. Persons with higher standing in terms of sex and occupation became the group members with higher status inside the group. They participated at a higher rate, were perceived as contributing more to the group's problem-solving efforts, and were more frequently chosen as the formal leader.

Although the findings in this study seem clear-cut, the interpretation in terms of status generalization is admittedly open to criticism. A critic might argue, for example, that a person's status inside a group is not a function of his or her status outside, but merely reflects the same qualities that determined that person's outside status. For example, people of high occupational status may be more intelligent, or possibly more experienced in leadership, than people of lower occupational status. One or both of these qualities could enable them to contribute heavily within the group.

To further our understanding of status generalization, several controlled studies have attempted to manipulate status characteristics experimentally. One of these studies (Moore 1968) investigated female subjects in small, two-person groups. Both women were shown

a series of large figures made up of smaller black and white rectangles. Their task was to judge which of the two colors, black or white, covered the greater area in each of the large figures. It was a difficult task because the areas were in fact approximately equal, making the figures ambiguous. The subjects, who were seated so that they could not see or talk with each other, indicated their preliminary judgments by pressing buttons on consoles in front of them. Each subject's answer was revealed to the other through a system of lights. After making their initial judgments, the subjects had been told that they should weigh their own answers against the answers of their partners, and that the goal was to make their final judgments correct. The subjects did not know, however, that the connections on the consoles were in fact controlled by the experimenter. He could manipulate how often one subject perceived that the partner disagreed with her. Between their first judgment and their final judgment, subjects were free to reverse their decisions when their partners appeared to disagree with them.

All of the subjects in this experiment were junior-college students. To manipulate status, one half were told that their partners were high-school students (low-status partner), whereas the other half were led to believe that their partners were from Stanford University (high-status partner). The results show that the women who believed their partners to be

TABLE 13.4
AVERAGE VOTES RECEIVED AS "HELPFUL JUROR" BY OCCUPATION AND SEX OF JUROR

Sex	Occupation				
	Proprietor	Clerical	Skilled	Laborer	Combined Average
Male	6.8	4.2	3.9	2.7	4.3
Female	3.2	2.7	2.0	1.5	2.3
Combined Average	6.0	3.4	3.5	2.3	3.6

Source: adapted from Strodtbeck, Simon, and Hawkins (1965).

Jury members listen to testimony by a witness. Although formally of equal status, some jury members may be more influential than others in determining the verdict. Characteristics such as occupation, gender, and race can affect the deliberations of jury members.

of higher status changed their answers on the judgmental task more often than those who thought themselves to have the higher status. In other words, group members were receptive to influence from a higher-status person, but relatively unreceptive to influence from a lower-status person. The random assignment of subjects to experimental treatments eliminates the possibility that subjects differed systematically in ability on the judgmental task. Thus, receptiveness to influence depended on status expectations, not task ability. These findings, like those from the mock jury research, support the case for status generalization.

Status Characteristics and Performance Expectations

Why does status generalization occur? That is, why do the status characteristics of group members affect the interaction occurring within the group?

The answer is that status characteristics cause group members to form expectations regarding one another's potential performance on the group's task. These performance expectations, which are to some degree based on cultural stereotypes, affect subsequent interaction among members. Group members are more likely to defer to and accept influence from those persons whom they expect to perform well than those they expect to perform poorly (Berger and Fisek 1974; Berger et al. 1977).

In order for status characteristics such as race, sex, or age to affect behavior, they must be salient to group members. Any circumstance that fosters this will increase the probability of status generalization. Thus, status generalization is most likely to occur when group members (1) have no prior history of interaction; (2) have no information about one another except for their standing on status characteristics; and (3) have no special experience or information about the group's task.

When generalizing from status characteristics, group members behave as though the burden of proof is placed on demonstrating that characteristics are *not* relevant to the task at hand, rather than showing that they are relevant. In the absence of such a demonstration, group members will treat status characteristics as relevant even when they are not. For example, suppose a group is developing plans to take a weekend trip. Although status characteristics (such as race, sex, and occupation) may not in fact be relevant to performance on this task, the group's members will behave as if they are relevant. The members will be willing to ignore these status characteristics only after there has been some explicit demonstration or proof that they are not relevant to performance in planning the trip. This may seem surprising, but the process has been tested and confirmed in several studies (Berger, Cohen, and Zelditch 1972; Freese 1974, 1976; Webster and Driskell 1978).

As already noted, each member in a newly forming group possesses a variety of status characteristics. How, then, do members combine information on two or more status characteristics to form performance expectations regarding a given person? What performance expectations result if that person's standing on one status characteristic is inconsistent with his or her standing on another?

For example, consider the case of a female physician. Such a person has inconsistent status characteristics. On one hand, she is a female, and many studies show that this is perceived as a lower-status characteristic than being male (Zimmerman and West 1975; Deaux and Emswiller 1974; Megargee 1969; Berger, Rosenholtz, and Zelditch 1980). On the other hand, she is a physician and this is a high-status characteristic. How would group members respond to her? Clearly there are several possibilities. They might ignore one of the status characteristics and focus on the other. In other words, they might respond to her only as a woman or only as a physician. Alter-natively, they might combine both status characteristics to form some kind of intermediate expectation. Studies have shown that, in general, members form an intermediate expectation in these cases, rather than focusing on only one or another of these status characteristics (Berger and Fisek 1970; Freese 1974; Webster and Driskell 1978). Thus, confronted with a female physician, group members would consider her more competent than female nonphysicians, but less competent than male physicians.

Overcoming Status Generalization

Status generalization often works to an individual's disadvantage. For example, in a mixed setting with both males and females, the females may find that they are not permitted to participate fully or to influence the group's decision significantly even though they are as qualified as males with respect to the problem under discussion. Likewise, in interracial interactions between blacks and whites, the blacks may feel that they are treated as low-status minority members. Because irrelevant status characteristics can so easily place someone at a disadvantage, we might ask whether status generalization can be overcome or eliminated in face-to-face interaction.

Some persons have suggested that the best way to overcome status generalization is by direct methods—that is, to raise the expectations of lower-status persons regarding their own performance, so that they can in turn force a change in other people's expectations regarding their performance on group tasks. Unfortunately, this approach does not work especially well. In one study, for example, blacks at a northern university were trained in assertiveness techniques. They then participated with whites in biracial groups. The training raised the blacks' expectations for themselves, and they behaved in an assertive and confident manner. But because the whites' expectations regarding the blacks' performance were not affected by the training, what ensued was not smooth interaction but a status struggle. From the whites' viewpoint, the black members behaved inappropriately considering their "low ability." From the blacks' viewpoint, the whites behaved inappropriately by refusing to recognize the blacks' equal ability. The whites thought the blacks seemed arrogant, whereas the blacks viewed the whites as racist bigots (Katz and Cohen 1962; Katz 1970).

This demonstrates that, to overcome status generalization, one must change not only the expectations of minority members, but also those of majority members. Although this is not always easy, it can be accomplished. Studies of black and white boys have shown that by modifying the expectations of *both* it is possible to create status-equal interaction. For instance, in one study (Cohen and Roper 1972), investigators taught black junior-high school students how to build a radio, then showed them how to teach another pupil to build a radio. This created two specific status characteristics inconsistent with students' conceptions of race. They then had the blacks train white pupils to build a radio, thereby establishing the relative superiority of the blacks on this task. Finally, they informed some of their students that the skills involved in building the radio and teaching others to build it were relevant to another, entirely different task. This task was a decision-making game called "Kill the Bull," which the boys subsequently played. Results of the study indicated that this pattern of training modified the performance expectations held by both black and white boys. The change in expectations produced a significant increase in equality between blacks and whites, as indicated by who exercised influence over decisions when the boys played Kill the Bull. The general conclusion is that status generalization can be prevented, provided that the expectations of both minority and majority persons are modified simultaneously. Similar findings appear in related studies (Cohen, Lockheed, and Lohman 1976; Riordan and Ruggiero 1980).

Even when direct methods are not applicable, there are indirect methods of overcoming status generalization. One of these is to block the burden-of-proof assumption noted earlier. That is, to convince group members that a status characteristic is not relevant to the task at hand. In some settings, this can be accomplished by having a credible authority say something like, "We know from experience that race is not relevant to the task at hand. That is, some whites do well and some do poorly, and some blacks do well and some do poorly." Such methods have been shown to prevent members from forming task expectations on the basis of such status characteristics as race or sex (Webster and Driskell 1978; Berger, Rosenholtz, and Zelditch 1980).

Equity and Reward Distribution

So far we have considered the *sources* of status differences among group members. It is clear that status differences arise from variations in skill and motivation that affect group goal attainment, as well as from various characteristics (age, sex, race, or occupation) that create expectations regarding performance in group contexts. This next section will focus on the *consequences* that result from status differences. In particular, we will discuss the distribution of rewards and benefits among group members.

When members contribute to the attainment of group goals, they typically receive benefits in return. This form of exchange occurs in many groups. It is especially evident in work situations, where group members contribute their labor and skill to produce the group's product, and receive rewards such as money and approval in return.

Although all members obtain some benefits in exchange for their contributions, not everyone receives the same amount. In a work group, for example, higher rewards are often allotted to the high-status members—that is, higher rewards go to those persons who have higher levels of skill relevant to the group's task and who contribute more toward goal attainment (Parcel and Cook 1977). The distribution of rewards within a group is a matter of concern to all members because it raises questions of justice and fairness. Most individuals care not only about their own rewards, but also about the rewards their fellow members receive.

There are many criteria that members might use in judging the fairness and appropriateness of the distribution of rewards (Deutsch 1975; Leventhal 1976). They might follow the *equity principle* and distribute rewards in proportion to members' contributions. Alternatively, they might use the *equality principle* and distribute rewards equally among members, regardless of members' contributions. Or, they could follow the *needs principle* and distribute rewards in accordance with members' personal needs. Although there are other possible criteria, the principles of equity, equality, and need are especially important in reward distribution (Lamm and Schwinger 1980).

A group may rely exclusively on one of these principles when allocating rewards among members, or it may apply several of them simultaneously. These principles appear contradictory in the sense that they would lead to different distributions of rewards, but what really matters is the relative importance (or weighting) accorded each principle. Not surprisingly, their relative importance varies from group to group and from situation to situation. For instance, the equity principle may be very important in work situations where persons are concerned with receiving their share of the profit. The equality principle often prevails in situations where members are concerned with solidarity and wish to avoid conflict (Leventhal, Michaels, and Sanford 1972). There is some evidence that females favor the equality principle more than do males (Leventhal and Lane 1970; Bond and Vinacke 1961). The needs principle is frequently salient in intimate relationships involving friends, lovers, and relatives. However, this principle has also been invoked in other contexts—Karl Marx, for example, advocated the adoption of the needs principle in communist societies where individuals would contribute according to their abilities and receive according to their needs.

Equity Theory

The principle of equity has been discussed by many theorists (Homans 1961, 1974; Adams 1963, 1965; Walster, Walster, and Berscheid 1978; Blalock and Wilken 1979). By definition, **equity** occurs when members receive rewards in proportion to the contributions they make to the group. This principle is very important because, among other things, its application fosters high levels of task performance. There is substantial evidence that group productivity is strengthened when high rewards are given to good performers and low rewards are given to poor performers (Burnstein 1969; Lawler 1971; Leventhal 1976).

The equity principle is applicable to many settings. For example, in a work setting, one person would expect to receive better outcomes (salary, benefits) than another person if his or her job required more input (higher skill, more hours per week, and so on). In a marriage, a wife would feel that the outcomes are inequitable if she contributes more to the relationship than her husband, but receives little help or love in return. As these examples show, equity judgments are made when one group member compares his or her own outcomes and inputs with the outcomes and inputs of another member. This comparison can be expressed in terms of the following equation:

$$\frac{\text{Person A's outcomes}}{\text{Person A's inputs}} = \frac{\text{Person B's outcomes}}{\text{Person B's inputs}}$$

This equation states that equity exists when the ratio of person A's outcomes to inputs is equal to the ratio of person B's outcomes to inputs. What matters is not merely the level of outcomes or inputs but the equality in the ratio of outcomes to inputs.

To make this concrete, consider the case of two women employed by the same industrial corporation. One of the women (person A) receives a high outcome: a salary of $45,000 a year, four weeks of paid vacation, reserved parking in the company's lot, and a fancy corner office with thick rugs and a nice view. The other woman (person B) is about the same age but gets fewer rewards. She earns $14,000 per year, receives no paid vacation, has no reserved parking, and works in a cramped office with no windows and a lot of noise.

Will persons A and B feel that this distribution of rewards is equitable? They may or they may not—it depends on their relative inputs. If their inputs to the company are identical, then the arrangement will almost certainly be experienced as inequitable, especially by person B. For example, if both A and B work a 40-hour week, have only high-school educations, and are equally lacking in experience, there is little basis for paying person A more than person B. Person B will feel angry because the reward distribution is inequitable. Person A may also sense the inequity and feel guilty or uncomfortable.

Suppose instead that person A's inputs are much greater than B's. Let's say that person A works 60 hours per week, holds an advanced degree such as an MBA, and has 12 years of relevant experience in the industry. Suppose also that the work being done by person A involves a high level of stress because it entails the risk of serious failure and financial loss for the company. In this event, A not only has greater "investments" (that is, education and experience) but is also bearing greater immediate "costs" (60 hours of work per week, including stress). Person A may receive better outcomes, but she also contributes more to the company. Under these conditions, both A and B may feel that their outcomes, while not equal, are nevertheless equitable.

Although this illustrates the basic difference between an equitable and an inequitable relationship, precise calculations regarding equity can be difficult to make in everyday life. Two persons may view the same situation in different ways. They may disagree, for instance, over how to evaluate particular inputs and outcomes. If one worker holds an advanced university degree while another worker has seven years' job seniority, who is contributing the more important input? Persons may also disagree over which inputs and outcomes are to be included in the equity calcuation. This issue arises, for example, with respect to pay for women in our society. In some jobs, women perform the same activities as men, but they receive less pay for their efforts; in short, they do not receive equal pay for equal work. Many people feel such an arrangement is inequitable. They argue that a worker's gender should be irrelevant (not considered as an input) in the equity calculation. As these examples show, equity may be difficult to measure.

Responses to Inequity

Inequity produces strong emotional reactions (anger, guilt), as well as direct attempts to change the conditions that produce it. By eliminating inequity, group members can rid themselves of emotional distress. There are two distinct types of inequity: **underreward** and **overreward.** Underreward occurs when a person's outcomes are too small relative to inputs; overreward occurs when a person's outcomes are too large relative to inputs.

RESPONSES TO UNDERREWARD. Persons who are underrewarded usually become dissatisfied or angry (Austin and Walster 1974; Leventhal, Weiss, and Long 1969). The greater the degree of underreward, the greater the dissatisfaction and the desire to restore equity. To illustrate, suppose that person A is underrewarded in a relationship. In this case, inequity may be expressed as follows:

$$\frac{\text{Person A's outcomes}}{\text{Person A's inputs}} < \frac{\text{Person B's outcomes}}{\text{Person B's inputs}}$$

This states that person A's ratio of outcomes to inputs is less than B's ratio. Given this situaion of underreward, any of various actions ould restore equity between A and B. These nclude: (1) increase the outcomes received by A; (2) reduce the inputs from A; (3) reduce the outcomes received by B; or (4) increase the inputs from B.

Studies show that most underrewarded people take direct steps to reduce inequity. If the situation permits, they will attempt to reduce inequity by increasing their outcomes. This would occur, for example, if the person had the ability to reallocate rewards in the group directly (Leventhal, Allen, and Kemelgor 1969; Schmitt and Marwell 1972). A related method of reducing inequity is sometimes used by industrial workers paid on a piece rate basis. A worker who feels underrewarded might reduce the quality of his effort on each piece in order to increase the total number of pieces produced per hour. This will allow the worker to increase his outcomes without increasing his input (Andrews 1967; Lawler and O'Gara 1967).

RESPONSES TO OVERREWARD. What happens when someone receives more than a fair share in a relationship? Would he be content just to enjoy the benefits? Indeed, overreward is apparently less troubling to people than is underreward. However, people who feel guilty and/or indebted may attempt to rectify the inequity (Pritchard, Dunnette, and Jorgensen 1972; Austin and Walster 1974).

Suppose that person A is overrewarded in a relationship. In this case, inequity is expressed as follows:

$$\frac{\text{Person A's outcomes}}{\text{Person A's inputs}} > \frac{\text{Person B's outcomes}}{\text{Person B's inputs}}$$

This states that person A's ratio of outcomes to inputs is greater than person B's ratio. Given this situation, any of the following changes could restore equity: (1) reduce the outcomes received by A; (2) increase the inputs from A; (3) increase the outcomes received by B; and (4) reduce the inputs from B.

Research findings indicate that, in some situations, overrewarded individuals will sacrifice some of their rewards to increase those of others. Frequently, however, the extent of the redistribution will not be complete, and equity will be only partially restored (Leventhal, Weiss, and Long 1969). Other times, overrewarded persons may prefer to restore equity by increasing their inputs. In a work situation, for example, overrewarded members may strive to produce more or better products as a means of reducing inequity (Goodman and Friedman 1971).

This process was demonstrated in a classic study (Adams and Jacobson 1964) in which students were hired to work as proofreaders. In one condition, subjects were told that they were not really qualified for the job (due to inadequate experience and poor test scores), but they were nevertheless paid the same rate as professional proofreaders (30 cents per page). In a second condition, subjects were told that, due to their lack of qualifications, they would be paid a reduced rate (20 cents per page). In a third condition, subjects were told they had adequate experience and ability for the job, and they were paid the full 30-cent rate. Subjects in the first condition were overrewarded, whereas those in the second and third conditions saw the pay as fair. Measures of the quality of students' work showed that significantly more errors were caught by the overrewarded students than by the equitably paid students. In fact, the overrewarded students were so vigilant that they often challenged the accuracy of material that was correct. These results show that overrewarded students increased their inputs, thereby restoring equity. Similar findings appear in related studies (Adams and Rosenbaum 1962; Goodman and Friedman 1969).

OTHER RESPONSES TO INEQUITY. We have noted that inequity—both underreward and overreward—can be resolved by changing outcomes and/or inputs. There are other ways of coping

Equality in marriage can mean various things. For this couple, it means sharing the housework. What might happen to their relationship if the husband insisted on doing less around the house?

with inequity, however. Although these methods do not rectify the conditions producing the inequity, they make it more tolerable. As one method, a person who is underrewarded might choose a different person for comparison. Instead of comparing her inputs and outcomes with those of person B, she might compare them with person C. By adjusting her frame of reference, A may see the situation in a different light and experience less inequity.

Another way to cope with inequity is to withdraw from the situation entirely. An individual may choose to resign from her job, for example, rather than continue to perform under severe inequity. This may lead to behavior that seems economically irrational. For

instance, one study found that workers were often willing to accept an alternative position that paid less in order to remove themselves from severe inequity (Schmitt and Marwell 1972).

Still another way to reduce inequity is through perceptual distortion. By distorting inputs and outcomes, equity may be reestablished in a psychological sense. For example, an employer might convince himself that his overworked and underpaid secretary is in fact being treated equitably by minimizing the secretary's inputs ("You wouldn't believe how incompetent she is!") or exaggerating the outcomes ("Work gives her a chance to socialize with all her friends"). This distortion precludes any need to reduce the secretary's work load or increase her salary (Walster, Berscheid, and Walster 1973).

Perceptual distortion is especially convenient for those who are overrewarded. If someone is receiving more than he deserves, he might simply conclude that his inputs are greater than he originally believed. This will eliminate any need to reallocate rewards. Perceptual distortion of this type has been observed in task situations (Gergen, Morse, and Bode 1974).

Equity in Intimate Relationships

So far most of our examples regarding equity have involved work and business settings. However, equity theory may also be applied to intimate relationships. Initially one might think that the concept of equity is not especially relevant in intimate relationships, or that these relationships are somehow above considerations of give and take (Clark and Mills 1979). Nevertheless, theorists (Blau 1964) have argued that equity is relevant to personal relationships and that, indeed, people end up paired only with partners with whom they can establish equitable exchanges. In dating and marital relationships, as in work situations, people make contributions and receive outcomes. Thus, we might expect that persons will be happier and more content if they believe their intimate relationship is equitable, rather than inequitable.

This hypothesis was tested in a study of 500 undergraduates involved in heterosexual dating relationships (Walster, Walster, and Traupmann 1978). These individuals were asked to evaluate their inputs in the relationship, including personal contributions (physical attractiveness, intelligence), emotional contributions (being loving and understanding), and day-to-day contributions (taking care of housework, helping to make decisions). Individuals were also asked to evaluate the outcomes they were receiving from the relationship. Results indicated that students who believed their relationship was equitable (that is, involved a balance between their own and their partner's outcomes and inputs) were more content and happy with the relationship. Students who felt their relationship was inequitable (because they were putting more into it than they received) were more resentful and angry. The results also show that persons with equitable relationships were more physically intimate and sexually involved than persons with inequitable relations.

Just as equity is relevant to dating relationships, it is also a significant variable in marriage. Each spouse contributes some things to the relationship, including financial support, parenting, day-to-day maintenance of the household, emotional companionship, and love. Suppose that one member feels that he or she is contributing more than is being returned. A wife, for example, may feel that she is giving far more to the family than she is receiving. When she compares herself with her husband—who brings home a small paycheck, doesn't help with the housework, and refuses to spend much time with the kids—the relationship may seem inequitable. A situation like this can induce not only anger, but also psychological depression.

In one study investigating the relationship between inequity and depression (Schafer and Keith 1980), 333 married couples responded to questions about equity/inequity in the performance of five family roles (cooking, housekeeping, provider, companion, and parent). The study also measured symptoms of depression, including the frequency with which respondents experienced poor appetite, lack of enthusiasm, boredom, loss of sexual interest, trouble sleeping, crying easily, feeling downhearted or blue, feeling low in energy, feeling lonely, and feeling hopeless about the future. Results indicate that psychological depression was related to marital inequity. In other words, husbands and wives who felt there was equity in the performance of family roles were less depressed than respondents who felt either underbenefited or overbenefited.

Authority and Obedience

In many groups, high-status persons exercise a substantial amount of influence over other members. Typically, this influence is based in authority, rather than in the direct use of threats and promises. By definition, **authority** refers to the capacity to influence other members by invoking rights that are vested in one's role.

Obedience to authority is an everyday matter. Orders issued by policemen, decisions rendered by judges, directives specified by corporate executives, and exhortations made by clergymen all involve the invocation of norms. A person can exercise authority only when, by virtue of the role that he or she occupies in a group, other members accept his or her right to prescribe behavior for the issue at hand (French and Raven 1959; Raven and Kruglanski 1970). In essence, the person exercising authority activates an obligation that requires the target person(s) to comply. The more persons that can be directly or indirectly influenced in this manner, the greater a person's authority within the group (Homans 1974; Zelditch 1972; Michener and Burt 1974).

Because it involves invocation of norms, authority can be exercised only within certain contexts. If you happen to observe a military parade on the 4th of July, for example, and you hear the commanding officer issue an order to "About face," the troops will turn around and face the opposite direction, but you yourself will not obey the order. The officer's authority does not extend to you, because you are not a member of the military unit. You are outside the group's boundaries and beyond the officer's influence.

Milgram's Study of Obedience

One issue regarding authority concerns its limits. Although obedience to authority frequently produces beneficial results, it sometimes produces negative consequences, especially when orders are morally questionable. The Third Reich of Nazi Germany provides a chilling example. In complying with the dictates of Hitler's authoritarian government, German citizens committed what most people consider morally unconscionable actions— beatings, torture, confiscation of property, even murder—against millions of others.

A series of classic experiments by Milgram (1963, 1965a, 1974) explored the limits of obedience to legitimate authority. In a controlled setting, these studies created a situation in which one person (the authority) directed another person (the subject) to engage in actions that hurt a third person (the victim). Subjects in these experiments, recruited through newspaper advertisements, were adults, aged 20 to 50 years, with diverse occupations (laborers, blue-collar, white-collar, and professional). Subjects were paid a small monetary fee for participating in the study.

When a subject arrived for the experiment, he found that another person (a gentle, 47-year-old accountant) had also responded to the newspaper advertisement. The experimenter, dressed in a lab coat, indicated that the purpose of the research was to study the effects of punishment (that is, electric shock) on learning. One of the subjects was to occupy the role of teacher, and the other of learner. A random drawing was held, and the accountant was selected to be the learner. He was then taken into the adjacent room and strapped into an

"electric chair." During this process, the accountant mentioned that he had some heart trouble and expressed concern that the shock might prove excessively dangerous. The experimenter replied that the shock would be painful but would not cause permanent damage.

The other subject, now in the role of teacher, was taken into a separate room and seated in front of an electric shock generator. This generator was equipped with 30 voltage levels ranging from 15 to 450 volts. The lowest voltage level was labelled *slight shock*; a higher level read *danger: severe shock*; the highest level was ominously marked *XXX*. The experimenter gave the teacher a sample shock of 45 volts to show him how the generator worked. Even at this low level, the shock was painful.

The learning session was structured somewhat like a multiple-choice exam. The teacher read word pairs over an intercom system to the accountant in the adjacent room. After reciting the entire list, the teacher then read aloud the first word of a pair and four alternatives for the second word of the pair. The learner's task was to select the correct alternative response. In accordance with directives from the experimenter, the teacher was to shock the learner whenever he gave an incorrect response. The first shock was to begin at the lowest level (15 volts) and then increase to the next higher voltage with each successive error. Thus, the voltages were to increase from 15 to 30 to 45 on up to the 450-volt maximum.

The accountant proved to be a slow learner. Although getting a few answers right, he responded incorrectly on numerous trials. The required level of shock moved up quickly. Although a few subjects serving in the teacher role refused to administer high levels of shock, most were willing to proceed with the task.

When the shock level reached 75 volts, the victim grunted loudly. At 120 volts, he shouted that the shocks were becoming painful. At 150 volts, he demanded to be let out of the experiment ("Get me out of here! I won't be in the experiment anymore! I refuse to go on!") When the shock level reached 180 volts, he cried out that he could not withstand the pain. At 270 volts, his response to the shock was an agonized scream. Whenever a subject administering the shock expressed concern about the procedure, the experimenter calmly instructed him to persist ("You have no other choice, you must go on").

At the 300-volt level, the accountant shouted in desperation that he wanted to be released from the electric chair and would not provide any further answers to the test. The experimenter, however, instructed the subject to treat any refusal to answer as an incorrect response. At the 315-volt level, the learner gave out a violent scream. At the 330-volt level, he fell completely silent. The experimenter directed the subject to continue routinely toward the 450-volt maximum even though the learner did not respond.

The focus of this experiment by Milgram concerns the subject's compliance to the experimenter's directives. What percentage of the subjects in the teacher's role continued to administer shock up to the 450-volt maximum? That is, how effective is legitimate power?

As you may have guessed, the accountant receiving the shock was a professional actor hired by the experimenter. He was not actually receiving any shocks. The shouts and screams that subjects heard from the adjacent room were from carefully crafted tape recordings. Nevertheless, the actor's performance was extremely realistic, and post-experimental interviews show that subjects believed they were administering shocks to the learner.

The results of this study are astonishing. Milgram (1963, 1974) ran several variations of the basic research design described here. Hundreds of subjects were involved, and more than 60 percent of those in the basic experimental situation continued to administer shock up to the highest possible level (450 volts). These results are shown in Figure 13.3. Despite the tortured reaction of the victim, subjects complied with the experimenter's directives.

Although they followed orders and continued to administer shocks, this situation was extremely stressful for subjects. Most were concerned about the victim's welfare. As the shock level rose, subjects grew increasingly worried and agitated. Some laughed nervously. Many requested that the experimenter check the victim to make sure he was all right. A few subjects became so distressed that they disobeyed the experimenter and refused to follow his orders. The overall level of compliance on this study, however, was extremely high, which illustrates the enormous impact of directives from a legitimate authority.

Factors Affecting Obedience to Authority

Authorities customarily attain compliance to their directives, in part because these are often backed by the threat of coercive power, but exceptions do occur. Although most subjects in Milgram's study obeyed the experimenter's orders, some did not. Other studies have also shown that, although obedience to authority is more common, defiance does occur in some cases (French, Morrison, and Levinger, 1960; Michener and Burt 1975). This raises a general question: Under what conditions will people comply with authority, and under what conditions will they refuse to comply?

Extensions of the basic study by Milgram offer some insights. Some general factors affecting compliance include: (1) the amount of surveillance maintained by the authority, (2) the role a person occupies within a network of authority, and (3) the level of peer support favoring or opposing the authority.

First, obedience depends on the extent to which the subject is under surveillance by the authority. In a series of experiments, Milgram (1965a, 1974) varied the physical closeness (degree of surveillance) maintained by the experimenter. In one condition, the experimenter sat just a few feet away from the subject. In another condition, after giving preliminary instructions, the experimenter departed

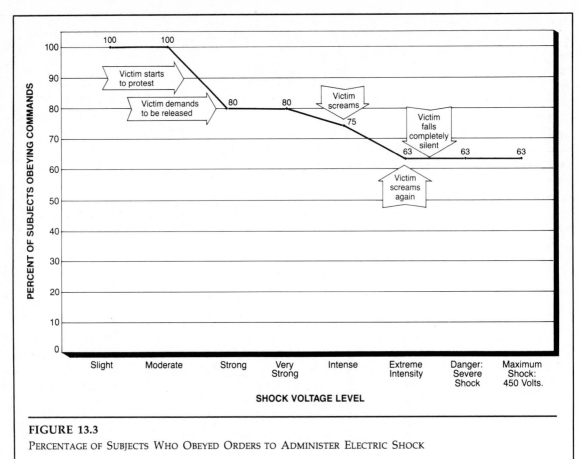

FIGURE 13.3

PERCENTAGE OF SUBJECTS WHO OBEYED ORDERS TO ADMINISTER ELECTRIC SHOCK

Neither protests nor screams by the victim were sufficient to deter subjects from complying with orders from an authority to administer an electric shock. Although more subjects were willing to administer low-voltage shocks than high-voltage shocks, as many as 63 percent administered the most severe level (450 volts).

Source: adapted from Milgram (1974, experiment 2).

from the laboratory and issued orders by telephone. Obedience was greatest when subjects were under close surveillance; it dropped sharply as the experimenter was physically removed from the situation. The number of obedient subjects in the face-to-face condition was almost three times as great as in the order-by-telephone condition. During the telephone conversations, some subjects specifically assured the experimenter that they were raising the shock level when in actuality they were using only the lowest shock. This tactic permitted them to ease their conscience, and at the same time avoid an open break with authority.

Another factor affecting obedience to authority is the subject's position in a larger chain of command. One study (Kilham and Mann 1974) used a Milgram-like situation in which a subject (the executant) actually pushed the buttons to administer shock, while another subject (the transmitter) simply conveyed the orders from the experimenter. Results show that the obedience rates were

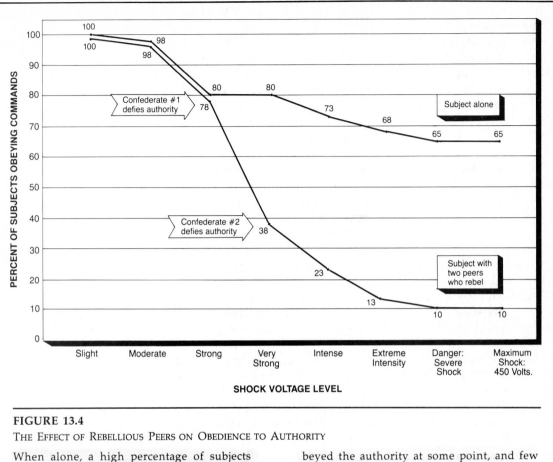

FIGURE 13.4

THE EFFECT OF REBELLIOUS PEERS ON OBEDIENCE TO AUTHORITY

When alone, a high percentage of subjects administered the maximum shock (450 volts) to the victim. In the presence of two peers who defy orders, however, most subjects disobeyed the authority at some point, and few administered the highest level of shock.

Source: adapted from Milgram (1974, experiments 5 and 17).

approximately twice as high among transmitters as among executants. In other words, persons positioned closer to the authority but farther from the unhappy task of throwing the switch were more obedient.

Another variable affecting compliance to authority is pressure from peers. If peers of the subject comply with and support the authority, this increases the pressure on the subject to comply. However, if peers resist orders from authority, the subject will also tend to disobey. To investigate the propensity to defy authority, Milgram (1965b, 1974) set up a situation involving five people: one experimenter, three teachers, and one learner. Two of the teachers as well as the learner (victim) were confederates. The third teacher was the subject. Teacher 1 (a confederate) read aloud the list of word pairs. Teacher 2 (a confederate) indicated whether the victim's answer was correct or incorrect. Teacher 3 (the naive subject) administered punishment. As usual, the experimenter directed the subject to raise the level of shock with each wrong answer.

The confederates followed the experimenter's orders to the 150-volt level, at which point Teacher 1 indicated that he would not participate further because of the victim's complaints. Despite the authority's insistence, he got up from his chair in front of the shock generator and moved to another part of the room. The experiment continued until the 210-volt level, at which point Teacher 2 refused to participate further.

Figure 13.4 shows the level of obedience by subjects in the company of two defiant peers. Note that most subjects disobeyed the experimenter at some point, and that only 10 percent administered shock to the highest level (450 volts). The average maximum shock was approximately 240 volts. These findings contrast with the experiments in which subjects were alone with the authority, which showed that approximately 65 percent of subjects administered shock to the highest level and that the average maximum shock was 370 volts. The activity of the defiant peers had a liberating effect on subjects, for it showed that refusal to comply with authority was a behavioral possibility. Moreover, the activity of defiant peers intensified the moral pressure on subjects to break away from the experimenter's demands.

Stability and Change in Status Hierarchies

Transactional View of Leadership

Imagine a band without a conductor or a ball club without a manager. Both groups will have something in common—a lack of leadership. Without a leader, the ball club would have no game plan, and the band would be nothing but a collection of individuals, each literally marching to a different drummer.

By definition, **leadership** is the enactment of several functions necessary for successful group performance; these functions include planning, organizing, and controlling the activity of group members (Stogdill 1974). In established groups, in which roles are sharply defined in a status hierarchy, leadership functions are typically fulfilled by high-status members. These members have both the right and the responsibility to provide leadership for the group. Once in place, leadership usually remains stable over time—members serving as leaders today will probably also be leaders tomorrow. Leadership is perhaps the most stable aspect of group structure (Crosbie 1975).

Nevertheless, an individual can exercise leadership only by the consent of group members. A group cannot be led toward any arbitrary goal; it can only be moved in directions where members are willing to go. Moreover, a leader cannot easily stay in power for an extended period of time without the active support of the other members. The basic question addressed in this section is: What must a person do to perform successfully as a leader and to obtain continuing support from members?

LEADERSHIP AS EXCHANGE. In essence, leadership involves a tacit exchange between the person serving as leader and the other group members. By fulfilling the planning, organizing, and controlling functions in a group, the leader helps the members attain their personal and collective objectives. In return, the leader receives support for continued control, as well as special rewards and privileges. This perspective, which characterizes leadership as an exchange between the leader and group members, is termed the **transactional view of leadership** (Homans 1974; Hollander and Julian 1969).

Exactly what do leaders contribute to groups in exchange for support from other members? The behavior of leaders has been investigated in many settings, including military units, industrial work groups, training groups, and laboratory groups (Halpin and Winer 1952; Gibb 1969; Wofford 1970). As might be expected, the behavior of leaders depends on situational factors such as the size of the group and the communication structure.

Nevertheless, certain behaviors are universal to leadership, including planning, organizing, and controlling. Specifically, leaders are expected to (1) formulate a clear conception of the group's goals and objectives; (2) develop specific strategies for the attainment of group goals; (3) specify role assignments and standards of performance for members; (4) establish and maintain channels of communication among members; (5) train members in needed skills; (6) interact with members personally to maintain good relations; (7) resolve conflict among members to reduce tension and maintain harmony; (8) monitor the group's progress toward goal attainment; (9) influence the activities of group members by means of rewards and punishments; and (10) represent the group to outside agencies and organizations.

In any group, some of these leadership behaviors will be more important than others. To perform successfully, leaders must have technical and interpersonal skills, as well as decision-making and problem-solving abilities.

In return for their performance, leaders receive not only rewards and benefits but also support for their continued control over the group's activities. This support is referred to as endorsement. By definition, **endorsement** is an attitude held by a group member indicating the extent to which he or she supports the leader (Hollander and Julian 1969, 1970; Michener and Tausig 1971). Endorsement can be measured in various ways. The following scale (Michener and Lawler 1975) is one approach:

1. Consider the person occupying the position of leadership. How legitimate is it for that person to occupy this position?

2. How satisfied are you with the leader's use of power in arriving at group decisions?

3. How satisfied are you with the performance of the leader in directing the group?

4. To what extent do you support or oppose the leader?

5. How willing would you be to have the person serving as leader continue to head the group?

A group member responding favorably to most or all of these items endorses the group's leader. Group members are not always unanimous in their attitude; they may endorse a leader to different degrees. Moreover, the endorsement accorded a leader fluctuates over time. A leader may enjoy high levels of endorsement on some occasions but have to endure lower levels on other occasions.

With a high level of endorsement from members, a leader may proceed vigorously and confidently. With a low level, leadership may be difficult if not impossible to exercise. History is full of leaders who gained and subsequently lost endorsement from their followers. One notable example is Richard Nixon, who enjoyed a high level of political support in the first years of his presidency— enough to win reelection in 1972. In the declining days of his presidency, Nixon lost the endorsement not only of the American people, but of his own political party, Congress, and even some members of his cabinet. His level of endorsement dropped so low that he could no longer lead the country effectively, and he chose to resign rather than face the possibility of impeachment.

FACTORS AFFECTING ENDORSEMENT. Why do some leaders receive high levels of endorsement from members, while others receive only low levels? According to the transactional view of leadership, leaders will receive endorsement in proportion to the benefits they deliver to group members Thus, the extent to which a group attains its objectives is one factor. If members perceive the group as moving toward the attainment of its goals, endorsement of leadership will remain high; if members see the group as failing, endorsement will decline. A distinction must be drawn, however, between initial failure and repeated failure on group objectives. When a group fails initially, members may actually

Without a strong game plan, this team would have little chance of winning. A coach performs several leadership functions, including planning and organizing team activities.

increase their endorsement and "rally around" the leader in hopes of improving the situation (Hollander, Fallon, and Edwards 1977). Repeated failure, however, indicates that something is fundamentally wrong. If the responsibility for failure is attributed to faulty leadership, endorsement will certainly decline and group members may even attempt to change leaders (Julian, Hollander, and Regula 1969; Michener and Lawler 1975). Situations of this type sometimes arise in voluntary associations and industrial work groups. They also occur in military organizations (especially during wartime) and in professional sports (especially at the end of a losing season).

Failure to attain collective goals leads to low endorsement primarily because members infer that the leader is incompetent. Repeated failure is strong evidence that the leader is not sufficiently skilled to move the group in the direction of its goals. In addition, group members may construe other unrelated behaviors such as difficulty on high-skill tasks or failure on written tests as evidence of leader incompetence. Thus, behavior of this type by the leader will also produce low levels of endorsement (Julian and Hollander 1966; Julian, Hollander, and Regula 1969; Suchner and Jackson 1976).

Another determinant of endorsement is the level of consideration a leader shows toward group members. If the leader treats members equitably, this will help create a climate of high endorsement. For instance, if a leader controls the allocation of rewards and decides to share these rewards equitably, this will show concern for the welfare of other group members, and induce high levels of endorsement (Michener and Lawler 1975). A selfish leader—even one who is very competent—will suffer reduced levels of endorsement.

Revolutionary and Conservative Coalitions

When group members agree on their relative status, and especially on that of their leader, a condition of **status consensus** is said to exist (Shelley 1960; Heslin and Dunphy 1964). Although a moderate-to-high level of status consensus is common in established groups, consensus may collapse under certain conditions. For example, if a group experiences unexpected difficulty in attaining its goals, some members may continue to endorse the existing leadership, whereas others may prefer to change leaders. This difference of opinion would indicate a lack of consensus regarding the status order.

MOBILIZATION OF REVOLUTIONARY COALITIONS. Lack of status consensus poses serious problems for an established leader. He will experience his position as very precarious. Under certain conditions, a lack of consensus may lead to the formation of a **revolutionary coalition,** which is a union of some medium- and low-status members who oppose the existing leader (Caplow 1968; Crosbie 1975). By combining forces, members of a revolutionary coalition hope to displace the leader and his supporters.

Revolutionary coalitions are difficult to mobilize. Members must first have reason to end their allegiance to the established order, and then agree to take joint action to overthrow that order. For example, before a mutiny on shipboard can occur, the seamen must have a serious basis for discontent with the ship's captain. They must feel that existing channels provide no remedy for their discontent, and must be willing to face the punishment involved if the mutiny fails. Finally, they must agree who will be the new commander if the mutiny succeeds.

Nevertheless, various factors increase the likelihood that a revolutionary coalition will form and take action against an established leader. These are the same factors that produce low levels of endorsement. For instance, when a group fails repeatedly to achieve its goals, a revolutionary coalition may try to reverse the group's fortunes by removing the formal leader from his position. The coalition will reallocate important responsibilities among group members and/or change some of the group's operational procedures (Michener and Lawler 1971).

Another contributing factor is inequitable treatment of group members by high-status persons. If a leader shows extreme selfishness or favoritism in allocating rewards among group members, a coalition may attempt to restore equity (Ross, Thibaut, and Evenbeck, 1971; Michener and Lyons 1972).

Similarity of interest and opinions among lower-status members is still another important factor in the emergence of a revolutionary coalition. Sharing common interest heightens members' expectations of support from other members. This in turn increases the probability that individuals will join an emerging revolutionary coalition (Lawler 1975a, 1975b).

REACTIONS TO REVOLUTIONARY COALITIONS. Established leaders have a lot to lose by the emergence of a revolutionary coalition, and they seldom sit idly by during the upheaval. The revolt by some of Hitler's generals during World War II led only to their own death, not Hitler's. A leader will typically engage in various counterstrategies to thwart the coalition. For example, a leader might threaten to punish insurgent members. This may work if the threats are sufficiently large and credible. A second counterstrategy would be to mobilize a **conservative coalition,** a union of medium- and low-status members who support the existing status order against revolutionaries.

A third counterstrategy available to a leader is the use of co-optation. By definition, **co-optation** is a strategic attempt to weaken the bond among potential revolutionaries by singling out one or several lower-status members for favored treatment. Co-optation might be used by a calculating leader who anticipates a future upheaval. For instance, a leader could offer several low-status members the possibility of future promotion. This will increase their investment in the existing status order, thereby making it more difficult for a revolutionary coalition to recruit them as members (Lawler, Youngs, and Lesh 1978).

Summary

In any group, members occupy positions having different value or importance. As a result, each member's social status is determined by the position in the group that he or she occupies. In this chapter, we have discussed both the origins and the consequences of status differences among members.

STATUS EMERGENCE IN TASK GROUPS. In task-oriented groups, status differences among members usually develop during the course of interaction. (1) Interaction Process Analyses (IPA) is a technique for investigating interaction and communication in groups. Studies using this technique have shown not only that some group members consistently send and receive more messages than others, but also that patterns of communication stabilize over time. (2) Studies using IPA have also analyzed the emergence of status differences in groups. Differentiation of leadership functions—task versus social-emotional—appears regularly in problem-solving groups.

STATUS CHARACTERISTICS AND SOCIAL INTERACTION. A status characteristic is any property of a person around which beliefs about that person come to be organized. Age, race, sex, and occupation are important status characteristics. (1) When groups are composed of persons having different status characteristics, this can have a significant effect on interaction. Studies of juror interactions, for example, have shown that characteristics such as occupation and sex affect which members participate the most, exert the most influence, and hold positions of leadership. (2) This phenomenon, known as status generalization, occurs because group members base their expectations regarding one another's performance on status characteristics. Status generalization is most likely to occur when members have no prior history of interaction and no experience with the group's task. (3) To eliminate or reduce status generalization, one must change not only the expectations of minority (or low-status) members, but also those of majority (high-status) members. Status generalization can be eliminated only when both minority and majority members believe that the characteristic is not relevant to the group's task.

EQUITY AND REWARD DISTRIBUTION. Status differences in a group determine the amount of rewards that each member will receive. (1) A state of inequity exists if group members receive rewards that are not proportional to their contributions. (2) If inequity prevails within a group, members may react emotionally (with anger or guilt) and initiate efforts to restore equity. These efforts usually entail increasing the rewards or reducing the inputs of underrewarded members, or increasing the inputs or reducing the rewards of overrewarded members. (3) Considerations of equity apply not only to task situations, but also to intimate relations. Couples in inequitable dating relationships, for example, are less satisfied and more likely to break up than those in equitable relationships.

AUTHORITY AND OBEDIENCE. Authority is influence based on invocation of group norms; it can be exercised only by particular persons in certain contexts. (1) Research on obedience to authority has shown that subjects will comply with orders to administer extreme levels of electric shock to an innocent victim. (2) Obedience to authority is more likely to occur when subjects are under direct surveillance, when they are transmitters rather than executants of a command, and when counterpressure from defiant peers is absent.

STABILITY AND CHANGE IN STATUS HIERARCHIES. A group member can exercise leadership only by the consent of group members. (1) The transactional view of leadership maintains that leadership involves a tacit exchange. In return for helping the group achieve its objectives, a leader receives endorsement as well as special rewards and privileges. Endorsement will decline if the group fails repeatedly to achieve its goal(s), if the leader is judged incompetent, or if the level of consideration shown members by the leader is low. (2) Without status consensus, discontented members may attempt to oust the established leadership by forming a revolutionary coalition. Coalitions of this type are most likely to emerge when the group fails to achieve its goals or when the leader distributes rewards inequitably among members. Revolutionary coalitions are not always successful, because they may be thwarted by conservative coalitions or by a leader's use of co-optation.

Key Terms and Concepts
Social Status
Interaction Process Analysis (IPA)
Social-Emotional Acts
Task Acts
Social-Emotional Leader
Task Leader
Status Characteristic
Status Generalization
Equity
Underreward
Overreward
Authority
Leadership
Transactional View of Leadership
Endorsement
Status Consensus
Revolutionary Coalition
Conservative Coalition
Co-optation

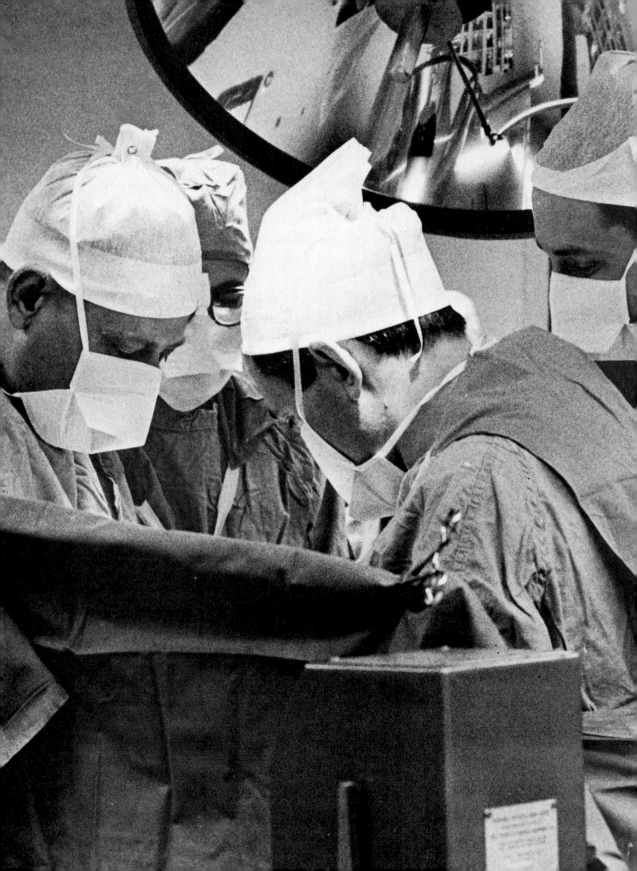

Chapter 14

Group Productivity and Leadership Effectiveness

Introduction

Many groups in society exist primarily to attain specific goals. A work group in a clothing factory strives to meet its production quotas for swimsuit apparel; an airline crew seeks to transport passengers to their specified destination on time; a police detective squad may work around the clock to crack an urgent case; a professional ball club tries to win games and take the league championship. Not every group, however, is concerned with producing something tangible. Some groups—such as a Wednesday night poker club—exist for their own sake, for simple pleasure. But many groups in society—work groups especially—exist to produce something valuable or to bring about some end state.

What Is Group Productivity?

The term **group productivity** refers to the output or end state resulting from group activity. A group's productivity is always measured in terms of products or outcomes, rather than group activities themselves. The unit of measurement depends on the goals of the group. An industrial work group that manufactures clothing, for example, might be concerned with the number of units produced, the amount of material wasted, the number of "seconds" or rejects, the speed of production, and so on. Problem-solving groups such as a police detective squad may base productivity on the percentage of cases successfully cleared by arrest, the quality or thoroughness of the solutions, the speed with which the problems were solved, and the number of errors or dead ends.

All measures of productivity are based on outcomes or end states of group activity. For this reason, a group's productivity can be assessed even after the members have "gone home for the day." The need to directly observe group activity arises only when **troubleshooting**—that is, determining why a particular group is performing poorly (Gilbert 1978). For example, if a baseball team has a low league standing and is losing a lot of games, we might troubleshoot by examining its pitching record (the earned-run average), its fielding performance (errors), or its batting statistics (overall batting average and percentage of extra-base hits). If the pitching and fielding are good but the hitting is poor, we may then want to observe the players while they bat in order to determine what is wrong with their stance, their grip on the bat, their swing, and so on.

Frequently we observe differences in productivity among groups, even when they are similar in size and talent. Some groups produce more than others, win more frequently, achieve better solutions, work at higher speed, commit fewer errors, and create less waste. From this basic observation stem some questions regarding group productivity:

1. In what ways is productivity governed by the task(s) confronting a group?

2. To what extent is productivity affected by a group's organization? Can factors such as group size, cohesiveness, reward structure, and communication structure affect the level of group performance?

3. Does a group's organization affect the quality of its decisions? Under what conditions do pressures for conformity lead to poor decisions?

4. Does the style of leadership in a group determine productivity? Are some styles more effective than others in fostering a high level of performance by the group?

The remainder of this chapter will discuss these issues in detail.

Factors Affecting Group Productivity

Group Tasks

Any analysis of group productivity should begin with the task at hand. The nature of the task facing a particular group affects its performance, both directly and indirectly, by interacting with other group attributes. For example, to understand how group size or communication structure affect group performance we must first understand what the group is trying to accomplish.

UNITARY VERSUS DIVISIBLE TASKS. A task has many different characteristics, including its difficulty, the rules or method for carrying it out, and the criteria that specify when it is completed. Another important quality is a task's divisibility (Steiner 1972, 1974; Shiflett 1979). **Unitary tasks** (sometimes called nondivisible tasks) are those in which all group members perform identical activities. A typing pool at an insurance company is one example. Typically, all the persons in the pool sit at computer terminals and type insurance policies for new customers. They also retrieve and revise information on existing policies to keep the company's records current. This is a unitary task because all members in the typing pool have similar skills and perform the same activities.

In contrast, **divisible tasks** are those in which members perform different, although complementary, activities. Because divisible tasks can be broken into various subtasks, they involve a division of labor among group members. One example would be flying a commercial aircraft. The pilot, copilot, navigator, flight attendants, and baggage handlers all perform different activities between takeoff and landing. Both unitary and divisible tasks are shown schematically in Figure 14.1.

Unitary tasks can be further divided into three types: conjunctive, disjunctive, or additive. A **conjunctive task** is a unitary task in which the group's performance depends entirely on that of its weakest or slowest member. A **disjunctive task** is one in which the group's performance depends entirely on that of its strongest or fastest member, and an **additive task** is one in which the group's

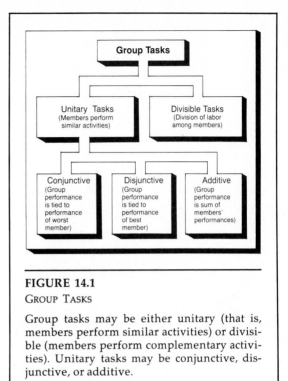

FIGURE 14.1
GROUP TASKS

Group tasks may be either unitary (that is, members perform similar activities) or divisible (members perform complementary activities). Unitary tasks may be conjunctive, disjunctive, or additive.

Source: adapted from Steiner (1972).

performance is equal to the sum of the performances of its members (Steiner 1972).

A conjunctive task may be illustrated by a mountain climbing expedition. Although all members of the expedition may have experience, they will nevertheless differ in dexterity and strength. Because all members of the expedition are held together by a rope, the group's performance (as measured by speed and height of ascent) will be constrained by its slowest member. Because the expedition can move no faster than the slowest member, the group's performance depends entirely on this person.

A disjunctive task is one in which the group's performance depends entirely on its strongest or fastest member. A solution by any member is tantamount to a solution by the entire group. Suppose we gave the following problem to a five-person group and measured group performance in terms of the speed with which a solution is found:

> Three missionaries and three cannibals are standing on one side of a wide river. The missionaries want to cross the river to the other side. One rowboat is available, but it can hold no more than two persons at a time. All of the missionaries and one of the cannibals can row the boat. The cannibals pose a danger to the missionaries, because if more cannibals than missionaries are placed on either bank of the river, those cannibals will eat the missionaries. Problem: How can all six persons cross the river alive?*

Only one member is needed to solve this problem. As soon as a member has found a solution, he or she can show it to the other members. The group's score is the solution time of its fastest member. The task is disjunctive, because solutions by slower members do not affect the group's performance.

An additive task is illustrated by the insurance typing pool mentioned earlier. The number of policies typed for new customers in a day (a measure of group productivity) is simply the sum of policies typed by individual members. If the eight members of the pool type 27, 41, 43, 34, 52, 40, 29, and 46, respectively, the group's overall performance is 312 policies (the sum). A group of five men using shovels to clear a snowy driveway is another example of an additive task. Each man performs a similar activity. The group's performance can be measured in terms of total time required to clear the drive.

GOOD VERSUS POOR PERFORMANCE. As these examples illustrate, all unitary tasks—whether conjunctive, disjunctive, or additive—require similar skills and resources from group members. For a group to perform well on a unitary task, several conditions must be met. First, the group members must have the necessary abilities and talents to perform the task. Second, the group members must have sufficient motivation—they must want to do the task. Third, members must know what is expected of them and have feedback indicating the quality of their performance.

The absence of any of these conditions may result in poor performance. A typing pool, for example, will obviously produce at a low level if some of its members are terrible typists. Productivity will also be poor if members do not want to work; this might happen if they are paid poorly or inequitably. And performance will be below par if group members do not know what level of performance is expected of them. Typists at the insurance company might be quite happy with a total of 312 policies per day—until the typing supervisor points out that every other typing pool in the company produces at least 400 per day.

Divisible tasks pose even greater hurdles to successful performance than do unitary tasks. Group members must have ability, motivation, and information, and the group also must match skills with task requirements—that is, put the right member in the right job. Beyond this, the group must establish coordination among its members. It takes careful planning to blend a number of subtasks into a group effort. Coordination becomes increasingly important as the task becomes more complex (Sorenson 1971). One sure way to lose a football game is to assign members to the wrong positions—make the team's weakest thrower the quarterback, the slowest runners the deep receivers, and the smallest players the linemen. Another sure route to defeat is to neglect coordination—run plays without informing each of the players beforehand what formation has been chosen.

Group Size

How does the size of a group affect its productivity and performance? Are large groups superior to smaller ones? Large groups

---

*The answer to the missionaries (M) and cannibals (C) problem is: (1) M1 and C1 cross; M1 returns. (2) M1 and C2 cross; C2 (who can row) returns. (3) M2 and C2 cross; C2 returns. (4) C2 and C3 cross; C2 returns. (5) M3 and C2 cross. Everyone is now on the other side of the river.

generally have the advantage of greater resources (information, skills, muscle), which may lead to greater productivity. On the other hand, large groups require extensive organization and coordination among members, which may inhibit performance.

To understand the effects of group size on performance, we must look closely at the type of task facing the group (Thomas and Fink 1963). For example, a five-person group could shovel the snow from a driveway faster than a two-person team, and eight people could probably do the job even faster. On this additive task, larger size is clearly an advantage. But can 30 chefs prepare a better soup than two? Certainly the coordination problems among 30 chefs would be enormous. And if the soup's quality is limited by the least skilled person in the kitchen (a conjunctive task), then too many cooks may literally spoil the broth.

DISJUNCTIVE AND CONJUNCTIVE TASKS. According to one theorist (Steiner 1972), a group's size affects its performance in one of two ways. Performance will (1) increase directly with group size when the task is disjunctive, and (2) decrease with group size when the task is conjunctive.

Consider these predictions for a moment. When the task is disjunctive, the group's performance is determined by the most competent member. Assuming that groups are composed at random, a large group would have more chance of containing members of very high ability. The larger the group, the more likely it is to contain the necessary skills. Therefore, as size increases, performance should also improve. There may, however, be a limit to this effect—some maximum point beyond which additional members will have relatively little or no added impact. If a group already has 20 members, for example, the 21st member may not add very much.

When the group's task is conjunctive the effects of size should be quite different. Group performance will be no better than that of its weakest member. Again assuming that groups

In a relay race, teams of runners face a unitary additive task. Each team member must complete a lap, and the team with the fastest total time wins.

are composed at random, a large group will be more likely to have very weak members than a small group. These weak members will be slower or less competent on their task than other group members. Consequently, large groups should perform less well than small ones on conjunctive tasks.

To test these predictions, one study (Frank and Anderson 1971) investigated the effects of group size on conjunctive and disjunctive tasks by comparing the performances of groups with two, three, five, and eight members. Each group worked on a series of tasks for 15 minutes; performance was measured by the number of tasks completed successfully. The tasks were intellectual in nature, requiring group members to generate ideas or images.

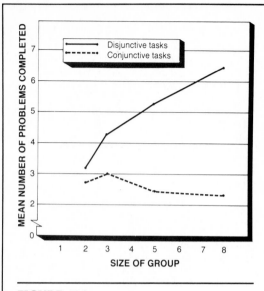

FIGURE 14.2

EFFECTS OF DISJUNCTIVE AND CONJUNCTIVE
TASKS ON GROUP PRODUCTIVITY

On disjunctive tasks—tasks in which a
group's performance depends on the performance of its best member—large groups were
shown to perform better than small ones.
However on conjunctive tasks—tasks in
which a group's performance is restricted by
the performance of its worst member—large
groups performed slightly less well than
small ones.

Source: adapted from Frank and Anderson (1971).

(For example: "Write three points pro and con
on the issue of legalizing gambling.") These
tasks were made either disjunctive or conjunctive by manipulating the instructions. Some
groups received disjunctive instructions,
which stated that the group was to work on
various tasks in sequence. As soon as *any*
member had completed the task, the group
could move on to the next task. Other groups
received conjunctive instructions, which
stated that the group was not permitted to
move to the next task until *every* member had
completed the task. Thus a group in the disjunctive condition could perform at the level
of its most competent member, whereas a
group in the conjunctive condition could
move no faster than its slowest member. The

observed outcomes of this study support the
predictions made earlier (Steiner 1972). On
disjunctive tasks, large groups perform better
than small ones. On conjunctive tasks, large
groups perform worse than small ones,
although this difference was not particularly
marked. These findings are shown in Figure
14.2.

ADDITIVE TASKS. What is the effect of group
size when the group faces an additive task, one
that depends on the sum of the performances
of all members? When the task is additive,
Steiner (1972) suggests that total productivity
will increase with group size but that productivity per member may decline. For example,
consider the task of pulling a heavy object by
means of a rope. In a classic study conducted
more than a half-century ago, Ringelmann
investigated the effects of group size on the
total pulling power exerted by the members of
a group (Moede 1927). Members pulled on a
rope as hard as they could, trying to move
heavy weights attached to the rope. Results
showed that, although a group of eight men
could pull harder than a smaller group or a
single individual, the average contribution of
members declined as group size increased.
Thus a single individual in this study pulled
63 kilograms, a two-person group pulled 118, a
three-person group pulled 160, and an eight-
person group pulled 248 (see Table 14.1).
Although the total performance of the group
increased with size, the efficiency of each
member declined. Working alone, each individual pulled at 100 percent of his capacity; but
working as members of an eight-person team,
each used only 49 percent of his individual
capacity in pulling the 248 kilograms. Had the
group used 100 percent of the capacity of each
member, it would have pulled 8 × 63 = 504
kilograms. Overall these results indicate that
on additive tasks group productivity increases
with group size, although the efficiency per
person declines.

This phenomenon—termed the "Ringelmann effect"—has been observed again in
recent studies with the rope-pulling task

TABLE 14.1
ACTUAL AND POTENTIAL PULLING POWER OF GROUPS OF VARIOUS SIZES

Group Size	Actual Pull (kilograms)	Potential Pull (kilograms)	Ratio of Actual Pull to Potential Pull (percent)
1	63	63	100
2	118	126	94
3	160	189	85
8	248	504	49

Source: adapted from Moede (1927).

(Ingham et al. 1974). The findings in this research were similar to Ringelmann's, although the per capita loss in the larger groups was not quite as sharp as in the original study. The Ringelmann effect has also been observed with respect to activities such as cheering and clapping (Latané, Williams, and Harkins 1979). Here again, diminishing returns occur: although larger groups made more noise than smaller ones, output per member in the larger groups was lower than in the smaller groups.

There are two reasons for this discrepancy between a group's potential productivity and its actual productivity on additive tasks. The first is faulty coordination. In the case of Ringelmann's rope-pull task, for instance, the possibility of poor coordination (pulling in different directions at different times) increases with group size. The second reason is what may be termed "social loafing"—that is, a decrease in individual effort due to the presence of other members. Workers tend to slack off slightly on additive tasks, which causes the group's output to fall short of its potential (Latané, Williams, and Harkins 1979).

Group Cohesiveness

Is a highly cohesive group more productive than a less cohesive one? The relationship here is complex. Highly cohesive groups are not always more productive. Yet, in conjunction with other factors such as group norms and task structure, cohesiveness does have an impact on group productivity.

COHESIVENESS AND GROUP NORMS. The more cohesive a group, the more attraction it exerts on its members (Lott and Lott 1965). If a task group is highly cohesive and has norms of high productivity, the group will be highly productive. On the other hand, if the group is highly cohesive but has norms of low productivity, its members may spend more time socializing than producing. This hypothesis was tested in several experiments that manipulated both group production standards and cohesiveness (Schachter et al. 1951; Berkowitz 1954). Results indicated that in highly cohesive groups with low production norms, productivity was markedly suppressed. In general, cohesiveness does not affect group productivity directly. Instead it amplifies the effects of whatever productivity norms prevail within the group.

COHESIVENESS AND TASK TYPE. Group cohesiveness interacts not only with group norms but also with task structure to affect performance. (Nixon 1976, 1977a). Consider the performance of an athletic team. What we call "team sports" involves divisible tasks—a division of labor among team members. One example is a football team, which consists of different squads (offensive team, defensive team, specialty team) and also requires specialization within those squads (on the offensive team there are linemen, wide receivers, a quarterback, running backs, and so on). Success in football requires individual skills as well as careful integration of the individual performances. Thus group cohesiveness is positively related to successful team performance (Stogdill 1963). This is also true of volleyball (Vos and Brinkman 1967), basketball (Nixon 1977b), and baseball (Landers and Crum 1971)—all sports that require coordination among team members. Harmonious personal relationships enhance effective teamwork, and the team's success tends to make its members friendlier toward each other.

Other sports, like singles tennis, involve unitary additive tasks. They do not entail a division of labor because the players perform more or less independently on identical tasks. If a team is assembled to compete in such a sport, its score is simply the sum of the individual members' scores. Studies of rifle teams (McGrath 1962) and bowling teams (Landers and Luschen 1974) indicate a negative relationship between cohesiveness and successful team performance. In activities not requiring much coordination among members, teams that have many individual stars will tend to do best. Although the stars may dislike each other, their rivalry can motivate higher levels of individual excellence. Thus in sports involving unitary additive tasks, low levels of personal harmony (increased rivalry) may actually lead to greater success in competition against other teams.

Interdependence and Reward Structure

Nicoletti and Strauss are moving their law offices across town and they want the move completed quickly. They have hired four young men from Personpower Inc. to load their office equipment into a rented truck, drive it to the new building, and unload it there. If the men finish the job in one day or less, Nicoletti has promised them each a $25 bonus on top of the regular fee for the work. If they take more than one day, nobody gets a bonus.

In this case, a **cooperative** reward structure

exists among the four workers (Deutsch 1973). A cooperative structure has several hallmarks. First, the members are functionally interdependent in the sense that they rely on one another's efforts to accomplish the overriding goal. No one person could complete the task of moving the office equipment in one day by himself. Second, the members' interests are linked in the sense that each man can get a reward if, and only if, the others also get rewards. If one man earns a $25 bonus from Nicoletti, the other three will earn theirs.

A cooperative reward structure induces open communication, mutual trust, and a readiness on the part of each person to consider the suggestions of his fellows. Research shows that members of a cooperative structure are prone to trust one another and to coordinate their energies, provided they believe the group will eventually succeed in its task (Thomas 1957; Myers 1962; Steiner 1972, p.150).

In contrast to cooperation, a **competitive** reward structure is one that pits group members against one another in an attempt to gain scarce rewards for themselves. A competitive structure involves a low level of functional interdependence and a high level of differential reward (rewards distributed unequally), with the best performers receiving the greatest rewards. For example, a competitive situation occurs in university classes when the professor decides to grade members on a curve. If only the top 10 percent of the class is allowed to receive A's, successful actions by one student will obstruct goal attainment by others. Thus classmates' interests are clearly opposing.

What type of reward structure—cooperative or competitive—assures the best possible group performance? On one hand, a competitive structure within a group often produces a breakdown of coordination and lack of trust among members (Deutsch 1949; Hammond and Goldman 1961). We might therefore expect lower levels of group productivity if group members are competing rather than cooperating. On the other hand, a competitive structure may heighten members' motivation and cause them to try harder in hopes of attaining superior rewards. This might lead to higher levels of productivity under competition than under cooperation. In fact, research findings have been ambiguous: some studies show that group performance is better under cooperation than under competition (Deutsch 1949; Smith, Madden, and Sobol 1957; Raven and Eachus 1963), whereas others show the opposite (deCharms 1957).

Some theorists have suggested that what affects group performance is not cooperation or competition per se, but the degree of underlying task interdependence and differential rewarding. The effect of these variables on group performance was demonstrated vividly in a study (Miller and Hamblin 1963) in which groups of three members were asked to work on a series of problems. Members were placed in separate booths connected by a system of electrical lights and switches. The group's task was to determine which one of 13 numbers had been selected by the experimenter. Each member was privately informed of four numbers that had *not* been selected by the experimenter. These sets of four numbers were different for each member; thus, if the three members pooled their information (by the electrical signaling system), they would immediately see the correct answer. The task was completed only when all three members knew the answer. The group's performance was measured in terms of time: the faster it discovered the correct answer, the higher score it received.

Two independent variables were manipulated in the study. One was the degree of task interdependence among group members. In the high-interdependence condition, guessing was discouraged by a substantial penalty. Group members were therefore forced to coordinate their efforts and share information in order to solve the problem. In the low-interdependence condition, there was no restriction on guessing, making coordination among members unnecessary. To solve the problem, individuals merely continued to guess until they hit the correct solution.

The other independent variable in the study was the degree of differential rewarding among group members. Rewards for group members were based both on their own efforts and on those of the group as a whole. Each group started with 90 points, and 1 point was subtracted for every second that elapsed before all three members had solved the problem. For example, if the group took 60 seconds to reach a solution, it scored 30 points. The group's points were then distributed among its members. In one experimental condition (no differential rewarding), each member received one-third of the group reward. In a second condition (medium differential rewarding), the member who solved the problem first received one-half of the group's points, the member who finished second received one-third, and the one who finished third received one-sixth. In a third condition (high differential rewarding), the member who solved the problem first received two-thirds of the group's points, the member who finished second received one-third, and the one who finished third received none.

The results of this study are depicted in Figure 14.3. Under conditions of low interdependence (in which all three individuals could freely guess at the answer), differential rewarding did not significantly affect group productivity. Under conditions of high interdependence (in which guessing was prohibited and members had to share information), higher levels of differential rewarding sharply reduced the group's level of productivity.

To interpret these results, note that under conditions of high task interdependence and no differential rewarding, members realized their best strategy for achieving higher rewards was to cooperate with each other. Thus they shared information quickly and, as a result, had high productivity scores. Under conditions of high task interdependence and high differential rewarding, however, members realized that they could achieve high rewards for themselves only by outperforming others in their group. This created a competitive atmosphere in which members tried to hinder one another. For example, a member

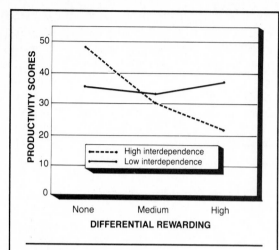

FIGURE 14.3

GROUP PRODUCTIVITY AS A FUNCTION OF
INTERDEPENDENCE AND DEGREE OF
DIFFERENTIAL REWARDING

Under low task interdependence, differential
rewarding (that is, unequal reward distribution) had little effect on group performance.
However under high task interdependence, a
high level of differential rewarding induced
low group productivity as well as competition
among members, and a low level of differential rewarding induced high productivity and
cooperation.

Source: adapted from Miller and Hamblin (1963).

might try to obtain information from others
without yielding information in return,
thereby blocking others' performance. This
engendered a lack of coordination and inevitably resulted in poor overall group productivity.

Under conditions of low task interdependence, in contrast, group members could not
use a blocking strategy on one another (because guessing was permitted). To increase
their rewards, they were forced to raise their
own performance independently. This led to
moderate group productivity regardless of the
degree of differential rewarding. Related
research shows similar results (Rosenbaum et
al. 1980).

Communication Structure

We frequently hear about the frustrations
of working within a large organization like a
military or industrial bureaucracy, where communication must go through prescribed channels designed to restrict who can talk with
whom. To some degree, this holds true for
smaller groups as well. Free communication
among members of a group is also affected by
the nature of a group's task, its status patterns,
and even the physical distance between members.

Years ago a method was developed for
investigating the effects of alternative communication structures on a group's performance
(Bavelas 1948, 1950). The method involves
placing the members of a group in separate
cubicles. These members are not permitted to
talk to one another; they can communicate
only by passing notes through slots in the
cubicle walls. When all of these slots are
opened simultaneously, each member can
communicate directly with every other member. Closing some of the slots eliminates certain channels and restricts the flow of information. By manipulating the flow of information,
investigators can use this method to study the
effects of alternate communication networks.
The term **communication network** refers to
the pattern of communication opportunities
within a group. Figure 14.4 displays a variety
of communication networks for a group of five
persons. The *comcon* (or "completely *connected*") network allows each member to talk
freely with all the others. The other networks
restrict communication. For example, in the
wheel network, one person is at the hub, and all
communication must pass through him or her.
In a *chain* network, all information transmitted
from the person at either end must pass
through a number of others to reach the other
end; people located nearer the middle of the
chain will therefore be more central to the
flow of communication than those located at
the extremes.

Does the type of communication network

affect a group's productivity? This question arises partly from practical considerations. People want to know how to organize work groups, committees, teams, and other task-oriented groups in the most efficient way. In typical research studies on this issue, each group is assigned a task which, to be resolved successfully, requires communication among members. In some cases these are simple tasks, such as identifying which of various symbols (stars, triangles, circles, and so on) appear on cards. In other cases these are more complex tasks that require the members to transform information, such as arranging words, constructing sentences, and performing arithmetic. Whether the task is simple or complex, a group's efficiency in problem solving is measured by the time it takes to achieve a solution, by the number of messages sent by members in order to achieve a solution, or by the number of errors made while attempting to solve the problem.

A group's problem-solving efficiency depends in part on its communication network, because the network restricts how group members can behave when attempting to solve problems. An early study (Leavitt 1951) compared the relative efficiency of the wheel, chain, Y, and circle networks in five-person groups. Results indicate that members of groups having wheel, chain, and Y networks adopt a centralized organization in which the person occupying the central position (for example, the "hub" in the wheel) is likely to emerge as highly influential. Those occupying the more peripheral positions are unlikely to emerge as influential. In contrast, members of groups having a circle network tend to adopt a decentralized organization in which all members actively communicate with and influence one another. Studies of comcon groups have also found that members adopt a decentralized organization (Shaw and Rothschild 1956; Guetzkow and Dill 1957). In general, a group's communication network determines whether its organization is centralized or decentralized.

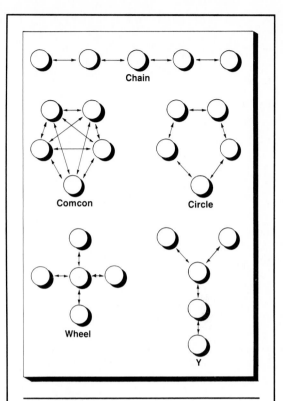

FIGURE 14.4

COMMUNICATION NETWORKS IN FIVE-PERSON GROUPS

This figure shows different types of communication networks that can exist within five-person groups. Three of the networks shown—the wheel, the chain, and the Y— are centralized. That is, messages flowing from one end of the network to the other must pass through a central person (or "hub"). The other two networks—the circle and the comcon—are decentralized because messages need not pass through a single hub.

Source: adapted from Leavitt (1951).

This point is important because centrality of organization in turn affects a group's problem-solving efficiency. This was demonstrated by a compilation of findings from numerous experiments on communication networks (Shaw 1964). Each study was classified as involving either centralized networks (wheel, chain, Y) or decentralized networks (circle,

TABLE 14.2

COMPARISONS OF CENTRALIZED (WHEEL, CHAIN, Y) AND DECENTRALIZED (CIRCLE, COMCON) NETWORKS' EFFICIENCY AS A FUNCTION OF TASK COMPLEXITY

	Simple problems[a]	Complex problems[b]	Total
Time			
Centralized faster	14	0	14
Decentralized faster	4	18	22
Messages			
Centralized sent more	0	1	1
Decentralized sent more	18	17	35
Errors			
Centralized made more	0	6	6
Decentralized made more	9	1	10
No difference	1	3	4
Satisfaction			
Centralized higher	1	1	2
Decentralized higher	7	10	17

[a]Simple problems: symbol-, letter-, number-, and color-identification tasks.

Source: adapted from Shaw (1964).

[b]Complex problems: arithmetic, word arrangement, sentence construction, and discussion problems.

comcon), and as entailing either simple tasks (collating information) or complex tasks (carrying out operations on the information). The results of this compilation are shown in Table 14.2. Notice that for simple problems, centralized communication networks lead to superior performance. Groups with centralized networks solved simple problems faster, sent fewer messages, and made fewer errors than groups with decentralized networks. For complex problems, however, the findings are reversed: groups with decentralized networks were more efficient. Even though they sent more messages, they were faster and tended to make fewer errors than groups with centralized networks.

Numerous studies support the generalization that centralized networks are more efficient for simple tasks whereas decentralized networks are more efficient for complex ones (Shaw 1954; Guetzkow and Simon 1955; Law-

son 1964; Morrissette, Switzer, and Crannell 1965; Morrissette 1966). One explanation for this pattern lies in the concept of **saturation,** which refers to the degree of communication overload experienced by group members occupying the central positions within communication networks (Gilchrist, Shaw, and Walker 1954; Shaw 1978). The level of saturation depends not only on the communication requirements imposed by the network, but also on factors such as the data manipulation and decisions required by the task. In general, the greater the level of saturation, the less efficient a group is at solving problems.

As an example, consider the wheel network (see Figure 14.4). In this structure, the hub position is central. When the group is working on a simple task, communication requirements are not very demanding. The hub position does not become saturated, and the person occupying this position can work

Box 14.1
COMMUNICATION NETWORKS IN AN ORGANIZATION

Communication networks have a significant impact not only in laboratory groups, but also in organizational settings. In one case study (Mears 1974), a group of division representatives within an aerospace firm tried out several different communication networks. This group consisted of an administrative officer and representatives from several divisions such as manufacturing, quality control, procurement, contracts, and engineering. At first this group was organized in a *comcon network*. This permitted virtually unrestricted communication among all members. Satisfaction was very high, but only a modest amount of work was accomplished because members wasted a great deal of time in useless discussion and debate.

Top management grew dissatisfied with the group's performance and restructured it in a *wheel network* with the administrative officer in a position of authority at the hub. This restriction in communication reduced worker motivation and satisfaction. It also lowered productivity because the hub position became saturated, which caused many errors in relaying complex information.

Finally, the group was again reorganized in a *modified comcon network*, which permitted each member to communicate only with persons who were directly involved in the task at hand. This reduced the communication overload on the administrative officer and also protected the time of members who did not need to be consulted. As a result, the group experienced high levels of satisfaction and performance.

As this case study shows, communication networks are not theoretical abstractions found only in research laboratories. They come into existence—either through natural evolution or by intentional design—in real-world work groups and organizations. And, just as with laboratory groups, they can significantly affect the productivity and satisfaction of workers in industry.

quickly and efficiently. When the group confronts a more complex problem, however, the communication requirements placed on the hub are substantial, and the person occupying that position may become saturated and overburdened. When this happens, the group's problem-solving efficiency will be low. Decentralized networks do not have this problem because no position in the network is subject to extreme saturation.

Group Decision Making

Collective decisions are important outcomes resulting from group interaction. Family members decide where to travel on their vacation; managers of a business firm decide which new products to develop; experts on a review committee decide whether to support a research proposal; a group of basketball coaches decides what games to schedule for the upcoming season. In every instance, the end product resulting from interaction among group members is a decision—a choice among alternative courses of action.

Deliberations by a group must follow certain steps if a good decision is to result. Alternative courses of action must be developed in detail, the potential consequences of each option must be explored, and the relative value of each option must be weighed. In many cases, decisions made by groups are based on these steps, resulting in good outcomes.

Nevertheless, group decision making is fraught with special hazards. The decision-making process can go awry for a variety of reasons. Perhaps group members differ in the value they place on various options—a circumstance that can lead to a compromise decision that satisfies nobody. Or perhaps conformity

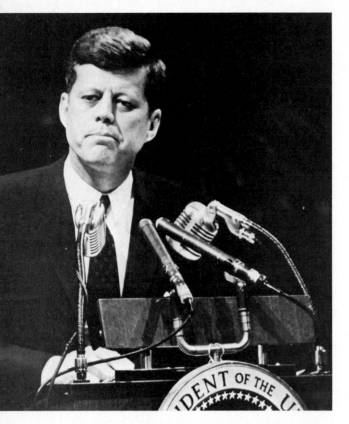

In an awkward moment President John F. Kennedy tries to explain the Bay of Pigs Fiasco. Even the "best and the brightest" can be victimized by groupthink.

pressures within the group may force members to bypass or short-circuit the decision-making process. If this happens, group deliberations can produce poor or unrealistic decisions.

Groupthink

Aberrations in decision making can plague any group, even those at the highest levels of business and government. The history of American foreign policy provides numerous examples. The decisions by the United States to invade the Cuban Bay of Pigs, to cross the 38th parallel in the Korean War, and to escalate the war in Vietnam—all were made by committees. The Bay of Pigs invasion, for example, was planned by a small group of top

government officials immediately after President Kennedy took office in 1961. The group included the nation's best and brightest: McGeorge Bundy, Dean Rusk, Robert McNamara, Douglas Dillon, Robert Kennedy, Arthur Schlesinger, Jr., and President Kennedy himself, together with representatives of the Pentagon and the Central Intelligence Agency. The decision was made to invade Cuba in April, 1961, with a small band of 1,400 Cuban exiles. The invasion was to be staged at the Bay of Pigs, assisted covertly by the U.S. Navy and Air Force and the CIA. As it turned out, the invasion was poorly conceived. The materiel and reserve ammunition on which the exiles were depending never arrived, because Castro's air force sank the supply ships. The exiles were promptly surrounded by 20,000 well-equipped Cuban soldiers, and within three days virtually all were captured or killed. The United States suffered a humiliating defeat in the eyes of the world, and the Castro government became more strongly entrenched in the Caribbean.

How could it happen? How could a group of such capable and experienced men make a decision that turned out so poorly? One post hoc analysis offered by Irving Janis (1982) suggests that high levels of group cohesiveness and conformity pressures can produce inferior outcomes. In a detailed study of cases in which government policymakers made poor decisions, Janis coined the term **groupthink.** This term refers to a mode of thinking within a cohesive group whereby pressures for unanimity overwhelm the members' motivation to appraise alternative courses of action realistically. In their effort to preserve cohesiveness and consensus, detailed critical thought, inspection of alternatives, weighing of pros and cons—all the requirements of carefully reasoned decisions—are neglected.

Groupthink is more likely to occur under some conditions than others. Four conditions that increase the probability of groupthink are (1) a crisis situation; (2) a highly cohesive group; (3) the insulation of group members from the judgments and criticisms of qualified outsiders; and (4) a leader who actively promotes his or her own favored solution to the problem facing the group. According to Janis, the simultaneous occurrence of these conditions is likely to produce groupthink.

How can the presence of groupthink be detected? Janis (1982, pp. 174–175) suggests there are a number of symptoms including:

1. An illusion of invulnerability shared by most or all of the members that produces excessive optimism and encourages taking extreme risks.

2. An unquestioned belief in the group's inherent morality, inclining the members to ignore the ethical consequences of their decisions.

3. Collective efforts to rationalize in order to discount warnings that might lead the members to reconsider their assumptions.

4. In the political sphere, a stereotyped view of enemy leaders as too evil to warrant genuine attempts to negotiate, or as too weak and stupid to counter whatever attempts are made to defeat their purposes.

5. Self-censorship of deviation from the apparent group consensus, with each member inclined to minimize the importance of doubts and counterarguments.

6. A shared illusion of unanimity concerning judgments conforming to the majority view.

7. Direct pressure on any member who expresses strong arguments against any of the group's stereotypes, illusions, or commitments, making clear that dissent is contrary to what is expected of all group members.

8. The emergence of self-appointed "mindguards"—members who protect the group from adverse information that might shatter their shared complacency about the effectiveness and morality of their decisions.

Some of these symptoms were present during the Bay of Pigs decision. For example, there was an assumed air of consensus that caused members of the group to ignore some glaring defects in their plan. Although several of Kennedy's senior advisors had strong doubts about the planning (which they expressed later), the group atmosphere inhibited them from voicing criticism. Several members emerged as "mindguards" within the group; they suppressed the views of opponents by arguing that the decision to invade had already been made and that everyone should help the president instead of distracting him with dissension. Open inquiry and clearheaded exploration were discouraged. Even the contingency planning was unrealistic. If the exiles did not succeed in their prime military objective at the Bay of Pigs, they were supposed to join the anti-Castro guerrillas known to be operating in the Escambray Mountains. Apparently no one was concerned that 80 miles of swamp and jungle stood between the mountains and the invasion site.

There are several ways to prevent groupthink from occurring, even in highly cohesive groups (Janis 1982). Basically these methods increase the probability that a group will obtain all the information relevant to the decision and evaluate that information with great care. First, the group's leader should encourage dissent and call on each member to express any objections and doubts. Second, the leader should be impartial and not state preferences for a favorite plan at the outset. By describing a problem, rather than recommending a solution, the leader can foster an atmosphere of open inquiry and impartial exploration. Third, the group might establish several independent subgroups to work on the same problem, each carrying out its deliberations independently. This will prevent the premature development of consensus. Finally, after a tentative consensus has been reached, the group might hold a "second chance" meeting at which each member can express any remaining doubts before a firm decision is taken.

Polarization in Decisions Involving Risk

Groupthink is not the only problem that can occur in group decision making. Interaction in groups may also cause individuals to favor courses of action that are riskier than what they would choose if they made the decision alone. This was demonstrated in an early study (Stoner 1962) in which subjects responded individually to a series of 12 problems called "choice dilemmas." In each problem, the subjects were asked to advise a fictional character how much risk he or she should assume. The following item (from Kogan and Wallach 1964) illustrates this task:

Mr. A, an electrical engineer who is married and has one child, has been working for a large electronics corporation since graduating from college five years ago. He is assured of a lifetime job with a modest, although adequate, salary and liberal pension benefits upon retirement. On the other hand, it is very unlikely that his salary will increase much before he retires. While attending a convention, Mr. A is offered a job with a small, newly founded company which has a highly uncertain future. The new job would pay more to start and would offer the possibility of a share in the ownership if the company survived the competition of the larger firms.

Imagine that you are advising Mr. A. Listed below are several probabilities or odds of the new company proving financially sound. Please check the lowest probability that you would consider acceptable to make it worthwhile for Mr. A to take the new job.

_____ The chances are 1 in 10 that the company will prove financially sound.
_____ The chances are 3 in 10 that the company will prove financially sound.
_____ The chances are 5 in 10 that the company will prove financially sound.
_____ The chances are 7 in 10 that the company will prove financially sound.
_____ The chances are 9 in 10 that the company will prove financially sound.
_____ Place a check here if you think Mr. A should not take the new job no matter what the probabilities.

After individually offering their advice on this and other items, the participants assembled in groups of six and discussed each item until they reached a unanimous decision. Each subject was then asked to review each item and, once again, to make an individual decision. The basic finding was that the decisions made after group discussion were on the average riskier than the decisions made by individual members prior to discussion. This phenomenon, called the **risky-shift**, has been observed in numerous studies (Pruitt and Teger 1967; Dion, Baron, and Miller 1970; Cartwright 1971; Clark 1971).

A number of other studies, however, indicate that although group discussion frequently produces a shift in individual opinions, this shift is not necessarily toward greater risk. In some circumstances, members shift toward a more conservative position. This is known as a _cautious-shift_ (Fraser, Gouge, and Billig, 1971; Baron et al. 1971; Knox and Safford 1976).

Risky-shift and cautious-shift are part of a more general phenomenon called group polarization. By definition, **group polarization** occurs when group members shift their opinions toward a position that is similar to, but more extreme than, their initial pregroup responses. For instance, if members initially advocated a moderately risky position prior to group discussion, they will shift toward greater risk following discussion. If they initially advocated a moderately cautious position, they will shift in the direction of even greater caution after discussion.

Group polarization is a widespread phenomenon. It occurs not only on the choice dilemma questionnaire, but also in other contexts. It has been observed with respect to political attitudes (Moscovici and Zavalloni

A group of investors plans for a new building. In circumstances like this, group polarization may lead to ill-considered—and costly—decisions.

1969; Paicheler and Bouchet 1973), jury decisions (Myers and Kaplan 1976), satisfaction with new consumer products (Johnson and Andrews 1971), judgments of physical dimensions (Vidmar 1974), ethical decisions (Horne and Long 1972), perception of other persons (Myers 1975), and interpersonal bargaining and negotiation (Rabbie and Visser 1972; Lamm and Sauer 1974).

Why does group polarization occur? That is, what causes group members to shift their risk-taking responses toward an extreme position? Two basic explanations have been proposed (Myers and Lamm 1976). According to

one, group polarization results from a process of *social comparison* (Jellison and Riskind 1970; Pruitt 1971). This theory suggests that people often value opinions that are more extreme than those they personally advocate. They fail to adopt these ideal (extreme) positions as their own because they fear being labelled extremist or deviant. However, during a group discussion in which members compare their positions, these persons may discover that other members hold opinions closer to their ideal positions than they do themselves. This realization motivates the moderate members to adopt more extreme positions. The overall result is a polarization of opinions. Although controversial, this explanation has been supported by various studies (Myers 1973; Jellison and Davis 1973; Baron and Roper 1976; Sanders and Baron 1977).

The other explanation of group polarization emphasizes *persuasive argumentation* (Burnstein and Vinokur 1973, 1977). According to this view, group polarization occurs whenever the preponderance of compelling arguments advanced during group discussion favors a position more extreme than that held initially by the average member. Discussion within the group serves to persuade members who, because they were unaware of the arguments, initially chose relatively moderate positions. Consequently, the moderate members shift their opinions in the direction of the most compelling, and relatively extreme, arguments. This produces group polarization.

Research supports the persuasive arguments explanation. It has been shown, for instance, that the greater the proportion of arguments favoring a particular point of view, the greater the shift of opinion in its direction (Morgan and Aram 1975; Ebbesen and Bowers 1974). Thus, subjects who are exposed to mostly risky arguments become more risk-taking, whereas those who hear mostly conservative arguments become more cautious.

Leadership Effectiveness

As we have seen, group performance depends on several factors, including the nature of the task, group communication structure, and cohesiveness. Still another factor affecting group performance is the type of leadership exercised within the group.

By definition, a *leader* is any person who directs and coordinates activities of other members in the pursuit of group goals. In exchange for their support, a leader provides guidance, specialized skills, and contacts with the environment that are valuable to members. Some of the factors that determine whether or not a person will become a leader were discussed in Chapter 13. Here, we will consider the attributes and behaviors that determine whether a leader will be effective or ineffective in helping a group achieve its goals.

Authoritarian and Democratic Leadership Styles

Depending on the situation and on their personalities, leaders use different techniques to influence group members. For example, some leaders adopt an authoritarian style: they make most of the decisions and issue orders to members. Other leaders adopt a democratic style: they allow the group as a whole to make important decisions and act primarily to coordinate activities. Which style—authoritarian or democratic—produces better group performance?

One of the pioneer studies on leadership style was conducted by Lewin, Lippit, and White (1939). In this study and later work (Lippitt 1940; Lippitt and White, 1943, 1952), groups of 10-year-old boys met after school for three six-week periods. The groups performed various activities such as painting and lettering signs, building box furniture out of wood, and carving soap. These activities were directed by adult leaders using specific leadership styles. The **authoritarian leader** exercised a great deal of control. He determined all policies, dictated techniques and work activities, assigned tasks and work partners, and administered praise and criticism without explaining his reasons. Moreover, he intentionally kept the group uninformed about many matters, and remained aloof from group participation. The **democratic leader** behaved quite differently. He encouraged group members to discuss policy issues, and he collaborated with them in making decisions. He suggested alternatives, but did not give orders. His group members chose their own tasks and working companions. He was friendly and tried to be "one of the group" as much as possible. He also tried to be objective, and to explain his praise and criticism. A third type of leader, the **laissez-faire leader,** adopted a "hands off" approach. He was friendly but extremely passive, keeping his participation to an absolute minimum. The laissez-faire leader supplied information when asked, but otherwise left the group pretty much to itself. He made no attempt to evaluate or regulate the group's activities.

While the groups were at work, observers kept extensive records of members' behavior. The results show that leadership style had a marked influence not only on group productivity, but also on the interpersonal relationships of members.

The lowest level of group productivity was associated with the laissez-faire leadership style. The groups with a laissez-faire leader were not very goal-oriented, and the members engaged in a lot of horseplay. As a result, the work was of relatively poor quality, although the boys were friendly with the laissez-faire leader.

Groups with an authoritarian leader displayed the highest level of productivity in terms of quantity of output. Groups responded submissively to their leader's directives, spent more time at work, and as a result produced more than other groups. However, their members showed a high level of hostility and negative feelings. Hostility was expressed as anger toward the leader, and in the destruction of property and scapegoating of other group members. Despite the relatively high output, these group members did not internalize the motivation to work. When the leader was called away from the room, for example, they stopped producing.

Groups with a democratic leader proved superior in some respects to those with authoritarian or laissez-faire leaders. Not only were they highly productive, they also enjoyed good interpersonal relations. Although the quantity of work completed under the democratic leader was slightly lower than that completed under the authoritarian leader, the quality and originality of the work were

superior. Boys in the democratically led groups manifested less submissive and dependent behavior than in the authoritarian groups. Work motivation was also high; when the leader left the room in a democratic group, the boys continued to work. The groups were cohesive and the boys engaged in friendly playfulness, offered mutual praise, and readily shared group property.

Many studies since this one have investigated the effects of authoritarian versus democratic leadership style on group performance. In general, findings show that members of groups under democratic leadership express more satisfaction with their group and its leaders than members of groups under authoritarian leadership. This is supported by both laboratory experiments (Preston and Heintz 1949; Shaw 1955) and field studies of work groups within larger organizations (Morse and Reimer 1956; Likert 1961). Although a few studies have shown that members prefer authoritarian to democratic leadership, these findings pertain primarily to military or bureaucratic settings where people have no expectation of sharing in decision making (Scott 1952; Berkowitz 1953; Gibb 1969).

The effects of leadership style on group productivity is less clear, however. Neither authoritarian nor democratic leadership is regularly associated with higher levels of group performance (Anderson 1963). Although some studies have found that a democratic style promotes higher levels of productivity and effectiveness (Kahn and Katz 1960; McGregor 1960), other studies show the opposite effect—with authoritarian groups having higher performance levels (Gekoski 1952; Shaw 1955). Authoritarian leadership is more effective, for example, among a group of sailors on shipboard. Clearly a democratic leader would be inefficient and potentially dangerous in a crisis at sea. Thus the relationship between leadership style and group performance is complex. As we shall see, the effectiveness of a leadership style depends on a variety of factors.

A drill instructor uses the strict authoritarian leadership style to command his troops. Would the instructor's leadership style be effective in another setting, such as conducting a symphony orchestra (next page)?

The Contingency Model of Leadership Effectiveness

A leader's effectiveness in directing a group depends not only on style, but also on characteristics of the situation. Someone with a specific leadership style might be effective in one situation, but not in another. This basic notion underlies the **contingency model of leadership effectiveness** (Fred Fiedler 1964, 1971, 1978). The contingency model pertains primarily to groups working on divisible tasks that require coordination among members for successful performance. This model is highly general, and has been applied to a variety of groups in military, educational, and industrial settings.

THE LPC SCORE. There are four independent variables in the contingency model. One of these is leadership style; the other three are properties of the situation in which a leader performs. The contingency model characterizes leadership style as being either relationship-oriented or task-oriented. To determine leadership style, a leader is first asked to recall all the people with whom he or she has ever worked in a group setting, and to select the one who was most difficult to get along with. This person is designated the least-preferred co-worker (LPC). Next the leader is asked to rate this person on dimensions such as pleasant–unpleasant, helpful–frustrating, cooperative–uncooperative, and efficient–inefficient.

Some leaders give very low, negative ratings to their least-preferred co-worker; these are called "low-LPC leaders." Other leaders find positive qualities even in their least-preferred co-worker; these are "high-LPC leaders." It has been found that low-LPC leaders are oriented toward achieving successful task performance, whereas high-LPC leaders are primarily concerned with establishing congenial interpersonal relations with others (Fiedler 1978; Rice 1978).

SITUATIONAL FACTORS. As already noted, a leader's effectiveness depends not only on leadership style, but on various characteristics of the situation. According to the contingency model, three characteristics of the situation are crucial. In order of importance these are (1) the leader's personal relationship with other group members (good or poor), (2) how highly structured the group's task is (structured or unstructured), and (3) the leader's position of power in the group (strong or weak).

A leader's *personal relationships* with other members is assumed to be the most important factor determining the leader's influence in the group. A leader whom the other members trust, like, and respect is in a more favorable situation than one with poor rapport, and will usually have the support of group members. The second factor, *task structure,* refers to how clearly defined the task requirements of a group are. Is their goal clearly defined? Is there a single path by which this goal can be achieved? Is there only one correct solution or decision? Is there some method of verifying

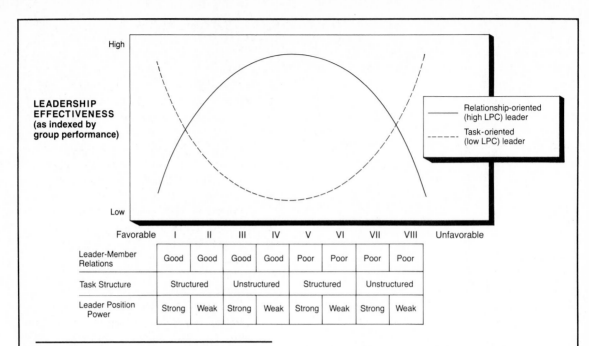

FIGURE 14.5

LEADERSHIP EFFECTIVENESS AS A FUNCTION OF LEADERSHIP STYLE AND SITUATIONAL FACTORS

The contingency model predicts that group performance depends on both leadership style and situational factors. According to this model, task-oriented (low-LPC) leaders will be most effective in situations that are either highly favorable (that is, good leader-member relations, structured task, strong leader pow-er) or that are highly unfavorable (poor lead-er-member relations, unstructured task, weak leader power). In contrast, relationship-oriented (high-LPC) leaders will be most effective in situations that are of medium favorableness.

Source: adapted from Fiedler (1978).

the accuracy of the solution or decision? The more these things are true, the greater the degree to which the task is structured, and the more favorable the situation for the lead-er. The third factor, *power,* has to do with the leader's formal authority over group members and the degree to which he can buttress his directives with rewards and punishments. The leader who wields more power is in a more favorable situation.

For convenience, each of these factors is considered to be dichotomous: leader-member relations are either good or poor, the task is either structured or unstructured, and the

leader's power is either strong or weak. Taken together, these three dichotomies produce eight possible situations. These situations are shown in Figure 14.5, listed according to their overall favorableness for the leader.

From a leader's standpoint, a situation is favorable if it enables him or her to exercise a great deal of influence. Thus, a situation involving good leader-member relations, a highly structured task, and strong leader power is favorable. At the other extreme, a situation involving poor leader-member rela-tions, an unstructured task, and weak leader power is very unfavorable for the leader.

PREDICTIONS. According to the contingency model, task-oriented (low-LPC) leaders will be effective in situations that are either highly favorable or highly unfavorable, and ineffective in other situations. In contrast, relationship-oriented (high-LPC) leaders will be effective in situations that are moderately favorable, and ineffective in the other situations. These predictions are shown in Figure 14.5.

When conditions are extremely unfavorable, the group will need strong task leadership, and it is the task-oriented (low-LPC) leader who best provides this. A low-LPC leader will be willing to overlook interpersonal conflicts in order to concentrate on the group's task. A high-LPC leader will attempt to smooth over interpersonal problems rather than to work on the group's fundamental task. However, when conditions for leadership are intermediate in favorableness, the high-LPC leader is the one who will provide what the group needs. Under these conditions, some situational factors will be positive and others negative. Interpersonal problems may come to the surface and the relationship-oriented (high-LPC) leader will be more effective than the task-oriented (low-LPC) leader. Finally, when conditions are highly favorable, the low-LPC leader will again emerge as most effective. Under these circumstances, low-LPC leaders will feel they can relax because goal attainment is not very problematic. They will turn their attention to interpersonal relations with their co-workers because they know that the task will get done. Thus, low-LPC leaders undergo a change in behavior that causes them to be highly effective when conditions are favorable. Under these same conditions, however, relationship-oriented (high-LPC) leaders are relatively ineffective and behave, as someone once remarked, like "underemployed mothers." They start looking for things to do and become bossy and unconcerned with the feelings and opinions of their co-workers, which diminishes their effectiveness (Fiedler 1978; Fiedler, Meuwese, and Oonk 1961; Chemers 1969; Larson and Rowland 1973).

TESTS OF THE CONTINGENCY MODEL. Although there are some exceptions, research generally supports the contingency model's predictions (Fiedler and Chemers 1974). One study (Chemers and Skrzypek 1972; Shiflett 1973), using West Point cadets as subjects, manipulated all three dimensions of situational favorableness. Four-man groups were assembled on the basis of previously attained information regarding the relations among members. In half of the groups, the leader-member relations were good, whereas in the other half they were poor. Each group performed one structured task (transforming blueprints from metric units to inches) and one unstructured task (discussing an issue and making policy recommendations). In half of the groups the leader had strong power—that is, members believed that the leader would assess their performance and this would affect their standing in the Academy. In the other half, the leader had only weak power—members believed he could have little effect on their standing. As predicted by the contingency model, the task-oriented low-LPC leaders proved to be more effective when the situation was either very unfavorable or very favorable. In contrast, the relationship-oriented high-LPC leaders were more effective when the situation was of intermediate favorableness. Similar findings have emerged in studies of college and elementary-school students (Hardy 1971, 1975; Hardy, Sack, and Harpine 1973) and naval personnel (Fielder 1966).

Summary

This chapter has discussed both group productivity and group decision making. That is, it has focused on outcomes from group interaction rather than on the processes of interaction per se.

FACTORS AFFECTING GROUP PRODUCTIVITY. Group productivity refers to the output or end state resulting from the activity of group members. Several factors determine how productive a group will be. (1) First, group tasks can be categorized as unitary (that is, members perform similar activities) or divisible (members perform complementary activities). Unitary tasks may be conjunctive, disjunctive, or additive. Performance on conjunctive tasks depends on the group's slowest or worst member; performance on disjunctive tasks depends on the fastest or best member; performance on additive tasks depends on the sum (or average) of members' performances. (2) Group size also affects performance. On disjunctive tasks, group performance increases directly with group size; on conjunctive tasks, it decreases with group size. On additive tasks, the Ringelmann effect occurs: total productivity increases directly with group size, but productivity per member decreases. (3) Group cohesiveness interacts with group norms to determine productivity. Highly cohesive groups will be more productive than less cohesive groups, but only when they have norms favoring high productivity. (4) The group's reward structure affects productivity, especially when members make equal contributions toward group performance. Under low task interdependence, differential rewarding has little effect on group productivity. Under high task interdependence, a high level of differential rewarding induces low group productivity as well as competition among members, whereas a low level of differential rewarding induces high group productivity and cooperation. (5) The structure of a group's communication network also affects performance. Centralized communication networks lead to faster, more accurate performance then decentralized ones on simple problems. Decentralized networks lead to superior performance on complex problems, because they prevent excessive saturation.

GROUP DECISION MAKING. Another product of interaction among group members is decision-making—that is, choices among alternative courses of action. Group decision making is fraught with potential hazards that can lead to poor or inferior choices. (1) One of these haz-

ards is groupthink, a mode of thinking that occurs when pressures for unanimity overwhelm members' motivation to realistically appraise alternative actions. Groupthink is most likely to occur in groups that are highly cohesive, facing a crisis situation, and insulated from outside criticism. Groupthink can be prevented or reduced if group leaders strive not only to obtain all information relevant to the decision but also to encourage an atmosphere of open inquiry and impartial exploration of alternatives. (2) Another hazard in group decision making is polarization, which occurs when group members shift the opinions they held earlier toward a more extreme position following group discussion. Polarization is especially significant when the decision involves some risk, for it may cause the group to shift its choice toward higher or lower levels of risk. The underlying cause of group polarization has been traced to two distinct processes, social comparison and persuasive argumentation.

LEADERSHIP EFFECTIVENESS. An important factor affecting group decision making and performance is the style of leadership. (1) Although findings are somewhat inconsistent, research shows that authoritarian-led groups produce large quantities of moderate quality output, whereas democratically-led groups produce moderate-to-large quantities of high quality output. (2) The contingency model of leadership effectiveness maintains that group performance is a function not only of leadership style but also of the situation in which the leader performs. According to this model, task-oriented (low-LPC) leaders are most effective in situations that are highly favorable (that is, good leader-member relations, structured task, strong leader power position) and in situations that are highly unfavorable (that is, poor leader-member relations, unstructured tasks, weak leader power position). In contrast, relationship-oriented (high-LPC) leaders are most effective in situations that are moderately favorable. A number of studies support the contingency model.

Key Terms and Concepts
Group Productivity

Troubleshooting

Unitary Task

Divisible Task

Conjunctive Task

Disjunctive Task

Additive Task

Cooperation

Competition

Communication Network

Saturation

Groupthink

Risky-Shift

Group Polarization

Authoritarian Leadership

Democratic Leadership

Laissez-Faire Leadership

Contingency Model of Leadership
Effectiveness

Part 4
Society and Social Behavior

Chapter 15

Intergroup Conflict

Introduction

Kanawha County, West Virginia, contains the state capital of Charleston as well as a number of smaller communities. The county school board has five members, elected at large. In early 1974, the school board became embroiled in a controversy regarding the selection of 325 language arts textbooks (English, composition, journalism, and speech). The conflict was instigated by a member of the school board, the articulate wife of a fundamentalist minister. She opposed the new books on the grounds that they were excessively liberal in viewpoint. At the April 11 meeting of the school board, she objected to the method of textbook selection. At the June 2 meeting, she again objected to the new books, and observed that there was little in the texts to support a traditional, fundamentalist conception of God, the Bible, and religion. On June 23, she spoke in opposition to the books to the congregation of a local Baptist church. All these events were covered by the local news media.

On June 27, over 1,000 textbook protestors appeared at the regularly scheduled school board meeting. Nevertheless, after hours of testimony, the board voted formally to adopt the disputed books.

During the months of July and August, the textbook protestors organized their ranks and developed strategy. There were several distinct protest groups within the movement. One of these, The Concerned Citizens of Kanawha County, was a large coalition of church congregations. A second group was the Businessmen and Professional People's Alliance for Better Textbooks, a middle-class group composed mainly of businessmen, teachers, and other professionals. A third protest group was the Christian American Parents. These groups held marches and rallies, circulated petitions, appealed to elected officials, and planned a boycott of the school system for September. Opposing these groups were the Kanawha County School Board and the Citizens for Quality Education. Further support

for the textbooks came from such liberal organizations as the American Civil Liberties Union (ACLU), the National Association for the Advancement of Colored People (NAACP), and from teachers and school administrators.

On September 3, the new school term started for some 45,000 students. Protesting parents withheld their children from the schools (10,000 by some estimates), and prevented school and city buses from operating. On September 12, the school board closed the schools for a three-day cooling-off period. The controversial textbooks were removed from the classrooms pending review by a special citizens' committee.

During this period, some violence broke out. Random gunfire and sniping were reported. Vandalism of school property was commonplace. The protestors demanded that the board members and the superintendent resign and that the books be banned permanently. On October 28, the citizens' review committee recommended that all but 35 of the 325 books be returned to the classroom. In reaction, the county board building was dynamited and partially destroyed the night of October 30.

On November 9, the school board voted 4–1 to reintroduce most of the textbooks in the classrooms. In response, the protestors had the police arrest the school superintendent and four board members on November 15 for "contributing to the delinquency of minors." Many parents continued to withhold their children from public schools, while other students were enrolled in newly created private Christian schools stressing a fundamentalist curriculum.

By the end of the year, the protestors appeared to have won a number of concessions from the school board. New guidelines were issued for textbook selection, and a number of "alternative" elementary schools with a more traditional approach to education were planned for the following semester. Although the vehemence of the protest subsided, the anger of protestors lingered on (Page and Clelland 1978).

Intergroup Conflict

The Kanawha County textbook controversy is an instance of **intergroup conflict,** a situation in which groups take antagonistic actions toward one another in order to control some outcome important to them. The major participants in the textbook controversy are groups—the Concerned Citizens of Kanawha County, the Businessmen and Professional People's Alliance for Better Textbooks, and the Christian American Parents on one side, and the Kanawha County School Board and the Citizens for Quality Education on the other. The textbook controversy shows many features typical of intergroup conflict. The issues at stake become more apparent as the conflict progresses. Distrust and hostility grow, and members of opposing groups develop antagonistic attitudes toward each other. Overt hostility becomes increasingly severe and destructive. Groups commit themselves to various positions, and the conflict becomes more difficult to resolve.

Intergroup conflict often involves confrontation between competing beliefs and norms. Thus, a concerned mother who intentionally blocks the movement of a school bus may, in the eyes of the school board, be performing an unlawful and deviant act. But, in fact, she may be conforming to a different set of norms—those of the anti-textbook coalition. In most intergroup conflicts, behavior viewed as appropriate by members of one group is considered unacceptable by members of another. The conflict is rooted not merely in individual behavior, but in the different goals, norms, and belief systems of opposing groups.

Although peaceful relationships among groups are probably more widespread than conflicting ones, it is intergroup conflict that receives the most attention on television and in newspaper headlines. Every day in the media we encounter intergroup conflict in many forms. Street fights between teen gangs, hostilities between the KKK and the black

The Kanawha County textbook controversy began with disagreements about the selection of textbooks. It escalated into a classroom boycott by students and parents, attacks on the Board of Education building, and even the creation of alternative schools.

community, labor strikes against management, strife between religious groups, economic competition and rivalry among ethnic groups, and long-standing family feuds—these are all examples of intergroup conflict.

In discussing intergroup conflict, this chapter will address the following questions:

1. What causes groups to shift from peaceful to hostile relations? That is, what factors cause the development and escalation of intergroup conflict?

2. What sustains the conflict? When intergroup conflict persists over a long period of time—as it often does—what mechanisms support its persistence?

3. What effect does intergroup conflict have on relationships among members within each of the groups? In other words, when a group is involved in conflict with another, what impact does this have on the group's structure and on the way its members relate to one another?

4. How can intergroup conflict be reduced or stopped before it escalates to extreme levels?

Development of Intergroup Conflict

There are several basic causes of intergroup conflict. Conflict may develop (1) because groups have directly opposing goals (that is, a real opposition of interest), (2) because one group suddenly threatens or deprives the other, provoking an aggressive reaction, or (3) because members of one group act in an ethnocentric and prejudicial way toward members of another group. These factors are not mutually exclusive; in fact, they often work simultaneously to foster intergroup conflict. We shall consider each of them in turn.

Realistic Group Conflict Theory

A number of years ago, Muzafer Sherif and his co-workers conducted an important study on intergroup conflict at Robbers Cave, Oklahoma (Sherif 1966; Sherif and Sherif 1953; Sherif et al. 1961). The participants in this experiment were well-adjusted, academically successful, white, middle-class American boys ages 11 and 12. These boys attended a two-week experimental summer camp and participated in camp activities, unaware that their behavior was under observation. Throughout the two-week period, the boys were organized into two groups, the Eagles and the Rattlers. The overall objective of the research was to investigate conditions that cause intergroup conflict, as well as conditions that reduce conflict.

The experiment consisted of several stages. The first stage, which lasted about a week, was intended to produce a high level of cohesiveness within each of the two groups. The boys arrived at the camp on two separate buses and settled in cabins located a considerable distance apart. Contact between the two groups was minimal.

The boys within each cabin engaged in numerous activities, many of which were interdependent in character and required cooperative effort for achievement. They camped out, cooked, worked on improving swimming holes, transported canoes over rough terrain to the water, and played various games. As they worked together, the boys in each group pooled their efforts, organized duties, and divided up tasks of work and play. Eventually, the boys in each unit developed a high degree of group cohesiveness.

The next stage of the experiment induced conflict between the two groups. Several competitive situations were set up in which one group could attain its goal only at the other's expense. The camp staff arranged a tournament of games—baseball, touch football, tug-of-war, a treasure hunt, and so on—in which prizes were awarded only to the victorious group.

The tournament started in the spirit of good sportsmanship, but as it progressed, the good feeling began to fade. The "good sportsmanship" cheer customarily given after a game, "2–4–6–8, who do we appreciate" followed by the name of the other group, turned into "2–4–6–8, who do we appreci-*hate*." Intergroup hostility intensified, and members of each group began to call their rivals "sneaks" and "cheats." After suffering a defeat in one game, the Eagles burned a banner left behind by the Rattlers. The next morning, the Rattlers seized the Eagles' flag when they arrived on the athletic field. Name-calling, threats, physical scuffling, and cabin raids became increasingly frequent. When asked by the experimenter to rate each other's characters, a large proportion of the boys in each group gave negative ratings to all boys in the other group. When the tournament was over, members of the two groups refused to have anything to do with each other.

In later stages of the experiment when the level of antagonism was quite high, various strategies for reducing strife were introduced. Several techniques failed, but by introducing goals that were valued by both groups and that required intergroup cooperation for attainment, the experimenters did succeed in reducing conflict (Sherif et al. 1961; Sherif 1966).

This study is a classic illustration of **realistic group conflict theory,** which is the most firmly established theory for explaining the development of intergroup conflict. It explains the development of intergroup conflict in terms of the goals of each group. Its central hypothesis is that groups will engage in conflictive behavior when their goals run head-on. It was precisely under these conditions that conflict erupted between the Eagles and the Rattlers. It was also under these conditions that conflict erupted in Kanawha County regarding the content of textbooks and the social values to be taught in public schools. The realistic group conflict theory has received support from Sherif's study as well as various others (Blake and Mouton 1961b; Diab 1970).

The basic propositions of realistic group conflict theory are as follows: First, when groups engage in competitive activities so that one group's victory necessarily results in the other's loss, they are by definition involved in a "real opposition of interest." Second, this real opposition of interest causes members of each group to experience frustration and develop antagonistic attitudes and unfavorable stereotypes regarding members of the other group. Third, as members of one group develop negative attitudes toward the other group, they become more strongly identified with and attached to their own group. As solidarity and cohesiveness within each group increases, it intensifies the conflict, making this increasingly difficult to resolve.

Aversive Events and Escalation

Sometimes a single event will trigger open conflict where none existed previously. For example, several years ago an unexpected defeat in an important high-school basketball game on Long Island, New York, led to an argument between fans that quickly escalated into a serious brawl. These fans had different racial and ethnic identities—those supporting the losing home team were largely black, whereas those supporting the visitors were mostly Irish and Italian. Persons were beaten and school buses were overturned. Squads of police arrived, and eventually suppressed the brawl, but the conflict continued for several weeks among groups of teen-agers from each community.

This example shows how a single aversive event can provoke open hostilities between groups (Berkowitz 1972; Konečni 1979). By definition, an **aversive event** is a situation caused by (or attributed to) an outside group that produces negative or undesirable outcomes for members of the target group. The unexpected loss of the basketball game was an aversive event for fans of the home team, and it provoked wider conflict. In general, aversive events are situations that most people would avoid, such as being physically or verbally attacked, being slighted or humiliated, or facing a loss of income or property.

In addition to provoking new conflicts, aversive events can also activate latent conflicts between groups. Consider a situation in which several groups have an underlying opposition of interest, but have managed to avoid open hostilities over the issue. Should an aversive event occur, it may activate the latent conflict. In the Kanawha County textbook controversy, for example, a latent conflict existed between fundamentalist church groups and the liberal board of education. But it took an aversive event—the adoption of the new textbooks—to provoke demonstrations and overt hostility. Once this event occurred, groups mobilized in terms of ideologies and real interests; the conflict quickly escalated.

The idea that aversive events lead to intergroup conflict is one form of the psychological hypothesis that frustration leads to aggression. When group members respond to an aversive event, they often develop antagonistic attitudes and negative stereotypes. In extreme cases, the group under attack will mobilize and counterattack its adversary. This is most likely to happen when an underlying opposition of interest already exists between groups and/or when obvious differences (such as language, religion, or skin color) serve as a basis for differentiation between them.

In-Group Identification and Ethnocentrism

So far we have seen how such factors as an underlying opposition of interest or an aversive event can cause intergroup conflict. Another factor in intergroup conflict is the extent to which members identify with the group to which they belong. In conjunction with aversive events or opposition of interest, strong group identification can greatly intensify the conflict between groups.

ETHNOCENTRISM. Years ago, William Graham Sumner (1905) noted that people tend to like their own group (the **in-group**) and to dislike competing or opposing groups (the **out-groups**). He hypothesized that persons having strong group identification are especially prone to favor the in-group and to hold negative sentiments toward out-groups. Sumner's term for this phenomenon was **ethnocentrism**—regarding one's own group as the center of everything and evaluating other groups with reference to it. In its purest form, ethnocentrism is based on a pervasive and rigid distinction between in-group and out-group. It entails stereotyped negative imagery and hostile attitudes regarding out-groups and stereotyped positive imagery and favorable attitudes regarding one's own group (Adorno et al. 1950). Ethnocentrism can be expressed in many ways. A summary of the in-group and out-group orientations in ethnocentrism is presented in Table 15.1 (LeVine and Campbell 1972).

Ethnocentrism involves a generalized prejudice against the out-group and glorification

TABLE 15.1

ETHNOCENTRIC ORIENTATIONS TOWARD THE IN-GROUP AND THE OUT-GROUP

Orientations toward In-group	Orientations toward Out-group
See selves as virtuous and superior	See out-group as contemptible, immoral, and inferior
See own standards of value as universal, intrinsically true	Rejection of out-group values
See selves as strong	See out-group as weak
Sanctions against theft	Sanctions for theft
Sanctions against murder	Sanctions for murder
Cooperative relations with other group members	Absence of cooperation
Obedience to authorities	Absence of obedience
Willingness to retain membership in group	Rejection of membership
Willingness to fight and die for group	Virtue in killing out-group members in warfare
	Maintenance of social distance
	Negative affect, hate Use as bad examples in training children
	Blame for in-group troubles
	Distrust and fear

Source: adapted from LeVine and Campbell (1972).

of the in-group. Thus, many specific attitudes comprising the ethnocentrism syndrome occur simultaneously in a given setting—seeing the in-group as superior and the out-group as inferior, viewing the in-group as strong and the out-group as weak, and construing the in-group as honest and peaceful and the out-group as treacherous and hostile. Note, however, that not all facets of ethnocentrism manifest themselves in every conflict. In some instances, only a portion of the orientations listed in Table 15.1 occur (Brewer and Campbell 1976; Brewer 1979). Nor is it necessary that all members of the in-group hold ethnocentric prejudices regarding out-groups. Members who identify less strongly with the in-group may hold a more objective viewpoint (Merton 1968; Turner 1975).

Nevertheless, ethnocentrism in one form or another often occurs in intergroup relations. Combined with aversive events or a real opposition of interest, ethnocentric attitudes can create ill will and a hostile interpretation of the motives of out-group members. These attitudes devalue and demean out-group members, causing them to be seen as something less than human. In turn, this makes them ready targets for hostile action. When out-group members fight back, they are seen as the source of all the problems.

INTERGROUP DISCRIMINATION. Bias favoring the in-group is very likely to come into play during situations of direct competition between groups. More remarkable, several studies have shown that even when an underlying opposition of interest is not present, the mere awareness that an out-group exists can provoke discriminatory responses by in-group members. In some cases, the simple process of social categorization—dividing people arbitrarily into groups—is sufficient to trigger intergroup discrimination (Tajfel et al. 1971; Tajfel 1978; Brewer and Silver 1978).

This was demonstrated in an experimental paradigm (Tajfel et al. 1971; Tajfel and Billig 1974), in which subjects—English schoolboys aged 14–16, who knew each other well—were brought into a laboratory. The boys were divided into two groups based on their performance on a trivial task, such as estimating the number of dots flashed onto a screen. Although subjects were told what group they themselves were in, they did not know who else was in their group or who was in the other group. Next, the boys were told to distribute points worth money to other subjects. They did not know personal identities of those to whom they were awarding money—only their group membership. The boys received no directions how to award these points, but merely were told that at the end of the experiment each of them would receive amounts of money allotted by the other subjects.

Results of these studies show that subjects awarded more money to anonymous in-group members than to anonymous out-group members. The effect was widespread; approximately 75 percent of the subjects showed a clear bias favoring the in-group. This occurred in spite of the fact that: (1) such responses had no utilitarian value for the subjects themselves, because they were giving money to other people; (2) there was no social interaction, either within a group or between groups; (3) there was neither an opposition of interest nor any previously existing hostility between the groups.

In natural settings, there is a much stronger basis for intergroup discrimination than in laboratory settings. Salient factors such as skin color or language make group membership easily recognizable. Members of groups based on such sharp distinctions will often show strong in-group bias. In this sense, the process of categorization itself can be important in intergroup conflict.

Persistence of Intergroup Conflict

Probably the most famous family feud in the history of the United States is the long-enduring conflict between the Hatfields and the McCoys. In the early days, these mountain people lived peacefully on opposite sides of a narrow river, the Hatfields in West Virginia and the McCoys in Kentucky. The feud began one day in 1873 when Floyd Hatfield drove a

The Ku Klux Klan has long symbolized racial hatred and conflict in the United States. More recently, the activities of the Klan have met with increasing opposition.

razorback sow and her piglets into his pigsty on the McCoy side of the river. The pigs settled in comfortably, but trouble broke out a few days later when Randolph McCoy, Floyd's brother-in-law, came up beside the pigsty and accused Floyd of stealing the pigs. A furious argument broke out, and the family bond was suddenly shattered. The dispute eventually wound up in a backwoods court. Witness upon witness went to the stand to testify regarding the ownership of the pigs. All those witnesses named Hatfield swore that Floyd owned the pigs and all those named McCoy pointed to Randolph as the rightful owner. When the trial finally ended, Floyd Hatfield retained possession of the animals.

This was only the beginning, however. The McCoys were very angry and familial affection quickly turned to hatred. The feud deepened in intensity. Time passed and the pigs were forgotten, but the entire McCoy family joined the fight against the Hatfield clan. Several months later Ellison Hatfield was

murdered, and three McCoy boys were shot in retaliation. Eventually, civil authorities of West Virginia and Kentucky were drawn into the fight as they attempted to maintain order and protect human rights. According to one estimate, more than 100 persons lost their lives during the course of the feud. It was not until 1928, when Tennis Hatfield and Uncle Jim McCoy shook hands in public, that the conflict finally ended (Jones 1948).

The Hatfield-McCoy feud is an interesting—and puzzling—event. It began as a simple disagreement over ownership of a pig, and escalated into an enduring conflict that lasted 55 years and cost many lives. The feud illustrates a fundamental point about intergroup conflict: even without outside provocation, processes *internal* to a conflict can cause it to escalate and persist over time. Conflicts often feed on themselves.

What processes support the persistence of intergroup conflict? Researchers have identified several, including (1) biased perception regarding the intentions and performance of out-group members, and (2) changes in the structure of the relationship between adversaries. We will consider each of these below.

Biased Perception of the Out-Group

STEREOTYPIC DISTORTION.   One striking feature of intergroup conflict is the apparent irrationality of group members. In-group members often hold extremely negative and distorted stereotypes of out-group members. In part these stereotypes result from the fact that in-group members have less information about the out-group than about their own group (Linville and Jones 1980). Yet these stereotypes are very resistant to change. Even close contact between members of hostile sides often fails to modify stereotypes and prejudices.

How can group members maintain their negative stereotypes despite evidence to the contrary? One answer, based on *attribution theory*, suggests that stereotypes are maintained by a perceptual bias on the part of the in-group. If an in-group observer sees a member of an out-group engaging in undesirable behavior, the observer will ascribe it to the personal or dispositional characteristics of the out-group member. If, however, the behavior happens to be desirable or to have positive consequences for the in-group, the prejudiced in-group observer will ascribe it to situational pressures, accident, or luck. Thus, the out-group will be blamed for negative behaviors, but not given credit for positive behaviors (Pettigrew 1979; Cooper and Fazio 1979).

There are many ways that the in-group can explain away or discount positive behavior by out-group members. For example, the out-group member may be viewed as an "exceptional case," someone who differs from other out-group members ("He's really very capable—not like the rest of those stupid Arabs"). Likewise, the positive behavior by the out-group member may be ascribed to situational pressures ("It's true that mercenary Jew offered us a good price on this business deal, but what else could he do with four of our accountants looking over his shoulder?").

One study illustrating this phenomenon was conducted in India, where Hindus and Muslims have a long history of severe conflict (Taylor and Jaggi 1974). In this study, researchers observed Hindu office clerks making attributions regarding positive or negative behaviors involving either Hindus or Muslims. The behaviors in the study included situations such as a shopkeeper either behaving generously or cheating, and a person either helping or ignoring an injured individual. Results indicated that negative behavior by an out-group member (a Muslim) was attributed more to internal (personality) factors than positive behavior, whereas negative behavior by an in-group member (a Hindu) was only rarely attributed to personal dispositions and was usually viewed as caused by external pressures. These attributions enabled the Hindus to maintain their prevailing stereotypes regarding Muslims. Biased perception of this kind is widespread in intergroup conflict.

BIASED EVALUATION OF PERFORMANCE.   Another common bias that feeds intergroup conflict involves the in-group's evaluation of its own performance. Members tend to overrate the performance of their own group relative to that of the out-group. The Robbers Cave study discussed earlier in this chapter clearly demonstrates this bias (Sherif et al 1961). When antagonism between the two groups of boys was at its peak, investigators arranged a bean collecting contest. Beans were scattered on the ground, and the boys collected as many as they could in one minute. Each person stored his beans in a sack with a narrow opening, so he could not check the number of beans in it. Later, the beans gathered by each boy were projected on a screen in a large room, and all persons were asked to estimate the number in each boy's collection. The projection time was very short and prohibited counting. In reality, the same number of beans (35) was projected on the screen each time. The boys' estimates revealed a strong in-group bias. They overesti-

Box 15.1

GROUP MEMBERSHIP AND BIASED PERCEPTION

Group membership can bias the way in which a situation is perceived. Thus, a single event may be perceived and evaluated differently by in-group members and out-group members. This is illustrated in a classic case study of student reaction to an Ivy League football game between perennial rivals, Princeton and Dartmouth (Hastorf and Cantril 1954). It was the last game of the season for both teams. A few minutes after the opening kickoff, it was obvious that the game was going to be rough. Referees were kept busy blowing their whistles, calling penalties on both teams. Tempers flared. In the second quarter, Princeton's star back left the game with a broken nose and a mild concussion. In the third quarter, a Dartmouth player was taken off the field with a broken leg.

After the game (which Princeton won), accusations and recriminations were made by persons at both schools. What was interesting from the investigators' standpoint was that the discussions of the game on each campus, and particularly the coverage in the school newspapers, described starkly different versions of the contest. Four days after the game, the *Daily Princetonian* is quoted as saying: "This observer has never seen quite such a disgusting exhibition of so-called 'sport.' Both teams were guilty but the blame must be laid primarily on Dartmouth's doorstep. Prince-

ton, obviously the better team, had no reason to rough up Dartmouth. . . ." Meanwhile, Dartmouth students were seeing a different game through the editorial eyes of the *Dartmouth*. That paper asserted that, after Princeton's star player had been injured early in the game, the Princeton coach "instilled the old see-what-they-did-go-get-them attitude into his players. His tale got results. . . . Results: one bad leg and one leg broken."

Investigators administered a questionnaire to both Dartmouth and Princeton undergraduates one week after the game. The table shown here displays some of their responses. Nearly all the Princeton students judged the game as "rough and dirty"—not one respondent thought it was "clean and fair." Eighty-six percent of them thought that Dartmouth's team started the rough play during the game. A plurality of Dartmouth students also felt the game was "rough and dirty," although 13 percent thought the game was "clean and fair" and 39 percent described it as "rough and fair." Although some Dartmouth students felt that their own team initiated the rough play, the majority of Dartmouth students thought both sides were to blame.

In addition to the questionnaire, the investigators arranged to show a film of the game to a group of students at each school.

---

mated the number of beans collected by members of their own group and underestimated the out-group's performance. This bias was more pronounced among members of the group that had won the preceding tournament of competitive sports events. This phenomenon also has been demonstrated in other studies. For instance, research on competing industrial work groups reveals a clear tendency for members to judge their own group's performance as superior to that of an out-group (Blake

and Mouton 1961a, 1962a, 1962b).

What causes this bias in the evaluation of in-group performance? One explanation is based on *cognitive balance theory*, discussed in Chapter 6. An individual's cognitions are "balanced" when that person holds a high evaluation of products from a group whose members he or she likes and to which he or she personally belongs. It would obviously be difficult to hold a low or negative evaluation of in-group products while identifying with group members. Several

DIFFERING OPINIONS OF DARTMOUTH AND PRINCETON STUDENTS

Question	% Dartmouth Students	% Princeton Students
From your observations of what went on at the game, or from what you have heard and read about the game, do you believe the game was clean and fairly played, or that it was unnecessarily rough and dirty?		
Clean and fair	13	0
Rough and dirty	42	93
Rough and fair	39	3
Don't know	6	4
From what you saw in the game or the movies, or from what you have read, which team do you feel started the rough play?		
Dartmouth started it	36	86
Princeton started it	2	0
Both started it	53	11
Neither	6	1
No answer	3	2

Source: adapted from Hastorf and Cantril (1954).

These viewers were asked to report any infractions they noticed. Princeton students "saw" the Dartmouth team commit more than twice as many infractions as their own team. Dartmouth students "saw" the Princeton team commit slightly more infractions than the Dartmouth team.

This study clearly demonstrates the effect of group membership on the students' perceptions of the event. Perceptual distortion made one's own group appear in a favorable light and the out-group in an unfavorable one. In these conflictual situations, a vicious circle is established in which the in-group expects the worst from the out-group, looks for the worst, and consequently finds it.

studies have confirmed this hypothesis (Hinkle 1975; Ferguson and Kelley 1964).

Changes in Relations Between Adversaries

Once a conflict is under way, a change occurs in the relationship between conflicting groups. Often there is expansion of the issues under dispute and polarization of relations. These changes may, in turn, lead to further escalation of the conflict (Kriesberg 1973).

EXPANSION OF THE ISSUES. When groups are disputing a particular matter, they often compound the conflict by introducing additional issues. Typically, the process of expansion moves from very specific issues to more general ones. The Kanawha County textbook controversy discussed at the beginning of this chapter provides a good illustration. The initial issue concerned what textbooks should be adopted by the school system. This quickly expanded to the larger issue of what curriculum should be taught. Soon the conflict broadened to include the issue of who should be members of the school board and what behaviors are appropriate for board members. Opposing sides also raised a larger philosophical issue: What viewpoint—liberal or traditional—should be taught in the public schools? The conflict quickly expanded to include another issue: Should schools teaching the "wrong" viewpoint be permitted to operate without interference, or should they be shut down by force? Many persons raised still another issue: Should legitimacy be withdrawn entirely from the public school system and invested instead in a new system of "alternate" schools?

Expansion of issues occurs for several reasons. First, as relations between conflicting groups deteriorate, latent issues that had previously been denied or ignored come to the fore. Conflicting parties feel less need to deny the repressed issues. Indeed, they may view the overt conflict as a good occasion to get even or "settle accounts" (Ikle 1971). Second, as one group in the conflict imposes punishment on another, those actions become issues themselves. In the Kanawha County conflict, various actions by the participants—blocking the passage of school buses, arresting the school board members, and dynamiting the board's building—were highly provocative. These actions became issues in themselves and drew new participants into the fray.

POLARIZATION OF RELATIONS. As a conflict expands, the relationship between adversaries often becomes polarized. There is an increase in interaction among members within each of the conflicting groups and a decrease in communication between the groups. At the same time, adversaries become increasingly isolated from each other. This feeds the conflict further; as the number of nonconflicting relations declines, opposing groups are less constrained by cross pressures and increasingly free to utilize coercion.

The polarization of relations between con-

flicting groups means that there are fewer opportunities to communicate openly about issues. Consequently, people on one side will lack accurate information about the plans and desires of the other side. Even if one group wants to de-escalate the conflict, it becomes increasingly difficult to signal that intention. Tentative efforts to reduce the conflict may, under conditions of low communication, be viewed by the other side as a trick or trap. When groups are polarized, stereotypes come heavily into play and guide behavior. Thus, polarization and the accompanying lack of communication between groups further perpetuate the conflict.

Effects of Conflict on Group Structure

So far we have discussed the effect of intergroup conflict on the relationship *between* groups. However, intergroup conflict also restructures the relationships among members *within* a given group. Once a struggle has begun, each group in the conflict undergoes changes that contribute to further escalation. This next section will consider (1) the effects of conflict on group cohesiveness, (2) the effects of conflict on the behavior of group leaders, and (3) the effects of conflict on the normative structure of the in-group, particularly on standards defining fairness.

Group Cohesiveness

Social theorists have long recognized that external threats and conflict affect the internal structure of groups. Lewis Coser (1956, 1967) proposed that conflict with an outside group heightens in-group cohesiveness and reaffirms members' identification with the ingroup. He also suggested that conflict can provide a "safety valve" whereby members release tension by directing aggression and hostility toward outside groups, rather than toward each other.

Various studies have documented the effects hypothesized by Coser, and have shown that intergroup conflict increases cohesiveness within each of the opposing groups.

For instance, consider again the Robbers Cave study in which groups of preadolescent boys at a summer camp engaged in competitive activities (Sherif et al. 1961; Sherif 1966). As conflict between the Eagles and the Rattlers escalated, various measures of in-group cohesiveness— such as cooperativeness and friendship choice—rose to high levels. These groups became more cohesive internally and more antagonistic externally as they participated in the win-or-lose competition.

Why does intergroup conflict lead to high levels of in-group cohesiveness? First, as conflict escalates, members endow their cause with additional significance and increase their commitment to it. This in turn leads to higher levels of cohesiveness. Second, the threat posed by the out-group can intensify hatred of a common enemy, and this also heightens in-group cohesiveness (Holmes and Grant 1979). In one study (Samuels 1970) researchers varied the degree of cooperation and competition within groups separately from the presence or absence of competition between groups. The results indicated that groups facing intergroup competition were more cohesive than those not facing intergroup competition, regardless of whether members within a given group related cooperatively or competitively with each other. Thus, the common antagonism of in-group members toward an opposing group overshadowed any friction within the in-group and produced greater cohesiveness.

Leadership Rivalry

The actions of group leaders are especially important under conditions of conflict. Leaders plan and direct the group's strategic moves, allocate resources applicable to the conflict, and serve as spokespersons for the group *vis-à-vis* outside agencies or persons. Activities of this type can have an important impact on a group's success or failure in intergroup conflict.

When a group is embroiled in conflict, its members may disagree as to whether the fight is worth the effort. Even if there is general agreement to pursue the conflict, there may nevertheless be disagreement regarding the best strategy to use. If action against an opposing group is not progressing favorably, rival leaders will probably emerge within the in-group, and attempt to displace the existing leaders and to change their policies. Frequently, the rivals are more militant than existing leaders. The threat of being outflanked by more militant rivals can cause established leaders to adopt an increasingly hard line and to intensify the action against the out-group. Leaders are especially prone to react in this manner when their own position is unstable or insecure (Rabbie and Bekkers 1978). Thus, competition for leadership can actually intensify the conflict between groups (Kriesberg 1973).

This was illustrated in a study of civil rights leaders in 15 U.S. cities in the mid-1960s (McWorter and Crain 1967). At that time, civil rights organizations were trying to bring about changes favoring blacks and other minorities. Interviews were conducted with civil rights leaders to determine the extent to which there was rivalry for leadership within civil rights groups. Results showed that organizations with higher levels of rivalry also had greater militancy. Militancy was measured both in terms of attitudinal responses and in terms of the frequency of civil rights demonstrations conducted in the cities. Rivalry for leadership within these civil rights groups created pressure to escalate intergroup conflict.

In-Group Normative Structure

Intergroup conflict affects not only cohesiveness and leadership, but also group norms. With the onset of conflict, a group will become more concerned with winning (or surviving) the conflict and less concerned with the rights and liberties of individual members. Greater emphasis will be placed on behavior that helps the entire group and less on what is best for individual members (Korten 1962).

Demonstrators blocking a city street are removed physically by police. During intergroup conflict, conformity to group standards may lead to actions that violate the law.

Consequently, there will be less tolerance of dissent. Enforcement of norms will stiffen and penalties will increase. When internal dissent does occur, attempts will be made to suppress it or to force the dissidents out. Pressure for conformity will increase not only in small groups and organizations, but even at the national level. During the Vietnam War, for example, automobile bumper stickers illustrated this point: "America: Love It or Leave It."

In some cases, group members may turn against each other if they suspect their fellows of sympathizing with the adversary or of engaging in behaviors that reduce the chances of victory. Allegedly dangerous members may find their rights reduced and their civil liberties abridged. This was demonstrated during World War II, when the U.S. government relocated many American citizens of Japanese ancestry into detention centers (Miyamoto 1973).

Not only will the enforcement of norms intensify under conditions of conflict, but the norms themselves will change. This is particularly evident with respect to standards of equity and fairness. As conflict intensifies, the in-group will reorder its priorities and then reallocate task assignments and resources to achieve a strategic advantage (Zaleznik 1966; Lewis 1968). Actions that were previously considered valuable may suddenly be judged useless or even harmful. As a result, the distribution of status and rewards among members will shift in a direction that may not appear fair.

The reallocation of tasks and resources will have additional ramifications. First, there may be an unequal or disproportionate sharing of costs and hardships. If a nation becomes involved in a conventional war, for example, the persons conscripted into military combat service may pay costs greater than those producing munitions back home. Second, the group may disregard members' past contributions and seniority. The nation will favor members who can help win the war, not persons who contributed heavily during peacetime. Finally, some persons may resent the reordering of values produced by the external conflict. Certain groups within the nation may feel that the war is unjust and should not be waged. Each of these concerns may become a serious source of tension within the in-group (Leventhal 1979).

Reduction of Intergroup Conflict

Every conflict ends, sooner or later. Of course, the termination of one conflict may coincide with the start of another—there is almost always a war being waged somewhere on the face of the earth—but each conflict leads to some specific outcome.

Full-blown conflicts can end in a number of ways. One way is by *withdrawal*—one side decides to withdraw or pull out of the conflict. The group may feel the conflict is not worth the effort and therefore drop its demands and abandon the fight. As a result, the situation may return gradually to what it had been before the conflict started. A second way that conflicts end is by *domination*—one side wins the conflict and imposes its will on the other. In this case, there is a clear victory for one group and a loss for the other. Domination entails a shift in the balance of power: the order prevailing after the conflict is different from what existed before. A third way that conflicts end is by *compromise*—the opposing groups each yield on certain points and reach a compromise. For instance, opponents may decide to "split the difference" or to accept mutual trade-offs. When a compromise is reached, however, neither party achieves everything that it wants (Kriesberg 1973).

Conflicts consume—and ultimately dissipate—time, energy, and resources. Even worse, they have the capacity to expand beyond rational limits, as illustrated by the Kanawha County textbook controversy and the Hatfield-McCoy family feud. Conflicts begin as small disagreements that grow in scope, pulling in new participants and escalating in intensity. Because intergroup conflicts are potentially very dangerous and costly, many theorists have wondered how to bring them to a halt in the early or middle stages, before they escalate beyond all control. The solution to this problem is surprisingly complex, however. One cannot reduce intergroup conflict merely by reversing the processes that initially caused it. In a practical sense, it is often impossible to eliminate underlying opposition of interest, to prevent aversive events, or to diminish ethnocentric identification with the in-group.

Nevertheless, a number of ways to reduce conflict have been proposed. These include:

(1) establish an overriding, superordinate goal to induce collaborative action between the in-group and the out-group; (2) increase contact and communication between the in-group and the out-group; (3) deploy group representatives to negotiate a settlement; and (4) initiate unilateral conciliatory moves in the hope that the out-group will respond in a manner that lessens hostility. Each of these approaches merits consideration, and each will be discussed in detail below.

Superordinate Goals

One of the most effective techniques for reducing intergroup conflict is to interpose superordinate goals. By definition, **superordinate goals** are objectives held in common by all groups in a conflict that cannot be achieved by any group without the supportive efforts of the others.

The Robbers Cave study discussed earlier provides a clear demonstration that superordinate goals can reduce conflict. After a high level of conflict had developed between two groups of twelve-year-old boys, researchers introduced a series of superordinate goals. First, they arranged for the system that supplied water to both groups to break down, so that groups had to work together to restore water to the camp. Next, the food delivery truck became stuck along the roadway. If the boys were to eat, they all had to work together to free the vehicle. These overriding goals induced cooperation between the groups and eventually decreased hostility (Sherif et al. 1961).

The impact of superordinate goals is not immediate, but gradual and cumulative. Results are most effective when a series of goals is introduced one after another, rather than a single goal on a one-shot basis. Under these conditions, the effects of superordinate goals are cumulative and their impact greater (Sherif et al. 1961; Blake, Shepard, and Mouton 1964).

Superordinate goals are not always introduced by outside agents as they were in the

Robbers Cave study. Sometimes they occur naturally. For instance, when the airline industry was deregulated a few years ago, competition among airlines increased dramatically. Some went into bankruptcy and others came close to it. One of the companies in financial trouble was Republic Airlines. Despite its enormous size, some persons seriously questioned whether Republic would survive. These circumstances created a new superordinate goal for Republic's management and the various unions representing pilots, mechanics, and attendants. Instead of an adversarial relationship between management and the unions—with management trying to increase profits and the unions trying to increase wages—the situation at Republic shifted toward greater cooperation. The unions accepted wage cuts and higher productivity requirements, and management agreed to protect workers' jobs and prevent avoidable layoffs. The superordinate goal of keeping the airline alive reduced conflict and heightened collaboration between management and the unions.

Superordinate goals reduce intergroup conflict because they serve as a basis for restructuring the relationship between groups. By changing a hostile win-lose situation into one of collaborative problem solving, a superordinate goal reduces friction. Members of conflicting groups will consider a range of alternative actions rather than a fixed position, and they are likely to look for points of similarity as well as differences. In the presence of a superordinate goal, the activities of the out-group members assume greater value for in-group members, and vice versa. All of this leads to reduced hostility and conflict between groups.

The Intergroup Contact Hypothesis

Some theorists have suggested that intergroup conflict will be reduced by establishing contact and opening communication between members of opposing groups. They maintain that increased contact will eradicate stereotypes and reduce prejudice, and consequently reduce antagonism between groups. This concept, called the **intergroup contact hypothesis,** has been proposed primarily with respect to racial and ethnic groups (Amir 1969, 1976; Cook 1972).

Although intergroup contact does reduce prejudice and conflict between groups in some cases, it does not do so in all cases. This raises the question: Under what conditions will intergroup contact lead to favorable outcomes? Usually it depends on whether the persons involved in the contact are of equal status, whether the contact is intimate rather than casual, and whether the contact has institutional and normative support.

EQUAL STATUS CONTACT. Intergroup contact is more likely to reduce prejudice when in-group and out-group members occupy positions of equal status than when they occupy positions of unequal status. The effect of equal status contact is demonstrated, for instance, by a classic study conducted in the military during World War II (Mannheimer and Williams 1949). This study showed that white soldiers changed their attitudes toward black soldiers after the two racial groups fought together in combat side by side. When asked how they felt about their company including black as well as white platoons, only 7 percent of the white soldiers from integrated units had a negative reaction. In contrast, 62 percent of the soldiers in completely segregated units indicated a negative reaction at the prospect of having black platoons in their unit.

Equal status contact has been effective in reducing prejudice in other situations as well. It has been shown to operate among black and white children at interracial summer camps (Clore et al. 1978) and in interracial housing situations (Hamilton and Bishop 1976). To reduce prejudice through contact, members of the different groups should ideally enter the situation on an equal footing (Pettigrew 1969). This establishes norms of equality from the very start of interaction and helps to assure that members of both groups will view one another as having equal status.

Box 15.2

EQUAL STATUS CONTACT AND INTERRACIAL ATTITUDES

According to various theorists (Allport 1954; Amir 1969), contact between ethnic and racial groups is likely to reduce prejudice when members of different groups have *equal status* during the encounter. Because blacks do not enjoy the same economic position as whites in American society, interracial contacts are often structured in terms of status inequality instead of status equality. Nevertheless, contacts that can be structured in terms of equal status have the potential to change interracial attitudes. One clear demonstration of this occurred in an experimental interracial summer camp for children (Clore et al. 1978).

This camp was structured to foster equal status contact among children, who were aged 8 to 12. Half of the children were white and half were black. Likewise, half of the counselors and administrative staff were white and half were black. Living assignments in the camp assured that each unit was half white and half black. The living situation provided an opportunity for intimate acquaintances rather than casual associations typical of many integrated social settings. All children had equal privileges and duties around the camp. Moreover, counselors provided tasks—such as firebuilding and cooking—that required cooperative efforts among the children.

Approximately 200 children attended the camp during the summer. They attended in groups of 40, with each group staying at the camp for one week. Interracial attitudes were measured in several ways. First, researchers asked the children how they felt toward persons of the opposite race; responses were recorded in terms of evaluation scales such as good–bad, clean–dirty, pleasant–unpleasant, valuable–worthless, and so on. In addition, researchers assessed the extent of interracial liking and selection of friends by means of games that required the children to indicate their interpersonal choices. For instance, in the "name game," children designated the others they knew well by circling their names on a card with a pencil. At the end of the week, children indicated the names of three other campers whose telephone numbers and addresses they wanted to have.

Results show that a change in attitude occurred for girls, although not for boys. Boys began the camp sessions with neutral attitudes toward persons of the opposite race, and did not have much room to change. Girls began with negative attitudes and shifted in a positive direction as a function of the interracial contact. Similarly, there was a significant increase in cross-race interpersonal choices from the beginning of the camp to the end. This increase was more pronounced for girls than for boys. Overall, the results of this study suggest that changes in interracial attitudes can be brought about by prolonged, intimate, equal status contact across the races.

INTIMATE VERSUS CASUAL CONTACT. Another factor affecting reduction in prejudice via intergroup contact is whether the contact is intimate rather than superficial in character. Social contact that fosters high levels of acquaintance and intimacy between members of different racial and ethnic groups can reduce prejudice, whereas social contact that involves lower levels of intimacy has little effect (Yarrow, Campbell, and Yarrow 1958; Segal 1965).

There is some evidence that intergroup contact in work situations produces only limited attitude change, if any (Harding and Hogrefe 1952). One explanation is that work situations frequently involve relatively impersonal or superficial contact, and even if a work relationship becomes more personal, it is generally confined to the job setting. In contrast, intergroup contact in housing or residential settings is more intimate and personal. Thus racially intermixed housing provides an opportunity for reducing negative racial attitudes and stereotypes. In one study (Deutsch and Collins 1951), researchers compared segregated versus integrated occupancy patterns. Segregation was favored by approximately 70 percent of the tenants in segregated projects, but only by 40 percent of the tenants in the integrated projects. Much greater intimacy between black and white housewives was found in the integrated projects. When contact between the races was more intimate, the stereotyping of blacks by whites was less common.

INSTITUTIONAL SUPPORT. Intergroup contact is more likely to reduce stereotyping and create favorable attitudes if the contact is regulated by positive social norms. If the norms support openness, friendliness, and mutual respect, the contact is more likely to produce a change in attitudes. Thus, intergroup contacts sanctioned by an outside authority or by established law or custom are also more likely to produce a change in attitudes.

In the absence of institutional support, members of the in-group may be reluctant to interact with outsiders because they feel it is deviant or simply inappropriate. But in the presence of institutional support, contact between groups may be viewed as appropriate and possible. Several studies have demonstrated that institutional support increases the probability that intergroup contact will lead to positive attitude change (Wilner, Walkley, and Cook 1952; James 1955).

In sum, intergroup contact tends to reduce conflict under the following conditions: (1) when there is equal status contact between members of the in-group and the out-group, (2) when the contact is of an intimate rather than a superficial nature, and (3) when the contact is based on institutional or authoritative support.

Group Representatives

In conflicts between large groups or organizations, it may be impossible to bring together all members of the contending sides for face-to-face negotiations. Even with smaller groups, efforts to resolve conflict are frequently more effective when they involve only a few persons. For these reasons, groups frequently rely on representatives to negotiate a settlement with the opposing side. Representatives have been used to resolve a wide variety of conflicts, ranging from community arguments regarding land use and rezoning to labor-management negotiations or familial disputes over inheritances.

The role of a group representative, or spokesperson, is difficult to perform effectively, because this person must deal with a range of cross pressures (McGrath 1966; Adams 1976). Consider the pressures confronting a negotiator representing a union during a strike over wages. First, he faces the demands of the opposing negotiator, who represents management. Pressure to agree with management's terms may stem from the conditions prevailing in the economy, from the intrinsic logic of management's position, or from positive personal bonds with representatives of management. At the same time, the union negotiator faces pressure to meet the expectations of his own group. Any agreement reached with management on the wage issue must ultimately be acceptable to the union; this constraint will determine whether he can accede to demands from the other side. Finally, the negotiator must cope with external pressures from the community, the government, and others who demand a speedy, constructive resolution to the ongoing strike.

Although the role is complex, certain conditions increase the likelihood that a group representative will succeed in resolving intergroup conflict. First of all, if the representative treats the conflict as a problem to be solved rather than as a battle to be won, he or she is more likely to bring about a lasting resolution (Kelman and Cohen 1976; Fisher and Ury 1981). By adopting a problem-solving orientation, the representative will be able to think creatively about alternative resolutions or compromises. However, if the representative approaches the conflict on a win-or-lose basis, adopting a rigid position or defensive reaction, this may doom negotiations to failure.

Unfortunately, representatives do not always have a free hand in negotiations, and they may not be able to adopt a problem-solving orientation. Groups often constrain their representatives by giving them detailed instructions prior to negotiations. Studies show that if a group develops rigid positions and strategies rather than studying and discussing the issues broadly, the level of conflict between groups is likely to increase at the negotiation stage (Bass 1966; Druckman 1968; Kahn and Kohls 1972).

Another factor that may prevent a representative from adopting a problem-solving orientation is loyalty. Because representatives spend a lot of time in contact with opposing groups, their loyalty may be questioned by members of their own group. Persons in their own group may desire to monitor what they are doing and to limit their freedom of action. These pressures reduce the possibility of collaborative problem solving with the opposing side. A negotiator whose behavior is being monitored by his own group is more likely to adopt a competitive, tough orientation when his job is at risk than when it is not (Walton and McKersie 1965; Bartunek, Benton, and Keyes 1975); or when constituents control the level of monetary rewards he receives (Benton 1972). Thus, the imposition of surveillance and sanctions may inhibit the representative from adopting a problem-solving orientation, and ultimately preclude a realistic, lasting resolution of the impasse.

The GRIT Strategy

Some intergroup conflicts are very difficult to resolve. When goals are directly opposed or severe distrust prevails between groups, the participants may become locked into conflict. Under these conditions, superordinate goals will not be discernible, and representatives on each side are sure to be pressured by their groups to adopt a tough stance in any negotiations. When there is little prospect that mutual efforts will resolve the conflict, a group wishing to lessen the tensions is limited to taking steps unilaterally.

One approach to unilateral conflict reduction is a strategy called **GRIT** which stands for Graduated and Reciprocated Initiatives in Tension-reduction (Osgood 1959, 1962, 1979). The GRIT strategy pertains primarily to conflicts in which opposing sides have approximately equal power. Originally a product of the Cold War between the United States and the Soviet Union during the 1950s and 1960s, GRIT was inspired by a fear of nuclear holocaust and a desire to find a way to reduce tension between the superpowers. GRIT has a renewed relevance during the 1980s, in view of the current tensions between the United States and the Soviet Union (Granberg 1978). Moreover, the GRIT proposal is general in character; it applies not only to conflicts between nations but also to those between smaller groups.

The basic idea underlying GRIT is a sort of arms race in reverse: one side initiates de-escalatory steps in the hope that they will eventually be reciprocated by the other side. GRIT is based on the assumption that each side in the conflict has an interest in reducing tension, so that resources devoted to the conflict can be committed to other, more productive purposes. The principles comprising the GRIT strategy are designed to build trust and reduce tension. By acting on these principles, one group in the conflict assumes the initiative, rather than merely responding to the moves of the other.

The principles in the GRIT strategy are as follows (Osgood 1962, 1979):

1. The group initiating the strategy issues a public statement describing its plan to reduce tension through subsequent actions.

2. The initiating group publicly announces each unilateral move in advance, and indicates that it is part of the overall strategy.

3. Each announcement of a unilateral move explicitly invites reciprocation in some form by the out-group.

4. Each unilateral move is carried out on schedule to demonstrate credibility.

5. Initiatives are continued for some time, even in the absence of reciprocation. This entails risk, but it also intensifies pressure on the out-group to reciprocate.

6. The initiatives are unambiguous and open to verification by the out-group.

7. Conciliatory initiatives are structured so that they do not seriously impair the capacity of the in-group to retaliate against any attack that may be launched by the out-group. The GRIT strategy is not intended as a method of unilateral disarmament.

8. Further moves by the initiating group are graduated to match the responses by the out-group. If the out-group responds in a friendly manner, the in-group reacts by assuming further risk. If the out-group responds in a hostile manner, the in-group responds in like fashion, but avoids excessive retaliation.

9. Unilateral moves by the initiating group are diversified in nature. This protects against developing a large gap in defenses, and it also illustrates to the out-group that a variety of moves might be made in reciprocation.

The GRIT strategy attempts not only to change the out-group's perceptions of the initiating group, but also to change its behavior through the principles of reinforcement. If the out-group reciprocates, it is rewarded with further conciliatory initiatives, but if the out-group takes aggressive action, it is punished with retaliation.

How effective is the GRIT stretegy in practice? In the context of East-West relations, no one knows whether GRIT really works. Neither the United States nor the Soviet

Union has ever seriously used it, although there have been many instances in which minor conciliatory initiatives have been reciprocated. Perhaps the closest approximation to a real test of GRIT was the so-called Kennedy Peace Offensive (Etzioni 1967). On 10 June 1963, President John Kennedy spoke on "A Strategy for Peace" at the American University. He suggested that the policies of the United States be restructured to give the Soviet Union some stake in building a genuine peace. Taking the initiative, Kennedy announced that atmospheric nuclear tests by the United States were to be halted immediately and would not be resumed unless some other country conducted a test. In response, the Soviet Union stopped jamming broadcasts by the Voice of America so that Kennedy's speech could be heard behind the Iron Curtain. A day later at the United Nations, the Soviet Union withdrew its objection to dispatching U.S. observers to war-torn Yemen. In response, the United States agreed to give full status to the Hungarian delegation at the United Nations. A week later, Khrushchev reciprocated by announcing a halt in production of Soviet strategic bombers. A number of other conciliatory moves soon followed, but the Peace Offensive stalled in late 1963 because Kennedy faced mounting criticism within the United States for failure to oppose communism. Political support for Kennedy's policies was thin, and he could not risk losing the next year's election.

According to some critics, the Kennedy Peace Offensive was not a real test of the GRIT strategy because not all conciliatory moves were genuine (Etzioni 1967). They argue that the United States, already ahead of Russia in atmospheric testing, needed time to assess the data on hand before conducting further tests. Likewise, the Russian strategic bombers were obsolete and likely to be phased out in any event. Nevertheless, the 1963 Peace Offensive is the closest thing the world has seen to an international-scale application of the GRIT strategy.

Unilateral application of GRIT may lead, in the later stages, to face-to-face negotiations, as in this meeting held between Soviet Foreign Minister Andrei Gromyko and U.S. Secretary of State George Schultz.

Further evidence on the effectiveness of GRIT comes from research on smaller-scale conflicts, as well as from simulation studies and experimental games. These studies indicate that some of the points in the strategy are more important than others in reducing conflict (Lindskold 1978, 1979).

Various studies support points 1 and 2 (announcing intentions). By issuing a public statement, the initiating group makes clear its goals. Conciliatory moves without such announcements may be incorrectly construed by the out-group as indicating weakness or passivity, and may lead to exploitation (Oskamp 1971). Studies show that repeated truthful announcements that one will cooperate on the next move produced greater cooperation from the other side than does the same rate of cooperation when unannounced (Voissem and Sistrunk 1971; Lindskold and Finch 1981). These findings suggest that, if a group's strategy is conciliation, it should announce this fact to minimize ambiguity.

Little evidence is available regarding point 3 of the GRIT strategy (inviting reciprocation), although point 4 (carrying out initiatives as announced) has been amply supported. Carrying out initiatives as announced increases the credibility of the initiator (Ayers, Nacci, and Tedeschi 1973; Schlenker, Helm, and Tedeschi 1973), whereas failure to carry out initiatives makes the strategy ineffective in bringing about reciprocation (Gahagan and Tedeschi 1968).

Point 5 (continuing initiatives without reciprocation) is complex, because its effectiveness depends on the relative power positions of the two sides. Initiatives from a strong party are likely to be met with concessions by the other side, whereas initiatives from a weak party are not likely to be met with concessions by a stronger opponent (Michener et al. 1975; Lindskold and Aronoff 1980). In general, the GRIT strategy will bring about reciprocity only when the initiatives come from a group having equal or superior power in the conflict.

Several studies have tested point 6 (making initiatives unambiguous and open to inspection). These studies have not offered much support for this step, suggesting that it might not be crucial to the overall strategy (Pilisuk and Skolnick 1968; Pilisuk et al. 1967). In contrast, point 7 of GRIT (maintaining capacity to retaliate) has received substantial support in experimental studies. If one side makes conciliatory moves but fails to maintain the capacity to retaliate, it will quickly weaken itself and create an imbalance of power. Studies have shown that cooperation drops off when power imbalance is created (Aronoff and Tedeschi 1968; Michener and Cohen 1973). The GRIT strategy is viable only under conditions of approximate power equality.

The remaining principles in the GRIT strategy are point 8 (matching the response by the out-group) and point 9 (diversifying initiatives). Although there is not much evidence with respect to point 9, findings provide some support for point 8, which holds that once the out-group responds, the initiating group should match the action of the out-group. Thus, if the out-group responds in a cooperative manner, the initiating group should make further concessions. If the out-group responds with hostility, the initiating group should retaliate, but at moderate intensity so as not to escalate. Studies regarding reciprocity show that there is a tendency for one side in a conflict to match concessions by the other side in frequency although not in size (Pruitt and

Drews 1969; Lindskold and Collins 1978). This suggests that it may be unrealistic to expect precise matching because of biases in perception and differences in values between the groups.

In general, available evidence supports most steps in the GRIT strategy. Although GRIT is not likely to be effective between groups of very unequal power, it is a promising strategy of conciliation when the groups are closely matched in strength. Each point in GRIT contributes to reduction of tension, but the real value of GRIT lies in its unity as a strategy. Perhaps the 1980s will provide an opportunity to further test its effectiveness in international relations.

Summary

Intergroup conflict is a situation in which groups take antagonistic actions toward one another in order to control some outcome important to them.

DEVELOPMENT OF INTERGROUP CONFLICT. Three major sources of intergroup conflict can be identified. (1) Conflicting groups usually will have an underlying opposition of interest. This prevents them from achieving their goals simultaneously, and leads to friction, hostility, and overt conflict. (2) One group, by threatening or depriving another, may create an aversive event that turns latent antagonism into overt conflict. (3) High level of in-group identification, accompanied by ethnocentric attitudes, may create ill will between groups and foster actions that escalate conflict. In many intergroup conflicts, two or more of these sources occur simultaneously.

PERSISTENCE OF INTERGROUP CONFLICT. Although some conflicts between groups are resolved quickly, others extend for a long period of time. Several mechanisms support the persistence of intergroup conflict. (1) In-group members typically hold biased impressions regarding the out-group. Stereotypic distortion, caused by insufficient information regarding the out-group, creates biased perception concerning the intentions and performances of out-group members. (2) Once the conflict escalates, it changes the relationship between the conflicting sides. The number of issues under dispute may expand, and the number of parties in the conflict may increase. Relations between adversaries will polarize, communication across groups will decline, trust will become harder to establish, and the conflict more difficult to resolve.

EFFECTS OF CONFLICT ON GROUP STRUCTURE. Intergroup conflict changes the internal structure of the in-group. (1) Conflict increases the level of cohesiveness of the in-group, as members endow their cause with increased commitment, and unite to face a common enemy. (2) Conflict may increase rivalry for leadership among in-group members, especially if the group appears to be losing the conflict. Rivalry can exert pressure on existing leaders to become more militant, which in turn may escalate the conflict. (3) Conflict increases the demands for conformity and often changes the normative structure of the in-group. Standards of fairness may shift as the in-group reorders its priorities to achieve a strategic advantage in the conflict.

REDUCTION OF INTERGROUP CONFLICT. Intergroup conflict has the potential to escalate to severe levels, dissipating resources and imposing large losses. Several techniques have been suggested to reduce intergroup conflict before it escalates seriously. These include: (1) Introduce superordinate goals into the conflict. Because goals of this type cannot be achieved without the joint efforts of opposing sides, they promote cooperative behavior and serve as a basis for restructuring the relationship between groups. (2) Increase intergroup contact in order to limit stereotyping and prejudice. This approach is more effective when group contact is intimate rather than superficial in nature and is based on equal status. (3) Deploy group representatives to negotiate a settlement between opposing sides. This technique is most effective when representatives have a free hand to adopt a problem-solving orientation in the negotiations. (4) In severe conflicts, one group may adopt a unilateral strategy modelled after the GRIT approach, in which one side initiates de-escalatory steps in the hope that the other side will reciprocate. The GRIT approach works best when the initiating group is at least as strong as its opponent.

Key Terms and Concepts
Intergroup Conflict

Realistic Group Conflict Theory

Aversive Event

In-Group

Out-Group

Ethnocentrism

Superordinate Goals

Intergroup Contact Hypothesis

GRIT

Chapter 16
Social Structure and Personality

Introduction

Fred is 38, married, the father of two children, and sells pacemakers and artificial joints to hospitals. He travels two or three days a week and works at home the rest of the time in his $150,000 house in the suburbs. He earns $65,000 a year. Because his income is based entirely on commission, Fred worries about his sales falling off, but on the whole he is satisfied with his life. His values are conservative and he votes for Republican candidates.

Larry is also 38 and has a wife and two children. He runs a service station, and works six days a week from eary morning until 6 or 7 P.M. Larry and his family live in a small, three bedroom house. Last year he made about $16,000. He worries a lot about money and has been very tense the past year. He has liberal values and usually votes for Democratic candidates.

Marie is 39. She is head nurse in the pediatric ward in the hospital. Although she enjoys her patients, she hates all the paperwork and the personnel problems. Some of her values are conservative whereas others are liberal; she considers herself an Independent.

Fred, Larry, and Marie are three very different people. Each has a different occupation, which produces differences in income and life style. They differ in their values—in what they believe is important—and in the amount of stress they feel.

Where do these differences come from? Often they are the result of one's location in society. Every person occupies a **position,** a designated location in a social system (Biddle and Thomas 1966). The ordered and persisting relationships among these positions in a social system make up the **social structure** (House 1981a).

This chapter is concerned with the impact of social structure on the individual. There are three ways in which social position influences various aspects of a person's life. First, every position in the social structure carries a set of expectations about the behavior of occupants of that position, called a **role** (Rommetveit 1955). Role expectations are anticipations of how people will behave based on knowledge of their position. Through socialization and personal experience, each of us knows the role expectations associated with our positions (Heiss 1981). For example, Fred enacts several roles, including salesman, husband, and father. The expectations associated with these roles are a major influence on Fred's behavior.

A second influence on the individual are **social networks,** the sets of relationships associated with the various positions a person occupies. Each of us is woven into several networks, including those involving coworkers, family, and friends. Two examples are depicted in Figure 16.1. The network on the left depicts the pattern of relationships among a group of friends that evolved out of their shared experience. For example, the ties between Mary and Margie and Mary and John developed because they took classes together, whereas Mary got to know Kathy at work. Mary produced this network when asked to name the people to whom she is closest, excluding relatives. When asked to include relatives, Mary produced the network on the right of Figure 16.1. The most striking difference is the greater number of direct ties between the persons in the network on the right. This network is dense—most of the persons in it are close to Mary and to each other. Each of the ties between Mary and another person reflects a **primary relationship,** one that is personal, emotionally involving, and of long duration. Such relationships have a substantial effect on one's behavior and self-image (Cooley 1902).

A third way that social structure influences the individual is through **status,** the social ranking of a person's position. In every society, some positions are accorded greater prestige than others; this differential ranking comprises the stratification system. Each of us occupies several positions of differing status. In the United States, occupational status is especially influential in determining life style

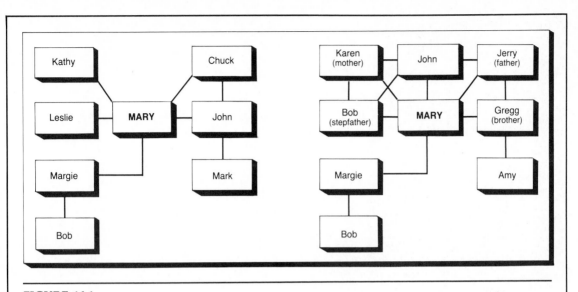

FIGURE 16.1

SOCIAL NETWORKS

These two networks are focused on Mary. When asked to name her best friends, and to exclude relatives, Mary described the network on the left. John is her boyfriend, whereas Mark is John's roommate. Mary met Chuck through John, and since then she and Chuck have become friends. Mary's three best women friends are Kathy (a coworker), Leslie (whose parents are friends of Mary's parents) and Margie (a classmate). Margie has recently married Bob. This is a loosely knit network because few of Mary's friends are close to each other. The network on the right represents the people to whom Mary feels closest, including her relatives. Notice that only Margie and John remain from the friendship network. Mary's intimates now include Gregg (her brother) and Amy (Gregg's girlfriend). They also include her mother (Karen), stepfather (Bob), and her father (Jerry). This network is dense because most of its members are close to Mary and to each other.

and values. Occupation is the major determinant of income, which has a substantial effect on one's life style. One of the obvious differences between Fred and Larry, for instance, is their annual income.

This chapter will focus on how social structure influences the individual—via roles, social networks, and status. It considers the impact of social structure on four areas: achievement, values, physical and mental health, and a person's sense of belonging. Specifically, it considers four questions:

1. How does location in society affect educational and occupational achievement?

2. How does social position influence people's values?

3. How does social location influence a person's physical and mental health?

4. How does position influence a person's sense of belonging in society, or the lack thereof?

Status Attainment

The individual's location in the stratification system of the society, or status, is perhaps the single most important influence on a person's life. Status determines access to resources—to money, and influence over others. In the

Uniforms are a very efficient way of communicating one's role. We can tell at a glance what role this woman is enacting, and as a result, we know how to behave toward her.

United States, occupation is the main determinant of status. This section will consider the nature of occupational status, the determinants of the status that particular individuals achieve, and the impact of social networks on the achievement of status.

Occupational Status

Occupational status is a key component of social standing, and a major determinant of income and life style. Fred is a sales representative for a company that makes artificial hip and elbow joints, pacemakers, and other medical equipment. These items are in great demand, and few companies make them. Fred sells a single pacemaker for $3,000, and keeps half of the money as his commission. He only needs to be on the road two or three days per

week to earn $65,000 each year. He has a beautiful suburban home and two cars. Larry, by contrast, owns a service station. He works from morning until night pumping gas and repairing cars. His station is in a good location, but his overhead is high; he only earned $16,000 last year, and he worries that this year will be worse. Larry and his family live in a smaller, older house and have a six-year-old car.

The benefits Fred and Larry receive from their occupational statuses are clearly different. First, Fred earns four times as much money as Larry. This determines the quality of housing, clothing, and medical care his family receives. Fred also has much greater control over his own time. Within limits, he can choose which days he works and how much; this in turn affects the time he can spend with family and friends. Larry doesn't have much free time. Finally, Fred receives a great deal of respect from the people he works with. He controls a scarce resource, so doctors and hospital personnel generally treat him well. Larry, however, deals with people who are usually preoccupied or angry because their cars are not running properly.

In addition to these tangible benefits, occupational status is associated with prestige. Several surveys in the United States and numerous studies in other countries have found that there is widespread agreement about the prestige ranking of specific occupations. Typically, respondents are given a list of occupations and asked to rate each occupation in terms of its "general standing" or "social standing." The average rating is often used as a measure of relative prestige. The scores shown in Table 16.1 were taken from the Standard International Occupational Prestige Scale, which ranges from 10 to 90.

The social structure of the United States consists of several groups or social classes. One type of analysis of social class emphasizes occupational prestige in conjunction with income and education. This approach ordinarily classifies people into upper-upper,

upper-lower, upper-middle, lower-middle, working, and lower classes (Coleman and Neugarten 1971). A variation on this approach, called the *reputational method*, asks persons to classify members of their community into one of these classes (Warner and Lunt 1941). A very different approach emphasizes the control, or lack thereof, an individual has over one's work and coworkers as the main determinant of class standing (Wright et al. 1982).

Intergenerational Mobility

The means by which people improve their status is **upward mobility,** the movement from an occupation lower in prestige and income to one higher in prestige and income. To what extent is upward mobility realistically possible in the United States? On the one hand, we have the Horatio Alger rags-to-riches imagery. Anyone who is determined and works hard can achieve economic success. This imagery is fueled by stories about the astonishing success of the man who invented the transistor, the woman who founded Mary Kay cosmetics, and the man who borrowed from his friends to establish Motown Records. On the other hand, some argue that America is not an open society, that our eventual occupational and economic achievements are fixed at birth by our parent's social class, our ethnicity, and gender. To be sure, every city includes families who have been wealthy for generations, and families who have been poor for just as long. This suggests that the United States is characterized by *castes,* groups whose members are prevented from changing their social status.

These two views of upward mobility are concerned with *intergenerational mobility,* the extent of change in social status from one generation to the next. To determine intergenerational mobility, we would compare the social status of persons with that of their parents. If the rags-to-riches image is accurate, we should find that a substantial number of adults attain a social status significantly higher than their parents. If the caste-society image is cor-

TABLE 16.1

Occupational Prestige in the United States

Occupation	Prestige
Physician	78
College or University Professor	78
Lawyer	72
Dentist	70
Airplane Pilot	66
Electronic Engineer	65
Sales Representative	61
Clergy	60
Elementary Schoolteacher	57
Social Worker	56
Office Manager	55
Registered Nurse	54
Legal Secretary	53
Computer Programmer	51
Radio/TV Announcer	50
Airline Stewardess	50
Athlete	49
Dental Hygienist	44
Insurance Sales	44
Auto Mechanic	43
Farmer	40
Salesclerk	38
Carpenter	37
Hairdresser	35
Mail Carrier	33
Streetcar Operator	29
Waiter	23
Gas Station Attendant	22
Garbage Collector	13

Source: adapted from the Standard International Occupational Prestige Scale (Treiman 1977).

rect, we should find little or no vertical mobility, though there may be considerable horizontal movement to an occupation similar in prestige.

Occupational attainment in American society rests on educational achievement. In order to be a doctor, dental assistant, computer programmer, lawyer, or business executive, one needs to complete the required education. In order to be a registered nurse, Marie (whom we met at the beginning of the chapter) had to complete nursing school. Fred, our medical equipment salesman, completed a bachelor's degree in business. Thus, movement to an occupation with higher prestige often requires additional education.

SOCIOECONOMIC BACKGROUND. Beyond education, what other factors influence occupational attainment? To answer this question effectively we need to trace the occupational careers of individuals over their life course. Such longitudinal data are available in a study that began by surveying large samples of high-school students (Sewell and Hauser 1980). In 1957, all high-school seniors in Wisconsin were surveyed regarding their post-high-school plans. From this sample, a random sample of 10,317 were selected for more intensive analysis. In 1964, researchers obtained information from students' parents about post-high-school education, military service, marital status, and current occupation. Subsequently, they obtained information about students' earnings and about colleges/universities they attended. In 1975, 97 percent of the original sample were located and most were interviewed by telephone. The interview focused on post-high-school education, work history, and family characteristics. Data from this study enabled researchers to trace the impact of characteristics of high-school seniors on subsequent education, occupation, earnings, and work experience.

Figure 16.2 presents a diagram of the relationships found among the variables studied. The arrows indicate causal impacts. Variables are arranged from left to right reflecting the order in which the variables affect the person through time. For example, socioeconomic background influences ability which in turn influences educational attainment. Specifically, these results indicate that children from more affluent homes have greater ability, higher aspirations, and receive more education. Children with higher ability get better grades which reward them for their academic work and reinforce their aspirations. Children

who do well are also encouraged by significant others, such as teachers and relatives, which also contributes to high aspirations. These children are likely to choose courses that will prepare them for college. They are likely to spend more time on academic pursuits and less time on dating and social activities (Jessor et al. 1983). As a result they are likely to continue their education beyond high school and perhaps beyond college. Finally, high ability, encouragement of significant others, and high educational attainment lead to greater occupational status and earnings.

Note that socioeconomic background and grades have an indirect effect on occupational status, and a direct influence on educational attainment. This does not mean that parental socioeconomic status and an individual's grades are unrelated to occupational status. Rather, it indicates that status and grades influence occupational attainment through other variables—like aspirations—which have a direct impact on occupational attainment (Sewell and Hauser 1975).

The experiences of Fred and Larry clearly reflect the importance of these processes. Fred's parents were upper-middle class; they sent him to preschool at age four and encouraged him to learn to read. Larry's parents were working class; they encouraged him to get out and play, not to waste time reading. Fred did well in school; his grades were always high. Larry struggled with his schoolwork, especially math. By eighth grade, Fred had an excellent record and his teachers gave him lots of encouragement; Larry's teachers, on the other hand, didn't pay much attention to him. Fred worked hard in high school, got good grades, and, with the support of his teachers and family, went to the university. After finishing high school, Larry went into the army where he learned vehicle mechanics. When Fred finished college, he got a job in a medical equipment firm. Ten years after he graduated from high school, Fred was selling $200,000 worth of equipment per year and earning 10

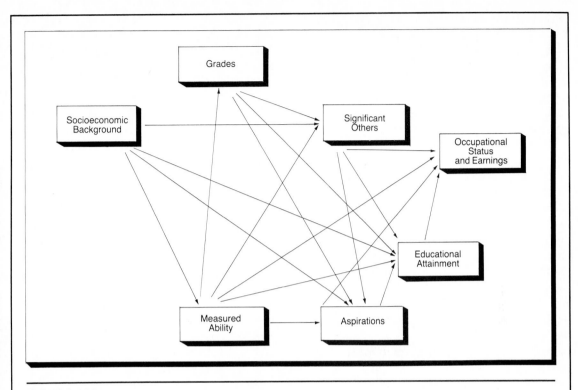

FIGURE 16.2

THE DETERMINANTS OF OCCUPATIONAL STATUS ATTAINMENT

This figure summarizes the influences that determine educational and the occupational status over the life course. Socioeconomic background (parents' education, occupation, and income) influences ability, aspirations, and educational attainment. Ability influences grades, which in turn affects encouragement from significant others, and aspirations for educational attainment. Occupational status is affected by education and also by ability, aspirations, and significant others.

Source: adapted from Sewell and Hauser (1980).

percent commissions. After he finished his military service, Larry went to work in a gas station. Ten years after Larry graduated from high school, he was earning $11,000 per year working in a gas station.

Mobility studies like the one described earlier indicate there *is* upward mobility, and that socioeconomic background does not fix one's occupational attainment and earnings. Through greater education, many persons achieve an occupational status and income substantially greater than would be expected based solely on their background. Thus, America is not a caste society. At the same time, socioeconomic background is not irrelevant to one's educational and occupational attainment. Not everyone has the ability to be a doctor, lawyer, or engineer. Thus, not everyone has unlimited opportunities.

GENDER. Is the process of status attainment different for men and women? According to the data obtained on Wisconsin high-school students, the determinants of occupational status as depicted in Figure 16.2, are the same for both men and women, although the size of some of the relationships varies.

Most striking were the findings with regard to occupational status. Using a prestige scale ranging from 0 to 100, the first jobs held by women were, on the average, six points higher on the scale than the first jobs held by men. That is, women in general started out in higher prestige jobs than men. Women's first jobs were concentrated within a narrow range of prestige, whereas there was much greater variation in the prestige scores of first jobs held by males (Sewell, Hauser, and Wolf 1980). Table 16.1 reveals how this occurred. The first jobs women held included schoolteacher, social worker, registered nurse, airline stewardess, dental hygienist, and salesclerk. The prestige scores of these jobs range from 57 to 38, respectively. In contrast, men's first jobs ranged from garbage collector (13) to physician (78).

When the researchers looked at 1975 occupations, they found men had gained an average of nine points in status. Women, on the other hand, had actually lost status; the average prestige of current occupations for women was two points lower than the average prestige of their first jobs. Men experience upward mobility because they work continuously. In addition, they are in occupations with possibilities of promotion and advancement. Women's work careers are often interrupted by marriage, moving (due to spouses being transferred), and by raising children; when they return to work, they often take up the same job. Thus, women are often unable to build up enough continuous experience to gain promotion. Advancement is also more limited in occupations held largely by women. The top positions in schools, social work, airlines, and sales are more often held by men than women. So the occupational status achieved by men and women differs over the course of their careers.

These differences are evident in the lives of Fred, Larry, and Marie who were introduced at the beginning of this chapter. After college, Fred began in sales and his income increased substantially every year. If he wanted, he could move up in the company to regional sales manager, national sales manager, and perhaps vice-president of sales. Larry has moved from gas station attendant (prestige score = 22) to owner of a service station (prestige score = 50). Like Fred, Marie went to college and earned a bachelor's degree. Her first job involved working on a surgical unit in a large hospital (prestige score = 54). As head nurse in pediatrics she works days now, gets weekends off, and earns more—but her occupation is basically unchanged. She could move up to director of nursing, but she is unlikely to do so because the added responsibility isn't balanced by added pay.

Social Networks

We have seen that socioeconomic background, ability, educational attainment, and earlier jobs influence occupational attainment over the life course. In part, this is because differences in experiences create differences in an individual's aspirations and abilities to cope with the occupational world. Varied experiences also move people into different social networks. This exposes them to important social contacts, which can have an important effect on their upward mobility. This section will consider the ways in which position in social networks promotes entry into specific jobs.

Networks provide channels for the flow of information, including information about employment opportunities. What types of networks are likely to provide information on finding new jobs? You might think it is networks characterized by strong ties, such as families or peer groups. Surprisingly, employment opportunities are often found through networks characterized by *weak ties*—infrequent interaction, low intensity, and little exchange of services. Weak ties are more likely to characterize relationships involving members of two different groups. Those to whom our ties are weak are involved in different groups and activities. Consequently, they will be exposed to information that is different from the information we already have. For this reason, new information is more likely to come via a weak tie than a strong one.

In one study (Granovetter 1973), a random sample of persons who had recently changed jobs was asked how they found out about their new job. Those who heard about their job through another person were asked how often they had seen that contact. If the person saw the contact at least twice a week, this was considered a strong tie; if the person saw the contact less often, it was considered a weak tie. Of those who found jobs through contacts, only 17 percent were obtained through people considered strong ties. The remainder found jobs through people they saw less than twice a week. The contacts were often friends from school, former coworkers, or former employers, people with whom they had had little recent interaction. It was often a chance meeting or a reintroduction by a mutual friend which led to the individual learning about the job. Thus, people were more likely to hear about jobs from those to whom they were weakly tied.

We noted earlier that women are less likely than men to experience upward occupational mobility during their careers. Might this be because men and women differ in their access to networks that carry job information? Our ties to networks grow out of the activities we share with others. The organizations we belong to are a major setting for such activities (Feld 1981). The larger the organization, the larger the potential number of weak rather than strong ties. If men belong to larger organizations than women, they would be likely to have more weak ties, and hence better access to information useful in finding jobs.

To examine this possibility, a sample of 1,799 adults were asked the name and size of each organization to which they belonged (Miller-McPherson and Smith-Lovin 1982). On the average, men belonged to organizations three times larger than those women did. Men were also more likely to belong to organizations such as business and professional groups and labor unions, whereas women were more likely to belong to smaller charitable, church, neighborhood, and community groups. Thus men were likely to develop a larger number of weak ties. Moreover, job-related contacts are more likely to develop in business/professional/union groups. Findings showed that males had an average of 170 job-related potential contacts, whereas females had an average of less than 35. Apparently, men are in networks that allow greater access to information about, and opportunities for, advancement.

Although finding a job is influenced by social networks, the status of the job one finds is influenced by the contact's status. You are more likely to get a management job at the phone company, for example, if your friend's father is a vice-president than if he is a line-man. In a study of males aged 21–64 in the Albany, New York area (Lin, Ensel, and Vaughn 1981) 57 percent of the men reported using contacts to get their first job. The higher the contact's occupational status, the greater the prestige of the position the job-seeker obtained.

Individual Values

Last year, Fred, Larry, and Marie were each approached by a labor union organizer. Fred, the sales representative, was approached by a member of Retail Clerks International. She explained that under a union contract he would spend fewer days on the road and be entitled to a travel allowance from his employer. Larry was approached by a representative of the Teamsters. The organizer sympathized with the problems of independent service station owners, and urged Larry to let the Teamsters represent his interests in dealing with his supplier. Marie was approached by the president of United Health Care Workers; he promised her higher wages and greater respect from physicians if she would join.

Fred flatly rejected the invitation, believing that a union contract would limit his freedom and perhaps reduce his income. What about Larry? On the one hand, he does feel at the mercy of "big oil," although he is also a self-employed businessman. Like Fred, he doesn't want to join a labor organization which might limit his ability to determine his prices and the pace at which he works. Marie reacted very favorably to the invitation, and began to attend union meetings "to see what they are like." She felt that a union might lead to higher pay, and might force the hospital to give her more freedom in determining the pace at which she worked.

In making their decisions, Fred, Larry, and Marie all used their **values**—enduring beliefs that certain patterns of behavior or end states are preferable to their opposites (Rokeach 1973). All three were concerned with protecting or enhancing their freedom and their wealth or income. These values provided criteria for making decisions. Thus, each person weighed the potential effect of joining a union on freedom and income. Fred felt the effect on both of these would be negative. Larry was sure union membership would limit his freedom but uncertain about its effect on his income. Marie perceived a potential gain in both freedom and income, so she decided to explore union membership.

Each of us has his or her own values. Each of us believes that particular goals and modes of behavior are more desirable than others. Although our values are general, they influence many specific attitudes, behaviors, and choices. How do value systems arise? To some extent, they are influenced by our location in the social structure. This section will examine three aspects of social position that

affect individual values, including occupational role, education, and social class.

Occupational Role

Because we spend up to half of our waking hours at work, we would expect our work to influence our values. But occupational experiences vary tremendously. To determine their effect on values, it is necessary to identify the basic differences between occupations. Three important characteristics have been suggested (Kohn 1969). The first is closeness of supervision—the extent to which the worker is under the direct surveillance and control of a supervisor. As a traveling salesman, Fred is rarely under close supervision, whereas Marie's work is supervised quite closely by the director of nursing and various physicians. The second occupational characteristic is routinization of work—the extent to which tasks are repetitive and predictable. Much of Larry's work is quite routine—pumping gas, checking oil levels, washing windshields. But Larry's work is not highly routinized. From one day to the next he never knows what kind of auto breakdown he will encounter or what unusual request some customer may make. The third characteristic is substantive complexity of the work—how complicated the work tasks are. Work with people is usually more complex than work with data and work with things. Marie's occupation as a nurse is especially complex because she must constantly cope with the problems posed by doctors, patients, and families.

All three of these characteristics were measured in several studies of employed men to determine the impacts of occupational role on values and personality (Kohn and Schooler 1983). Results of these studies show a relationship between particular occupational characteristics and particular values: Men whose jobs were less closely supervised, less routine, and more complex placed especially high value on responsibility, good sense, and curiosity. Men whose work was closely supervised, routine,

Workers on an assembly line often experience alienation. Assembly-line jobs are monotonous, do not allow workers to exercise initiative, and give them no influence over working conditions.

and not complex were more likely to value conformity. Thus, the occupational conditions that encourage self-direction—less supervised, nonroutine, complex tasks—are associated with valuing individual qualities that facilitate adjustment and success in a self-directed environment—responsibility, curiosity, and good sense. Occupational conditions that encourage adherence to a prescribed routine—close supervision, and routine and simple tasks such as bolting bumpers on new cars—are associated with qualities that facilitate success in that environment, such as neatness and obedience. This pattern has emerged in studies of employed men and women (Miller et al. 1979), and in studies conducted in several countries including the United States, Japan, and Poland (Slomczynski, Miller, and Kohn, 1981).

Early studies of the relationships between workers' values and their occupational conditions reveal that workers exposed to particular conditions tended to hold particular values. However, these studies were unable to determine with certainty whether adjustment to occupational conditions actually *caused* people to value particular qualities. Perhaps men who value curiosity and desire responsibility select occupations that allow them to exercise these traits (Kohn and Schooler 1973). In attempting to identify the causal order, researchers compared the men's values and occupational conditions in 1974 with their values and occupational conditions 10 years earlier (Kohn and Schooler 1982). What they found indicated causal impacts in *both* directions between values and occupational conditions. Men who had valued self-direction highly in 1964 were more likely to be in work roles that were more complex, less routine, and less closely supervised 10 years later. Thus, values influenced job selection. At the same time, men who were in occupations that allowed or required self-direction in 1964 tended to place greater value on responsibility, curiosity, and good sense in 1974. Thus, their earlier job conditions influenced their later values.

Another perspective on the impact of work on individual values emphasizes the organizational setting of the work place (Inkeles and Smith 1974). Many people work in complex, bureaucratic organizations. The study described above shows that, within complex organizations, variation in work roles is related to variation in values. What characteristics enable people to function effectively in modern organizational settings? That is, how do people become "modern"?

Inkeles and his colleagues developed a profile of the characteristics that distinguish "modern" workers from traditional workers (Inkeles 1975). Among these were openness to new experience, a belief in one's personal efficacy, autonomy and independence from familial or religious authority, interest in public affairs, and positive attitudes toward use of birth control and greater equality for women. Using these characteristics, the researchers constructed a scale that measures the degree to which a person is "modernized." A survey including questions about these characteristics was distributed to samples of men in six countries. Each sample included several hundred industrial workers, 100 or more recent migrants to a city, and 100 or more rural agricultural workers.

What variables correlate with being "modern"? One was working in a large-scale organization such as a factory. There was a strong positive correlation between individuals' modernity scores and the number of months they had worked in factories. In contrast, employment in agriculture did not correlate with individuals' modernization. Thus employment in a factory had a substantial and cumulative modernizing effect on people's values compared to working on a farm. Differences in average modernity scores across the six countries—Argentina, Chile, India, Israel, Nigeria, and East Pakistan—reflect in part national differences in the degree of industrialization and the amount of factory work available (Inkeles 1978).

Education

A second influence on individual values is education. According to the above profile, a "modern man" is characterized by an openness to new experience, independence from authority, and an interest in public affairs. Intuitively, these should be affected by the amount of education one has. Analysis of the relationship between several variables and individual modernity scores support this hypothesis (Inkeles 1975). Each additional year of education was associated with an increase in modernity scores. Months of work in a factory was generally second in importance to education.

Are differences in education also related to differences in an individual's values? The study in the preceding section demonstrated that men in jobs that are not closely supervised, nonroutine, and substantively complex value self-direction, whereas men in jobs with the opposite characteristics value conformity. Education is also associated with the value one places on these characteristics.

Substantively complex occupations involve working independently with people, things, or data. Such work requires intellectual flexibility, the ability to evaluate data or situations and to solve problems. Assuming these abilities are influenced by education, education should be related to intellectual flexibility. Statistical analyses of the data relating men's values to occupational conditions confirm this hypothesis (Kohn and Schooler

1973). Thus intellectual flexibility is associated with both the substantive complexity of occupation and the value placed on self-direction. These relationships are summarized in Figure 16.3.

Social Class

How important is each of the following to you: a comfortable life, a sense of accomplishment, an exciting life, family security, salvation? What order of importance would you place them in? According to research, the order in which people rank these and other values depends on their position in the social structure (Rokeach 1973). Evidence suggests that there is a systematic difference in the way people of different social classes order a number of values—including the five listed above. Persons who are of high status give high ratings to a sense of accomplishment and family security, whereas persons low in education and income give high ratings to a comfortable life and salvation. At the same time, there was no relationship between social class and the importance of an exciting life, which was given a low rating by most respondents (Rokeach 1973).

These differences probably reflect the social conditions experienced by rich and poor in the United States. Persons with low incomes perhaps aspire to a comfortable life because they don't have it, or at least cannot count on having it. Their economic situation may also make religion an important source of comfort, and thus lead to a concern with salvation. High-status persons already have a comfortable life; for them, maintaining the family is important because it contributes to their social standing in the community. Those with high status also have the time and resources available to make individual accomplishment possible.

The five values mentioned above are "terminal values," enduring beliefs about desirable end states. Two other terminal values are

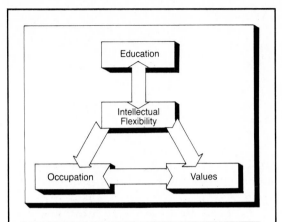

FIGURE 16.3

THE RELATIONSHIP BETWEEN EDUCATION, OCCUPATION, AND VALUES

Occupations vary in the degree to which they allow for self-direction. Jobs that are routine, simple, and closely supervised encourage placing a high value on conformity and obedience, whereas jobs that are nonroutine and complex encourage placing a high value on self-direction. Education provides skills that are essential to intellectual flexibility—the ability to evaluate complex information and solve problems. Thus intellectual flexibility is associated with both the ability to perform work requiring self-direction, and valuing curiosity, good sense, and responsibility. A study of 3,101 men supports the existence of these relationships.

Source: adapted from Kohn and Schooler (1973).

freedom and equality. A survey of 1,397 adults revealed systematic differences in the average rankings of freedom and equality by whites and blacks (Rokeach 1973). Each respondent was asked to rank a list of 18 values in order of importance. Whereas white respondents ranked freedom as more important (5.6) than equality (9.6), blacks ranked them about equally important (5.0 and 4.6 respectively). On the whole, whites in the United States have more education and income than blacks. Many blacks believe that discrimination or racism prevents them from achieving higher levels of education and income. Perhaps they rank equality higher than whites because they view equality as essential to improving their status in American Society.

Social Influences on Health

Most of us attribute diseases to biological rather than social factors. But the transmission of disease obviously depends on people's interactions, while our physical susceptibility to disease is influenced by our life styles. Likewise, our mental health is influenced by our relationships with relatives, friends, lovers, professors, supervisors, and so on. Thus, social position affects both physical and mental health. This section examines the impact of occupation, gender, and marital roles on physical health. It also considers the relationship between social networks, gender and occupational roles, and social class on mental health.

Physical Health

OCCUPATIONAL ROLES. What do the physician addicted to demerol, the executive with an ulcer, the coal miner with black lung disease, and the salesclerk who is an alcoholic all have in common? The answer is a health problem that may largely be due to occupational role.

Occupational roles affect physical health in two ways. First, some occupations directly expose workers to health hazards. For example, exposure to coal dust damages lung tissue, causing a condition known as black lung disease. Workers whose jobs involve direct contact with asbestos are more likely to contract lung cancer. Workers who manufacture polyvinyl chloride used in making plumbing fixtures are particularly susceptible to cancer of the liver (Epstein 1976).

Second, many occupational roles expose individuals to stresses that affect physical health indirectly. Each of the roles we play carries a set of obligations or duties. We experience **role overload** when the demands of our roles exceed the amount of time, energy, and

other resources we have to meet them (Goode 1960).

Many physicians are subject to role overload. They are expected to carefully diagnose each patient's condition, make sure each is treated correctly, react professionally to emergencies, keep up with advances in their areas of specialization, and be active in the medical society and on hospital boards. At the same time, a physician is expected to spend time with family members, to keep the house in good repair, and to travel with the children when they are out of school. Many physicians seek relief from role overload through narcotics such as demerol, to which they may become addicted (Winick 1964). Physicians and nurses are more likely to use narcotics than other professionals, simply because the drugs are readily available to them. Availability alone is not enough to explain addiction, however; pharmacists also have access to narcotics but rarely use them. Pharmacists, however, are less likely to experience role overload. It is the combination of role overload and availability that promotes drug use.

The most widely studied relationship between job characteristics and physical health is the impact of occupational stress on coronary heart disease. As work load increases—including perceived demands on one's time, number of hours worked, and feelings of responsibility—so does the risk of coronary heart disease (House 1974). One acute source of overload is an important deadline, especially when the failure to meet the deadline may have negative consequences. Heart attacks are associated with a high level of serum cholesterol in the blood. Several studies report that the level of serum cholesterol rises among medical students as the day of their examinations approaches (Sales 1969). This suggests one tangible link between role demands and physical health.

People are not necessarily at the mercy of occupational and other role demands. There are three common strategies for coping with role overload. First, people set priorities, deciding on the relative importance of obligations to family, work or school, friends, and other activities. They establish a *queue,* an order in which they will complete tasks or occupy various roles (Schwartz 1978). Once established, the queue takes on moral and psychological significance. We have all experienced the feeling that we "have to" do something even though a much more attractive opportunity is offered. Thus, we turn down an invitation to a party because we have to study, visit parents or other relatives, or do some volunteer task for a club or neighborhood organization. Although limiting, queues reduce the pressures associated with role overload.

A second strategy is to renegotiate the role expectations causing the overload (Handel 1979). A student with two important exams on the same day may be able to arrange to take one of them earlier or later. An overworked doctor may substantially reduce the number of patients she is seeing; alternatively, she may add a nurse-clinician or a partner to her practice to achieve the same goal. A third solution is to exit from one or more of the roles (Goode 1960). A college student who finds that he is unable to meet the school's performance standards may quit school and go to work. A heart attack victim will assume a slower pace, and may even resign from some of his roles.

GENDER ROLES. Who is more likely to experience coronary heart disease, lung cancer, or cirrhosis of the liver—men or women? You probably picked men, and if you did, you are right. Men are two to six times more likely than women to die from these conditions. Although there is evidence that genetic and hormonal factors play a role, traditional role expectations for males and females in our society are another significant factor (Waldron 1976).

Earlier we mentioned that role overload is associated with coronary heart disease. Professionals such as physicians, lawyers, accountants, and so on, are especially vulnerable to overload, and the persons holding these positions are primarily male. Other studies have shown that heart attacks are correlated with certain personality traits known as Coronary Prone Behavior Patterns (Jenkins, Rosenman, and Zyzanski 1974). People who exhibit this behavior pattern are work-oriented, aggressive, competitive, and impatient. Males are much more likely to be characterized by this behavior pattern than females.

Men are more likely to contract lung cancer and emphysema because they are much more likely to smoke cigarettes. They are more prone to cirrhosis because they are four times as likely as women to be heavy drinkers (Cahalan 1970). They are more likely to die in auto accidents, both because of higher rates of driving under the influence of alcohol, and because of poor driving habits (Waldron 1976).

MARITAL ROLES. A recent study compares single, married, divorced, separated, and widowed persons on a variety of health-related measures (Verbrugge 1979). Divorced and separated persons had the highest rates of illness and disability, followed by widowed and single persons. Married persons were healthiest. Other data indicated that rates of hospital *residence* were highest for singles and lowest for married persons. Mortality rates at a given age were also correlated with marital status (Kobrin and Hendershot 1977). A study of 20,000 deaths revealed that singles had the highest death rate in any age group. Following singles were single "heads of households" (people with others dependent on them), followed by married persons without children, and married persons with children. Among married persons, the death rate of males and females is virtually the same (Waldron 1976).

Why is it that being married and having children protects people against illness and accidents? The most likely explanation is that married persons are less likely to engage in behaviors that expose them to illness and accidents (Verbrugge 1979). They probably eat and sleep better than unmarried persons. They are perhaps less likely to smoke and drink. They may take fewer risks, reducing the likelihood they will be involved in accidents. Finally, they may be more likely to seek medical care when ill (Verbrugge 1979). Thus, being married is associated with a life style that reduces the risk of illness and death.

Mental Health

At the beginning of the chapter, we introduced Larry who owns a service station, works long hours, and earns about $16,000 per year. He has two children, owns his own home, and has trouble making ends meet. He comes home from work every day exhausted. He worries about the economy and whether or not there will be another energy crisis leading to inadequate supplies of gasoline, or an oil glut leading to gasoline price wars. Either one would ruin his business, because more than one-half of his income is from gasoline sales.

Like many Americans, Larry finds that his life situation is very demanding. His customers expect him to do high quality repair work at low prices, his wife expects him to support the family and spend time with her, and his children want more toys than he can afford. Other life events that can be demanding including moving, serious conflict with a parent, lover, or spouse, changing jobs, getting married, and having a child (Holmes and Rahe 1967). Each person develops techniques to cope with such demands. At times, the demands made on a person exceed the individual's ability to cope with them; such a discrepancy is referred to as **stress** (Dohrenwend 1961).

People who are under stress often engage in behavior designed to reduce the discrepancy. They may also become tense, anxious, worried, generally unhappy—or all of these. A typical questionnaire used to measure stress-related symptoms is reproduced in Box 16.1. Other measures of mental health focus on happiness and satisfaction with various aspects of life.

Stress is often temporary. A move from one apartment to another, for example, will be stressful during the weeks all the arrangements are made, and during the move itself. As one becomes settled, however, the demands will decline. At the same time, the ability to respond to the demands of moving may increase as one learns how to cope with packing, disconnecting the old phone and getting a new one, and so on.

On the other hand, stress may be continuous as it is for Larry, who constantly experiences tension and anxiety due to his economic worries. Chronic stress may lead to persistent physical and psychological problems. Neuroses, schizophrenia, and affective disorders such as depression are among the mental illnesses associated with severe stress. The experience of stress and impaired psychological functioning varies by gender, by marital and work roles, by membership in social networks, and by social class.

GENDER ROLES. Adult women in the United States have somewhat poorer mental health than men. On symptom scales such as the one shown in Box 16.1, women attain significantly higher scores than men (Warheit et al. 1976). Women also have higher rates of two types of mental illness, neuroses (which involve high levels of anxiety) and depression (Dohrenwend and Dohrenwend 1976).

Are there differences in the social roles that men and women typically enact that might account for the higher level of psychological impairment among women? The majority of people in these studies were married. Traditional marital roles require men to provide financially for the family, and women to take care of the home and to provide emotional support for their husbands. Thus traditional marriages may reduce stress for men because they provide a supportive environment. For women, however, being married may increase stress. Women in a traditional marriage may be subordinate to their husbands and thus have less control over their

Family members play an important part in helping us to cope with stressful events, such as the death of a relative or close friend. They are an important source of emotional support, and may help by temporarily taking over some of our role responsibilities.

lives. A lack of control is, in itself, stressful. Until recently, married women also tended to remain in the home, isolated from social networks outside the family that could provide support. The responsibility of married women to care for husbands and children may also reduce their ability to respond adaptively to stress—for example, to take care of themselves when they are ill (Gove and Hughes 1979).

Is greater social isolation and the presence of children associated with greater stress among married women? This hypothesis was tested using data from interviews with more than 2,300 men and women (Pearlin and Johnson 1977). The study measured three potential sources of stress, including economic hardship, social isolation, and parental responsibility. Economic hardship was assessed by asking the persons how often they lacked enough money for food, clothing, and medical care. Social isolation was measured by membership in voluntary associations, number of "really good friends," and length of time the person had lived in the neighborhood. Parental responsibility was measured by the number of children in the home. The study also measured symptoms associated with depression. The results indicated that economic strain was the major variable associated with depression scores. Neither social isolation nor having children was related to depression. Both married men and women were less depressed than singles under equivalent conditions of hardship, social isolation, or parental responsibility. Thus marriage appears to help both men and women cope with stress.

MARITAL AND WORK ROLES. Although marriage appears to benefit both men and women, the conflicting demands of family and work roles may cause stress. Evidence for and against this view is presented in various studies.

Box 16.1
HOW DO YOU RESPOND TO STRESS?

Stress is a discrepancy between the demands on a person and the ability to successfully respond to those demands. Individuals under stress often react with a variety of physical and psychological symptoms. One of the most common measures of stress was developed by Langner (1963). His original scale consists of the 22 questions reproduced below. As you read each question, circle the appropriate response.

Question	Response Categories
1. I feel weak all over much of the time.	1. yes 2. no
2. I have had periods of days, weeks, or months when I couldn't take care of things because I couldn't "get going."	1. yes 2. no
3. In general, would you say that most of the time you are in high (very good) spirits, good spirits, low spirits, or very low spirits?	1. high 2. good 3. low 4. very low
4. Every so often I suddenly feel hot all over.	1. yes 2. no
5. Have you ever been bothered by your heart beating hard? Would you say: often, sometimes, or never?	1. often 2. sometimes 3. never
6. Would you say your appetite is poor, fair, good, or too good?	1. poor 2. fair 3. good 4. too good
7. I have periods of such great restlessness that I cannot sit long in a chair (cannot sit still very long).	1. yes 2. no
8. Are you the worrying type (a worrier)?	1. yes 2. no
9. Have you ever been bothered by shortness of breath when you were *not* exercising or working hard? Would you say: often, sometimes, or never?	1. often 2. sometimes 3. never
10. Are you ever bothered by nervousness (irritable, fidgety, tense)? Would you say: often, sometimes, or never?	1. often 2. sometimes 3. never

11. Have you ever had any fainting spells (lost consciousness)? Would you say: never, a few times, or more than a few times?

1. never
2. a few times
3. more than a few times

12. Do you ever have any trouble in getting to sleep or staying asleep? Would you say: often, sometimes, or never?

1. often
2. sometimes
3. never

13. I am bothered by acid (sour) stomach several times a week.

1. yes
2. no

14. My memory seems to be all right (good).

1. yes
2. no

15. Have you ever been bothered by "cold sweats"? Would you say: often, sometimes, or never?

1. often
2. sometimes
3. never

16. Do your hands ever tremble enough to bother you? Would you say: often, sometimes, or never?

1. often
2. sometimes
3. never

17. There seems to be a fullness (clogging) in my head or nose much of the time.

1. yes
2. no

18. I have personal worries that get me down physically (make me physically ill).

1. yes
2. no

19. Do you feel somewhat apart even among friends (apart, isolated, alone)?

1. yes
2. no

20. Nothing ever turns out for me the way I want it to (turns out, happens, comes about, that is, my wishes aren't fulfilled).

1. yes
2. no

21. Are you ever troubled with headaches or pains in the head? Would you say: often, sometimes, or never?

1. often
2. sometimes
3. never

22. You sometimes can't help wondering if anything is worthwhile anymore.

1. yes
2. no

These questions measure response to stress. To determine your stress score, give yourself one point if you circled 3 or 4 on item 3, if you answered 3 on item 11, and if you answered 2 on item 14. For each of the other items, give yourself 1 point if you circled a 1.

Langner collected data using this and other measures from 1,660 adults living in Manhattan. He found that adults who scored 0 to 3 on this scale appeared to be "normal" on various other indices of mental health. Those who scored 4 to 6 on the scale also showed some psychological impairment on other indices. Adults who scored 7 or more were very likely to be diagnosed as severely impaired. Thus, according to Langner, as response to stress increases, mental health deteriorates.

Source: adapted from Langner (1963).

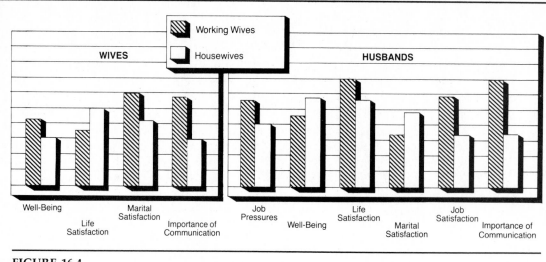

FIGURE 16.4

THE EFFECTS OF WORKING WIVES ON THE MENTAL HEALTH OF WIVES AND HUSBANDS

For women, the effects of working outside the home were generally positive. Those who worked reported greater mental and physical well-being, greater satisfaction with their marriages, and ranked communication as more important than wives who did not work outside the home. On the other hand, working wives reported lower overall satisfaction with their lives. The effects of working wives on their husbands were mixed. The husbands reported greater job pressures, lower mental and physical well-being, and lower marital satisfaction. At the same time, these men reported greater overall satisfaction with life, job satisfaction, and communication with their wives. In general, the impact of wives working is different for husbands and wives. *Source: adapted from Burke and Weir (1976).*

First, consider the conflict between work and family roles for men. Marital roles actually encompass four narrower roles: housekeeper, therapeutic (discussing and helping with problems), recreational, and sexual. The more time a man spends working, the less time he has to fulfill each of these marital roles. This is especially likely to pose a problem for men whose jobs are not limited to a specific number of hours, such as doctors, lawyers, sales representatives, professors, and business executives. In a study of role conflict (Clarke, Nye, and Gecas 1978), 390 married couples were asked about the degree to which each spouse participated in each of the four marital roles, about their competence in each of the roles, and about the number of hours the husband worked. The amount of time husbands spent working had no effect either on participation or on competence in the housekeeper, therapeutic, or sexual roles, although it significantly reduced the time they devoted to the recreational role.

Now consider conflict between work and family roles for women. In the past 20 years, increasing numbers of married women have taken full or part-time employment outside the home. To what extent does working outside the home cause stress for married women? Note that if married women are subjected to increased stress, this could prove stressful to their husbands as well. If a working wife has less time to fulfill her spouse's needs, he may become dissatisfied.

These questions were explored in a study of 189 professional men (engineers and accountants) and their wives (Burke and Weir 1976). Spouses were interviewed separately about satisfaction with their jobs, marriage, and life, about pressures experienced at work and in their lives, about communication with spouse, and about mental and physical well-being. The results, illustrated in Figure 16.4, indicate that working wives are more satisfied with their marriage and communicate more with their husbands than nonworking wives. By contrast, husbands of working women are less satisfied with their marriages, but more satisfied with their jobs and lives. When both spouses work, the relationship is subjected to greater stress. Women seem to cope better, partly because they gain extrafamilial networks that provide social support and help them cope with the stresses they experience. Men, on the other hand, lose some emotional and physical supports, and may have to undertake tasks that women traditionally performed (Kessler and McRae 1981).

Who is happier, housewives or working wives? An analysis of data from six national surveys found no correlation between reported happiness and whether or not wives were employed (Wright 1978).

What if a couple has children? Does that increase the stress associated with a woman's employment? Child care is traditionally considered to be primarily the woman's role obligation. Employment outside the home is thought to reduce a woman's ability to fulfill this obligation. A study of 122 college-educated women confirmed this expectation. Married career women with children scored higher on a stress scale than married housewives with children (Stewart and Salt 1981).

A survey study of 1,800 adults (Gove and Geerken 1977) examined the effects of women's employment on couples with children. Among the four variables measured were: feeling "incessant demands" (overworked); the desire to be alone; loneliness; and the frequency with which respondents experienced 14 psychiatric symptoms over the past two weeks. Married men scored the lowest on each

of these four measures whereas unemployed wives scored the highest and employed wives scored in between these two groups. The presence of children was associated with feeling more demands, desire to be alone, and loneliness for both men and women. Higher scores on these three measures were associated with psychiatric symptoms. Thus, for married women, employment is associated with greater psychological well-being, whereas having children is associated with increased stress and reduced psychological well-being.

These results indicate that the relationships between work, marital and parental roles, and psychological well-being are complex. Among professional men, work and family roles may conflict. Employment of wives appears to improve their mental health, although it may decrease their husband's well-being and satisfaction with marriage. The demands of child care appear to increase stress on both parents, especially working mothers.

SOCIAL NETWORKS. Although relationships can be a major source of stress, they also serve as an important resource in coping with stress. Social networks can reduce stress in several ways. First, a network of close friends and kin eases the impact of stressful events by providing various types of support (House 1981b). Their trust and affection reduce our feelings of vulnerability, and positive feedback about our abilities helps us deal with occasional negative feedback. A poor grade, for example, is less stressful if our friends let us know they think we are a good student. Informational support from others prepares us to avoid problems or to handle them when they arise. Advice from friends on how to handle job interviews, for example, improves our ability to cope with this situation. Finally, network members provide each other with instrumental support—money, labor, and time. For instance, in a study of 1,212 married couples from the Philadelphia area women were more likely to be employed full-time if they had relatives living within 10 minutes of their home (Ericksen, Yancey, and

Ericksen 1979). The availability of kin to provide child care can reduce the stress of women working outside the home.

A second way social networks reduce stress is by helping people cope with stressful events or crises when they occur. A student who has an accident or illness requiring hospitalization will be in trouble if she has no one around to contact her teachers, bring assignments and needed books to the hospital, and deliver papers. A roommate or close friend can assist her in such a crisis. Similarly, when the death of a relative occurs our friends and relatives provide emotional support, and may even help with the arrangements that must be made.

Third, network members influence how we react to stress. When we experience anxiety or tension for a prolonged period, we often discuss it with friends or family in an attempt to define the problem (Emerson and Messinger 1977). The reactions of others often influence how we handle our problem. A student experiencing chronic tension, for example, might talk it over with a close friend. A friend with strong religious beliefs might suggest that the student be "born again" and find renewed purpose in life. Another friend might say that a ski trip to Colorado is the necessary tonic.

Membership in a social network can help women cope with the stresses that typically occur during pregnancy. Women experience many physical and psychological changes during pregnancy, some of them ambiguous. These changes may put stress on a couple; their reaction to this stress depends in part on the nature of their social networks. For example, women who live with relatives or have relatives living nearby, are more likely to rely on these kin for information about the meaning of these changes and for emotional support. Women who do not have kin close by are more likely to rely on support from health care clinics. The density of the social network—the extent to which friends and relatives know each other—is also influential. Women in dense, interlocking networks are more likely to get similar advice from each network member, whereas women in loose knit networks are more likely to get conflicting information, and to seek the advice of health care clinics (McKinlay 1973). Thus, social networks not only help women cope with the stress of pregnancy but influence how they react to it.

SOCIAL CLASS. The lower a person's socioeconomic status, the greater the amount of stress reported (Langner and Michael 1963). Socioeconomic status is jointly determined by a person's education, occupation, and income. Does each of these components contribute to stress independently? Or is stress the result of only one or two of these components?

An analysis of data from surveys of eight quite diverse samples (Kessler 1982) shows a consistent pattern: low education, low occupational attainment, and low income contribute separately to stress. The relative importance of these three components as sources of stress is not the same for men as for women, however. For men, income appears most important; for women (employed or not) education appears to be the most important component. Occupational attainment is the least important determinant of stress for both sexes.

Further analyses attempted to identify the causes of the negative relationship between social status and stress. Are lower class persons exposed to greater stress, or are they simply less able to cope effectively with stressful events? The answer is both (Kessler and Cleary 1980). On the one hand, lower-class persons are more likely to experience economic hardship—not having enough money to provide adequate food, clothing, and medical care (Pearlin and Radabaugh 1976). They also experience higher rates of a variety of physical illnesses (Syme and Berkman 1976). Both economic hardship and illness increase the stress an individual experiences. At the same time, persons who are low in income, education, and occupational attainment lack the resources that would enable them to cope with these stresses effectively. Low income reduces their ability to cope with illness. In addition, low-status persons are less likely to have a sense of control over their environment, and less access to political power or influence. For this reason, they are less likely to attempt to change stressful conditions or events.

If stress increases as socioeconomic status decreases, we would expect persons lower in status to have poorer mental health. Research over the past 30 years has consistently confirmed this expectation; there is a strong correlation between social class and serious mental disorders (Eaton 1980). This correlation has been found in studies conducted in numerous countries (Dohrenwend and Dohrenwend 1974). In general, persons in the lowest socioeconomic class have the highest rates of mental illness.

A study of first admissions to mental hospitals in Maryland (Eaton 1980) analyzed the relationship between class (measured by education) and schizophrenia. Individuals with only an elementary-school education were 10 times as likely to be diagnosed as schizophrenic upon admission as those with a college education. This finding involves persons who reach mental hospitals. What of the rate of schizophrenia among those who remain in the community? In community surveys—which included psychiatric assessments of persons who are not institutionalized—the same concentration of schizophrenia in the lowest class is found. With respect to the less serious conditions such as neuroses, the results are less consistent. In some studies the rate of neurosis is highest among lower class persons, whereas other studies show no pattern (Dohrenwend and Dohrenwend 1974). In the case of the affective psychoses (manic, depressive, and manic-depressive disorders) there appears to be no relationship between class and incidence of the illness (Eaton 1980).

There are three explanations for why membership in the lower class might cause mental disorders (Eaton 1980). The first suggests that lower-class infants are more likely to have suffered damage during the pregnancy, and that this damage may contribute to later psychiatric illness (Mednick and Schulsinger 1969). There is no direct evidence to support this explanation, however. The major indirect evidence is the higher rate of infant mortality in the lower class. By extension, it is argued that conditions which are not fatal, but which could cause later psychological disorders, are more common in this class. A study of first admissions to mental hospitals revealed that the negative relationship between class and illness was strongest for disorders with an organic cause, which are often due to hereditary factors (Rushing and Ortega 1979). These results are consistent with the hypothesis that lower-class infants are more often physically damaged during pregnancy.

Another explanation contends that personality characteristics vary by social class, and that socialization patterns typical of lower-class families contribute to mental illness. These patterns may reduce people's ability to deal successfully with stress. As we have seen, the values taught to children by parents differ by social class (Kohn 1969, 1977). The values for conformity and obedience to authority that lower-class persons tend to acquire may reduce their flexibility, make them less able to respond adaptively to new situations. There is no direct evidence, however, that these differences produce differential rates of mental illness.

Finally, it has been proposed that the different rates of mental disorder are caused by differences in stress. Both low socioeconomic class (Warheit et al. 1976) and economic hardship (Pearlin and Radabaugh 1976; Mirowksy and Ross 1980) are positively associated with stress. Perhaps the highest rates of schizophrenia and personality disorders among the lower class are a consequence of the greater stress associated with poverty, low education, low occupational status, and other deprivational aspects of lower-class life. Evidence for such an association is based on a survey of 1,660 adults living in Manhattan (Langner and Michael 1963). Results of this study, illustrated in Figure 16.5, show a strong association

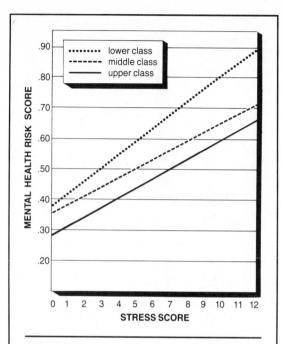

FIGURE 16.5

SOCIAL CLASS, STRESS, AND MENTAL HEALTH RISK

The Midtown Manhattan study investigated the relationship between social class, stress, and mental health. Respondents completed an early version of the Langner scale (see Box 16.1) and were questioned in detail about their lives. Based on the interviews, two psychiatrists independently rated the mental health of each person; these ratings were averaged, and transformed into mental health risk scores, which ranged from .00 to 1.0. The risk score for the average person in the study was .50; the higher the score above .50, the greater the risk. The results show that both social class and stress score are related to the Mental Health Risk Score: As socioeconomic status declines and stress increases, a person's risk of mental health impairment increases dramatically.

Source: adapted from Langner and Michael (1963, Fig. 14.2).

between social class, stress, and the incidence of mental disorder.

Alienation

Jim dragged himself out of bed and headed for the shower. As the water poured over him he thought: "Thursday . . . another 10-hour shift . . . if the line doesn't shut down, I'll bolt 500 bumpers . . . sick of car frames . . . I'd rather do almost anything else . . . if only I'd finished high school . . . damn the money! . . . Let 'em take the job and shove it . . . but what else pays a guy who quit school $11.28 an hour?"

Jim is experiencing **alienation,** the sense that one is uninvolved in the social world or lacks control over it. Many types of alienation have been identified (Seeman 1975). Two of the most important are self-estrangement and powerlessness. We will consider both of these in detail as well as four additional types: normlessness, meaninglessness, social isolation, and cultural estrangement.

Self-Estrangement

Jim's hatred for his job reflects **self-estrangement,** the awareness that he is engaging in activities that are not rewarding in themselves. Work is an important part of one's daily life, often involving more than half of one's waking hours. When work is meaningless, the individual perceives the self as devoting time and energy to something unrewarding—that is, something "alien."

What makes a job intrinsically rewarding? One feature is variety in the specific tasks the person performs; another is that the work gives the individual a sense of mastery and self-respect. Work that requires the individual to use judgment, make decisions, and surmount obstacles contributes to one's sense of mastery and self-respect. Jim's job has no variety; it is monotonous and boring. It is also cut and dried. He does the same set of tasks 50 times per hour with little opportunity to exercise judgment or initiative.

Four features of industrial technology tend to produce self-estrangement. First, the worker has no connection with the finished product; Jim will never see that car after it leaves the plant. Second, he has no control over company policies. Third, he has little influence over the conditions of employment, over which days, which hours, or how long he works. Finally, he has no control over the

The graffiti gracing subway trains in some American cities are responses by urban youth to alienation. Spray-painted messages reflect the lack of control over their lives that disadvantaged youths feel.

work process—for example, the speed with which cars pass his work station (Blauner 1964).

These features are especially characteristic of assembly-line work, in which each person performs the same highly specialized task dozens or hundreds of times per day. Thus workers on assembly lines should be more likely to experience self-estrangement than other workers. A study testing this hypothesis (Blauner 1964) compared assembly-line workers in textile and automobile plants with skilled printers and technicians in the chemical industry. As expected, assembly-line workers were more alienated than skilled workers, who had jobs that were more varied and involved the exercise of judgment and initiative.

It has also been argued that work in bureaucratic organizations—like large insurance companies or government agencies—may produce self-estrangement. In many bureaucratic organizations workers have little or no control over the work process and do not participate in organizational decision making. Thus workers at the lowest levels of such organizations should experience self-estrangement or dissatisfaction with their work. Supervisors, on the other hand, should be more satisfied because they have greater control (Bachrach and Aiken 1979).

According to the theory developed by Karl Marx (*Early Writings,* published 1964), a person's relationship to the means of production determines whether he or she will experience self-estrangement. The most alienated employees are hypothesized to be those who have no autonomy, who do not have the freedom to solve nonroutine problems, and who have no subordinates. Marx referred to such workers as the *proletariat.* In contemporary society,

TABLE 16.2

A MEASURE OF POWERLESSNESS

	Strongly Agree	Agree	Disagree	Strongly Disagree
1. People like me can change the course of world events if we make ourselves heard.	SA	A	D	SD
2. I think each of us can do a great deal to improve world opinion of the United States.	SA	A	D	SD
3. There's very little that persons like myself can do to improve world opinion of the United States.	SA	A	D	SD
4. The average citizen can have an influence on government decisions.	SA	A	D	SD
5. This world is run by the few people in power, and there is not much the little guy can do about it.	SA	A	D	SD
6. It is only wishful thinking to believe that one can really influence what happens in society at large.	SA	A	D	SD
7. A lasting world peace can be achieved by those of us who work toward it.	SA	A	D	SD
8. More and more, I feel helpless in the face of what's happening in the world today.	SA	A	D	SD

Note: Agreement with items 3, 5, 6 and 8 indicates a sense of powerlessness, as does disagreement with statements 1, 2, 4 and 7. How powerless do *you* feel?

Source: adapted from Zeller, Neal, and Groat (1980).

assembly-line workers, salesclerks, file clerks, and laborers are all in occupations which have these characteristics. A survey of 1,499 working adults found that 46 percent were in jobs of this type (Wright et al. 1982). Another survey found that men whose jobs were characterized by lack of autonomy and complexity attained high scores on a measure of self-estrangement (Kohn 1976).

It has been suggested that the widespread alienation of workers has resulted in poorer quality and lower productivity in the automobile and other assembly-line industries. However, self-estrangement does not necessarily lead to dissatisfaction with work. Satisfaction is influenced not only by the presence or absence of intrinsic gratification, but also by extrinsic factors like pay, hours, and job security. Finally, there is no evidence that self-estrangement of workers affects the person's familial or other nonwork roles (Seeman 1975).

Powerlessness

Consider the fact that vandalism is widespread in certain sections of large cities, that many middle- and upper-class adults do not vote in presidential elections, and that some people on welfare make no effort to find a job. These facts all have something in common. They reflect, at least in part, people's sense of **powerlessness,** the sense of having little or no control over events.

Powerlessness is a generalized orientation toward the social world. People who feel powerless believe they have no influence on political affairs and world events—this is different from feeling a lack of control over events in day-to-day life. A typical measure of powerlessness is reproduced in Table 16.2. Interestingly, a sense of powerlessness is not associated with social class—that is, income, occupation, or education. Most people's scores on measures of powerlessness are quite stable over a period of eight years (Neal and Groat

1974). There is some evidence that our sense of powerlessness develops during childhood.

For example, a positive correlation exists between the powerlessness scores of mothers and their sons (Goodwin 1972). Another study reports a significant positive association between the scores of male and female college students and their parents (Renshon 1974). The relationship probably reflects the use of particular socialization techniques that have not yet been determined (Seeman 1975).

Although the sense of powerlessness is common to all classes, upper and lower classes may have different means of expressing it. Whereas middle- and upper-class persons may be more likely to stay home on election day, or to feel apathetic about political affairs or organizations that influence public policy, lower-class persons may be more likely to have a hostile attitude toward city officials and to vandalize city buses, subway trains, and businesses in their neighborhoods. How the individual expresses frustration over lack of influence on the world may depend on social position.

Other Varieties of Alienation

What other ways might people feel estranged from society? Four other varieties of alienation are identified as follows.

NORMLESSNESS. Conformity to social norms is a major feature of social life. Not everyone feels that conformity will help them to get ahead, however. People characterized by **normlessness** believe that socially disapproved behavior is necessary to achieve their goals (Neal and Groat 1974). Like powerlessness, normlessness is measured using an attitude scale. The most common scale is Srole's (1956) *anomia scale.* One item on this scale states "Nowadays, a person has to live pretty much for today and let tomorrow take care of itself." Persons low in education, income, or occupational prestige attain higher scores on scales measuring normlessness. The association of normlessness with

low status probably reflects the fact that persons of low status often lack socially approved means of achieving their goals (Merton 1957). They may in fact have to use disapproved methods, such as theft, to earn a living. The relationship between social class and normlessness may also reflect the difference in the availability of education and jobs among the upper and lower classes.

MEANINGLESSNESS. Have you ever felt that things have become so complicated in the world today that you don't understand what is going on? If so, you have experienced **meaninglessness,** a sense that what is going on around you is incomprehensible. Meaninglessness refers to the absence of a definition of the situation, to the lack of a set of meanings that the individual can use as guidelines for behavior. Meanings arise out of interaction with others. Thus meaninglessness may be a consequence of lack of group ties and the absence of the familial and other roles that reflect such ties.

SOCIAL ISOLATION. Closely related to meaninglessness is **social isolation,** the lack of involvement in meaningful relationships. Critics of American society frequently argue that social isolation is the primary source of alienation in the United States. Is isolation from family and community common? According to research, the answer is no. Most adults are embedded in networks of primary relationships that include family and close friends (Shulman 1975; Wellman 1979). Even weak ties (short-term, nonintimate relationships) appear to be a source of social support for the individual.

At the same time, some people are isolated and have virtually no ties. For example, some cities have sizable populations of the chronically mentally ill, former mental patients who have been released to the community. Many of these persons were released from mental hospitals in the late 1970s, in an attempt to reintegrate them into society. Often they have no friends or family to help them, and many are unable to find employment. Large metropolitan areas like New York City have "bag ladies"—women who live on the streets with all their belongings and sleep in railroad and bus terminals. These people are truly alienated. They have been cut off from familial, work, and other roles, either by their own illness, or by the death of or desertion by other persons.

CULTURAL ESTRANGEMENT. A final variety of alienation is **cultural estrangement,** the rejection of the basic values and life styles available in society. Whereas self-estrangement is alienation from one's self, cultural estrangement is alienation from society. Cultural estrangement was the basis for the counterculture movement of the late 1960s and early 1970s and for the founding of various "utopian" communities. Such a rejection promotes either a lack of commitment to established cultural values and a withdrawal from organized social life, or militant attempts to change the society. The former leads to deviant behavior whereas the latter is a source of social protest and social movements. The consequences of cultural estrangement will be examined in detail in the next two chapters.

Summary

There are three ways that social structure influences the individual: through the expectations associated with one's roles, the social networks to which one belongs, and the status associated with one's positions.

STATUS ATTAINMENT. An individual's status determines access to resources—to money, life style, and influence over others. Three generalizations can be made about status in the United States: (1) Status is closely tied to occupation. (2) Occupational attainment is influenced directly by the individual's educational attainment and ability and indirectly by socioeconomic background. (3) Information about employment opportunities is often obtained via social networks.

INDIVIDUAL VALUES. Three aspects of the individual's position in society influence his or her values. (1) Certain occupational characteristics are associated with certain values. Men and women whose jobs are closely supervised, routine, and not complex value conformity, whereas those whose jobs are less closely supervised, less routine, and more complex value self-direction. (2) A formal education influences values. Higher education is associated with more modern values and with greater intellectual flexibility. (3) Social class standing influences the relative importance of such values as sense of accomplishment, a comfortable life, freedom and equality.

SOCIAL INFLUENCES ON HEALTH. Physical health is influenced by occupation, gender, and marital roles. (1) Occupational roles determine the health hazards individuals are exposed to and whether they experience role overload. (2) The traditional role expectations for males and females make males more vulnerable than females to illnesses such as coronary heart disease. (3) Marriage seems to protect both men and women from illness and premature death.

Mental illness is also influenced by social factors. (1) Women have somewhat higher rates of mental illness than men, although marriage is associated with reduced stress for both men and women. (2) Although working outside the home may conflict with marital role obligations, it does not necessarily lead to unhappiness or stress. The mental health of working wives tends to improve, although husbands may experience a decrease in well-being and marital satisfaction. (3) Social networks are an important resource in coping with stress. (4) Lower-class persons report greater stress and experience a higher incidence of mental illness.

ALIENATION. There are several types of alienation. (1) Self-estrangement is associated with work roles that are not intrinsically rewarding, such as assembly-line jobs. (2) Powerlessness, which seems to develop in childhood, is a generalized sense that one has little or no control over the world. (3) Other varieties of alienation include normlessness, meaninglessness, social isolation, and cultural estrangement.

Key Terms and Concepts

Position

Social Structure

Role

Social Network

Primary Relationship

Status

Upward Mobility

Values

Role Overload

Stress

Alienation

Self-Estrangement

Powerlessness

Normlessness

Meaninglessness

Social Isolation

Cultural Estrangement

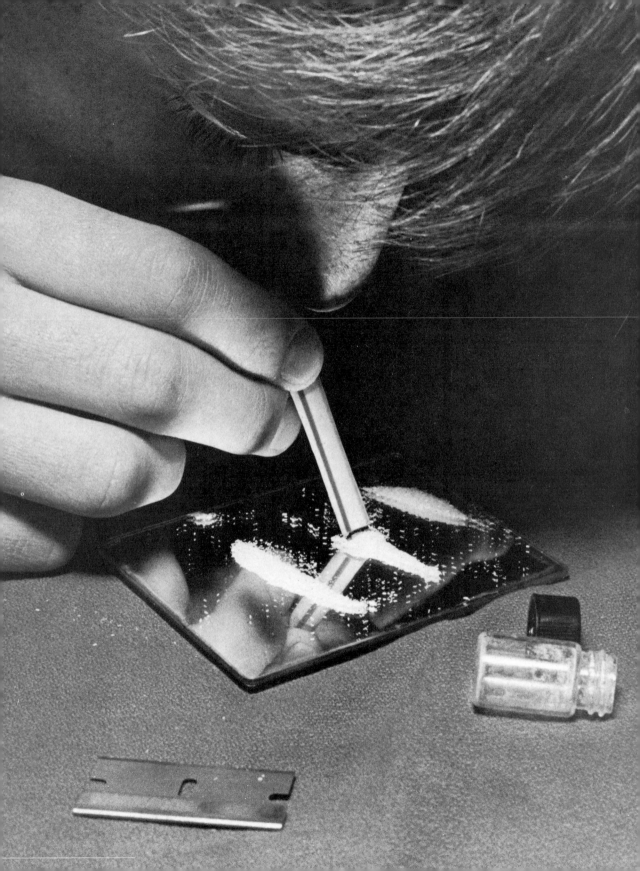

Chapter 17
Deviant Behavior and Social Reaction

Introduction

Virginia and Susan wandered through the department store, stopping briefly to look at blouses, and then going to the jewelry counter. Each looked at several bracelets and necklaces. Susan kept returning to a 24 karat gold bracelet with several jade stones priced at $139.50. Finally she picked it up, glanced quickly around her, and dropped the bracelet into her shopping bag.

The only other shopper in the vicinity, a well-dressed man in his forties, saw Susan take the bracelet. He too looked around the store, spotted a security guard, and walked toward him. Virginia stammered "I, uh, I don't think we should do this." Susan replied, "Oh, it's okay. Nothing will happen." Susan walked quickly out of the store. Moments later, Virginia followed her. As Susan entered the mall, the security guard stepped up to her, took her by the elbow, and said, "Come with me, please."

Episodes like this one occur dozens of times every day in the United States. Shoplifting is only one type of **deviant behavior**, behavior that violates the norms that apply in a given situation. Other types include such varied behaviors as "knavery, skulduggery, cheating, unfairness, crime, sneakiness, malingering, cutting corners, immorality, dishonesty, betrayal, graft, corruption, wickedness, and sin" (Cohen 1966).

There are two reasons why social psychologists study deviant behavior, one theoretical and one practical. First, social norms and conformity are the basic means by which the orderly social interaction necessary to maintain society is attained. By studying nonconformity, we learn about the processes that produce social order. For example, we might conclude that Susan took the bracelet because there were no store employees nearby, suggesting the importance of surveillance in maintaining order. The practical reason for studying deviant behavior is to better understand its causes. Deviant behaviors such as alcoholism, drug addiction, and crime are perceived as serious threats to society. Once we

understand its causes, we may be able to develop better programs that reduce or eliminate deviance or that help people change their deviant behavior.

The shoplifting incident described above raises several questions to be addressed in this chapter:

1. Why did Susan take the bracelet? In short, what are the causes of deviant behavior?

2. How important was the reaction of the male observer? Does someone have to react to behavior in particular ways in order for it to be considered deviant?

3. Why do some people engage in deviance regularly? Why do they adopt a life style that involves participation in deviant activities?

4. How will the security guard and other officials deal with Susan and Virginia? Will their behavior be influenced by Susan's behavior, or by her gender, social status, or other characteristics of the situation?

The Violation of Norms

Norms

Most people would regard Susan's behavior as deviant because it violates social norms. Specifically, she violated laws which define taking merchandise from stores without paying for it as a criminal act. Deviance is thus a social construction; whether a behavior is deviant or not depends on the norms or expectations for behavior in the situation in which it occurs.

In any situation, our behavior is governed by norms derived from three sources (Suttles 1968). First, there are purely "local" or group norms. Thus roommates and families develop norms about what personal topics can and cannot be discussed. Second, there are subcultural norms that apply to large numbers of persons who share some characteristic. For example, there are racial or ethnic group norms governing the behavior of blacks or persons of Slavic descent that do not apply to all Americans. Third, there are societal norms, such as those requiring certain types of dress or those limiting sexual activity to certain relationships and situations. Thus, the norms that govern our daily behavior have a variety of origins, including family, friends, socioeconomic or religious or ethnic subcultures, and the society in general.

The repercussions of deviant behavior depend on which of the three types of norms the individual violates. Violations of local norms may be of concern only to a certain group. Failing to do the dishes when it is your turn may result in a scolding from your roommate, although your friends may not care about that deviance. Subcultural norms are often held in common by most of those with whom we interact, whether friends, family members, or co-workers. Violation of these can affect most of one's day-to-day interactions. Violations of societal norms may subject the person to action by formal agencies of control such as police and the courts. So far we have discussed the violation of "local" norms (Chapter 9), and group norms (Chapter 12). In this chapter we will focus on the violation of societal norms and reactions to norm violations.

Perspectives on Norm Violation

When we read or hear that someone is accused of murder, or embezzling money from the bank, we often ask, "Why?" In Susan's case, we would ask "Why did she take that bracelet?" There are several theories about the causes of deviant behavior including anomie, control, and differential association theories.

ANOMIE. The **theory of anomie,** developed by Robert Merton (1938, 1957), suggests that deviance arises when people who strive to achieve culturally valued goals such as wealth find they do not have any legitimate way to attain these goals. These people then break the rules, often in an attempt to attain the goal illegitimately.

Every society provides its members with goals to aspire to. If the members of a society value religion, they are likely to socialize their youth and adults to aspire to salvation. If the members value power, they will teach people to seek positions in which they can dominate others. Merton argued that American culture extolls wealth as the appropriate goal for most members of society. In every society, there are also norms that define acceptable ways of striving for goals, called **legitimate means.** In America, legitimate means for attaining wealth include learning and acquiring roles which serve as routes to success (such as student or apprentice), working hard at a job to earn money, and making wise investments.

A person socialized into American society will most likely desire material wealth and will strive to succeed in a desirable occupation—to become a teacher, nurse, business executive, or doctor. The legitimate means of attaining this goal are to obtain a formal education and to climb the ladder of occupational prestige. The person who has access to these means—who can afford to go to college and has the accepted skin color, ethnic background, and gender—will attain the socially desirable goals.

What about those who do not have access to the legitimate means? As Americans, these people will desire material wealth like everyone else, but at the same time they will be blocked in their strivings. Because of the way society is structured, certain members will be denied access to legitimate means. Government decisions regarding budgeting and building or closing schools will determine the availability of education to individuals and the availability of jobs for teachers. When money is invested in bilingual education, it increases access to legitimate means for Hispanics. If it is invested in upper-middle class high schools, it furthers the access of the already advantaged.

A person who strives to achieve the goal but is denied access to legitimate means of attaining success experiences *anomie*, which reduces commitment to norms and the pursuit of goals. There are four ways a person may respond to anomie; each is a type of deviance. First, an individual may reject the goals, give up trying to achieve success, but continue to conform to social norms; this adaptation is termed *ritualism*. The poorly paid stock clerk who never misses a day of work in 45 years is a ritualist. He is deviant because he has given up the struggle for success. Second, the individual might reject the goals *and* the means, withdrawing from active participation in society by *retreatism*. This may take the form of drinking, drug use, withdrawal into mental illness, or other kinds of escape. Third, one might remain committed to the goals but turn to disapproved or illegal ways of achieving success through *innovation*. Earning a living as a burglar, fence, or loan shark is an innovative means of attaining wealth. Finally, one might attempt to overthrow the existing system and create different goals and means through *rebellion*. Examples include such large-scale events as the Russian revolution and the countercultural movement of the late 1960s and early 1970s.

Shoplifting is a form of innovation. Like other types of economic crime, it represents a rejection of the normatively prescribed means (buying what you want) while continuing to strive for the goal (possessing merchandise). According to anomie theory, Susan has been socialized to desire wealth, but does not have access to a well-paying job due to her poor education. As a result, she steals what she wants because she cannot pay for it.

Why is Susan an innovator? Why didn't she accept her lack of wealth and become a ritualist? The adaptation of the individual depends partly on the relative strength of socialization to the goals and to the means. Given that Susan does not have access to legitimate means to success, she will become an innovator if her socialization to the goals is stronger than her socialization to the means. If her socialization to the means is stronger, however, she will become a ritualist. Withdrawal is the likely outcome when socialization to both goals and means is weak.

Another influence on the individual's adaptation is access to deviant roles. Utilizing

a means of goal achievement—whether legitimate or illegitimate—requires access to two structures (Cloward 1959). The first is a **learning structure,** an environment in which the individual can learn the information and skills required; a shoplifter needs to learn how to quickly conceal objects, to spot plainclothes detectives, and so forth. The second is an **opportunity structure,** opportunities to play the role, which usually requires the assistance of those in complementary roles. Anomie theory assumes that anyone can be an innovator—through shoplifting, prostitution, or professional theft—but not everyone has access to the special knowledge and skills needed to succeed as a prostitute (Heyl 1977) or a professional thief (Sutherland 1937). Just as access to legitimate means to achieve goals is limited, so is access to illegitimate means. Only those who have both the learning and opportunity structures necessary to become a shoplifter, prostitute, or embezzler can utilize these alternative routes to success.

The opportunities available to a person also depend on age, sex, kinship, ethnicity, and social class (Cloward 1959). All these characteristics, with the possible exception of class, are beyond the individual's control. Thus, prostitution in our society primarily involves young, physically attractive persons. People who do not have access to the necessary learning or opportunity structures are double failures; they can succeed neither via legitimate nor via illegitimate means. Double failure often produces retreatism. Drug addicts, alcoholics, and mentally ill persons may be losers in both the conventional and criminal worlds.

According to anomie theory, then, deviant behavior is indirectly a consequence of one's social position. A white female from a wealthy family is more likely to get a good education, enter a profession such as law, and attain wealth through occupational success. A black female from a poor family may not have access to a good education and is unlikely to be able to get a good job. As a result she may experience despair and frustration and decide the struggle isn't worth it and turn to drugs. Or she may observe other attractive black women earning a good living via prostitution, and decide to learn the trade. Her deviance is a response to anomie, which in turn is due to her position in American society.

Anomie theory directs our attention to the importance of education and employment in attaining wealth. Because lower-class persons are more frequently excluded from quality education and jobs, the theory predicts that they will commit more crimes. Data collected by police departments and the Federal Bureau of Investigation in the 1950s and 1960s confirmed this prediction, showing that a disproportionate number of crimes occurred in lower-class neighborhoods. Similarly, a disproportionate number of those arrested for crimes were poor and minority males. This led to the conclusion that crime and social class are inversely related—that "the highest crime rates are to be found in the lower social strata" (Cloward 1959, p. 174).

More recently it has become apparent that there is a class bias built into official statistics on crime. For example, not all illegitimate activities are included in these statistics. While data on burglary, robbery, and theft are compiled by police departments, data on income tax evasion, price-fixing, and stock swindles are not. Police and FBI statistics are much more likely to include crimes committed by the lower classes than the kinds of economic ("white collar") crimes committed by members of the middle and upper classes.

Another bias in official statistics is the fact that many crimes are never reported. In the past, store employees rarely turned shoplifters over to the police. It has been suggested that they were unlikely to call the police if the person was middle or upper class. If in fact police were more likely to be notified when the suspect was from a lower socioeconomic class, then this, too, would suggest a relationship between class and crime.

In response to these limitations in official statistics, researchers began to gather information using self-report measures of crime. Such studies ask persons—frequently high-school

Most Americans are socialized to strive for economic success. But some people do not have access to legitimate employment, so they seek wealth via alternative, sometimes illegal, means.

or college students—whether they have engaged in various behaviors in the recent past. Typically the questionnaire asks whether they have taken things that did not belong to them; damaged, destroyed, or mistreated others' property; smoked marijuana; or committed a variety of other crimes (See Box 17.1). These studies have found little or no relationship

Box 17.1
HOW DEVIANT ARE YOU?

Researchers frequently use self-report to study the incidence of deviant behavior. By asking people direct questions, researchers hope to avoid the biases found in official statistics that suggest crime is concentrated in the lower class. Below is a typical questionnaire on deviance. Take a few minutes and fill it out.

Most people have done at least a few things that others would consider wrong. For each item below, circle the number of times you have engaged in the activity in the *past two years*.

1. Taken an item from a store without paying for it	0	1	2	3	4	5+
2. Taken things from someone else's room or home that did not belong to you, without permission	0	1	2	3	4	5+
3. Bought, kept, or used something that you knew had been stolen from someone else	0	1	2	3	4	5+
4. Damaged, destroyed, or mistreated property on purpose	0	1	2	3	4	5+
5. Beaten up or hurt someone on purpose	0	1	2	3	4	5+
6. Threatened to beat up or hurt someone unless they did what you wanted	0	1	2	3	4	5+
7. Smoked or used marijuana	0	1–2	3–5	6–10	11–24	25+
8. Used cocaine	0	1	2	3	4	5+
9. Used drugs such as LSD, pep pills ("uppers," "speed"), tranquilizers ("downers"), or sleeping pills without a doctor's prescription	0	1	2	3	4	5+
10. Cheated on an exam or quiz in class	0	1	2	3	4	5+
11. Worked with other students on homework or a take-home project when you weren't supposed to	0	1	2	3	4	5+

Source: adapted from Tittle and Villemez (1977).

between social class and self-report measures of crime (Tittle and Villemez 1977).

How can we reconcile these differences? Are lower-class people more likely to commit crimes as anomie theory predicts and official statistics seem to verify? Or is there no relationship as self-report studies indicate? These questions assume that self-reports of behavior and official statistics measure the same thing—"crime"—or in studies where the sample consists of adolescents, "delinquency." This assumption may be false (Hindelang, Hirschi, and Weis 1979). Arrest statistics compiled by police departments include seven crimes: homicide, forcible rape, robbery, aggravated assault, burglary, larceny/theft, and auto theft. Self-report measures ask about assault, theft, auto theft, receiving stolen property, use of drugs such as marijuana, cocaine and tranquilizers, and academic cheating. Thus official statistics include serious and relatively infrequent crimes, whereas self-report measures include less serious, much more common offenses. Both sets of results appear to be valid. Lower-class persons may be more likely to commit the serious, officially tabulated crimes,

The answers of a sample of college sophomores, juniors, and seniors (97 males and 106 females) are reproduced below. The sample was obtained from a survey of two large undergraduate classes at the University of Wisconsin (Zimmerman and DeLamater 1983). These responses indicate that students commit some crimes frequently, such as taking things without permission, vandalism, and the use of marijuana. Compare your own responses to the questionnaire with theirs.

Behavior		*Number of Times*					
		0	**1**	**2**	**3**	**4**	**5+**
1. Taken something from a store	males	81%	8	4	3	0	3
	females	85	7	4	2	0	3
2. Taken something from a room or home	males	56	12	12	10	2	7
	females	54	17	14	5	2	8
3. Bought or used stolen property	males	61	20	15	2	1	1
	females	85	6	4	1	1	4
4. Vandalized property	males	58	16	13	6	1	5
	females	77	14	6	1	0	2
5. Beat up someone	males	86	8	2	2	1	1
	females	89	8	3	0	0	0
6. Threatened someone	males	79	7	8	2	1	2
	females	91	1	4	0	1	3
7. Used marijuana	males	36	10	9	6	8	29
	females	34	16	8	12	9	20
8. Used cocaine	males	69	5	2	2	2	19
	females	75	5	3	4	3	11
9. Used other drugs	males	72	5	4	0	0	19
	females	66	8	6	6	1	15
10. Cheated in class	males	55	25	8	3	4	5
	females	58	18	12	7	5	1
11. Worked with other students	males	65	12	10	4	3	5
	females	59	19	13	4	2	3

but no more likely than middle-class persons to commit less serious violations of the law (Elliott and Ageton 1980).

Indeed, if persons are asked to report their involvement in all of the seven crimes included in official statistics, there is a negative relationship between social class and crime in this self-report data (Thornberry and Farnsworth 1982). It appears that persons of lower socioeconomic status are more likely to commit serious crimes as anomie theory predicts.

CONTROL THEORY. If you were asked why you

don't shoplift tapes or records from stores, you might reply "Because my parents (or lover or friends) would kill me if they found out." According to control theory, social ties influence our behavior. We often conform to social norms because we are sensitive to the wishes and expectations of others. This sensitivity creates a bond between the individual and other persons; the stronger the bond, the less likely the individual is to engage in deviant behavior.

According to Hirschi (1969), there are four components of this social bond. The first is *attachment*, ties of affection and respect to others. Attachment to parents is especially important because they are the primary socializing agents of a child; a strong attachment leads the child to internalize social norms. The second component is *commitment* to long-term educational and occupational goals. Someone who aspires to go to law school is unlikely to commit a crime because a criminal record would be an obstacle to a career in law. The third component is *involvement.* People who are involved in sports, scouts, church groups, and other conventional activities have less time to engage in deviance. The fourth component is *belief*, a respect for the law and persons in positions of authority.

We can apply control theory to the shoplifting incident described in the introduction. If Susan does not feel attached to law-abiding adults, she will not be concerned about their reactions to her behavior. Nor does she seem deterred by commitment, when she says, "Nothing will happen." Susan's deviant act seems to reflect the absence of a strong bond with conventional society.

The relationship between delinquency and the components of the social bond has been the focus of numerous studies. Several have found a relationship between lack of attachment and delinquency—young people from homes characterized by lack of parental supervision, communication, and support report more delinquent behavior (Hirschi 1969; Jensen 1972). Attachment to school, measured by grades, is also associated with delinquency; boys and girls who do well in school are less likely to be delinquent. Regarding commitment to long-term goals, research indicates that youths who are committed to educational and career goals are less likely to engage in property crimes such as robbery and theft (Johnson 1979; Shover et al. 1979). Findings relevant to the third component are mixed. Whereas involvement in studying and homework is negatively associated with reported delinquency, participation in athletics, hobbies, and work is unrelated to reported delin-

quency. Finally, evidence suggests that a person's beliefs are less important than other influences on delinquency (Jenson 1972).

DIFFERENTIAL ASSOCIATION. Are all types of deviance explained by the absence of a social bond? Perhaps not. Sometimes people deviate from one set of norms because they are being influenced by a contradictory set of norms. American society is composed of many groups with different values, norms, and behavior patterns. With respect to many behaviors there is no single, society-wide set of norms. An adolescent's use of marijuana may deviate from her parents' norms, for example, but may conform to her friends' norms. Hence the deviance involved in marijuana use reflects a conflict between the norms of two groups, rather than an insensitivity to the expectations of others. In fact, the use of marijuana may reflect a high degree of sensitivity to the expectations of one's peers.

This view of deviance was first expressed in the *theory of differential association,* developed by Edwin Sutherland (1939). Sutherland argued that even though the law provides a uniform standard for deviance, one group may define that behavior as deviant whereas another defines it as desirable. Shoplifting, for example, is legally defined as a crime. Some groups believe it is wrong because (1) it leads to increased prices which hurts everyone; (2) it violates the moral principle against stealing; and (3) it constitutes lawbreaking. Other groups, in contrast, believe shoplifting is acceptable because (1) businesses deserve to have things taken because they overcharge; (2) the loss is covered by insurance; and (3) the shoplifter won't be caught. Susan's comment, "It's okay. Nothing will happen" reflects the latter belief.

These beliefs or attitudes about behaviors are learned through associations with others, usually in primary group settings. People learn motives, drives, and techniques of engaging in specific behaviors. What they learn depends on whom they interact with—

that is, on their differential associations. Whether someone engages in a specific behavior depends on how frequently one is exposed to attitudes and beliefs that are favorable toward that behavior.

The principle of differential association states that "A person becomes delinquent because of an excess of definitions favorable to violation of the law over definitions unfavorable to violation of the law" (Sutherland and Cressey 1978). Studies designed to test this principle typically ask individuals questions about their attitudes toward a specific behavior, and about their participation in that behavior. A study on delinquency revealed that the number of definitions unfavorable to delinquency accurately predicted which young people reported delinquent behavior (Matsueda 1982).

Another study involving several hundred college students found systematic differences in the beliefs of those who had engaged in shoplifting and those who had not (Kraut 1976). Those who had taken merchandise without paying for it believed that they would not be caught or that they would not be severely punished even if they were caught. On a measure of self-image, the ratings they gave themselves were similar to the ratings they gave in describing a "typical shoplifter." Students who had not taken things defined the risk of getting caught as high, and believed the consequences would be serious. They were especially concerned about informal sanctions and reactions of friends and family. They rated themselves as quite different from the "typical shoplifter."

The theory of differential association does not specify the process by which people learn criminal or deviant behavior. For this reason, a modified theory of differential association was developed (Burgess and Akers 1966). Unlike the original theory which emphasizes the influence of interactions with others, this newer version emphasizes the influence of positive and negative reinforcement on the acquisition of behavior. If beliefs are learned

through interaction with others, especially in primary relationships, then people whose attitudes are favorable toward a behavior should have friends who also have favorable attitudes toward that behavior. Alternatively, people whose attitudes are opposed to the activity should have friends who share those negative views.

A survey of 3,056 high-school students was conducted to test these hypotheses. It assessed the relationship between differential association, reinforcement, and adolescents' drinking behavior and marijuana use (Akers et al. 1979). Differential association was measured by three questions: How many of your (1) best friends, (2) friends you spend the most time with, and (3) friends you have known the longest, smoke marijuana and/or drink? The survey also assessed students' definitions of drug and alcohol use, and attitudes toward drug and alcohol laws and laws in general. Both social reinforcement (whether the adolescent expected praise or punishment for use from parents and peers) and nonsocial reinforcement (whether effects of substance use were positive or negative) were measured. Findings of this survey show that differential association is closely related to use of alcohol and/or drugs—that is, the larger the number of friends who drank/smoked grass, the more likely the student was to drink/smoke grass. Reinforcement was also related to behavior; those who used a substance reported that it had positive effects. The students' definitions were also related to whom they associated with; if their friends drank (used marijuana), they were more likely to have positive attitudes toward the behavior and negative attitudes toward laws defining that behavior as criminal. Finally, students' attitudes were consistent with their behavior; those who opposed marijuana use and supported the marijuana laws were much less likely to use grass.

Another study of high-school students in New York state found a strong correlation between use of marijuana and drug use by one's best friends (Kandel et al. 1976). The

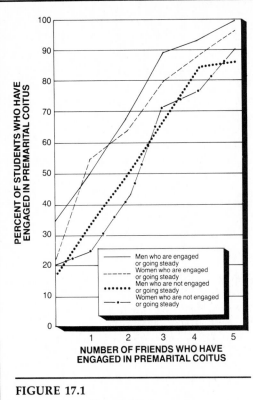

FIGURE 17.1

PERCEPTION OF FRIENDS' PARTICIPATION IN
PREMARITAL SEX AND INDIVIDUAL
PREMARITAL BEHAVIOR

More than 1,800 college seniors were asked
whether they had engaged in premarital
intercourse as well as how many of their five
best friends of the same sex had engaged in
premarital intercourse. Note that as the number of best friends who were sexually experienced increased, the likelihood that the student was sexually experienced increased dramatically. For each additional friend who is
experienced, the number of sexually active
persons increases 12 percent. Note that going
steady or being engaged was also associated
with an increased likelihood of premarital
intercourse.

Source: adapted from Schulz et al. (1977).

pression, were found to be correlated with
extensive use of hard drugs but not marijuana.
Thus, in this study, marijuana use was associated with group influences, not psychological factors within the individual.

Because drinking and smoking often occur
in group settings, it is not surprising that these
behaviors are influenced by the norms of the
group. Even more interesting is the fact that
the attitudes and behavior of our friends
influence very private behaviors. For example,
studies have found that whether and how
frequently single persons engage in various
sexual activities reflect differential association.
One survey of college seniors found that
whether individuals engaged in premarital sex
was related to how many of their best friends
had engaged in that behavior (Schulz et al.
1977). Results of the survey are illustrated in
Figure 17.1. If none of their best friends were
sexually experienced, only 15 to 35 percent of
the students reported engaging in sexual intercourse; if all five of their best friends were
sexually experienced, more than 80 percent of
the respondents reported they were also.

Of course, we don't simply conform to the
norms of whatever group we happen to be in.
Our behavior is also influenced by our own
beliefs. For example, researchers in this survey
found that the more a person endorsed "conventional religious values," the less likely he
or she was to have engaged in sexual intercourse, regardless of how many friends had
done so. The least religious students were 18
percent more likely to be sexually experienced
than the most religious students.

Differential association theory emphasizes
learning through social interaction. The modified version of differential association based
on reinforcement theory argues that the principles of reinforcement identified by psychologists are involved in the acquisition of
deviant behavior. As an example, consider
imitation, in which the individual observes
the behavior of another person and subsequently engages in that behavior. Imitation is
one type of learning that can occur without
social interaction.

study measured not only social and family
characteristics, but also psychological characteristics. Psychological traits, particularly de-

Box 17.2
THE POWER OF SUGGESTION

Rape, robbery, murder, and other types of deviant behavior receive a substantial amount of coverage in newspapers and on radio and television. One function of publicizing deviance is to remind us of norms—in short, to tell us what we should not do (Erikson 1964). But is this the only consequence? Could the publicity given particular deviant activities increase the frequency with which they occur? In two cases, the answer appears to be yes.

A study of the relationship between the publicity given suicides and suicide rates suggests that the two are positively correlated (Phillips 1974). This study identified every time a suicide was publicized in three major American daily papers from 1947 to 1968. Next, the study calculated the number of expected suicides for the following month by averaging the suicide rates for that same month for the year before and the year after. For example, researchers noted that the suicide of a Ku Klux Klan leader on 1 November 1965 was widely publicized. They then obtained the expected number of suicides (1,652) by averaging the total number of suicides for November 1964 (1,639) and November 1966 (1,665). In fact, there were 1,710 suicides in November 1965; the difference between the observed and expected rates (58) could be due to suggestion.

Results of this study showed that suicides increase in the month following reports of a suicide in major daily papers. Moreover, the more publicity given the story—as measured by number of days the story is on the front page—the larger the rise in suicides. If a story was published locally—in Chicago but not in New York, for example, the rise in suicides occurred only in the area where it was publicized.

Why should such publicity lead other persons to kill themselves? Most people don't; there must be some factor that predisposes a small number of persons to take their own lives following a publicized suicide. That predisposing factor may be anomie. According to this theory, suicide is a form of retreatism, of withdrawal from the struggle for success. Persons who don't have access to legitimate means are looking for some way to adapt to their situation. Publicity given to a suicide may suggest a solution to their problem.

When we think of suicide, we think of shooting oneself, taking poison, or jumping off a building. We distinguish suicide from accidents when we presume the person didn't intend to harm himself. But the critical difference is the person's intent, not the event itself. Some apparent accidents may be suicides, whereas some apparent suicides may be accidents. For example, when a car hits a bridge abutment well away from the pavement on a clear day with no evidence of mechanical malfunction, this may be suicide.

If some auto accidents are in fact suicides, we should observe an increase in the number of deaths in motor vehicle accidents following newspaper stories about a suicide. In fact, data from newspapers and motor vehicle deaths in San Francisco and Los Angeles verify this hypothesis (Phillips 1979). Statistics show a marked increase in the number of deaths in automobile accidents two and three days after a suicide is published—especially accidents involving one vehicle. In the Detroit metropolitan area, an analysis of motor vehicle fatalities between 1973 and 1976 revealed an average increase in fatalities of 35 to 40 percent the third day after a suicide story appeared in the daily papers (Bollen and Phillips 1981). Again, the more publicity, the greater the increase. Finally, if the person whose suicide is publicized was young, deaths of young drivers increase, whereas if the person killing himself was older, the increase in fatalities involves more older drivers.

Thus media reports of suicides may suggest behavioral responses to anomie, suggestions that are acted upon by some persons.

As noted at the beginning of this chapter, some people who study deviance are looking for ways to reduce criminal behavior. According to differential association theory, deviant behavior should decrease when people are exposed to attitudes unfavorable to deviant behavior (Johnson and Cressey 1963). This reasoning has frequently been used in programs designed to reduce some form of deviance.

The state of Wisconsin, for example, developed an antishoplifting campaign that relied on advertisements that disparage shoplifting. The first phase publicized the slogan "Shoplifters take everybody's money," to counter the belief that only the store is economically harmed by this behavior. The acronym, STEM, was subsequently printed on decals that appeared on the doors of many retail establishments to provide a constant reminder to shoppers.

To combat the image of shoplifting as a minor offense, public officials and business leaders commonly refer to it as "retail theft." In early 1981, full-page advertisements ran in newspapers featuring mug shots of suspects and the headline "Shoplifters: Come in for a free portrait." These ads are clear attempts to remind people of the risks of retail theft, and to counter statements like Susan's at the beginning of this chapter that "Nothing will happen." State officials and business leaders believe that the campaign reduced retail theft by 4 to 8 percent. Thus the relationship between attitudes toward deviance and the behavior itself may help explain why some people engage in shoplifting, drug use, and other forms of deviance, and also provide ways to reduce the likelihood that people will engage in such behaviors.

The anomie, control, and differential association perspectives are not incompatible. Anomie theory suggests that culturally valued goals, and the opportunities available to achieve these goals, are major influences on behavior. Opportunities to learn and occupy particular roles are influenced by age, social class, gender, race, and ethnic background. According to control theory, we are also influenced by our attachments to others and our commitment to attaining success. Our position in the social structure and our attachments to parents and peers determine our differential associations—the kinds of groups to which we belong. Within these groups we learn definitions favorable to particular behaviors and that we face sanctions when we choose behaviors group members define as deviant.

Reactions to Norm Violations

When we think of murder, robbery, or rape, we think of cases we have read about, or heard of through radio or television. We frequently refer to police and FBI statistics as measures of the number of crimes that have occurred in our city or county. Our knowledge of alcohol or drug abuse and homosexual behavior depends on knowing or hearing about persons who engage in these behaviors. All of these instances of deviance share another important characteristic as well. In every case, the behavior was discovered by someone who called it to the attention of others.

Does it matter that these instances involve both an action and a reaction? Isn't an act just as deviant whether others find out about it or not? Let's go back to our introduction and Susan's theft of the bracelet. Suppose Susan had left the store without being stopped by the security guard. In this case, she and Virginia would know she took the bracelet, but she would not experience sanctions from others. She would not experience the embarrassment of being confronted by a store detective and accused of deviance. Moreover, she would have a beautiful bracelet. But she was stopped by the guard. She will be questioned, the police will be called, and she may be arrested. Thus the consequences for committing a deviant act are quite different when certain reactions follow. This reasoning is the basis of **labelling theory,** the view that reactions to a norm violation are a critical element in deviance. Only after an act is discovered and labelled "deviant" is the act recognized as such. If the same act is not discovered and labelled, it is not deviant (Becker 1963).

If deviance depends on the reactions of others to an act rather than on the act itself, the key social psychological question becomes: Why do particular audiences choose to label an act deviant? Labelling theory is an attempt to understand how and why acts are labelled deviant. In the case of the stolen bracelet, labelling analysts would not be concerned with Susan's behavior. Rather, they would be interested in Virginia's *response* to Susan's act, and the reaction of the male customer and security guard. Only if an observer challenges Susan's behavior or alerts a store employee does the act of taking the bracelet become deviant. In this case, the action taken by the security guard clearly defines her act as a violation of norms.

Reactions to Rule-Breaking

Labelling theorists refer to behavior that violates norms as **rule-breaking,** to emphasize that the act by itself is not deviant. Most rule violations are "secret" in the sense that no one other than the actor (and on occasion the actor's accomplices) is aware of them. Many cases of theft and tax evasion, many violations of drug laws, and some burglaries are never detected; these activities can be carried out by a single person. Other acts, such as robberies, assaults, and various sexual activities, involve other people and will be known about.

How will members of the audience respond to a rule violation? It depends on the circumstances, but various studies suggest that *very often, people ignore it.* When wives of men hospitalized for psychiatric treatment were asked how they had reacted to their husbands' bizarre behavior, for example, they generally replied that they had not considered their husbands ill or in need of help (Yarrow et al. 1955). People react to isolated episodes of unusual behavior in one of four ways. A common response is *denial*, in which the person simply

The reactions of others to rule-breaking behavior depend on the characteristics of the actor. The dress and grooming of this shoplifter will influence whether her behavior is reported by the man observing it.

does not recognize that a rule violation occurred. Denial was typically the first response of women to their husband's excessive drinking (Jackson 1954). A second response is *normalization*, in which the observer recognizes that the act occurred but defines it as normal or common. Thus, wives often reacted to excessive drinking as normal, assuming that many men drink a lot. Third, the person may excuse the act, recognizing it as a rule violation but attributing its occurrence to situational or transient factors; such a reaction is known as *attenuation* (Goode 1978).

Thus, some of the wives of men who were later hospitalized believed that the episodes of bizarre behavior were caused by unusually high levels of stress or by physical illness. Finally, people may respond to the rule violation by *balancing* it, recognizing it as a violation but deemphasizing its significance due to the actor's good qualities.

The man who had witnessed Susan's behavior could not deny it. He was looking directly at her. He might have normalized the act, believing that Susan intended to go to a cashier's counter and pay for the bracelet before she left the store. He could have excused the act, noting that both girls' clothes were worn, suggesting that they were not well-off. Finally, he could have balanced the fact that Susan was stealing against the fact that both girls were young; perhaps they reminded him of his daughters. In this case, he might have felt that the theft was not serious enough to have them apprehended, questioned, and perhaps charged with a crime.

In fact, the man did not react in these ways; he looked around, spotted a security guard, and reported the act. In doing so, he labelled the actor. Labelling involves a redefinition of the actor's social status; the man placed Susan into a category of "shoplifter" or "thief." The security guard in turn probably defined Susan as a "typical shoplifter." Although labelling is triggered by a behavior, it results in a redefinition or typing of the actor. As we shall see, this has a major impact on people's perceptions of and behavior toward the actor.

Determinants of the Reaction

What determines how an observer reacts to rule-breaking? Reactions depend on three aspects of the rule violation, including the nature of the actor, the audience, and the situation (Goode 1978).

ACTOR CHARACTERISTICS. Reaction to a rule violation often depends on who performs the behavior. People are more tolerant of rule-breaking by family members than by strangers. The research cited above reveals extraordinary tolerance of spouses for bizarre, disruptive, and even physically abusive behavior. Many of us probably know of a family who is attempting to care for a member whose behavior creates problems for them. In addition, people are more tolerant of rule violations by persons who make positive contributions in other ways. In small groups, tolerance is greater for persons who contribute to the achievement of group goals (Hollander and Julian 1970). We seem to tolerate deviance when we are dependent on the person committing the act, perhaps because if we punish the actor it will be costly for us.

Does gender affect reactions to behavior? An ingenious field experiment suggests that gender does not affect an audience's response to shoplifting. With the cooperation of store employees, shoplifting events were staged in the presence of customers who could see the event. The experiment was conducted in a small grocery store, a large supermarket in a shopping mall, and a large discount department store. Three aspects of the situation were varied: the gender of the shoplifter, the appearance of the shoplifter, and the gender of the observer. Neither the shoplifter's nor the customer's gender had an effect on the frequency with which the customer reported the apparent theft. The appearance of the shoplifter, however, had a substantial effect. If the man or woman who took an item was wearing soiled, patched clothing and had unkempt hair, the customer was much more likely to report the theft than if the shoplifter was neatly dressed and well-groomed. Perhaps the customers balanced the theft against what they presumed were the good qualities of the well-dressed shoplifter (Steffensmeier and Terry 1973).

Traditionally, males have been expected to exhibit higher levels of ability at instrumental tasks than females. We may therefore be more sensitive to signs of lack of competence in men. For example, we might expect that males are more likely to be labelled retarded than females of the same age and ability. Research indicates that gender does seem to affect reactions to incompetent behavior. Retarded males are more likely to be institutionalized than retarded females, and at earlier ages; males are also more likely to be institutionalized for mild levels of retardation (Tudor et al. 1979). With regard to crime, numerous authors have suggested that we are less likely to label women than men for violations of the law (Pollak 1961; Ward and Kassebaum 1965; Haskell and Yablonsky 1983). One study reports that police treated older, white, and deferential women leniently, but not young, black, or hostile women (Visher 1981).

AUDIENCE CHARACTERISTICS. The reaction to a violation of rules also depends on who witnesses it. Because groups vary in their norms, audiences vary in their expectations. People enjoying a city park on a warm day will react quite differently to a nude man walking through the park than will a group of nudists in a nudist park. Recognizing this variation in reaction, people who contemplate breaking the rules often make sure no one is around who will punish them—as before smoking marijuana, drinking in public, or jaywalking.

Citizens react very differently to suspected criminals than do police and other officials who routinely deal with suspects. A study of various officials working in a court-affiliated unit who evaluated suspected murderers following arrest found that these officials had a stereotyped image of the type of person who commits murder, called the "normal primitive" (Swigert and Farrell 1977). When lower-class male members of ethnic minorities committed murder, these officials believed that it was in response to a threat on their masculinity. For example, they would be more likely to assume that an Italian had killed another man in response to verbal insults and taunts. This labelling based on a stereotype had important consequences. Suspects who fit this image were less likely to be defended by a private attorney, more likely to be denied bail, to plead guilty, and more likely to be convicted on more severe charges.

Consider another example. When a student with a drinking problem seeks help at the university's counseling center, her treatment will depend on how counselors view student "troubles." In one study, the staff of a university clinic believed that all students' problems could be classified into one of the following categories: problems in studying, choosing a career, achieving sexual intimacy, or handling personal finances; conflict with family or friends; and stress arising from sociopolitical activities. When a student came to the clinic because of excessive drinking, the therapist decided which of these categories applied to this particular person's troubles, that is, which type of problem might cause the student to drink excessively. How the problem is defined in turn determines what the therapist does to try to help the student (Kahne and Schwartz 1978).

Because audiences vary in their standards, conditions or experiences defined as deviant by one audience may be considered normal by another. A woman in rural Wisconsin claimed that the Virgin Mary appeared and spoke with her on eight occasions. To many, such experiences are hallucinations, a symptom of serious mental illness. But to tens of thousands, these were genuine religious experiences, and thousands made pilgrimages to the woman's farm (Scheff 1967).

SITUATIONAL CHARACTERISTICS. Whether a behavior is defined as normal or labelled deviant also depends on the definition of the situation. Marijuana and alcohol use, for example, are much more acceptable at a party than at work (Orcutt 1975). Various sexual activities expected between married persons in the privacy of their home would elicit condemnation if performed in a public park.

Another important influence on reactions is the role an audience assumes. For example, in a documentary on drug use a pusher was

The reaction to rule-breaking behavior depends on characteristics of the observer. Mary Ann Van Hoof, a Catholic, claimed that the Virgin Mary appeared and spoke to her on several occasions, and thousands of Catholics believed her. On October 7, 1956, an estimated 100,000 people gathered to listen to Mrs. Van Hoof relay messages from the Virgin. Catholic officials reacted with disbelief and placed Van Hoof under interdict, denying her the sacraments of the Church.

asked if he worried about being "busted"; he replied, "Cops buy like everybody else." Thus the same person (the audience) can enact the role of police officer or drug purchaser. While enacting the police officer role, the person will label the sale a criminal act and arrest the pusher; while enacting the drug user role, the person will be pleased that he found a supplier.

We often rely on the behavior of others to help us define situations. Our reaction to a rule violation may be influenced by the reactions of other members of the audience. Suppose you are in a chemistry lab trying to make

sulfuric acid with two other students. The instructor gave you careful directions and has moved on to another group. While you are working, one of your co-workers violates one of the directions you were given. You might well observe the other co-worker's reaction before you react. The third person might react in a neutral or friendly way, indicating he did not perceive the violation as serious. On the other hand, he might react angrily and criticize the rule-breaker for his behavior. An experiment modelled after this situation was conducted with one naive subject and two confederates. The results indicated that the third party's reaction did influence whether the subject sanctioned the rule-breaker (Dedrick 1978).

In sum, labelling a person as deviant does not automatically or routinely follow a violation of rules. Witnesses are more likely to label behavior deviant if it is performed (1) by a stranger rather than an acquaintance, (2) by a person whose characteristics fit our stereotypes of a deviant person, and (3) in a situation where that act is defined as inappropriate.

Consequences of Labelling

Assume that an audience defines an act as deviant. What are the consequences for the actor and the audience? We will consider four possible outcomes.

INSTITUTIONALIZATION OF DEVIANCE. In some cases, individuals who label a behavior deviant may decide that it is in their own interest for the person to continue the behavior. They may in fact reward that person for the deviant behavior. If you learn that a good friend is selling drugs, you may decide to use this person as a source, and purchase drugs from him. Over time, your expectations will change; you will come to expect him to sell drugs. If your drug-selling friend decided to stop dealing, you might treat him as a rule-breaker. The process by which members of a group come to expect and support deviance by another member over time is called **institutionalization of deviance** (Dentler and Erikson 1959).

Consider prostitution, which has been a fixture in most societies throughout history. Despite attempts of religious and political leaders to stamp it out, why does the impersonal exchange of sexual gratification for money persist? Institutionalization is partly the answer. Every society specifies the legitimate means of achieving sexual gratification; in American society, adult, heterosexual, voluntary relationships are the appropriate means. Not everyone has access to these means, however, and prostitution provides an alternative (Davis 1937). Houses of prostitution developed rapidly on the West Coast in the 1880s where there was a tremendous surplus of Chinese men relative to the number of Chinese women. These brothels became widely known, and were patronized by large numbers of men, including whites (Light 1977). Brothels continue to operate legally in parts of Nevada, perhaps because there is an excess of men relative to women in those counties.

BACKTRACKING. Even when the audience reacts favorably to a rule violation, the actor may decide to discontinue the behavior. This second consequence of labelling is called *backtracking*. It may occur after the actor learns that others label her act deviant. Even though some audiences react favorably, the actor may wish to avoid the reaction of those who would not react favorably and the resulting punishment. Consequently, the actor may terminate the behavior.

EFFECTIVE SOCIAL CONTROL. An audience that reacts negatively to rule-breaking and attempts to punish the actor or threatens to do so may force the actor to give up further involvement in the activity. This third consequence of labelling is known as *effective social control.* This reaction is common among friends or family members who often threaten to end their association with the actor who continues to engage in deviance. Similarly, they may threaten to break off their relationship if the person does not seek professional help. In these instances, the satisfaction of the actor's needs is contingent on changing his behavior. Members of the audience may also insist that the actor renounce aspects of her life that they see as contributing to future deviance (Sagarin 1975). If excessive drinking is due to job-related stresses, for example, family members may demand that the person find a different type of employment.

UNANTICIPATED DEVIANCE. Still another possibility is that the individual may engage in further or unanticipated deviance. Note the use of the term "unanticipated." Negative reactions by members of the audience are intended to terminate rule-breaking activity. However, such reactions may in fact produce further deviance. This occurs when the audience's response sets in motion a process that leads to greater involvement in deviance. This process and its outcomes are the focus of the next section.

Labelling and Secondary Deviance

Societal Reaction

Earlier in this chapter we mentioned that labelling is a process of redefining a person. By categorizing a person as a particular kind of deviant, we place that person in a stigmatized social status. The deviant (addict, pimp, thief) is defined as undesirable, not fully acceptable in conventional society, and frequently treated as inferior. Two important consequences of this stigmatized status follow.

CHANGES IN THE BEHAVIOR OF OTHERS. When we learn that someone is an alcoholic, homosexual, or mentally ill, our perceptions and behavior toward that person change. For example, if we learn that someone has a "drinking problem," we may respond to his request for a drink with, "Do you think you should?" or "Do you really need it?" to convey our own objections. We may avoid jokes about drinking in the person's presence, or we may stop inviting such a person to parties or dinners.

A more severe behavioral reaction involves withdrawal from the stigmatized person (Kitsuse 1964). The labelled shoplifter, alcoholic, or homosexual may be fired from his or her job. This has the unintended effect of reducing the individual's interaction with nondeviant persons by removing legitimate opportunities for the deviant to perform in nondeviant ways (Cohen 1965). Behavioral changes may occur because of hostility toward the deviant (Kitsuse 1964), or they may reflect a sincere desire to help the person. For example, the employer who fired the alcoholic may have done so because he dislikes alcoholics or because he believes that relief from work obligations will reduce stress that may be causing the drinking problem.

Paradoxically, our reaction to deviance may produce additional rule-breaking by the labelled person. We expect people who are psychologically disturbed to be irritable or unpredictable, so we avoid them in order to avoid an unpleasant interaction. The other person will sense that he is being avoided, and respond with anger or distrust. His anger may cause co-workers to talk about him behind his back; he may respond with suspicion and become paranoid. When members of the audience behave toward the person according to a label and cause the person to respond in ways that confirm the label, they have produced a **self-fulfilling prophecy** (Merton 1957). Lemert (1962) documents a case in which just such a sequence led to a man's hospitalization for paranoia.

SELF-PERCEPTION OF THE DEVIANT. Another consequence of stigmatized social status is that it changes the deviant's self-image. A person labelled deviant often comes to identify with the label. This redefinition of oneself is due partly to feedback from others, to the extent that they treat the person as a deviant. The new self-image may be reinforced by the individual's own behavior. Repeated participation in shoplifting, for example, may lead the person to define herself as a thief.

Redefinition is facilitated by the institutions that deal with specific types of deviant persons. Such institutions pressure persons to acknowledge that they are deviant. Admitting that one is a thief will often lead police and prosecutors to go easy on a shoplifter, especially if it is a first offense. Failure to acknowledge this may lead to a substantial prison sentence. Many social programs also help shape the deviant's self-image. Admitting that one is mentally ill is often a prerequisite for psychiatric treatment (Goffman 1959). Mental health professionals often believe that a patient cannot be helped until he "recognizes his problem." A number of agencies that serve blind persons view getting the blind person to admit and accept his limitations as a major part of their job. These agencies try to convince the blind that their disability imposes "enormous obstacles to independence—obstacles seen as insurmountable by a majority of people" (Scott 1969).

Thus, there are numerous pressures on the deviant to accept a stigmatized identity. As deviants find themselves encouraged and rewarded for engaging in behavior consistent with the label, they will do so increasingly. At the same time, others may punish or prevent opportunities for behavior inconsistent with the label. Efforts by the blind person to navigate without a Seeing Eye dog, for example, may elicit chiding for not accepting his incapacity. People come to expect activity consistent with the label. In response, the deviant behaves in ways that are expected. Such behavior reinforces others' beliefs that the label applies to the person. In short, the process becomes a cycle in which changes in behavior produce changes in other people's behavior which changes the deviant's self-image and subsequent behavior.

Secondary Deviance

A frequent outcome of the societal reaction process is **secondary deviance,** in which the person employs deviant behavior as a means of defense against or adjustment to others' reactions (Lemert 1951). Usually the individual becomes openly and actively involved in the deviant role, adopting the clothes, speech, and mannerisms associated with it. For example, initially a person with a drinking problem may drink only at night and on weekends to

prevent drinking from interfering with his work. Once he adopts the role of "alcoholic," however, he may drink continuously. For male homosexuals, "coming out" constitutes an act of self-labelling and a public commitment to homosexuality (Dank 1971). Prior to coming out, the homosexual tries to limit his homosexual involvement, whereas after coming out he engages in sexual activity with males more frequently.

As individuals become openly and regularly involved in deviance, they increasingly associate with others who routinely engage in the activity. They become members of a **deviant subculture,** a group of people whose norms encourage participation in the deviance and who regard those who engage in it positively. Subcultures provide not only acceptance, but also the opportunity to enact deviant roles. Through a deviant subculture the would-be drug dealer or prostitute will gain access to customers more readily.

Subcultural groups are an attractive alternative for deviants for two reasons. First, these people are often forced out of straight relationships and groups through others' reactions. As family and friends progressively break off relationships with them, they are compelled to seek acceptance from others. Second, membership in subcultural groups may result from the deviants' desire to associate with people who are similar and who can provide them with feelings of social acceptance and self-worth (Cohen 1966). Deviants are no different from others in their need for such interpersonal rewards.

Deviant subcultures help persons cope with the stigma associated with deviant status. We have already noted that deviants are often treated with disrespect and sanctioned by others for their activity. Such treatment threatens self-esteem and produces fear of additional sanctions. Subcultures help the deviant cope with these feelings. They provide a *vocabulary of motives*—beliefs that explain and justify the individual's participation in the behavior.

FIGURE 17.2

IMAGES OF THE DEVIANT

We often have very negative images or stereotypes of many types of deviant persons. Because these labels are widely shared, persons who engage in some form of deviant behavior are usually aware that others look down on them. To counter this stigma, deviants attempt to create a positive self-image, which is reinforced by members of deviant subcultures. It is easier to view oneself as "normal" when others support that view.

The norms and belief systems of subcultures support the deviant's self-conceptions. A study of a group of black male heroin addicts (Finestone 1964) found that these men valued being "cool" and earning a living through a "hustle"—such as gambling, being a pickpocket, or running a "stable" of prostitutes. These "cats" in turn disdained the "square" who worked hard at a repetitive, boring, legitimate job. Similarly, many people think that nudists are exhibitionists who take off their clothes in order to get sexual kicks. Nudists consider themselves morally respectable and hold several beliefs designed to enhance that claim: (1) nudity and sexuality are unrelated, (2) there is nothing shameful about the human body, (3) nudity promotes a feeling of freedom and natural pleasure, and (4) nude exposure to the sun promotes physical, mental and spiritual well-being. There are also specific norms—"no staring," "no sex talk," and "no body contact"—designed to sustain these general beliefs (Weinberg 1976). The contrast between the stigmatized image of the deviant and the deviant's self-image is illustrated in Figure 17.2. The belief systems of deviant subcultures provide the social support the person needs to maintain a positive self-image.

Joining a deviant subculture may not only stabilize participation in one form of deviance, it may also lead to involvement in additional forms of deviant behavior. Black heroin users, for example, were encouraged by group norms and values to engage in a variety of other illegal, money-making activities. Similarly, many prostitutes become drug users through participation in the subculture.

Formal Social Controls

So far this chapter has been concerned with **informal social control**—the reactions of family, friends, and acquaintances to rule violations by individuals. Informal controls are probably the major influence on individual behavior. In modern societies, however, there are often elaborate systems set up specifically to treat deviants. Collectively, these are called **formal social controls,** agencies given responsibility for dealing with violations of rules or laws. Typically the rules enforced are written, and, in some cases, punishments may also be specified. The most prominent system of formal social control in our society is the criminal justice system—which includes police, courts, jails, and prisons. A second form of control is the juvenile justice system, which includes police, social workers, and probation officers, courts, and treatment or detention facilities. A third formal control system deals with mental illness. It includes mental health professionals, commitment procedures, and institutions for the mentally ill and mentally impaired.

Formal Labelling and the Creation of Deviance

Most of us think of formal agencies as reactive—as simply processing individuals who have already committed crimes, who are mentally retarded, or in need of psychiatric treatment. But these agencies do much more than take care of persons already known to be deviant. It can be argued that the function of formal social control agencies is to select members of society and identify or certify them as deviant (Erikson 1964). Of what value is labelling people "criminals," "delinquents," or "mentally ill"?

FUNCTIONS OF LABELLING. One function of public identification of deviance is to provide concrete examples of how we should not behave (Cohen 1966). We are constantly reminded of social norms in expressions like "Don't take things that don't belong to you." What exactly does this mean in terms of everyday behavior? Arresting someone for shoplifting dramatizes the possible consequences of taking things that don't belong to us.

According to the **deterrence hypothesis,** the arrest and punishment of some individuals for violation of laws deters other persons from committing the same violations. To what extent does general deterrence really affect people's behavior? Most analysts agree that the objective possibility of arrest and punishment does not deter people from breaking the law. Rather, conformity is based on people's perceptions of the likelihood of punishment and the severity of punishment. Thus, youths who perceive a higher probability that they will be caught, and that the punishment will be severe, are less likely to engage in delinquent behavior (Jensen, Erickson, and Gibbs 1978).

In general, perceived certainty of sanctions has a much greater effect on persons who have low levels of moral commitment (Silberman 1976). People whose own morals define the behavior as wrong are not as affected by the threat of punishment. For example, a person's moral beliefs are a more important influence on whether adults use marijuana than fear of legal sanctions (Meier and Johnson 1977). Adults who believe that use of marijuana is wrong do not use it, regardless of their perception of the likelihood that they will be sanctioned for its use. Thus, by itself, deterrence is not a primary influence on whether or not people break the law. The perceived threat of legal sanctions deters mainly those who are not morally opposed to an activity.

Many people face threats to the stability and security of their daily lives. Some fear the failure of others to conform to norms—the

Public identification of a person as deviant involves mass media coverage, such as this magazine photo of former U.S. government official Paul Thayer, who was convicted of giving false information to the Securities and Exchange Commission. One important function of such publicity is to provide concrete examples of how *not* to behave.

possibility that they will be victimized by aggressive behavior or the criminal activity of others. The existence of threats arouses tension. Thus a second function of public identification of deviants is to provide a scapegoat for the release of tension. Such persons provide a

focus for these fears and insecurities. The deviant becomes the concrete threat which we can deal with decisively. The Puritans came to New England in order to establish a community based on a specific Christian theology. As time passed, groups within the community periodically challenged the ministers' claims that they were the sole interpreters of the theology. In addition, they faced the threat of Indian attacks, and the problems of daily survival in a harsh environment. In 1692, when a group of young women began to behave in such bizarre ways as screaming, convulsing, crawling on all fours, and barking like dogs, the community focused attention on these women. The physician defined them as "witches," representatives of Satan, and the entire community banded together in search of others who were under the "devil's influence." The community imprisoned many persons suspected of sorcery and sent 22 persons to death. Thus the witch hunt provided a scapegoat, an outlet for people's fears and anxieties (Erikson 1966).

A third function of public identification of deviants is to increase the cohesion and solidarity of society. "Nothing unites the members of a group like a common enemy" (Cohen 1966). Deviants, in this context, are "internal enemies," persons whose behavior threatens the morale and efficiency of the group. Should the solidarity of a group be threatened, it can be restored by identifying one member as deviant and imposing appropriate sanctions. Suppose you are given the case study of a boy with a history of delinquency who is to be sentenced for a minor crime. You are asked to discuss the case with three other persons and decide what should be done. One member argues for extreme discipline, while you and the other two favor leniency. Suddenly, an expert in criminal justice who has been sitting quietly in the corner announces that your group should not be allowed to reach a decision. How might you deal with this threat to the group's existence? The reasoning above

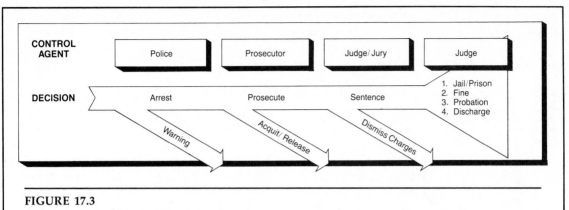

FIGURE 17.3

Formal Social Control: Processing Criminal Defendants

Formal social control often involves several control agents, each of whom makes one or more decisions. The first step in the criminal justice system is an encounter with a law enforcement officer. If you are arrested, the case is passed to a prosecutor who decides whether to prosecute. If your case goes to court, the judge or jury decides whether you are guilty. Finally, the judge renders a sentence. Each of these decision makers is influenced by their own personal attitudes, attributional processes, role expectations, and the attitudes of others regarding their decisions. Much research is devoted to the social psychological aspects of decision making in the criminal justice system.

suggests that the person who took the extreme position will be identified as the cause of the group's poor performance and that other members will try to exclude him from future group meetings. A laboratory study used exactly this setup, contrasting the reaction of threatened groups to the person taking the extreme position with the reaction of non-threatened groups. In the former condition, the person taking the extreme position was more likely to be stigmatized and rejected (Lauderdale 1976).

Thus, controlled amounts of deviant behavior serve an important function and may in fact contribute to the effective operation of groups or societies. Deviance clarifies the rules, provides scapegoats for the release of tension, and maintains social integration. If deviance is useful, we might expect control agencies to "create" deviance when the functions it serves are needed. In fact, the number of persons who are publicly identified as deviant seems to reflect the levels of stress and integration in society (Scott 1976). When integration declines, there is an increased probability of deviance. Eventually, the level and severity of deviance will reach a point where citizens will demand a "crackdown," and social control agencies will increase their activity, increasing the number of publicly identified deviants. This in turn will increase solidarity and lower stress, leading to an increase in the amount of informal control and a reduction in deviance.

THE PROCESS OF LABELLING. Labelling is not a simple, one-step procedure for formal agencies. The processing of rule-breakers usually involves a sequence of decisions. At each step, someone has to decide whether to terminate the process at that step, or to pass the rule-breaker on to the next one. Figure 17.3 portrays the sequence of steps involved in processing criminal defendants.

Each of these controlling agents—police officers, prosecutors, and judges—has to make many decisions every day. Like anyone else, they develop cognitive categories and rules that simplify their decision making. A very common police–citizen encounter occurs when an officer stops a motorist who has been drinking. What determines whether a driver who has been drinking becomes a "drunk driver"? Research suggests that police officers develop a series of informal guidelines that they use in deciding whether to arrest the motorist. Officers on the street have to rely on a variety of subjective data, when the breathalyzer or blood or urine test may only be available at the police station. The decision to arrest also depends on situational circumstances. In one study of 195 police encounters with persons who had been drinking, arrests were more likely if the encounter occurred downtown and if the citizen was disrespectful (Lundman 1974).

Prosecutors also develop informal rules that govern their decisions. For example, in one large midwestern city, taking an object worth less than $100 is a misdemeanor, and conviction normally results in a fine. Theft of a more valuable object is a felony and results in a prison sentence. Because felony theft cases require much more time and effort, the prosecutor charged virtually all persons arrested for shoplifting with misdemeanors, even if they took jewelry worth hundreds of dollars.

BIASES IN SOCIAL CONTROL. Not all persons who violate the rules are necessarily labelled. Most social control agencies process only some of the persons who violate the rules. In the study of police encounters with drunken persons only 31 percent were arrested (Lundman 1974). In some cases, control agents may be influenced by the demeanor of the rule-breaker, by the agent's stereotypes, or by where the violation occurs. This leads us to ask whether systematic biases exist in the social control system.

It has been suggested that control agents are more likely to label people who have the least power to resist certification as deviant (Quinney 1970). This hypothesis predicts that people from the lower class and members of racial and ethnic minorities are more likely to be certified as deviant than upper-class, middle-class, and white persons. This hypothesis offers a radically different explanation for the correlation between crime and social class. Earlier in this chapter, we suggested that crime rates are higher for lower-class persons because they do not have access to nondeviant means of economic and social success. Here we are suggesting that crime rates are higher among lower-class persons because they are more likely to be arrested, prosecuted, and found guilty.

Does social class or race influence how an individual is treated by control agents? One way to answer this question is by studying police–citizen contacts through the "ride-along" method, in which trained observers ride in squad cars and systematically record data about police contacts. In the largest study of this kind, observers rode with some officers on all shifts every day for seven weeks. Data were collected in Boston, Washington, and Chicago and included 5,713 contacts. There was no evidence that blacks were more likely to be arrested than whites. Arrests were more likely when a third party demanded an arrest, when the evidence was strong, and when the crime was serious (Black 1980).

What about decisions by prosecutors? Do they result in discrimination based on race or class? Prosecutors are generally motivated to maximize the ratio of convictions to trials. This may be one criterion citizens use in evaluating the performance of a district attorney. Prosecutors develop beliefs about which cases are "strong"—those likely to result in conviction. A study of a random sample of 980 defendants charged with felonies found that prosecutors are more likely to prosecute cases involving serious crimes where the evidence is strong

Whether or not a police officer gives a citizen a traffic ticket will depend partly on the demeanor of the citizen. Officers are more likely to ticket or arrest hostile, argumentative persons than polite and submissive ones.

and the defendant has a serious prior record. Race was not generally influential (Myers and Hagan 1979).

Does the social class of an arrested person influence how he or she is treated by the courts? Research on this question offers no straightforward answer. A study of the handling of juvenile cases by the courts in Philadelphia revealed that dispositions of cases involving both lower-class and black males were more severe than those of middle-class and white males (Thornberry 1973). A more recent study found no evidence of class or race bias in the processing of juvenile cases in Denver and Memphis. In most cases, the seriousness of the offense and prior record were the major determinants of severity of sentence (Cohen and Kluegel 1978).

A common practice in adult criminal cases is *plea bargaining,* in which both the prosecutor and the defendant's lawyer negotiate a plea to avoid the time and expense of a trial. A single action frequently violates several laws. Thus, if a driver who has been drinking runs a red light, and hits a pedestrian who later dies, that incident involves at least three crimes: drunken driving, failure to obey a signal, and vehicular manslaughter. These offenses vary in seriousness, and thus in their associated sentences. The prosecutor may offer not to indict the driver for manslaughter if a plea of guilty is entered to a drunken driving charge; the attorney may accept the offer, provided the prosecutor also recommends a suspended sentence. The judge then accepts the plea and sets the sentence.

Are members of certain groups more likely to be tried or to get bigger reductions in sentences through plea bargaining? An analysis of charge reduction or plea bargaining in a sample of 1,435 criminal defendants found that women and whites received slightly more favorable reductions than men and blacks. There was also evidence that certain characteristics of judges—such as their attitudes toward particular crimes—were related to the outcome of the case (Bernstein et al. 1977). Another study of 3,941 adult arrests found that blacks and persons with lower-status occupations were charged with more serious offenses (Burke and Turk 1975). Another study of 1,213 men charged with felonies focused on three outcomes: dismissal, probation, and sentence length. Characteristics of the offense—especially the seriousness of the crime and the strength of the evidence against the defendant—were most important in determining the disposition. Neither age, ethnicity, nor employment status were shown to be related to outcome of the case (Bernstein, Kelly, and Doyle 1977).

Among persons convicted, do we find a class or racial bias in the length of sentences given? One study focused on the sentences received by 10,488 persons in 3 southern states: North Carolina, South Carolina, and Florida (Chiricos and Waldo 1975). Research-

ers examined sentences for 17 different offenses and found no relationship between socioeconomic status or race and sentence length. Once again, the individual's prior record was the principal variable related to sentence length. A study of 816 cases in Chicago reveals the opposite, however. Results indicated that persons with low-status occupations and nonwhites received longer sentences than other persons for the same offense (Lizotte 1978).

Thus, decisions by social control agents are based on characteristics of offenders, of the situation in which the offense occurs, and decision rules that agents develop. There is some evidence that black males may be more likely to be charged with serious offenses and to receive longer sentences. Cases involving serious deviance and strong evidence are more likely to be prosecuted, and to lead to punishment.

Long-Term Effects of Formal Labelling

How long does the official label of deviant stick to a person? Can it be shaken? In contrast to the setting in which a person is formally certified as deviant, there is no formal ceremony terminating one's deviant status (Erikson 1964). People are simply released from prison or a mental hospital, or the final day of probation passes, with no fanfare. Does this mean that deviant status in our society tends to be for life?

Some argue that ex-convicts, ex-patients, and others who have been labelled face continuing pressures from family and friends that could prevent them from readjusting to normal life; it constitutes a reminder of their former stigmatized status. However, two studies of former psychiatric patients (Sampson et al. 1964; Greenley 1979) found no evidence of continuing stigmatization by members of their families.

Another area in which former prison inmates and mental patients might face discrimination is employment. This may occur

TABLE 17.1

EFFECTS OF LEGAL RECORD ON EMPLOYMENT OPPORTUNITIES

Percent of employers who responded:	Applicant's Legal Record				
	Convicted (N = 25)	*Acquitted w/o letter* (N = 25)	*Acquitted w/ letter* (N = 25)	*Control* (N = 25)	*Total*
Positively	4	12	24	36	19
Negatively	96	88	76	64	81

Source: adapted from Schwartz and Skolnick (1964).

because others continue to perceive these persons as deviant and expect them to behave in ways consistent with that label. In a widely cited study (Schwartz and Skolnick 1964), researchers prepared four versions of a job application. All four applications were identical; all applicants had had a succession of short-term jobs. The only variable was their legal record. In one condition, the applicant had been convicted of assault; in a second, he had been charged and acquitted. In the third condition, he had been acquitted and the application included a letter from the trial judge. In the fourth (control) condition, he had no legal record. Twenty-five employers were shown each of the four versions. The employer's responses are summarized in Table 17.1. Compared to the control condition, employers were less likely to respond favorably when the person had been arrested. Employers were about equally likely to respond negatively whether the man had been acquitted or convicted. When the letter from the judge was included, the employer's interest was higher.

The impact of mental illness on occupational careers has also been studied (Huffine and Clausen 1979). A study of psychiatrically disturbed persons compared the income and

employment status of those who had been treated (labelled) with the income and status of those who had not been treated. Treatment was negatively associated with both income and employment (Link 1982). The impact seemed to depend partly on whether occupational competence was developed prior to the onset of the illness, or later. Men who had no history of competent work performance had more difficulty obtaining employment following hospitalization, whereas men who had a history of occupational competence usually kept their jobs, even during periods when their work performance was seriously affected.

Thus, according to the available evidence, people do not stigmatize former deviants uniformly. Families do not necessarily stigmatize ex-patients. Similarly, persons who have a history of occupational competence do not usually experience job discrimination following hospitalization for psychiatric illness. In cases where the person does not have an established work record, stigma does seem to affect the reactions of prospective employers. In this situation, prospective employers may feel uncertain about whether the person is competent and reliable and may be unwilling to take a chance by giving him a job.

Summary

Deviant behavior is any act that violates the social norms that apply in a given situation.

THE VIOLATION OF NORMS. Several theories account for why people engage in deviant behavior. (1) Anomie theory asserts that deviance occurs when persons do not have legitimate means available for attaining cultural success goals. Possible responses to anomie include ritualism, retreatism, innovation, and rebellion. (2) Control theory states that deviance occurs when the individual is not responsive to the expectations of others. This responsiveness, or social bond, includes attachment to others, commitment to long-term goals, involvement in conventional activities, and a respect for law and authorities. (3) Differential association theory emphasizes the importance of learning through interaction with others. Individuals often learn the motives and actions that constitute deviant behavior just as they learn socially approved behavior.

REACTIONS TO NORM VIOLATIONS. Deviant behavior involves not only acts that violate social norms but also the societal reactions to these acts. (1) There are numerous possible responses to rule-breaking. Very often we ignore it. At other times, we define the act as normal, or excuse the perpetrator. Only after an act is discovered and labelled "deviant" is it recognized as such. (2) Our reaction to rule-breaking depends on the character of the actor, the audience, and the situation. People often have a stereotyped image of deviant persons; these stereotypes influence how audiences react to rule violations. (3) The consequences of rule-breaking depend on the reactions of the audience and the response of the rule-breaker. If members of the audience reward the person, the deviance may become institutionalized. Alternatively, the person may decide to avoid further deviance, in spite of others' encouragement. If the person is punished, he or she may give up the behavior, or respond with additional rule violations.

LABELLING AND SECONDARY DEVIANCE. The process of labelling has two important consequences. (1) It leads members of the audience to change their perceptions of and behavior toward the actor. If they withdraw from the stigmatized person, they may create a self-fulfilling prophecy, and elicit the behavior by the person they expected. (2) Labelling often causes the actor to change his or her self-image and come to define the self as deviant. This in turn may lead to secondary deviance, open and active involvement in a life style based on deviance. Such life styles are often embedded in deviant subcultures.

FORMAL SOCIAL CONTROLS. Every society gives certain agents the authority to respond to deviant behavior. (1) In American society, the major formal social control agents are the criminal justice and mental health systems. These agencies select persons and identify them as deviant through a sequence of decisions. Within the criminal justice system, the sequence includes the decisions to arrest, prosecute, and sentence the person. Various factors influence each step in decision making, including the strength of the evidence, the seriousness of the rule violation and the individual's prior record. (2) Contrary to popular belief, people do not systematically stigmatize former deviants. Most families do not continue to stigmatize relatives following their release from mental hospitals, and most employers do not stigmatize ex-patients and ex-convicts who have established work records.

Key Terms and Concepts

Deviant Behavior

Anomie Theory

Legitimate Means

Learning Structure

Opportunity Structure

Labelling Theory

Rule-Breaking

Institutionalization of Deviance

Self-Fulfilling Prophecy

Secondary Deviance

Deviant Subculture

Informal Social Control

Formal Social Control

Deterrence Hypothesis

Chapter 18

Collective Behavior and Social Movements

Introduction

—Following a victory by the home football team, hundreds of excited spectators pour onto the field and tear down the goalposts.

—Rumors that a major auto manufacturer is bankrupt set off waves of panicky selling on Wall Street, completely disrupting the stock market.

—In the wake of the shooting of a black teenager by white police officers, thousands of blacks march through the streets to City Hall, and a series of speakers demand changes in police practices.

Such events occur daily and sometimes receive national media coverage. In part because they are so common, they have been of interest to social scientists since the turn of the century.

Collective behavior refers to "emergent and extrainstitutional" behavior (Lofland 1981). By *emergent,* we mean behavior that is spontaneous and often subject to norms created by the participants themselves. By *extrainstitutional,* we mean that the norms involved are not derived from and may even be opposed to those of society (Turner and Killian 1972).

Collective behavior has three dimensions: the underlying goals, the degree of organization among participants, and the duration. First, the goal of collective behavior may be expressive—to release tension or publicly display emotions such as patriotism or hostility— or it may be instrumental—to achieve some concrete outcome such as escape from danger or a change in the distribution of power. Many collective behaviors have expressive as well as instrumental aspects. Second, collective behavior varies from unorganized (if the event is spontaneous with no formal leaders) to highly organized (with formal leaders and a planned program of activities). Degree of organization is closely associated with the third dimension, duration. Some collective activities, such as victory celebrations, last only a few hours. Others last several days, such as the racial disturbances which have occurred in large cities. Still other activities may persist for years, such as the Pentecostal movement within various religions.

The diagram shown in Figure 18.1 compares various forms of collective behavior in terms of these three dimensions. Most research focuses on either relatively short, unorganized events—often referred to as crowds—or on long-term, relatively organized social movements.

The first part of this chapter is concerned with crowds. Specifically, it addresses the following questions:

1. What social processes occur within a crowd situation?
2. What causes crowd events to occur?
3. What influences the activities of members of a crowd?

The second part of this chapter discusses social movements, and considers the following questions:

4. How do social movements develop? What are the processes by which they define issues and attract members?
5. How do movement organizations motivate people to participate in their activities?
6. How do social movements affect the larger society?

Collective Behavior

Crowds

A **crowd** refers to a substantial number of persons, usually strangers, who engage in behavior recognized as unusual by participants and observers. Crowd events are characterized by unanimity of feeling (Turner and Killian 1972). Examples include a victory celebration, a mass looting of retail stores during a blackout, a stampede of people waiting to be admitted to a theater, and epidemics in which physical symptoms or behaviors spread rapidly.

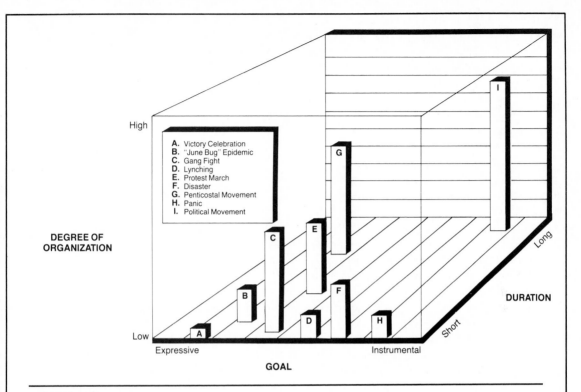

DEGREE OF ORGANIZATION

High

A. Victory Celebration
B. "June Bug" Epidemic
C. Gang Fight
D. Lynching
E. Protest March
F. Disaster
G. Penticostal Movement
H. Panic
I. Political Movement

Low

Expressive   Instrumental

GOAL

Long

DURATION

Short

FIGURE 18.1

FORMS OF COLLECTIVE BEHAVIOR

Collective behaviors differ on three dimensions: (1) goals, (2) degree of organization, and (3) duration. The goal may be expressive, as in the celebration of an athletic victory, or it may be instrumental, as in the panic selling of stock in response to a rumor that a company is going bankrupt. Some collective behaviors have almost no organization, as in the aimless wandering of hundreds of people after a natural disaster, whereas others have a high degree of organization, such as a Pentecostal religious movement. Finally, some collective behaviors involve only one event such as a lynching, whereas others involve numerous activities over an extended period of time, such as a political movement.

Crowds sometimes behave in ways that seem bizarre or irrational. Thus, when the doors opened at a theater in Cincinnati where a well-known rock group was appearing, those waiting in line could have filed in slowly and found seats. Instead, persons in the middle and back of the line pushed forward, and the resulting stampede killed several persons in front. Such tragedies, and the desire to prevent them, have led many people to study what happens within crowds.

LE BON. One of the first social scientists to analyze crowds was Gustave Le Bon (1895). Le Bon proposed the crowd mind, or "psychological crowd," to explain people's behavior in such settings. In 1895, he wrote: "The sentiments and ideas of all the persons in the gathering take one and the same direction, and their conscious personality vanishes. A collective mind is formed. . . ." According to Le Bon, this "mental unity of the crowd" determines behavior. The best evidence for the existence of the crowd mind is that members of the aggregation "feel, think, and act in a manner quite different from that in which each individual of them would feel, think, and act were he in a state of isolation."

Le Bon identified three mechanisms that bring about the crowd mind. First, a crowd provides anonymity. When the individual is among others, often strangers, there is a decline in the sense of responsibility for one's own behavior. This makes it easier for the person to act on impulse, and to engage in behavior that violates the norms of society—such as looting, vandalism, or assault. Second, contagion occurs; behavior or ideas expressed by one person spread quickly through a crowd. This process gives direction to the crowd's activity; it is the mechanism through which uniformity of behavior is produced. The third mechanism is suggestibility. Le Bon believed that individuals in crowds lose conscious awareness of their behavior, and that unconscious aspects of their personalities come to the fore. This accounts for the seemingly irrational or bizarre character of some crowd behavior.

Le Bon's analysis of crowd behavior has had considerable influence on subsequent research. The same mechanisms he identified in 1895 are often used by social psychologists today, though often under different names.

DEINDIVIDUATION. Le Bon's view of anonymity is very similar to the contemporary concept of **deindividuation,** a reduction in awareness of one's individuality and feelings of personal responsibility.

In one study of deindividuation (Festinger et al. 1952), students participated in a group discussion under one of two conditions. In one condition (public identity), participants were seated in a well-lit room wearing their own clothing. In the other condition (deindividuation), each person put on a gray coat and the discussion was conducted in a dimly lit room. Each group was asked to make hostile remarks about their parents. Such remarks were much more frequent in the deindividuation condition. In another study (Zimbardo 1969), subjects were asked to administer electric shocks to a confederate. In one condition, they wore hoods, were forbidden to use names, and were placed in a dimly lit room. In the other condition, subjects wore large name tags in a well-lit room. Not surprisingly, deindividuated subjects administered electric shocks for longer periods to the target person. Of course, the equipment was wired so that the target person did not receive the shocks.

Thus it appears that an increase in anonymity (deindividuation) produces an increase in antisocial behavior. This evidence, however, comes from experiments in which participants performed the behavior in small groups. Thus, the extent to which it applies to crowd settings is not clear. In a crowd, activities are initiated by one member and then spread to others.

CONTAGION. A second process identified by Le Bon is **contagion,** the rapid spread through a group of visible and often unusual symptoms or behavior. In any interaction, one person acts and witnesses the reaction of others to that behavior. Usually, others respond in different but related ways. In a crowd, however, others respond by engaging in the *same* behavior. If one person shouts a hostile message, others will do likewise. Their reaction reinforces that person's behavior, making it more likely that it will be repeated. This *circular reaction* is a fundamental mechanism of collective behavior (Blumer 1969).

Contagion is illustrated by the "June bug" epidemic, which occurred in a clothing manufacturing plant in the South in 1962. Within one week, 62 employees received medical attention for what they said were insect bites. Typical symptoms reported by the persons affected included feeling faint, nausea, severe pain, or feeling disoriented. Almost all of those affected were white women who worked the same shift in the same area of the plant. A thorough investigation could not identify any insect or chemical that could have produced these symptoms.

The "June bug" epidemic is an example of *hysterical contagion* (Kerckhoff, Back, and Miller 1965). We are all frequently exposed to models of hysterical behavior, such as people expressing fears of insect bites. We generally ignore these behaviors completely, or define persons who display them as deviant. However, when two other conditions are met, contagion may occur: (1) the persons involved must be experiencing tension, and (2) the behavior must be relevant to their situation. It appears that both of these conditions were present in the clothing plant. Pressures to produce were great, and many of the employees were working overtime. At the same time there was the possibility of layoffs at the end of the peak period. The behavior was also relevant because insects are common in clothing plants.

Analysis of friendship patterns revealed that the sociometric structure of workers in the plant affected the spread of the "epidemic." People considered isolates—those who had no friends at the plant—were most likely to be affected at the beginning of the epidemic. As the contagion spread, however, it increasingly affected friends of those who had already been affected. These results suggest that contagion initially occurs among those most susceptible to tension, the isolates; as it spreads, group influences appear to become increasingly important (Kerckhoff, Back, and Miller 1965).

Closely related to hysterical contagion is *behavioral contagion* (Wheeler 1966) in which the behavior of one person reduces constraints that prevent others from performing the same behavior. For example, many people in a crowd may have thought of rushing onto the playing field but restrained themselves for fear of being arrested. Seeing others run onto the field without interference from security police shows observers that they will not be punished for that behavior.

Although contagion is useful in understanding why persons engage in the same

Behavioral contagion often occurs in a crowd. One person acts, liberating others from the restraints that have prevented them from performing the act. Behavioral contagion can produce something trivial like a "wave" at a football game—or something serious like this attack on a spectator at a soccer match.

behavior, it does not explain why some people in a crowd engage in various other behaviors, and why others do not act at all (Turner and Killian 1972). By itself, contagion is not a complete explanation of crowd behavior.

CONVERGENCE. So far we have assumed that a crowd is composed of dissimilar persons, and that its initial makeup depends simply on who happens to be in the vicinity. Next, conditions such as deindividuation reduce the effectiveness of self-control. Finally, through contagion, some behavior spreads through the crowd. But suppose that the crowd shares certain qualities that predispose them to act in some ways and not others (Milgram and Toch 1969).

When this happens, similar behavior may reflect the convergence of those with similar predispositions, not reduction in self-control and contagion. For example, electronic media often rapidly spread word of an event. The news of John Lennon's death in December of 1980 was transmitted nationally within hours. While millions heard the news, only a few hundred converged at the apartment building where he lived in New York City. These were people for whom his death was especially meaningful. Their behavior—the singing of his songs, lighting candles, and various other memorial rituals at the scene of his murder—reflected their shared sense of loss.

EMERGENT NORMS. Deindividuation, contagion, and convergence provide only a partial explanation of collective behavior. Most crowds include some people who know each other; in fact many participants arrive and remain with family, friends, or acquaintances (McPhail and Wohlstein 1983). In addition, crowds involve various types of persons engaging in a variety of related but different actions. A much more general perspective on crowd activity is provided by the *emergent norm theory*, derived from the symbolic interactionist perspective (see Chapter 1).

According to emergent norm theory, collective behavior occurs when people find themselves in an undefined or unanticipated situation (Turner and Killian 1972). The situation may be novel, so that there are no cultural norms or directives for action. Consider the aircraft hijackings of the late 1960s. These hijackings were completely unexpected and there were no behavioral guidelines for passengers, crew, or authorities. Alternatively, the social structure may be temporarily disrupted by a natural disaster such as a tornado, or by an event such as a city-wide strike by police officers. Another possibility is that there are conflicting definitions of how people should behave. In order to act in these situations, those present must develop a shared definition of the situation and the associated behavioral norms.

In circumstances such as these, people are unable to find out what is going on or what they should do. Because of the need for information, conventional barriers to communication break down. Strangers talk to each other or to members of groups they usually avoid. In addition, the usual standards of judgment and morality may be suspended. **Rumor**—communication via informal and often novel channels that cannot be validated—exerts a major influence on the emerging definition of the situation. *Milling*—the movement of persons within the setting and the consequent exchange of information between crowd members—is the major method through which information is transmitted.

As noted earlier, a crowd usually consists of a variety of people, many of whom will have a different definition of the situation. Thus, diverse action tendencies are present in any crowd situation (Turner and Killian 1972). Each person will have some sense of the likelihood that others will support his or her own disposition (Johnson and Feinberg 1977). Those most likely to initiate acts are those who believe others will support them. Once a person initiates an act, the support of those around him will determine whether that person persists in attempts to influence others. If enough people reinforce that person's position or behavior, a consensus will emerge. The definition of the situation which results from interaction in an initially ambiguous situation is termed an **emergent norm.** The emergent norm is usually not completely novel; it involves a modification or transformation of preexisting norms (Killian 1984).

Once a definition of the situation develops, people are able to act. In a crowd, behaviors consistent with the emergent norm are encouraged, whereas behaviors inconsistent with the norm are discouraged. Thus, there are normative limits on the behavior of crowd participants. Crowds celebrating a football championship do not engage in looting; conversely, looters usually do not congregate in

Box 18.1
REACTIONS TO DISASTERS

A **disaster** is an event that produces widespread physical damage or destruction of property accompanied by social disruption (Quarantelli and Dynes 1977). Many disasters occur with no warning. Sometimes, however, there may be prior warning, such as increasingly strong tremors prior to an earthquake, or warnings by authorities prior to an enemy attack. There are three types of reactions to the threat of disaster (Perry and Pugh 1978). Denial is the most common when the likelihood of the disaster is perceived as small, or the warning is ambiguous. Extreme emotion such as terror and hysteria are likely if the threat is accurately perceived but not imminent. Effective adaptation is most likely if there are repeated accurate warnings which include information about what people can do to enhance their survival. Research shows that reactions to threat are more appropriate and effective when information is communicated via official channels; inappropriate and ineffective behavior is more likely when information is via unofficial, interpersonal channels such as rumor.

Little is known about how people behave at the time a disaster hits. What data there are indicate that most people do not panic (Perry and Pugh 1978). Panic in response to disaster occurs only under certain conditions. First, the situation must be defined as dangerous. Panic will not occur if most people deny that there is any threat to themselves. Second, the danger must be perceived as escapable by some action. If there is a fire in a building, for example, at least some of those present must believe there are doors or windows through which they can escape. People often remain calm when it is obvious that there is no possibility of escape, for example, in an emergency on an airplane at high altitudes. Third, at least some of those present must believe that escape routes are inadequate or will be cut off. Under these conditions, people are influenced by the behavior of others. If there is an emergency during a concert, and the emcee calmly announces the procedures to be followed, everyone may leave in an orderly fashion. On the other hand, if several people suddenly run toward the exits, others may attempt to do the same. This clearly illustrates the emergent norm model. An experiment in which all three conditions were simulated revealed that people were more likely to escape when the threat was low rather than high, and when the group was small (3 or 4) rather than large (5 or 6) (Kelley et al. 1965).

What happens after the disaster depends in part on the ability of existing, emergency organizations to respond, including police and fire departments, hospitals, utility companies, and civil defense agencies (Quarantelli and Dynes 1977). Such organizations often have drills to prepare their personnel to respond to emergencies rapidly and efficiently. At the scene of a disaster, an "emergency social system" emerges (Perry and Pugh 1978). At first, residents of the impact area may work together in informal groups. They will take responsibility for the recovery of victims, removal of debris, and the initial assessment of damages. A tremendous sense of community and high morale often develop. Gradually, the emergency organizations move in to supplement or supplant the emergency social system.

bars for several hours and drink alcoholic beverages.

The emergent norm model incorporates all of the ideas discussed earlier in this section. It emphasizes the situational character of collective behavior, without assuming that participants behave in the same way or that they are all strangers. In fact, the pressure to conform to the emergent norm may be more effective when participants know each other.

Underlying Causes of Collective Behavior

Having considered the internal dynamics of crowds, we turn now to the causes of collective behavior. In some instances, collective behavior is a response to a precipitating event like a natural disaster, an athletic victory, or an assassination. Other types of collective behavior—demonstrations, boycotts, lynchings, lootings, and epidemics—frequently involve not only a precipitating event but also more basic causes that can be traced to underlying conditions in the larger society. Three such conditions are strain, relative deprivation, and grievances.

STRAIN. Society may be viewed as normally in a state of equilibrium, maintaining a balance between the emphasis on achieving society's goals and the provision of means to achieve them—education and jobs (Merton 1957). At times, however, social change may disrupt this equilibrium, so that one aspect of society is no longer in balance with other aspects. Advances in technology, for example, demand changes in occupational structure. Machines and robots have increasingly replaced many blue-collar workers in automobile plants. This has produced high unemployment in cities like Detroit which depend heavily on the auto industry. Such change produces strains in society affecting some individuals more than others. Although those who are affected may not recognize the source (for example, automation) they experience discontent or frustration which could result in an outbreak of collective behavior.

Historically, economic issues have frequently been at the heart of collective protest (Rude 1964). "Food riots" to protest the lack of sufficient food, attacks on factories and businesses to prevent mechanization, and sabotage to disable machinery and other property are frequently economically motivated. These activities were common in preindustrial England and France. More recently, we have seen farmers in the United States dump milk and slaughter beef cattle rather than sell them at depressed prices. Such protests seek to maintain or improve an area's standard of living by reducing supplies and thus keeping prices high.

RELATIVE DEPRIVATION. In the eighteenth century, the revolt against the feudal socioeconomic structure occurred first in France. Yet France had already lost many feudal characteristics by the time the French Revolution began in 1789. The French peasant was free to travel, to buy and sell goods, and to contract services. In Germany, however, the feudal social structure was still intact. Thus, based on objective conditions, one would have expected a revolution to occur in Germany before it did in France. Why didn't it? One analyst (de Tocqueville 1800/1955) argues that the decline of medieval institutions in France caused peasants to become obsessed with the ownership of land. In short, the improvement in their objective situation created subjective expectations for further improvement. Peasant participation in the French Revolution was motivated by the desire to fulfill subjective expectations—obtain land—not by a desire to eliminate oppressive conditions.

This basic insight on the causes of revolutions was expanded into a more systematic theory called the *J-Curve theory* (Davies 1962, 1971). According to this view, the "state of mind" of citizens determines whether there is political stability or revolution. On the basis of external conditions, individuals develop expectations regarding the satisfaction of their needs. Expectations may be derived from one's own past experience or from comparison with the experiences of other groups. Under certain conditions, persons expect continuing improvement in the satisfaction of their needs. As long as these expectations are met, people will be content and political stability will result. But if the gap between expectations and reality becomes too great, people become frustrated and engage in protest and rebellious activity.

Revolutions usually occur when the level of actual satisfaction declines following a period of rising expectations and their relative satisfaction (Davies 1971). These relationships are summarized in Figure 18.2. Note the J shape of the actual need satisfaction curve; as satisfaction declines, an intolerable gap between expected and actual satisfaction is created. The J-Curve theory applies well to several major revolutions, including the Russian Revolution of 1917, the Cairo Riots of 1952, and the Hungarian Uprising of 1956.

The gap between expected and actual need satisfaction is called **relative deprivation.** As relative deprivation becomes greater, the likelihood of protests and social movements increases. As noted earlier, expectations regarding need satisfaction may be based on comparisons with one's own past experience, or with the current experiences of other groups. The French peasant experienced deprivation because, even though his freedom had increased dramatically, he had not gained the freedom to own land like the aristocracy. Recent research confirms that it is the feeling that members of one's own group are deprived relative to members of other groups that is associated with collective protest (Begley and Alker 1982; Guimond and Dubé-Simard (1983).

Labor union members, on the other hand, base their expectations regarding contract provisions on past experiences. Strikes are more likely when economic conditions are good and there is a large gap between the wage increases workers expect and what management offers—that is, a high relative deprivation (Snyder 1975). Relative deprivation only becomes significant when people have the capacity to protest effectively. For this reason, unions require a large, stable membership, institutionalized collective bargaining, and influence in the national political system.

There have been numerous attempts to study the relationship between collective behavior and relative deprivation. Many have attempted to measure people's subjective evaluation of their level of need satisfaction using

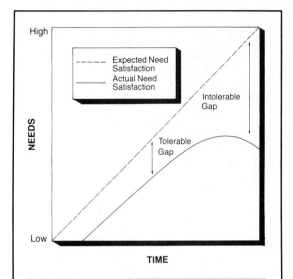

FIGURE 18.2
THE J-CURVE MODEL

One theory of the causes of revolutions is the J-Curve theory. According to this model, revolutions occur when there is an intolerable gap between people's expectations of need satisfaction and the actual level of satisfaction they experience. In response to improved economic and social conditions, people expect continuing improvement in the satisfaction of their needs. As long as they experience satisfaction, there will be political stability, even if there is a gap between expected and actual satisfaction (called "relative deprivation"). If the level of actual satisfaction declines, the gap gets bigger; at some point it becomes intolerable, and revolution occurs.

Source: adapted from Davies (1962).

questionnaires. Results indicate that while relative deprivation is associated with collective behavior, it is not the only determinant of participation (Marx and Wood 1975).

GRIEVANCES. In any society, certain resources will be highly valued but scarce; these resources include income or property, skills of certain types, and power and influence over others. Because of their scarcity, such resources are unequally distributed. Some groups have

Civil disorders or riots occur periodically in American cities. As in this disturbance in Miami, they often involve members of minority groups and sometimes result in widespread vandalism and destruction of property.

more access to a given resource than others. When one group has a *grievance*—is discontented with the existing distribution of resources—collective behavior may occur in order to change that distribution (Oberschall 1973). Attempts to change the existing arrangement frequently elicit responses by other groups designed to preserve the status quo.

Generally there are three types of collective action (Tilly et al. 1975). *Competitive* activity involves conflict between communal groups, usually on a local scale. Gang fights in cities, long-standing feuds between ethnic or kin groups, and similar phenomena are concerned with dominance. The high rates of lynching of blacks in the South in the 1890s is another example. From 1865 to 1890, blacks enjoyed substantial gains in political influence. By 1890, however, the white middle and upper classes were attempting to regain

political control. Between 1890 and 1900, several state legislatures discussed laws taking the vote away from blacks. During these years, the number of blacks lynched in Alabama, Georgia, Louisiana, Mississippi, and South Carolina reached a peak (Wasserman 1977). Both disenfranchisement and lynchings can be seen as a reassertion of white dominance over blacks. Historical data at the parish level from Louisiana show that the percentage of blacks in a parish was positively associated with the number of lynchings in that parish between 1889 and 1896 (Inverarity 1976). Thus, whites were more concerned about reestablishing their control in areas with a more concentrated black population.

A second type of collective action, called *reactive*, involves a conflict between a local group and agents of the national political system. Tax rebellions, draft resistance movements, and protests of governmental policy are reactive. Such behavior is a response to attempts by the state to enforce its rules (regarding military service, for example), or extend its control (imposing a new tax). Thus, such events represent resistance to centralization of authority.

A third type of collective action, called *proactive*, involves demands for material resources, rights, or power. Unlike reactive behavior, it is an attempt to influence rather than resist authority. Strikes by workers, demonstrations in favor of equal rights or equal opportunity, and various nonviolent protest activities are all proactive. Most proactive situations involve broad coalitions rather than one or two locally based groups.

The three underlying conditions discussed in this section differ in their emphasis. The strain model emphasizes the individual's emotional state in explaining collective behavior, whereas the relative deprivation viewpoint emphasizes the person's subjective assessment of need satisfaction. The grievance model suggests that collective behavior results from rational attempts to redistribute resources in society (Zurcher and Snow 1981).

Precipitating Events

Conditions of strain, relative deprivation, and grievances may be present in a society over extended periods of time. By contrast, incidents of collective behavior are often sporadic. Frequently, there are warning signals that a group is frustrated or dissatisfied. Members of the dissatisfied group or third parties may attempt to convince those in power to make changes (Oberschall 1973). If changes are not made, members will increasingly perceive legitimate channels as ineffective, leading to marches, protests, or other activities. Eventually, an incident occurs that adversely affects members of the group and symbolizes the problem, triggering collective behavior by group members; such an incident is termed a **precipitating event.**

An incident is more likely to trigger collective behavior if it occurs in an area accessible to many members of the affected group at a time when social controls are weak (Turner and Killian 1972). It is also more likely to become a precipitating event if it occurs in a location that has special significance to group members (Oberschall 1973). An event that occurs in such a place may produce a stronger reaction than would the same incident in a less meaningful location.

Empirical Studies of Crowds

Because they are unpredictable, hostile crowd incidents are difficult to study empirically. Nevertheless, extensive and sophisticated research has been conducted on the racial disturbances that occurred in many American cities between 1965 and 1969. These studies support many of the theories presented earlier in this chapter on collective behavior. In the first nine months of 1967 there were 164 racial disturbances. In response, President Lyndon Johnson appointed the National Advisory Commission on Civil Disorders to study the causes of these incidents. In its report (1968), the commission concluded that the racial disturbances were caused by the underlying social and economic conditions affecting blacks in our society. It pointed to the high rates of unemployment, poverty, poor health and sanitation conditions in black ghettos, exploitation of blacks by retail merchants, and the experience of racial discrimination, all of which produced a sense of deprivation and frustration among blacks.

The commission studied 24 disorders in 23 cities in depth. It concluded:

> Disorder was generated out of an increasingly disturbed social atmosphere, in which typically a series of tension-heightening incidents over a period of weeks or months became linked in the minds of many in the Negro community with a reservoir of underlying grievances. At some point in the mounting tension, a further incident—in itself often routine or trivial—became the breaking point and the tension spilled over into violence. Violence usually occurred almost immediately following the occurrence of the final precipitating incident, and then escalated rapidly. Disorder generally began with rock and bottle throwing and window breaking. Once store windows were broken, looting usually followed.
> —*Report of the National Advisory Commission on Civil Disorders*, p. 6.

The precipitating incident frequently involved contacts between police officers and blacks. In Tampa, Florida, a disturbance began after a policeman shot a fleeing robbery suspect. A rumor quickly spread that the black suspect was surrendering when the officer shot him. In other cities, disorder was triggered by incidents involving police attempts to disperse a crowd in a shopping district or to arrest patrons of a tavern selling alcoholic beverages after the legal closing time. To many blacks, police officers symbolize white society and are therefore a readily available target for grievances and frustration. When a police officer arrests or injures a black under ambiguous circumstances, it provides a concrete focus for discontent.

SEVERITY OF DISTURBANCES. Of particular concern to researchers was the intensity or severity of these disturbances. Numerous studies were based on the assumption that severity was determined by the degree of deprivation experienced by blacks.

In one study of racial disorders in 42 American cities during 1967 (Morgan and Clark 1973), a "racial disorder" was defined as four or more persons engaging in behavior involving personal injury, property damage, or civil disobedience. A distinction was drawn between the intensity of a disorder and the extent of participation in it. Four empirical measures of intensity were employed: duration in days, number of injuries, estimated property damage, and a militancy index. Measures of extent included the number of participants, number of police, and number of arrests. The data showed that measures of intensity and extent were highly correlated, so they were combined into an overall index of severity.

Researchers hypothesized that the more widespread the grievances among blacks, the greater the number of persons who would support disorders, and hence, the more severe the disorder. A high level of grievance may result from experience with racial discrimination, and from relative deprivation. Deprivation was measured by comparing the situation of blacks with that of whites on several dimensions, including housing and employment. Severity of disturbances was positively associated with housing inequality and a city's population size. This suggests that greater relative deprivation in housing produces greater dissatisfaction, and that the larger the black population, the greater the number of potential participants (Morgan and Clark 1973).

Although underlying frustrations may account for the severity of disturbances, they do not explain why disorders occur in some cities and not others (Spilerman 1976). Presumably, blacks in most American cities were experiencing the same types of deprivations in the 1960s. Yet disturbances occurred in only 170 of the 673 cities whose 1960 population

exceeded 25,000. Thus, there must be factors other than grievance level that differentiate those cities where disturbances occur.

One possibility is that disturbances occurred in cities where the deprivation experienced by blacks was greatest. This hypothesis was tested in an analysis of 322 incidents that occurred in 1967 and 1968 (Spilerman 1976). The study measured both absolute and relative levels of deprivation. The absolute level of deprivation was measured by unemployment rate, average income, and average education of nonwhites in each city. Relative deprivation was measured by the differences between white and nonwhite unemployment rates, average income, average education, and average occupational status. To measure severity of disorders, the study used the composite riot severity scale reproduced in Table 18.1. This scale distinguishes four degrees of severity based on the amount of personal injury, property damage, crowd size, and number of arrests.

Both severity and frequency of disturbances were associated with size of the nonwhite population of a city, rather than a city's overall population. But, in sharp contrast to earlier research, the level of deprivation was not associated with the severity of disorders. These results suggest that black protests were not due to local community conditions, but to general features of the society such as increased black consciousness, heightened racial awareness, and greater identification with other blacks due to the civil rights movement. Television may have contributed to the disorders of the late 1960s by providing role models. Films of other blacks engaged in vandalism, looting, and other collective behavior served as a model for blacks experiencing deprivation.

Thus, although deprivation was an underlying cause of black protest, disorders were facilitated by the civil rights movement and increased black consciousness. The magnitude of deprivation was not related to the location or severity of disturbances. Rather, severity was associated with the number of people experiencing deprivations, that is, the number of people available to participate in disorders.

AMBIENT TEMPERATURE AND COLLECTIVE VIOLENCE. It is often suggested that high temperatures are a contributing factor in large-scale racial disturbances. In its report (1968), the National Advisory Commission noted that 60 percent of the 164 racial disorders that occurred in 1967 took place in July during hot weather. Of the 24 serious disturbances studied in detail, "in most instances, the temperature during the day on which violence first erupted was quite high" (National Advisory Commission, p. 123).

One study of the relationship between temperature and collective violence focused on 102 incidents that occurred between 1967 and 1971 (Baron and Ransberger 1978). Results showed a strong relationship between the mean temperature on the days the incidents occurred and the occurrence of violence. This relationship is depicted in Figure 18.3.

A serious problem with this correlation is that there are many more days when the temperature is between 70 and 85 than when it is greater than 85. If we estimated the probability of a disturbance controlling for the number of days in each temperature range, the results show a similar direct relationship (Carlsmith and Anderson 1979). In other words, the higher the temperature the more likely a disturbance. One interpretation of this relationship is that, in high-density neighborhoods, the number of people on the streets increases with the temperature. Large street crowds facilitate the transmission of rumors, increase the likelihood of supportive responses by others to acts initiated by a single individual, and increase the number affected by the "circular reaction" process.

SELECTION OF TARGETS. Looting during a civil disturbance does not occur in a random fashion. During the racial disorders of the 1960s,

TABLE 18.1

RIOT SEVERITY SCALE

0	*Low intensity*—rock and bottle throwing, some fighting, little property damage. Crowd size <125; arrests <15; injuries <8.
1	Rock and bottle throwing, fighting, looting, serious property damage, some arson. Crowd size 75–250; arrests 10–30; injuries 5–15.
2	Substantial violence, looting, arson and property destruction. Crowd size 200–500; arrests 25–75; injuries 10–40.
3	*High intensity*—major violence, bloodshed, and destruction. Crowd size >400; arrests >65; injuries >35.

Source: adapted from Spilerman (1976).

property damage was almost always confined to retail stores. Residences, public buildings such as schools, and medical facilities like clinics and hospitals were usually unaffected. In addition, the looting and vandalism of businesses was selective. Some stores were cleaned out whereas others in the same block were untouched.

According to one survey (Berk and Aldrich 1972), the reason for this discrepancy is businesses with higher average prices of goods sold (that is, more attractive merchandise) were more likely to be attacked. A second factor was familiarity with the interior of the store; the larger the percentage of black customers, the more likely the store was to be looted. Retaliation was also a factor; stores whose owners refused to cash checks and give credit to blacks were more likely to be attacked. White ownership by itself was the least important factor.

Thus the selection of targets during a riot is far from random. Rather, it reflects the desire of participants to obtain expensive consumer goods, and to retaliate against antiblack owners. This may reflect the operation of social control within the crowd; emergent

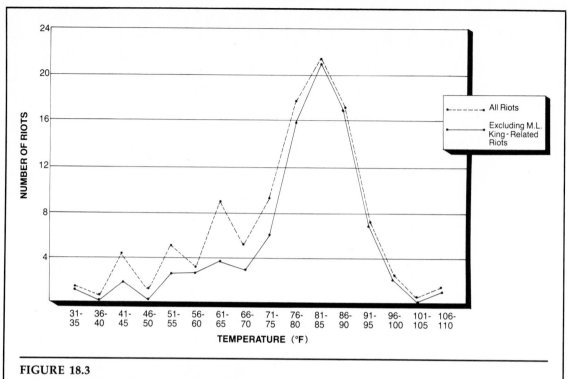

FIGURE 18.3

AMBIENT TEMPERATURE AND COLLECTIVE VIOLENCE

There is a strong relationship between mean temperature and the occurrence of collective disturbances. An analysis of 102 incidents between 1967 and 1971 generated this graph. As the temperature increased, the frequency of riots also increased. As the temperature increases, so does the number of people who are outside. Large numbers of people on the streets facilitates the development of a crowd.

Source: adapted from Baron and Ransberger (1978).

norms may define some buildings and types of stores as appropriate targets and others as inappropriate targets. These norms are probably enforced by members of the crowd itself (Oberschall 1973).

SOCIAL CONTROL AND COLLECTIVE BEHAVIOR. Social control agents such as police officers strongly influence the course of a collective incident. In some cases, the mere appearance of authorities at the scene of an incident will set off collective action. Police–citizen encounters were frequently the precipitating factor in the racial disturbances of the 1960s (National Advisory Commission 1968).

The importance of control agents is especially clear in protest situations. Protesters usually enter a situation with (1) beliefs about the efficacy of violence, and (2) norms regarding its use (Kritzer 1977). If participants' norms do not oppose violence, and if they believe violence may be effective, they are predisposed to choose violent tactics. Similarly, control agents enter the situation with (1) beliefs about what tactics the protesters are likely to use, and (2) informal norms regarding violence. If the police anticipate violence, they will prepare for violence by bringing specially trained personnel and special equipment. Based on these beliefs and expectations, either

Box 18.2
WIRE SERVICES AND RACIAL DISTURBANCES

Investigators of the racial disorders in the 1960s relied on one of four sources for information about the location and severity of each disturbance. These were *The New York Times Index*, the *Congressional Quarterly Civil Disorder Chronology* (based on newspaper reports), the *Riot Data Review* published at Brandeis University, and the *Report* of the National Advisory Commission. All four of these sources were based on reports by the wire services—Associated Press and United Press International—and only events reported by one or both of these services were included in the data available to researchers. Is it possible that reliance on wire service reports might bias these studies?

One way to answer this question is to determine whether the cities which reportedly experienced disorders all had a wire service office. Earlier research indicates that the size of the black population had a strong relationship with the frequency of conflict. Subsequent work, however, reveals that this relationship may reflect the presence of a wire service office (Danzger 1975). Danzger analyzed all civil rights incidents that occurred between 1955 and 1965 in 644 cities with populations over 25,000. He found that cities with a wire service office were characterized by more frequent disorders. Thus the earlier correlation between black population and number of incidents was probably due to the fact that larger cities (cities with a larger black population) were more likely to have a wire service office, and so incidents in these cities were more likely to be reported.

Whereas small-scale, isolated events are more likely to be reported in cities with wire service offices, severe disturbances will be reported no matter where they occur. Their magnitude alone will attract media personnel. Therefore, the study of protests should concentrate on cities that experience substantial conflict, where the data are probably complete. If we reanalyze the data, looking only at these major incidents, the effect of the location of wire service offices disappears, and the size of the nonwhite population reemerges as a significant factor in the occurrence of racial conflict.

Another factor that determines whether or not an incident will be reported is "media sensitivity." Sensitivity is influenced by several factors, including frequency of the type of event and political climate. In an extension of Danzger's analysis, researchers hypothesized that the more frequent an event, the *less* likely it is to be reported. For example, interracial assaults in large cities are more common, and therefore less likely to be reported. An analysis of racial disorders occurring in 673 cities between 1965 and 1969 verified this hypothesis. Disorders occurring in 1969 were more likely to be included in the *Congressional Quarterly Chronology* if the city had not experienced disorders in the preceding four years. Thus, a city experiencing its first disorder in five years is more newsworthy than a city experiencing its fifth disorder in five years.

In effect, both of these studies confirm earlier findings that the size of the black urban population is associated with the incidence of racial protest. At the same time, the analyses remind us that media reports and data files do not necessarily provide complete information. For this reason, empirical data concerning racial protest in the United States in the 1960s appear to be most accurate for events that are large scale and relatively infrequent.

the control agents or the protesters may initiate violence. Violence by one group is likely to produce a violent response from the other. Data from 126 protest events support this view (Kritzer 1977).

In some instances, the response of authorities determines the severity and duration of disorders (Spiegel 1969). In any disturbance, there are two critical points at which under- or over-control can cause a protest to escalate. First, there is the authorities' response to the initial or "street confrontation" phase. Undercontrol by police in reaction to the initial disorder may be interpreted by protesters as "an invitation to act"; it suggests that illegal behavior will not be punished. Overcontrol at this point—such as an unnecessary show of force or large numbers of arrests—may arouse moral indignation which may attract new participants and increase violence. The second critical point in a disturbance is the response to widespread disorder and looting during the later "Roman Holiday" phase. As it progresses, participants gradually become physically exhausted. Undercontrol by authorities may facilitate the collapse of the protest, whereas overcontrol may result in incidents that fuel hostility, draw in new participants, and move the disturbance into the final "siege" phase.

The response of authorities to one incident may also affect the severity of subsequent disorders in the same city (Spilerman 1976). One study investigating incidents of collective violence in France, Germany, and Italy between 1830 and 1930 (Tilly et al. 1975) found that episodes involving violence were often preceded by nonviolent collective action. Moreover, a substantial amount of the violence consisted of the forcible *reaction* of authorities (often military or police forces employed by the government) to the nonviolent protests of citizens. Thus, violence was not necessarily associated with attempts to influence authority; if anything, it was associated with reactions to such attempts by the agents of authority. The data also suggest that

repression—violent penalties such as damage or seizure of persons or property—diminished the frequency and intensity of collective action—witness the history of the Solidarity Workers' Union in Poland.

Smelser's Theory of Collective Behavior

The most ambitious theory of collective behavior was proposed by Neil Smelser (1963). Because it is very comprehensive, it can be used to summarize our discussion. According to Smelser, there are six determinants of collective behavior which occur in order. Each stage depends on those which precede it, and each adds its own ingredient to the final product. To illustrate this process, Smelser describes the process of making cars from iron. Included in this process are mining, smelting, shaping, combining steel with other parts, assembling the car, delivering it to the dealer, and selling it. These stages must occur in this order. If the order varied, one would not get the final product. In addition, at each stage the possible outcome is progressively narrowed, until a car is the only possible product.

The determinants of collective behavior are as follows. First, certain social conditions called *structural conduciveness* are necessary in order for certain types of collective behavior to occur. A financial panic can only occur in a money economy. A protest march can only occur in a political system that permits such activity. The second determinant, called *structural strain*, involves ambiguous situations, relative deprivation, and intergroup conflict. The third determinant is the growth and spread of a *generalized belief* among participants. This identifies the cause of the strain and specifies appropriate actions for those afflicted by it.

Together, conduciveness, strain, and generalized beliefs constitute the underlying causes of collective behavior. The fourth condition, a *precipitating factor*, is necessary to produce a collective episode. Once the episode begins, it is necessary to *mobilize participants* of the affected group. A collective episode provides a concrete focus for behavior. In response, *social controls* are mobilized; authorities act in ways designed to interrupt, deflect, or inhibit the collective activity. This in turn determines the intensity and direction of the episode.

It is the occurrence of each of these determinants in order and the particular strain, belief, precipitating factor, mobilization, and control effects that determine the character of any particular incident.

There is widespread agreement among critics that structural conduciveness plays a major role in influencing collective behavior. Moreover, there is agreement that specific events do serve to crystalize discontent and trigger collective action, and that the responses of authorities play a major role in determining the course of the incident. However, with respect to strain as the underlying cause, like other analysts, Smelser does not specify how much is necessary. Nor does he offer a precise statement of the relationship between strain and collective behavior. There is less agreement that a generalized belief is necessary; incidents such as victory celebrations and responses to disasters do not seem to require a generalized belief. Finally, it is very difficult to identify good empirical measures for each determinant. For this reason, the predictive validity of Smelser's theory is not yet known (Marx and Wood 1975).

Social Movements

The difference between collective behavior and social movements is one of degree. Both involve extrainstitutional behavior—behavior that is not consistent with the norms of society. Both are caused by social conditions which generate strain, frustration, or grievances. Their differences lie in degree of organization. Crowd incidents are relatively unorganized; they occur spontaneously, with no widely recognized leaders, and no specific goals.

This demonstration is part of the social movement aimed at producing a nuclear weapons freeze. Organizers of such events hope to attract the mass media, for reports of movement activities may attract additional supporters.

A **social movement** is collective activity that expresses a high level of concern about some issue (Zurcher and Snow 1981). Its members are people who feel strongly enough about an issue to take action. Persons involved in a movement do a tremendous variety of things—talk to family or friends, sign petitions, participate in demonstrations, campaign in particular elections, or donate time and money to their cause. In this sense, a social movement involves a very broad segment of society. Within the movement a **movement organization** may emerge—a group of persons with defined roles who engage in sustained activity to promote or resist social change (Turner and Killian 1972).

The Development of a Movement

PRECONDITIONS. By itself, strain or frustration cannot create a social movement. For a movement to occur, people must perceive their discontent as the result of an inability of society to satisfy their needs. In addition, people must believe they have a moral right to the satisfaction of their unmet expectations (Oberschall 1973). The moral principles used to legitimate their demand may be taken from the culture or from a specific ideology or philosophy. Thus at the core of any social movement are beliefs rooted in the larger society.

A current social movement taking place in the United States involves abortion. On one side are persons who believe that a woman has the right to choose to obtain an abortion under a wide variety of circumstances. This belief is based on the value of individual freedom and a liberal theology. In the late 1960s, an organized social movement attempted to change laws that restricted the availability of abortion. This movement culminated in the Supreme Court decision *Roe* v. *Wade* on January 22, 1973, which held that the state cannot interfere in an abortion decision by a woman and her physician during the first three months of pregnancy. The increasingly widespread availability of abortion created strain for others in our society. Many people view a fetus as a person, and thus define abortion as murder. These people, drawing primarily on conservative Christian theology, organized a countermovement in the mid-1970s to obtain legislation that would sharply restrict a woman's right to abortion.

In addition, people in a social movement must believe that the satisfaction of their needs cannot be achieved through established

channels. Frequently this perception is based on the failure of prior attempts to bring about change via those channels. Studies of the civil rights disturbances in the late 1960s document the importance of this perception.

Given a large population experiencing deprivation, there are four structural conditions that increase the probability a social movement will emerge (Morrison 1971). The first is proximity and interaction among members of that population. This facilitates the emergence of shared definitions and beliefs. Second, people experiencing the same deprivation must be similar in social status; otherwise, the individual is likely to attribute the problem to himself rather than the social environment. Third, there must be a social hierarchy with "visible power differences between the strata" (Morrison 1971). This increases the likelihood that the problem will be attributed to the social structure. Finally, the existence of considerable collective activity creates the perception that concerted effort may help.

IDEOLOGY. As affected individuals interact, an ideology or generalized belief emerges. **Ideology** is a conception of reality that emphasizes certain values and justifies the movement (Turner and Killian 1972; Zurcher and Snow 1981).

The antiabortion or prolife ideology rests on several assumptions. First, each conception is an act of God; abortion thus violates God's will. Second, the fetus is an individual who has a constitutional right to life. Third, every human life is unique, and should be valued by every other human being. Prolife forces view the current status of abortion as temporary, a departure from the past when it was morally unacceptable. Persons and programs (such as sex education) are evaluated in terms of whether they support or undermine these beliefs. Any person or group who favors continued legal abortion is defined as immoral; in many communities, a candidate's position on abortion has been a major political issue. Prolife activists believe that by opposing people and programs that encourage abortion, they

Box 18.3
WHO PARTICIPATES IN RIOTS?

A popular view of disturbances is the so-called "riff-raff theory," which holds that the most alienated persons in society—the young, unemployed, and others with few ties to the community—are the principal participants in riots.

A more systematic analysis (Paige 1971) suggests there are two dimensions that determine an individual's political activity. The first is efficacy, the degree to which people believe they can influence the political system. The second is trust, the degree to which people believe the government will act in their best interest. The combination of these two dimensions produces four different political orientations as depicted below:

		Trust	
		High	*Low*
Efficacy	*High*	Allegiant	Dissident
	Low	Subordinate	Alienated

A person who is high in both trust and efficacy (allegiant) will actively support the existing political system. A person who is high in trust but low in efficacy (subordinate) believes the government is acting in his or her interest, and is a passive supporter of the system. A person who is low on both dimensions (alienated) is unlikely to join social movements due to the belief that he cannot influence the political system. It is the *dissident*—the person who does not trust the present government but believes that he or she can influence political events—who is likely to participate in protest activities.

In order to test this model, Paige studied the racial disturbances that occurred in Newark, New Jersey, in 1967. Interviews were conducted with 233 black males ages 15 to 35. The sample was drawn from areas in which violence and property damage occurred during the disturbance. Within these areas, respondents were randomly selected. They were asked a series of questions designed to measure their degree of trust and efficacy. Those who reported active involvement were most often dissident in orientation. Thus it is not the alienated who are likely to protest, but the persons who distrust the government and believe they can influence the system.

will bring about a sharp decline in its availability, and redefine it as illegitimate.

Such an ideology fulfills a variety of functions (Turner and Killian 1972). First, it provides a way of identifying people and events, and a set of beliefs regarding appropriate behavior toward them. Ideology is usually oversimplified, because it emphasizes one or a small number of values at the expense of others. A second function of ideology is that it gives the movement a temporal perspective. It provides a history (what caused the present undesirable situation), and a conception of the future (what goals can be attained by the movement). Third, it defines group interests and gives preference to them. Finally, it creates villains; it identifies certain persons or aspects of society as responsible for the discontent. This latter function is essential, because it provides the rationale for activity designed to produce change (Oberschall 1973).

Because supporters of a movement share a common ideology, it might seem that they will be very similar in many beliefs. For example, we might expect someone who is opposed to abortion to be opposed to all killing, whether in war or in the context of capital punishment. We would also expect that person to value individual freedom less highly than some other values. We might even expect the person to be Catholic, Republican, and opposed to the Equal Rights Amendment. In fact, such consistency within the person's beliefs is rare. Many feminists are opposed to abortion. Indeed, studies of movement supporters find considerable heterogeneity in their personal beliefs (Marx and Wood 1975). So although movement ideology is important, not all aspects of it are necessarily held by every supporter.

RECRUITMENT. The continuing existence of any movement depends on *recruitment*—the process of attracting supporters. A number of people will be attracted to the movement because they share some distinctive attributes (Zurcher and Snow 1981). In many instances, these are persons who experience the discontent or grievances at the base of the movement. A study comparing people who participated in the movement to prevent the reopening of Three Mile Island nuclear power plant with a group of nonparticipants found that activists had opposed commercial and military uses of nuclear energy before the accident and that the accident served to substantially increase their discontent (Walsh and Warland, 1983). There are limitations to this "grass roots" view of recruitment, however (Turner and Killian 1972). Many studies have found that supporters of a movement are not the most deprived or frustrated. Second, the goals of a movement may not be aimed at removing the sources of the discontent. The content of the ideology reflects several influences, not just a desire to eliminate a particular source of frustration. Once developed, people may be attracted by the ideology who do not share the discontent.

Recruitment depends on two catalysts, the ideology and existing social networks (Zurcher and Snow 1981). The content of the ideology is what attracts supporters. The ideology spreads, at least in part, through existing social networks—supporters communicate the ideology to their friends, families, and co-workers in the course of their ongoing relationships.

The patterns of recruitment in religious movements document the importance of friendship and kinship ties (Stark and Bainbridge 1980). Adherents to the Mormon religion, for example, establish friendship ties with nonmembers, then gradually introduce their beliefs to their friends. Likewise, members of a doomsday cult who believed that the earth would soon be destroyed were in many cases relatives of other members. Those with kinship ties were less likely to leave the cult.

In the past decade, many persons have been "born again,"—that is, become Pentecostals. A recent study compared 150 converts to Catholic Pentecostalism with a control group of non-Pentecostal Catholics who were similar in age, social class, and gender (Heirich 1977). The major difference between the two groups was their social networks. Converts reported that they were introduced to Pentecostalism by a "trusted person," often a teacher, priest, or nun. Catholics who had not converted, however, had not been introduced to Pentecostalism by such a person. Converts were more likely to have received positive or neutral reactions to their initial participation from family and friends. Following their introduction to the Pentecostal movement, converts also tended to seek out other converts and spend less time with friends who were not part of the movement.

Sometimes entire groups are recruited all at once (Oberschall 1973). The civil rights movement in the South in the 1950s is one example. Because of their religious views, black ministers were predisposed to support a movement whose ideology emphasized freedom and equality. These ministers recruited their congregations and communicated the ideology to other ministers. As a consequence, the movement spread rapidly. More recently, the prolife movement has grown by recruiting entire congregations of Catholics and Mormons. Such bloc recruitment is much more efficient than recruiting individuals (Jenkins 1983).

An alternative mechanism of recruitment is the mass media. On 3 October 1970, an estimated 15,000 to 20,000 persons participated in Reverend Carl McIntire's March for Victory

Social movements vary greatly in their impact. The American Nazi Party, led by George Lincoln Rockwell, has never attracted more than a handful of supporters, whereas the Southern Christian Leadership Conference, led by Martin Luther King, Jr., attracted a broad spectrum of people and organizations, and was a major force in bringing about increased opportunity for blacks in American society.

in Washington. McIntire, a fundamentalist pastor who supported the war in Vietnam, communicated his views via a weekly radio program carried by 600 stations and a weekly newsletter. Interviews with 201 March for Victory demonstrators revealed that they held conservative political attitudes. Most had come from outside the Washington area, and the overwhelming majority learned of the march through McIntire's radio program or newsletter (Lin 1974–1975).

Thus, the media play an important role in social movements. In the McIntire case, prior political beliefs appear to have led persons to seek specific information about the organizational program and the march. Media reports convey the movement's ideology, and attract members by providing role models, or by providing information about the time and place of activities. It is no accident that movement groups devote considerable effort in getting television camera crews to cover their activities.

The Development of a Movement Organization

Having attracted supporters, a movement must induce some of them to become committed members (Zurcher and Snow 1981). Commitment involves the creation of links between the individual's interests and those of the movement so that the individual will be willing to contribute actively to the achievement of movement goals. Committed members are necessary if the movement is to become active and self-sustaining. This involves the creation of a movement organization.

A group of persons engaged in sustained activity that reflects the movement's ideology is called a *movement organization.* It occurs through the mobilization of resources to carry out certain tasks.

RESOURCE MOBILIZATION. **Mobilization** is the process through which individuals surrender personal resources and commit them to the pursuit of group goals (Oberschall 1978). Resources can be many things: money or other material goods, time and energy, leadership or other skills, or moral or political authority. From the individual's viewpoint, mobilization involves a rational decision about investing one's resources. The person weighs the costs and benefits of various actions; if the potential rewards seem to outweigh the potential risks, a particular course of action is undertaken.

Leadership is obviously essential to an organization. Taking a leadership role may be risky, but potentially very rewarding (Oberschall 1973). If the movement organization is successful, leaders may attain substantial prestige, visibility, a permanent well-paid position with the organization, and opportunities to interact with powerful, high-status members of society. Leaders are frequently persons with substantial education (such as lawyers, writers, professors, and students) and at least moderate status in society. They are frequently people whose skills cannot be taken away by authorities, who can expect social support, and who will be dealt with leniently if arrested. Thus, their risk–reward ratio is favorable to involvement.

For a movement to succeed, others must also be induced to work actively in the organization (Zurcher and Snow 1981). One basis of commitment is moral, anchoring the individual's world view in the movement's ideology. Members who are attracted primarily by the content of the ideology tend to see their own interests as furthered by the achievement of organizational goals. Many women become involved in proabortion organizations because preserving freedom of choice for all women will benefit them. A second basis of commitment is a sense of belonging. This is facilitated by collective rituals in which members participate. One advantage of recruiting preexisting groups, such as church congregations, is that this sense of belonging is already developed. A third basis of commitment is instrumental. If the organization has enough resources at its disposal, it can provide utilitarian rewards for committed members. These rewards may be distributed equally among members, or selectively to members who make particular contributions (Oliver 1980).

Depending on its overall strategy, a movement organization can use moral, affective, or instrumental rewards as bases for building commitment. These are sufficient for most organizations to induce members to contribute time, materials, and other resources. Still other organizations demand that members commit themselves to exclusive participation. They require that members renounce other roles and commitments, and undergo **conversion,** the process through which an ideology becomes the individual's fundamental perspective. This degree of commitment is required by some religious movements, such as the Unification Church of Reverend Moon. It is also required by "utopian" communities. Conversion is usually accomplished during a period of intensive interaction with other movement members.

ORGANIZATIONAL GROWTH. The social environment is another influence on the development of a movement organization. First, changes in the environment can increase or decrease the size of the movement and the probability of its success. This is illustrated in a study comparing the evolution of the National Farm Labor Union Movement in 1946–55 and the United Farm Workers Movement in 1965–72 (Jenkins and Perrow 1977). Both movements had very similar ideologies and organizational structures. However, whereas the NFLU was generally unsuccessful, the UFW achieved major benefits for many farm workers. The difference was the amount of resource support from the environment, due to a change in the political climate in the United States. An analysis of newspaper articles published during each period indicates that government, liberal political organizations, and organized labor gave much greater support to the United Farm Workers. Thus, challenges to the established order succeed when there is sustained support from the environment and the absence of organized opposition.

Other organizations may cooperate or compete with a movement organization. Cooperation is rare. If organizations have distinct ideologies—for example, if they differ in their acceptance of violence—they will tend to distrust each other. Under some circumstances, however, coalitions may occur, especially when achievement of a major goal seems at hand, and the potential benefits of coordination outweigh the costs (Zald and Ash 1964).

Other influences on the development of a movement organization are internal processes. For example, a movement may experience *factionalization,* the emergence of identifiable subgroups that oppose other subgroups. This in turn may lead to **schismogenesis,** which occurs when a faction splits off or leaves the movement organization. These outcomes are particularly likely when the social base is heterogeneous and when organizational authority is based on doctrine. When the support base is heterogeneous, there is a tendency for persons to seek out others within the movement who are similar and form factions. Similarly, when a movement is based on doctrine, whether religious or political, there is a tendency for disputes over doctrinal issues to result in schisms.

The Seventh Day Adventist Church provides one example of factionalization. The church draws all of its theology from many books written in the 1800s by Ellen G. White.

Most Adventists interpret her books literally, just as many other fundamentalists interpret the Bible as literal truth. Recently, several young Adventist ministers began to question the authenticity of White's writings, in some cases suggesting she borrowed freely from other sources. In 1981, established church leaders demanded that these ministers and their followers leave the church.

Another internal process involves changes in leadership. Over time, as the organization develops, it is subject to increasing routinization. The organization develops an administrative structure. Roles are increasingly filled by secretaries, accountants, and lawyers, rather than by volunteers committed to the movement. This is likely to produce an increasingly conservative stance among the movement's leadership, which may alienate members who are more radical in orientation.

There are several other reasons why social movements often become more conservative over time (Myers 1971). First, the leader–follower relationship is characterized by increasing distance and formality. Second, there is increased bureaucracy—including a role hierarchy, rules and procedures, and membership criteria. Third, there is a tendency for goal displacement to occur; leaders become increasingly concerned with maintaining the organization and less concerned with the goals of the broader movement.

Much more rare is the movement that experiences *radicalization,* like the Committee of 100 in Great Britain (Myers 1971). The Committee was formed to protest the increasing reliance of the British government on nuclear weapons for national defense. From the beginning, the group was committed to the use of civil disobedience to achieve its goals, and this commitment led to greater radicalization rather than conservatism. In general, groups committed to illegal tactics tend to attract members who are more radical. This commitment also produces extreme demands on the time and energy of leaders, which leads to a predominance of younger leaders, who tend to have more energy and fewer competing commitments. Organizations of this type are less likely to achieve their goals, for use of illegal tactics tends to alienate the larger society and reduces the amount of support received. Such tactics may even elicit violence by control agents (Kritzer 1977).

The Consequences of Social Movements

Once a movement has established an ideology, attracted supporters, and developed an organization that embodies its ideals, its ultimate success or failure depends on the reaction of authorities. Those in positions of power—whether political, economic, or religious—can use various strategies in dealing with a social movement (Oberschall 1973).

One obvious strategy is to exercise social control. For example, authorities can control access to social roles; they determine the educational, occupational, or religious roles available. A protesting student may be expelled from school by administrators; a Catholic priest challenging the celibacy rule may be removed from his parish by the bishop. Second, authorities can manipulate material benefits and punishments, which may affect the risk–reward assessments of movement members. Third, authorities can use physical power in the form of police or troops. Of course, in most cases, this method results in violence.

A second general strategy is conciliation. Authorities may open up channels of communication and negotiate in an attempt to resolve grievances. Conciliation is more likely when the movement is relatively powerful and has the support of large numbers or influential members of society. It is also more likely if both sides are highly organized, united internally, and have strong leadership.

Through conciliation, a movement may achieve at least some of its objectives. As a result of negotiation, there may be changes in the distribution of resources or in power relationships. A movement that succeeds in this sense may itself become institutionalized. The changes it brings may ensure a continuing flow of resources that perpetuate the move-

ment organization. This is what happened to the labor, civil rights, and women's movements in the United States.

Summary

Collective behavior is spontaneous, and is subject to norms developed by the participants; these norms are often different from those of society.

COLLECTIVE BEHAVIOR. Most instances of collective behavior involve crowds. Four processes that contribute to crowd behavior are (1) deindividuation: reduced awareness of one's individuality and feelings of responsibility; (2) contagion: the rapid spread through the crowd of visible and often unusual behavior; (3) convergence: the attraction of persons with similar traits to the scene; and (4) emergent norms that define the situation for participants.

Several generalizations can be made about collective behavior. (1) There are three underlying causes: strain, relative deprivation, and grievances. (2) Collective behavior is often triggered by a precipitating event that adversely affects those experiencing strain, deprivation, or grievances. (3) Empirical studies suggest that the severity of a disturbance is influenced by the extent of relative deprivation and the number of potential participants. (4) Once it begins, the course of a collective incident and the likelihood of future disorders are influenced by the behavior of police and other social control agents.

According to Smelser, there are six determinants of collective behavior. They occur in a series of stages and determine the outcome of any collective incident.

SOCIAL MOVEMENTS. A social movement is collective activity that expresses a high level of concern about some issue.

The development of a social movement rests on several factors. (1) People must experience strain or deprivation, believe that they have a right to the satisfaction of their unmet needs, and believe that satisfaction cannot be achieved through established channels. (2) As participants interact, an ideology emerges that justifies collective activity. (3) To sustain the movement, additional people must be recruited by spreading the ideology, often through existing social networks.

A movement organization is a group of persons engaged in sustained activity that reflects the movement ideology. The development of a movement organization depends on: (1) resource mobilization—getting individuals to commit personal resources to the group; (2) the external environment, especially the extent to which outside groups and individuals support the movement; (3) internal processes, such as factionalization and the nature of group leadership.

The ultimate success or failure of a social movement depends on the reactions of authorities—whether those in positions of power attempt to exercise control, or to negotiate and attempt to ameliorate the sources of strain or deprivation.

Key Terms and Concepts

Collective Behavior

Crowd

Deindividuation

Contagion

Rumor

Emergent Norm

Disaster

Relative Deprivation

Precipitating Event

Social Movement

Movement Organization

Ideology

Mobilization

Conversion

Schismogenesis

Appendix

Research Methods in Social Psychology

The purpose of this Appendix is to acquaint you with the research process in contemporary social psychology. Of necessity, it is limited to a few basic issues, and covers only three types of research. The following discussion is oriented toward those who have not had a course in research methods. Its purpose is to provide information that can be used to better understand and evaluate the empirical studies discussed in the text.

Characteristics and Goals of Research

Like other behavioral scientists, social psychologists rely on systematic observation of behavior as a means of better understanding human social relationships. The techniques used to obtain information are numerous and varied. At the same time, they share certain characteristics and objectives. We will discuss these characteristics and objectives in turn.

Characteristics of Social Psychological Research

There are three characteristics of the research conducted by a social psychologist, or by any scientist. First, he or she relies on empirical information. Social scientists attempt to gather information that reflects external events in an accurate and unbiased form. Frequently this information is quantitative, and is used by researchers to evaluate descriptions of or theories about social behavior.

Second, the information is usually gathered according to a *methodology*, a set of systematic procedures. Social psychologists plan in advance how the information will be collected, monitor the process of gathering it, and systematically analyze the data in order to arrive at certain conclusions. Throughout this process, the investigator follows specific procedures. It is very important that the procedures used to collect and analyze data be recorded, so that other researchers can collect information independently, following the same procedures, and attempt to replicate the

findings of the original research. Independent verification is one of the hallmarks of science. Through independent verification, scientific information becomes more reliable and less biased.

A third characteristic of scientific research is the dissemination of scientific data and theories and the consequent scrutiny of this information by others. Scientists share their research and their ideas, both orally at meetings, and in writing. To the extent that people with differing perspectives evaluate their work, biases will be identified and eliminated.

Objectives of Social Psychological Research

Social science research has four specific objectives: description, identification of relationships, determining causal relationships, and the construction and testing of theory.

DESCRIPTION. Frequently the social psychologist wants to learn more about some behavior or social process, and to identify its basic characteristics. The researcher may begin by simply observing ongoing social behavior, noting, for example, the extent to which persons take turns in verbal interaction and how they signal each other that they are finished speaking. Alternatively, the researcher may conduct a survey to determine what percentage of some population holds a particular attitude or engages in particular behaviors. Public opinion polls are used to learn how Americans feel about political candidates and issues, and to study changes in these attitudes over time. Several surveys of sexual behavior in the 1970s have been designed to learn how frequently various sexual activities occur (Hunt 1974).

IDENTIFICATION OF RELATIONSHIPS. A second goal of research is to study the relationship between two or more behaviors or characteristics. We are often interested, for example, in whether one behavioral attribute is associated with others. For example, is engaging in sexual intercourse before marriage more common among Protestants than among Catholics? If the behavior occurs more frequently among members of one religious group compared to others, does it suggest that religion may be related to sexual activity? In fact, Catholics are less likely to have intercourse before marriage than are Protestants (DeLamater and MacCorquodale 1979); this is a descriptive finding from which we could construct an explanation or theory.

DETERMINING CAUSAL RELATIONSHIPS. Perhaps the most common goal of research is to identify the causes of some behavior or social process—such as engaging in premarital intercourse, identifying with the Republican party, or assuming a leadership role in a group. Generally, the social psychologist develops a **hypothesis,** a statement that a specific behavior or event is caused by some other event or social process. Then he or she collects data that can be used to test or evaluate this hypothesis. The best test of a hypothesis is an experiment that manipulates the presumed causal condition, randomly assigns subjects to two or more conditions, and then measures the effect of the manipulation on the behavior in question. Such an ideal test is not always possible, however.

Hypotheses may be drawn from the researcher's intuition. More frequently, however, specific hypotheses are derived from a general theory. For example, several social psychologists have developed theories stating that socioeconomic differences cause major differences in social behavior. One such theory asserts that employment conditions determine a person's values (Kohn 1969). From this general theory, the researcher derives and tests specific hypotheses. One hypothesis, for example, is that working-class men tend to hold more conservative attitudes. This can be used to explain why working-class men are more likely to be Republicans and less likely to engage in premarital intercourse.

CONSTRUCTION AND TESTING OF A THEORY. The ultimate objective in science is to construct a theory that will account for a wide variety of observed relationships. A **theory** is a network of interrelated hypotheses that both explains observed phenomena and can be used as a basis for predictions. We gain confidence in a theory when the predictions it makes are confirmed by empirical data.

The identification of causal relationships and the development of valid theories are important because they allow us to predict future events accurately. That ability, in turn, is essential if we are to have greater control over social events. Some people, for example, wish to increase the frequency of altruistic and conflict-reducing behavior, or to decrease the frequency of interpersonal exploitation and aggression. As social psychological research and theory become more sophisticated, they provide knowledge that can be used to increase control over social behavior, and to improve the social conditions in people's lives.

Research Methods

There are numerous ways of collecting data about social behavior. Social psychologists rely heavily on three methods: surveys, observational procedures, and experiments. We will discuss each of these methods in turn.

Surveys

A **survey** is the gathering of information by asking members of some group of persons a number of questions. Many research projects in social psychology are based on surveys. For example, to test the hypothesis that working-class men have more conservative attitudes, a group of men was asked questions about their occupation and their attitudes (Kohn 1969). The researcher compared the attitudes of white-collar workers such as lawyers with those of blue-collar workers such as automobile assembly-line workers.

TYPES OF SURVEYS. There are two basic types of surveys, the interview and the questionnaire. In the **interview,** one person asks each question and records each of the respondent's answers. The advantage of using an interviewer is that he or she can adjust the questioning to the individual; the interviewer can be alert for both verbal and nonverbal signs that the respondent does not understand a question, and repeat or clarify as necessary. It is also important to be sure that each respondent is asked the same questions. Thus the interviewer usually works from an "interview schedule," which specifies the order and exact wording of questions in advance. In some studies, however, the interviewer is instructed to make sure that certain topics are covered, but is given flexibility in determining the exact order and wording of questions.

In a **questionnaire,** the questions are printed and the respondents read through and answer them at their own pace. No interviewer is used. A major advantage of the questionnaire is that no one else sees the respondent's answers. Thus, a respondent may be more likely to answer truthfully, particularly when the questions deal with embarrassing or threatening topics (Sudman and Bradburn 1974). However, data from two studies suggest that questionnaires do not really have this advantage (Johnson and DeLamater 1976). Using well-trained age peers as interviewers, investigators found no significant differences in the reported sexual behavior of those who were interviewed and those who completed a questionnaire containing identical questions.

There is a clear advantage of questionnaires over interviews in terms of cost. The cost of a national survey, using trained personnel to conduct face-to-face interviews, is about $300 per completed interview. The same survey using questionnaires would cost $50 per completed form. The major disadvantage of questionnaires is in **response rate,** the percentage of those contacted who complete the survey. Whereas an interview study can obtain response rates as high as 80 or 85 percent, mailed questionnaires rarely attain more than a 50 percent response rate. A compromise is the telephone interview, which is becoming more common. It is cheaper than the face-to-face technique (about $75 per interview), but typically achieves a 70 percent response rate.

THE PURPOSE OF A SURVEY. The purpose of a survey is to obtain information from individuals about their own attributes—their attitudes, behavior, and experiences. Surveys are commonly used to determine (1) the frequency (or distribution) of an attribute in the population of interest, and (2) the relationship between two or more attributes of individuals.

Public opinion surveys have become very common in the United States. Several organizations specialize in conducting surveys that are designed to measure the frequency and strength of favorable or unfavorable attitudes toward political figures or candidates. As some observers have pointed out (Halberstam 1979), these polls play a major role in American politics, as public policy and the positions taken by political figures are increasingly influenced at least in part by their results.

Surveys are also used to obtain data relevant to various social problems. Government agencies and individual researchers have conducted surveys on the effects of exposure to pornography, on frequency and patterns of alcohol and other drug use, and on teen-age pregnancy and contraceptive use among teenagers (Zelnik and Kantner 1977). Gathering information about the extent of such phenomena and the social characteristics of persons involved in them is a necessary prerequisite to developing effective social policy.

Finally, surveys have also made significant theoretical contributions to social psychology. Many studies of socialization processes and outcomes, attitude structure and attitude-behavior relationships, psychological well-being, discrimination and prejudice, and collective behavior have used survey methodology.

RELIABILITY AND VALIDITY. Two basic considerations in surveys—as in any type of measurement—are reliability and validity. **Reliability** is the extent to which the same methods and measures produce the same results each time they are employed. Reliability produces consistent results across independent measurements of the same phenomenon. In order for other researchers to carry out the same study, and to replicate the results, investigators must record their research methods exactly. If measures are reliable, they should yield the same results when two independent researchers use them. We obviously need reliable measures if we are to obtain data that are unbiased. There are several ways to assess reliability. The *test-retest method* uses the same measuring instrument on the same population at two different times. A second technique uses several forms of measurement on the same population. For example, to study the psychological well-being of students at one college, we could have one-third of a sample take a personality test, interview another third asking questions about their mental health, and for the remaining third, use health center records to determine how often they seek psychological counseling. In order to assess reliability by comparing the results of the three forms, each must actually measure well-being.

Assuming that a measure is reliable, the next concern is its *validity*; that is, does it measure what we wish to measure? It is relatively easy to determine the validity of a measure of a specific behavior. If a researcher is interested in measuring the frequency of sexual intercourse, for example, the question "How often do you engage in sexual intercourse?" is a valid measure. "How often do you make love?" might not be a valid measure, because some people will not understand that "make love" refers to sexual intercourse. Validity is more problematic when one is attempting to measure an abstract concept such as group cohesiveness. In such cases there is no readily observable referent (no behavior or physical object we can point to); what one measures depends on his or her definition of the concept.

There are two basic aspects of validity, internal and external (Campbell and Stanley 1963). **Internal validity** is the extent to which the measurement technique influences the results. For example, we noted earlier that the presence of an interviewer might influence how a respondent answers questions in a survey. Obviously we wish to minimize such influences, so that measures reflect the actual characteristics of what is being studied and not our procedures for studying it. **External validity** is the extent to which we can generalize the results of a study to other populations and settings. Even though our results may be reliable and internally valid, they may be valid only for the specific group studied. For example, they may apply only to students at a major university, and not to part-time students, or even to students in two-year colleges.

THE QUESTIONS. A major influence on the reliability and validity of a survey is the character of the questions asked. Generally, the more precise the question, the more reliable and valid it will be. A public opinion pollster is often interested in an overall assessment of the president's peformance. Thus, an obvious question would be, "How would you rate President X's performance?" Many people, however, may think of the president's performance in more specific or concrete ways. For example, they may have one evaluation of his performance in foreign affairs ("poor"), a different evaluation of his handling of the economy ("very good"), and yet a third evaluation of his relations with Congress ("average"). If the pollster asks only the general question, the answer will depend on which dimension a respondent has in mind, and different respondents may spontaneously think of different dimensions. Such uncontrolled variation would reduce the reliability of the item and affect its internal validity.

Another consideration is the wording of questions. In general, it is desirable to avoid jargon or specialized terminology unless one is interviewing a group of specialists. Also, the words and grammar employed should be appropriate to the educational level of the respondents. Finally, there is evidence that questions of moderate length elicit more complete answers than very short ones (Sudman and Bradburn 1974).

THE SAMPLE. One of the most important aspects of any survey is the sample of persons questioned. Typically the researcher selects a sample that is representative of some larger group. Suppose the researcher is interested in learning the extent of prejudice toward blacks among white adults in the United States; these white adults constitute the *population* of interest. Because it would be impossible to question all white adults, the researcher must select a *sample*, or subset of that population. The selection process affects the extent to which the results of the survey can be applied to the general population. The type of sample is therefore a major influence on the external validity of the results.

Three types of samples are common in social psychological research. One is the **convenience sample** (also referred to as a "haphazard sample"), which is selected on the basis of availability; the researcher questions persons who happen to be handy. Collecting data from a class of students, for example, yields a convenience sample. Collecting information from students who happen to be in a dormitory or a student union is another example. Street interviews are also common. Here, the researcher may decide to question the first 50 persons who walk by. The appeal of convenience samples is clear. The disadvantage is that the researcher cannot know how representative such a sample is of some larger population. For example, when data are collected from students enrolled in social psychology courses, we do not know whether they differ in important ways from students who do not take such courses. If all of the persons sampled are undergraduates, we may not be able to generalize to graduate students or to persons in the labor force.

In order to ensure that a sample is representative, one can employ a technique called simple random sampling. In drawing a **simple random sample,** the researcher selects units, usually individuals, from the population in such a way that every unit is equally likely to be selected. In order to use this technique, the researcher needs a complete list of members of the population. At a university, for example, a list of all persons taking classes can frequently be obtained from the registrar. At the city or county level, voter registration lists might be employed. A frequent problem, especially when the population being sampled is large, is the absence of a complete list. Under these circumstances, researchers usually fall back on some substitute, such as a telephone directory, but this may introduce bias into the sample. Persons who are poor or who move frequently may not have telephones, and some people choose not to list their numbers in the directory.

Once a complete list is obtained, the researcher selects a sample. A common way to do this is to number the people on the list consecutively and then use a table of random numbers to determine which persons will be in the sample. Once a random sample has been chosen, the researcher must take steps to assure that all the members of the sample are interviewed. In other words, the researcher must maximize the response rate; otherwise, bias may be introduced by differences between people who participate in the study and those who refuse to do so.

In a very large population, there may be too many units to list them all. Under these conditions, researchers frequently employ *stratified sampling* techniques. They group the population according to characteristics known or thought to be important, select a random sample from each group, and then sample some units within the selected groups. Public opinion polls, for example, are designed to represent the entire adult population of the United States. The population is first stratified on the basis of region (South, Northeast, Midwest, Southwest, and West). Next, the population within each region is stratified into urban versus rural; within urban areas, there may be further stratification by size of urban area. The result is a large number of *sampling units*—population groups of known regional and residential type. Some units are then sampled in proportion to their frequency in the population as a whole. Thus one would sample more urban units from the Northeast than from the South or Midwest; conversely, one would select more rural units in the latter regions. Within each unit, persons are selected at random. Using this technique, one can represent the adult population of the United States with a sample of 750 to 1,500 persons.

The stratified sampling technique allows the researcher to obtain data from a large population that is both reliable and valid. Such data have become important sources of information on political attitudes, economic behavior, and other characteristics of Americans. The disadvantage of this method is that only a handful of specific types of persons will be included in the sample. Thus, it will be impossible to compare the attitudes of rural and urban blacks who live in the South using the typical stratified sampling technique.

ADVANTAGES AND DISADVANTAGES OF SURVEYS. Surveys are particularly useful in studying attitudes and social characteristics of populations or of subgroups within populations. They can also be used to develop and test theories about phenomena such as attitude structure and change, and the impact of the mass media. Researchers have frequently used surveys in the study of intergroup relations, ethnicity, and social movements.

We have already discussed the use of surveys in studying social behavior. Here, a word of caution is in order. First, some people do not respond truthfully to questions about their behavior, particularly if the questions deal with their participation in activities that are illegal or otherwise embarrassing to reveal. Although researchers found no significant difference between the reporting of premarital sexual behavior on questionnaires and in interviews (Johnson and DeLamater 1976), they found that 14 percent of the respondents admitted after the interview that they had not told the truth "all of the time." Interestingly, about equal numbers indicated that they had overreported or underreported their sexual activity, so that on the whole, the results were not changed by leaving out the data from the noncandid respondents.

Finally, the relationship between attitudes and behavior is not one of perfect correspondence. In particular, attitudes do not always predict behavior; answers to questions about what the respondent would do in some hypothetical situation cannot be assumed to be a valid indication of behavior. For example, surveys investigating black-white relations have often asked a white respondent what he or she would do if a black family moved into the neighborhood, or if the neighborhood school were integrated. The answers to such questions are more properly considered attitudes, and may not accurately predict what would actually happen if the anticipated event actually occurred.

Observational Research

In contrast to surveys, observational research involves collecting data about ongoing or naturally occurring events. Typically it involves an observer or witness who makes observations of social behavior and records these systematically. Whereas a survey often intrudes on or interrupts ongoing activity, observational research attempts to minimize or eliminate such intrusion, and to study the events of interest *in situ,* as they occur naturally. We will discuss two types of observational research, the case study and the field study.

CASE STUDIES. On a Friday afternoon, at 5:30 P.M., a tornado roared through White County, Arkansas, completely destroying a town of 1,100 people. Altogether, there were 46 deaths, more than 600 injuries, and 3½ million dollars in property damage. Such tragedies are of great interest to some social scientists, who, by studying these events, hope to learn how communities can effectively cope with disaster. Accordingly, a team of four researchers arrived in the area three days later. They interviewed county and other governmental officials. They conducted a survey of residents of the affected areas, and of a control group of people in nonaffected areas. They talked to representatives of various organizations about how their organization was affected by and responded to the disaster. The resulting data from this case study constitutes one of the most comprehensive descriptions available of a community disaster (Barton 1969).

A **case study** is an intensive investigation of one incident or event that seeks to obtain multiple sources of information about the event in question. Interviews may be conducted with key participants, or with some or all of the affected persons, as in the tornado study. Documents such as newspaper and media articles and official records may also be studied. When the event is contemporary, trained observers may record information about it as it occurs. The resulting data are usually rich in detail and reflect a variety of perspectives on what has taken place. Because of this detail, the case study is a good method for obtaining descriptive information. It is often used to initiate research about a topic that has not been extensively studied.

Case studies have frequently been em-

ployed in the study of natural disasters (Drabeck and Stephenson 1978), collective behavior (Kerckhoff, Back, and Miller 1965), and other social phenomena that are unpredictable and of relatively short duration. One of the advantages of this method is that it also can be used to study events that occurred in the past. Thus, it allows the researcher to determine whether a hypothesis or explanation based on current social events can be applied to similar phenomena in historical settings. At the same time, the researcher must recognize that the information available may be highly selective, and may reflect particular biases.

There are two disadvantages to the case study. First, the investigator has little or no control over the type of data available, and is often forced to rely on information collected by others—newspaper and media personnel, public or organizational officials, and the diaries or informal records of participants. Other research methods give the investigator much greater control over what information is collected and in what form.

The other disadvantage is a result of studying only one unit. In most case studies, like the investigation of the tornado disaster, there is no way to determine whether a particular case is representative, so the external validity of any conclusions is essentially unknown. In order to overcome this limitation, a detailed case study may be combined with a survey of a sample of similar events. The case study provides detailed information and the survey helps in assessing the external validity of the findings.

FIELD STUDIES. A **field study** involves collecting data about ongoing activity in everyday settings—in the "field." Most of the data come from one or more "observers," members of the research team who have been trained to observe the activity and record information about it. For example, researchers have observed and recorded data about social interaction among couples in informal settings (Zimmerman and West 1975), between judges and attorneys in the courtroom (Maynard 1983), and between police and juveniles (Piliavin and Briar 1964). One study (Suttles 1968) observed the use of stores, churches, and parks by members of different ethnic groups in one neighborhood, and was able to demonstrate that ethnicity was a major determinant of utilization patterns. Still other studies have observed the reactions of bystanders to emergencies (Piliavin, Rodin, and Piliavin 1969).

Field studies vary in how systematically the information is collected and recorded. In some, observers watch carefully while the phenomenon of interest is occurring and record the information later. The advantage here is that the observer does not arouse the curiosity of participants; the disadvantage is that selective perception and memory may influence what is later recorded. In studies of police-citizen encounters (Black and Reiss 1970) observers coded the interaction—classified each interaction into one of a small number of categories as it occurred. The use of coding categories provides systematic and quantitative data for later analysis. More recently, researchers have used audio or video tape recorders to record interactions, and subsequently coded and analyzed them. Such recordings maximize the information obtained, although interactions may be influenced if participants are aware that they are being recorded.

One specific type of field study is referred to as *participant observation research.* Here, members of the research team play an active role in the ongoing activity and do not engage in coding or other activity that would intrude into the interaction. This approach is preferred by some researchers, particularly those who are interested in the influence of group membership on individuals. These investigators point out that active participation can make the researcher aware of dimensions and meanings that a nonparticipant would overlook. The drawback is that the researchers' own behavior may influence the activity, producing outcomes that would not otherwise occur.

Another type of field study relies on **unobtrusive measures,** techniques that do not intrude on the activity being studied and do not run the risk of eliciting reactions that otherwise might not occur (Webb et al. 1966). For example, physical evidence can be collected relatively unobtrusively. This was demonstrated in an unpublished work by Duncan, who discovered that the rate at which vinyl tiles needed replacement in the Chicago Museum of Science and Industry was a good indicator of the relative popularity of exhibits. These unobtrusive measures may be combined with the more standard techniques for studying social behavior.

Thus, observational techniques allow us to study ongoing activity in real-world settings. They can provide a wealth of information, although their reliability depends on the specific recording techniques used; observations recorded after the fact are generally less reliable than those based on audio or video tape recording on the spot. The internal validity of observational research can be quite high, since the investigator is studying the activity as it occurs in natural settings. The external validity, however, can be problematic, since this type of research frequently employs only one group or organization, or a sample of interactions selected on the basis of convenience.

Experiments

The experiment is the most highly controlled of the research methodologies available to the social psychologist. Two characteristics are essential to experimentation. The first is the researcher's ability to manipulate one or more variables to study their effects; such a variable is referred to as an **independent variable.** The experimenter creates at least two levels of the independent variable(s)—either presence versus absence, or one amount versus another amount. The second characteristic of experimentation is the random assignment of subjects to the "treatment" conditions—that is, to the different levels of the independent variable. **Random assignment** is the placement of subjects in experimental conditions on the basis of chance, such as flipping a coin. It creates groups of subjects that are equivalent, and removes the possibility that the groups will differ in intelligence, personality, motivation, or other qualities that may influence the outcome of the experiment. With random assignment, the investigator can infer that differences in outcome between the groups are due to the differing levels of the independent variable.

In conducting an experiment, both subjects and research team members must be "blind" to the hypothesis of the study and to the treatment condition to which each subject belongs. Experimental subjects bring various motives of their own to the research setting. If they are aware of the hypothesis or of their experimental condition, they may tend either to "cooperate" and behave as they think they are expected to, or to behave contrary to the investigator's expectations. Thus, many experimenters now disguise the nature of the research, providing a plausible but false description of its purpose. In addition, the research team's own expectations can affect outcomes (Rosenthal 1966). They may behave in ways that influence the subjects to confirm their expectations, or they may be influenced in their perceptions of whether the subjects have confirmed them. Thus, it is important either to keep the members of the research team blind to the hypothesis, or to prevent them from communicating with (and inadvertently influencing) the subjects.

In an experiment, researchers manipulate the independent variable in order to observe the effect on another variable—called the **dependent variable**—that they believe will be influenced by this manipulation. Dependent variables can be measured in many ways—through monitors of physiological arousal, by short questionnaires assessing subjects' attitudes, by recording of interactions occurring between subjects, or by scoring the performance of subjects on tasks that are part of the experimental setting. The internal validity of these measures is always of concern to the researcher. In experimental research, there is a good possibility of obtaining valid measures because of the high degree of control exercised by the experimenter. If multiple measures of the dependent variable(s) are taken, and are positively related, the investigator can have greater faith in their internal validity.

Experiments are designed to control all factors other than the independent variable that might affect the outcome. Some factors are controlled by the random assignment of subjects to experimental conditions. Others may be controlled by holding them constant; for example, many experiments employ subjects of the same gender, to eliminate any possible effects of male-female differences. A third type of control is to measure possibly confounding variables. A common measure of performance in experiments is the number of math problems solved correctly; since this measure is influenced by intelligence, the experimenter may measure this confounding variable by giving subjects a brief intelligence test. Any variation in such confounding factors should be taken into account when analyzing the influence of the independent variables.

LABORATORY EXPERIMENTS. Much of the experimentation in social psychology is conducted in the **laboratory,** a setting where the investigator has essentially complete control over the physical surroundings and the subjects' activity. In the laboratory, the investigator can determine what stimuli, tasks, or situations will be presented to subjects and then measure the subjects' responses. In studies of social interaction or group processes, the researcher often restricts or limits the interaction among subjects. Communication may be limited to written notes, whose contents can later be analyzed. This practice eliminates the influence of nonverbal communication. Another common technique is to have each subject interact with the same person(s), a trained "confederate" of the experiment, who the subject believes is another subject. Systematic variation in the behavior of the confederate can then be used to manipulate the independent variable.

Results of laboratory experiments are generally highly reliable. The high degree of control means that the procedures can readily be reproduced, and there is a high probability that the results will be replicated. As noted earlier, laboratory experiments are also characterized by high internal validity because investigators can choose the best measures of the phenomena of interest. Given these characteristics, laboratory experimentation is the best method for testing causal hypotheses. With other variables controlled, the independent variable can be carefully manipulated, and its effects reliably measured. Thus differences between treatment groups on the dependent variable measures can be unambiguously attributed to the independent variable.

External validity is a concern in many laboratory experiments. In order to control and measure variables, the experimenter creates an artificial situation for which there are no comparable real-life settings. Consider the following experiment which sought to determine the influence of certain independent variables on whether one person will help another in an emergency (Darley and Latané 1968). Men and women were recruited to come to the laboratory to participate in a discussion of problems encountered by students in adjusting to the university. Each subject was placed in a separate room, and asked to communicate with other subjects via intercom. The independent variable was the number of other persons

who the subject believed were participating in the discussion. Subjects were told there were one, two, or five other participants; this was the manipulation of the independent variable. The discussion proceeded with each "participant" speaking in turn; in fact, the subject was hearing a tape recording of the appropriate number of persons speaking. One of these recorded voices admitted that he was subject to nervous seizures. In his second turn, he started to speak normally, but his speech suddenly became disorganized, there were choking sounds, and then silence. The dependent variable was whether the subject would leave the room to help, and how quickly he or she did so. The results verified the hypothesis that the larger the number of witnesses, the less likely a subject was to offer help.

This carefully controlled experiment allows an unambiguous test of the hypothesis. However, most people rarely encounter a situation in which they interact via intercom with others located in individual rooms. Thus it is not clear whether we can generalize these findings to everyday situations. The relationship between the number of others present and the person's reaction may be different in more complex situations, where other variables may influence behavior. In this sense, external validity is problematic for many laboratory experiments.

FIELD EXPERIMENTS. To obtain greater external validity, researchers turn to the **field experiment,** which involves manipulating one or more independent variables in an everyday setting and measuring one or more dependent variables. The advantage of this technique is that it allows manipulation of variables to occur within ongoing natural situations.

Following the laboratory experiment by Darley and Latané, a team of researchers conducted a field experiment on helping behavior to determine in part whether laboratory findings could be generalized to "real-life" settings (Piliavin, Rodin, and Piliavin 1969). In this field experiment, researchers staged the collapse of a "victim" on subway trains in New York City. Independent variables included race of victim (black or white) and whether the victim appeared to be drunk or ill. Two observers on the train recorded data about the characteristics and reactions of passengers. One of the variables they considered was the number of bystanders, which is analogous to number of participants in the laboratory experiment described earlier. Results of this field study did *not* show a decrease in the likelihood of someone's helping as the number of bystanders increased. Both this and other data from their experiment did not confirm those obtained in the laboratory. An important difference in this experiment, however, was the fact that both the victim and the other bystanders were visible to the "subject," whereas there was no visual contact in the laboratory study.

The comparison of these two studies is instructive. First, we see that results obtained in the field may be different from those obtained in the laboratory. Thus, there are apparent limits to the external validity of the findings of the laboratory experiment. Second, the difference may or may not be due to the difference in control which characterizes the two settings. If the high degree of control in the laboratory happens to eliminate a variable that is important in natural settings (like the visibility of the "victim"), then, in order to generalize to other settings, researchers will need to take the eliminated variable into account. Third, the researchers on the subway had much less control over who participated in their study. Their subjects were New York subway riders, who may differ in important but unmeasured ways from college students.

In addition to greater external validity, field experiments sometimes have the advantage of employing unobtrusive measures. That is, in some field experiments, participants are unaware that they are subjects, so they respond naturally to experimental conditions, including the manipulation of variables. At

the same time, there are several problems inherent in field experiments. First, the experimenter is usually not able to randomly assign subjects to conditions. Second, because subjects are usually a convenience sample, care must be taken to try to obtain typical groups. Third, the researcher has much less control over the situation than would be the case in a laboratory setting. For this reason, experimenters must carefully analyze the field setting in advance and plan their research to make sure it fits appropriately into the natural setting. The nature of the setting and of the activity will limit the manipulations and measurements that can be carried out. Finally, the investigators in the field are limited to recording overt behavior; they frequently cannot utilize precise measurement techniques such as physiological measures and attitude scales. This may reduce both the reliability and the internal validity of the resulting measures.

Ethical Issues in Social Psychological Research

In the past 20 years there has been growing concern about ethical issues in research. Specifically, a consensus has developed among investigators and other persons and agencies affiliated with the scientific community that subjects who participate in research have certain rights that must be protected. In some cases, protecting those rights requires investigators to limit or modify research practices.

Discussion of ethical issues focuses on several sources of potential harm to subjects—both physical and psychological—and on steps that can or should be taken to minimize its occurrence.

Potential Sources of Harm

PHYSICAL HARM. Exposure to physical harm is usually not a factor in social psychological research, although there are exceptions. Studies designed to measure the effects of stress sometimes utilize the exercise treadmill or the cold pressor test, where subjects immerse one hand in a mixture of ice and water, as means of inducing stress. As precautions, prospective subjects should be thoroughly screened for relevant medical problems, and any risks should be made known to them so that they can decide whether they might be harmed by participating in the experiment. Finally, in experiments involving physical stress, investigators should carefully monitor participants for adverse effects throughout the research.

PSYCHOLOGICAL HARM. A more common risk in social psychological research is psychological harm to subjects. This is most likely to occur as a result of subjects receiving negative information about themselves in the course of the study. For example, a common experimental manipulation is to give subjects false feedback about their physical attractiveness, others' reactions to them, or their performance on experimental tests or tasks. Such feedback can be used to raise or lower self-esteem, induce feelings of acceptance or rejection by others, or create perceptions of success or failure on important tasks. These are powerful manipulations precisely because they do affect the subject's self-perception. Negative feedback may cause psychological stress or harm, at least temporarily. For this reason, some investigators believe that such techniques should not be employed in research. Others, however, believe that they should be used only where alternative, less potentially harmful manipulations are not available. When false feedback is provided, it is important to minimize the time between providing it and giving the subject a thorough *debriefing*, providing him or her with a full description of the experiment and emphasizing the falsity of the feedback.

Another potential source of psychological harm lies in inducing a subject to engage in behavior which, upon reflection, may have a negative impact on his or her self-image. A commonly cited example is Milgram's research (1965), in which subjects were asked to follow the experimenter's instructions and administer what they believed to be increasingly strong electric shocks to another person. Many subjects persisted even after the victim indicated that he had a heart condition and demanded to be released from the apparatus. Even though subjects were subsequently debriefed and informed that no shocks were actually received by the "victim," they were faced with the recognition that they did comply with the experimenter's orders to administer shock. Some people have suggested that it may have caused these subjects considerable anguish to be made aware of their capacity to behave in this manner (Baumrind 1964). Again, a postexperimental debriefing that emphasizes the ways in which the subject was *induced* to comply, as well as checkups on subjects following the experiment, are recommended safeguards.

BREACH OF CONFIDENTIALITY. Confidentiality is a special issue in survey and observational research. Interviewers and observers are frequently in a position to identify participants, and may recall details of their answers to questions or of their behavior. It is important that they maintain the confidentiality of such data, especially in surveys inquiring about sexual or other behaviors whose disclosure could be damaging to respondents, or in observational studies of deviant or criminal activities. An important precaution is to avoid using as research team members persons who are apt to have social contacts with respondents. In addition, it is desirable not to attach identifying information such as names and addresses to data after it has been collected. Identifying information should also be kept separate from questionnaires or behavioral records to prevent later breaches of confidentiality.

Observational and case study research often deals with a specific group or organization. In the course of their investigations, researchers may gather a great deal of information both about the organization itself and about various members. When the findings are reported, the organization is typically assigned a pseudonym, and members are referred to by role only. This usually suffices to prevent outsiders from identifying the unit and its members, although it may not prevent members from identifying each other. There are obvious risks to members' positions, reputations, or jobs within the organization if certain kinds of information become known to other members.

SOCIAL HARM. Still another area of concern is the potential of research to harm entire groups or segments of society. There has been a great deal of research in recent years on ethnic minorities in the United States. Research on differences between blacks and whites in intelligence, family structure, and academic success is potentially useful as a basis for social policy. But there is no guarantee that data on blacks or other minorities will be used to design better educational and job training programs. This data could also be used to *restrict* the access of blacks to better educational institutions and jobs. Although no one has yet advocated curtailing research that may adversely affect some groups, there is heated debate over researchers' responsibilities for the utilization of their findings.

Minority groups are also becoming increasingly aware of the potential for social science data to cause them harm. Both blacks and American Indians have become much more concerned about the researcher's purposes and the possible consequences of participating in a study. In some cases, members of these groups are demanding greater or even primary control of the dissemination of results and the process of data gathering.

Informed Consent

Increasingly, the major safeguard against risk is the requirement that informed consent be obtained from all individuals, groups, or organizations who participate in research studies. **Informed consent** means that potential participants have been told what their participation will involve, and that researchers have obtained their voluntary consent to participate. Specifically, six elements are essential to informed consent. First, potential subjects are entitled to a brief description of the procedures to be employed; they need not be told the purpose or hypothesis of the research. Second, they should be given information about foreseeable risks that participation may entail, as well as about any benefits they may receive. Third, participants should be told to what extent the information they provide will be kept confidential; if possible, they should be given a guarantee that confidentiality or anonymity will be maintained. Fourth, investigators should include information about what medical or psychological resources, if any, are available to subjects who are adversely affected by participation. Fifth, researchers should offer to answer questions, whenever possible. Finally, potential subjects should be informed that they have the right to terminate their participation at any time. In many survey and case-study settings, informed consent is implemented by orally providing subjects with this information. In experiments, especially those involving some risk to subjects, investigators often obtain written consent from each participant.

There is increasing acceptance in the social sciences of the principle that all potential participants in research should be given the opportunity to exercise judgment about whether to participate. In general, the mechanisms of documenting informed consent have served to make investigators more aware that their relationships with participants are interactive rather than unilateral, and that participants have rights that cannot be ignored in the interest of science.

Key Terms and Concepts

Hypothesis

Theory

Survey

Interview

Questionnaire

Response Rate

Reliability

Internal Validity

External Validity

Convenience Sample

Simple Random Sample

Case Study

Field Study

Unobtrusive Measures

Independent Variable

Random Assignment

Dependent Variable

Laboratory Experiment

Field Experiment

Informed Consent

Glossary

Access Display A signal (verbal or nonverbal) by one person to another that further social interaction is permissible.

Accounts Explanations people offer in order to repair damaged identities and disrupted interactions after they have performed acts that threaten their social identities. Accounts take two forms—excuses that minimize one's responsibility, and justifications that redefine acts in a more socially acceptable manner.

Achievement Motive A conscious or unconscious desire to reach high standards of excellence.

Activation (of an attitude) The bringing of an attitude from memory into conscious awareness.

Active Minority In groups, a set of individuals who adopt a distinct viewpoint on some important issue(s) and who try to persuade the majority to change its position.

Actor-Observer Difference The bias in attribution in which actors tend to see their own behavior as due to characteristics of the external situation, whereas observers tend to attribute actors' behavior to the actors' internal, personal characteristics.

Additive Model Theoretical model for combining information about individual traits in order to predict how favorable the overall impression people form of another person will be. This model adds together the favorability values of all the single traits people associate with the person. (See *averaging model* and *weighted averaging model*.)

Additive Task A type of unitary group task in which the group's performance is equal to the sum (or average) of the performances of its members.

Ageism Prejudice and discrimination against the elderly based on negative beliefs about aging.

Aggression Behavior intended to harm another person; behavior the target would want to avoid.

Alienation The sense that one is uninvolved in the social world or lacks control over it.

Aligning Actions Actions people use to define their apparently questionable conduct as actually in line with cultural norms, thereby repairing social identities, restoring meaning to situations, and reestablishing smooth interaction.

Altercasting The tactics people use to impose roles and identities on others that complement the roles and identities they wish to claim for themselves.

Altruism Voluntary, self-sacrificing behavior intended to benefit another with no expectation of external reward.

Anomie Theory The view that deviant behavior occurs when people striving to attain culturally valued goals find that they do not have access to the legitimate means of achieving these goals.

Anticipatory Socialization Activities that provide people with knowledge, skills, and values of a role they have not yet assumed. Anticipatory socialization differs from explicit training because it is not intentionally designed as role preparation by socialization agents.

Attachment A warm, close relationship with an adult that provides infants with a sense of security and stimulation.

Attitude A predisposition to respond to a particular object in a generally favorable or unfavorable way.

Attitudinal Similarity The sharing by two people of beliefs, opinions, likes, and dislikes.

Attractiveness Stereotype The belief that "what is beautiful is good"; the assumption than an attractive person possesses other desirable qualities.

Attribution The processes of judgment that link behavior to its causes—to the intentions, dispositions, and events that explain why people act as they do.

Authoritarian Leadership A style of leadership in which the leader exercises a great deal of control; this may include determining policies, selecting goals, assigning tasks, and administering rewards.

Authority The capacity to influence group members by invoking rights that are vested in one's role.

Autokinetic Effect A physical phenomenon in which a stationary pinpoint of light in a dark room appears to move.

Availables Those persons with whom we come into contact, however fleeting, who constitute the pool of potential friends and lovers.

Averaging Model A theoretical model for combining information about individual traits in order to predict how favorable the overall impression people form of another person will be. This model averages the favorability values of all the single traits people associate with a person. (See *additive model* and *weighted averaging model*.)

Aversive Event In intergroup relations, a situation or event caused by (or attributed to) an outside group that produces negative or undesirable outcomes for members of the target group.

Back Channel Feedback The small vocal and visual comments a listener makes while a speaker is talking, without taking over the speaking turn. It includes responses such as "Yeah," "Huh?," head nods, brief smiles, and completions of the speaker's words. Back channel feedback is crucial in order to coordinate conversation smoothly.

Balanced State The state in which the relationships among three cognitive elements are all positive, or in which one is positive and the other two are negative.

Bargaining A process of interaction in which two or more persons with different preferences make a sequence of concessions in an attempt to reach an agreement that is mutually acceptable.

Bargaining Range In bargaining, the difference between the limit of person A and the limit of person B; the set of possible outcomes that might result from bargaining.

Bilateral Threat In bargaining, a situation in which both bargainers can issue threats and inflict punishments on one another.

Birth Cohort A group of people born during the same period of one or several years who are consequently exposed to particular historical events at approximately the same age.

Body Language (kinesics) Communication through the silent motion of the face and body—scowls, smiles, nods, gazing, gestures, leg movements, postural shifts, caressing, slapping, and so on.

Bystander Effect The tendency for each bystander in an emergency to help less often and less quickly as the number of bystanders present increases.

Career A sequence of roles, each with its own set of activities. People's most important careers are in the domains of work, family and friends, and education.

Case Study An intensive investigation of one incident or event, that seeks to obtain multiple sources of information about the event in question.

Catharsis The reduction of aggressive arousal brought about by performing aggressive acts. The catharsis hypothesis states that we can purge ourselves of hostile emotions by intensely experiencing these emotions while performing aggressive acts.

Causal Schemata Preconceptions of "what causes what" that people use to fill in missing information in order to make causal attributions.

Cognitions The elements of cognitive structure.

Cognitive Dissonance A state of psychological tension induced by dissonant relationships between cognitive elements.

Cognitive Process The mental activities of an individual, including perception, memory, reasoning, problem solving, and decision making.

Cognitive Structure Any form of organization among a person's cognitions.

Cognitive Theory A theoretical perspective based on the premise that an individual's mental activities (perception, memory, reasoning) are important determinants of behavior.

Collective Behavior Emergent and extrainstitutional behavior; behavior that is often spontaneous and subject to norms created by the participants.

Communication The process whereby people transmit information about their ideas and feelings to each other.

Communication Network The pattern of communication opportunities in groups; typical communication networks include the comcon, the wheel, the circle, the chain, and so on.

Communicator Credibility In persuasion, the extent to which the communicator is perceived by the target audience as a believable source of information.

Comparison Level A standard used to evaluate the outcomes of a relationship, based on an average of the person's experiences in past relevant relationships.

Comparison Level for Alternatives The level of profit available to an individual in his or her best alternative relationship. A standard specifying the lowest level of outcomes a person will accept in light of available alternatives.

Competition In groups, a reward structure that pits members against one another in an attempt to gain scarce rewards for themselves.

Concession Magnitude In bargaining, the average size of a bargainer's concessions.

Conditioning A process of learning in which a person performs a particular response and, through reinforcement, the response is strengthened.

Conformity Adherence to group norms; behavior within the range of tolerable behavior.

Conjunctive Task A type of unitary group task in which the group's performance depends entirely on that of its weakest or slowest member.

Connotative meaning The personal associations and emotional responses than an individual has to a word or object.

Consensus In person perception, information used in making attributions about a behavior that refers to whether all or only a few people perform that behavior. Consensus among actors is high when everyone performs the behavior, suggesting that the particular actor is not causally important.

Conservative Coalition In groups, a union of medium- and low-status members who support the existing leadership and status order against revolutionaries.

Consistency Information used in making attributions about a behavior that refers to whether the actor behaves the same way at different times and in different settings. Consistency is high when the actor performs the same behavior regardless of conditions, suggesting that the context is not causally important.

Consistency Theory The view hypothesizing that if inconsistency develops among cognitions, people are motivated to restore harmony among them.

Contagion In a group, the rapid spread of visible and often unusual symptoms or behavior.

Contingency Model of Leadership Effectiveness A theory of leadership effectiveness (proposed by Fiedler) which maintains that group performance is a function of the interaction between a leader's style (task-oriented or relationship-oriented) and various situational factors such as the leader's personal relationships with members, the degree of task structure, and the leader's position power.

Convenience Sample A set of respondents or subjects selected on the basis of ready availability, such as students enrolled in a class.

Conversion The process by which the ideology of a social movement becomes the individual's fundamental perspective.

Cooling Out A response to an individual's repeated or glaring failures to present an appropriate identity, in which the offender is eased into accepting a less desirable, though reasonable, alternative identity.

Cooperation In groups, a reward structure in which group members are functionally interdependent (no member can achieve the group goal alone) and in which members' interests are linked in the sense that no one achieves a reward unless they all do.

Cooperative Principle An assumption conversationalists ordinarily make that a speaker is behaving cooperatively by trying to be (1) informative (giving as much information as is necessary and no more), (2) truthful, (3) relevant to the aims of the ongoing conversation, and (4) clear (avoiding ambiguity and wordiness).

Co-optation In groups, a strategy by which an existing leader singles out one or several lower-status members for favored treatment; this is done to weaken the bonds among lower-status persons who might otherwise form revolutionary coalitions.

Crowd A substantial number of persons, usually strangers, who engage in behavior recognized as unusual by participants and observers.

Cultural Estrangement The rejection of the basic values and life styles available in a culture.

Death Instinct According to Freud, the innate urge to destroy that constantly generates hostile impulses demanding release. This is an instinctual basis for aggression.

Deficit Theories The view that members of disadvantaged groups are cognitively inferior and bound to perform poorly on intellectual tasks because their style of speech is less suited to logical reasoning and abstract thought.

Definition of the Situation In symbolic interactionist theory, a person's interpretation of a situation and the objects in it; an agreement among interacting persons about who they are, what their behaviors mean, and what actions are appropriate in the setting.

Deindividuation The temporary loss of self-awareness and of a sense of personal identity brought on by such situational conditions as anonymity, an undifferentiated crowd, darkness, and consciousness-altering drugs.

Democratic Leadership A style of leadership in which the leader encourages group discussion and shares decision-making prerogatives with members.

Denotative Meaning The literal, explicit properties associated with a word as defined in a dictionary. Unlike the connotative meaning of a word, which varies depending on who is defining it, the denotative meaning is shared by most people.

Dependent Variable In an experiment, the variable that is measured to determine whether it is affected by the manipulation of one or more other (independent) variables.

Deterrence Hypothesis The view that the arrest and punishment of some individuals for violation of laws deters others from committing the same violations.

Deviant Behavior Any behavior that violates the norms that apply to a given situation or that define a given role.

Deviant Subculture A group of people whose norms encourage participation in a specific form of deviance and who regard positively those who engage in such deviance.

Diffusion of Responsibility The process of accepting less personal responsibility to act because that responsibility is with others. Diffusion of responsibility among bystanders in an emergency is one reason why bystanders sometimes fail to help.

Disaster An event that produces widespread physical damage or destruction of property, accompanied by social disruption.

Disclaimers Verbal assertions people use before acting in ways they anticipate will be disruptive, in order to deflect any negative implications the actions may have for their social identities. Disclaimers plead that the situation is extraordinary or that the actions do not reflect importantly on one's crucial identities.

Discrepant Message In persuasion, a message advocating a position that is different from what the target believes.

Discrimination Actions which harm members of another group or bar them from opportunities.

Disengagement Theory A theory of adjustment to aging asserting that withdrawal from social commitments is inevitable with aging, and that withdrawal promotes satisfaction with life because it frees up time and energy for introspection.

Disjunctive Task A type of unitary group task in which the group's performance depends entirely on that of its strongest or fastest member.

Displacement The release of pent-up anger in the form of aggression against a target other than the original source of anger.

Display Rules Culture-specific norms for modifying facial expressions of emotion to make them compatible with the social situation.

Dissonance Effect The greater the reward or incentive for engaging in counterattitudinal behavior, the less the resulting attitude change.

Distinctiveness Information used in making attributions about a behavior that refers to whether the actor behaves toward an object in a manner similar to or different from his or her behavior toward other objects. Distinctiveness is low when the actor behaves in the same manner toward various objects, suggesting that the particular object is not causally important.

Divisible Task A group task in which members perform different, although complementary, activities.

Dyadic Withdrawal Increasing reliance on one person for gratifications and decreasing reliance on others.

Elaborated Code A relatively abstract speech style attuned to the characteristics of the particular listener that allows for subtle differences in meaning by employing qualifications and extended perspectives on time and events. Used in relationships that tend toward flexible, personal social control.

Eligibles Persons who are both appropriate (as defined by social norms) and desirable (as defined by personal preferences) for a particular kind of relationship.

Embarrassment The feeling people experience when interaction is disrupted because the identity they have claimed in an encounter is discredited.

Emergent Norm The definition of the situation that results from interaction in an initially ambiguous situation.

Emotion Work Attempts to change the intensity or quality of one's feelings to bring them in line with the requirements of the occasion. Emotion work may be used to evoke feelings that are not present but should be (psyching oneself up), or to suppress feelings that are present but should not be (calming oneself down).

Empathy Responding emotionally to another person as if we ourselves were in his or her situation; feeling pleasure at another's pleasure or pain at another's pain.

Endorsement An attitude held by a group member indicating the extent to which he or she supports the group's leader.

Equitable Relationship A relationship in which the outcomes received by each person are equivalent.

Equity A state of affairs that prevails in a dyad or group when people receive rewards in proportion to the contributions they make.

Ethnocentrism In intergroup relations, the tendency to take one's own group as the center of everything and to evaluate other groups with reference to it.

Evaluation Apprehension Concern about what others expect of one and how others will evaluate one's behavior. Evaluation apprehension inhibits helping by bystanders when they fear others will view their intervention as foolish. It promotes helping when bystanders believe others expect them to help.

Exchange An interaction in which person A gives person B something that B values in exchange for B giving A something that A values.

External Validity The extent to which we can generalize the results of one study to other populations and settings.

Extrinsic Motivation Motivation to engage in behavior in order to obtain an external reward such as food or money or praise.

Feedback The information received by a person or group indicating whether progress toward goal attainment is satisfactory.

Feeling Rules Social rules that dictate what a person with a particular public identity ought to feel in a given situation.

Field Experiment An experiment that involves manipulating one or more independent variables in an everyday setting and measuring one or more dependent variables.

Field Study Research involving the collection of data about ongoing activity in everyday settings.

Focus of Attention Bias The tendency to overestimate the causal impact of whomever or whatever our attention is focused on.

Formal Social Control Agencies that are given responsibility for dealing with violations of rules or laws.

Frame The type of social occasion people recognize they are engaged in as they interact. Weddings, job interviews, and archeological digs are examples of frames of interaction. Each frame is governed by a set of stable, widely known rules or conventions.

Front and Back Regions Settings used in managing appearances. In front regions people carry out interaction performances and exert efforts to maintain appropriate appearances. In back regions they allow themselves to violate appearances while they prepare, rehearse, and rehash performances

Frustration The blocking of goal-directed activity. According to the frustration-aggression hypothesis, frustration leads to aggression.

Fundamental Attribution Error The tendency to underestimate the importance of situational influences and to overestimate personal, dispositional factors as causes of behavior.

Gender Role The behavioral expectations associated with gender.

Generalized Other A conception of the attitudes held in common by the members of the organized groups with whom one interacts.

Goal Consensus In groups, a state of affairs in which a substantial portion of members agree on the group's goal and accept the desirability of trying to achieve it.

GRIT A strategy for reducing intergroup conflict whereby one side initiates de-escalatory steps in the hope that the other side eventually will reciprocate; GRIT is an acronym for Graduated and Reciprocal Initiatives in Tension-reduction.

Group A set of persons who are related to one another as parts of a system.

Group Cohesiveness The extent to which persons are attracted to a group and want to be members of it.

Group Goal A desirable outcome that group members strive collectively to bring about.

Group Polarization In group decision making, the tendency for group members to shift their opinions toward a position that is similar to, but more extreme than, the position they held prior to group discussion; both the risky shift and the cautious shift are instances of group polarization.

Group Productivity The output or end state resulting from group activity.

Groupthink A mode of thinking within a cohesive group whereby pressures for unanimity overwhelm the members' motivation to appraise alternative courses of action realistically.

Halo Effect The tendency to perceive personalities as clusters of either good or bad traits that leads people to generalize that individuals are good or bad based on knowing only about one or a few of their traits.

Helping Any behavior intended to benefit another person. Also called *prosocial behavior,* because helping has positive social consequences and is approved by prevailing social standards.

Hypothesis A statement that a specific behavior or event is caused by some other event or social process.

Identification Display A signal (verbal or nonverbal) that we believe the other person is a potential partner in a specific kind of relationship.

Identities The categories people use to specify their sense of who they are, their position in the world relative to others, and what they can do.

Identity Degradation A response to repeated or glaring failures to present an appropriate identity in which the offender's current identity is destroyed and he or she is transformed into a "lower" social type.

Ideology In the study of social movements, a conception of reality that emphasizes certain values and justifies the movement.

Imbalanced State The state in which the relationships among three cognitive elements are all negative, or in which two are positive and one is negative.

Imitation A process of learning in which the learner watches another person's response and observes whether that person receives any reinforcement.

Implicit Personality Theories Assumptions people hold about how personality traits are related to one another, which ones go together and which do not. These theories are implicit because people do not subject them to explicit examination nor do they ordinarily know their contents.

Impression Management The intentional use of tactics aimed at manipulating the images others form of us.

Incentive Effect The greater the incentive for engaging in counterattitudinal behavior, the greater the resulting attitude change.

Independent Variable In an experiment, the variable manipulated by the investigator in order to study the effect on one or more other (dependent) variables.

Informal Social Control The reactions of family, friends, and acquaintances to rule violations by individuals.

Informational Influence In groups, a form of influence that occurs when a group member relies on other members to provide information about reality.

Informed Consent Voluntary consent by an individual to participate in a research project based on information about what participation will entail.

Ingratiation The deliberate use of deception to increase a target person's liking for us in hopes of gaining tangible benefits the target person controls. It includes such techniques as flattery, expressing agreement with the target person, and exaggerating one's admirable qualities.

In-Group In intergroup relations, one's own membership group; contrasted with the out-group.

Institutionalization of Deviance The process by which members of a group come to expect and support deviance in another member.

Instrumental Learning The acquisition of behavior based on the rewards or punishments that the learner experiences following performance of the behavior.

Integrative Proposal In bargaining, a proposition or alternative that reconciles bargainers' divergent interests by providing high benefits to both of them.

Interaction Process Analysis (IPA) A coding system of 12 categories used to measure and analyze communication patterns and processes in groups.

Intergroup Conflict A situation in which groups take antagonistic actions toward one another in order to control some outcome important to them.

Intergroup Contact Hypothesis A theoretical perspective asserting that, in intergroup relations, increased interpersonal contact between groups will reduce stereotypes and prejudice, and consequently reduce antagonism between groups.

Internalization The process through which behavioral standards initially external to the person become internal and subsequently guide the person's behavior.

Internal Validity The extent to which the measurement techniques employed in a study influences the results obtained.

Interpersonal Attraction The development of a relationship based on liking, loving, and mutual respect.

Interpersonal Spacing (proxemics) The ways people position themselves at varying distances and angles from others. Interpersonal spacing communicates feelings and ideas nonverbally. It is also known as *proxemics* because it refers to the proximity of people to each other.

Interview A research method in which one person asks questions of another and records each of the respondent's answers.

Intrinsic Motivation The motivation to engage in a behavior in order to achieve an internal state that an individual finds rewarding.

Labelling Theory The view that reactions by others to a rule violation are an essential element in deviance.

Laboratory Experiment An experiment conducted in a setting where the investigator has essentially complete control over the physical surroundings and the subject's activity.

Laissez-faire Leadership A style of leadership in which the leader adopts a "hands off" aproach and relates to members in a friendly but nondirective manner.

Leadership In groups, the enactment of several functions necessary for successful group performance; these functions include planning, organizing, and controlling the activity of group members.

Learning Structure An environment in which the individual can learn the information and skills required to enact a role.

Level of Aspiration In bargaining, the highest price that a person realistically hopes to get for his or her product or service. In group decision making, the level of difficulty of the goal(s) that group members agree to pursue.

Life Cycle Squeeze Periods in the life course when financial and family burdens are great while job status and rewards are low, producing an unfavorable balance between aspirations and resources. Life cycle squeeze tends to be greatest for couples with preschool children.

Life Event An event marking a transition point in the life course (such as leaving home for college) that activates coping and readjustment.

Likert Scale A measure of attitudes which asks the respondent to indicate the extent to which he or she agrees with each of a series of statements about the object.

Limit In bargaining, the lowest price that a person will accept for his product or service.

Linguistic Competence Knowing the associations among sounds and meanings in a language and the implicit rules for generating and understanding grammatically acceptable sentences.

Linguistic Relativity Hypothesis The hypothesis proposed by Whorf (1956) that language shapes ideas and guides the individual's mental activity. In a strong form it holds that people cannot perceive distinctions absent from their language. In a weak form it holds that languages facilitate thinking about events and objects that are easily codable or symbolized in them.

Linguistic Universals Features that are present in all languages, such as nouns, verbs, terms for distance, and time.

Matching Hypothesis The view that each person seeks a mate who is of approximately the same level of desirability.

Meaning In symbolic interactionist theory, the implications that an object or thing has when judged in terms of a person's plan of action.

Meaninglessness The sense that what is going on around us is incomprehensible; the absence of a definition of the situation.

Media Campaign A systematic attempt by an influencing source to use the mass media to change attitudes and beliefs of a target audience.

Mere Exposure Effect Repeated exposure to the same stimulus produces positive attitude toward it.

Midlife Crisis A stage in the transition into middle age when people presumably become aware that time is running short, that they must make changes in their personal relationships, their work, and themselves now, or else it will be too late.

Mobilization The process through which individuals surrender personal resources and commit them to the pursuit of group or organizational goals.

Moral Development The process through which children become capable of making moral judgments.

Motive A disposition within the person that produces behavior directed toward goals.

Motive Talk Verbal statements people make to explain the motives that supposedly underlie their behavior.

Movement Organization A group of persons with defined roles who engage in sustained activity to promote or resist social change.

Norm In groups, a statement or rule specifying how members are expected to behave under given circumstances. Expectations concerning which behaviors are acceptable and which behaviors are unacceptable for specific persons in specific situations.

Normative Influence In groups, a form of influence that occurs when someone conforms to group norms in order to receive the rewards and/or avoid the punishments that are contingent on adherence to these norms.

Normative Life Stage A discrete period in the life course during which individuals are expected to perform the set of activities associated with a distinct age-related role.

Normlessness The belief that socially disapproved behavior is necessary to achieve one's goals.

Norm of Homogamy A social norm requiring that friends, lovers, and spouses be characterized by similarity in age, race, religion, and socioeconomic status.

Observational Learning The acquisition of behavior based on observation of another person's behavior and of its consequences for that person.

Opinion Molecule An isolated cognitive unit consisting of a fact, a feeling (evaluation), and a following (a sense that others agree with the fact).

Opportunity Structure Opportunities to enact a role, which usually involve the assistance of those in complementary roles.

Outcomes The rewards expected from an interpersonal relationship minus the expected costs.

Out-Group In intergroup relations, a group of persons different from one's own group.

Overreward In equity theory, a condition of inequity in which a group member receives more rewards than would be justified on the basis of his or her contribution to the group.

Paralanguage All the vocal aspects of speech other than words, including vocal pitch, speed of speaking, pauses, sighs, laughter, and so on.

Passionate Love An intense state of absorption in and physiological arousal associated with another person.

Personal Norms Feelings of moral obligation to perform specific actions that are generated by an individual's unique system of internalized values.

Persuasion An effort by a source to change the beliefs or attitudes of a target person through the use of information or argument.

Position A designated location in a social system.

Powerlessness The sense of having little or no control over events.

Precipitating Event An incident that adversely affects members of a group and symbolizes their discontent, triggering collective behavior by group members.

Prejudice A strong like or strong dislike for members of a specific group.

Primacy Effect The tendency to be influenced in forming an impression by the earliest information received. Because of the primacy effect, first impressions are especially powerful. (See *recency effect*.)

Primary Group A small group in which members develop strong emotional ties with one another.

Primary Reinforcement The reduction or satisfaction of a biological need, such as the need for food, water, or sexual gratification.

Primary Relationship An interpersonal relationship that is personal, emotionally involving, and of long duration.

Principle of Consistency In cognitive theory, a principle maintaining that if a person holds several ideas that are incongruous or inconsistent with each other, he or she will experience discomfort or conflict and will subsequently change one or more of the ideas to render them consistent.

Principle of Covariation The view that behavior should be attributed to the potential cause that is present when the behavior occurs and absent when the behavior fails to occur.

Principle of Determinism The principle that there are discoverable causes for all events in a science's domain of interest.

Promise An influence technique that is a communication taking the general form: "If you do X (which I want), then I will do Y (which you want)."

Psychological Reactance An unpleasant emotional state that motivates efforts to regain control and to restore freedom when a person's freedom of action is threatened.

Punishment An unpleasant event that follows a response and reduces the frequency with which the response occurs.

Questionnaire A research method in which individuals read through a series of printed questions and record their own answers.

Random Assignment In an experiment, the placement of subjects in experimental conditions on the basis of chance.

Range of Tolerable Behavior With respect to group norms, that portion or segment of the behavior dimension that group members approve and evaluate positively; the range of behavior that group members find acceptable.

Realistic Group Conflict Theory A theoretical perspective regarding intergroup conflict that explains the development and the resolution of conflict in terms of the goals of each group; its central hypothesis is that groups will engage in conflictive behavior when their goals involve opposition of interest.

Recency Effect The tendency to be most influenced in forming an impression by the latest information received. Though the opposite, *primacy effect*, is more common, a recency effect occurs when there is reason for the perceiver to attend especially to later information.

Reciprocity Norm A widely accepted social norm stating that people should help those who help them and avoid hurting those who help them.

Reinforcement In reinforcement theory, anything that strengthens a response.

Reinforcement Theory A theoretical perspective based on the premise that social behavior is governed by external events, especially rewards and punishments.

Relative Deprivation A gap between the expected level and the actual level of satisfaction of the individual's needs, in which the level expected by the individual exceeds the level of need satisfaction experienced.

Reliability The extent to which the same research methods and measures produce the same results each time they are employed.

Response In reinforcement theory, a change in behavior induced by a stimulus.

Response Rate In a survey, the percentage of those who are contacted or receive a mailed questionnaire who complete the survey.

Restricted Code A concrete and egocentric speech style that is direct, rooted in the here and now, lacking qualifications, and emotionally expressive. Used in relationships that tend toward rigid, positional social control.

Revolutionary Coalition In groups, a union of medium- and low-status members who oppose the existing leader.

Risky Shift In group decision making, the tendency for decisions made after group discussion to be riskier than decisions made by individual members prior to discussion.

Rites of Passage Public ceremonies or rituals marking important normative transitions and affirming the individual's new status. Weddings, graduations, and christenings are examples of rites of passage.

Role A set of functions performed by a person on behalf of the group of which he or she is a member. The set of expectations governing the behavior of an occupant of a specific position within a social structure.

Role Discontinuity Movement into a role associated with values and identities that contradict those of earlier roles.

Role Identities The concepts people hold of who they are in each of their different, specific social roles.

Role Overload The condition in which the demands placed on the person by his or her roles exceed the amount of time, energy, and other resources available to meet those demands.

Role Taking In symbolic interactionist theory, a process wherein one person interacting with another imagines how he or she looks from the other person's standpoint; the process of imagining the other's attitudes and anticipating that person's responses.

Role Theory A theoretical perspective based on the premise that a substantial portion of observable, day-to-day social behavior is simply persons carrying out their roles.

Romantic Love Ideal Five beliefs regarding love, including the belief (1) in true love, (2) in love at first sight, (3) that love conquers all, (4) that there is one and only one true love for each person, and (5) that one should follow his or her heart.

Rule Breaking Behavior that violates social norms.

Rumor Communication via informal and often novel channels that cannot be validated.

Saturation The degree of overload experienced by members occupying central positions in group communication networks.

Scapegoating A method of deflecting responsibility for failure by blaming others.

Schismogenesis The splitting off of one or more factions from a social movement or a movement organization.

Scripts Learned sequences of behavior that people reel off virtually automatically with only minimal information processing.

Secondary Deviance Deviant behavior employed by the person as a means of defense or adjustment to the problems created by others' reactions to rule breaking by him or her.

Secondary Reinforcement The use of a stimulus that has become rewarding through association with a primary reinforcer to reward behavior.

Self The individual viewed as both the active source that initiates reflexive behavior and the passive object of this behavior.

Self-Awareness A state in which one takes the self as the object of one's attention and focuses on one's own appearance, actions, and thoughts.

Self-Concept The various thoughts and feelings a person has about himself or herself.

Self-Disclosure The act of revealing personal information about oneself to another person. Self-disclosure is sometimes used as an impression management tactic.

Self-Esteem The evaluative component of the self-concept, one's sense of how capable, successful, significant, worthy, and so on, one is.

Self-Estrangement The awareness that one is engaging in activities that are not rewarding in themselves.

Self-Fulfilling Prophecy When persons behave toward another person according to a label (impression), and cause the person to respond in ways that confirm the label (impression).

Self-Presentation All conscious and unconscious attempts by people to control the images of self they project in social interaction.

Self-Reinforcement The use of internalized standards to judge behavior and reward the self.

Self-Schema The active structure of ideas and knowledge that people have about themselves and use in processing information.

Semantic Differential Scale A measure of attitudes that asks the respondent to rate the object on each of a series of bipolar adjective scales, that is, scales whose ends are two adjectives having opposite meanings.

Sentiment Relations In balance theory, positive (liking, endorsing) or negative (disliking, opposing) relationships between two cognitive elements.

Sentiments Socially significant feelings that arise out of enduring social relationships, such as grief, love, jealousy, and indignation. Each sentiment is a pattern of sensations, emotions, actions, and cultural beliefs appropriate to a social relationship.

Shaping The learning process in which an agent initially reinforces any behavior that remotely resembles the desired response and subsequently requires increasing correspondence between the learner's behavior and the desired response before providing reinforcement.

Significant Other Another person whose views and attitudes are taken to be especially important and worthy of consideration. A person whose reflected views have great influence on a person's self-concepts and self-regulation.

Simple Random Sample A sample of individuals selected from a larger population in such a way that everyone in the population is equally likely to be selected.

Situated Self The subset of self-concepts that constitutes the self people recognize in a particular situation. Selected from the person's various identities, qualities, and self-evaluations, the situated self depends on the demands of the situation.

Situated Social Identity One's sense of who he or she is in relation to the other people in a specific situation, agreed upon for purposes of smooth social interaction.

Situational Constraint An influence on behavior due to the likelihood that other persons will learn about that behavior.

Small Group A group of persons, usually consisting of no more than 20 persons, who are able to interact face-to-face.

Social-Emotional Acts In interaction process analysis, emotional reactions (both positive and negative) directed by one member toward other members in a group.

Social-Emotional Leader In groups, a person who strives to keep emotional relationships pleasant among members; a person who initiates acts that ease the tensions and soothe hurt feelings.

Social Exchange Theory A theoretical perspective, based on the principle of reinforcement, which postulates that people choose whatever actions maximize rewards and minimize costs.

Social Influence An interaction process in which one person's behavior causes another person to change an opinion or to perform an action that he or she would not otherwise do.

Social Isolation The lack of involvement in meaningful relationships.

Socialization The learning of skills, knowledge, values, motives, and roles appropriate to the individual's position in a group or society.

Social Learning Theory A theoretical perspective based on the premise that a person acquires new responses (that is, learns) through the application of reinforcement.

Social Movement Collective activity that expresses a high level of concern about some issue; the activity may include participation in discussions, petition drives, demonstrations, or election campaigns.

Social Network The set of interpersonal relationships associated with the position(s) a person occupies.

Social Perception The process of constructing an understanding of the social world from the data obtained through one's senses. More narrowly defined, the processes through which one uses available information to form impressions of people.

Social Psychology That field which systematically studies the nature and causes of human social behavior.

Social Responsibility Norm A widely accepted social norm stating that individuals should help people who are dependent on them.

Social Status In groups, the evaluation by members of a social position in terms of its prestige, importance, or value to the group.

Social Structure The ordered and persisting relationships among the positions in a social system.

Sociolinguistic Competence A knowledge of the implicit rules for generating socially appropriate sentences that make sense because they fit with the listeners' cultural and social knowledge.

Source In social influence, the person who intentionally engages in some behavior (persuasion, threat, promise) to cause another person to behave in a manner different from the way he or she would ordinarily behave.

Speech Act The smallest unit of verbal social behavior intended to communicate a purpose such as to warn, inform, question, invite, and so on.

Spoken Language A socially acquired system of sound patterns with meanings agreed upon by the members of a group.

Status In groups, a member's relative standing vis-à-vis others. The social evaluation or ranking assigned to a position.

Status Characteristics Any property of a person (including race, occupation, age, sex, ethnicity, education, etc.) around which evaluations and beliefs about that person come to be organized.

Status Consensus A state of affairs in which group members agree on their relative status and especially on that of their leader.

Status Generalization A process through which differences in members' status characteristics lead to different performance expectations and affect patterns of interaction in groups.

Stereotype A fixed set of characteristics or traits that people attribute to all the members of a group. A simplistic and rigid perception of members of one group that is widely shared by others.

Stigma A characteristic widely viewed as an insurmountable handicap that prevents competent or morally trustworthy behavior. Stigmas include physical and characterological defects as well as membership in despised groups.

Stimulus In reinforcement theory, an event that leads to a change in behavior.

Stress A condition in which the demands made on the person exceed the individual's ability to cope with them.

Subjective Expected Value (SEV) With respect to threats, the product of a threat's credibility times its magnitude; with respect to promises, the product of a promise's credibility times its magnitude.

Summons-Answer Sequence The most common verbal method for initiating a conversation: one person summons the other as with a question or greeting, and the other indicates availability for conversation by responding. This sequence establishes the mutual obligation to speak and to listen that produces conversational turn taking.

Superordinate Goals In intergroup conflict, objectives held in common by all groups that cannot be achieved by any group without the supportive efforts of the others.

Survey A research method that involves the gathering of information by asking members of some group of persons a number of questions.

Symbol A form used to represent ideas, feelings, thoughts, intentions, or any other object. Symbols represent experience in ways that can be perceived through the sensory organs—through sounds, gestures, pictures, and so on.

Symbolic Interactionism A theoretical perspective based on the premise that human nature and social order are products of communication among people.

Target In social influence, the person who is impacted by a social influence attempt from the source.

Task Acts In interaction process analysis, instrumental behaviors that move the group toward realization of its goal.

Task Leader In groups, a member who pushes the group toward attainment of its goals; a person who contributes many ideas and suggestions to the group.

Theoretical Perspective A theory that makes broad assumptions about human nature and offers general explanations of a wide range of diverse behaviors.

Theory A set of interrelated propositions that organizes and explains a set of observed facts; a network of hypotheses that can be used as a basis for predictions.

Theory of Speech Accommodation The theory that people express or reject intimacy with others by adjusting their speech behavior (accent, vocabulary, language) during interaction. They make their own speech behavior more similar to their partner's in order to express liking, and more dissimilar in order to reject intimacy.

Threat An influence technique that is a communication taking the general form: "If you don't do X (which I want), then I will do Y (which you don't want)."

Transactional View of Leadership A theoretical perspective that characterizes leadership in groups as an exchange between the leader and other group members.

Troubleshooting An analytic process used to determine why a group is performing poorly.

Trust The belief that a person is both honest and benevolent.

Underreward In equity theory, a condition of inequity in which a group member receives fewer rewards than would be justified on the basis of his or her contribution to the group.

Unitary Task A group task in which all members perform identical activities.

Unit Relations In balance theory, the extent of perceived association between two cognitive elements.

Unobtrusive Measures Techniques of measurement that do not intrude on the activity being studied and do not run the risk of eliciting reactions that otherwise might not occur.

Upward Mobility Movement from an occupation that is lower in prestige and income to one that is higher in prestige and income.

Values Enduring beliefs that certain patterns of behavior or end states are preferable to their opposites.

Vocabularies of Motive Explanations of unsuitable behavior that particular groups accept as nullifying the negative implications of the behavior for the actor's identity.

Weighted Averaging Model A theoretical model for combining information about individual traits in order to predict how favorable the overall impression people form of another person will be. This model averages the favorable values of all the single traits people associate with a person after first weighting each trait according to criteria such as its credibility, negativity, and consistency with prior impressions. (See *additive model* and *averaging model*.)

References

Abeles, R.P., L. Steel, and L.L. Wise. 1980. Patterns and implications of life-course organization: Studies from project TALENT. In *Life-span development and behavior,* eds. P.B. Baltes and O.G. Brim, Jr. Vol. 3. New York: Academic Press.

Abelson, R.P. 1968. Computers, polls and public opinion—some puzzles and paradoxes. *Trans-action* 5:20–27.

———. 1976. Script processing in attitude formation and decision making. In *Cognition and social behavior,* eds. J.S. Carroll and J.W. Payne. Hillsdale, NJ: Erlbaum.

Abramson, L.Y., M.E.P. Seligman, and J. Teasdale. 1978. Learned helplessness in humans: Critique and reformulation. *Journal of Abnormal Psychology* 87:49–74.

Acock, A. and W. Scott. 1980. A model for predicting behavior: the effect of attitude and social class on high and low visibility political participation. *Social Psychology Quarterly* 43:59–72.

Adamek, R.J. and J.M. Lewis. 1975. Social control violence and radicalization: Behaviorial data. *Social Problems* 22:633–74.

Adams, J.S. 1963. Toward an understanding of inequity. *Journal of Abnormal and Social Psychology* 67:422–36.

———. 1965. Inequity in social exchange. In *Advances in experimental social psychology,* ed. L. Berkowitz. Vol. 2. New York: Academic Press.

———. 1976. The structure and dynamics of behavior in organization boundary roles. In *Handbook of industrial and organizational psychology,* ed. M.D. Dunette. Chicago: Rand McNally.

Adams, J.S. and P.R. Jacobsen. 1964. Effects of wage inequities on work quality. *Journal of Abnormal and Social Psychology* 69:19–25.

Adams, J.S. and W.B. Rosenbaum. 1962. The relationship of worker productivity to cognitive dissonance about wage inequities. *Journal of Applied Psychology* 46:161–64.

Adorno, T.W., E. Frenkel-Brunswik, D.J. Levinson, and R.N. Sanford. 1950. *The authoritarian personality.* New York: Harper and Row.

Ainsworth, M. 1973. The development of infant-mother attachment. In *Review of child development research,* eds. B. Caldwell and H. Ricciuti. Vol 3. Chicago: Univ. of Chicago Press.

Ainsworth, M. 1979. Infant-mother attachment. *American Psychologist* 34:932–37.

Ainsworth, M. 1980. Attachment and child abuse. In *Child abuse,* eds. G. Gerbner, G. Ross, and E. Zigler. New York: Oxford Univ. Press.

Ajzen, I. 1982. On behaving in accordance with one's attitudes. In *Consistency in social behavior: The Ontario symposium,* eds. M. Zanna, E. Higgins, and C. Herman. Vol. 2. Hillsdale, NJ: Erlbaum.

Ajzen, I. and M. Fishbein. 1977. Attitude–behavior rela-

tions: A theoretical analysis and review of research. *Psychological Bulletin* 84:888–918.

Ajzen, I. and W.H. Holmes. 1976. Uniqueness of behavioral effects in causal attribution. *Journal of Personality* 44:98–108.

Ajzen, I., C. Timko, and J. White. 1982. Self-monitoring and the attitude behavior relation. *Journal of Personality and Social Psychology* 42:426–35.

Akers, R., M. Krohn, L. Lanza-Kaduce, and M. Radosevich. 1979. Social learning and deviant behavior: A specific test of a general theory. *American Sociological Review* 44:636–55.

Alexander, C.N. and P. Lauderdale. 1977. Situated identities and social influence. *Sociometry* 40:225–33.

Allen, H. 1972. Bystander intervention and helping on the subway. In *Beyond the laboratory: Field research in social psychology,* eds. L. Bickman and T. Henchy. New York: McGraw-Hill.

Allen, V.L. and J.M. Levine. 1968. Social support, dissent and conformity. *Sociometry* 31:138–49.

———. 1969. Consensus and conformity. *Journal of Experimental Social Psychology* 5:389–99.

———. 1971. Social support and conformity: The role of independent assessment of reality. *Journal of Experimental Social Psychology* 7:48–58.

Allport, F.H. 1924. *Social psychology.* Cambridge, MA: Houghton Mifflin.

Allport, G.W. 1935. Attitudes. In *Handbook of social psychology,* ed. C. Murchison. Worcester, MA: Clark Univ. Press, 798–844.

———. 1954. *The nature of prejudice.* Reading, MA: Addison-Wesley.

———. 1961. *Pattern and growth in personality.* New York: Holt Rinehart and Winston.

Altman, I. and D.A. Taylor. 1973. *Social penetration: The development of interpersonal relationships.* New York: Holt Rinehart and Winston.

Alvarez, R. 1968. Informal reactions to deviance in a simulated work organization: A laboratory study. *American Sociological Review* 33:895–912.

Amir, Y. 1969. Contact hypothesis in ethnic relations. *Psychological Bulletin* 71:319–42.

———. 1976. The role of intergroup contact in change of prejudice and ethnic relations. In *Towards the elimination of racism,* ed. P.A. Katz. New York: Pergamon.

Anderson, A.B. 1975. Combined effects of interpersonal attraction and goal-path clarity on the cohesiveness of task oriented groups. *Journal of Personality and Social Psychology* 31:68–75.

Anderson, N.H. 1968. Likeableness ratings of 555 personality trait words. *Journal of Personality and Social Psychology* 9:272–79.

————. 1981. *Foundations of information integration theory.* New York: Academic Press.

Anderson, N.H. and S. Hubert. 1963. Effects of concomitant verbal recall on order effects in personality impression formation. *Journal of Verbal Learning and Verbal Behavior* 2:379–91.

Anderson, R., S.T. Manoogian, and J.S. Reznick. 1976. The undermining and enhancing of intrinsic motivation in preschool children. *Journal of Personality and Social Psychology* 34:915–22.

Anderson, R.C. 1963. Learning in discussions: A resumé of the authoritarian-democratic studies. In *Readings in the social psychology of education,* eds. W.W. Charters, Jr. and N.L. Gage. Boston: Allyn and Bacon.

Andrews, I.R. 1967. Wage inequity and job performance: An experimental study. *Journal of Applied Psychology* 51:39–45.

Angrist, S.S. and E. Almquist. 1975. *Careers and contingencies: How college women juggle with gender.* New York: Dunellen.

Appleton, W. 1981. *Fathers and daughters.* New York: Doubleday.

Archer, D. and R.M. Akert. 1977. Words and everything else: Verbal and nonverbal cues in social interpretation. *Journal of Personality and Social Psychology* 35:443–49.

Argyle, M., M. Lalljee, and M. Cook. 1968. The effects of visibility on interaction in a dyad. *Human Relations* 21:3–17.

Aronfreed, J. 1968. *Conduct and conscience.* New York: Academic Press.

Aronfreed, J. and A. Reber. 1965. Internalized behavior suppression and the timing of social punishment. *Journal of Personality and Social Psychology* 1:3–16.

Aronoff, D., and J.T. Tedeschi. 1968. Original stakes and behavior in the prisoner's dilemma game. *Psychonomic Science* 12:79–80.

Aronson, E., J.A. Turner, and J.M. Carlsmith. 1963. Communicator credibility and communication discrepancy as determinants of opinion change. *Journal of Abnormal and Social Psychology* 67:31–36.

Asch, S.E. 1946. Forming impressions of personality. *Journal of Abnormal and Social Psychology* 41:258–90.

————. 1951. Effects of group pressure upon the modification and distortion of judgements. In *Groups, leadership, and men,* ed. H. Guetzkow. Pittsburgh: Carnegie Press.

————. 1952. *Social psychology.* Englewood Cliffs, NJ: Prentice-Hall.

————. 1955. Opinions and social pressure. *Scientific American* 193:31–35.

————. 1956. Studies of independence and conformity: I. A minority of one against a unanimous majority. *Psychological Monographs,* 70, whole No. 416.

————. 1957. An experimental investigation of group influence. Symposium on Preventive and Social Psychiatry. Walter Reed Army Institute of Research, Washington, DC: U.S. Government Printing Office.

Asch, S.E. and H. Zukier. 1984. Thinking about persons. *Journal of Personality and Social Psychology* 46:1230–40.

Atchley, R.C. 1980. *The social forces in later life.* Belmont, CA: Wadsworth.

Atkin, C.K. 1981. Mass media information campaign effectiveness. In *Public communication campaigns,* eds. R.E. Rice and W.J. Paisley. Beverly Hills, CA: Sage.

Austin, J.L. 1962. *How to do things with words.* Cambridge, MA: Harvard University Press.

Austin, W. and E. Walster. 1974. Participants' reactions to "equity with the world." *Journal of Experimental Social Psychology* 10:528–48.

Ayers, L., P. Nacci, and J.T. Tedeschi. 1973. Attraction and reactions to noncontingent promises. *Bulletin of the Psychonomic Society* 1(1B):75–77.

Bacharach, S.B. and M. Aiken. 1979. The impact of alienation, meaninglessness and meritocracy on supervisor and subordinate satisfaction. *Social Forces* 57:853–70.

Bacharach, S.B., and E.J. Lawler. 1980. *Power and politics in organizations.* San Francisco: Jossey-Bass.

Bachman, J.G. 1970. *Youth in transition,* Vol. 2. *The impact of family background and intelligence on tenth-grade boys.* Ann Arbor, MI: Institute for Social Research.

Back, K.W. 1951. Influence through social communication. *Journal of Abnormal and Social Psychology* 46:9–23.

Back, K.W., S. Bunker, and C.B. Dunnagen. 1972. Barriers to communication and measurement of semantic space. *Sociometry* 35:347–56.

Backman, C.W. 1981. Attraction in interpersonal relationships. In *Social psychology: Sociological perspectives,* eds. M. Rosenberg and R.H. Turner. New York: Basic Books.

Backman, C. and P.F. Secord. 1959. The effect of perceived liking on interpersonal attraction. *Human Relations* 12:379–84.

————. 1962. Liking, selective interaction, and misperception in congruent interpersonal relations. *Sociometry* 25:321–25.

————. 1968. The self and role selection. In *The self in social interaction,* eds. C. Gordon and K.J. Gergen. New York: Wiley.

Bagozzi, R.P. 1981. Attitudes, intentions and behavior: A test of some key hypotheses. *Journal of Personality and Social Psychology* 41:607–27.

Bales, R.F. 1950. *Interaction process analysis.* Reading, MA: Addison Wesley.

————. 1953. The equilibrium problem in small groups. In *Working papers in the theory of action,* eds. T. Parsons, R.F. Bales, and E.A. Shils. New York: Free Press.

————. 1970. *Personality and interpersonal behavior.* New York: Holt Rinehart and Winston.

Bales, R.F. and A.P. Hare. 1965. Diagnostic use of the interaction profile. *Journal of Social Psychology* 67:239–58.

Bales, R.F. and P.E. Slater. 1955. Role differentiation in small decision-making groups. In *Family, socialization, and interaction process,* eds. T. Parsons, R.F. Bales, and others. New York: Free Press.

Ball, D.W. 1967. An abortion clinic ethnography. *Social Problems* 14:293–301.

————. 1976. Failure in sports. *American Sociological Review* 41:726–39.

Baltes, P. and S.L. Willis. 1982. Plasticity and enhancement of intellectual functioning in old age: Penn State's adult development and enrichment project. In *Aging and cognitive processes*, eds. F. Craik and S. Trehub. New York: Plenum.

Baltes, R., H. Reese, and L. Lipsitt. 1980. Life-span developmental psychology. *Annual Review of Psychology* 3:65–100.

Bandura, A. 1962. Social learning through imitation. In *Nebraska symposium on motivation: 1962*, ed. M.R. Jones. Lincoln, NE: Univ. of Nebraska Press.

———. 1965. Influences of models' reinforcement contingencies on the acquisition of imitative responses. *Journal of Personality and Social Psychology*, 1:589–95.

———. 1969. Social-learning theory of identificatory processes. In *Handbook of socialization theory and research*, ed. D. Goslin. Chicago: Rand McNally.

———. 1973. *Aggression: A social learning analysis*. Englewood Cliffs, NJ: Prentice-Hall.

———. 1977. *Social learning theory*. Englewood Cliffs, NJ: Prentice-Hall.

———. 1977. Self-efficacy: Toward a unifying theory of behavioral change. *Psychological Review* 84:191–215.

———. 1978. The self system in reciprocal determinism. *American Psychologist* 33:344–58.

———. 1982. The self and the mechanisms of agency. In *Psychological perspectives on the self*, ed. J. Suls. Vol. 1. Hillsdale, NJ: Erlbaum.

———. 1982. The psychology of chance encounters and life paths. *American Psychologist* 37:747–55.

———. 1982. Self-efficacy mechanism in human agency. *American Psychologist* 37:122–47.

Bardwick, J.M. 1971. *The psychology of women*. New York: Harper and Row.

Barker, R.G., T. Dembo, and K. Lewin. 1941. Frustration and regression: An experiment with young children. *University of Iowa Studies in Child Welfare* 18:1–34.

Barnes, E.J. 1972. The black community as a source of positive self-concept for black children: A theoretical perspective. In *Black psychology*, ed. R.L. Jones. New York: Harper and Row.

Baron, R.A. 1971. Reducing the influence of an aggressive model: The restraining effects of discrepant modeling cues. *Journal of Personality and Social Psychology* 20:240–45.

———. 1977. *Human aggression*. New York: Plenum.

Baron, R.A. and C.R. Kepner. 1970. Model's behavior and attraction toward the model as determinants of adult aggressive behavior. *Journal of Personality and Social Psychology* 14:335–44.

Baron, R.A. and V. Ransberger. 1978. Ambient temperature and the occurrence of collective violence: The "Long, hot summer" revisited. *Journal of Personality and Social Psychology* 36:351–60.

Baron, R.S., K.L. Dion, P.H. Baron, and N. Miller. 1971. Group consensus and cultural values as determinants of risk-taking. *Journal of Personality and Social Psychology* 20:446–55.

Baron, R.S. and G. Roper. 1976. A reaffirmation of a social comparison view of choice shifts, averaging, and extremity effects in autokinetic situations. *Journal of Personality and Social Psychology* 33:521–30.

Bart, P.B. 1975. The loneliness of the long-distance mother. In *Women: A feminist perspective*, ed. J. Freeman. Palo Alto, CA: Mayfield.

Bar-Tal, D. 1976. *Prosocial behavior: Theory and research*. New York: Halsted.

Barton, A.H. 1969. *Communities in disaster: A sociological analysis of collective stress situations*. New York: Doubleday.

Bartos, O.J. 1974. *Process and outcome in negotiation*. New York: Columbia Univ. Press.

Bartunek, J.M., A.A. Benton, and C.B. Keys. 1975. Third party intervention and the bargaining behavior of group representatives. *Journal of Conflict Resolution* 19:532–57.

Bass, B.M. 1966. Effects on the subsequent peformance of negotiators of studying issues or planning strategies alone or in groups. *Psychological Monographs* 80 (whole no. 614).

Batson, C.D. and J.S. Coke. 1981. Empathy: A source of altruistic motivation for helping? In *Altruism and helping behavior*, eds. J.P. Rushton and R.M. Sorrentino. Hillsdale, NJ: Erlbaum.

Batson, C.D., K. O'Quin, J. Fultz, M. Vanderplas, and A.M. Isen. 1983. Influence of self-reported distress and empathy on egoistic versus altruistic motivation to help. *Journal of Personality and Social Psychology* 45:706–18.

Bauer, R. 1964. The obstinate audience: The influence process from the point of view of social communication. *American Psychologist* 19:319–28.

Bauer, R. and D. Cox. 1963. Rational vs. emotional communications: A new approach. In *Television and human behavior*, eds. L. Arons and M. May. Englewood Cliffs, NJ: Prentice-Hall.

Baum, A., M. Riess, and J. O'Hara. 1974. Architectural variants of reaction to spatial invasion. *Environment and Behavior* 6:91–100.

Baumeister, R. and E.E. Jones. 1978. When self-presentation is constrained by the target's knowledge: Consistency and compensation. *Journal of Personality and Social Psychology* 36:608–18.

Baumrind, D. 1964. Some thoughts on ethics of research: After reading Milgram's "Behavioral Study of Obedience." *American Psychologist* 19:421–23.

———. 1980. New directions in socialization research. *American Psychologist* 35:639–52.

Bavelas, A. 1948. A mathematical model for group structures. *Applied Anthropology*. 7:16–30.

Bavelas, A. 1950. Communication patterns in task-oriented groups. *Journal of the Acoustical Society of America* 22:725–30.

Beaman, A.L., B. Klentz, E. Diener, and S. Svanum. 1979. Objective self awareness and transgression in children: A field study. *Journal of Personality and Social Psychology* 37:1835–46.

Becker, H. 1963. *Outsiders: Studies in the sociology of deviance*. New York: Free Press.

———. 1964. What do they really learn at college? *Trans-Action* 1:14–17.

Beebe, L.M. and H. Giles. 1984. Speech accomodation theories: A discussion in terms of second language learning. *International Journal of the Sociology of Language* 46:5–32.

Begley, T. and H. Alker. 1982. Anti-busing protest: Attitudes and actions. *Social Psychology Quarterly* 45:187–97.

Bell, R. 1979. Parent, child and reciprocal influences. *American Psychologist* 34:821–26.

Bem, D.J. 1970. *Beliefs, attitudes and human affairs.* Belmont, CA: Brooks/Cole.

———. 1972. Self perception theory. In *Advances in experimental social psychology*, ed. L. Berkowitz. Vol. 6. New York: Academic Press.

Bem, D.J. and A. Allen. 1974. On predicting some of the people some of the time: The search for cross-situational consistency in behavior. *Psychological Review* 81:506–20.

Benassi, M. 1982. Effect of order of presentation, primacy and physical attractiveness on attributions of ability. *Journal of Personality and Social Psychology* 43:48–58.

Benedict, R. 1938. Continuities and discontinuities in cultural conditioning. *Psychiatry* 1:161–67.

Benham, T.W. 1965. Polling for a presidential candidate: Some observations of the 1964 campaign. *Public Opinion Quarterly* 29:185–99.

Bentler, P.M. and G. Speckart. 1981. Attitudes "cause" behaviors: A structural equation analysis. *Journal of Personality and Social Psychology* 40:226–38.

Benton, A.A. 1972. Accountability and negotiations between group representatives, *Proceedings of the 80th annual convention of the American Psychological Association*, 7.

Benton, A.A., H.H. Kelley, and B. Liebling. 1972. Effects of extremity of offers and concession rate on the outcomes of bargaining. *Journal of Personality and Social Psychology* 24:73–83.

Bereiter, C. and S. Engelmann. 1966. *Teaching disadvantaged children in the preschool.* Englewood Cliffs, NJ: Prentice-Hall.

Berelson, B., P.F. Lazarsfield, and W. McPhee. 1954. *Voting.* Chicago: Univ. of Chicago Press.

Berger, J., B.P. Cohen, and M. Zelditch, Jr. 1972. Status characteristics and social interaction. *American Sociological Review* 37:241–55.

Berger, J. and M.H. Fisek. 1970. Consistent and inconsistent status characteristics and the determination of power and prestige orders. *Sociometry* 33:287–304.

———. 1974. A generalization of the theory of status characteristics and expectations states. In *Expectation states theory*, eds. J. Berger, T.L. Conner, and M.H. Fisek. Cambridge, MA: Winthrop.

Berger, J., M.H. Fisek, R.Z. Norman, and M. Zelditch, Jr. 1977. *Status characteristics and social interaction: An expectation states approach.* New York: Elsevier.

Berger, J., S.J. Rosenholtz, and M. Zelditch, Jr. 1980. Status organizing processes. *Annual Review of Sociology* 6:479–508.

Berk, R.A. and H. Aldrich. 1972. Patterns of vandalism during civil disorders as an indicator of selection of targets. *American Sociological Review* 37:533–47.

Berkowitz, L. 1953. Sharing leadership in small, decision-making groups. *Journal of Abnormal and Social Psychology* 48:231–38.

Berkowitz, L. 1954. Group standards, cohesiveness and productivity. *Human Relations* 7:509–19.

Berkowitz, L. 1971. Social norms, feelings, and other factors affecting helping and altruism. In *Advances in experimental social psychology*, ed. L. Berkowitz. Vol. 6. New York: Academic Press.

———. 1972. Frustrations, comparisons, and other sources of emotion arousal as contributors to social unrest. *Journal of Social Issues* 28:77–91.

———. 1978. Whatever happened to the frustration-aggression hypothesis? *American Behaviorial Scientist* 21:691–708.

Berkowitz, L. and D.R. Cottingham. 1960. The interest value and relevance of fear-arousing communications. *Journal of Abnormal and Social Psychology* 60:37–43.

Berkowitz, L., S.B. Klanderman, and R. Harris. 1964. Effects of experimenter awareness and sex of subject and experimenter on reactions to dependency relationships. *Sociometry* 27:327–37.

Berkowitz, L. and A. LePage. 1967. Weapons as aggression-eliciting stimuli. *Journal of Personality and Social Psychology* 7:202–07.

Bernard, J.S. 1975. *The future of motherhood.* New York: Penguin.

———. 1981. *The female world.* New York: Free Press.

Bernstein, B. 1961a. Aspects of language and learning in the genesis of the social process. *Journal of Child Psychology and Psychiatry* 1:313–24.

———. 1961b. Social class and linguistic development: A theory of social learning. In *Education, economy and society*, eds. Halsey, A.H., J. Floud, and A. Anderson. New York: Free Press.

———. 1974. *Class, codes and control I*, revised edition. London: Routledge and Kegan Paul.

———. 1975. *Class, codes and control III.* London: Routledge and Kegan Paul.

Bernstein, I., W. Kelly, and P. Doyle. 1977. Societal reaction to deviants: The case of criminal defendants. *American Sociological Review* 42:743–55.

Bernstein, I., E. Kick, J. Leung, and B. Schulz. 1977. Charge reduction: An intermediary stage in the process of labelling criminal defendants. *Social Forces* 56:362–84.

Bernstein, W.M., W.G. Stephan, and M.H. Davis. 1979. Explaining attributions for achievement: A pathanalytic approach. *Journal of Personality and Social Psychology* 37:1810–21.

Berscheid, E. 1966. Opinion change and communicator-communicatee similarity and dissimilarity. *Journal of Personality and Social Psychology* 4:670–80.

Berscheid, E., K. Dion, E. Walster (Hatfield), and G. Walster. 1971. Physical attractiveness and dating choice: A test of the matching hypothesis. *Journal of Experimental Social Psychology* 7:173–89.

Berscheid, E. and E. Walster (Hatfield). 1974a. A little bit about love. In *Foundations of interpersonal attraction*, ed. T. Huston. New York: Academic Press, 355–81.

———. 1974b. Physical attractiveness. In *Advances in experimental social psychology*, ed. L. Berkowitz. New York: Academic Press.

———. 1978. *Interpersonal attraction*, 2nd ed. Reading, MA: Addison-Wesley.

Bertenthal, B.I. and K.W. Fischer. 1978. Development of self-recognition in the infant. *Developmental Psychology* 14:44–50.

Bickman, L. 1971. The effect of another bystander's ability

to help on bystander intervention in an emergency. *Journal of Experimental Social Psychology* 7:367–79.

Biddle, B.J. and E.J. Thomas. 1966. Eds. *Role theory: Concepts and research.* New York: Wiley.

Birdwhistell, R.L. 1970. *Kinesics in context: Essays on body motion communications.* Philadelphia: Univ. of Pennsylvania Press.

Birnbaum, J.A. 1975. Life patterns and self-esteem in gifted family-oriented and career-committed women. In *Women and achievement: Social and motivational analyses,* eds. M.T.S. Mednick, S.T. Schwartz, and L.W. Hoffman. New York: Halsted.

Black, D. 1980. *The manners and customs of the police.* New York: Academic Press.

Black, D. and A.J. Reiss Jr. 1970. Police control of juveniles. *American Sociological Review* 35:63–77.

Blake, R.R. and J.S. Mouton. 1961a. Reactions to intergroup competition under win-lose conditions. *Management Science* 7:420–35.

———. 1961b. Comprehension of own and of outgroup positions under intergroup competition. *Journal of Conflict Resolution* 5:304–10.

———. 1962a. The intergroup dynamics of win-lose conflict and problem-solving collaboration in union-management relations. In *Intergroup relations and leadership,* ed. M. Sherif. New York: Wiley.

———. 1962b. Overevaluation of own group's product in intergroup competition. *Journal of Abnormal and Social Psychology* 64:237–38.

Blake, R.R., H.A. Shepard, and J.S. Mouton. 1964. *Managing intergroup conflict in industry.* Houston: Gulf.

Blalock, H.M., Jr. and P.H. Wilken. 1979. *Intergroup processes: A micro-macro perspective.* New York: Free Press.

Blau, P. 1960. Patterns of deviation in work groups. *Sociometry* 23:245–261.

———. 1964. *Exchange and power in social life.* New York: Wiley.

Blauner, R. 1964. *Alienation and freedom.* Chicago: Univ. of Chicago Press.

Blom, J.P. and J.J. Gumperz. 1972. Social meaning and linguistic structure: Code-switching in Norway. In *Directions in sociolinguistics,* eds. J.J. Gumperz and D. Hymes. New York: Holt Rinehart and Winston.

Blumenthal, M., R.L. Kahn, F.M. Andrews, and K.B. Head. 1972. *Justifying violence: Attitudes of American men.* Ann Arbor, MI: Institute for Social Research.

Blumer, H. 1962. Society and symbolic interaction. In *Human behavior and social processes,* ed. A.M. Rose. Boston: Houghton Mifflin.

———. 1969. *Symbolic interactionism: Perspective and method.* Englewood Cliffs, NJ: Prentice-Hall.

———. 1969. Elementary collective groupings. In *Principles of sociology,* ed. A. McClung Lee. 3d. ed. New York: Barnes and Noble.

Blumler, J.G. and D. McQuail. 1969. *Television in politics: Its uses and influence.* Chicago: Univ. of Chicago Press.

Blumstein, P.W. 1975. Identity bargaining and self-conception. *Social Forces* 53:476–85.

———. 1974. The honoring of accounts. *American Sociological Review* 39:551–66.

Bochner, S. and C.A. Insko. 1966. Communicator discrepancy, source credibility, and opinion change. *Journal of Personality and Social Psychology* 4:614–21.

Bogardus, E. 1959. *Social distance.* Yellow Springs, OH: Antioch Press.

Bollen, K.A. and D.P. Phillips. 1981. Suicidal motor vehicle fatalities in Detroit: A replication. *American Journal of Sociology* 87:404–12.

Bond, J.R. and W.E. Vinacke. 1961. Coalitions in mixed-sex triads. *Sociometry* 24:61–75.

Bonoma, T.V., B.R. Schlenker, R.B. Smith, and J.T. Tedeschi. 1970. Source prestige and target reactions to threats. *Psychonomic Science* 19:111–13.

Bord, R.J. 1976. The impact of imputed deviant identities in structuring evaluations and reactions. *Sociometry* 39:108–16.

Boucher, J.D. and P. Ekman. 1975. Facial areas of emotional information. *Journal of Communication* 25:21–29.

Boulding, K.E. 1981. *Ecodynamics: A new theory of societal evolution.* Beverly Hills, CA: Sage.

Bourhis, R.Y., H. Giles, J.P. Leyens, and H. Tajfel. 1979. Psycholinguistic distinctiveness: Language diversity in Belgium. In *Language and social psychology,* eds. H. Giles and R.N. St. Clair. Oxford: Blackwell.

Bowlby, J. 1965. Maternal care and mental health (1953). In *Child care and the growth of love,* ed. J. Bowlby. London: Penguin.

Bradley, G.W. 1978. Self-serving biases in the attribution process: A reexamination of the fact or fiction question. *Journal of Personality and Social Psychology* 36:56–71.

Braine, M. 1963. The ontogeny of English phrase structure: The first phrase. *Language* 39:1–13.

Brehm, J.W. 1956. Postdecision changes in the desirability of alternatives. *Journal of Abnormal and Social Psychology* 52:384–89.

———. 1972. *Responses to loss of freedom: A theory of psychological reactance.* Morristown, NJ: General Learning Press.

Brehm, J.W. and A.R. Cohen. 1962. *Explorations in cognitive dissonance.* New York: Wiley.

Brenner, M.W. 1976. *Memory and interpersonal relations.* Doctoral dissertation, Ann Arbor, MI: Univ. of Michigan.

Brewer, M.B. 1979. In-group bias in the minimal intergroup situation: A cognitive-motivational analysis. *Psychological Bulletin* 86:307–24.

Brewer, M.B. and D.T. Campbell. 1976. *Ethnocentrism and intergroup attitudes: East African evidence.* New York: Halsted.

Brewer, M.B. and M. Silver. 1978. Ingroup bias as a function of task characteristics. *European Journal of Social Psychology* 8:393–400.

Brim, O.G., Jr. 1966. *Socialization through the life-cycle.* In *Socialization after childhood,* eds. O.G. Brim, Jr. and S. Wheeler. New York: Wiley.

———. 1976. Theories of the male mid-life crisis. *Counseling Psychologist* 6:2–9.

Brim, O.G., Jr. and C.D. Ryff. 1980. On the properties of life events. In *Life-span development and behavior,* eds. P.B. Baltes and O.G. Brim, Jr. Vol. 3. New York: Academic Press.

Bronfenbrenner, U. 1958. Socialization and social class

through time and space. In *Readings in social psychology,* eds. E.E. Maccoby, T.M. Newcomb, and E.L. Hartley. New York: Holt Rinehart and Winston.

———. 1961. The mirror-image in Soviet-American relations. *Journal of Social Issues* 17:45–6.

Brophy, J.E. and T.L. Good. 1974. *Teacher-student relationships: Causes and consequences.* New York: Holt Rinehart and Winston.

Broverman, I., S. Vogel, D. Broverman, F. Clarkson, and P. Rosenkrantz. 1972. Sex-role stereotypes: A current appraisal. *Journal of Social Issues* 28:59–78.

Brown, P. and R. Elliott. 1965. Control of aggression in a nursery school class. *Journal of Experimental Child Psychology* 2:103–107.

Brown, R.W. 1964. The acquisition of language. In *Disorders of communication,* eds. D.M. Rioch and E.A. Weinstein. Proceedings of the Association for Research in Nervous and Mental Disease. Vol. 42. Baltimore: Williams and Wilkins.

———. 1965. *Social psychology.* Glencoe, IL: Free Press.

Brown, R. and U. Bellugi. 1964. Three processes in the child's acquisition of syntax. *Harvard Educational Review* 34:133–51.

Brown, R. and C. Fraser. 1963. The acquisition of syntax. In *Verbal behavior and learning,* eds. C.N. Cofer and B.S. Musgrave. New York: McGraw-Hill.

Bruner, J.S. 1957. On perceptual readiness. *Psychological Review* 64:123–52.

———. 1958. Social psychology and perception. In *Readings in social psychology,* eds. E.E. Maccoby, T.M. Newcomb, and E.L. Hartley. New York: Holt Rinehart and Winston.

———. 1964. The course of cognitive growth. *American Psychologist* 19:1–15.

Bruner, J. and H. Kenney. 1966. The development of the concepts of order and proportion in children. In *Studies in cognitive growth,* ed. J. Bruner. New York: Wiley.

Bruner, J. and R. Tagiuri. 1954. The perception of people. In *Handbook of social psychology,* ed. G. Lindzey. Cambridge, MA: Addison-Wesley.

Bryan, J.H. and M. Davenport. 1968. *Donations to the needy: Correlates of financial contributions to the destitute.* (Research Bulletin No. 68-1). Princeton, NJ: Educational Testing Service.

Bugenthal, D.E. 1974. Interpretations of naturally occurring discrepancies between words and intonation: Modes of inconsistency resolution. *Journal of Personality and Social Psychology* 30:125–133.

Bugenthal, J.F.T. and S.L. Zelen. 1950. Investigations into the self-concept. *Journal of Personality* 18:483–98.

Burgess, R.L. and L.R. Akers. 1966. A differential association-reinforcement theory of criminal behavior. *Social Problems* 14:128–47.

Burke, P.J. 1968. Role differentiation and the legitimation of task activity. *Sociometry* 31:404–11.

———. 1972. Leadership role differentiation. In *Experimental social psychology,* ed. C.G. McClintock. New York: Holt Rinehart and Winston.

Burke, P.J. and D.C. Reitzes. 1981. The link between identity and role performance. *Social Psychology Quarterly* 44:83–92.

Burke, P.J. and A.T. Turk. 1975. Factors affecting post arrest dispositions: A model for analysis. *Social Problems* 22:313–32.

Burke, P.J. and J.C. Tully. 1977. The measurement of role/identity. *Social Forces* 55:881–97.

Burke, R. and T. Weir. 1976. Relationship of wives' employment status to husband, wife and pair satisfaction and performance. *Journal of Marriage and the Family* 38:279–87.

Burnstein, E. 1969. Interdependence in groups. In *Experimental social psychology,* ed. J. Mills. New York: Macmillan Co.

Burnstein, E. and A. Vinokur. 1973. Testing two classes of theories about group-induced shifts in individual choice. *Journal of Experimental Social Psychology* 9:123–37.

Burnstein, E. and A. Vinokur. 1977. Persuasive argumentation and social comparison as determinants of attitude polarization. *Journal of Experimental Social Psychology* 13:315–32.

Bush, D. and R. Simmons. 1981. Socialization processes over the life course. In *Social psychology: Sociological perspectives,* eds. M. Rosenberg and R. Turner. New York: Basic Books.

Buss, A. 1961. *The psychology of aggression.* New York: Wiley.

Byrne, D. 1971. *The attraction paradigm.* New York: Academic Press.

———. 1961a. The influence of propinquity and opportunities for interaction on classroom relationships. *Human Relations* 14:63–69.

———. 1961b. Interpersonal attraction and attitude similarity. *Journal of Abnormal and Social Psychology* 62:713–15.

Byrne, D. and G.L. Clore. 1970. A reinforcement model of evaluative responses. *Personality: An International Journal* 1:103–28.

Byrne, D., C. Ervin, and J. Lamberth. 1970. Continuity between the experimental study of attraction and real-life computer dating. *Journal of Personality and Social Psychology* 16:157–65.

Byrne, D. and D. Nelson. 1965. Attraction as linear function of proportion of positive reinforcements. *Journal of Personality and Social Psychology* 1:659–63.

Calahan, D. 1970. *Problem drinkers.* San Francisco: Jossey-Bass.

Calder, B.J., M. Ross, and C.A. Insko. 1973. Attitude change and attitude attribution: Effects of incentive, choice and consequences. *Journal of Personality and Social Psychology* 25:84–99.

Caldwell, M.A. and L.A. Peplau. 1982. Sex differences in same-sex relationships. *Sex Roles* 8:721–32.

Campbell, A., P.E. Converse, and W.L. Rodgers. 1976. *The quality of American life.* New York: Russell Sage Foundation.

Campbell, D.T. 1967. Stereotypes in the perception of group differences. *American Psychologist* 22:817–29.

Campbell, D.T. and D.W. Fiske. 1959. Convergent and discriminant validity by the multitrait-multimethod matrix. *Psychological Bulletin* 56:81–105.

Campbell, D.T. and J.C. Stanley. 1963. *Experimental and*

quasi-experimental designs for research. Chicago: Rand McNally.

Cantor, J., H. Alfonso, and D. Zillmann. 1976. The persuasive effectiveness of the peer appeal and a communicator's first-hand experience. *Communication Research* 3:293–310.

Caplan, F. 1973. *The first twelve months of life.* New York: Grosset and Dunlap.

Caplow, T. 1968. *Two against one: Coalitions in triads.* Englewood Cliffs, NJ: Prentice-Hall.

Carey, M. 1978. The role of gaze in the initiation of conversation. *Social Psychology* 41:269–71.

Carlsmith, J.M. and C. Anderson. 1979. Ambient temperature and the occurrence of collective violence. *Journal of Personality and Social Psychology* 37:337–44.

Carlsmith, J.M., P. Ellsworth, and J. Whiteside. 1968. Guilt, confession, and compliance, cited in Freedman, J.L. Transgression, compliance, and guilt. In *Altruism and helping behavior,* eds. J.R. Macaulay and L. Berkowitz. New York: Academic Press.

Carlson, E.R. 1956. Attitude change through modification of attitude structure. *Journal of Abnormal and Social Psychology* 52:256–61.

Carlston, D.E. and N. Shovar. 1983. Effects of performance attributions on others' perceptions of the attributor. *Journal of Personality and Social Psychology* 44:515–25.

Carrigan, W.C. and J.W. Julian. 1966. Sex and birth-order differences in conformity as a function of need affiliation arousal. *Journal of Personality and Social Psychology* 3:479–83.

Carroll, J. and J. Casagrande. 1958. The function of language classifications in behavior. In *Readings in social psychology,* eds. E.E. Maccoby, T.M. Newcomb, and E.L. Hartley. 3d ed. New York: Holt Rinehart and Winston.

Cartwright, D. 1971. Risk taking by individuals and groups: An assessment of research employing choice dilemmas. *Journal of Personality and Social Psychology* 20:361–78.

Cartwright, D.S. and R.J. Robertson. 1961. Membership in cliques and achievement. *American Journal of Sociology* 66:441–45.

Cartwright, D. and A. Zander. 1968. Motivation process in groups: Introduction. In *Group dynamics: Research and theory,* eds. D. Cartwright and A. Zander, 3d ed. New York: Harper and Row.

Cash, T.F., J.A. Kehr, J. Polyson, and V. Freeman. 1977. Role of physical attractiveness in peer attribution of psychological disturbance. *Journal of Consulting and Clinical Psychology* 45:987–93.

Centers, R. 1975. Attitude similarity-dissimilarity as a correlate of heterosexual attraction and love. *Journal of Marriage and the Family* 37:305–12.

Chaffee, S. 1981. Mass media in political campaigns: An expanding role. In *Public communication campaigns,* eds. R.E. Rice and W.J. Paisley. Beverly Hills, CA: Sage.

Chaiken, S. 1979. Communicator physical attractiveness and persuasion. *Journal of Personality and Social Psychology* 37:1387–97.

Chaiken, S. 1980. Heuristic versus systematic information processing and the use of source versus message cues in persuasion. *Journal of Personality and Social Psychology* 39:752–66.

Chemers, M.M. 1969. Cross-cultural training as a means for improving situational favorableness. *Human Relations* 22:531–46.

Chemers, M.M. and G.J. Skrzypek. 1972. An experimental test of the contingency model of leadership effectiveness. *Journal of Personality and Social Psychology* 24:172–77.

Cherlin, A.J. 1981. *Marriage, divorce, remarriage.* Cambridge, MA: Harvard Univ. Press.

Chertkoff, J.M. and M. Conley. 1967. Opening and frequency of concession as bargaining strategies. *Journal of Personality and Social Psychology* 7:181–85.

Chesterfield, Earl of (P.D. Stanhope). 1901 (orig. publ. 1774). In *Letters to his Son,* ed. W.M. Dunne. New York: Wiley.

Chiricos, T. and G. Waldo. 1975. Socioeconomic status and criminal sentencing: An empirical assessment of a conflict proposition. *American Sociological Review* 40:753–72.

Chomsky, N. 1965. *Aspects of the theory of syntax.* Cambridge, MA: MIT Press.

Cialdini, R.B. and D. Baumann. 1981. Littering: A new unobtrusive measure of attitudes. *Social Psychology Quarterly* 44:254–59.

Cialdini, R.B., R.J. Borden, A. Thorne, M.R. Walker, and S. Freeman. 1976. Basking in reflected glory: Three (football) field studies. *Journal of Personality and Social Psychology* 34:366–75.

Cialdini, R.B., B.L. Darby, and J.E. Vincent. 1973. Transgression and altruism: A case for hedonism. *Journal of Experimental Social Psychology* 9:501–16.

Cicourel, A.V. 1972. Basic and normative rules in the negotiation of status and role. In *Studies in social interaction,* ed. D. Sudnow. New York: Free Press.

Clark, B. 1956. The cooling-out function in higher education. *American Journal of Sociology* 65:569–76.

Clark, E.V. 1976. From gesture to word: On the natural history of deixis in language acquisition. In *Human growth and development,* eds. J.S. Bruner and A. Gartner. Oxford: Clarendon Press.

Clark, H.H. and E.V. Clarke. 1977. *Psychology and language.* New York: Harcourt Brace Jovanovich.

Clark, K.B. 1963. *Prejudice and your child,* 2d ed. New York: Beacon Press.

Clark, M.S. and J. Mills. 1979. Interpersonal attraction in exchange and communal relationships. *Journal of Personality and Social Psychology* 37:12–24.

Clark, R.A., F.I. Nye, and V. Gecas. 1978. Husband's work involvement and marital role performance. *Journal of Marriage and the Family* 40:9–21.

Clark, R.D. III. 1971. Group-induced shift toward risk: A critical appraisal. *Psychological Bulletin* 76:251–70.

Clark, R.D. III and L.E. Word. 1972. Why don't bystanders help? Because of ambiguity? *Journal of Personality and Social Psychology* 24:392–400.

Clarke-Stewart, K.A. 1978. Popular primers for parents. *American Psychologist* 33:359–69.

Clausen, J. 1966. Family structure, socialization and personality. In *Review of child development research,* eds. M.

Hoffman and L. Hoffman. Vol. 2. New York: Russell Sage.

———. 1968. *Socialization and society*. Boston: Little, Brown.

Clore, G.L., R.M. Bray, S.M. Itkin, and P. Murphy. 1978. Interracial attitudes and behavior at a summer camp. *Journal of Personality and Social Psychology* 36:107–16.

Cloward, R. 1959. Illegitimate means, anomie and deviant behavior. *American Sociological Review* 24:164–76.

Cohen, A. 1959. Some implications of self-esteem for social influence. In *Personality and persuasibility*, eds. C. Hovland and I. Janis. New Haven: Yale Univ. Press.

———. 1959. Situational structure, self-esteem, and threat-oriented reactions to power. In *Studies in social power*, ed. D. Cartwright. Ann Arbor, MI: Institute for Social Research.

———. 1965. The sociology of the deviant act: Anomie theory and beyond. *American Sociological Review* 30:9–14.

———. 1966. *Deviance and control*. Englewood Cliffs, NJ: Prentice-Hall.

Cohen, E.G., M.E. Lockheed, and M.R. Lohman. 1976. The center for interracial cooperation: A field experiment. *Sociology of Education* 49:47–58.

Cohen, E.G. and S. Roper. 1972. Modification of interracial interaction disability: An application of status characteristic theory. *American Sociological Review* 37:643–57.

Cohen, L. and J. Kluegel. 1978. Determinants of juvenile court dispositions: Ascriptive and achieved factors in two metropolitan courts. *American Sociological Review* 43:162–76.

Cohen, R. 1982. *In the end, this son is the father*. Washington Post Syndicate.

Cohn, R. 1978. The effect of employment status change on self-attitudes. *Social Psychology* 41:81–93.

Coleman, J.S. 1957. *Community conflict*. New York: Free Press.

Coleman, R.P. and B.L. Neugarten. 1971. *Social status in the city*. San Francisco: Jossey-Bass.

Collett, P. 1971. On training Englishmen in the nonverbal behavior of Arabs: An experiment in inter-cultural communication. *International Journal of Psychology* 6:209–15.

Comstock, G. 1984. Media influences on aggression. In *Prevention and control of aggression: Principles, practices and research*, ed. A. Goldstein. New York: Pergamon.

Condon, W.S. and W.D. Ogston. 1967. A segmentation of behavior. *Journal of Psychiatric Research* 5:221–35.

Condry, J. 1977. Enemies of exploration: Self-initiated versus other initiated learning. *Journal of Personality and Social Psychology* 35:459–77.

Cook, S.W. 1972. Motives in a conceptual analysis of attitude-related behavior. In *Racial attitudes in America: Analyses and findings of social psychology*, eds. J. Brigham and T. Weissbach. New York: Harper and Row.

Cooley, C.H. 1902. *Human nature and the social order*. New York: Scribner.

———. 1908. A study of the early use of self-words by a child. *Psychological Review* 15:339–57.

Cooper, H.M. 1979. Statistically combining independent studies: A meta-analysis of sex differences in confor-

mity research. *Journal of Personality and Social Psychology* 37:131–46.

———. 1981. Ubiquitous halo. *Psychological Bulletin* 90:218–44.

Cooper, J. and R.H. Fazio. 1979. The formation and persistence of attitudes that support intergroup conflict. In *The social psychology of intergroup relations*, eds. W.G. Austin and S. Worchel. Monterey, CA: Brooks/Cole.

Coopersmith, S. 1967. *The antecedents of self-esteem*. San Francisco: W. H. Freeman.

Coser, L.A. 1956. *The functions of social conflict*. Glencoe, IL: Free Press.

———. 1967. *Continuities in the study of social conflict*. New York: Free Press.

Coser, R.L. 1960. Laughter among colleagues. *Psychiatry* 23:81–95.

Costa, P.T., Jr. and R.R. McCrae. 1980. Still stable after all these years: Personality as a key to some issues in adulthood and old age. In *Life-span development and behavior*, eds. P.B. Baltes and O.G. Brim, Jr. Vol. 3. New York: Academic Press.

Cozby, P. 1972. Self-disclosure, reciprocity, and liking. *Sociometry* 35:151–60.

Crittenden, K.S. 1983. Sociological aspects of attribution. *Annual Review of Sociology* 9:425–86.

Croner, M.D. and R.H. Willis. 1961. Perceived differences in task competence and asymmetry of dyadic influence. *Journal of Abnormal and Social Psychology* 62:705–708.

Crosbie, P.V. 1972. Social exchange and power compliance: A test of Homans' proposition. *Sociometry* 35:203–22.

Crosbie, P.V., ed. 1975. *Interaction in small groups*. New York: Macmillan Co.

Cumming, E. and W.E. Henry. 1961. *Growing old: The process of disengagement*. New York: Basic Books.

Cunningham, J.D. and H.H. Kelley. 1975. Causal attributions for interpersonal events of varying magnitudes. *Journal of Personality* 43:74–93.

Cunningham, M., J. Steinberg, and R. Grev. 1980. Wanting to and having to help: Separate motivations for positive mood and guilt induced helping. *Journal of Personality and Social Psychology* 38:181–92.

Dabbs, J.M., Jr. and H. Leventhal. 1966. Effects of varying the recommendations in a fear-arousing communication. *Journal of Personality and Social Psychology* 4:525–31.

Daher, D. and P. Banikiotes. 1976. Interpersonal attraction and rewarding aspects of disclosure content and level. *Journal of Personality and Social Psychology* 33:492–96.

Danish, S.J., M.A. Smyer, and C.A. Nowak. 1980. Developmental intervention: Enhancing life-event processes. In *Life-span development and behavior*, eds. P.B. Baltes and O.G. Brim, Jr. Vol. 3. New York: Academic Press.

Dank, B. 1971. Coming out in the gay world. *Psychiatry* 34:180–97.

Danzger, M.H. 1975. Validating conflict data. *American Sociological Review* 40:570–84.

Darley, J.M. and C.D. Batson. 1973. From Jerusalem to Jericho: A study of situational and dispositional variables in helping behavior. *Journal of Personality and Social Psychology* 27:100–108.

Darley, J.M. and R.H. Fazio. 1980. Expectancy confirmation processes arising in the social interaction sequence. *American Psychologist* 35:867–81.

Darley, J.M. and G.R. Goethals. 1980. People's analyses of the causes of ability-linked performances. In *Advances in experimental social psychology*, ed. L. Berkowitz. Vol. 13. New York: Academic Press.

Darley, J.M. and B. Latané. 1968. Bystander intervention in emergencies: Diffusion of responsibility. *Journal of Personality and Social Psychology* 8:377–83.

Darley, J.M., A.I. Teger, and L.D. Lewis. 1973. Do groups always inhibit individuals' responses to potential emergencies? *Journal of Personality and Social Psychology* 26:395–99.

Darwin, C. 1872. *The expression of emotion in man and animals.* London: Murray.

Davidson, A.R. and J. Jaccard. 1979. Variables that moderate the attitude-behavior relation: Results of a longitudinal survey. *Journal of Personality and Social Psychology* 37:1364–76.

Davies, J.C. 1962. Toward a theory of revolution. *American Sociological Review* 27:5–19.

Davis, D. and W.T. Perkowitz. 1979. Consequences of responsiveness in dyadic interaction: Effects of probability of response and proportion of content-related responses on interpersonal attraction. *Journal of Personality and Social Psychology* 37:534–50.

Davis, F. 1961. Deviance disavowal: The management of strained interaction by the visibly handicapped. *Social Problems* 9:120–32.

Davis, J. 1976. Self-disclosure in an acquaintance exercise: Responsibility for level of intimacy. *Journal of Personality and Social Psychology* 33:787–92.

Davis, K. 1937. The sociology of prostitution. *American Sociological Review* 2:744–55.

———. 1947. Final note on a case of extreme isolation. *American Journal of Sociology* 52:432–37.

Davis, M.H. 1983. Empathic concern and the muscular dystrophy telethon. *Personality and Social Psychology Bulletin* 9:223–29.

Deaux, K. and T. Emswiller. 1974. Explanations of successful performance on sex-linked tasks: What is skill for the male is luck for the female. *Journal of Personality and Social Psychology* 29:80–85.

de Charms, R. 1957. Affiliation motivation and productivity in small groups. *Journal of Abnormal and Social Psychology* 55:222–26.

Deci, E. 1975. *Intrinsic motivation.* New York: Plenum.

Deci, E., J. Nezlek, and L. Sherman. 1981. Characteristics of the rewarder and intrinsic motivation of the rewardee. *Journal of Personality and Social Psychology* 40:1–10.

Dedrick, D.K. 1978. Deviance and sanctioning within small groups. *Social Psychology* 41:94–105.

DeLamater, J. and P. MacCorquodale. 1979. *Premarital sexuality: Attitudes, relationships, behavior.* Madison, WI: Univ. of Wisconsin Press.

DeLamater, J. and K. McKinney. 1982. Response-effects of question content. In *Response behavior in the survey-interview*, eds. W. Dijkstra and J. Van der Zouwen. London: Academic Press.

DeLozier, P. 1979. *An application of attachment theory to the study of child abuse.* Unpublished doctoral dissertation. California School of Professional Psychology.

Dentler, R. and K. Erikson. 1959. The functions of deviance in groups. *Social Problems* 7:98–107.

Denzin, N. 1977. *Childhood socialization: Studies in the development of language, social behavior, and identity.* San Francisco: Jossey-Bass.

———. 1983. *On understanding emotion.* San Francisco: Jossey-Bass.

DePaulo, B.M., K. Lanier, and T. Davis. 1983. Detecting the deceit of the motivated liar. *Journal of Personality and Social Psychology* 45:1096–1103.

DePaulo, B.M., G.D. Lassiter, and J.T. Stone. 1983. Attentional determinants of success at determining deception and truth. *Personality and Social Psychology Bulletin* 8:273–79.

DePaulo, B.M., A. Nadler, and J.D. Fisher. 1983. *New directions in helping: Help seeking.* Vol. 2. New York: Academic Press.

DePaulo, B.M., R. Rosenthal, R.A. Eisenstat, P.L. Rogers, and S. Finkelstein. 1978. Decoding discrepant nonverbal cues. *Journal of Personality and Social Psychology* 36:313–23.

Der-Karabetian, A. and A. Smith. 1977. Sex-role stereotyping in the United States: Is it changing? *Sex Roles* 3:193–98.

Derlega, V. and A. Chaiken. 1975. *Sharing intimacy: What we reveal to others and why.* Englewood Cliffs, NJ: Prentice-Hall.

Derlega, V. and J. Grzelak. 1979. Appropriateness of self-disclosure. In *Self-Disclosure*, ed. G.J. Cheleene. San Francisco: Jossey-Bass.

Dervin, B. 1981. Mass communicating: Changing conceptions of the audience. In *Public Communication Campaigns*, eds. R.E. Rice and W.H. Paisley. Beverly Hills, CA: Sage.

Deschamps, J.C. 1972–73. Attribution of responsibility for failure (or success) and social categorization. (French) *Bulletin de Psychologie* 26:794–806.

de Tocqueville, A. 1955. *The old regime and the French Revolution,* Translated by Stuart Gilbert. Garden City, NY: Doubleday. Originally published 1856.

Deutsch, M. 1949. An experimental study of the effects of cooperation and competition upon group process. *Human Relations* 2:199–232.

Deutsch, M. 1973. *The resolution of conflict: Constructive and destructive processes.* New Haven: Yale University Press.

Deutsch, M. 1975. Equity, equality, and need: What determines which value will be used as the basis of distributive justice? *Journal of Social Issues* 31:137–49.

Deutsch, M. and M.E. Collins. 1951. *Interracial housing: A psychological evaluation of a social experiment.* Minneapolis: Univ. of Minnesota Press.

Deutsch, M. and R.M. Krauss. 1960. The effect of threats upon interpersonal bargaining. *Journal of Abnormal and Social Psychology* 61:181–89.

———. 1962. Studies in interpersonal bargaining. *Journal of Conflict Resolution* 6:52–76.

Diab, L. 1970. A study of intragroup and intergroup relations among experimentally produced small groups. *Genetic Psychology Monographs* 82:49–82.

Dickoff, H. 1961. Reactions to evaluations by others as a function of self-evaluation and the interaction context. Ph.D. Dissertation, Raleigh, NC: Duke Univ. Press.

Diener, E. 1980. Deindividuation: The absence of self-awareness and self-regulation in group members. In *The psychology of group influence*, ed. P.B. Paulus. Hillsdale, NJ: Erlbaum.

Diener, E. and M. Wallbom. 1976. Effects of self-awareness on antinormative behavior. *Journal of Research in Personality* 10:107–11.

Dienstbier, R.A. 1978. Attribution, socialization, and moral decision making. In *New directions in attribution research*, eds. J. Harvey, W. Ickes, and R.F. Kidd. Vol. 2. Hillsdale, NJ: Erlbaum.

Dion, K., E. Berscheid, and E. Walster (Hatfield). 1972. What is beautiful is good. *Journal of Personality and Social Psychology* 24:285–90.

Dion, K., R. Baron, and N. Miller. 1970. Why do groups make riskier decisions than individuals? In *Advances in experimental social psychology*, ed. L. Berkowitz. Vol. 5. New York: Academic Press.

Dipboye, R.L. 1977. Alternative approaches to deindividuation. *Psychological Bulletin* 84:1057–75.

Dipboye, R.L., H.L. Fromkin, and K. Wiback. 1975. Relative importance of applicant sex, attractiveness and scholastic standing in evaluation of job applicant resumes. *Journal of Applied Psychology* 60:39–45.

Doering, C.H. 1980. The endocrine system. In *Constancy and change in human development*, eds. O.G. Brim, Jr. and J. Kagan. Cambridge, MA: Harvard Univ. Press.

Dohrenwend, B.P. 1961. The social psychological nature of stress: A framework for causal inquiry. *Journal of Abnormal and Social Psychology* 62:294–302.

Dohrenwend, B.P. and B.S. Dohrenwend. 1976. Sex differences and psychiatric disorders. *American Journal of Sociology* 81:1447–54.

———. 1974. Social and cultural influences on psychopathology. *Annual Review of Psychology* 25:417–52.

Doise, W., G. Csepeli, H.D. Dann, C. Gouge, K. Larsen, and A. Ostell. 1972. An experimental investigation into the formation of intergroup representations. *European Journal of Social Psychology* 2:202–04.

Dollard, J., J. Doob, N. Miller, O. Mowrer, and R. Sears. 1939. *Frustration and aggression*. New Haven: Yale Univ. Press.

Dollinger, S. and M. Thelen. 1978. Overjustification and children's intrinsic motivation: Comparative effects of four rewards. *Journal of Personality and Social Psychology* 36:1259–69.

Dornbusch, S., A. H. Hastorf, S.A. Richardson, R.E. Muzzy, and R.S. Vreeland. 1965. The perceiver and the perceived: Their relative influence on the categories of interpersonal cognition. *Journal of Personality and Social Psychology* 1:434–41.

Douvan, E. and J. Adelson. 1966. *The adolescent experience*. New York: Wiley.

Dovidio, J.F. and S.L. Ellyson. 1982. Decoding visual dominance: Attributions of power based on relative percentages of looking while speaking and looking while listening. *Social Psychology Quarterly* 45:106–13.

Drabeck, T.E. and J.S. Stephenson. 1978. When disaster strikes. *Journal of Applied Social Psychology* 1:187–203.

Drake, G.F. 1980. The social role of slang. In *Language: Social psychological perspectives*, eds. H. Giles, W.P. Robinson, and P.M. Smith. New York: Pergamon.

Dreben, E.K., S.T. Fiske, and R. Hastie. 1979. The independence of evaluative and item information: Impression and recall order effects in behavior-based impression formation. *Journal of Personality and Social Psychology* 37:1758–68.

Driver, E.D. 1969. Self-conceptions in India and the United States: A crosscultural validation of the twenty statements test. *The Sociological Quarterly* 10:341–54.

Druckman, D. 1968. Prenegotiation experience and dyadic conflict resolution in a bargaining situation. *Journal of Experimental Social Psychology* 4:367–83.

———. 1977. *Negotiations: A social psychological perspective*. Beverly Hills, CA: Sage-Halsted.

Duncan, S., Jr. and D.W. Fiske. 1977. *Face-to-face interaction: Research methods and theory*. Hillsdale, NJ: Erlbaum.

Dunphy, D. 1972. *The primary group*. New York: Appleton-Century-Crofts.

Dutton, D.G. and A. Aron. 1974. Some evidence for heightened sexual attraction under conditions of high anxiety. *Journal of Personality and Social Psychology* 30:510–17.

Dutton, D.G., and R.A. Lake. 1973. Threat of own prejudice and reverse discrimination in interracial situations. *Journal of Personality and Social Psychology* 28:94–100.

Dyck, R.J. and B.G. Rule. 1978. Effect on retaliation of causal attribution concerning attack. *Journal of Personality and Social Psychology* 36:521–29.

Eagly, A.H. 1978. Sex differences in influenceability. *Psychological Bulletin* 85:758–73.

———. 1983. Gender and social influence: A social psychological analysis. *American Psychologist* 38:971–81.

Eagly, A.H. and L.L. Carli. 1981. Sex of researchers and sex-typed communications and determinants of sex differences in influencibility. *Psychological Bulletin* 90:1–20.

Eagly, A.H. and S. Chaiken. 1975. An attribution analysis of the effect of communicator characteristics on opinion change: The case of communicator attractiveness. *Journal of Personality and Social Psychology* 32:136–44.

Eagly, A.H. and R. Warren. 1976. Intelligence, comprehension, and opinion change. *Journal of Personality* 44:226–42.

Eaton, W.W. 1980. *The sociology of mental disorders*. New York: Praeger.

———. 1978. Life events, social supports, and psychiatric symptoms: A reanalysis of the New Haven data. *Journal of Health and Social Behavior* 19:230–34.

Ebbesen, E.B. and R.J. Bowers. 1974. Proportion of risky to conservative arguments in a group discussion and choice shift. *Journal of Personality and Social Psychology* 29:316–27.

Edwards, A.D. 1976. *Language in culture and class: The sociology of language and education*. London: Heinemann Educational.

Efran, M.G. and J.A. Cheyne. 1974. Affective concomitants of the invasion of shared space: Behavioral, physiological and verbal indicators. *Journal of Personality and Social Psychology* 29:219–26.

Ehrlich, H. and D.B. Graeven. 1971. Reciprocal self-disclosure in a dyad. *Journal of Experimental Social Psychology* 7:389–400.

Ehrlich, H.J. 1973. *The social psychology of prejudice.* New York: Wiley.

Eibl-Eibesfeldt, I. 1979. Universals in human expressive behavior. In *Nonverbal behavior: Applications and cultural implications*, ed. A. Wolfgang. New York: Academic Press.

Eisen, S.V. 1979. Actor-observer differences in information inference and causal attribution. *Journal of Personality and Social Psychology* 37:261–72.

Eisenstadt, S.D. 1956. *From generation to generation: Age groups and social structure.* Glencoe, IL: Free Press.

Ekman, P. 1972. Universals and cultural differences in facial expression of emotion. In *Nebraska symposium on motivation, 1971*, ed. J.K. Cole. Lincoln, NE: Nebraska Univ. Press.

Ekman, P. and W.V. Friesen. 1969. Nonverbal leakage and clues to deception. *Psychiatry* 32:88–106.

———. 1975. *Unmasking the face.* Englewood Cliffs, NJ: Prentice-Hall.

Ekman, P., W.V. Friesen, and S.S. Tomkins. 1971. Facial affect scoring technique (FAST): A first validity study. *Semiotica* 3:37–58.

Ekman, P., E.T. Sorenson, and W.V. Friesen. 1969. Pan-cultural elements in facial displays of emotion. *Science* 164:86–88.

Elder, G.H., Jr. 1974. *Children of the great depression.* Chicago: Univ. of Chicago Press.

———. 1975. Age differentiation and the life course. In *Annual Review of Sociology*, eds. A. Inkeles, J. Coleman, and N. Smelser. Vol. 1. Palo Alto, CA: Annual Reviews.

———. 1980. Adolescence in historical perspective. In *Handbook of adolescent psychology*, ed. J. Adelson. New York: Wiley.

———. 1981. History and the life course. In *Biography and society*, ed. D. Bertaux. Beverly Hills, CA: Sage.

———. 1985. Perspectives on the life course. In *Life course dynamics: Trajectories and transitions, 1968–1980*, ed. G.H. Elder, Jr. Ithaca, NY: Cornell Univ. Press.

Elder, G.H., Jr. and C. Bowerman. 1963. Family structure and childbearing patterns: The effect of family size and sex composition. *American Sociological Review* 28:891–905.

Elder, G.H., Jr. and J.K. Liker. 1982. Hard times in women's lives: Historical influences across forty years. *American Journal of Sociology* 88:241–69.

Elder, G.H., Jr. and R.C. Rockwell. 1979a. The depression experience in men's lives. In *Kin and communities: Families in America*, eds. A.J. Lichtman and J.R. Challinor. Washington: Smithsonian Press.

———. 1979b. Economic depression and postwar opportunity in men's lives: A study of life patterns and health. In *Research in community mental health*, ed. R. Simmons. Vol. 1. Greenwich, CT: JAI Press.

Elig, T. and I.H. Frieze. 1979. Measuring causal attributions for success or failure. *Journal of Personality and Social Psychology* 37:621–34.

Elkin, F. and G. Handel. 1978. *The child and society.* 3d ed. New York: Random House.

Elkind, D. 1961. The child's conception of his religious denomination: I. The Jewish child. *Journal of Genetic Psychology* 99:209–25.

———. 1962. The child's conception of his religious denomination: II. The Catholic child. *Journal of Genetic Psychology* 101:183–93.

———. 1963. The child's conception of his religious denomination: III. The Protestant child. *Journal of Genetic Psychology* 103:291–304.

Elliott, D.S. and S.S. Ageton. 1980. Reconciling race and class differences in self-reported and official estimates of delinquency. *American Sociological Review* 45:95–110.

Ellsworth, P.C., J.M. Carlsmith, and A. Henson. 1972. The stare as a stimulus to flight in human subjects. *Journal of Personality and Social Psychology* 21:302–11.

Emerson, R.M. 1966. Mount Everest: A case study of communication feedback and sustained group goal-striving. *Sociometry* 29:213–27.

———. 1981. Social exchange theory. In *Social psychology: Sociological perspectives*, eds. M. Rosenberg and R.H. Turner. New York: Basic Books.

Emerson, R.M. and S. Messinger. 1977. The micro-politics of trouble. *Social Problems* 25:121–34.

Emswiller, T., K. Deaux, and J.E. Willis. 1971. Similarity, sex, and requests for small favors. *Journal of Applied Social Psychology* 1:284–91.

Endler, N.S. 1966. Conformity as a function of different reinforcement schedules. *Journal of Personality and Social Psychology* 4:175–80.

Entwistle, D.R. and S.G. Doering. 1981. *The first birth: A family turning point.* Baltimore: John Hopkins Univ. Press.

Epstein, S. 1976. The political and economic basis of cancer. *Technology Review* 78:34–43.

Ericksen, J., W. Yancey, and E. Ericksen. 1979. The division of family roles. *Journal of Marriage and the Family* 41:301–13.

Erikson, E.H. 1968. *Identity: Youth and crisis.* New York: W.W. Norton.

Erikson, K. 1964. Notes on the sociology of deviance. In *The other side*, ed. H. Becker. New York: Free Press.

———. 1966. *The wayward Puritans.* New York: Wiley.

Eron, L.D. 1980. Prescription for the reduction of aggression. *American Psychologist* 35:244–52.

———. 1982. Parent-child interaction, television violence, and aggression of children. *American Psychologist* 37:197–211.

Estes, R.L. and W.L. Wilensky. 1978. Life cycle squeeze and the morale curve. *Social Forces* 56:277–92.

Etaugh, C. 1980. Effects of nonmaternal care on children: Research evidence and popular views. *American Psychologist* 35:309–19.

Ettinger, R.F., C.J. Marino, N.S. Endler, S.H. Geller, and T. Natziuk. 1971. Effects of agreement and correctness on relative competence and conformity. *Journal of Personality and Social Psychology* 19:204–12.

Etzioni, A. 1967. The Kennedy experiment. *The Western Political Quarterly* 20:361–80.

Fafouti-Milenkovic, M. and I. Uzgiris. 1979. The mother-infant communication system. In *Social interaction and communication during infancy*, ed. I. Uzgiris. In *New directions for child development*, Vol. 4. San Francisco: Jossey-Bass.

Faley, T. and J.T. Tedeschi. 1971. Status and reactions to threats. *Journal of Personality and Social Psychology* 17:192–99.

Farina, A., D. Gliha, L.A. Boudreau, J.G. Allen, and M. Sherman. 1971. Mental illness and the impact of believing others know it. *Journal of Abnormal Psychology* 77:1–5.

Fazio, R., M. Powell, and P. Herr. 1983. Toward a process model of the attitude-behavior relation: Accessing one's attitude upon mere observation of the attitude object. *Journal of Personality and Social Psychology* 44:723–735.

Fazio, R.H. and M.P. Zanna. 1981. Direct experience and attitude-behavior consistency. In *Advances in experimental social psychology*, ed. L. Berkowitz. Vol. 14. New York: Academic Press.

Feather, N.T. 1967. A structural balance approach to the analysis of communication effects. In *Advances in experimental social psychology*, ed. L. Berkowitz. Vol. 3. New York: Academic Press.

Feather, N.T. and D.J. Armstrong. 1967. Effects of variations in source attitude, receiver attitude and communication stand on reactions to source and contents of communications. *Journal of Personality* 35:435–55.

Featherman, D.L. and R.M. Hauser. 1976. Sexual inequalities and socioeconomic achievement in the U.S., 1962–1973. *American Sociological Review* 41:462–83.

Fehrenbach, P., D. Miller, and M. Thelen. 1979. The importance of consistency of modeling behavior upon imitation: A comparison of single and multiple models. *Journal of Personality and Social Psychology* 37:1412–17.

Feld, S. 1981. The focused organization of social ties. *American Journal of Sociology* 86:1015–35.

Felipe, N.J. and R. Sommer. 1966. Invasions of personal space. *Social Problems* 14:206–14.

Felson, R.B. 1980. Communication barriers and the reflected appraisal process. *Social Psychology Quarterly* 42:223–33.

———. 1981. Ambiguity and bias in the self-concept. *Social Psychology Quarterly* 44:64–69.

Ferguson, C.K. and H.H. Kelley. 1964. Significant factors in overevaluation of own group's product. *Journal of Abnormal and Social Psychology* 69:223–28.

Ferree, M.M. 1976. Working-class jobs: Housework and paid work as sources of satisfaction. *Social Problems* 23:431–41.

Festinger, L. 1950. Informal social communication. *Psychological Review* 57:271–82.

———. 1954. A theory of social comparison processes. *Human Relations* 7:117–40.

———. 1957. *A theory of cognitive dissonance*. Stanford, CA: Stanford Univ. Press.

Festinger, L. and J.M. Carlsmith. 1959. Cognitive consequences of forced compliance. *Journal of Abnormal and Social Psychology* 58:203–10.

Festinger, L., A. Pepitone, and T. Newcomb. 1952. Some consequences of deindividuation in a group. *Journal of Abnormal and Social Psychology* 47:382–89.

Festinger, L., H.W. Riecken, and S. Schachter. 1956. *When prophecy fails*. Minneapolis: Univ. of Minnesota Press.

Festinger, L., S. Schachter, and K.W. Back. 1950. *Social pressures in informal groups*. New York: Harper and Row.

Fiedler, F.E. 1964. A contingency model of leadership effectiveness. In *Advances in experimental social psychology*, ed. L. Berkowitz. Vol. 1. New York: Academic Press.

———. 1966. The effect of leadership and cultural heterogeneity on group performance: A test of the contingency model. *Journal of Experimental Social Psychology*. 2:237–64.

———. 1971. Validation and extension of the contingency model of leadership effectiveness: A review of empirical findings. *Psychological Bulletin*. 76:128–48.

———. 1978. Recent developments in research on the contingency model. In *Group processes*, ed. L. Berkowitz. New York: Academic Press.

Fiedler, F.E. and M.M. Chemers. 1974. *Leadership and effective management*. Glenview, Illinois: Scott, Foresman and Co.

Fiedler, F.E., W. Meuwese, and S. Oonk. 1961. An exploratory study of group creativity in laboratory tasks. *Acta Psychologica* 18:100–19.

Finestone, H. 1964. Cats, kicks and color. In *The other side*, ed. H. Becker. New York: Free Press.

Firestone, J.M. 1972. Theory of the riot process. *American Behavioral Scientist* 15:859–82.

Fischer, C.S. 1976. *The urban experience*. New York: Harcourt Brace Jovanovich.

———. 1980. Friendship, gender and the life cycle. Unpublished Paper. Institute of Urban and Regional Development. Univ. of California, Berkeley.

Fisek, M.H. 1974. A model for the evolution of status structures in task-oriented discussion groups. In *Expectations states theory*, eds. J. Berger, T.L. Conner, and M.H. Fisek. Cambridge, MA: Winthrop.

Fisek, M.H. and R. Ofshe. 1970. The process of status evolution. *Sociometry*. 33:327–46.

Fishbein, M. 1980. A theory of reasoned action: Some applications and implications. In *Nebraska symposium on motivation*, eds. H. Howe and M. Page. Vol. 27. Lincoln, NE: Univ. of Nebraska Press.

Fishbein, M. and I. Ajzen. 1975. *Belief, attitude, intention and behavior*. Reading, MA: Addison-Wesley.

———. 1981. Acceptance, yielding and impact: Cognitive processes in persuasion. In *Cognitive responses in persuasion*, eds. R.E. Petty, T.M. Ostrom, and T.C. Brock. Hillsdale, NJ: Erlbaum.

Fisher, J.D., B.M. DePaulo, and A. Nadler. 1981. Extending altruism beyond the altruistic act: The mixed effects of aid on the help recipient. In *Altruism and helping behavior*, eds. J.P. Rushton and R.M. Sorrentino. Hillsdale, NJ: Erlbaum.

Fisher, R. and W. Ury. 1981. *Getting to yes: Negotiating agreement without giving in*. Boston: Houghton Mifflin.

Fishman, J. 1972. *The sociology of language: An interdisciplinary social science approach to language and society*. Rowley, MA: Newbury House.

Fishman, P.M. 1978. Interaction: The work women do. *Social Problems* 25:397–406.

Fishman, P.M. 1980. Conversational insecurity. In *Lan-*

guage: *Social psychological perspectives,* eds. H. Giles and W.P. Robinson. New York: Pergamon.

Fitz, D. 1976. A renewed look at Miller's conflict theory of aggression displacement. *Journal of Personality and Social Psychology* 33:725–32.

Flavell, J.H., S.G. Shipstead, and K. Croft. 1978. What young children think you see when their eyes are closed. Unpublished report. Stanford Univ., CA.

Form, W.H. and S. Nosow. 1958. *Community in disaster.* New York: Harper.

Forsyth, D.R., R.E. Berger, and T. Mitchell. 1981. The effects of self-serving vs. other serving claims of responsibility on attraction and attribution in groups. *Social Psychology Quarterly* 44:59–64.

Fouts, R. 1974. Language: origins, definitions and chimpanzees. *Journal of Human Evolution* 3:475–82.

Frank, F. and L.R. Anderson. 1971. Effects of task and group size upon group productivity and member satisfaction. *Sociometry* 34:135–49.

Franks, D.D. and J. Marolla. 1976. Efficacious action and social approval as interacting dimensions of self-esteem. *Sociometry* 39:324–41.

Fraser, C., C. Gouge, and M. Billig. 1971. Risky shifts, cautious shifts, and group polarization. *European Journal of Social Psychology* 1:7–30.

Fraser, C., U. Bellugi, and R. Brown. 1963. Control of grammar in imitation, comprehension and production. *Journal of Verbal Learning and Verbal Behavior* 2:121–35.

Fredricks, A. and D. Dossett. 1983. Attitude-behavior relations: A comparison of the Fishbein-Ajzen and the Bentler-Speckart models. *Journal of Personality and Social Psychology* 45:501–12.

Freedman, D.G. 1979. *Human sociobiology.* New York: Free Press.

Freese, L. 1974. Conditions for status equality. *Sociometry* 37:174–88.

———. 1976. The generalization of specific performance expectations. *Sociometry.* 39:194–200.

Freese, L. and B.P. Cohen. 1973. Eliminating status generalization. *Sociometry.* 36:177–93.

French, J.R.P., Jr., H.W. Morrison, and G. Levinger. 1960. Coercive power and forces affecting conformity. *Journal of Abnormal and Social Psychology.* 61:93–101.

French, J.R.P., Jr., and B. Raven. 1959. The bases of social power. In *Studies in social power,* ed. D. Cartwright. Ann Arbor, MI: Institute for Social Research.

Freud, S. 1905. Fragment of an analysis of a case of hysteria. *Collected Papers,* Vol. 3. New York: Basic Books.

———. 1930. *Civilization and its discontents.* London: Hogarth Press.

———. 1950. Why war? In *Collected papers,* ed. J. Strachey. Vol. 5. London: Hogarth.

Frey, D. 1978. Reactions to success and failure in public and private conditions. *Journal of Experimental Social Psychology* 14:172–79.

———. 1982. Different levels of cognitive dissonance, information seeking and information avoidance. *Journal of Personality and Social Psychology* 43:1175–83.

Frey, R.L., Jr. and J.S. Adams. 1972. The negotiator's dilemma: Simultaneous in-group and out-group conflict. *Journal of Experimental Social Psychology* 8:331–46.

Frideres, J. 1971. Situational and personality variables as influencing the relationship between attitudes and overt behavior. *Canadian Review of Social Anthropology* 8:91–105.

Frideres, J.S., L.G. Warner, and S.L. Albrecht. 1971. The impact of social constraints on the relationship between attitudes and behavior. *Social Forces* 50:102–12.

Frieze, I.H., J.E. Parsons, P.B. Johnson, D.N. Ruble, and G.L. Zellman. 1978. *Women and sex roles: A social psychological perspective.* New York: W.W. Norton.

Frodi, A. 1975. The effect of exposure to weapons on aggressive behavior from a cross-cultural perspective. *International Journal of Psychology* 10:283–92.

Frye, R.L. 1966. The effect of orientation and feedback of success and effectiveness on the attractiveness and esteem of the group. *Journal of Social Psychology* 70:205–11.

Gaertner, S. and L. Bickman. 1971. A nonreactive indicator of racial discrimination: The wrong number technique. *Journal of Personality and Social Psychology* 20:218–22.

Gahagen, J.P. and J.T. Tedeschi. 1968. Strategy and the credibility of promises in the Prisoner's Dilemma game. *Journal of Conflict Resolution* 12:224–34.

Gamson, W.A. 1968. *Power and Discontent.* Homewood, IL: Dorsey.

Gardner, R.A. and B.T. Gardner. 1980. Comparative psychology and language acquisition. In *Psychology: The state of the art,* eds. K. Salzinger and F. Denmark. Annals of the New York Academy of Science.

Garfinkel, H. 1956. Conditions of successful degradation ceremonies. *American Sociological Review* 61:420–24.

Gecas, V. 1971. Parental behavior and dimensions of adolescent self-evaluation. *Sociometry* 34:466–82.

———. 1979. The influence of social class on socialization. In *Contemporary theories about the family,* eds. W. Burr, R. Hill, F.I. Nye, and I. Reiss. Vol. 1. New York: Free Press.

———. 1981. Contexts of socialization. In *Social psychology: Sociological perspectives,* eds. M. Rosenberg and R.H. Turner. New York: Basic Books.

Gecas, V. and F.I. Nye. 1974. Sex and class differences in parent–child interaction: A test of Kohn's hypothesis. *Journal of Marriage and the Family* 36:742–49.

Gecas, V. and M.L. Schwalbe. 1983. Beyond the looking-glass self: Social structure and efficacy-based self-esteem. *Social Psychology Quarterly* 46:77–88.

Geen, R.G. 1978. Some effects of observing violence upon the behavior of the observer. In *Progress in experimental personality research,* ed. B.A. Maher. Vol. 8. New York: Academic Press.

Geen, R.G. and M.G. Quanty. 1977. The catharsis of aggression: An analysis of a hypothesis. In *Advances in experimental social psychology,* ed. L. Berkowitz. Vol. 10. New York: Academic Press.

Geen, R.G., L. Stonner, and G.L. Shope. 1975. The facilitation of aggression by aggression: A study in response inhibition and disinhibition. *Journal of Personality and Social Psychology* 31:721–26.

Gekoski, N. 1952. Predicting group productivity. *Personnel Psychology* 5:281–92.

Geller, V. 1977. The role of visual access in impression

management and impression formation. Unpublished doctoral dissertation, Columbia Univ., NY.

Gelles, R. 1980. A profile of violence toward children in the United States. In *Child abuse*, eds. G. Gerbner, C. Ross, and E. Zigler. New York: Oxford Univ. Press.

George, C. and M. Main. 1979. Social interactions of young abused children: Approach, avoidance and aggression. *Child Development* 50:306-18.

Gerard, H.B., R.A. Wilhelmy, and E.S. Conolley. 1968. Conformity and group size. *Journal of Personality and Social Psychology* 8:79-82.

Gerard, H.B., E.S. Conolley, and R.A. Wilhelmy. 1974. Compliance, justification, and cognitive change. In *Advances in experimental social psychology*, ed. L. Berkowitz. Vol. 7. New York: Academic Press.

Gergen, K.J. 1971. *The self-concept.* New York: Holt Rinehart and Winston.

Gergen, K.J., P. Ellsworth, C. Maslach, and M. Siepel. 1975. Obligation, donor resources and reactions to aid in three cultures. *Journal of Personality and Social Psychology* 31:390-400.

Gergen, K.J., M.M. Gergen, and K. Meter. 1972. Individual orientation to prosocial behavior. *Journal of Social Issues* 28:105-30.

Gergen, K.J., S.J. Morse, and K.A. Bode. 1974. Overpaid or overworked? Cognitive and behavioral reactions to inequitable rewards. *Journal of Applied Social Psychology.* 4:259-74.

Gerson, L.W. 1967. Punishment and position: The sanctioning of deviants in small groups. *Case Western Reserve Journal of Sociology* 1:54-62.

Gesell, A. and F. Ilg. 1943. *Infant and child in the culture of today.* New York: Harper and Row.

Gibb, C.A. 1969. Leadership. In *Handbook of social psychology*, eds. G. Lindzey and E. Aronson. Vol. 4. 2nd ed. Reading, MA: Addison-Wesley.

Gifford, R. 1982. Projected interpersonal distance and orientation choices: Personality, sex, and social situation. *Social Psychology Quarterly* 45:145-52.

Gilbert, G.M. 1951. Stereotype persistence and change among college students. *Journal of Abnormal and Social Psychology* 46:245-54.

Gilbert, T.F. 1978. *Human competence.* New York: McGraw-Hill.

Gilchrist, J.C., M.E. Shaw, and L.C. Walker. 1954. Some effects of unequal distribution of information in a wheel group structure. *Journal of Abnormal and Social Psychology.* 49:554-56.

Giles, H. 1980. Accommodation theory: Some new directions. In *Aspects of linguistic behavior*, ed. S. deSilva. York, England: York Univ. Press.

Giles, H., M. Hewstone, and R. St. Clair. 1981. Speech as an independent and dependent variable of social situations: An introduction and new theoretical framework. In *The social psychological significance of speech*, eds. H. Giles and R. St. Clair. Hillsdale, NJ: Erlbaum.

Giles, H. and P.F. Powesland. 1976. *Speech style and social evaluation.* London: Academic Press.

Gilligan, C. 1982. *In a different voice.* Cambridge, MA: Harvard Univ. Press.

Glaser, B.G. and A.L. Strauss. 1971. *Status passage: A formal theory.* Chicago: Aldine.

Goffman, E. 1952. Cooling the mark out: Some adaptations to failure. *Psychiatry: Journal for the Study of Interpersonal Processes* 15:451-63.

———. 1959a. *The presentation of self in everyday life.* Garden City, NY: Doubleday / Anchor.

———. 1959b. The moral career of the mental patient. *Psychiatry* 22:125-69.

———. 1963a. *Behavior in public places.* New York: Free Press.

———. 1963b. *Stigma: Notes on the management of spoiled identity.* Englewood Cliffs, NJ: Spectrum/Prentice-Hall.

———. 1967. *Interaction ritual.* Chicago: Aldine.

———. 1974. *Frame analysis.* New York: Harper and Row.

———. 1983. Felicity's condition. *American Journal of Sociology* 89:1-53.

Goldberg, C. 1974. Sex roles, task competence, and conformity. *Journal of Psychology* 86:157-164.

———. 1975. Conformity to majority type as a function of task and acceptance of sex-related stereotypes. *Journal of Psychology* 89:25-37.

Goldberg, P.A., N. Gottesdiener, and P.R. Abramson. 1975. Another put-down of women? Perceived attractiveness as a function of support for the feminist movement. *Journal of Personality and Social Psychology* 32:113-15.

Goldfarb, W. 1943. The effects of early institutional care on adolescent personality. *Journal of Experimental Education* 12:106-29.

Golembiewski, R.T. 1962. *The small group: An analysis of research concepts and operations.* Chicago: Univ. of Chicago Press.

Goodacre, D.M. III. 1951. The use of a sociometric test as a predictor of combat unit effectiveness. *Sociometry* 14:148-52.

Goode, E. 1978. *Deviant behavior: An interactionist approach.* Englewood Cliffs, NJ: Prentice-Hall.

Goode, W.J. 1960. A theory of role strain. *American Sociological Review* 25:483-96.

Goodman, P.S. and A. Friedman. 1969. An examination of quantity and quality of performance under conditions of overpayment in piece rate. *Organizational Behavior and Human Performance.* 4:365-74.

———. 1971. An examination of Adams' theory of inequity. *Administrative Science Quarterly.* 16:271-88.

Goodwin, C. 1979. The interactive construction of a sentence in natural conversation. In *Everyday language: Studies in ethnomethodology*, ed. G. Psathas. New York: Irvington.

Goodwin, L. 1972. *Do the poor want to work? A social psychological study of work orientations.* Washington, DC: Brookings Institute.

Gonos, G. 1977. "Situation" vs. "Frame": The "interactionist" and the "structuralist" analysis of everyday life. *American Sociological Review.* 42:854-67.

Gonzales, M., J. Davis, G. Loney, C. Lukens, and C. Junghans. 1983. Interactional approach to interpersonal attraction. *Journal of Personality and Social Psychology* 44:1192-97.

Goranson, R. and L. Berkowitz. 1966. Reciprocity and responsibility reactions to prior help. *Journal of Personality and Social Psychology* 3:227-32.

Gordon, C. 1968. Self-conceptions: Configurations of content. In *The self in social interaction*, eds. C. Gordon and K.J. Gergen. New York: Wiley.

———. 1976. Development of evaluated role-identities. In *Annual Review of Sociology*, eds. A. Inkeles, J. Coleman, and N. Smelser, 2:405–33.

Gordon, S.L. 1981. The sociology of sentiments and emotion. In *Social psychology: Sociological perspectives*, eds. M. Rosenberg and R.H. Turner. New York: Basic Books.

Gorfein, D.S. 1964. The effects of a nonunanimous majority on attitude change. *Journal of Social Psychology* 63:333–38.

Gould, R.L. 1978. *Transformations*. New York: Simon & Schuster.

Gouldner, A. 1960. The norm of reciprocity: A preliminary statement. *American Sociological Review* 25:161–78.

Gove, W. and M. Geerken. 1977. The effect of children and employment on the mental health of married men and women. *Social Forces* 56:66–76.

Gove, W. and M. Hughes. 1979. Possible causes of the apparent sex differences in physical health: An empirical investigation. *American Sociological Review* 44:126–46.

Gove, W., M. Hughes, and M.R. Geerken. 1980. Playing dumb: A form of impression management with undesirable effects. *Social Psychology Quarterly* 43:89–102.

Granberg, D. 1978. GRIT in the final quarter: Reversing the arms race through unilateral initiatives. *Bulletin of Peace Proposals* 9:210–21.

Granovetter, M.S. 1973. The strength of weak ties. *American Journal of Sociology* 78:1360–80.

Grayshon, M.C. 1980. Social grammar, social psychology, and linguistics. In *Language: Social psychological perspectives*, eds. H. Giles, W.P. Robinson, and P.M. Smith. New York: Pergamon.

Green, J.A. 1972. Attitudinal and situational determinants of intended behavior toward blacks. *Journal of Personality and Social Psychology* 22:13–17.

Greenbaum, P. and H. Rosenfeld. 1978. Patterns of avoidance in response to interpersonal staring and proximity: Effects of bystanders on drivers at a traffic intersection. *Journal of Personality and Social Psychology* 36:575–87.

Greenberg, J.H. 1966. *Language universals*. The Hague: Mouton.

Greenberg, M. 1980. A theory of indebtedness. In *Social exchange: Advances in theory and research*, eds. K.J. Gergen, M.S. Greenberg, and R.H. Willis. New York: Plenum.

Greenberg, M. and D. Frisch. 1972. Effect of intentionality on willingness to reciprocate a favor. *Journal of Experimental Social Psychology* 8:99–111.

Greenfield, L. 1972. Spanish and English usage self-ratings in various situational contexts. In *Advances in the sociology of language II*, ed. J.A. Fishman. The Hague: Mouton.

Greenley, J. 1979. Familial expectations, post-hospital adjustment and the societal reaction perspective on mental illness. *Journal of Health and Social Behavior* 20:217–27.

Greenwald, A.G. and A.R. Pratkanis. 1984. The self. In *Handbook of social cognition*, eds. R.S. Wyer and T.K. Srull. Hillsdale, NJ: Erlbaum.

Grice, P.H. 1975. Logic and conversation. In *Syntax and semantics, volume 3: Speech acts*, eds. P. Cole and J.L. Morgan. New York: Academic Press.

Grimshaw, A.D. 1973. On language in society. Part 1. *Contemporary Sociology* 2:575–85.

———. 1981. Talk and social control. In *Social psychology: Sociological perspectives*, eds. M. Rosenberg and R.H. Turner. New York: Basic Books.

Gross, E. and G.P. Stone. 1964. Embarrassment and the analysis of role requirements. *American Journal of Sociology* 70:1–15.

Guetzkow, H. and W.R. Dill. 1957. Factors in the organizational development of task-oriented groups. *Sociometry* 20:175–204.

Guetzkow, H. and H.A. Simon. 1955. The impact of certain communication nets upon organization and performance in task-oriented groups. *Management Science* 1:233–50.

Guimond, S. and L. Dubé-Simard. 1983. Relative deprivation theory and the Quebec nationalist movement: The cognition-emotion distinction and the personal-group deprivation issue. *Journal of Personality and Social Psychology* 44:526–35.

Gumperz, J.J. 1976. The sociolinguistic significance of conversational code-switching. In *Papers on language and context*, eds. J. Cook-Gumperz and J.J. Gumperz. Berkeley, CA: Univ. of California Language Behavior Research Laboratory.

Gurin, G., J. Veroff, and S. Feld. 1960. *Americans view their mental health*. New York: Basic Books.

Guttman, D. 1977. The cross-cultural perspective: Notes toward a comparative psychology of aging. In *Handbook of the psychology of aging*, eds. J.E. Birren and K.W. Schaie. New York: Van Nostrand Reinhold.

Guttman, L. 1944. A basis for scaling qualitative data. *American Sociological Review* 9:139–50.

Haan, N. 1978. Two moralities in action contexts: Relationships to thought, ego regulation, and development. *Journal of Personality and Social Psychology* 36:286–305.

Haan, N. and D. Day. 1974. A longitudinal study of change and sameness in personality development: Adolescence to later adulthood. *International Journal of Aging and Human Development* 5:11–39.

Haan, N., M.B. Smith, and J. Block. 1968. Moral reasoning of young adults: Political-social behavior, family background, and personality correlates. *Journal of Personality and Social Psychology* 10:183–201.

Hagstrom, W.O. and H.C. Selvin. 1965. Two dimensions of cohesiveness in small groups. *Sociometry* 28:30–43.

Halberstram, D. 1979. *The powers that be*. New York: Alfred Knopf.

Hall, E.T. 1966. *The hidden dimension*. Garden City, NJ: Doubleday.

Halpin, A.W. and B.J. Winer. 1952. *The leadership behavior of the airplane commander*. Research Foundation, Co: Ohio State Univ.

Hamilton, D.L. 1979. A cognitive-attributional analysis of stereotyping. In *Advances in experimental social psychology*, ed. L. Berkowitz. Vol. 12. New York: Academic Press.

Hamilton, D.L. and G.D. Bishop. 1976. Attitudinal and behavioral effects of initial integration of white suburban neighborhoods. *Journal of Social Issues* Vol. 32:47–56.

Hammond, L.K. and M. Goldman. 1961. Competition and non-competition and its relationship to individual and group productivity. *Sociometry* 24:46–60.

Handel, W. 1979. Normative expectations and the emergence of meaning as solutions to problems: Convergence of structural and interactionist views. *American Journal of Sociology* 84:855–81.

Hanni, R. 1980. What is planned during speech pauses? In *Language: Social psychological perspectives*, eds. H. Giles, W.P. Robinson, and P.M. Smith. New York: Pergamon.

Harding, J. and R. Hogrefe. 1952. Attitudes of white department store employees toward Negro coworkers. *Journal of Social Issues* 8:18–28.

Harding, J., H. Proshansky, B. Kutner, and I. Chein. 1969. Prejudice and ethnic relations. In *The handbook of social psychology*, eds. G. Lindzey and E. Aronson, 2d ed. Vol. 5. Reading, MA: Addison-Wesley.

Hardy, R.C. 1971. Effect of leadership style on the performance of small classroom groups: A test of the contingency model. *Journal of Personality and Social Psychology*. 19:367–74.

Hardy, R.C. 1975. A test of poor leader-member relations cells of the contingency model on elementary school children. *Child Development* 45:958–64.

Hardy, R.C., S. Sack, and F. Harpine. 1973. An experimental test of the contingency model on small classroom groups. *Journal of Psychology* 85:3–16.

Harnett, D.L. and J.P. Vincelette. 1978. Strategic influences on bargaining effectiveness. In *Contributions to experimental economics*, ed. H. Sauermann. Vol. 7. Tubingen: Mohr.

Harper, R.G., A.N. Wiens, and J.D. Matarazzo. 1978. *Nonverbal communication: The state of the art*. New York: Wiley.

Harris, L. et al. 1975. *The myth and the reality of aging in America*. Washington: National Council on Aging.

———. 1982. *Aging in the 80's*. Washington: National Council on Aging.

Harris, M.B. 1974. Mediators between frustration and aggression in a field experiment. *Journal of Experimental Social Psychology* 10:561–71.

Harris, M.B., S.M. Benson, and C. Hall. 1975. The effects of confession on altruism. *Journal of Social Psychology* 96:187–92.

Harrison, A. 1977. Mere exposure. In *Advances in Experimental Social Psychology*, ed. L. Berkowitz. Vol. 10. New York: Academic Press.

Harrison, A. and L. Saeed. 1977. Let's make a deal: An analysis of revelations and stipulations in lonely hearts advertisements. *Journal of Personality and Social Psychology* 35:257–64.

Harrison, J. 1978. Warning: The male sex role may be dangerous to your health. *Journal of Social Issues* 3:65–86.

Hart, R.J. 1978. Crime and punishment in the Army. *Journal of Personality and Social Psychology* 36:1456–71.

Harvey, J.H., K.L. Yarkin, J.M. Lightner, and J.P. Tolin. 1980. Unsolicited interpretation and recall of interpersonal events. *Journal of Personality and Social Psychology* 38:551–68.

Haskell, M.R. and L. Yablonsky. 1983. *Criminology: Crime and Criminality* 3d ed. Boston: Houghton Mifflin.

Hastorf, A.H. and H. Cantril. 1954. They saw a game: A case study. *Journal of Abnormal and Social Psychology* 49:129–34.

Hastorf, A.H., J. Wildfogel, and T. Cassman. 1979. Acknowledgement of a handicap as a tactic in social interaction. *Journal of Personality and Social Psychology* 37:1790–97.

Hatfield, E. 1982. What do women and men want from love and sex? In *Changing boundaries: Gender roles and sexual behavior*, eds. E.R. Allgeier and N.B. McCormick. Palo Alto, CA: Mayfield.

Hatfield, E. and G.W. Walster. 1983. *A new look at love*, 2d ed. Reading, MA: Addison-Wesley.

Havighurst. 1948. *Developmental tasks and education*. Chicago: Univ. of Chicago Press.

Hayduk, L.A. 1978. Personal space: An evaluation and orienting review. *Psychological Bulletin* 85:117–34.

Hearold, S.L. 1979. Meta-analysis of the effects of television on social behavior. Unpublished doctoral dissertation. Univ. of Colorado.

Heider, E.R. and D. Olivier. 1972. The structure of the color space in naming and memory of two languages. *Cognitive Psychology* 3:337–54.

Heider, F. 1944. Social perception and phenomenal causality. *Psychological Review* 51:258–374.

———. 1958. *The psychology of interpersonal relations*. New York: Wiley.

Heirich, M. 1977. Change of heart: A test of some widely held theories about religious conversion. *American Journal of Sociology* 83:653–80.

Heiss, J. 1981. Social roles. In *Social psychology: Sociological perspectives*, eds. M. Rosenberg and R.H. Turner. New York: Basic Books.

Heiss, J. and S. Owens. 1972. Self-evaluations of blacks and whites. *American Journal of Sociology* 78:360–70.

Henley, N.M. 1977. *Body politics: Power, sex, and nonverbal communication*. Englewood Cliffs, NJ: Prentice-Hall.

Hensley, V. and S. Duval. 1976. Some perceptual determinants of perceived similarity, liking, and correctness. *Journal of Personality and Social Psychology* 34:159–68.

Hepburn, C. and A. Locksley. 1983. Subjective awareness of stereotyping: Do we know when our judgements are prejudiced? *Social Psychology Quarterly* 45:311–18.

Heron, A. and S. Chown. 1967. *Age and function*. Boston: Little, Brown.

Heslin, R. and D. Dunphy. 1964. Three dimensions of member satisfaction in small groups. *Human Relations* 17:99–112.

Hess, A.L. and H.L. Bradshaw. 1970. Positiveness of self-concept and ideal self as a function of age. *Journal of Genetic Psychology* 117:57–67.

Hess, R. and V. Shipman. 1965. Early experience and the socialization of cognitive modes in children. *Child Development* 36:869–86.

Hewitt, J.P. 1976. *Self and society*. Boston: Allyn and Bacon.

Hewitt, J.P. and R. Stokes. 1975. Disclaimers. *American Sociological Review* 40:1–11.

Heyl, B.S. 1977. The madam as teacher: The training of house prostitutes. *Social Problems* 24:545–55.

Higbee, K.L. 1969. Fifteen years of fear arousal: Research on threat appeals 1953-1968. *Psychological Bulletin* 72:426–44.

Higgins, E.T. and G.A. King. 1981. Accessibility of social constructs: Information processing consequences of individual and contextual variability. In *Personality, cognitions, and social interaction*, eds. N. Cantor and J.F. Kihlstrom. Hillsdale, NJ: Erlbaum.

Higgins, E.T., G.A. King, and G.H. Mavin. 1982. Individual construct accessibility and subjective impressions and recall. *Journal of Personality and Social Psychology* 43:35–47.

Hill, C., Z. Rubin, and L. Peplau. 1976. Breakups before marriage: The end of 103 affairs. *Journal of Social Issues* 32(1):147–68.

Hill, C. and D. Stull. 1981. Sex differences in effects of social and value similarity in same-sex friendship. *Journal of Personality and Social Psychology* 41:488–502.

Hilton, T.L. and G.W. Berglund. 1974. Sex differences in mathematics achievement—a longitudinal study. *Journal of Educational Research* 67:231–37.

Hindelang, M., T. Hirschi, and J. Weis. 1979. Correlates of delinquency: The illusion of discrepancy between self-report and official measures. *American Sociological Review* 44:995–1014.

Hinkle, S. 1975. Cognitive consistency effects on attitudes toward ingroup and outgroups products. Unpublished doctoral dissertation, Univ. of North Carolina.

Hirschi, T. 1969. *Causes of Delinquency*. Berkeley: Univ. of California Press.

Hochschild, A.R. 1975. Disengagement theory: A critique and a proposal. *American Sociological Review* 40:553–69.

———. 1979. Emotion work, feeling rules, and social structure. *American Journal of Sociology* 85:551–75.

Hoelter, J.W. 1983. The effects of role evaluation and commitment on identity salience. *Social Psychology Quarterly* 46:140–47.

Hoffman, L.W. 1977. Changes in family roles, socialization, and sex differences. *American Psychologist* 32:644–57.

Hoffman, M.L. 1981a. Is altruism part of human nature? *Journal of Personality and Social Psychology* 40:121–37.

———. 1981b. The development of empathy. In *Altruism and helping behavior*, eds. J.P. Rushton and R.M. Sorrentino. Hillsdale, NJ: Erlbaum.

Hogan, D.P. 1981. *Transitions and social change*. New York: Academic Press.

Hollander, E.P. 1961. Some effects of perceived status on responses to innovative behavior. *Journal of Abnormal and Social Psychology* 63:247–50.

———. 1975. Independence, conformity and civil liberties: Some implications from social psychological research. *Journal of Social Issues* 31:55–67.

Hollander, E.P., B.J. Fallon, and M.T. Edwards. 1977. Some aspects of influence and acceptability for appointed and elected group leaders. *Journal of Psychology* 95:289–96.

Hollander, E.P. and J.W. Julian. 1969. Contemporary trends in the analysis of leadership processes. *Psychological Bulletin* 71:387–97.

———. 1970. Studies in leader legitimacy, influence and innovation. In *Advances in Experimental Social Psychology*, ed. L. Berkowitz. Vol. 5. New York: Academic Press.

Hollander, E.P. and R. Willis. 1967. Some current issues in the psychology of conformity and nonconformity. *Psychological Bulletin* 68:62–76.

Holmes, D.S. 1971. Compensation for ego threat: Two experiments. *Journal of Personality and Social Psychology* 18:234–37.

Holmes, J.G. and P. Grant. 1979. Ethnocentric reactions to social threats. In *Social psychology: East–west perspectives*, ed. L.H. Strickland. Oxford, England: Pergamon.

Holmes, T.H. and R.H. Rahe. 1967. The social readjustment rating scale. *Journal of Psychosomatic Research* 11:213–18.

Homans, G.C. 1950. *The human group*. New York: Harcourt Brace Jovanovich.

———. 1961. *Social behavior: Its elementary forms*. New York: Harcourt Brace Jovanovich.

———. 1974. *Social behavior: Its elementary forms*, 2d ed. New York: Harcourt Brace Jovanovich.

Hood, W.R. and M. Sherif. 1962. Verbal report and judgment of an unstructured stimulus. *Journal of Psychology* 54:121–30.

Hopmann, P.T. and T.C. Smith. 1977. An application of a Richardson-process model: Soviet-American interactions in the test ban negotiations 1962–3. *Journal of Conflict Resolution* 21:701–26.

Horai, J., N. Naccari, and E. Fatoullah. 1974. The effects of expertise and physical attractiveness upon opinion agreement and liking. *Sociometry* 37:601–06.

Horai, J. and J.T. Tedeschi. 1969. The effects of threat credibility and magnitude of punishment upon compliance. *Journal of Personality and Social Psychology* 12:164–69.

Horne, W.C. and G. Long. 1972. Effect of group discussion on universalistic-particularistic orientation. *Journal of Experimental Social Psychology* 8:236–46.

Hornstein, H.A. 1965. The effects of different magnitudes of threat upon interpersonal bargaining. *Journal of Experimental Social Psychology* 1:282–93.

———. 1978. Promotive tension and prosocial behavior. A Lewinian analysis. In *Altruism, sympathy and helping*, ed. L. Wispé. New York: Academic Press.

House, J.S. 1974. Occupational stress and coronary heart disease: A review and theoretical integration. *Journal of Health and Social Behavior* 15:17–21.

———. 1981a. Social structure and personality. In *Social psychology: Sociological perspectives*, eds. M. Rosenberg and R.H. Turner. New York: Basic Books.

———. 1981b. *Work stress and social support*. Reading, MA: Addison-Wesley.

Hovland, C.I. and W. Weiss. 1951. The influence of source credibility on communication effectiveness. *Public Opinion Quarterly* 15:635–50.

Hoyenga, K.B. and K.T. Hoyenga. 1979. *The question of sex differences: Psychological, cultural and biological issues*. Boston: Little, Brown.

Huesmann, L.R. 1982. Television violence and aggressive behavior. In *Television and behavior: Ten years of scientific progress and implications for the eighties*, eds. D. Pearl, L. Bouthilet, and J. Lazar. Vol. 2. Washington: U.S. Government Printing Office.

Huffine, C. and J. Clausen. 1979. Madness and work: Short- and long-term effects of mental illness on occupational careers. *Social Forces* 57:1049–62.

Hull, C.L. 1943. *Principles of behavior.* New York: Appleton-Century-Crofts.

Hultsch, D. and J. Plemons. 1979. Life events and life span development. In *Life-span development and behavior,* eds. P.B. Baltes and O.G. Brim, Jr. Vol. 2. New York: Academic Press.

Hunt, M. 1974. *Sexual behavior in the 1970s.* Chicago: Playboy Press.

Hurwitz, J.I., A.F. Zander, and B. Hymovitch. 1960. Some effects of power on the relations among group members. In *Group dynamics,* eds. D. Cartwright and A. Zander, 3d. ed. New York: Harper and Row.

Huston, A.C. and J.C. Wright. 1982. Effects of communication media on children. In *The child: Development in a social context,* eds. C.B. Kopp and J.B. Krakow. Boston: Addison-Wesley.

Huston-Stein, A. and A. Higgins-Trenk. 1978. Development of females from childhood through adulthood: Career and feminine role orientations. In *Life-span development and behavior,* ed. P.B. Baltes. Vol. 1. New York: Academic Press.

Hymes, D. 1974. *Foundations in sociolinguistics.* London: Tavistock.

Ikle, F.C. 1971. *Every war must end.* New York: Columbia Univ. Press.

Ingham, A.G., G. Levinger, J. Graves, and V. Peckham. 1974. The Ringelmann effect: Studies of group size and group performance. *Journal of Experimental Social Psychology* 10:371–84.

Inkeles, A. 1975. Becoming modern: Individual change in six developing countries. *Ethos* 3:323–42.

———. 1978. National differences in individual modernity. *Comparative Studies in Sociology* 1:47–72.

Inkeles, A. and D. Smith. 1974. *Becoming modern: Individual change in six developing countries.* Cambridge, MA: Harvard Univ. Press.

Insko, C.A., A. Arkoff, and V.M. Insko. 1965. Effects of high and low fear-arousing communications upon opinions toward smoking. *Journal of Experimental Social Psychology* 40:256–66.

Inverarity, J. 1976. Populism and lynching in Louisiana, 1889–1896: a test of Erikson's theory of the relationship between boundary crisis and repressive justice. *American Sociological Review* 41:262–80.

Isen, A.M. 1970. Success, failure, attention, and reaction to others: The warm glow of success. *Journal of Personality and Social Psychology* 15:294–301.

Isen, A.M., M. Clark, and M.F. Schwartz. 1976. Duration of the effect of good mood on helping: "Footprints on the sands of time." *Journal of Personality and Social Psychology* 34:385–95.

Isen, A.M. and P.F. Levin. 1972. Effect of feeling good on helping: Cookies and kindness. *Journal of Personality and Social Psychology* 21:384–88.

Isen, A.M. and S.F. Simmonds. 1978. The effect of feeling good on a helping task that is incompatible with good mood. *Social Psychology Quarterly* 41:346–49.

Jaccard, J. 1981. Toward theories of persuasion and belief change. *Journal of Personality and Social Psychology* 40:260–69.

Jackson, J. 1954. The adjustment of the family to the crisis of alcoholism. *Quarterly Journal of Studies on Alcohol* 15:564–86.

Jackson, J. 1965. Structural characteristics of norms. In *Current studies in social psychology,* eds. I.D. Steiner and M. Fishbein. New York: Holt Rinehart and Winston.

Jackson, J.N. and H.D. Saltzstein. 1958. The effect of person-group relationships on conformity processes. *Journal of Abnormal and Social Psychology* 57:17–24.

Jacques, J.M. and K.J. Chason. 1977. Self-esteem and low status groups: A changing scene? *Sociological Quarterly* 18:399–412.

Jahoda, M., M. Deutsch, and S.W. Cook, eds. 1951. *Research methods in social relations.* Vol. 2. New York: Holt Rinehart and Winston.

James, H.E.O. 1955. Personal contact in school and change in intergroup attitudes. *International Social Science Bulletin.* 7:66–70.

James, W. 1890. *Principles of psychology.* New York: Holt Rinehart and Winston.

Janis, I.L. 1954. Personality correlates of susceptibility to persuasion. *Journal of Personality* 22:504–18.

Janis, I.L. 1982. *Groupthink,* 2nd edition. Boston: Houghton Mifflin.

Jellison, J.M. and D. Davis. 1973. Relationships between perceived ability and attitude extremity. *Journal of Personality and Social Psychology* 27:430–36.

Jellison, J.M. and K.W. Gentry. 1978. A self-presentation analysis of the seeking of social approval. *Personality and Social Psychology Bulletin* 4:227–30.

Jellison, J.M. and J. Riskind. 1970. A social comparison of abilities interpretation of risk-taking behavior. *Journal of Personality and Social Behavior* 15:375–90.

Jenkins, C.D., R.H. Rosenman, and S. Zyzanski. 1974. Prediction of clinical coronary heart disease by a test for coronary prone behavior pattern. *New England Journal of Medicine* 290:1271–75.

Jenkins, J.C. 1983. Resource mobilization theory and the study of social movements. In *Annual Review of Sociology* 9, eds. R.H. Turner and J.F. Short.

Jenkins, J.C. and C. Perrow. 1977. Insurgency of the powerless: Farm worker movements (1946–1972). *American Sociological Review* 42:249–68.

Jensen, G. 1972. Parents, peers and delinquent action: A test of the differential association perspective. *American Journal of Sociology* 78:562–75.

Jensen, G., M. Erickson, and J. Gibbs. 1978. Perceived risk of punishment and self-reported delinquency. *Social Forces* 57:57–78.

Jessor, R., F. Costa, L. Jessor, and J.E. Donovan. 1983. Time of first intercourse: A prospective study. *Journal of Personality and Social Psychology* 44:608–26.

Johnson, D.L. and I.R. Andrews. 1971. The risky-shift hypothesis tested with consumer products as stimuli. *Journal of Personality and Social Psychology.* 20:382–85.

Johnson, M. and L. Leslie. 1982. Couple involvement and network structure: A test of the dyadic withdrawal hypothesis. *Social Psychology Quarterly* 45:34–43.

Johnson, M.M., J. Stockard, J. Acker, and G. Naffziger. 1975. Expressiveness reevaluated. *School Review* 83:617–44.

Johnson, N. and W. Feinberg. 1977. A computer simulation of the emergence of consensus in crowds. *American Sociological Review* 52:505–21.

Johnson, R.E. 1979. *Juvenile delinquency and its origins*. New York: Cambridge Univ. Press.

Johnson, R.V. and D.R. Cressey. 1963. Differential association and the rehabilitation of drug addicts. *American Journal of Sociology* 69:129–42.

Johnson, W.T. and J.D. DeLamater. 1976. Response effects in sex surveys. *Public Opinion Quarterly* 40:165–81.

Jones, E.E. 1964. *Ingratiation*. New York: Appleton-Century-Crofts.

———. 1979. The rocky road from acts to dispositions. *American Psychologist* 34:107–17.

Jones, E.E. and K.E. Davis. 1965. From acts to dispositions. In *Advances in experimental social psychology*, ed. L. Berkowitz. Vol. 2. New York: Academic Press.

Jones, E.E., K.E. Davis, and K.J. Gergen. 1961. Role playing variations and their informational value for person perception. *Journal of Abnormal and Social Psychology* 3:302–10.

Jones, E.E., K.J. Gergen, P. Gumpert, and J. Thibaut. 1965. Some conditions affecting the use of ingratiation to influence performance evaluation. *Journal of Personality and Social Psychology* 1:613–26.

Jones, E.E., K.J. Gergen, and R.G. Jones. 1963. Tactics of ingratiation among leaders and subordinates in a status hierarchy. *Psychological Monographs* 77:3. Whole No. 566.

Jones, E.E. and G.R. Goethals. 1971. *Order effects in impression formation: Attribution context and the nature of the entity*. Morristown, NJ: General Learning Press.

Jones, E.E. and E.M. Gordon. 1972. Timing of self-disclosure and its effects on personal attraction. *Journal of Personality and Social Psychology* 24:358–65.

Jones, E.E. and V.A. Harris. 1967. The attribution of attitudes. *Journal of Experimental Social Psychology* 3:1–24.

Jones, E.E. and D. McGillis. 1976. Correspondent inferences and the attribution cube: A comparative reappraisal. In *New directions in attribution research*, eds. J.H. Harvey, W.J. Ickes, and R.F. Kidd. Vol. 1. Hillsdale, NJ: Erlbaum.

Jones, E.E. and R. Nisbett. 1972. The actor and observer: Divergent perceptions of the causes of behavior. In *Attribution: Perceiving the causes of behavior*, eds. E.E. Jones et al. Morristown, NJ: General Learning Press.

Jones, E.E. and T.S. Pittman. 1982. Toward a general theory of strategic self-presentation. In *Psychological perspectives on the self*, Vol. 1. Hillsdale, NJ: Erlbaum.

Jones, E.E., L. Rock, K.G. Shaver, G.R. Goethals, and L.M. Ward. 1968. Pattern of performance and ability attribution: An unexpected primacy effect. *Journal of Personality and Social Psychology* 10:317–40.

Jones, E.E. and J.W. Thibaut. 1958. Interaction goals as a basis of inference in interpersonal perception. In *Person perception and interpersonal behavior*, eds. R. Tagiuri and L. Petrullo. Stanford, CA: Stanford Univ. Press.

Jones, V.C. 1948. *The Hatfields and the McCoys*. Chapel Hill: Univ. of North Carolina Press.

Jordan, N. 1953. Behavioral forces that are a function of attitudes and of cognitive organization. *Human Relations* 6:273–88.

Joseph, N. and N. Alex. 1972. The uniform: A sociological perspective. *American Journal of Sociology* 77:719–30.

Jourard, S.M. 1971. *Self-disclosure*. New York: Wiley.

Julian, J.W. and E.P. Hollander. 1966. *A study of some dimensions of leader-follower relations*. Technical report #3. ONR contract 4679. Buffalo, NY: State Univ. of New York.

Julian, J.W., E.P. Hollander, and C.R. Regula. 1969. Endorsement of group spokesman as a function of his source of authority, competence, and success. *Journal of Personality and Social Psychology* 11:42–49.

Kahne, M. and C. Schwartz. 1978. Negotiating trouble: The social construction and management of trouble in a psychiatric context. *Social Problems* 25:461–75.

Kalish, R.A. 1976. Death and dying in a social context. In *Handbook of aging and the social sciences*, eds. R.H. Binstock and E. Shanas. New York: Van Nostrand Reinhold.

Kahn, A.S. and J.W. Kohls. 1972. Determinants of toughness in dyadic bargaining. *Sociometry* 35:305–15.

Kahn, R.L. and D. Katz. 1960. Leadership practices in relation to productivity and morale. In *Group dynamics*, eds. D. Cartwright and A. Zander. 2d ed. Evanston, IL: Row, Peterson and Co.

Kandel, D. 1978. Similarity in real-life adolescent friendship pairs. *Journal of Personality and Social Psychology* 36:306–12.

Kandel, D., D. Treiman, R. Faust, and E. Single. 1976. Adolescent involvement in legal and illegal drug use: A multiple classification analysis. *Social Forces* 55:438–58.

Kanter, R.M. 1976. *Men and women of the corporation*. New York: Basic Books.

Karabenick, S.A. 1983. Sex-relevance of context and influenceability: Sistrunk and McDavid revisited. *Personality and Social Psychology Bulletin* 9:243–52.

Karlins, M. and H.I. Abelson. 1970. *How opinions and attitudes are changed*, 2d ed. New York: Springer.

Karlins, M., T.L. Coffman, and G. Walters. 1969. On the fading of social stereotypes: Studies on three generations of college students. *Journal of Personality and Social Psychology* 13:1–16.

Karniol, R. and M. Ross. 1976. The development of causal attributions in social perception. *Journal of Personality and Social Psychology* 34:455–64.

Katz, D. 1960. The functional approach to the study of attitudes. *Public Opinion Quarterly* 24:163–204.

Katz, D. and K. Braly. 1933. Racial stereotypes in one hundred college students. *Journal of Abnormal and Social Psychology* 28:280–90.

Katz, I. 1970. Experimental study in Negro-white relationships. In *Advances in experimental social psychology*, ed. L. Berkowitz. Vol. 5. New York: Academic Press.

Katz, I. and M. Cohen. 1962. The effects of training Negroes upon cooperative problem solving in biracial teams. *Journal of Abnormal and Social Psychology*. 64:319–25.

Kauffman, D.R. and I.D. Steiner. 1968. Some variables affecting the use of conformity as an ingratiation technique. *Journal of Experimental Social Psychology* 4:400–14.

Kelley, G.A. 1955. *The psychology of personal constructs.* New York: Norton.

Kelley, H.H. 1950. The warm-cold variable in first impressions. *Journal of Personality* 18:431–39.

———. 1967. Attribution theory in social psychology. In *Nebraska Symposium on motivation, 1967,* ed. D. Levine. Lincoln, NE: Univ. of Nebraska Press.

———. 1972. Causal schemata and the attribution process. In *Attribution: Perceiving the causes of behavior,* eds. E.E. Jones, D.E. Kanouse, H.H. Kelley, R.E. Nisbett, S. Valins, and B. Weiner. Morristown, NJ: General Learning Press.

———. 1973. The process of causal attribution. *American Psychologist* 28:107–28.

Kelley, H.H., E. Berscheid, A Christensen, H.H. Harvey, T. Huston, G. Levinger, E. McClintock, L.H. Peplau, D.R. Peterson. 1983. *Close relationships.* New York: W.H. Freeman.

Kelley, H.H., J.C. Condry, Jr., A.E. Dahlke, and A.H. Hill. 1965. Collective behavior in a simulated panic situation. *Journal of Experimental Social Psychology* 1:20–54.

Kelley, H.H. and J.L. Michela. 1980. Attribution theory and research. *Annual Review of Psychology* 31:457–501.

Kelley, H.H. and J.W. Thibaut. 1978. *Interpersonal relations: A theory of interdependence.* New York: Wiley.

Kelman, H.C. 1974. Attitudes are alive and well and gainfully employed in the sphere of action. *American Psychologist* 29:310–24.

Kelman, H.C. and S.P. Cohen. 1976. The problem-solving workshop: A social-psychological contribution to the resolution of international conflicts. *Journal of Peace Research* 13:79–90.

Kemper, T.D. 1973. The fundamental dimensions of social relationship: A theoretical statement. *Acta Sociologica* 16:41–57.

———. 1978. *A social interactional theory of emotions.* New York: Wiley.

Kendon, A. 1970. Movement coordination in social interaction. Some examples described. *Acta Psychologica* 32:100–25.

Kendon, A., R.M. Harris, and M.R. Key. 1975. *Organization of behavior in face-to-face interaction.* The Hague: Mouton.

Keniston, K. 1971. Psychological development and historical change. *The Journal of Interdisciplinary History* 2:329–45.

Kenney, D. and L. La Voie. 1982. Reciprocity of interpersonal attraction: A confirmed hypothesis. *Social Psychology Quarterly* 45:54–58.

Kent, G., J. Davis, and D. Shapiro. 1978. Resources required in the construction and reconstruction of conversations. *Journal of Personality and Social Psychology* 36:13–22.

Kerckhoff, A.C. 1966. Family patterns and morale in retirement. In *Social aspects of aging,* eds. I.H. Simpson and J.C. McKinney. Durham, NC: Duke Univ. Press.

———. 1974. The social context of interpersonal attraction. In *Foundations of interpersonal attraction,* ed. T. Huston. New York: Academic Press.

Kerckhoff, A.C., K.W. Back, and N. Miller. 1965. Sociometric patterns in hysterical contagion. *Sociometry* 28:2–15.

Kessler, R.C. 1982. A disaggregation of the relationship between socioeconomic status and psychological distress. *American Sociological Review* 47:752–64.

Kessler, R.C. and P.D. Cleary. 1980. Social class and psychological distress. *American Sociological Review* 45:463–78.

Kessler, R.C. and J.A. McRae, Jr. 1981. Trends in the relationship between sex and psychological distress: 1957–76. *American Sociological Review* 46:443–52.

———. 1982. The effects of wives' employment on the mental health of married men and women. *American Sociological Review* 47:216–26.

Kidd, R.F. and T.M. Amabile. 1981. Causal explanations in social interaction: Some dialogues on dialogue. In *New directions in attribution theory,* eds. J.H. Harvey, W. Ickes, and R.F. Kidd. Vol. 3. Hillsdale, NJ: Erlbaum.

Kiesler, C.A. and L.H. Corbin. 1965. Commitment, attraction, and conformity. *Journal of Personality and Social Psychology* 2:890–95.

Kiesler, C.A. and S.B. Kiesler. 1969. *Conformity.* Reading, MA: Addison-Wesley.

Kiesler, C.A., M. Zanna, and J. deSalvo. 1966. Deviation and conformity: Opinion change as a function of commitment, attraction, and presence of a deviate. *Journal of Personality and Social Psychology* 3:458–67.

Kilham, W. and L. Mann. 1974. Level of destructive obedience as a function of transmitter and executant roles in the Milgram obedience paradigm. *Journal of Personality and Social Psychology* 29:696–702.

Killian, L. 1984. Organization, rationality and spontaneity in the civil rights movement. *American Sociological Review* 49:770–83.

Kimberly, J.C. 1970. The emergence and stabilization of stratification in simple and complex social systems. *Sociological Inquiry.* 40:73–101.

Kiparsky, P. 1976. Historical linguistics and the origin of language. *Annals of the New York Academy of Sciences* 280:97–103.

Kitsuse, J. 1964. Societal reaction to deviant behavior: Problems of theory and method. In *The other side,* ed. H. Becker. New York: Free Press.

Klapper, J. 1960. *The effects of mass communication.* New York: Free Press.

Kleck, R.E. 1968. Physical stigma and nonverbal cues emitted in face-to-face interaction. *Human Relations* 21:19–28.

Kleck, R.E. and A. Strenta. 1980. Perceptions of the impact of negatively valued physical characteristics on social interaction. *Journal of Personality and Social Psychology* 39:861–73.

Knox, R.E. and R.K. Safford. 1976. Group caution at the race track. *Journal of Experimental Social Psychology.* 12:317–24.

Knudsen, D.D. 1969. The declining status of women. *Social Forces* 48:183–93.

Kobrin, F. and G. Hendershot. 1977. Do family ties reduce mortality? Evidence from the United States, 1966–68. *Journal of Marriage and Family* 39:737–45.

Koffka, K. 1935. *Principles of gestalt psychology.* New York: Harcourt Brace and World.

Kogan, N. and M.A. Wallach. 1964. *Risk taking: A study in*

cognition and personality. New York: Holt Rinehart and Winston.

Kohlberg, L. 1969. Stage and sequence: The cognitive-developmental approach to socialization. In *Handbook of socialization theory and research,* ed. D. Goslin. Boston: Houghton Mifflin.

Kohler, W. 1947. *Gestalt psychology.* New York: Liveright Press.

Kohn, M. 1969. *Class and conformity: A study in values.* Homewood, IL: Dorsey.

———. 1976. Occupational structure and alienation. *American Journal of Sociology* 82:111–30.

———. 1977. Reassessment, 1977. *Class and conformity: A study in values.* 2d ed. Chicago: Univ. of Chicago Press.

Kohn, M. and C. Schooler. 1973. Occupational experience and psychological functioning: An assessment of reciprocal effects. *American Sociological Review* 38:97–118.

———. 1982. Job conditions and personality: A longitudinal assessment of their reciprocal effects. *American Journal of Sociology* 87:1257–86.

Kohn, M. and C. Schooler, with the collaboration of J. Miller, K. Miller, S. Schoenbach, and R. Schoenberg. 1983. *Work and personality: An inquiry into the impact of social stratification.* Norwood, NJ: Ablex.

Komarovsky, M. 1946. Cultural contradiction and sex roles. *American Journal of Sociology* 52:184–89.

Konevcni, V.J. 1979. The role of aversive events in the development of intergroup conflict. In *The social psychology of intergroup relations,* eds. W.G. Austin and S. Worchel. Monterey, CA: Brooks/Cole.

Korten, D.C. 1962. Situational determinants of leadership structure. *Journal of Conflict Resolution* 6:222–35.

Kothandapani, V. 1971. Validation of feeling, belief and intention to act as three components of attitude and their contribution to prediction of contraceptive behavior. *Journal of Personality and Social Psychology* 19:321–33.

Kraus, S. ed. 1962. *The great debates.* Bloomington: Indiana Univ. Press.

Krauss, R.M. 1981. Impression formation, impression management, and nonverbal behaviors. In *Social cognition: The Ontario Symposium,* eds. E.T. Higgins, C.P. Herman, and M.P. Zanna. Hillsdale, NJ: Erlbaum.

Krauss, R.M., V. Geller, and C.T. Olson. 1976. Modalities and cues in the detection of deception. Paper presented at the meeting of the American Psychological Association, Washington, D.C.

Kraut, R. 1976. Deterrent definitional influences on shoplifting. *Social Problems* 23:358–68.

Kraut, R.E. 1978. Verbal and nonverbal cues in the perception of lying. *Journal of Personality and Social Psychology* 36:380–91.

Kraut, R.E., S.H. Lewis, and L.W. Swezey. 1982. Listener responsiveness and the coordination of conversation. *Journal of Personality and Social Psychology* 43:718–31.

Krebs, D. 1975. Empathy and altruism. *Journal of Personality and Social Psychology* 32:1134–46.

Krebs, R. 1967. Some relations between moral judgment, attention and resistance to temptation. Unpublished doctoral dissertation, Univ. of Chicago.

Krech, D. and R. S. Crutchfield, 1948. *Theory and problems of social psychology.* New York: McGraw-Hill.

Kremer, J.F. and L. Stephens. 1983. Attributions and arousal as mediators of mitigation's effect on retaliation. *Journal of Personality and Social Psychology* 45:335–343.

Kriesberg, L. 1973. *The sociology of social conflicts.* Englewood Cliffs, NJ: Prentice-Hall.

Kritzer, H. 1977. Political protest and political violence: A nonrecursive causal model. *Social Forces* 55:630–40.

Kruglanski, A.W. 1980. Lay epistemologic process and contents: Another look at attribution theory. *Psychological Review* 87:70–87.

Kuhlen, R.G. 1964. Developmental changes in motivation during adult years. In *Relations of development and aging,* ed. J.E. Birren. Springfield, IL: C.C. Thomas.

Kuhlman, C.E., M.H. Miller, and E. Gungor. 1973. Interpersonal conflict resolution: The effects of language and meaning. In *Human judgment and social interaction,* eds. L. Rappoport and D.A. Summers. New York: Holt Rinehart and Winston.

Kuhn, D., J. Langer, L. Kohlberg, and N. Haan. 1977. The development of formal operations in logical and moral judgement. *Genetic Psychology Monographs* 95:97–188.

Kuhn, M.H. 1964. Major trends in symbolic interaction theory in the past twenty-five years. *Sociological Quarterly* 5:61–84.

Kuhn, M.H. and T. S. McPartland. 1954. An empirical investigation of self-attitudes. *American Sociological Review* 19:68–76.

Kulick, J.A. and R. Brown. 1979. Frustration, attribution of blame, and aggression. *Journal of Experimental Social Psychology* 15:183–94.

Kun, A. 1978. Evidence for preschoolers understanding of causal direction in extended causal sequences. *Child Development* 49:218–22.

Labov, W. 1972a. *Language in the inner city. Studies in the Black English vernacular.* Philadelphia: Univ. of Pennsylvania Press.

———. 1972b. *Sociolinguistic patterns.* Philadelphia: Univ. of Pennsylvania Press.

Labov, W. and D. Fanshel. 1977. *Therapeutic discourse: Psychotherapy as conversation.* New York: Academic Press.

LaFrance, M. and C. Mayo. 1978. *Moving bodies: Nonverbal communication in social relationships.* Monterey, CA: Brooks/Cole.

Lakoff, R.T. 1979. Women's language. In *Women's language and style,* eds. O. Buturff and E.L. Epstein. Akron, OH: Univ. of Akron.

Lamb, M.E. 1979. Paternal influence and the father's role: A personal perspective. *American Psychologist* 34:938–43.

Lamm, H. and C. Sauer. 1974. Discussion-induced shift toward higher demands in negotiation. *European Journal of Social Psychology* 4:85–88.

Lamm, H. and T. Schwinger. 1980. Norms concerning distributive justice: Are needs taken into consideration in allocation decisions? *Social Psychology Quarterly* 43:425–29.

Landers, D.M. and T.F. Crum. 1971. The effects of team success and formal structure on inter-personal relations and cohesiveness of baseball teams. *International Journal of Sport Psychology* 2:88–96.

Landers, D.M. and G. Luschen. 1974. Team performance outcome and the cohesiveness of competitive coacting groups. *International Review of Sport Sociology* 2:57–69.

Landy, D. and H. Sigall. 1974. Beauty is talent: Task evaluation as a function of the performer's physical attractiveness. *Journal of Personality and Social Psychology* 29:299–304.

Langer, E.J. 1978. Rethinking the role of thought in social interaction. In *New Directions in attribution theory*, eds. J.H. Harvey, W. Ickes, and R.F. Kidd. Vol. 2. Hillsdale, NJ: Erlbaum.

Langner, T.S. 1963. A twenty-two item screening score of psychiatric symptoms indicating impairment. *Journal of Health and Human Behavior* 3:269–76.

Langner, T.S. and S. Michael. 1963. *Life stress and mental health: The midtown Manhattan study*. New York: Free Press.

Lantz, H., J. Keyes, and M. Schultz. 1975. The American family in the preindustrial period: From base lines in history to change. *American Sociological Review* 40:21–36.

Lantz, H., M. Schultz, and M. O'Hara. 1977. The changing American family from the preindustrial to the industrial period: A final report. *American Sociological Review* 42:406–21.

LaPiere, R. 1934. Attitudes versus actions. *Social Forces* 13:230–37.

Larson, L.L. and K. Rowland. 1973. Leadership style, stress, and behavior in task performance. *Organizational Behavior and Human Performance* 9:407–21.

Larzelere, R. and T. Huston. 1980. The dyadic trust scale: Toward understanding interpersonal trust in close relationships. *Journal of Marriage and the Family* 42:595–604.

Latané, B. and J.M. Darley. 1970. *The unresponsive bystander: Why doesn't he help?* New York: Appleton-Century-Crofts.

Latané, B. and J. Rodin. 1969. A lady in distress: Inhibiting effects of friends and strangers on bystander intervention. *Journal of Experimental Social Psychology* 5:189–202.

Latané, B., K. Williams, and S. Harkins. 1979. Many hands make light the work: The causes and consequences of social loafing. *Journal of Personality and Social Psychology* 37:822–32.

Lauderdale, P. 1976. Deviance and moral boundaries. *American Sociological Review* 41:660–76.

Lawler, E.E. 1971. *Pay and organizational effectiveness: A psychological view*. New York: McGraw-Hill.

Lawler, E.E. and P.W. O'Gara. 1967. Effects of inequity produced by underpayment on work output, work quality, and attitudes toward work. *Journal of Applied Psychology* 51:403–10.

Lawler, E.J. 1975a. An experimental study of factors affecting the mobilization of revolutionary coalitions. *Sociometry*. 38:163–79.

———. 1975b. The impact of status differences on coalitional agreements: An experimental study. *Journal of Conflict Resolution* 19:271–85.

Lawler, E.J. and M.E. Thompson. 1978. Impact of leader responsibility for inequity on subordinate revolts. *Social Psychology* 41:264–68.

Lawler, E.J., J.A. Youngs, Jr., and M.D. Lesh. 1978. Cooperation and coalition mobilization. *Journal of Applied Social Psychology* 8:199–214.

Lawson, E.B. 1964. Reinforced and non-reinforced four-man communication nets. *Psychological Reports* 14:287–96.

Lay, C.H. and D.N. Jackson. 1969. Analysis of the generality of trait-inferential relationships. *Journal of Personality and Social Psychology* 12:12–21.

Leavitt, H.J. 1951. Some effects of certain communication patterns on group performance. *Journal of Abnormal and Social Psychology* 46:38–50.

Le Bon, G. 1895. *Psychologie des Foules* (*The Crowd*). London: Unwin (1903).

Ledvinka, J. 1971. Race of interviewer and the language elaboration of Black interviewees. *Journal of Social Issues* 27:185–97.

Leffler, A., D.L. Gillespie, and J.C. Conaty. 1982. The effects of status differentiation on nonverbal behavior. *Social Psychology Quarterly* 45:153–61.

Lemert, E. 1951. *Social Pathology*. New York: McGraw-Hill.

Lemert, E. 1962. Paranoia and the dynamics of exclusion. *Sociometry* 25:2–20.

Lemon, N. 1973. *Attitudes and their measurement*. New York: Wiley.

Lenk, H. 1969. Top performance despite internal conflict. In *Sport, culture, and society*, eds. J.W. Loy, Jr. and G.S. Kenyon. London: Collier-MacMillan.

Lepper, M., D. Greene, and R. Nisbett. 1973. Undermining children's intrinsic interest with extrinsic reward: A test of the "overjustification" hypothesis. *Journal of Personality and Social Psychology* 28:129–37.

Leventhal, G.S. 1976. The distribution of rewards and resources in groups and organizations. In *Advances in experimental social psychology*, eds. L. Berkowitz and E. Walster. Vol. 9. New York: Academic Press.

———. 1979. Effects of external conflict on resource allocation and fairness within groups and organizations. In *The social psychology of intergroup relations*, eds. W.G. Austin and S. Worchel. Monterey, CA: Brooks/Cole.

Leventhal, G.S., J. Allen, and B. Kemelgor. 1969. Reducing inequity by reallocating rewards. *Psychonomic Sciences* 14:295–96.

Leventhal, G.S. and D.W. Lane. 1970. Sex, age, and equity behavior. *Journal of Personality and Social Psychology* 15:312–16.

Leventhal, G.S., J.W. Michaels, and C. Sanford. 1972. Inequity and interpersonal conflict: Reward allocation and secrecy about reward as methods of preventing conflict. *Journal of Personality and Social Psychology* 23:88–102.

Leventhal, G.S., T. Weiss, and G. Long. 1969. Equity, reciprocity, and reallocating the rewards in the dyad. *Journal of Personality and Social Psychology* 13:300–305.

Leventhal, H. 1970. Findings and theory in the study of fear communications. In *Advances in experimental social psychology*, ed. L. Berkowitz. Vol. 5. New York: Academic Press.

———. 1980. Toward a comprehensive theory of emotion. In *Advances in experimental social psychology*, ed. L. Berkowitz. Vol. 13. New York: Academic Press.

Leventhal, H. and R.P. Singer. 1966. Affect arousal and positioning of recommendations in persuasive communications. *Journal of Personality and Social Psychology* 4:137–46.

Levin, P.E. and A.M. Isen. 1975. Something you can still get for a dime: Further studies on the effects of feeling good on helping. *Sociometry* 38:141–47.

Levine, J.M. 1980. Reaction to opinion deviance in small groups. In *Psychology of group influence*, ed. P.B. Paulus. Hillsdale, NJ: Lawrence Erlbaum.

Levine, J.M., L. Saxe, and H.J. Harris. 1976. Reaction to attitudinal deviance: Impact of deviate's direction and distance of movement. *Sociometry* 39:97–107.

LeVine, R.A. and D.T. Campbell. 1972. *Ethnocentrism: Theories of conflict, ethnic attitudes and group behavior.* New York: Wiley.

Levinger, G. 1974. A three-level approach to attraction: Toward an understanding of pair-relatedness. In *Foundations of interpersonal attraction*, ed. T. Huston. New York: Academic Press, 100–20.

———. 1976. A social psychological perspective on marital dissolution. *Journal of Social Issues* 32:(1):21–47.

Levinson, D. 1978. *The seasons of a man's life.* New York: Knopf.

Levitin, T.E. 1975. Deviants as active participants in the labeling process: The visibly handicapped. *Social Problems* 22:548–57.

Lewin, K. 1951. *Field theory in social science.* New York: Harper and Row.

Lewin, K., R. Lippitt, and R.K. White. 1939. Patterns of aggressive behavior in experimentally created "social climates." *Journal of Social Psychology* 10:271–99.

Lewis, B.W. 1968. Price control and rationing. In *International encyclopedia of the social sciences*, ed. D.L. Sills. Vol. 12. New York: Macmillan Co.

Lewis, G.H. 1972. Role differentiation. *American Sociological Review* 37:424–34.

Lewis, M. and J. Brooks. 1975. Infants' social perception: A constructivist view. In *Infant perception: From sensation to cognition*, eds. L. Cohen and S. Salapatek. Vol. 2. New York: Academic Press.

Lewis, M. and J. Brookes-Gunn. 1979. Toward a theory of social cognition: The development of self. In *Social interaction and communication during infancy. New directions for child development*, ed. I. Uzgiris. Vol. 4. San Francisco: Jossey-Bass.

Lewis, S.A., C.J. Langan, and E.P. Hollander. 1972. Expectation of future interaction and the choice of less desirable alternatives in conformity. *Sociometry* 35:440–47.

Lieberman, P. 1975. *On the origins of human language: An introduction to the evolution of human speech.* New York: Macmillan.

Lieberman, S. 1965. The effect of changes of roles on the attitudes of role occupants. In *Basic studies in social psychology*, eds. H. Proshansky and B. Seidenberg. New York: Holt Rinehart and Winston.

Liebert, R.M., W.P. Smith, J.H. Hill, and M. Kieffer. 1968. The effects of information and magnitude of initial offer on interpersonal negotiation. *Journal of Experimental Social Psychology* 4:431–41.

Liebhart, E.H. 1972. Empathy and emergency helping: The effects of personality, self-concern and acquaintance. *Journal of Experimental Social Psychology* 8:404–11.

Light, I. 1977. The ethnic vice industry, 1880–1944. *American Sociological Review* 42:464–79.

Likert, R. 1932. A technique for the measurement of attitudes. *Archives of Psychology* (whole no. 142).

Likert, R. 1961. *New patterns of management.* New York: McGraw-Hill.

Lin, N. 1974–75. The McIntire march: A study of recruitment and commitment. *Public Opinion Quarterly* 38:562–73.

Lin, N., W.M. Ensel, and J.C. Vaughn. 1981. Social resources and strength of ties: Structural factors in occupational status attainment. *American Sociological Review* 46:393–405.

Linder, D.E., J. Cooper, and E.E. Jones. 1967. Decision freedom as a determinant of the role of incentive magnitude in attitude change. *Journal of Personality and Social Psychology* 6:245–54.

Lindskold, S. 1978. Trust development, the GRIT proposal, and the effects of conciliatory acts on conflict and cooperation. *Psychological Bulletin* 85:772–93.

———. 1979. Managing conflict through announced conciliatory initiatives backed with retaliatory capability. In *The social psychology of intergroup relations*, eds. W.G. Austin and S. Worchel. Monterey, CA: Brooks/Cole.

Lindskold, S. and J.R. Aronoff. 1980. Conciliatory strategies and relative power. *Journal of Experimental Social Psychology* 16:187–98.

Lindskold, S. and M.G. Collins. 1978. Inducing cooperation by groups and individuals: Applying Osgood's GRIT strategy. *Journal of Conflict Resolution* 22:679–90.

Lindskold, S., P. Cullen, J. Gahagan, and J.T. Tedeschi. 1970. Developmental aspects of reaction to positive inducements. *Developmental Psychology* 3:277–84.

Lindskold, S. and M.L. Finch. 1981. Styles of announcing conciliation. *Journal of Conflict Resolution* 25:145–55.

Lindskold, S. and J.T. Tedeschi. 1971. Reward power and attraction in interpersonal conflict. *Psychonomic Science* 22:211–13.

Link, B. 1982. Mental patient status, work and income: An examination of the effects of a psychiatric label. *American Sociological Review* 47:202–15.

Linton, R. 1936. *The study of man.* New York: Appleton-Century-Crofts.

Linville, P.W. and E.E. Jones. 1980. Polarized appraisals of out-group members. *Journal of Personality and Social Psychology* 38:689–703.

Lippitt, R. 1940. An experimental study of the effect of democratic and authoritarian group atmospheres. *University of Iowa Studies in Child Welfare* 16:43–195.

Lippitt, R. and R.K. White. 1943. The "social climate" of children's groups. In *Child behavior and development*, eds. R.G. Barker, J. Kounin, and H. Wright. New York: McGraw-Hill.

———. 1952. An experimental study of leadership and group life. In *Readings in social psychology*, eds. G.E. Swanson, T.M. Newcomb, and E.L. Hartley. New York: Holt.

Lippman, W. 1922. *Public opinion.* New York: Harcourt Brace Jovanovich.

Liska, A. 1984. A critical examination of the causal structure of the Fishbein-Ajzen attitude-behavior model. *Social Psychology Quarterly* 47:61–74.

Lizotte, A.H. 1978. Extra-legal factors in Chicago's criminal courts: Testing the conflict model of criminal justice. *Social Problems* 25:564–80.

Lofland, J. 1981. Collective behavior: The elementary forms. In *Social psychology: Sociological perspectives,* eds. M. Rosenberg and R.H. Turner. New York: Basic Books.

Lohr, J.M. and A.W. Staats. 1973. Attitude conditioning in Sino-Tibetan languages. *Journal of Personality and Social Psychology* 26:196–200.

Lopata, H.Z. 1971. *Occupation: Housewife.* New York: Oxford Univ. Press.

———. 1979. *Women as widows: Support systems.* New York: Elsevier.

Lord, C.G., M.R. Lepper, and D. Mackie. 1984. Attitude prototypes as determinants of attitude-behavior consistency. *Journal of Personality and Social Psychology* 46:1254–1266.

Lord, C.G., L. Ross, and M.R. Lepper. 1979. Biased assimilation and attitude polarization: The effects of prior theories on subsequently considered evidence. *Journal of Personality and Social Psychology* 37:2098–2109.

Lorenz, K. 1966. *On aggression.* New York: Harcourt Brace Jovanovich.

———. 1974. *Civilized man's eight deadly sins.* New York: Harcourt Brace Jovanovich.

Lott, A. and B. Lott. 1961. Group cohesiveness, communication level, and conformity. *Journal of Abnormal and Social Psychology* 62:408–412.

———. 1965. Group cohesiveness as interpersonal attraction: A review of relationships with antecedent and consequent variables. *Psychological Bulletin* 64:259–309.

———. 1974. The role of reward in formation of positive interpersonal attitudes. In *Foundations of interpersonal attraction,* ed. T. Huston. New York: Academic Press 171–92.

Lowenthal, M.F., M. Thurnher, and D. Chiriboga. 1975. *Four stages of life: A comparative study of women and men facing transitions.* San Francisco: Jossey-Bass.

Luchins, A.S. 1957. Experimental attempts to minimize the impact of first impressions. In *The order of presentation in persuasion,* ed. C.I. Hovland. New Haven: Yale Univ. Press.

Luckenbill, D.F. 1982. Compliance under threat of severe punishment. *Social Forces* 60:811–25.

Lundman, R.J. 1974. Routine police arrest practices: A commonweal perspective. *Social Problems* 22:127–41.

Luria, A. and F. Yudovich. 1971. *Speech and the development of mental processes in the child.* London: Penguin.

Lynch, J.C., Jr. and J.L. Cohen. 1978. The use of subjective expected utility theory as an aid to understanding variables that influence helping behavior. *Journal of Personality and Social Psychology* 36:1138–51.

Lynd, R.S. and H.M. Lynd. 1937. *Middletown in transition: A study in cultural conflicts.* New York: Harcourt Brace Jovanovich.

Lytton, H., D. Conway, and R. Sauvé. 1977. The impact of twinship on parental-child interaction. *Journal of Personality and Social Psychology* 35:97–107.

Maas, H.S. and J.A. Kuypers. 1974. *From thirty to seventy.* San Francisco: Jossey-Bass.

Macaulay, J.R. and L. Berkowitz. 1970. Eds. *Altruism and helping behavior.* New York: Academic Press.

Maccoby, E.E. and C.N. Jacklin. 1974. *The psychology of sex differences.* Stanford, CA: Stanford Univ. Press.

Mackie, M. 1983. The domestication of self: Gender comparisons of self-imagery and self-esteem. *Social Psychology Quarterly* 46:343–50.

Maddux, J.E. and R.W. Rogers. 1980. Effects of source expertness, physical attractiveness, and supporting arguments on persuasion: A case of brains over beauty. *Journal of Personality and Social Psychology* 39:235–44.

———. 1983. Protection motivation and self-efficacy: A revised theory of fear appeals and attitude change. *Journal of Experimental Social Psychology* 19:469–79.

Main, M. 1973. Exploration, play and level of cognitive functioning as related to child-mother attachment. Unpublished doctoral dissertation, Johns Hopkins Univ.

Mannheim, B.F. 1966. Reference groups, membership groups and the self-image. *Sociometry* 29:265–79.

Mannheim, K. 1952. The problem of generations. In *Essays in the sociology of knowledge,* translated by P. Keckskemeti. New York: Oxford Univ. Press (originally published 1928).

Mannheimer, D. and R.M. Williams, Jr. 1949. A note on Negro troups in combat. In *The American soldier,* eds. S.A. Stouffer, E.A. Suchman, L.C. DeVinney, S.A. Star, and R.M. Williams, Jr. Vol. 1. Princeton: Princeton Univ. Press.

Marini, M.M. 1978. Sex differences in educational attainment and age at marriage. *American Sociological Review* 43:483–507.

———. 1984. The order of events in the transition to adulthood. *Sociology of Education* 57:63–84.

Markus, H. 1977. Self-schemata and processing information about the self. *Journal of Personality and Social Psychology* 35:63–78.

Markus, H. and K. Sentis. 1982. The self in social information processing. In *Psychological perspectives on the self,* ed. J. Suls. Hillsdale, NJ: Erlbaum.

Markus, H. and R.B. Zajonc. 1985. The cognitive perspective in social psychology. In *The handbook of social psychology,* 3rd ed., eds. G. Lindzey and E. Aronson. Vol. 1. New York: Random House.

Marwell, G., K. McKinney, S. Sprecher, S. Smith, and J. DeLamater. 1982. Legitimizing factors in the initiation of heterosexual relationships. Paper presented at the International Conference on Personal Relationships, Madison, WI.

Marx, G.T. and J.L. Wood. 1975. Strands of theory and research in collective behavior. In *Annual Review of Sociology,* eds. A. Inkeles, J. Coleman, and N. Smelser. 1:363–428.

Marx, K. 1964. *Early writings.* Edited and translated by T.B. Bottomore. New York: McGraw-Hill.

Mason, K.O. and L.L. Bumpass. 1975. U. S. women's sex-role ideology, 1970. *American Journal of Sociology* 80:1212–19.

Mathes, E. 1975. The effects of physical attractiveness and anxiety on heterosexual attraction over a series of five encounters. *Journal of Marriage and the Family* 37:769–73.

Matsueda, D.L. 1982. Testing control theory and differential association: A causal modeling approach. *American Sociological Review* 47:489–504.

Matthews, S.H. 1977. *The social world of old women.* Beverly Hills, CA: Sage.

Mausner, B. 1954. The effect of prior reinforcement on the interaction of observer pairs. *Journal of Abnormal and Social Psychology* 49:65–68.

Maynard, D.W. 1978. Placement of topic changes in conversation. *Semiotica* 30-3/4:263–90.

———. 1983. Social order and plea bargaining in the court. *Sociological Quarterly* 24:215–33.

McArdle, J.B. 1972. Positive and negative communications and subsequent attitude and behavior change in alcoholics. Unpublished doctoral dissertation, Univ. of Illinois.

McArthur, L.Z. 1972. The how and what of why: Some determinants and consequences of causal attribution. *Journal of Personality and Social Psychology* 22:171–93.

———. 1976. The lesser influence of consensus than distinctiveness information on causal attributions: A test of the person-thing hypothesis. *Journal of Personality and Social Psychology* 33:733–42.

McArthur, L.Z. and D.L. Post. 1977. Figural emphasis and person perception. *Journal of Experimental Social Psychology* 13:520–35.

McCall, G.J. and J.L. Simmons. 1978. *Identities and interactions.* New York: Free Press.

McClelland, D. 1958. Risk-taking in children with high and low need for achievement. In *Motives in fantasy, action and society,* ed. J. W. Atkinson. Princeton, NJ: Van Nostrand.

———. 1961. *The achieving society.* Princeton, NJ: Van Nostrand.

McClelland, D. and D. Winter. 1969. *Motivating economic achievement.* New York: Free Press.

McFarland, C. and M. Ross. 1982. The impact of causal attributions on affective reactions to success and failure. *Journal of Personality and Social Psychology* 43:937–46.

McGrath, J.E. 1962. The influence of positive interpersonal relations on adjustment and effectiveness in rifle teams. *Journal of Abnormal and Social Psychology* 65:365–75.

McGrath, J.E. 1966. A social psychological approach to the study of negotiation. In *Studies on behavior in organizations,* ed. R.V. Bowers. Athens, GA: Univ. of Georgia Press.

McGregor, D.M. 1960. *The human side of enterprise.* New York: McGraw-Hill.

McGuire, W.J. 1964. Inducing resistance to persuasion: Some contemporary approaches. In *Advances in experimental social psychology,* ed. L. Berkowitz. Vol. 1. New York: Academic Press.

———. 1969. The nature of attitudes and attitude change. In *Handbook of social psychology,* eds. G. Lindzey and E. Aronson. Vol. 3. Reading, MA: Addison-Wesley.

———. 1972. Attitude change: The information-processing paradigm. In *Experimental social psychology,* ed. C.G. McClintock. New York: Holt Rinehart and Winston.

McGuire, W.J. and C.V. McGuire. 1982. Significant others in self-space: Sex differences and developmental trends in the social self. In *Psychological perspectives on the self,* ed. J. Suls. Hillsdale, NJ: Erlbaum.

McGuire, W.J. and D. Papageorgis. 1961. The relative efficacy of various types of prior belief-defense in producing immunity against persuasion. *Journal of Abnormal and Social Psychology* 62:327–37.

McGuire, W.J. and A. Padawer-Singer. 1976. Trait salience in the spontaneous self-concept. *Journal of Personality and Social Psychology* 33:743–54.

McHugh, P. 1968. *Defining the situation.* New York: Bobbs-Merrill.

McKinlay, J.B. 1973. Social networks, lay consultation and help-seeking behavior. *Social Forces* 51:275–92.

McLeod, J.M., K.O. Price, and E. Harburg. 1966. Socialization, liking and yielding of opinions in imbalanced situations. *Sociometry* 29:197–212.

McPhail, C. and R.T. Wohlstein. 1983. Individual and collective behavior within gatherings, demonstrations and riots. In *Annual Review of Sociology,* eds. R.H. Turner and J.F. Short. 9:579–600.

McWorter, G.A. and R.L. Crain. 1967. Subcommunity gladiatorial competition: Civil rights leadership as a competitive process. *Social Forces* 46:8–21.

Mead, G.H. 1934. *Mind, self, and society.* Chicago: Univ. of Chicago Press.

———. 1938. *The philosophy of the act.* Chicago: Univ. of Chicago Press.

Mears, P. 1974. Structuring communication in a working group. *Journal of Communication* 24:71–79.

Meddin, J. 1979. Chimpanzees, symbols and the reflective self. *Social Psychology Quarterly* 42:99–100.

Mednick, S.A. and F. Schulsinger. 1969. Factors related to breakdown in children at high risk for schizophrenia. In *Life history studies in psychopathology,* eds. M. Rolf and D.F. Rocks. Minneapolis: Univ. of Minnesota Press.

Meer, B. and E. Freedman. 1966. The impact of Negro neighbors on white house owners. *Social Forces* 45:11–19.

Megargee, E. 1969. Influence of sex roles on the manifestation of leadership. *Journal of Applied Psychology* 53:377–82.

Mehrabian, A. 1972. *Nonverbal communication.* New York: Aldine-Atherton.

Mehrabian, A. and S. Ksionzky. 1970. Models for affiliative and conformity behavior. *Psychological Bulletin.* 74:110–126.

Meier, R.F. and W.T. Johnson. 1977. Deterrence as social control: The legal and extralegal production of conformity. *American Sociological Review* 42:292–304.

Mendelsohn, H. 1973. Some reasons why information campaigns can succeed. *Public Opinion Quarterly* 37:50–61.

Merei, F. 1949. Group leadership and institutionalization. *Human Relations* 2:23–39.

Merton, R. 1938. Social structure and anomie. *American Sociological Review* 3:672–82.

———. 1948. The self-fulfilling prophecy. *Antioch Review* 8:193–210.

———. 1957. *Social theory and social structure.* Glencoe, IL: Free Press.

———. 1968. *Social theory and social structure.* Rev. ed. New York: Free Press.

Meyrowitz, J. 1985. *No sense of place: The impact of electronic media on social behavior.* New York: Oxford Univ. Press.

Michener, H.A. and M.R. Burt. 1974. Legitimacy as a base of social influence. In *Perspectives on social power,* ed. J.T. Tedeschi. Chicago: Aldine-Atherton.

———. 1975. Use of social influence under varying conditions of legitimacy. *Journal of Personality and Social Psychology* 32:398–407.

———. 1975. Components of "authority" as determinants of compliance. *Journal of Personality and Social Psychology* 31:605–14.

Michener, H.A. and E.D. Cohen. 1973. Effects of punishment magnitude in the bilateral threat situation: Evidence for the deterrence hypothesis. *Journal of Personality and Social Psychology* 26:427–38.

Michener, H.A. and E.J. Lawler. 1971. Revolutionary coalition strength and collective failure as determinants of status reallocation. *Journal of Experimental Social Psychology* 7:448–60.

———. 1975. Endorsement of formal leaders: An integrative model. *Journal of Personality and Social Psychology* 31:216–23.

Michener, H.A. and M. Lyons. 1972. Perceived support and upward mobility as determinants of revolutionary coalitional behavior. *Journal of Experimental Social Psychology* 8:180–95.

Michener, H.A., J.H. Plazewski, and J.J. Vaske. 1979. Integration tactics channeled by target values and threat capability. *Journal of Personality* 47:36–56.

Michener, H.A. and M. Tausig. 1971. Usurpation and perceived support as determinants of the endorsement accorded formal leaders. *Journal of Personality and Social Psychology* 18:364–72.

Michener, H.A., J.J. Vaske, S.L. Schleifer, J.G. Plazewski, and L.J. Chapman. 1975. Factors affecting concession rate and threat usage in bilateral conflict. *Sociometry.* 38:62–80.

Milardo, R.M. 1982. Friendship networks in developing relationships: Converging and diverging social environments. *Social Psychology Quarterly* 45:162–72.

Milardo, R.M., M. Johnson, and T. Huston. 1983. Developing close relationships: Changing patterns of interaction between pair members and social networks. *Journal of Personality and Social Psychology* 44:964–76.

Milavsky, J.R., R. Kessler, H. Stipp, and W. Rubens. 1983. *Television and aggression: A panel study.* New York: Academic Press.

Miles, R.H. 1975. An empirical test of causal inference between role perception of conflict and ambiguity and various personal outcomes. *Journal of Applied Psychology* 60:334–39.

Milgram, S. 1963. Behavioral study of obedience. *Journal of Abnormal and Social Psychology* 67:371–78.

———. 1965a. Some conditions of obedience and disobedience to authority. *Human Relations* 18:57–76.

———. 1965b. Liberating effects of group pressure. *Journal of Personality and Social Psychology* 1:127–34.

———. 1972. The lost-letter technique. In *Beyond the laboratory: Field research in social psychology,* eds. L. Bickman and T. Henchy. New York: McGraw-Hill.

Milgram, S. 1974. *Obedience to authority.* New York: Harper and Row.

Milgram, S. and H. Toch. 1969. Collective behavior: Crowds and social movements. In *The handbook of social psychology,* eds. G. Lindzey and E. Aronson. 2d. ed. Vol. IV. Reading, MA: Addison-Wesley. 507–610.

Miller, A.G. 1976. Constraint and target effects on the attribution of attitudes. *Journal of Experimental Social Psychology* 12:325–39.

Miller, G. and D. McNeill. 1969. Psycholinguistics. In *The handbook of social psychology,* eds. G. Lindzey and E. Aronson. 2d ed. Vol. 3. Reading, MA: Addison-Wesley.

Miller, G.H. 1981. *Language and speech.* San Francisco: W. H. Freeman.

Miller, J., C. Schooler, M. Kohn, and K. Miller. 1979. Women and work: The psychological effects of occupational conditions. *American Journal of Sociology* 85:66–94.

Miller, L.C., J. Berg, and R. Archer. 1983. Openers: Individuals who elicit intimate self-disclosure. *Journal of Personality and Social Psychology* 44:1234–44.

Miller, L.K. and R.L. Hamblin. 1963. Interdependence, differential rewarding, and productivity. *American Sociological Review* 43:193–204.

Miller, M. 1981. Parents or day care? The debate goes on. *Capital Times:* Madison, WI. Jan. 13, p. 13.

Miller-McPherson, J. and L. Smith-Lovin. 1982. Women and weak ties: Differences by sex in the size of voluntary organizations. *American Journal of Sociology* 87:883–904.

Mills, C.W. 1940. Situated actions and vocabularies of motive. *American Sociological Review* 5:904–13.

———. 1959. *The sociological imagination.* New York: Oxford Univ. Press.

Mills, J. and E. Aronson. 1965. Opinion change as a function of communicator's attractiveness and desire to influence. *Journal of Personality and Social Psychology* 1:173–77.

Mills, T.M. 1967. *The sociology of small groups.* Englewood Cliffs, NJ: Prentice-Hall.

Minnigerode, F. and J.A. Lee. 1978. Young adults' perceptions of sex roles across the lifespan. *Sex Roles* 4:563–69.

Mirowsky, J. and C.E. Ross. 1980. Minority status, ethnic culture and distress: A comparison of blacks, whites, Mexicans, and Mexican-Americans. *American Journal of Sociology* 86:479–95.

Mischel, W. and R.M. Liebert. 1966. Effects of discrepancies between deserved and imposed reward criteria on their acquisition and transmission. *Journal of Personality and Social Psychology* 3:45–53.

Miyamoto, S.F. 1973. The forced evacuation of the Japanese minority during World War II. *Journal of Social Issues* 29:11–31.

Miyamoto, S.F. and S.M. Dornbusch. 1956. A test of interactionist hypotheses of self-conception. *American Journal of Sociology* 61:399–403.

Modell, J., F.F. Furstenberg, Jr., and T. Hershberg. 1976. Social change and the transition to adulthood in historical perspective. *Journal of Family History* 1:7–32.

Modigliani, A. 1971. Embarrassment, face-work, and eye-contact: Testing a theory of embarrassment. *Journal of Personality and Social Psychology* 17:15–24.

Moede, W. 1927. Die richtlinien der leistungs-psychologie (Guidelines for a psychology of achievement). *Industrielle Psychotechnik.* 4:193–209.

Moen, P., E. Kain, and G.H. Elder, Jr. 1983. Economic conditions and family life: Contemporary and historical perspectives. In *The high art of living,* ed. R. Nelson. Washington: National Academy Press.

Money, J. and A. Ehrhardt. 1972. *Man and woman, boy and girl.* Baltimore: Johns Hopkins.

Moore, J.C., Jr. 1968. Status and influence in small group interaction. *Sociometry* 31:47–63.

Moore, K. and I. Sawhill. 1978. Implications of women's employment for home and family life. In *Women Working,* eds. A Stromberg and S. Harkness. Palo Alto, CA: Mayfield.

Moran, G. 1966. Dyadic attraction and orientational consensus. *Journal of Personality and Social Psychology* 4:94–99.

Moray, N. 1959. Attention in dichotic listening: Affective cues and the influence of instructions. *Quarterly Journal of Experimental Psychology* 12:56–60.

Moreno, J.L. 1934. *Who shall survive?* Washington, D.C.: Nervous and Mental Disease Publishing Co.

Morgan, C.J. and R.K. Leik. 1970. Simulation theory development: The bystander intervention case. In *Social science methods, Vol. 3: Theory construction,* eds. R.B. Smith and B. Anderson. New York: Halsted.

Morgan, C.P. and J.D. Aram. 1975. The preponderance of arguments in the risky shift phenomenon. *Journal of Experimental Social Psychology* 11:25–34.

Morgan, W., D. Alwin, and L. Griffin. 1979. Social origins, parental values and the transmission of inequality. *American Journal of Sociology* 85:156–66.

Morgan, W.R. and T. Clarke. 1973. Causes of racial disorders: A grievance-level explanation. *American Sociological Review* 38:611–24.

Morland, J.K. 1969. Race awareness among American and Hong Kong Chinese children. *American Journal of Sociology* 75:360–74.

Morley, I.E. and G.M. Stephenson. 1977. *The social psychology of bargaining.* London: Allen and Unwin.

Morris, W.N. and R.S. Miller. 1975. The effect of consensus-breaking and consensus-preempting partners on reduction of conformity. *Journal of Experimental Social Psychology* 11:215–23.

Morrison, D.E. 1971. Some notes toward theory on relative deprivation, social movements and social change. *American Behavioral Scientist* 14:675–90.

Morrissette, J.O. 1966. Group performance as a function of task difficulty and size and structure of groups, II. *Journal of Personality and Social Psychology* 3:357–59.

Morrissette, J.O., S.A. Switzer, and C.W. Crannell. 1965. Group performance as a function of size, structure, and task difficulty. *Journal of Personality and Social Psychology* 2:451–55.

Morsbach, H. 1973. Aspects of nonverbal communication in Japan. *Journal of Nervous and Mental Diseases* 157:262–77.

Morse, N.C. and E. Riemer. 1956. The experimental change of a major organizational variable. *Journal of Abnormal and Social Psychology* 52:120–29.

Morse, S. and K. Gergen. 1970. Social comparison, self-consistency, and the concept of self. *Journal of Personality and Social Psychology* 16:148–56.

Mortimer, J.T., M.D. Finch, and D. Kumka. 1982. Persistence and change in development: The multidimensional self-concept. In *Life span development and behavior,* eds. P.B. Baltes and O.G. Brim, Jr. Vol. 4. New York: Academic Press.

Mortimer, J.T. and R.G. Simmons. 1978. Adult socialization. In *Annual Review of Sociology,* eds. R.H. Turner, J. Coleman and R.C. Fox. 4:421–54.

Morton, T. 1978. Intimacy and reciprocity of exchange: A comparison of spouses and strangers. *Journal of Personality and Social Psychology* 36:72–81.

Moscovici, S. and C. Faucheux. 1972. Social influence, conformity bias, and the study of active minorities. In *Advances in experimental social psychology,* ed. L. Berkowitz. Vol. 6. New York: Academic Press.

Moscovici, S. and E. Lage. 1976. Studies in social influence III: Majority versus minority influence in a group. *European Journal of Social Psychology* 6:149–74.

Moscovici, S., E. Lage, and M. Naffrechoux. 1969. Influence of a consistent minority on the responses of a majority in a color perception task. *Sociometry* 32:365–80.

Moscovici, S. and M. Zavalloni. 1969. The group as a polarizer of attitudes. *Journal of Personality and Social Psychology* 12:125–35.

Moss, H. and J. Kagan. 1961. Stability of achievement and recognition seeking behavior from early childhood through adulthood. *Journal of Abnormal and Social Psychology* 62:504–13.

Muir, D. and E. Weinstein. 1962. The social debt: An investigation of lower-class and middle-class norms of social obligation. *American Sociological Review* 27:532–39.

Murray, J.P. and S. Kippax. 1979. From the early window to the late night show. International trends in the study of television's impact on children and adults. In *Advances in experimental social psychology,* ed. L. Berkowitz. Vol. 12. New York: Academic Press.

Murstein, B. 1976. *Who will marry whom?* New York: Springer.

———. 1980. Mate selection in the 1970s. *Journal of Marriage and the Family* 42:777–92.

Myers, A. 1962. Team competition, success, and the adjustment of group members. *Journal of Abnormal and Social Psychology.* 65:325–32.

Myers, D.G. 1973. Summary and bibliography of experiments on group-induced response shift. *Catalogue of Selected Documents in Psychology* 3:123.

———. 1975. Discussion-induced attitude polarization. *Human Relations* 28:699–714.

Myers, D.G. and M.F. Kaplan. 1976. Group-induced polarization in simulated juries. *Personality and Social Psychology Bulletin* 2:63–66.

Myers, D.G. and H. Lamm. 1976. The group polarization phenomenon. *Psychological Bulletin* 83:602–27.

Myers, F.E. 1971. Civil disobedience and organization change: The British Committee of 100. *Political Science Quarterly* 86:92–112.

Myers, M.A. and J. Hagan. 1979. Private and public trouble: Prosecutors and the allocation of court resources. *Social Problems* 26:439–51.

Nadler, A. and J.D. Fisher. 1984a. Effects of donor-recipient relationships on recipient's reactions to aid. In *Development and maintenance of prosocial behavior: International perspectives on positive morality*, eds. E. Staub, D. Bar-Tal, J. Karylowski, and J. Reykowski. New York: Plenum.

———. 1984b. The role of threat to self-esteem and perceived control in recipient reaction to aid: In *Advances in experimental social psychology*, ed. L. Berkowitz. Vol. 17. New York: Academic Press.

Nadler, A. and O. Mayseless. 1983. Recipient self-esteem and reactions to help. In *New directions in helping*, eds. J.D. Fisher, A. Nadler, and B.M. DePaulo. Vol. 1. New York: Academic Press.

Neal, A.G. and H.T. Groat. 1974. Social class correlates of stability and change in levels of alienation: A longitudinal study. *Sociological Quarterly* 15:548–58.

Neisser, U. 1967. *Cognitive psychology*. New York: Appleton-Century-Crofts.

Neugarten, B.L. 1968. *Middle age and aging*. Chicago: Univ. of Chicago Press.

Neugarten, B.L., and N. Datan. 1973. Sociological perspectives on the life cycle. In *Life-span developmental psychology: Personality and social processes*, eds. P. Baltes and K.W. Schaie. New York: Academic Press.

Neugarten, B.L. and G.O. Hagestad. 1976. Age and the life course. In *Handbook of aging and the social sciences*, eds. R.H. Binstock and E. Shanas. New York: Van Nostrand Reinhold.

Neugarten, B.L., J.W. Moore, and J.C. Lowe. 1965. Age norms, age constraints, and adult socialization. *American Journal of Sociology* 70:710–17.

Newcomb, T.M. 1943. *Personality and social change*. New York: Dryden.

———. 1961. *The acquaintance process*. New York: Holt, Rinehart and Winston.

———. 1968. Interpersonal balance. In *Theories of cognitive consistency: A sourcebook*, eds. R.P. Abelson et al. Chicago: Rand McNally.

———. 1971. Dyadic balance as a source of clues about interpersonal attraction. In *Theories of attraction and love*, ed. B. Murstein. New York: Springer.

Newsweek. 1978. Gold in the streets. January 9:56–57.

———. 1983. A portrait of America. January 17:18–29.

Newtson, D. and T. Czerlinsky. 1974. Adjustment of attitude and communications for contrasts by extreme audiences. *Journal of Personality and Social Psychology* 30:829–37.

Nisbett, R.E., C. Caputo, P. Legant, and J. Maracek. 1973. Behavior as seen by the actor and as seen by the observer. *Journal of Personality and Social Psychology* 27:154–64.

Nisbett, R.E. and A. Gordon. 1967. Self-esteem and susceptibility to social influence. *Journal of Personality and Social Psychology* 27:154–164.

Nixon, H.L. II. 1976. *Sport and social organization*. Indianapolis: Bobbs-Merrill.

———. 1977a. "Cohesiveness" and team success: A theoretical reformulation. *Review of Sport and Leisure* 2:36–57.

———. 1977b. Reinforcement effects of sports teams success on cohesiveness-related factors. *International Review of Sport Sociology* 4:17–38.

Nizer, L. 1973. *The implosion conspiracy*. New York: Doubleday.

Norman, R. 1975. Affective-cognitive consistency, attitudes, conformity, and behavior. *Journal of Personality and Social Psychology* 32:83–91.

O'Barr, W. and B. Atkins. 1980. Women's language or powerless language. In *Women and language in literature and society*, eds. S. McConnell-Ginet, R. Borker, and N. Furman. New York: Praeger.

Oberschall, A. 1973. *Social Conflict and Social Movements*. Englewood Cliffs, NJ: Prentice-Hall.

———. 1978. Theories of social conflict. In *Annual Review of Sociology*, eds. R.H. Turner, J. Coleman, and R. Fox. 4:291–315.

Ogbu, J. 1974. *The next generation: An ethnography of education in an urban neighborhood*. New York: Academic Press.

Oliver, P. 1980. Rewards and punishments as selective incentives for collective action: Theoretical investigations. *American Journal of Sociology* 85:1356–75.

Olver, R. 1961. Developmental study of cognitive equivalence. Unpublished doctoral dissertation. Radcliffe College.

Oppenheimer, V.K. 1970. The female labor force in the United States. *Population monograph series, no. 5*. Berkeley, CA: Institute of International Studies.

Orcutt, J.D. 1973. Societal reaction and the response to deviation in small groups. *Social Forces* 52:259–67.

———. 1975. Deviance as a situated phenomenon: Variations in the social interpretation of marijuana and alcohol use. *Social Problems* 22:346–56.

Orvis, B.R., J.D. Cunningham, and H.H. Kelley. 1975. A closer examination of causal inference: The roles of consensus, distinctiveness, and consistency information. *Journal of Personality and Social Psychology* 32:605–16.

Orwell, G. 1949. *Nineteen eighty-four*. New York: Harcourt Brace Jovanovich.

Osgood, C.E. 1959. Suggestions for winning the real war with Communism. *Journal of Conflict Resolution* 3:295–352.

———. 1962. *An alternative to war or surrender*. Urbana, IL: Univ. of Illinois Press.

———. 1979. GRIT for MBFR: A proposal for unfreezing force-level postures in Europe. *Peace Research Review* 8,2:77–92.

Osgood, C.E., G.J. Suci, and P.H. Tannenbaum. 1957. *The measurement of meaning*. Urbana, IL: Univ. of Illinois Press.

Oskamp, S. 1971. Effects of programmed strategies on cooperation in the Prisoner's Dilemma and other mixed-motive games. *Journal of Conflict Resolution* 15:225–59.

Paicheler, G. and J. Bouchet. 1973. Attitude polarization, familiarization, and group process. *European Journal of Social Psychology* 3:83–90.

Page, A.L. and D.A. Clelland. 1978. The Kanawha County textbook controversy: A study of the politics of lifestyle concern. *Social Forces* 57:265–81.

Paige, J.M. 1971. Political orientation and riot participation. *American Sociological Review* 36:810–20.

Palmore, E. 1981. *Social patterns in normal aging.* Durham, NC: Duke Univ. Press.

Parcel, T.L. and K.S. Cook. 1977. Status characteristics, reward allocation, and equity. *Sociometry.* 40:311–24.

Parke, R. 1967. Nurturance, nurturance withdrawal, and resistance to deviation. *Child Development* 38:1101–10.

———. 1969. Effectiveness of punishment as an interaction of intensity, timing, agent nurturance and cognitive structuring. *Child Development* 40:213–35.

———. 1970. The role of punishment in the socialization process. In *Early experiences and the processes of socialization,* eds. R. Hoppe, G. Milton, and E. Simmel. New York: Academic Press.

Parke, R.D., L. Berkowitz, J.P. Leyens, S. West, and R.J. Sebastian. 1977. Some effects of violent and nonviolent movies on the behavior of juvenile delinquents. In *Advances in experimental social psychology,* ed. L. Berkowitz. Vol. 10. New York: Academic Press.

Patterson, M.L., S. Mullens, and J. Romano. 1971. Compensatory reactions to spatial intrusion. *Sociometry* 34:114–21.

Patterson, T.E. 1980. *The mass media election: How Americans choose their president.* New York: Praeger.

Pavlov, I.P. 1897. *The work of the digestive glands,* 2d ed. Trans. W.H. Thompson. 1910. London: Griffin.

Pearlin, L.I. and M. Kohn. 1966. Social class, occupation and parental values: A cross-national study. *American Sociological Review* 31:466–79.

Pearlin, L.I. and C. Radabaugh. 1976. Economic strains and the coping functions of alcohol. *American Journal of Sociology* 82:652–63.

Pearlin, L.I. and J. Johnson. 1977. Marital status, life-strains and depression. *American Sociological Review* 42:704–15.

Pearlin, L.I., M.A. Lieberman, E.G. Menaghan, and J.T. Mullan. 1981. The stress process. *Journal of Health and Social Behavior* 22:337–56.

Pennebaker, J.W. 1980. Self-perception of emotion and internal sensation. In *The self in social psychology,* eds. D.W. Wegner and R.R. Vallacher. New York: Oxford Univ. Press.

Pennybaker, J., M. Dyer, R. Caulkins, D. Litowitz, P. Ackerman, D. Anderson, K. McGraw. 1979. Don't the girls get prettier at closing time: A country and western application to psychology. *Personality and Social Psychology Bulletin* 5:122–25.

Peplau, L., Z. Rubin, and C. Hill. 1977. Sexual intimacy in dating relationships. *Journal of Social Issues* 33(2):86–109.

Perinbanayagam, R.S. 1974. The definition of the situation. *The Sociological Quarterly* 15:531–37.

Perry, J.B. and M.D. Pugh. 1978. *Collective behavior: Response to social stress.* St. Paul: West Publishing Company.

Petrunik, M. and C.D. Shearing. 1983. Fragile facades: Stuttering and the strategic manipulation of awareness. *Social Problems* 31:125–38.

Pettigrew, T.F. 1969. Racially separate or together? *Journal of Social Issues* 25:43–69.

———. 1979. The ultimate attribution error: Extending Allport's cognitive analysis of prejudice. *Personality and Social Psychology Bulletin* 5:461–76.

Petty, R.E. and J.T. Cacioppo. 1979. Issue involvement can increase or decrease persuasion by enhancing message-relevant cognitive responses. *Journal of Personality and Social Psychology* 37:1915–26.

———. 1981. *Attitudes and persuasion: Classic and contemporary approaches.* Dubuque, IA: William C. Brown.

Petty, R.E., J.T. Cacioppo, and R. Goldman. 1981. Personal involvement as a determinant of argument-based persuasion. *Journal of Personality and Social Psychology* 41:847–55.

Petty, R.E., J.T. Cacioppo, and M. Heesacker. 1981. Effects of rhetorical questions on persuasion: A cognitive response analysis. *Journal of Personality and Social Psychology* 40:432–40.

Phelps, E.S. 1975. Ed. *Altruism, morality and economic theory.* Chicago: Russell Sage.

Phillips, D.P. 1974. The influence of suggestion on suicide: Substantive and theoretical implications of the Werther effect. *American Sociological Review* 39:340–54.

———. 1979. Suicide, motor vehicle fatalities and the mass media: Evidence toward a theory of suggestion. *American Sociological Review* 84:1150–74.

Piaget, J. 1954. *The construction of reality in the child.* New York: Basic Books.

———. 1965. *The moral judgement of the child.* New York: Free Press.

Piliavin, I.M., and S. Briar. 1964. Police encounters with juveniles. *American Journal of Sociology* 70:206–14.

Piliavin, I.M., J. Rodin, and J.A. Piliavin. 1969. Good samaritanism: An underground phenomenon? *Journal of Personality and Social Psychology* 13:289–99.

Piliavin, J.A., J.F. Dovidio, S.L. Gaertner, and R.D. Clark III. 1981. *Emergency intervention.* New York: Academic Press.

Pilisuk, M. and P. Skolnick. 1968. Inducing trust: A test of the Osgood proposal. *Journal of Personality and Social Psychology* 8:121–33.

Pilisuk, M., J.A. Winter, R. Chapman, and N. Haas. 1967. Honesty, deceit, and timing in the display of intentions. *Behavioral Science* 12:205–15.

Piper, D. 1979. American Indian ethnicity as expressed in urban voluntary associations. Unpublished dissertation: Univ. of Wisconsin.

Plastic Surgery Now Commonplace. *Wisconsin State Journal* Madison, WI. July 15, 1979.

Pleck, J. 1976. The male sex role: Definitions, problems and sources of change. *Journal of Social Issues* 32:155–64.

Pollack, O. 1961. *The criminality of women.* New York: Perpetua Books.

Poloma, M. 1972. Role conflict and the married professional women. In *Toward a sociology of women,* ed. C. Safilios-Rothschild. Lexington, MA: Xerox College Publishing.

Poyatos, F. 1983. *New perspectives in nonverbal communication: Studies in cultural anthropology, social psychology, linguistics, literature and semantics.* Oxford: Pergamon.

Premack, D. and A. Premack. 1984. *The mind of an ape.* New York: Norton.

Prentice-Dunn, S. and R.W. Rogers. 1980. Effects of

deindividuating situational cues and aggressive models on subjective deindividuation and aggression. *Journal of Personality and Social Psychology* 13:289–99.

Preston, M.G. and R.K. Heintz. 1949. Effects of participatory versus supervisory leadership on group judgment. *Journal of Abnormal and Social Psychology* 44:345–55.

Price, K.O., E. Harburg, and T.M. Newcomb. 1966. Psychological balance in situations of negative interpersonal attitudes. *Journal of Personality and Social Psychology* 3:265–70.

Priest, R.T. and J. Sawyer. 1967. Proximity and peership: Bases of balance in interpersonal attraction. *American Journal of Sociology* 72:633–49.

Pritchard, R., M. Dunnette, and D. Jorgenson. 1972. Effects of perception of equity and inequity on worker performance and satisfaction. *Journal of Applied Psychology.* 56:75–94.

Pruitt, D.G. 1968. Reciprocity and credit building in a laboratory dyad. *Journal of Personality and Social Psychology* 8:143–47.

———. 1971. Choice shifts in group discussion: An introductory review. *Journal of Personality and Social Psychology* 20:339–60.

———. 1981. *Negotiation Behavior.* New York: Academic Press.

Pruitt, D.G. and P.J.D. Carnevale. 1980. The development of integrative agreements in social conflict. In *Living with other people: Theories and research on cooperation and helping behavior*, eds. V.J. Derlega and J. Grzelak. New York: Academic Press.

Pruitt, D.G. and J.L. Drews. 1969. The effects of time pressure, time elapsed, and the opponent's concession rate on behavior in negotiation. *Journal of Experimental Social Psychology* 5:43–60.

Pruitt, D.G. and C.A. Insko. 1980. Extension of the Kelley attribution model: The role of comparison-object consensus, target-object consensus, distinctiveness, and consistency. *Journal of Personality and Social Psychology* 39:39–58.

Pruitt, D.G. and S.A. Lewis. 1977. The psychology of integrative bargaining. In *Negotiations: A social-psychological perspective*, ed. D. Druckman. Beverly Hills, CA: Sage-Halsted.

Pruitt, D.G. and A.I. Teger. 1967. Is there a shift toward risk in group discussion? If so, is it a group phenomenon? If so, what causes it? In Braun, J.R. (Chair) The risky shift phenomenon: Current status. Symposium presented at the meeting of the American Psychological Association.

Prus, R.C. 1975. Resisting designations: An extension of attribution theory into a negotiated context. *Sociological Inquiry* 45:3–14.

Quarentelli, E.L. and J. Cooper. 1966. Self-conceptions and others: A further test of the Meadian hypothesis. *Sociological Quarterly* 7:281–97.

Quarentelli, E.L. and R.R. Dynes. 1977. Response to social crisis and disaster. In *Annual Review of Sociology*, eds. A. Inkeles, J. Coleman, and N. Smelser. 3:23–49.

Quinney, R. 1970. *The social reality of crime.* Boston: Little, Brown.

Rabbie, J.M. and F. Bekkers. 1978. Threatened leadership and intergroup competition. *European Journal of Social Psychology* 8:9–20.

Rabbie, J.M. and L. Visser. 1972. Bargaining strength and group polarization in inter-group polarization. *European Journal of Social Psychology* 2:402–16.

Radloff, L.S. 1980. Depression and the empty nest. *Sex Roles* 67:775–81.

Raven, B.H. and H.T. Eachus. 1963. Cooperation and competition in means-interdependent triads. *Journal of Abnormal and Social Psychology* 67:307–16.

Raven, B.H. and A.W. Kruglanski. 1970. Conflict and power. In *The structure of conflict*, ed. P. Swingle. New York: Academic Press.

Raven, B.H. and J. Rietsema. 1957. The effects of varied clarity of group goal and group path upon the individual and his relation to the group. *Human Relations* 10:29–44.

Ray, M. 1973. Marketing communication and the hierarchy of effects. In *New models for communication research*, ed. P. Clarke. Beverly Hills, CA: Sage.

Reeder, L.G., G.A. Donahue, and A. Biblarz. 1960. Conceptions of self and others. *American Journal of Sociology* 66:153–59.

Regan, D.T. and R.H. Fazio. 1977. On the consistency between attitudes and behavior: Look to the method of attitude formation. *Journal of Experimental Social Psychology* 35:21–30.

Regan, J.W. 1971. Guilt, perceived injustice, and altruistic behavior. *Journal of Personality and Social Psychology* 18:124–47.

Reis, H.T., L. Wheeler, M. Spiegel, M. Kernis, J. Nezlek, and M. Perri. 1982. Physical attractiveness in social interaction: II. Why does appearance affect social experience? *Journal of Personality and Social Psychology* 43:979–96.

Renshon, S.A. 1974. *Psychological needs and political behavior: A theory of personality and political efficacy.* New York: Free Press.

Report of the National Advisory Commission on Civil Disorders. 1968. New York: Bantam Books.

Rhine, R.J. and L.J. Severance. 1970. Ego-involvement, discrepancy, source credibility, and attitude change. *Journal of Personality and Social Psychology* 16:175–90.

Rice, R.W. 1978. Psychometric properties of the esteem for least preferred coworker (LPC) scale. *Academy of Management Review* 3:106–18.

Rigney, J. 1962. A developmental study of cognitive equivalence transformations and their use in the acquisition and processing of information. Unpublished honors thesis, Radcliffe College.

Riley, M.W., A. Foner, B. Hess, and M.L. Tobin. 1969. Socialization for the middle and later years. In *Handbook of socialization theory and research*, ed. D. Goslin. Chicago: Rand McNally.

Riley, M.W., M. Johnson, and A. Foner. 1972. Eds. *Aging and society, Vol. 3: A sociology of age stratification.* New York: Russell Sage Foundation.

Ring, K. and H.H. Kelley. 1963. A comparison of augmentation and reduction as modes of influence. *Journal of Abnormal and Social Psychology* 66:95–102.

Riordan, C.A., N.A. Marlin, and R.T. Kellogg. 1983. The

effectiveness of accounts following transgression. *Social Psychology Quarterly* 46:213–19.

Riordan, C. and J. Ruggiero. 1980. Producing equal-status interracial interaction: A replication. *Social Psychology Quarterly.* 43:131–36.

Rizzo, J.R., R.J. House, and S.E. Lirtzman. 1970. Role conflict and ambiguity in complex organizations. *Administrative Science Quarterly* 15:150–63.

Robinson, W.P. and S.J. Rackstraw. 1972. *A question of answers.* London: Routledge and Kegan Paul.

Robson, P. 1982. Patterns of mobility and activity among the elderly. In *Geographical perspectives on the elderly,* ed. E.M. Warnes. New York: Wiley.

Roethlisberger, F.J. and W.J. Dickson. 1939. *Management and the worker.* Cambridge, MA: Harvard Univ. Press.

Rogers, M., N. Miller, F.S. Mayer, and S. Duvall. 1982. Personal responsibilty and salience of the request for help: Determinants of the relation between negative affect and helping behavior. *Journal of Personality and Social Psychology* 43:956–70.

Rogers, R.W. 1975. A protection motivation theory of fear appeals and attitude change. *Journal of Psychology* 91:93–114.

Rogers, T.B. 1977. Self-reference in memory: Recognition of personality items. *Journal of Research in Personality* 11:295–305.

Rokeach, M. 1973. *The nature of human values.* New York: Free Press.

Rollins, B. and D. Thomas. 1979. Parental support, power and control techniques in the socialization of children. In *Contemporary theories about the family,* eds. W. Burr, R. Hill, I. Reiss, and F. I. Nye. Vol. 1. New York: Free Press.

Rommetveit, R. 1955. *Social norms and roles.* Minneapolis: Univ. of Minnesota Press.

Rosen, B. 1959. Race, ethnicity and the achievement syndrome. *American Sociological Review* 24:47–60.

Rosen, B. and R. D'Andrade. 1959. The psychological origins of achievement motivation. *Sociometry* 22:185–218.

Rosen, S. 1984. Some paradoxical status implications of helping and being helped. In *Development and maintenance of prosocial behavior: International perspectives on positive morality,* ed. E. Staub et al. New York: Plenum.

Rosenbaum, M.E., D.L. Moore, J.L. Cotton, M.S. Cook, R.A. Hieser, M.N. Shovar, and M.J. Gray. 1980. Group productivity and process: Pure and mixed reward structures and task interdependence. *Journal of Personality and Social Psychology* 39:626–42.

Rosenberg, L.A. 1961. Group size, prior experience, and conformity. *Journal of Abnormal and Social Psychology* 63:436–37.

Rosenberg, M. 1965. *Society and the adolescent self–image.* Princeton, NJ: Princeton Univ. Press.

———. 1973. Which significant others? *American Behavioral Scientist* 16:829–60.

———. 1979. *Conceiving the self.* New York: Basic Books.

———. 1981. The self-concept: Social product and social force. In *Social psychology: Sociological perspectives,* eds. M. Rosenberg and R.H. Turner. New York: Basic Books.

Rosenberg, M. and L.I. Pearlin. 1978. Social class and self esteem among children and adults. *American Journal of Sociology* 84:53–77.

Rosenberg, M. and R.G. Simmons. 1972. *Black and white self-esteem: The urban school child.* Washington: American Sociological Association.

Rosenberg, M.J. 1960. Cognitive reorganization in response to the hypnotic reversal of attitudinal affect. *Journal of Personality* 28:39–63.

Rosenberg, M.J. and R.P. Abelson. 1960. An analysis of cognitive balancing. In *Attitude organization and change,* eds. C.I. Hovland and M.J. Rosenberg. New Haven: Yale Univ. Press.

Rosenberg, S.V. 1977. New approaches to the analysis of personal constructs in person perception. In *Nebraska symposium on motivation,* ed. A.W. Landfield 1976. Lincoln, NE: Univ. of Nebraska Press.

Rosenberg, S.V., C. Nelson, and P.S. Vivekananthan. 1968. A multidimensional approach to the structure of personality impressions. *Journal of Personality and Social Psychology* 9:283–94.

Rosenberg, S.V. and A. Sedlak. 1972. Structural representations in implicit personality theory. In *Advances in experimental social psychology,* ed. L. Berkowitz. Vol. 6. New York: Academic Press.

Rosenfeld, H. 1978. Conversational control functions of nonverbal behavior. In *Nonverbal behavior and communication,* eds. A. Seigman and S. Feldstein. Hillsdale, NJ: Erlbaum.

Rosenhan, D.L. 1973. On being sane in insane places. *Science* 179:250–58.

Rosenhan, D.L., P. Salovey, and K. Hargis. 1981. The joys of helping: Focus of attention mediates the impact of positive affect on altruism. *Journal of Personality and Social Psychology* 40:899–905.

Rosenhan, D.L., P. Salovey, J. Karylowski, and K. Hargis. 1981. Emotion and altruism. In *Altruism and helping behavior,* eds. J.P. Rushton and R.M. Sorrentino. Hillsdale, NJ: Erlbaum.

Rosenthal, R. 1966. *Experimenter effects in behavioral research.* New York: Appleton-Century-Crofts.

———. 1973. *On the social psychology of the self-fulfilling prophecy: Further evidence for pygmalion effects and their mediating mechanisms.* New York: MSS Modular Publication, Module 53.

Rosenthal, R. and D.B. Rubin. 1978. Interpersonal expectancy effects: The first 345 studies. *The Behavioral and Brain Sciences* 3:377–86.

Rosow, I. 1974. *Socialization to old age.* Berkeley: Univ. of California Press.

Ross, A.S. 1971. Effect of increased responsibility on bystander intervention: The presence of children. *Journal of Personality and Social Psychology* 19:306–10.

Ross, C.E. and J. Mirowsky. 1984. Men who cry. *Social Psychology Quarterly* 47:138–46.

Ross, L. 1977. The intuitive psychologist and his shortcomings: Distortions in the attribution process. In *Advances in experimental social psychology,* ed. L. Berkowitz. Vol. 10. New York: Academic Press.

Ross, L., T. Amabile, and J. Steinmetz. 1977. Social roles, social control and biases in social perception processes. *Journal of Personality and Social Psychology* 35:485–94.

Ross, M. and G. Fletcher. 1985. Attribution and social

perception. In *The handbook of social psychology*, G. Lindzey and E. Aronson. 3d ed. Reading, MA: Addison-Wesley.

Ross, M. and H. Lumsden. 1982. Attributions of responsibility in sports settings: It's not how you play the game but whether you win or lose. In *Social Psychology*, eds. H. Hiebsch, H. Brandstatter, and H.H. Kelley. East Berlin: VEB Deutcher Verlag der Wissenschaften.

Ross, M. and F. Sicoly. 1979. Egocentric biases in availability and attribution. *Journal of Personality and Social Psychology* 37:322–36.

Ross, M., J. Thibaut, and S. Evenbeck. 1971. Some determinants of the intensity of social protests. *Journal of Experimental Social Psychology.* 7:408–18.

Rossi, A.S. 1980. Parenthood in the middle years. In *Life-span development and behavior*, eds. P.B. Baltes and O.G. Brim, Jr. Vol. 3. New York: Academic Press.

Rothbart, M., S. Fulero, C. Jensen, J. Howard, and B. Birrell. 1978. From individual to group impressions: Availability heuristics in stereotype formation. *Journal of Experimental Social Psychology* 14:237–255.

Rubenstein, E.A. 1983. Television and behavior: Research conclusions of the 1982 NIMH report and their policy implications. *American Psychologist* 38:820–25.

Rubin, J. 1962. Bilingualism in Paraguay. *Anthropological Linguistics* 4:52–68.

Rubin, J.Z. and B.R. Brown. 1975. *The Social Psychology of Bargaining and Negotiation.* New York: Academic Press.

Rubin, J.Z. and R.J. Lewicki. 1973. A three-factor experimental analysis of promises and threats. *Journal of Applied Social Psychology* 3:240–57.

Rubin, L. 1979. *Women of a certain age: The midlife search for self.* New York: Harper and Row.

———. 1983. *Intimate strangers.* New York: Harper and Row.

Rubin, Z. 1970. Measurement of romantic love. *Journal of Personality and Social Psychology* 16:265–73.

———. 1974. From liking to loving: Patterns of attraction in dating relationships. In *Foundations of interpersonal attraction*, ed. T. Huston. New York: Academic Press.

Rubin, Z., C. Hill, L. Peplau, and C. Dunkel-Scheker. 1980. Self-disclosure in dating couples: Sex roles and the ethic of openness. *Journal of Marriage and the Family* 42:305–17.

Rude, G. 1964. *The crowd in history.* New York: Wiley.

Rule, B.F., T.J. Ferguson, and A.R. Nesdale. 1980. Emotional arousal, anger, and aggression: The misattribution issue. In *Advances in communication and affect*, eds. P. Pliner, K. Blankstein, and T. Speigel. Hillsdale, NJ: Erlbaum.

Rusbult, C.E. 1980. Commitment and satisfaction in romantic associations: A test of the investment model. *Journal of Experimental Social Psychology* 16:172–86.

———. 1983. A longitudinal test of the investment model: The development (and deterioration) of satisfaction and commitment in heterosexual involvements. *Journal of Personality and Social Psychology* 45:101–17.

Rusbult, C.E., I.M. Zembrodt, and L.K. Gunn. 1982. Exit, voice, loyalty, and neglect: Responses to dissatisfaction in romantic involvement. *Journal of Personality and Social Psychology* 43:1230–42.

Rushing, W.A. and S.T. Ortega. 1979. Socioeconomic status and mental disorders: New evidence and a sociomedical formulation. *American Journal of Sociology* 84:1175–1200.

Ryder, N.B. 1965. The cohort as a concept in the study of social change. *American Sociological Review* 30:843–61.

Sabath, G. 1964. The effect of disruption and individual status on person perception and group attraction. *Journal of Social Psychology* 64:119–30.

Sacks, H., E. Schegloff, and G. Jefferson. 1978. A simplest systematics for the organization of turn-taking in conversations. In *Studies in the organization of conversational interaction*, ed. J. Schenkein. New York: Academic Press.

Saegert, S.C., W. Swap, and R.B. Zajonc. 1973. Exposure, context, and interpersonal attraction. *Journal of Personality and Social Psychology* 25:234–42.

Sagarin, E. 1975. *Deviants and deviance.* New York: Praeger.

Sakurai, M.M. 1975. Small group cohesiveness and detrimental conformity. *Sociometry* 38:340–57.

Sales, E. 1978. Women's adult development. In *Women and sex roles: A social psychological perspective*, eds. I.H. Frieze, J.E. Parsons, P.B. Johnson, D.N. Ruble, and G.L. Zellman. New York: W.W. Norton.

Sales, S. 1969. Organizational roles as a risk factor in coronary heart disease. *Administrative Science Quarterly* 14:325–36.

Salzter, E.B. 1981. Cognitive moderation of the relationship between behaviorial intentions and behavior. *Journal of Personality and Social Psychology* 41:260–271.

Sample, J. and R. Warland. 1973. Attitude and the prediction of behavior. *Social Forces* 51:292–304.

Sampson, E.E. and A.C. Brandon. 1964. The effects of role and opinion deviation on small group behavior. *Sociometry* 27:261–81.

Sampson, H., S. Messinger, R. Towne, D. Russ, F. Livson, M. Bowers, L. Cohen, and K. Dorst. 1964. The mental hospital and marital family ties. In *The other side*, ed. H. Becker. New York: Free Press.

Samuels, F. 1970. The intra- and inter-competitive group. *Sociological Quarterly* 11:390–96.

Sanders, G.S. and R.S. Baron. 1977. Is social comparison irrelevant for producing choice shifts? *Journal of Experimental Social Psychology* 13:303–14.

Santa, J.L. and H.B. Ranken. 1972. Effects of verbal coding on recognition memory. *Journal of Experimental Psychology* 93:268–78.

Santee, R.T. and S.E. Jackson. 1979. Commitment to self-identification: A socio-psychological approach to personality. *Human Relations* 32:141–58.

———. 1978. Similarity and positivity of self-description as determinants of estimated appraisal and attraction. *Social Psychology* 41:162–65.

Sarason, S.B. 1977. *Work, aging and social change: Professionals and the one life-one career imperative.* New York: Free Press.

Sarbin, T.R. and V.L. Allen. 1968. Role theory. In *The handbook of social psychology*, eds. G. Lindzey and E. Aronson. Vol 1, 2d. Reading, MA: Addison-Wesley.

Sarbin, T. and B.G. Rosenberg. 1955. Contributions to role-taking theory IV: A method for obtaining a qualitative estimate of the self. *Journal of Social Psychology* 42:71–81.

Sawyer, A. 1973. The effects of repetition of refutational and supportive advertising appeals. *Journal of Marketing Research* 10:23–33.

Schachter, S. 1951. Deviation, rejection and communication. *Journal of Abnormal and Social Psychology* 46:190–207.

———. 1964. The interaction of cognitive and physiological determinants of emotional state. In *Advances in experimental social psychology*, ed. L. Berkowitz. Vol. 1. New York: Academic Press.

Schachter, S., N. Ellertson, D. McBride, and D. Gregory. 1951. An experimental study of cohesiveness and productivity. *Human Relations* 4:229–38.

Schachter, S. and J. Singer. 1962. Cognitive, social and physiological determinants of emotional state. *Psychological Review* 69:379–99.

Schafer, R.B. and P.M. Keith. 1980. Equity and depression among married couples. *Social Psychology Quarterly.* 43:430–35.

Schatzman, L. and A. Strauss. 1955. Social class and modes of communication. *American Journal of Sociology* 60:329–38.

Scheff, T.J. 1966. *Being mentally ill.* Chicago: Aldine.

———. 1967. Introduction. In *Mental illness and social processes*, ed. T.J. Scheff. New York: Harper and Row.

Schegloff, E. 1968. Sequencing in conversational openings. *American Anthropologist* 70:1075–95.

Scheier, M.F. and C.S. Carver. 1981. Public and private aspects of the self. In *Review of personality and social psychology*, ed. L. Wheeler. Vol. 2. Beverly Hills, CA: Sage.

———. 1983. Two sides of the self: One for you and one for me. In *Psychological perspectives on the self*, eds. J. Suls and A.G. Greenwald. Vol. 2. Hillsdale, NJ: Erlbaum.

Schelling, T.C. 1960. *The strategy of conflict.* Cambridge, MA: Harvard Univ. Press.

Scherer, K.R. 1979. Nonlinguistic indicators of emotion and psychopathology. In *Emotions in personality and psychopathology*, ed. C.E. Izard. New York: Plenum.

Scherer, S.E. 1974. Proxemic behavior of primary school children as a function of their socioeconomic class and subculture. *Journal of Personality and Social Psychology* 29:800–05.

Schiffenbauer, A. and R.S. Schiavo. 1976. Physical distance and attraction: An intensification effect. *Journal of Experimental Social Psychology* 12:274–82.

Schiffrin, D. 1977. Opening encounters. *American Sociological Review* 42:679–91.

Schlenker, B.R. 1980. *Impression management: The self-concept, social identity, and interpersonal relations.* Belmont, CA: Brooks/Coles.

———. 1975. Self-presentation: Managing the impression of consistency when reality interferes with self-enhancement. *Journal of Personality and Social Psychology* 32:1030–37.

Schlenker, B.R., B. Helm, and J.T. Tedeschi. 1973. The effects of personality and situational variables on behavioral trust. *Journal of Personality and Social Psychology* 25:419–27.

Schmitt, D.R. and G. Marwell. 1972. Withdrawal and reward reallocation as responses to inequity. *Journal of Experimental Social Psychology* 8:207–21.

Schneider, D.J. 1973. Implicit personality theory: A review. *Psychological Bulletin* 79:294–309.

Schneider, D.J., A.H. Hastorf, and P.C. Ellsworth. 1979. *Person perception.* Reading, MA: Addison-Wesley.

Schoenbach, R. and R. Schoenbach. 1983. *Work and personality: An inquiry into the impact of social stratification.* Norwood, NJ: Ablex Publishing.

Schrauger, J.S. and T.J. Schoeneman. 1979. Symbolic interactionist view of self-concept: Through the looking glass darkly. *Psychological Bulletin* 86:549–73.

Schulz, B., G. Bohrnstedt, E. Borgatta, and R. Evans. 1977. Explaining premarital sexual intercourse among college students: A causal model. *Social Forces* 56:148–65.

Schuman, H. and M. Johnson. 1976. Attitudes and behavior. In *Annual Review of Sociology*, eds. A. Inkeles, J. Coleman, and N. Smelser, 2:161–203.

Schutte, J. and J. Light. 1978. The relative importance of proximity and status for friendship choices in social hierarchies. *Social Psychology* 41:260–64.

Schwartz, B. 1978. Queues, priorities, and social process. *Social Psychology* 41:3–12.

Schwartz, R. and J. Skolnick. 1964. Two studies of legal stigma. In *The other side*, ed. H. Becker. New York: Free Press.

Schwartz, S., K. Feldman, M. Brown, and A. Heingartner. 1969. Some personality correlates of conduct in two situations of moral conflict. *Journal of Personality and Social Psychology* 37:41–57.

Schwartz, S.H. 1977. Normative influences on altruism. In *Advances in experimental social psychology*, ed. L. Berkowitz. Vol. 10. New York: Academic Press.

———. 1978. Temporal instability as a moderator of the attitude-behavior relationship. *Journal of Personality and Social Psychology* 36:715–24.

Schwartz, S.H. and R. Ames. 1977. Positive and negative referent others as sources of influence: A case of helping. *Sociometry* 40:12–20.

Schwartz, S.H. and G.T. Clausen. 1970. Responsibility, norms, and helping in an emergency. *Journal of Personality and Social Psychology* 16:299–310.

Schwartz, S.H. and J. Fleishman. 1978. Personal norms and the mediation of legitimacy effects on helping. *Social Psychology* 41:306–315.

Schwartz, S.H. and A. Gottlieb. 1976. Bystander reactions to a violent theft: Crime in Jerusalem. *Journal of Personality and Social Psychology* 39:418–30.

Schwartz, S.H. and J.A. Howard. 1980. Explanations of the moderating effect of responsibility denial on the personal norm-behavior relationship. *Social Psychology Quarterly* 43:441–46.

———. 1981. A normative decision-making model of altruism. In *Altruism and helping behavior*, ed. J.P. Rushton and R.M. Sorrentino. Hillsdale, NJ: Erlbaum.

———. 1984. Internalized values as motivators of altruism. In *The development and maintenance of prosocial behavior: International perspectives on positive morality*, eds. E. Staub, D. Bar-Tal, J. Karylowski, and J. Reykowski. New York: Plenum.

Scott, E.L. 1952. *Perceptions of organization and leadership behavior.* Columbus, OH: Ohio State University Research Foundation.

Scott, M. and S. Lyman. 1968. Accounts. *American Sociological Review* 33:46–62.

Scott, R. 1969. *The making of blind men: A study of adult socialization.* New York: Russell Sage.

———. 1976. Deviance, sanctions and social integration in small-scale societies. *Social Forces* 54:604–20.

Scotton, C.M. 1983. The negotiation of identities in conversation. *International Journal of the Sociology of Language* 44:115–36.

Searle, J.R. 1979. *Expression and meaning: Studies in the theory of speech acts.* Cambridge: Cambridge Univ. Press.

Sears, D.O. and J.L. Freedman. 1967. Selective exposure to information: A critical review. *Public Opinion Quarterly* 31:194–213.

Sears, D.O. and R.E. Whitney. 1973. Political persuasion. In *Handbook of communication*, eds. I. deSola Pool, W. Schramm et al. Chicago: Rand McNally.

Sears, R.R., E. Maccoby, and H. Levin. 1957. *Patterns of child rearing.* New York: Harper and Row.

Sears, R.R., J. Whiting, V. Nowlis, and P. Sears. 1953. Some child-rearing antecedents of aggression and dependency in young children. *Genetic Psychology Monograph* 47:135–234.

Seashore, S.E. 1954. *Group cohesiveness in the industrial work group.* Ann Arbor, MI: Univ. of Michigan Press.

Sebeok, T.A. and J. Umiker-Sebeok. 1980. *Speaking of apes.* New York: Plenum.

Secord, P.F. and C.W. Backman. 1974. *Social psychology.* 2 ed. New York: McGraw-Hill.

Seedman, A.A. and P. Hellman. 1975. *Chief.* New York: Avon Books.

Seeman, M. 1975. Alienation studies. In *Annual Review of Sociology*, eds. A. Inkeles, J. Coleman, and N. Smelser, 1:91–123.

Segal, B.E. 1965. Contact, compliance and distance among Jewish and non-Jewish undergraduates. *Social Problems* 13:66–74.

Serbin, L.A. and K. O'Leary. 1975. How nursery schools teach girls to shut up. *Psychology Today* 9:56–58ff.

Sewell, W.H. and R.M. Hauser. 1975. *Education, occupation and earnings: Achievement in the early career.* New York: Academic Press.

———. 1980. The Wisconsin longitudinal study of social and psychological factors in aspirations and achievements. *Research in Sociology of Education and Socialization* 1:59–99.

Sewell, W.H., R.M. Hauser, and W.C. Wolf. 1980. Sex, schooling, and occupational status. *American Journal of Sociology* 86:551–83.

Shanas, E. 1979. The family as a support system in old age. *Gerontologist* 19:169–74.

Shaver, P. and J. Freedman. 1976. Your pursuit of happiness. *Psychology Today* 10:26–32, August.

Shaw, M. and P. Costanzo. 1982. *Theories of social psychology.* 2d. ed. New York: McGraw-Hill.

Shaw, M.E. 1954. Some effects of problem complexity upon problem solution efficiency in different communication nets. *Journal of Experimental Psychology* 48:211–17.

———. 1955. A comparison of two types of leadership in various communication nets. *Journal of Abnormal and Social Psychology* 50:127–34.

———. 1964. Communication networks. In *Advances in experimental social psychology*, ed. L. Berkowitz. Vol. 1. New York: Academic Press.

———. 1978. Communication networks fourteen years later. In *Group processes*, ed. L. Berkowitz. New York: Academic Press.

Shaw, M.E. and G.H. Rothschild. 1956. Some effects of prolonged experience in communication nets. *Journal of Applied Psychology* 40:281–86.

Shaw, M.E. and L.M. Shaw. 1962. Some effects of sociometric grouping upon learning in a second grade classroom. *Journal of Social Psychology* 57:453–58.

Sheehy, G. 1976. *Passages: Predictable crises of adult life.* New York: Dutton.

Shelley, H.P. 1960. Status consensus, leadership, and satisfaction with the group. *Journal of Social Psychology* 51:157–64.

Sherif, M. 1936. *The psychology of social norms.* New York: Harper and Row.

Sherif, M., O.J. Harvey, B.J. White, W.R. Hood, and C.W. Sherif. 1961. *Intergroup cooperation and competition: The Robbers Cave experiment.* Norman, OK: Univ. Book Exchange.

Sherif, M. and C.W. Sherif. 1953. *Groups in harmony and tension.* New York: Harper Brothers.

———. 1956. *An outline of social psychology.* Revised. New York: Harper and Row.

———. 1964a. *Exploration into conformity and deviation of adolescents.* New York: Harper and Row.

———. 1964b. *Reference groups.* New York: Harper and Row.

———. 1966. *In common predicament.* Boston: Houghton Mifflin.

———. 1967. Group processes and collective interaction in delinquent activities. *Journal of Research in Crime and Delinquency* 4:43–62.

———. 1969. *Social psychology.* Revised edition. New York: Harper and Row.

Sherman, S.J. 1970. Effects of choice and incentive on attitude change in a discrepant behavior situation. *Journal of Personality and Social Psychology* 15:245–52.

Sherwood, J.J. 1965. Self-identity and referent others. *Sociometry* 28:66–81.

Shibutani, T. 1961. *Society and personality.* Englewood Cliffs, NJ: Prentice-Hall.

Shiflett, S. 1979. Toward a general model of small group productivity. *Psychological Bulletin* 86:67–79.

Shiflett, S.C. 1973. The contingency model of leadership effectiveness: Some implications of its statistical and methodological properties. *Behavioral Science* 18:429–40.

Shover, N., S. Novland, J. James, and W. Thornton. 1979. Gender roles and delinquency. *Social Forces* 58:162–75.

Shulman, N. 1975. Life-cycle variations in patterns of close relationships. *Journal of Marriage and the Family* 37:813–21.

Shweder, R.A. 1977. Likeness and likelihood in everyday thought: Magical thinking in judgments about personality. *Current Anthropology* 18:637–58.

Sigall, H. and D. Landy. 1973. Radiating beauty: The effects of having a physically attractive partner on person perception. *Journal of Personality and Social Psychology* 28:218–24.

Sigall, H. and N. Ostrove. 1975. Beautiful but dangerous: Effects of offender attractiveness and nature of crime on juridic judgement. *Journal of Personality and Social Psychology* 31:171–74.

Sigall, H. and R. Page. 1971. Current stereotypes: A little fading, a little faking. *Journal of Personality and Social Psychology* 18:247–55.

Silberman, M. 1976. Toward a theory of criminal deterrence. *American Sociological Review* 41:442–61.

Simmons, R.G., L. Brown, D.M. Bush, and D.A. Blyth. 1978. Self-esteem and achievement of black and white adolescents. *Social Problems* 26:86–96.

Simons, L.S. and C.W. Turner. 1974. A further investigation of the weapons effect. In *Proceedings of Division 8 of the American Psychological Association.* New Orleans.

Simpson, R.L. and I.H. Simpson. 1959. The psychiatric attendant: Development of an occupational self-image in a low status occupation. *American Sociological Review* 24:389–92.

Singer, J.L. and D.G. Singer. 1981. *Television, imagination and aggression: A study of preschoolers.* Hillsdale, NJ: Erlbaum.

———. 1983. Psychologists look at television: Cognitive, developmental, personality, and social policy implications. *American Psychologist* 38:826–34.

Sinnott, J.D. 1977. Sex-role inconstancy, biology, and successful aging. *Gerontologist* 17:459–63.

Sistrunk, F. and J.W. McDavid. 1971. Sex variable in conforming behavior. *Journal of Personality and Social Psychology* 17:200–07.

Sivacek, J. and W. Crano. 1982. Vested interest as a moderator of attitude-behavior consistency. *Journal of Personality and Social Psychology* 43:210–21.

Skinner, B.F. 1953. *Science and human behavior.* New York: Macmillan.

———. 1957. *Verbal behavior.* New York: Appleton-Century-Crofts.

———. 1971. *Beyond freedom and dignity.* New York: Knopf.

Slater, P.E. 1955. Role differentiation in small groups. *American Sociological Review* 20:300–10.

———. 1963. On social regression. *American Sociological Review* 28:339–64.

Slomczynski, K.M., J. Miller, and M. Kohn. 1981. Stratification, work and values: A Polish-United States comparison. *American Sociological Review* 46:720–44.

Smelser, N. 1963. *Theory of collective behavior.* New York: Free Press.

Smith, A.J., H.E. Madden, and R. Sobol. 1957. Productivity and recall in cooperative discussion groups. *Journal of Psychology* 43:193–204.

Smith, W.P. and A. Anderson. 1975. Threats, communication, and bargaining. *Journal of Personality and Social Psychology* 32:76–82.

Smith, W.P. and W.A. Leginski. 1970. Magnitude and precision of punitive power in bargaining strategy. *Journal of Experimental Social Psychology* 6:57–76.

Snodgrass, S.E. and R. Rosenthal. 1982. Teacher suspiciousness of experimenter's intent and the mediation of teacher expectancy effects. *Basic and Applied Social Psychology* 3:219–30.

Snow, D.A. and C.L. Phillips. 1982. The changing self-orientations of college students: From institution to impulse. *Social Science Quarterly* 63:462–76.

Snyder, D. 1975. Institutional setting and industrial conflict: Comparative analyses of France, Italy, and the United States. *American Sociological Review* 40:259–78.

Snyder, D. and W. Kelly. 1977. Conflict intensity, media sensitivity and the validity of newspaper data. *American Sociological Review* 42:105–23.

Snyder, M. 1979. Self-monitoring. In *Advances in experimental social psychology,* ed. L. Berkowitz. Vol. 12. New York: Academic Press.

———. 1982. When believing means doing: Creating links between attitudes and behavior. In *Consistency in social behavior: The Ontario symposium.* Vol. 2. eds. M. Zanna, E. Higgins, C. Herman. Hillsdale, NJ: Erlbaum.

Snyder, M., S. Gangestad, and J. Simpson. 1983. Choosing friends as activity partners: The role of self-monitoring. *Journal of Personality and Social Psychology* 45:1061–72.

Snyder, M. and E.D. Tanke. 1976. Behavior and attitude: Some people are more consistent than others. *Journal of Personality* 44:501–17.

Snyder, M., E.D. Tanke, and E. Berscheid. 1977. Social perception and interpersonal behavior: On the self-fulfilling nature of social stereotypes. *Journal of Personality and Social Psychology* 35:656–66.

Solomon, R.L. 1964. Punishment. *American Psychologist* 19:239–53.

Solomon, S. and L. Saxe. 1977. What is intelligent, as well as attractive, is good. *Personality and Social Psychology Bulletin* 3:670–73.

Sommer, R. 1969. *Personal space.* Englewood Cliffs, NJ: Prentice-Hall.

Sorenson, J.R. 1971. Task demands, group interaction and group performance. *Sociometry* 34:483–95.

Sorokin, P. 1947. *Society, culture, and personality.* New York: Harper.

Spiegel, J.P. 1969. Hostility, aggression and violence. In *Patterns in American racial violence,* ed. A.D. Grimshaw. Chicago: Aldine.

Spilerman, S. 1976. Structural characteristics of cities and severity of racial disorders. *American Sociological Review* 41:771–93.

Spitz, R. 1945. Hospitalism. *The Psychoanalytic Study of the Child* 1:53–72.

———. 1946. Hospitalism: A follow-up report. *The Psychoanalytic Study of the Child* 2:113–17.

Spitze, G.D. and J. Huber. 1980. Changing attitudes toward women's nonfamily roles: 1938 to 1978. *Sociology of Work and Occupations* 7:317–35.

Srole, L. 1956. Social integration and certain corollaries. *American Sociological Review* 21:709–16.

Staats, A. 1968. *Learning, language and cognition.* New York: Holt Rinehart and Winston.

Staats, A.W. and C.K. Staats. 1958. Attitudes established by classical conditioning. *Journal of Abnormal and Social Psychology* 57:37–40.

Stang, D.J. 1972. Conformity, ability, and self-esteem. *Representative Research in Social Psychology* 3:97–103.

Stark, R. and W.S. Bainbridge. 1980. Networks of faith: Interpersonal bonds and recruitment in cults and sects. *American Journal of Sociology* 85:1376–95.

Staub, E. 1978. *Positive social behavior and morality.* Vol. 1. New York: Academic Press.

Steele, C.M., L.L. Southwick, and B. Critchlow. 1981. Dissonance and alcohol: Drinking your troubles away. *Journal of Personality and Social Psychology* 41:831–46.

Steere, G.H. 1981. The family and the elderly. In *The dynamics of aging*, eds. F.J. Berghorn, D.E. Schafer, and Associates. Boulder, CO: Westview Press.

Steffensmeier, D.J. and R.M. Terry. 1973. Deviance and respectability: An observational study of reactions to shoplifting. *Social Forces* 51:417–26.

Steiner, I.D. 1972. *Group process and productivity.* New York: Academic Press.

Steiner, I.D. 1974. *Task-performing groups.* Morristown, NJ: General Learning Press.

Steiner, I.D. and E.D. Rogers. 1963. Alternative responses to dissonance. *Journal of Abnormal and Social Psychology* 66:128–36.

Stephan, F.F. and E.G. Mishler. 1952. The distribution of participation in small groups: An exponential approximation. *American Sociological Review* 17:598–608.

Stephenson, W. 1953. *The study of behavior.* Chicago: Univ. of Chicago Press.

Sternthal, B., R. Dholakia, and C. Leavitt. 1978. The persuasive effect of source credibility: A test of cognitive response analysis. *Journal of Consumer Research* 4:252–60.

Stewart, A. and P. Salt. 1981. Life stress, life style, depression and illness in adult women. *Journal of Personality and Social Psychology* 40:1063–69.

Stockard, J. and M.M. Johnson. 1980. *Sex roles: Sex inequality and sex role development.* Englewood Cliffs, NJ: Prentice-Hall.

Stogdill, R.M. 1963. Team achievement under high motivation. Ohio State University, Bureau of Business Research, Monograph no. R-113.

Stogdill, R.M. 1974. *Handbook of leadership: A survey of theory and research.* New York: Free Press.

Stoll, C.S. 1978. *Female and male: Socialization, social roles, and social structure.* Dubuque, IA: W.C. Brown.

Stone, G.P. 1962. Appearances and the self. In *Human behavior and social processes*, ed. A. Rose. Boston: Houghton Mifflin.

Stoner, J.A.F. 1961. A comparison of individual and group decisions involving risk. Master's Thesis, M.I.T. Cited in Marquis, D.G. 1962. Individual responsibility and group decisions involving risk. *Industrial Management Review* 3:8–23.

Storms, M.D. 1973. Videotape and attribution process: Reversing actors' and observers' points of view. *Journal of Personality and Social Psychology* 27:165–75.

Stotland, E. 1969. Exploratory investigations of empathy. In *Advances in experimental social psychology*, ed. L. Berkowitz. Vol. 3. New York: Academic Press.

Streufert, S. and S.C. Streufert. 1969. Effects of conceptual structure, failure, and success on attribution of causality and interpersonal attitudes. *Journal of Personality and Social Psychology* 11:138–47.

Streufert, S., S.C. Streufert, and C.H. Castore. 1969. Complexity, increasing failure, and decision making. *Journal of Experimental Research in Personality* 3:293–300.

Stricker, L.J., P.I. Jacobs, and N. Kogan. 1974. Trait interrelations in implicit personality theories and questionnaire data. *Journal of Personality and Social Psychology* 30:198–207.

Strodtbeck, F.L., R.J. Simon, and C. Hawkins. 1965. Social status in jury deliberations. In *Current studies in social psychology*, eds. I.D. Steiner and M. Fishbein. New York: Holt Rinehart and Winston.

Stroebe, W. and M. Diehl. 1981. Conformity and counterattitudinal behavior: The effect of social support on attitude change. *Journal of Personality and Social Psychology* 41:876–89.

Stroebe, W., V.D. Thompson, C.A. Insko, and S.R. Reisman. 1970. Balance and differentiation in the evaluation of linked attitude objects. *Journal of Personality and Social Psychology* 16:38–47.

Stryker, S. 1980. *Symbolic interactionism: A social structural version.* Menlo Park, CA: Benjamin/Cummings.

Stryker, S. and A. Gottlieb. 1981. Attribution theory and symbolic interactionism: A comparison. In *New directions in attribution theory*, eds. J.H. Hawes, W. Ickes, and R.F. Kidd. Vol. 3. Hillsdale, NJ: Erlbaum.

Stryker, S. and R.T. Serpe. 1981. Commitment, identity salience and role behavior: Theory and research example. In *Personality, roles and social behavior*, eds. W. Ickes and E. Knowles. New York: Springer-Verlag.

———. 1982. Towards a theory of family influence in the socialization of children. In *Research in sociology of education and socialization*, ed. A. Kerckhoff. Vol. 4. Greenwich, CT: J.A.I. Press.

Suchner, R.W. and D. Jackson. 1976. Responsibility and status: A causal or only a spurious relationship? *Sociometry* 39:243–56.

Sudman, S. and N.M. Bradburn. 1974. *Response effects in surveys.* Chicago: Aldine.

Suls, J.M. and R.L. Miller. Eds. 1977. *Social comparison processes: Theoretical and empirical perspectives.* New York: Wiley.

Sumner, W.G. 1906. *Folkways.* New York and Boston: Ginn.

Sussman, N.M. and H.M. Rosenfeld. 1982. Influence of culture, language and sex on conversational distance. *Journal of Personality and Social Psychology* 42:66–74.

Sutherland, E. and D. Cressey. 1978. *Principles of criminology.* 10th ed. New York: J.B. Lippincott.

Sutherland, E.H. 1937. *The professional thief.* Chicago: Univ. of Chicago Press.

Suttles, G. 1968. *The social order of the slum.* Chicago: Univ. of Chicago Press.

Swadesh, M. 1971. *The origin and diversification of language*, ed. J. Sherzer. Chicago: Aldine-Atherton.

Swanson, D.L. 1979. Ed. The uses and gratifications approach to mass communications research. *Communication Research* 3:3–111.

Sweet, J.A. The changing transition to adulthood. Unpublished manuscript.

Swigert, V. and R. Farrell. 1977. Normal homicides and the law. *American Sociological Review* 42:16–32.

Swinth, R.L. 1967. The establishment of the trust relationship. *Journal of Conflict Resolution* 11:335–44.

Syme, S.L. and L.F. Berkman. 1976. Social class, susceptibility and sickness. *American Journal of Epidemiology* 104:1–8.

Tajfel, H. 1978. Social categorization, social identity and social comparison. In *Differentiation between social groups: Studies in the social psychology of intergroup relations*, ed. H. Tajfel. London: Academic Press.

Tajfel, H. and M.G. Billig. 1974. Familiarity and categorization in intergroup behavior. *Journal of Experimental Social Psychology* 10:159–70.

Tajfel, H., M.G. Billig, R.P. Bundy, and C. Flament. 1971. Social categorization and intergroup behavior. *European Journal of Social Psychology* 1:149–78.

Takala, M., T.A. Pihkanen, and T. Markkanen. 1957. The effects of distilled and brewed beverages: A physiological, neurological and psychological study. *The Finnish Foundation for Alcohol Studies 4*.

Tavris, C. and C. Offir. 1984. *The longest war: Sex differences in perspective*. 2d ed. New York: Harcourt Brace Jovanovich.

Taylor, D.M. and V. Jaggi. 1974. Ethnocentrism and causal attribution in a South Indian context. *Journal of Cross-Cultural Psychology* 5:162–71.

Taylor, D.M. and L. Royer. 1980. Group processes affecting anticipated language choice in intergroup relations. In *Language: Social psychological perspectives*, eds. H. Giles, W.P. Robinson, and P.M. Smith. New York: Pergamon.

Taylor, S.E. and S.T. Fiske. 1978. Salience, attention and attribution: Top of the head phenomena. In *Advances in experimental social psychology*, ed. L. Berkowitz. Vol. 11. New York: Academic Press.

Taylor, S.E., S.T. Fiske, N.L. Etcoff, and A.J. Ruderman. 1978. The categorical and contextual bases of person memory and stereotyping. *Journal of Personality and Social Psychology* 36:778–93.

Taylor, S.P. 1967. Aggressive behavior and physiological arousal as a function of provocation and the tendency to inhibit aggression. *Journal of Personality* 35:297–310.

Tedeschi, J.T., T.V. Bonoma, and B.R. Schlenker. 1972. Influence, decision, and compliance. In *The Social Influence Processes*, ed. J. Tedeschi. Chicago: Aldine-Atherton.

Tedeschi, J.T. and M. Reiss. 1981. Predicaments and verbal tactics of impression management. In *Ordinary language explanations of social behavior*, ed. C. Antaki. London: Academic Press.

Tedeschi, J.T., B.R. Schlenker, and S. Lindskold. 1972. The exercise of power and influence: The source of influence. In *The Social Influence Processes*, ed. J. Tedeschi. Chicago: Aldine-Atherton.

Terrace, H. 1984. *Language in apes*. New York: Academic Press.

Terwilliger, R.F. 1968. *Meaning and mind*. New York: Oxford Univ. Press.

Tesser, A. and J. Campbell. 1983. Self-definition and self-evaluation maintenance. In *Psychological perspectives on the self*, eds. J. Suls and A.G. Greenwald. Vol. 2. Hillsdale, NJ: Erlbaum.

Tessler, R.C. and S.H. Schwartz. 1972. Help-seeking, self-esteem, and achievement motivation: An attributional analysis. *Journal of Personality and Social Psychology* 38:291–300.

Tetlock, P.E. 1980. Explaining teacher explanations of pupil performance: A self-presentation interpretation. *Social Psychology Quarterly* 43:282–90.

———. 1981. The influence of self-presentational goals on attributional reports. *Social Psychology Quarterly* 44:300–11.

Thakerar, J.N., H. Giles, and J. Cheshire. 1982. Psychological and linguistic parameters of speech accomodation theory. In *Advances in the social psychology of language*, eds. C. Fraser and K.R. Scherer. Cambridge: Cambridge Univ. Press.

Thibaut, J. and H. Kelley. 1959. *The social psychology of groups*. New York: Wiley.

Thomas, E.J. 1957. Effects of facilitative role interdependence on group functioning. *Human Relations* 10:347–66.

Thomas, E.J. and C.F. Fink. 1963. Effects of group size. *Psychological Bulletin* 60:371–84.

Thomas, W.I. and F. Znaniecki. 1918. *The Polish peasant in Europe and America*. Vol. 1. Boston: Badger.

Thompson, W., C. Cowan, and D. Rosenhan. 1981. Focus of attention mediates the impact of negative affect on altruism. *Journal of Personality and Social Psychology* 38:291–300.

Thornberry, T. 1973. Race, socioeconomic status and sentencing in the juvenile justice system. *Journal of Criminal Law and Criminology* 64:90–98.

Thornberry, T.P. and M. Farnsworth. 1982. Social correlates of criminal involvement: Further evidence on the relationship between social status and criminal behavior. *American Sociological Review* 47:505–18.

Thorndike, E.L. 1913. *The psychology of learning*. New York: Teachers College, Columbia Univ.

———. 1920. A constant error in psychological ratings. *Journal of Applied Psychology* 4:25–29.

Thorne, B., C. Kramerae, and H. Henley. 1983. Eds. *Language, gender and society*. Rowley, MA: Newbury.

Thornton, A. and D. Freedman. 1979. Changes in sex-role attitudes of women, 1962–1977: Evidence from a panel study. *American Sociological Review* 44:831–42.

Thornton, R. and P.M. Nardi. 1975. The dynamics of role acquisition. *American Journal of Sociology* 80:870–85.

Tilly, C., L. Tilly, and R. Tilly. 1975. *The rebellious century, 1830–1930*. Cambridge, MA: Harvard Univ. Press.

Tittle, C. and W. Villemez. 1977. Social class and criminality. *Social Forces*. 56:474–502.

Tittle, C., W. Villemez, and D. Smith. 1978. The myth of social class and criminality: An empirical assessment of the empirical evidence. *American Sociological Review* 43:643–56.

Tobin, S. 1980. Institutionalization of the aged. In *Transitions of aging*, eds. N. Datan and N. Lohman. New York: Academic Press.

Toch, H. 1969. *Violent men: An inquiry into the psychology of violence*. Chicago: Aldine.

Toi, M. and C.D. Batson. 1982. More evidence that empathy is a source of altruism. *Journal of Personality and Social Psychology* 43:289–292.

Touhey, J. 1979. Sex-role stereotyping and individual differences in liking for the physically attractive. *Social Psychology Quarterly* 42:285–89.

Treiman, D. 1977. *Occupational prestige in comparative perspective*. New York: Academic Press.

Triandis, H.C. 1980. Values, attitudes and interpersonal behavior. In *Nebraska symposium on motivation*, eds. H. Howe and M. Page. Vol. 27. Lincoln, NE: Univ. of Nebraska Press.

Trowbridge, N.T. 1972. Self-concept and socioeconomic status in elementary school children. *American Educational Research Journal* 9:525–37.

Tuddenham, R.D. 1958. The influence of a distorted group norm upon individual judgement. *Journal of Psychology* 46:227–41.

Tudor, W., J. Tudor, and W. Gove. 1979. The effect of sex role differences on the societal reaction to mental retardation. *Social Forces* 57:870–86.

Turner, G.J. 1974. Social class and children's language of control at ages five and seven. In *Class, codes and control II*, revised edition, ed. B. Bernstein. London: Routledge and Kegan Paul.

Turner, J.C. 1975. Social comparison and social identity: Some prospects for intergroup behaviour. *European Journal of Social Psychology* 5:5–34.

Turner, R.H. 1956. Role-taking, role standpoint, and reference group behavior. *American Journal of Sociology* 61:316–28.

———. 1962. Role-taking: Process vs. conformity. In *Human behavior and social process*, ed. A. Rose. Boston: Houghton Mifflin, 22–40.

———. 1970. *Family interaction*. New York: Wiley.

———. 1976. The real self: From institution to impulse. *American Journal of Sociology* 81:989–1016.

———. 1978. The role and the person. *American Journal of Sociology* 84:1–23.

Turner, R.H. and L.M. Killian. 1972. *Collective behavior*. 2d ed. Englewood Cliffs, NJ: Prentice-Hall.

Turner, R.H. and N. Shosid. 1976. Ambiguity and interchangeability in role attribution. *American Sociological Review* 41:993–1006.

Tversky, A. and D. Kahneman. 1974. Judgment under uncertainty: Heuristics and biases. *Science* 185:1124–31.

Tyler, T.O. and D.O. Sems. 1977. Coming to like obnoxious people when we must live with them. *Journal of Personality and Social Psychology* 35:200–11.

Ubell, E. 1985. Can changing your looks change your life? *Parade Magazine*, February 17, 1985.

Udry, J.R. 1974. *The social context of marriage*. Philadelphia: Lippincott.

Ungar, S. 1980. The effects of certainty of self-perceptions on self-presentation behaviors: A test of the strength of self-enhancement motives. *Social Psychological Quarterly* 43:165–72.

Valle, V.A. and I.H. Frieze. 1976. Stability of causal attributions as a mediator in changing expectations for success. *Journal of Personality and Social Psychology* 33:579–89.

Van Gennep, A. 1960, 1908. *The rites of passage*. Chicago: Univ. of Chicago Press.

Van Maanen, J. 1976. Breaking in: Socialization to work. In *Handbook of work, organization and society*, ed. R. Dubin. Chicago: Rand McNally.

Van Zelst, R.H. 1952a. Sociometrically selected work teams increase production. *Personnel Psychology* 5:175–86.

———. 1952b. Validation of a sociometric regrouping

procedure. *Journal of Abnormal and Social Psychology* 47:299–301.

Verbrugge, L. 1979. Marital status and health. *Journal of Marriage and the Family* 41:267–85.

Verplanck, W.S. 1955. The control of the content of conversation: Reinforcement of statements of opinion. *Journal of Abnormal and Social Psychology* 51:668–76.

Vidmar, N. 1974. Effects of group discussion on category width judgments. *Journal of Personality and Social Psychology* 29:187–95.

Visher, C. 1981. Sex and arrest: A test of the chivalry hypothesis. Unpublished paper presented at American Sociological Association Meeting.

Voissem, N.H. and F. Sistrunk. 1971. Communication schedule and cooperative game behavior. *Journal of Personality and Social Psychology* 19:160–67.

von Baeyer, C.L., D.L. Sherk, and M.P. Zanna. 1981. Impression management in the job interview: When the female applicant meets the male (chauvinist) interviewer. *Personality and Social Psychology Bulletin* 7:45–51.

Vos, K. and W. Brinkman. 1967. Success and cohesion in sports groups. *Sociologische Gids* 14:30–40.

Vygotsky, L.S. 1962. *Thought and language*. Cambridge, MA: MIT Press.

Wahrman, R. 1970. High status, deviance and sanctions. *Sociometry* 33:485–504.

Waldron, I. 1976. Why do women live longer than men? *Social Science and Medicine* 10:349–62.

Walker, E.L. and R.W. Heyns. 1962. *An anatomy for conformity*. Englewood Cliffs, NJ: Prentice-Hall.

Wall, J.A., Jr. 1975. Effects of constituent trust and representative bargaining orientation on intergroup bargaining. *Journal of Personality and Social Psychology* 31:1004–12.

———. 1977. Intergroup bargaining: Effects of opposing constituent's stance, opposing representative's bargaining, and representatives' locus of control. *Journal of Conflict Resolution* 21:459–74.

Wallin, P. 1950. Cultural contradictions and sex roles: A repeat study. *American Sociological Review* 15:288–93.

Walsh, E.J. and M.C. Taylor. 1982. Occupational correlates of multidimensional self-esteem: Comparisons among garbage collectors, bartenders, professors and other workers. *Sociology and Social Research* 66:252–58.

Walsh, E.J. and R.H. Warland. 1983. Social movement involvement in the wake of a nuclear accident: Activists and free riders in the TMI area. *American Sociological Review* 48:764–80.

Walster (Hatfield), E., E. Aronson, and D. Abrahams. 1966. On increasing the persuasiveness of a low prestige communicator. *Journal of Experimental Social Psychology* 2:325–42.

Walster (Hatfield), E., E. Berscheid, and G.W. Walster. 1973. New directions in equity research. *Journal of Personality and Social Psychology*. 25:151–76.

Walster (Hatfield), E., G.W. Walster, and E. Berscheid. 1978. *Equity: Theory and research*. Boston: Allyn and Bacon.

Walster (Hatfield), E., G.W. Walster, and J. Traupman. 1978. Equity and premarital sex. *Journal of Personality and Social Psychology*. 36:82–92.

Walster (Hatfield), E., V. Aronson, D. Abrahams, and L.

Rottman. 1966. The importance of physical attractiveness in dating behavior. *Journal of Personality and Social Psychology* 4:508–16.

Walster (Hatfield), E., G.W. Walster, J. Piliavin, and L. Schmidt. 1973. Playing hard-to-get: Understanding an elusive phenomenon. *Journal of Personality and Social Psychology* 26:113–21.

Walters, J. and L. Walters. 1980. Parent-child relationships: A review, 1970–1979. *Journal of Marriage and the Family* 42:807–22.

Walton, R.E. and R.B. McKersie. 1965. *A behaviorial theory of labor negotiations: An analysis of a social interaction system.* New York: McGraw-Hill.

Ward, D.A. and G. Kassebaum. 1965. *Women's prison: Sex and social structure.* Chicago: Aldine.

Warheit, G., C. Holzer III, R. Bell, and S. Arey. 1976. Sex, marital status and mental health: A reappraisal. *Social Forces* 55:459–70.

Warner, L.C. and M.L. DeFleur. 1969. Attitude as an interactional concept: Social constraint and social distance as intervening variables between attitudes and action. *American Sociological Review* 34:153–69.

Warner, W.L. and P.S. Lunt. 1941. *The social life of a modern community.* New Haven: Yale Univ. Press.

Warwick, C.E. 1964. Relationship of scholastic aspiration and group cohesiveness to the academic achievement of male freshman at Cornell Univ. *Human Relations* 17:155–68.

Wasserman, I. 1977. Southern violence and the political process. *American Sociological Review* 42:359–62.

Watson, R.I. 1973. Investigation into deindividuation using a cross-cultural survey technique. *Journal of Personality and Social Psychology* 25:342–45.

Webb, E.J., D.J. Campbell, R.D. Schwartz, and L. Sechrest. 1966. *Unobtrusive measures: Nonreactive research in the social sciences.* Chicago: Rand McNally.

Weber, M. 1958. *The Protestant ethic and the spirit of capitalism.* Translated by T. Parsons. New York: Scribners.

Weber, R. and J. Crocker. 1983. Cognitive processes in the revision of stereotypic beliefs. *Journal of Personality and Social Psychology* 45:961–77.

Webster, M., Jr., and J.E. Driskell, Jr. 1978. Status generalization: A review and some new data. *American Sociological Review* 43:220–36.

Weigel, R.H. and L.S. Newman. 1976. Increasing attitude-behavior correspondence by broadening the scope of the behaviorial measure. *Journal of Personality and Social Psychology* 33:793–802.

Weinberg, M. 1976. The nudist management of respectability. In *Sex research: Studies from the Kinsey Institute,* ed. M. Weinberg. New York: Oxford Univ. Press.

Weiner, B. 1974. *Achievement motivation and attribution theory.* Morristown, NJ: General Learning Press.

Weiner, B., D. Russell, and D. Lehrman. 1978. Affective consequences of causal ascriptions. In *New directions in attribution theory,* eds. J.H. Harvey, W. Ickes, and R.F. Kidd. Vol. 2. Hillsdale, NJ: Erlbaum.

Weinstein, E.A. and P. Deutschberger. 1963. Some dimensions of altercasting. *Sociometry* 26:454–66.

Weitzman, L.J., D. Eifler, E. Hokada, K. Ross. 1972. Sex role socialization in picture books for pre-school children. *American Journal of Sociology* 77:1125–50.

Wellman, B. 1979. The community question: The intimate networks of east Yorkers. *American Journal of Sociology* 84:1201–31.

Wells, L.E. and G. Marwell. 1976. *Self-esteem: Its conceptualization and measurement.* Beverly Hills, CA: Sage.

Werner, C. and P. Parmelee. 1979. Similarity of activity preferences among friends: Those who play together stay together. *Social Psychology Quarterly* 42:62–66.

Weyant, J.M. 1978. Effects of mood states, costs and benefits on helping. *Journal of Personality and Social Psychology* 36:1169–76.

Wheeler, L. 1966. Toward a theory of behavioral contagion. *Psychological Review* 73:179–92.

White, B. 1975. *The first three years of life.* Englewood Cliffs, NJ: Prentice-Hall.

White, C. 1975. Moral development in Bahamian school children: A cross-cultural examination of Kohlberg's stages of moral reasoning. *Developmental Psychology* 11:535–36.

White, C., N. Bushnell, and J. Regnemer. 1978. Moral development in Bahamian school children: A 3-year examination of Kohlberg's stages of moral development. *Developmental Psychology* 14:58–65.

White, G. 1980. Physical attractiveness and courtship progress. *Journal of Personality and Social Psychology* 39:660–68.

Whorf, B.L. 1956. *Language, thought and reality,* ed. J.B. Carroll. Cambridge, MA: MIT Press.

Wicker, A.W. 1969. Attitudes versus actions: The relationship of verbal and overt behavioral responses to attitude objects. *Journal of Social Issues* 25:41–78.

Wicklund, R.A. 1975. Objective self-awareness. In *Advances in experimental social psychology,* ed. L. Berkowitz. Vol. 8. New York: Academic Press.

Wicklund, R.A. and J.W. Brehm. 1976. *Perspectives on cognitive dissonance.* Hillsdale, NJ: Erlbaum.

Wicklund, R.A. and D. Frey. 1980. When the self makes a difference. In *The self in social psychology,* eds. D.M. Wegner and R.R. Vallacher. New York: Oxford University Press.

Wiggins, J.A., F. Dill, and R.D. Schwartz. 1965. On "status-liability". *Sociometry* 28:197–209.

Wilensky, H.L. 1961. Life cycle, work situation, and participation in formal associations. In *Aging and leisure,* ed. R. Kleemeier. New York: Oxford Univ. Press.

Wiley, M.G. 1973. Sex roles in games. *Sociometry* 36:526–41.

Wilke, H. and J.T. Lanzetta. 1970. The obligation to help: The effects of amount of prior help on subsequent helping behavior. *Journal of Experimental Social Psychology* 6:488–93.

Wilkinson, T. 1980. Gaining access. In *Child abuse,* eds. G. Gerbner, C. Ross, and E. Zigler. New York: Oxford Univ. Press.

Wilner, D.M., R.P. Walkley, and S.W. Cook. 1952. Residential proximity and intergroup relations in public housing projects. *Journal of Social Issues* 8:45–69.

Winch, R. 1958. *Mate selection: A study of complementary needs.* New York: Harper and Row.

Winick, C. 1964. Physician narcotic addicts. In *The other side,* ed. H. Becker. New York: Free Press.

Winterbottom, M. 1958. The relation of need for achievement to learning experiences in independence and mastery. In *Motives in fantasy, action and society*, ed. J.W. Atkinson. Princeton, NJ: D. Van Nostrand.

Wofford, J. 1970. Factor analysis of managerial behavior variables. *Journal of Applied Psychology* 54:169–73.

Worchel, S., E. Lind, and K. Kaufman. 1975. Evaluations of group products as a function of expectations of group longevity, outcome of competition, and publicity of evaluations. *Journal of Personality and Social Psychology* 31:1089–97.

Wortman, C., P. Adesman, E. Herman, and R. Greenberg. 1976. Self-disclosure: An attributional perspective. *Journal of Personality and Social Psychology* 33:184–91.

Wright, E.O., C. Costello, D. Hachen, and J. Sprague. 1982. The American class structure. *American Sociological Review* 47:709–26.

Wright, J. 1978. Are working women *really* more satisfied? Evidence from several national surveys. *Journal of Marriage and the Family* 40:301–13.

Wrightsman, L.S. 1969. Wallace supporters and adherence to "law and order." *Journal of Personality and Social Psychology* 13:17–22.

Wyer, R.S., Jr. 1966. Effects of incentive to perform well, group attraction, and group acceptance on conformity in a judgmental task. *Journal of Personality and Social Psychology* 4:21–26.

Wyer, R.S., Jr. and T.K. Srull. 1981. Category accessibility: Some theoretical and empirical issues concerning the processing of social stimulus information. In *Social cognition: The Ontario symposium*, eds. E.T. Higgins, C.P. Herman, and M.P. Zanna. Hillsdale, NJ: Erlbaum.

Wylie, R.C. 1979. *The self-concept: Theory and research on selected topics.* Rev. ed. Vol. 2. Lincoln, NE: Univ. of Nebraska Press.

Yancey, W.L., L. Rigsby, and J.D. McCarthy. 1972. Social position and self-evaluation: The relative importance of race. *American Journal of Sociology* 78:338–59.

Yarrow, M.R., J.P. Campbell, and L.J. Yarrow. 1958. Acquisition of new norms: A study of racial desegregation. *Journal of Social Issues* 14:8–28.

Yarrow, M.R., C. Schwartz, H. Murphy, and L. Deasy. 1955. The psychological meaning of mental illness in the family. *Journal of Social Issues* 11:12–24.

Younger, J.C., L. Walker, and A.J. Arrowood. 1977. Post decision dissonance at the fair. *Personality and Social Psychology Bulletin* 3:284–87.

Yukl, G.A. 1974a. Effects of situational variables and opponent concessions on a bargainer's perception, aspirations, and concessions. *Journal of Personality and Social Psychology* 29:227–36.

———. 1974b. Effects of opponent's initial offer, concession magnitude, and concession frequency on bargaining behavior. *Journal of Personality and Social Psychology* 30:323–35.

Zajonc, R.B. 1968. The attitudinal effects of mere exposure. *Journal of Personality and Social Psychology*, 9 (monograph supplement no. 2), Part 2, 1–27.

Zald, M. and R. Ash. 1964. Social movement organization growth, decay and change. *Social Forces* 44:327–41.

Zaleznick, A. 1966. *Human dilemmas of leadership.* New York: Harper and Row.

Zand, D.E. 1972. Trust and managerial problem solving. *Administrative Science Quarterly* 17:229–39.

Zander, A. 1971. *Motives and goals in groups.* New York: Academic Press.

———. 1977. *Groups at work.* San Francisco: Jossey-Bass.

Zanna, M. and R. Fazio. 1982. The attitude-behavior relation: Moving toward a third generation of research. In *Consistency in social behavior: The Ontario symposium*, eds. M. Zanna, E. Higgins, and C. Herman. Vol. 2. Hillsdale, NJ: Erlbaum.

Zanna, M.P. and D.L. Hamilton. 1977. Further evidence for meaning change in impression formation. *Journal of Experimental Social Psychology* 13:224–38.

Zelditch, M., Jr. 1972. Authority and performance expectations in bureaucratic organizations. In *Experimental social psychology*, ed. C.G. McClintock. New York: Holt Rinehart and Winston.

Zeller, R.A., A.G. Neal, and H.T. Groat. 1980. On the reliability and stability of alienation measures: A longitudinal analysis. *Social Forces* 58:1195–1204.

Zellner, M. 1970. Self-esteem, reception and influenceability. *Journal of Personality and Social Psychology* 15:87–93.

Zelnick, M. and J. Kantner. 1977. Sexual and contraceptive experience of young unmarried women in the United States, 1971. *Family Planning Perspectives* 9:55–71.

Zillman, D. 1978. Attribution and misattribution of excitatory reactions. In *New directions in attribution research*, eds. J. Harvey, W. Ickes, and R.F. Kidd. Vol. 2. Hillsdale, NJ: Erlbaum.

———. 1979. *Hostility and aggression.* Hillsdale, NJ: Erlbaum.

Zillman, D. and J.R. Cantor. 1976. Effects of timing of information about mitigating circumstances on emotional responses to provocation and retaliatory behavior. *Journal of Experimental Social Psychology* 12:38–55.

Zillman, D., A.H. Katcher, and B. Milavsky. 1972. Excitation transfer from physical exercise to subsequent aggressive behavior. *Journal of Experimental Social Psychology* 8:247–59.

Zimbardo, P.G. 1969. The human choice: Individuation, reason and order versus deindividuation, impulse and chaos. In *Nebraska symposium on motivation* 1969, eds. W.J. Arnold and D. Levine. Lincoln, NE: Univ. of Nebraska Press.

Zimmerman, D.H. and C. West. 1975. Sex roles, interruptions and silences in conversations. In *Language and sex: Difference and dominance*, eds. B. Thorne and N. Henley. Rowley, MA: Newbury House.

Zimmerman, R. and J. DeLamater. 1983. Threat of topic, social desirability, self-awareness and accuracy of self-report. Unpublished manuscript.

Zipf, S.G. 1960. Resistance and conformity under reward and punishment. *Journal of Abnormal and Social Psychology* 61:102–09.

Zuckerman, D.M. 1981. Family background, sex-role attitudes, and life goals of technical college and university students. *Sex Roles* 7:1109–26.

Zuckerman, M. 1978. Actions and occurrences in Kelly's cube. *Journal of Personality and Social Psychology* 36: 647–56.

———. 1979. Atttribution of success and failure revisited,

or: The motivational bias is alive and well in attribution theory. *Journal of Personality* 47:245–87.

Zuckerman, M., M.D. Amidon, S.E. Bishop, and S.D. Pomerantz. 1982. Face and tone of voice in the communication of deception. *Journal of Personality and Social Psychology* 43:347–57.

Zuckerman, M., B.M. DePaulo, and R. Rosenthal. 1981. Verbal and nonverbal communication of deception. In *Advances in experimental social psychology*, ed. L. Berkowitz. Vol. 14. New York: Academic Press.

Zuckerman, M. and R.E. Driver. 1984. Telling lies: Verbal and nonverbal correlates of deception. In *Nonverbal communication: An integrated perspective*, eds. A.W. Siegman and S. Feinstein. Hillsdale, NJ: Erlbaum.

Zuckerman, M., M.R. Kernis, R. Driver, and R. Koestner. 1984. Segmentation of behavior: Effects of actual deception and expected deception. *Journal of Personality and Social Psychology* 46:1173–82.

Zuckerman, M., N.H. Spiegel, B.M. DePaulo, and R. Rosenthal. 1980. Nonverbal strategies for decoding deception. *Journal of Nonverbal Behavior* 17:506–24.

Zurcher, L.A. 1977. *The mutable self: A self-concept for social change.* Beverly Hills, CA: Sage.

Zurcher, L.A. and D.A. Snow. 1981. Collective behavior and social movements. In *Social Psychology: Sociological Perspectives*, eds. M. Rosenberg and R.H. Turner. New York: Basic Books.

Credits

Photographs

Chapter 1 p. 2, Rudolph Robinson; **11,** Paul Conklin, Monkemeyer Press Photo Service; **14,** © Bill Strode, Woodfin Camp and Associates; **16,** © Laimute E. Druskis, Taurus Photos; **19,** Jean-Marie Simon, Taurus Photos.

Chapter 2 p. 28, © Loren Santow, Click/Chicago; **33,** Gatewood/Image Works; **36,** © Robert Kalman, The Image Works, Inc.; **44,** Black Star; **51,** UPI; **55,** © Loren Santow, Click/Chicago.

Chapter 3 p. 61, © Ellis Herwig, Stock, Boston; **66,** © Erika Stone, Peter Arnold, Inc.; **72,** Robert V. Eckert, EKM-Nepenthe; **78,** James L. Shaffer; **85,** © Peter Menzel, Stock, Boston.

Chapter 4 p. 94, © Les Mahon, Monkemeyer Press Photo Service; **104,** Paul Conklin; **106,** © E. J. Saur; **109,** Frank Siteman, EKM-Nepenthe; **113,** © Eric Kroll, Taurus Photos; **121,** © Marilyn M. Pfalz, Taurus Photos.

Chapter 5 p. 132, © Robert Beckhard, Taurus Photos; **136,** © Van Nostrand, from the National Audubon Society, Photo Researchers; **146,** Image Works; **150,** Courtesy of Dr. Paul Ekman; **153,** Mimi Forsyth, Monkemeyer Press Photo Service; **156,** © Will Rhyns, Woodfin Camp and Associates.

Chapter 6 p. 166, Mark Antman/The Image Works, Inc.; **172,** © Barbara Alper, Stock, Boston; **185,** Courtesy of the American Cancer Society; **185,** Courtesy of R. J. Reynolds Tobacco Co.; **191,** © Michael Siluk, EKM-Nepenthe; **191,** © Michael Siluk, EKM-Nepenthe; **196,** © Peter Menzel, Stock, Boston.

Chapter 7 p. 198, © Sepp Seitz, Woodfin Camp and Associates; **203,** © Rhoda Sidney, Monkemeyer Press Photo Service; **212,** © Bill Anderson, Monkemeyer Press Photo Service; **216,** Tim Carlson, Stock, Boston; **220,** Ray Young/Photo Genesis.

Chapter 8 p. 226, Lee Snider, Photo Images; **231,** © Michael Siluk, EKM-Nepenthe; **240,** Don Smetzer, © Click/Chicago; **247,** Steve Allen, © Peter Arnold, Inc.; **251,** Michael Sullivan; **256,** Patrick Ward, Stock, Boston.

Chapter 9 p. 260, © Ron Cooper, EKM-Nepenthe; **264,** © Sybil Shelton, Monkemeyer Press Photo Service; **267,** Tim Carlson, Stock, Boston; **272,** Richard Younker, © Click/Chicago; **279,** Union-Tribune Publishing Co.

Chapter 10 p. 286, Sygma; **292,** © Alon Reininger, Woodfin Camp and Associates; **294,** AP/Wide World; **296,** © Bob Daemmrich, Michael Sullivan Associates; **308,** The Museum of Modern Art Film Library; **311,** Bob Pacheco, EKM-Nepenthe.

Chapter 11 p. 320, © Andrew Gillespie, Click/Chicago; **324,** © Michael Kagen, Monkemeyer Press Photo Service; **333,** © Eric Kroll, Taurus Photos; **333,** Peter Menzel, Stock, Boston; **344,** © Sylvia Johnson, Woodfin Camp and Associates.

Chapter 12 p. 354, © Mike L. Wannemacher, Taurus Photos; **359,** © Ellis Herwig, Stock, Boston; **362,** Monkemeyer Press Photo Service; **370,** © Jean-Pierre Laffont, Sygma; **370,** © Peter Vandermark, Stock, Boston.

Chapter 13 p. 378, Donald L. Miller, Monkemeyer Press Photo Service; **386,** Rick Smolan, Stock, Boston; **390,** Jim Shaffer; **396,** Mark Antman, The Image Works; **404,** Bob Daemmrich, Michael Sullivan, Inc.

Chapter 14 p. 408, Hugh Rogers, Monkemeyer Press Photo Service; **413,** AP/Wide World; **422,** AP/Wide World; **425,** Phillis Graber Jensen, Stock, Boston; **428,** © R. Eckert, EKM-Nepenthe; **429,** © Carolyn A. McKeone.

Chapter 15 p. 436, © Michael Siluk, EKM-Nepenthe; **439,** AP/Wide World; **444,** Owen Franken, Stock, Boston; **444,** Paul Conklin, Monkemeyer Press Photo Service; **450,** Daniel Brody, Stock, Boston; **457,** Sygma.

Chapter 16 p. 460, Ben Lyon, Monterey Peninsula Herald; **464,** Ruth Block, Monkemeyer Press Photo Service; **471,** © Eric Kroll, Taurus Photos; **477,** © Alon Reininger, Woodfin Camp and Associates; **485,** Hugh Rogers, Monkemeyer Press Photo Service.

Chapter 17 p. 490, © Margaret Thompson, Picture Cube; **495,** Robert Eckert, Stock, Boston; **503,** © Bohdan Hrynwice, Southern Light; **506,** AP/Wide World; **512,** AP/Wide World; **515,** Harvey Barad, Monkemeyer Press Photo Service.

Chapter 18 p. 520, © Klaus D. Franke, Peter Arnold, Inc.; **525,** © Allsport/Dave Cannon; **530,** Sygma; **537,** © Loren Santow, Click/Chicago; **541,** AP/Wide World.

Figures

2.1 © 1976 by the American Psychological Association. Adapted by permission of McGuire and Padawer-Singer; **2.2** © 1973 by the American Psychological Association. Adapted by permission of Dutton and Lake; **6.4** Gerard, R. A. Wilhelmy and E. S. Conolley, *Advances in Experimental Social Psychology*, Vol. 7, ed. L. Berkowitz, Academic Press, Inc., 1974; **6.5** © 1979 by the American Psychological

Tables

Author Index

Subject Index